漢 英 小 字 典

CHINESE-ENGLISH DICTIONARY

Cantonese in Yale Romanization
Mandarin in Pinyin

植 漢 民
Chik Hon Man

吳 林 嬋 玉
Ng Lam Sim Yuk

New Asia - - Yale-in-China Chinese Language Center
The Chinese University of Hong Kong

ISBN 962-7141-14-3

First edition 1989
Second edition 1994
Second printing 1996

Published by
New Asia- -Yale-in-China Chinese Language Center
The Chinese University of Hong Kong
Shatin, N.T., Hong Kong

Printed in Hong Kong by Don Bosco Printing Co. Ltd.
B8, 4/F., Mai Hing Industrial Building,
Block B, 16-18 Hing Yip Street,
Kwun Tong, Kowloon

Contents

Preface

Although Chinese-English Dictionaries have become increasingly available on the market, one with Cantonese-Romanization is still relatively rare. For several years, teachers and students of Chinese, and in particular of the Cantonese dialect, have expressed a strong desire for having at their disposal a practical Chinese-English Dictionary which uses the well tried and now widely adopted Yale Cantonese Romanization system.

Having had over twenty years of first-hand experience in teaching Chinese to foreign students at the New Asia--Yale-in-China Chinese Language Center of the Chinese University of Hong Kong, we believe that the compilers Chik Hon-man (Section Head) and Ng Lam Sim-yuk (Chairperson of the Editorial board) are well qualified to undertake a work of this nature. After having studied numerous reference books and other dictionaries they eventually selected over six thousand of the most commonly used characters for inclusion in this dictionary. Moreover, two or more expressions are given to illustrate the use of each character, in this way bringing the character to life. Besides the Yale Romanization and the English meaning, Mandarin Pinyin has also been given for the characters thereby opening the door to a much wider use of the dictionary.

The many years of research and toil required to compile this dictionary will have been justified if students of Chinese find it helpful, enjoyable and stimulating. We believe they will.

Since any dictionary can be improved upon, we would welcome any constructive criticism.

We wish to take this opportunity to thank Mr. Ho Cheuk Sang (Assistant Director), Mr. Eddie Sin (Executive Assistant) and Brother Patrick Tierney (St. Joseph's College, Hong Kong) for their invaluable assistance in producing this dictionary.

"Dictum sapienti sat est."
"A word to the wise is sufficient."

Liu Min,
Director

July, 1989.

Introduction

1. This dictionary contains 6160 single-characters and about 12,000 terms.

2. The single-character is printed in **boldface**, simplified and/or variant forms are given in brackets after the single-character.

   e.g. 倫（伦）lèuhn

3. Cantonese and mandarin romanization are given to each single-character.

   (1) Cantonese romanization: The Yale system is used and is placed right after each single-character.

   (2) Mandarin romanization: The Han-Yu Pin-Yin system is used and is placed after the Cantonese romanization. (Md) denotes Mandarin.

   e.g. 人 yàhn (Md) rén

4. Two or three terms are given to illustrate the use of each single-character along with Cantonese romanization and English meaning.

5. If a single-character has more than one English meaning, the meanings are listed by using ①, ② etc. under each single-character.

6. Characters which have more than one pronunication will be listed, according to their different meanings, under each single-character as in the following example:

   行 hàhng (Md) xíng   to walk

   行 hahng (Md) xìng   one's conduct or behavior

   行 hòhng (Md) háng   a row, a line; a series

7. English meanings are given to the single-character and illustrative terms in the following two ways:

   (1) Equative translation:
       e.g. 書 — book, 河 — river

(2) Explanatory translation:

     e.g. 遲暮 — the later years of one's life

8. There are three indexes in this dictionary, namely:
   (1) Radical index
   (2) Number of strokes index
   (3) Cantonese romanization index

9. Three different ways may be used to look up a character in this dictionary:
   (1) By the radical
   (2) By the number of strokes
   (3) By the Cantonese romanization

10. Appendices:
   (1) Introduction to the Yale Romanization System
   (2) Introduction to the Han-Yu Pin Yin
   (3) A comparative chart for four different kinds of Cantonese Romanization System.

                                The Compilers

July 1989

勹	包	43	尸	尻	112	用	用	305		优	10		吐	53
	匀	145		尼	112		甩	305		伊	11		向	53
匕	北	43	工	左	120	田	田	305		伍	11		吒	53
匚	匹	44		巧	120		由	305		伎	11	囗	囡	74
十	半	45		巨	120		甲	306		伕	11		囟	74
卜	占	46	巾	市	122		申	306		伏	11		因	74
	卡	46		布	122	疋	疋	308		伐	11		回	74
卩	危	46	干	平	126	白	白	314		休	11	土	在	76
	卯	46	幺	幼	126	皮	皮	315		伙	11		圳	76
厶	去	48	广	庀	127	皿	皿	315	儿	兆	28		圬	76
口	叨	50	廾	弁	131	目	目	317		兇	28		圭	76
	古	50	弋	弍	132	矛	矛	322		充	28		圯	76
	句	50	弓	弗	133	矢	矢	323		先	28		地	76
	另	51		弘	133	石	石	323		光	28	夕	夙	86
	叩	51	心	必	140	示	示	329	入	全	29		多	86
	只	51	戈	戉	161	禾	禾	333	八	共	30	大	夷	88
	叫	51	手	扎	165	穴	穴	337	冂	再	31		夸	88
	召	51		打	165	立	立	340	冫	冰	32	女	奸	91
	叭	51		扔	165					決	32		她	91
	叮	51	斤	斥	199	**六畫**				冲	32		妁	91
	可	51	日	旦	202	、	兵	1	刂	刎	36		好	91
	台	51	木	末	213	一	丟	2		划	36		如	91
	叱	52		未	213		丞	2		列	36		妃	92
	史	52		本	213	丿	乒	4	力	劣	40		妄	92
	右	52		札	213	乙	乩	5	勹	匈	43	子	字	102
	叵	52	止	正	240	二	互	6	匚	匠	44		存	102
	司	52	毋	母	244		亙	6		匡	44	宀	宅	104
	叶	52	氏	民	246	亠	交	7	十	卉	45		守	104
	叼	52	水	永	247		亥	7	卩	印	47		安	104
囗	囚	74		氷	32		亦	7		危	47	寸	寺	110
	四	74		汀	247	人	仰	10	口	合	52	小	尖	111
夕	外	86		汁	247		仲	10		呼	52	山	屹	114
大	失	88		氾	247		仳	10		吃	52		屺	114
	央	88	犬	犯	293		件	10		各	52	巛	州	119
女	奴	91	玄	玄	298		价	10		吉	53	巾	帆	122
	奶	91	玉	玉	298		任	10		时	53	干	年	126
子	孕	102	瓜	瓜	303		仿	10		同	53	弓	弛	133
宀	宄	103	瓦	瓦	303		份	10		名	53	心	忖	141
	它	104	甘	甘	304		企	10		后	53		忙	141
	宄	104	生	生	304					吏	53	戈	戌	161

	侶	16	口	哎	58		姨	95	
	侷	16		咤	58		姪	95	
	便	16		咦	58		姱	95	
	係	16		咨	58		姹	95	
	促	16		咪	58		姻	95	
	俄	16		咫	58		姿	95	
	俎	16		咬	58		威	95	
	俏	16		咯	58		姣	95	
	俊	16		咧	59		娃	95	
	俐	17		咱	59	子	孩	103	
	俚	17		咳	59	宀	宣	105	
	俑	17		咸	59		客	105	
	俗	17		咽	59		宥	105	
	俘	17		呷	59		室	105	
	俟	17		哀	59		宦	106	
	保	17		哇	59	寸	封	109	
	俠	17		品	59	尸	屋	112	
	信	17		哂	59		屍	113	
儿	兗	29		哄	59		屎	113	
入	俞	29		哆	60	山	峒	115	
冂	胄	31		哈	60		峙	115	
	冒	31		哉	60		峋	115	
一	冠	31	囗	囿	75	己	巷	121	
刀	則	38	土	垠	78	巾	帥	123	
	剎	38		垢	78		帝	123	
	到	38		垣	78	幺	幽	127	
	削	38		垤	78	广	度	128	
	剋	38		垮	78		庠	128	
	剌	38	大	奎	89		麻	128	
	前	38		奔	89	廴	建	131	
力	勁	41		奕	89		廼	131	
	勃	41		奐	89		廻	131	
	勇	41		契	89	廾	弇	132	
	勉	41	女	妍	94		弈	132	
勹	匍	43		姚	94	弓	弭	133	
十	南	46		姜	94	彡	形	135	
卩	卽	47		姝	94		彥	135	
	卻	47		姥	94	彳	待	137	
厂	厚	48		姦	95		徇	137	
又	叛	50					很	137	

	律	137		挖	173
	後	137		拽	173
	徉	137		拾	174
	徊	137	攴	故	196
心	怎	144	斤	斫	200
	怒	144	方	施	201
	思	144	日	星	204
	息	144		映	204
	急	145		春	204
	怨	145		昧	205
	忽	145		昨	205
	恆	145		昭	205
	恂	145		是	205
	恃	145		昱	205
	恓	145		映	205
	恍	145		昂	205
	恢	146		昶	205
	恤	146		昫	205
	恨	146		昵	209
	恪	146	曰	曷	210
	恫	146	木	架	217
	恬	146		柜	218
	恰	146		枯	218
戶	扁	164		柱	218
	扃	164		枰	218
手	拜	171		柿	218
	括	172		柒	218
	拭	172		枳	218
	拮	172		柺	218
	拱	172		枷	218
	拯	172		枸	218
	挓	172		柁	218
	拴	172		柄	218
	挼	173		柏	219
	拷	173		某	219
	持	173		柑	219
	指	173		染	219
	挎	173		柔	219
	挑	173		柘	219
	按	173			

	暗 208		溝 266		煖 285		睦 320		筋 344
曰	會 211		溟 266		煙 285		睥 320	米	粱 349
木	極 228		溢 266		煇 285		睨 320		粲 349
	椰 228		溥 266	父	爺 290		睪 320		粳 349
	棗 228		溧 267	片	牒 291		睫 320	糸	絛 361
	楮 228		溪 267	牛	犍 293		睬 320		絹 355
	椽 228		溯 267	犬	猷 296	矢	矮 323		綃 355
	椿 228		滔 267		猻 296	石	硼 326		綆 355
	楂 228		溴 267		猿 296		碰 326		梯 355
	楊 228		溶 267		獅 296		碇 326		綁 355
	楓 228		溷 267		猾 296		碉 326		綏 355
	楚 229		溺 267	玉	瑋 301		碌 326		經 355
	楔 229		滓 267		瑕 301		碎 326		綑 175
	楝 229		滂 267		瑜 301		硼 326	网	罪 364
	楡 229		瀚 267		瑛 301		碑 326		罩 364
	楠 229		滄 267		瑚 301		碓 326		置 364
	楣 229		滅 268		瑞 301		碘 326	羊	羣 366
	楨 229		滇 268		瑟 301		碡 328		羨 366
	楫 229		滋 268		瑙 301		碁 225		義 366
	楬 229		滓 268		瑁 301	示	稟 335	耒	耡 468
	業 229		滔 268	瓦	瓶 304		祺 331	耳	聖 370
	楷 229		滙 268	田	畹 307		禁 331		聘 370
	楸 229	火	煮 283		當 308		祿 331	聿	肆 371
	楹 229		煉 283		畸 308	内	禽 332		肆 371
欠	歇 238		煌 283	广	廗 311	禾	稔 335		肅 371
	歃 238		煎 283		痰 311		稗 335	肉	腥 376
	歆 238		煒 284		痳 311		稚 335		腮 376
止	歲 240		煜 284		痼 311		稞 335		腦 376
歹	殛 242		煞 284		矮 311		稠 335		腴 376
	殣 493		煢 284		瘀 311		稜 227		腩 376
殳	殿 244		煥 284		痿 311	穴	窟 338		腫 376
	毀 244		煤 284	白	皙 315		窠 339		腰 376
毛	毽 245		煦 284	皿	盟 316	立	竪 430		腱 376
水	滑 265		煆 284		盞 316	竹	筠 343		腳 376
	溫 266		照 284	目	睞 319		筥 343		腸 377
	源 266		煨 284		睛 319		筱 343		腹 377
	溲 266		煩 284		睜 319		筲 343		腺 377
	溜 266		煬 285		睡 320		筵 343		腯 377
	準 266		煲 285		睢 320		筷 343		腭 377
	溢 266		煠 285		督 320		筦 343	臼	舅 380

	澮	274		瘼	312		縞	359		衡	408	足	踹	442
	澱	274	皿	盥	317		縟	359	衣	褪	413		踴	442
	澳	274		盧	317		縢	359		褲	413		蹂	442
	澶	274	目	瞞	321		縣	359		襯	413		蹀	442
	潰	274		瞠	321		繀	359		褰	413		踵	442
	澹	274		瞯	321	缶	罃	363		褌	413		踹	442
	潾	274		瞟	321	网	罹	364		褵	413		蹀	442
	激	275	石	磨	328	羽	翰	367	見	覦	320		踽	442
	濁	275		磧	328		翱	367		覩	415		蹂	442
	濂	275		磬	328	肉	膳	378		親	415		蹄	442
	濃	275		磡	328		膨	378	言	諛	424	車	輯	447
	澼	275		磚	328		膩	378		諸	424		輸	447
火	燈	286		磜	328	至	臻	380		謔	426		輻	447
	熹	286	示	禤	332	臼	舉	381		諭	424		頓	446
	燃	286		禦	332	舌	舘	495		諼	424	辛	辦	449
	熾	287	禾	穆	336	舟	艘	383		諝	425		辨	449
	燎	287		穌	336		艙	383		諜	425	辵	遅	457
	燉	287		積	336	艸	蔬	395		諞	425		遴	457
	燒	287		穎	336		蕈	395		諢	425		遵	457
	燔	287	穴	窺	339		蔽	395		諤	425		遷	457
	燁	287	竹	篝	345		蕃	396		諦	425		選	457
	燕	287		築	345		蕉	396		諧	425		遺	457
	燙	287		篙	345		蕊	396		諫	425		遼	458
	燜	287		篡	345		蕎	396		諮	425	邑	鄴	461
	燊	287		篤	345		蕙	396		諱	425	酉	醒	463
	燐	287		篦	345		蕺	396		譜	425		醐	463
	燄	287		篩	345		蕨	396		諶	425		醒	463
犬	獨	297		篲	394		蕩	396		諷	425	金	鋸	468
	獪	297	米	糕	349		蕪	396		諾	425		鋼	469
玉	璜	302		糍	350		蕭	396		謀	425		錄	469
	璞	302		糖	350	虫	螅	404		謁	426		錐	469
	璣	302	糸	縉	359		螃	404		謂	426		錘	469
	璘	302		緻	358		融	404		諺	426		錙	469
	璐	302		縈	359		螂	405		諡	426		錚	469
瓜	瓢	303		縊	359		螞	405	豕	豬	431		錠	469
瓦	甌	304		緼	359		螟	405		豫	431		錢	469
广	瘴	312		緝	359		螢	405	豸	貓	432		錦	469
	瘳	312		縐	359		螣	405	貝	賴	436		錕	469
	癃	312		縛	359		螽	401		賭	436		錫	469
	瘻	312		繽	359	行	衛	408	赤	赭	438		錮	469

	錯	469	魚	鮑	503	彳	徽	140	水	濟	275		瞭	321
	錳	470	鳥	鴕	505	心	懇	159		濕	275		瞰	322
	錶	470		鴛	505		懇	159		濘	275		瞳	322
門	閣	475		鴣	505		應	159		濠	275		瞶	322
	閣	475		鴦	505		懋	159		濡	275	矢	矯	323
	關	475		鴨	505		薏	159		濤	276	石	礦	328
	閣	475	黑	黔	509		懷	159		濫	276		磯	328
阜	隨	480		默	509		懺	159		濬	276		磴	328
	隆	480	龍	龍	512		懦	159		濮	276		磷	328
	陳	481	龜	龜	512	戈	戲	163		濯	276		礁	328
	險	481				手	擎	190		濰	276		磽	328
隹	雖	482	**十七畫**				擊	191		濱	276	示	禪	332
雨	霍	484	人	償	26		擘	191		濛	276		禧	332
	霎	484		傭	27		擯	192		澗	287	禾	穗	337
	霏	485		優	27		擠	192	火	燧	288		穉	335
	霑	485	力	勵	42		擢	192		營	288	穴	窿	339
	霓	485	口	嚎	72		擦	192		燠	288	竹	歉	346
	霖	485		嚅	72		撐	192		燥	288		篷	346
靑	靜	486		嚐	72		擬	193		燦	288		篼	346
	靛	486		嚀	72		擱	193		燬	288		簏	343
面	靦	487		嚇	72		擄	193		燭	288		篠	346
革	鞝	487		嚏	72	攴	斂	198		燮	288		簍	346
頁	頤	490	土	壓	84		斂	198		燴	288		簀	346
	頭	490		壎	84	日	暴	209	片	牆	290		簇	346
	頰	490		壑	84		暖	209	犬	獰	297		簁	346
	領	490		壕	84	木	檀	234		獲	297		簍	346
	頸	491	女	嬪	101		檄	234	玉	璨	302		簁	346
	頹	491		嬰	101		檜	235		環	302		簇	346
	頻	491		嬲	101		檉	235	瓦	甑	304	米	糙	350
食	餐	494		孀	101		檔	235		甏	304		糜	350
	餚	494	子	孺	103		檜	235	广	癆	312		糞	350
	餒	494	尢	尷	111		檟	235		療	312		糟	350
	餓	494	山	嵥	118		檻	235		癌	313		糠	350
	餘	494		嶺	119		檢	235		癇	313	糸	縭	360
馬	駭	497		嶼	119		檔	235		癉	313		縱	360
	駱	497		嶽	119		檸	235	皿	盪	317		縫	360
骨	骸	500	巾	幬	125		檗	235	目	瞥	321		縮	360
	骼	500		幫	125	歹	殭	243		瞬	321		縲	360
髟	髻	501		幪	125		殮	243		瞧	321		縴	360
	鬃	501	弓	彌	134	毛	氈	245		瞪	321		縹	360

	麿	360		薔	397	豕	豳	431	門	闐	475	齊 齋 511
	總	360		薤	397	豸	貕	432		闇	475	侖 侖 512
	績	360		薛	397	貝	賺	436		闊	475	
	繁	360		薦	397		賻	437		闋	475	**十八畫**
	繃	361		薨	397		購	437		闊	475	人 儲 27
	繆	361		薪	397		賽	437		闌	476	儡 27
	繰	361		嬬	397		臏	39		闔	476	厂 龎 131
	縫	361	虍	虧	400	走	趨	439	阜	隱	481	又 叢 50
	鯀	361	虫	螢	405	足	蹈	443		隢	481	口 嚕 72
	縐	413		孟	405		蹇	443	隶	隸	481	土 壙 84
缶	罄	363		螯	405		蹉	443	隹	雖	482	壘 84
	罅	363		螳	405		蹋	443	雨	霜	485	女 嬸 101
羊	義	366		螺	405		蹊	443		霞	485	巾 幮 125
羽	翳	367		螻	405		蹌	443	革	鞠	488	彐 彝 135
耳	聱	370		蟀	405	車	輾	447	韋	韓	488	心 懣 159
	聯	370		蟄	405		輿	448	頁	顆	491	懨 160
	聰	370		蟆	405		轂	448	風	颶	492	懟 160
	聲	370		蟋	405		轄	448	食	餛	494	戈 戴 163
	聳	371		蟑	405		轅	448		餞	494	戳 163
肉	膺	378		蟎	405	辵	避	458		餅	495	手 擲 193
	膾	378	衣	褶	413		邁	458		館	495	擴 193
	膿	378		褸	413		邃	458		餡	495	擷 193
	臀	378		襄	413		邀	458		鮓	373	擺 193
	臂	378		褻	413		邂	458	馬	騁	497	擻 193
	臆	378		褳	413		還	458		駿	498	擾 193
	臊	378	見	覬	415		邅	458	骨	骾	500	擤 193
	膰	378	言	謄	426	酉	醯	463	魚	鮫	503	攄 193
	膽	378		謊	426		醜	464		鮭	503	攴 斃 198
	臉	378		謫	426	金	錨	470		鮮	503	斤 斷 200
	臃	379		謎	426		鍋	470	鳥	鴿	505	日 曙 209
	膷	379		謇	426		鍍	470		鴻	505	曜 209
臣	臨	379		謐	426		鍛	470	鹿	麋	507	矇 210
艮	艱	383		誘	426		鍾	470	麥	麵	508	曛 210
艸	薄	396		謙	426		鍱	470	黍	黏	508	月 朦 212
	蕾	396		謚	426		鍬	470	黑	點	509	木 檬 235
	薇	397		講	426		錯	470		黛	509	檯 235
	鮜	397		謝	427		鍊	470		黜	509	檳 235
	蕙	397		謠	427		鍵	470		黝	509	檸 236
	薐	397	谷	豁	430		鎂	470	黹	黻	510	檻 236
	薑	397		谿	430		鏱	465	鼻	鼾	511	櫃 236

部	字	頁	部	字	頁	部	字	頁	部	字	頁	部	字	頁
欠	歟	239		簞	346		蟠	406		鎗	231		鵠	505
止	歸	241		簣	347	襾	覆	414		鑄	448	麥	麨	507
夕	殯	243		簡	347	見	覦	415	門	闖	476	黑	點	509
水	瀑	276		簀	347	角	觸	416		闐	476	電	黿	205
	濺	276		簪	347	言	謾	427		闓	476	鼓	鼕	510
	濼	277	米	糧	350		謨	427		闕	476	鼠	鼬	510
	濾	277	糸	繚	361		謫	427		闔	476			
	瀆	277		繕	361		謬	427	隹	雙	482	**十九畫**		
	瀉	277		織	361		謳	427		雛	483	口	嚮	72
	瀋	277		繙	361		謹	427		雜	483		嚦	72
	瀏	277		繞	361	豆	豐	430		雞	483		嚥	72
	瀅	277		繡	361	貝	贅	437	革	鞭	488		嚨	72
火	燼	288		繢	361	足	蹣	443		鞦	488	土	壟	84
	燹	288	缶	罇	234		蹬	443	韋	韙	488		壘	85
	燾	288		罈	85		蹤	443	頁	額	491		壞	85
爪	爵	289	羽	翼	367		蹢	443		題	491	子	孿	103
犬	獵	297		翹	367		蹠	443		顎	491	宀	寵	109
	獷	297		翔	367		蹦	443		顏	491	广	廬	130
玉	璧	302		翻	368		蹟	451	風	颺	492		龐	131
	璿	302	耳	職	371	身	軀	445	食	餬	495	心	懲	160
瓦	甕	304		聵	371	車	轉	448		饅	495		懷	160
疒	癘	313		聶	371		轆	448	香	馥	496		懵	160
	癖	313	肉	臍	379		轇	448	馬	騎	498		懶	160
	癒	313	臼	舊	381	辵	邇	458		騅	498	手	攀	194
目	瞻	322	舟	艟	383		邃	458		騈	498		攏	194
	瞽	322	艸	薩	397		邀	458	骨	髀	500	日	曠	210
	瞿	322		薈	397	邑	廓	461	彡	鬆	501		曝	210
	瞼	322		薰	397	酉	醫	464		鬃	501	木	櫓	236
石	礎	328		薺	397		醪	464		鬌	501		櫚	236
	礛	327		藉	397		醬	464	鬥	鬩	501		櫛	236
	礓	328		藍	398	里	釐	465	鬼	魑	502		櫝	236
示	禮	332		藏	398	金	鎖	470		魍	502		櫥	236
禾	穠	337		貌	398		鎊	470		魏	502		櫟	236
	穡	337	虫	蟮	406		鎧	470	魚	鯀	503	水	瀝	277
	穢	337		蟠	406		鎬	471		鯁	500		瀦	277
穴	竇	339		蟪	406		鎮	471		鯉	503		瀨	277
	竅	339		蟬	406		鎰	471		鯢	503		瀘	277
竹	簧	346		蟯	406		鎳	471		鯊	503		瀚	277
	簫	346		蟲	406		鎢	471	鳥	鵑	505		瀛	278
	簹	346		蟛	406		鎔	286		鵝	505		瀟	278

			baahk	蔔	395	bah	吧	56
à	呀	55	baahn	爿	290	bah	罷	364
à	啊	61	baahn	扮	166	bahn	笨	341
á	嘠	67	baahn	辦	449	bahng	蹦	443
a	呀	55	báai	捭	176	baht	拔	171
a	阿	477	báai	擺	193	baht	鈸	466
a	啊	61	baai	拜	171	baht	跋	440
aái	欸	238	baai	湃	265	baht	弼	134
aai	隘	480	baaih	敗	197	bài	跛	440
āak	扼	166	baaih	憊	158	bai	箄	344
aat	押	169	baaih	稗	335	bai	閉	474
aat	戛	162	baak	百	314	bai	蔽	395
aat	遏	455	baak	佰	15	baih	幣	125
aau	坳	78	baak	伯	11	baih	弊	132
ai	縊	359	baak	柏	219	baih	敝	197
àm	諳	425	baak	舶	382	baih	斃	198
àm	鵪	505	baak	擘	235	baih	狴	294
ám	黯	509	bāak	迫	451	baih	薜	397
ām	庵	128	bàan	班	299	baih	陛	478
ām	菴	128	bàan	斑	199	bāk	北	43
àng	罌	363	bàan	瘢	313	bām	泵	251
āng	鶯	363	bàan	頒	490	bām	乓	1
au	慪	156	báan	坂	77	bàn	賓	435
			báan	板	216	bàn	濱	276
bà	巴	121	báan	舨	382	bàn	檳	235
bà	芭	384	báan	版	290	bàn	鬢	501
bà	爸	289	báan	阪	477	bàn	賁	434
bà	疤	309	báan	闆	475	bàn	邠	459
bà	萡	392	baan	扮	166	bàn	彬	135
bá	把	167	baat	八	29	bàn	斌	199
bá	靶	487	baat	捌	176	bàn	瀕	277
ba	霸	485	bàau	包	43	bàn	奔	89
ba	壩	85	bàau	胞	373	bàn	犇	292
ba	灞	279	bàau	苞	385	bàn	闧	431
bā	叭	51	bàau	炮	280	bán	品	59
bā	吧	56	bàau	鮑	503	bán	稟	335
baahk	白	314	báau	飽	493	ban	儐	26
baahk	帛	123	baau	爆	288	ban	嬪	101
baahk	蔔	43	baauh	鮑	503	ban	擯	192

ban	繽	362	beih	備	23	bìng	冰	32
ban	殯	243	beih	憊	158	bíng	丙	2
bàng	崩	117	beih	莄	393	bíng	炳	281
bàng	嘣	69	beih	箆	345	bíng	秉	333
bàng	繃	361	béng	餅	495	bíng	屏	115
báng	甭	305	beng	柄	218	bing	并	126
bāt	不	2	bihn	弁	131	bing	併	18
bāt	筆	342	bihn	卞	46	bing	迸	454
bāt	畢	307	bihn	抃	166	bing	柄	218
bāt	嗶	68	bihn	汴	248	bing	摒	187
bè	啤	62	bihn	忭	142	bīt	必	140
behng	病	310	bihn	便	16	bit	憋	157
bèi	卑	45	bihn	諞	425	bìu	標	232
bèi	裨	412	bihn	辨	449	bìu	鏢	471
bèi	碑	326	bihn	辯	449	bìu	鑣	473
bèi	陂	477	bihng	並	3	bìu	彪	135
bèi	悲	150	bihng	病	310	bìu	杓	215
bèi	羆	365	biht	別	36	bìu	飆	493
béi	匕	43	biht	蟞	443	bíu	表	409
béi	比	244	biht	弊	134	bíu	俵	18
béi	妣	93	biht	鼈	510	bíu	裱	412
béi	彼	136	bīk	迫	451	bíu	婊	98
béi	媲	99	bīk	逼	454	bìu	表	409
béi	俾	18	bīk	愎	152	bìu	錶	470
béi	畀	306	bīk	碧	326	bìu	驃	499
béi	髀	500	bīk	辟	449	bò	陂	477
bei	惫	245	bīk	壁	83	bò	玻	299
bei	庇	127	bīk	壁	302	bò	波	253
bei	泌	252	bìn	邊	458	bò	坡	77
bei	秘	334	bìn	鯿	503	bò	菠	390
bei	費	434	bìn	鞭	488	bò	簸	347
bei	痹	311	bìn	辮	362	bò	嶓	118
bei	賁	434	bín	扁	164	bó	跛	440
bei	轡	449	bín	匾	44	bo	播	190
bei	臂	378	bín	貶	433	bo	簸	347
beih	匕	43	bin	變	429	bohk	泊	252
beih	鼻	510	bìng	乒	4	bohk	舶	382
beih	避	458	bìng	兵	30	bohk	鉑	466
beih	被	410	bìng	并	126	bohk	箔	344

bohk	磚	329	bouh	簿	347	bun	半	45
bohk	薄	396	bouh	暴	208	but	鉢	467
bohk	雹	484	bouh	曝	210			
bohk	魄	502	bouh	埠	79	chà	叉	49
bohk	濼	277	buhk	瀑	276	chà	差	120
bohng	傍	22	buhk	曝	210	chà	杈	166
bohng	鎊	470	buhk	僕	24	chà	杈	214
bok	博	46	buhk	濮	276	chà	炆	238
bok	搏	184	buhk	幞	125	cha	侘	15
bok	膊	377	buhn	伴	11	cha	姹	95
bok	縛	359	buhn	拌	170	cha	岔	114
bok	駁	496	buhn	畔	306	cha	汊	247
bok	亳	7	buhn	絆	354	cha	衩	409
bok	剝	38	buhn	胖	373	cha	銌	468
bòng	梆	223	buhn	叛	50	cha	詫	420
bòng	邦	459	buht	孛	102	chaahk	扠	166
bòng	幫	125	buht	勃	41	chaahk	賊	435
bòng	浜	256	buht	浡	256	chàahm	翟	367
bóng	榜	230	buht	渤	264	chàahm	讒	429
bóng	膀	377	buht	脖	375	chàahm	饞	496
bóng	綁	355	buht	荸	388	chàahm	攙	194
bòu	保	285	buht	餑	494	chàahm	巉	119
bòu	褒	413	buht	撥	188	chàahm	慚	156
bóu	保	17	bùi	杯	215	chàahm	蠶	407
bóu	堡	80	bui	貝	432	chàahn	殘	242
bóu	褓	413	bui	狽	295	chàahng	倀	18
bóu	圃	75	bui	背	373	chàahng	根	226
bóu	補	411	bui	褙	413	chàai	差	120
bóu	寶	109	bui	揹	183	chàai	猜	295
bóu	鴇	504	bui	輩	447	chàai	釵	466
bou	布	122	būi	杯	215	chaai	搋	184
bou	佈	12	buih	孛	102	cháai	踹	441
bou	怖	143	buih	悖	148	chàaih	踹	442
bou	報	80	buih	焙	282	chàaih	柴	220
bou	埔	79	būk	卜	46	chàaih	豺	431
bouh	步	240	bùn	般	382	chàaih	儕	26
bouh	部	460	bùn	搬	185	chaak	策	343
bouh	哺	60	bún	本	213	chaak	冊	31
bouh	捕	176	bún	苯	386	chaak	柵	220

chaak	拆	170	chàhn	陳	479	chāp	葺	393
chàam	坼	78	chàhn	塵	82	chāp	緝	357
chàam	攙	194	chàhng	曾	211	chāp	輯	447
chàam	參	48	chàhng	嶒	118	chāp	戢	162
cháam	慘	155	chàhng	層	114	chāt	七	1
chaam	懺	160	chài	妻	93	chāt	柒	220
chaam	杉	214	chài	凄	33	chāt	漆	269
chàan	餐	494	chài	悽	149	chàu	抽	169
cháan	產	305	chài	淒	260	chàu	秋	333
cháan	剷	39	chài	萋	391	chàu	楸	229
cháan	鏟	471	chài	栖	223	chàu	鰍	503
chaan	粲	349	chài	棲	228	chàu	鞦	488
chaan	燦	288	chai	切	35	chàu	瘳	312
chaan	璨	302	chai	傺	24	chàu	搊	184
chàang	撐	189	chai	砌	324	cháu	丑	2
chàang	瞠	321	chai	沏	250	cháu	瞅	320
cháang	鐺	472	chàih	齊	511	cháu	醜	464
cháang	橙	234	chàih	薺	397	chau	臭	380
chaap	插	182	cháih	薺	397	chau	嗅	67
chaat	刷	37	chāk	測	265	chau	溴	267
chaat	察	108	chāk	側	152	chau	湊	34
chaat	擦	192	chàm	參	49	chau	湊	263
chàau	獺	297	chàm	侵	16	chàuh	仇	8
chàau	抄	167	chám	寢	108	chàuh	囚	74
chàau	鈔	466	cham	讖	429	chàuh	泅	252
cháau	炒	280	chàn	嗔	68	chàuh	惆	150
cháau	吵	55	chàn	瞋	321	chàuh	稠	335
chàauh	巢	120	chàn	親	415	chàuh	裯	412
chàh	茶	387	chán	哂	59	chàuh	綢	356
chàh	搽	185	chán	抿	180	chàuh	酋	462
chàh	查	220	chán	診	419	chàuh	遒	456
chàh	碴	327	chán	殄	241	chàuh	酬	462
chàhm	槎	231	chán	疹	309	chàuh	雛	429
chàhm	尋	110	chán	畛	307	chàuh	籌	347
chàhm	噚	71	chán	軫	446	chàuh	儔	26
chàhm	潯	272	chan	親	415	chàuh	幬	125
chàhm	沉	249	chan	襯	413	chàuh	躊	444
chàhm	撏	188	chan	儭	236	chàuh	疇	308
cháhm	蕈	395	chan	趁	438	chè	車	455

chè	奢	90	cheui	淬	261	chèung	菖	390
ché	尺	111	cheui	翠	367	chèung	倀	18
ché	且	2	cheui	脆	374	chèung	嗆	67
ché	扯	166	cheui	趣	439	chèung	囪	74
chèh	邪	459	cheui	毳	245	chèung	菖	390
chèh	斜	199	cheui	覷	415	chèung	鏘	471
chèh	崋	446	chèuih	徐	137	chèung	搶	185
chek	尺	111	chèuih	除	478	cheung	唱	62
chek	呎	56	chèuih	蜍	403	cheung	倡	20
chèng	青	486	chèuih	椎	227	cheung	熗	163
chèuhn	秦	334	chèuih	隋	479	cheung	戧	285
chèuhn	旬	202	chèuih	隨	480	cheung	暢	208
chèuhn	循	139	chèuih	蔚	130	cheung	鬯	501
chèuhn	巡	120	chèuih	捶	181	chēung	槍	231
chèuhng	長	473	chèuih	錘	469	chēung	鏘	471
chèuhng	伜	14	chèuih	箠	344	chēung	窗	338
chèuhng	牂	162	chèuih	捶	183	chēut	出	35
chèuhng	祥	330	chèuih	槌	230	chēut	齣	511
chèuhng	詳	421	cheuk	勺	42	chì	差	120
chèuhng	庠	128	cheuk	灼	279	chì	蚩	401
chèuhng	翔	367	cheuk	芍	384	chì	嗤	68
chèuhng	場	81	cheuk	桌	222	chì	媸	99
chèuhng	腸	377	cheuk	卓	45	chì	螭	405
chèuhng	牆	290	cheuk	倬	20	chì	魑	502
chèuhng	薔	397	cheuk	焯	283	chì	郗	460
chèuhng	嬙	101	cheuk	逴	453	chì	笞	341
chèuhng	檣	235	cheuk	踔	442	chì	疵	310
chèui	吹	55	cheuk	綽	357	chì	癡	313
chèui	炊	280	cheuk	戳	163	chì	雌	482
chèui	崔	117	cheuk	鵲	505	chí	豕	431
chèui	催	23	cheuk	瀉	273	chí	矢	323
chèui	摧	187	chèun	春	204	chí	此	240
chèui	璀	302	chèun	椿	228	chí	恥	147
chèui	衰	409	chèun	鶉	506	chí	侈	14
chèui	縗	359	chéun	蠢	407	chí	始	93
chèui	趣	439	chèung	昌	203	chí	柿	218
chéui	取	50	chèung	倡	20	chí	摛	184
chéui	娶	97	chèung	娼	97	chí	褫	413
cheui	啐	63	chèung	猖	295	chí	齒	511

chi	次	237	chíhn	踐	441	chìng	青	486
chi	恣	147	chíhn	濺	276	chìng	菁	389
chi	刺	37	chìhng	呈	54	chìng	清	262
chi	眥	64	chìhng	程	335	chìng	蜻	403
chi	廁	129	chìhng	裎	411	chìng	稱	335
chi	熾	287	chìhng	情	149	chìng	檉	235
chi	幟	125	chìhng	晴	207	chìng	蟶	406
chi	翅	366	chìhng	澄	273	chíng	請	424
chi	賜	435	chìhng	懲	160	chíng	逞	453
chi	懘	159	chìk	彳	136	chíng	拯	172
chìh	池	248	chìk	叱	52	chíng	騁	497
chìh	弛	133	chìk	斥	199	ching	秤	334
chìh	馳	496	chìk	戚	162	ching	稱	335
chìh	茲	387	chìk	慼	157	chip	妾	93
chìh	磁	327	chìk	槭	232	chit	切	35
chìh	糍	350	chìk	敕	197	chit	設	418
chìh	慈	155	chìk	飭	493	chit	澈	273
chìh	茨	387	chik	赤	438	chit	撤	189
chìh	治	252	chìm	僉	24	chit	徹	140
chìh	瓷	304	chìm	簽	347	chit	轍	448
chìh	持	173	chìm	殲	243	chìu	昭	205
chìh	墀	83	chìm	纖	363	chìu	超	439
chìh	匙	43	chìm	籤	348	chìu	繰	362
chìh	祠	330	chím	謟	423	chìu	釗	465
chìh	詞	420	chìm	僭	25	chìu	鍬	470
chìh	臍	379	chìm	暹	209	chíu	愀	152
chìh	跙	442	chìm	槧	231	chíu	肖	372
chìh	辭	449	chìm	塹	82	chiu	俏	16
chìh	遲	457	chìn	千	45	chiu	悄	147
chíh	恃	145	chìn	仟	9	chiu	誚	422
chíh	柿	218	chìn	扦	165	chiu	峭	116
chíh	汜	247	chìn	阡	476	chiu	鞘	487
chíh	似	11	chìn	芊	383	chìuh	樵	233
chíh	姒	93	chìn	玔	304	chìuh	瞧	321
chihm	潛	271	chìn	遷	457	chìuh	憔	157
chìhn	前	38	chìn	轞	488	chìuh	朝	212
chìhn	錢	469	chín	淺	262	chìuh	潮	272
chìhn	廛	130	chín	闡	476	chìuh	晁	205
chìhn	纏	363	chín	濺	276	chò	初	36

chò	磋	327	chòng	蒼	393	chúhng	重	465
chò	嵯	118	chòng	艙	383	chūk	束	215
chò	搓	183	chóng	敞	197	chūk	速	453
chò	蹉	443	chóng	惝	150	chūk	涑	258
chò	芻	385	chóng	廠	130	chūk	促	16
chò	雛	483	chóng	昶	205	chūk	齪	511
chó	楚	229	chóng	氅	245	chūk	蹙	443
chó	礎	328	chóng	闖	476	chūk	蹴	444
cho	挫	174	chong	創	39	chūk	俶	18
cho	銼	468	chong	愴	154	chūk	畜	307
cho	錯	469	chong	闖	476	chūk	搐	186
chòh	鋤	468	chōng	瘡	312	chūk	蓄	394
chòh	雛	483	chòu	操	191	chūk	嗽	346
chòhng	床	127	chòu	粗	348	chūk	簇	346
chòhng	牀	290	chóu	草	388	chūk	蠹	322
chòhng	幢	125	chou	措	180	chùng	充	28
chòhng	藏	398	chou	厝	48	chùng	憧	157
chói	采	464	chou	噪	71	chùng	聰	370
chói	彩	135	chou	澡	274	chùng	沖	250
chói	採	179	chou	燥	288	chùng	衝	408
chói	踩	442	chou	譟	428	chùng	樅	232
chói	綵	356	chou	躁	444	chùng	衷	409
chói	睬	320	chou	糙	350	chùng	忽	145
chói	睞	441	chou	愺	156	chùng	蔥	392
choi	采	464	chou	酢	462	chùng	傯	22
choi	菜	390	chou	醋	463	chùng	囪	74
choi	蔡	395	chòuh	曹	211	chùng	涌	258
choi	塞	82	chòuh	岨	242	chùng	沖	32
choi	賽	437	chòuh	徂	136	chùng	仲	141
chòih	才	164	chòuh	嘈	69	chúng	塚	81
chòih	材	214	chòuh	槽	231	chúng	冢	32
chòih	財	432	chòuh	漕	271	chúng	寵	109
chòih	裁	410	chùhng	松	216	chyú	褚	412
chok	錯	469	chùhng	淞	260	chyu	處	400
chòng	倉	18	chùhng	從	138	chyùh	廚	130
chòng	傖	23	chùhng	重	465	chyùh	幮	125
chòng	創	39	chùhng	琮	300	chyùh	櫥	236
chòng	滄	267	chùhng	蟲	406			
chòng	蹌	443	chùhng	叢	50			

chyùh	蹰	444	chyun	吋	53	dàam	擔	192
chyùh	蹄	444	chyun	串	3	dáam	膽	378
chyùh	蛛	403	chyun	釧	466	daam	石	324
chyúh	佇	12	chyun	竄	339	daam	担	172
chyúh	苧	386	chyun	攛	194	daam	擔	192
chyúh	貯	430	chyun	爨	289	dàan	丹	1
chyúh	紵	353	chyut	捽	177	dàan	單	66
chyúh	署	364	chyut	撮	190	dàan	簞	346
chyúh	曙	209				dàan	鄲	461
chyúh	儲	27	dá	打	165	dàan	彈	243
chyúh	杵	216	dā	打	165	daan	旦	202
chyúh	杼	216	daahm	淡	260	daan	誕	422
chyúh	柱	218	daahm	氮	246	daap	搭	185
chyúh	楮	228	daahm	萏	391	daap	答	343
chyùhn	躇	443	daahm	澹	274	daat	妲	93
chyùhn	遄	455	daahm	啖	63	daat	怛	143
chyùhn	泉	254	daahn	但	12	daat	笪	342
chyùhn	存	102	daahn	蛋	402	daat	靼	487
chyùhn	全	29	daahn	撣	190	dahk	特	292
chyùhn	荃	388	daahn	憚	158	dahn	炖	280
chyùhn	筌	342	daahn	彈	134	dahn	炖	287
chyùhn	痊	310	daahp	沓	250	dahng	戥	162
chyùhn	詮	421	daahp	踏	441	dahng	澄	273
chyùhn	銓	467	daahp	蹋	443	dahng	鄧	461
chyùhn	傳	23	daaht	笪	342	dahng	瞪	321
chyùhn	椽	228	daaht	達	456	dahng	蹬	444
chyùhn	攢	194	daaht	韃	488	daht	凸	34
chyùn	川	119	daaih	獃	296	daht	突	338
chyùn	穿	338	dáai	歹	241	dài	氐	245
chyùn	村	214	daai	帶	123	dài	低	13
chyùn	釧	466	daai	戴	163	dài	胝	373
chyùn	邨	214	dāai	呆	56	dái	氐	245
chyún	竄	339	daaih	大	87	dái	底	127
chyún	忖	141	dàam	眈	318	dái	柢	220
chyún	喘	65	dàam	聃	369	dái	抵	169
chyún	惴	152	dàam	耽	369	dái	骶	169
chyún	揣	182	dàam	酖	462	dái	邸	459
chyún	舛	382	dàam	担	172	dái	牴	292
chyun	寸	109	dàam	儋	26	dái	詆	419

dái	砥	324	dehk	糴	350	dihn	甸	306
dai	帝	123	deih	地	76	dihn	鈿	466
dai	禘	331	dèng	釘	465	dihn	奠	90
dai	蒂	393	deuhk	諑	424	dihn	電	484
dai	締	358	deuhn	沌	249	dihn	淀	259
dai	諦	425	deuhn	囤	74	dihn	靛	486
daih	弟	133	deuhn	肫	318	dihn	殿	244
daih	悌	148	deuhn	頓	490	dihn	澱	274
daih	娣	96	deuhn	鈍	466	dihn	墊	82
daih	第	342	deuhn	遁	454	dihng	定	105
daih	棣	226	deuhn	燉	287	dihng	訂	417
daih	逮	454	dèui	堆	80	dihp	喋	65
daih	隸	481	deui	兌	28	dihp	碟	326
daih	遞	456	deui	碓	326	dihp	牒	291
dāk	德	139	deui	對	110	dihp	蝶	404
dāk	得	138	deuih	敦	197	dihp	諜	425
dàn	磴	328	deuih	憝	158	dihp	蹀	442
dán	蕈	444	deuih	隊	480	dihp	疊	308
dàng	登	314	deuih	懟	160	diht	垤	78
dáng	等	342	deuk	涿	259	diht	昳	205
dang	戥	162	deuk	啄	63	diht	帙	122
dang	凳	34	deuk	琢	300	diht	迭	451
dang	磴	328	deuk	椓	228	diht	耋	368
dang	鐙	472	deuk	斲	200	diht	秩	334
dāng	燈	286	dèun	惇	150	diht	峡	303
dàu	兜	29	dèun	墩	83	dīk	的	314
dàu	篼	346	dèun	敦	197	dīk	嫡	99
dáu	斗	199	dèun	頓	72	dīk	蹢	443
dáu	抖	167	dèun	蹾	443	dīk	滴	269
dáu	阣	478	dihk	狄	294	dìm	掂	178
dáu	蚪	401	dihk	荻	388	dím	點	509
dau	鬥	501	dihk	迪	451	dim	店	128
dauh	豆	430	dihk	滴	269	dim	惦	150
dauh	痘	310	dihk	嘀	69	dim	玷	298
dauh	逗	453	dihk	啲	69	dim	墊	82
dauh	讀	429	dihk	敵	198	dìn	滇	268
dauh	竇	339	dihk	滌	268	dìn	巔	119
dè	爹	290	dihk	翟	367	dìn	顛	491
dehk	笛	341	dihn	佃	12	dín	典	30

dín	碘	326	dohk	踱	442	douh	悼	149
din	墊	82	dohk	鐸	472	douh	道	456
dīn	癲	313	dohng	宕	104	douh	導	110
dìng	丁	1	dohng	蕩	396	douh	度	128
dìng	仃	8	dohng	盪	317	douh	渡	263
dìng	叮	51	doi	怠	144	douh	鍍	470
dìng	盯	317	doih	殆	242	douh	稻	336
dìng	疔	308	doih	待	137	douh	蹈	443
dìng	酊	461	doih	代	9	douh	盜	316
dìng	釘	465	doih	岱	115	douh	燾	288
díng	頂	489	doih	玳	299	douh	幬	125
díng	酊	461	doih	袋	410	duhk	毒	244
díng	鼎	510	doih	黛	509	duhk	頓	490
ding	碇	326	dòng	當	308	duhk	瀆	277
ding	訂	417	dòng	噹	72	duhk	櫝	236
ding	錠	469	dòng	襠	414	duhk	犢	293
dīng	町	306	dòng	鐺	472	duhk	牘	291
dit	跌	440	dóng	擋	191	duhk	讀	429
dìu	刁	35	dóng	檔	235	duhk	黷	509
dìu	叼	52	dóng	黨	509	duhk	獨	297
dìu	丢	2	dóng	讜	430	duhk	髑	500
dìu	凋	33	dong	當	308	duhng	洞	256
dìu	彫	135	dong	擋	191	duhng	恫	146
dìu	碉	326	dòu	圳	140	duhng	峒	115
dìu	雕	482	dòu	叨	50	duhng	胴	374
dìu	鵰	505	dòu	都	460	duhng	動	42
dìu	貂	431	dóu	島	116	duhng	慟	155
diu	弔	132	dóu	搗	184	dūk	督	320
diu	釣	466	dóu	倒	19	dūk	篤	345
diuh	調	423	dóu	堵	80	dùng	冬	32
diuh	掉	178	dóu	睹	320	dùng	佟	14
dò	多	86	dóu	賭	436	dùng	咚	58
dò	哆	60	dou	妒	92	dùng	東	216
dó	朵	213	dou	到	37	dùng	鼕	510
dó	躲	445	dou	倒	19	dúng	董	392
dó	剁	37	dou	歎	198	dúng	懂	159
dó	跺	441	dou	蠹	407	dúng	踵	442
doh	惰	151	dōu	刀	35	dung	凍	33
dohk	度	128	douh	杜	215	dung	棟	226

dyuhn	段	243		fàan	旛	125		fai	芾	385
dyuhn	煅	284		fàan	繙	361		fai	肺	373
dyuhn	緞	358		fàan	翻	368		fai	怫	144
dyuhn	斷	200		fáan	反	49		fai	沸	251
dyuht	奪	90		fáan	返	450		fai	費	434
dyùn	耑	369		faan	氾	247		fai	廢	130
dyùn	端	340		faan	汎	248		faih	吠	54
dyún	短	323		faan	泛	250		fàn	分	35
dyun	鍛	470		faan	販	433		fàn	芬	384
dyun	斷	200		faat	法	253		fàn	吩	54
				faat	珐	299		fàn	氛	246
eih	欸	238		faat	砝	324		fàn	紛	352
				faat	發	314		fàn	雰	483
fà	花	384		faat	髮	500		fàn	熏	285
fa	化	43		fàhn	棼	227		fàn	曛	210
fàahn	凡	34		fàhn	汾	249		fàn	薰	397
fàahn	帆	122		fàhn	濆	274		fàn	醺	464
fàahn	梵	225		fàhn	坟	83		fàn	勳	42
fàahn	煩	284		fàhn	墳	83		fàn	昏	204
fàahn	樊	232		fàhn	焚	282		fàn	惛	150
fàahn	蕃	396		fàhn	忿	143		fàn	婚	97
fàahn	旛	287		fáhn	僨	25		fàn	闇	475
fàahn	藩	398		fáhn	憤	158		fàn	葷	393
fàahn	膰	318		fáhn	奮	91		fán	粉	348
fàahn	繁	360		fahn	分	35		fan	訓	417
fàahn	攀	329		fahn	份	10		fan	糞	350
faahn	犯	293		faht	乏	4		fāt	芾	385
faahn	范	387		faht	伐	11		fāt	弗	133
faahn	飯	493		faht	筏	343		fāt	拂	169
faahn	梵	225		faht	閥	474		fāt	彿	136
faahn	範	345		faht	佛	13		fāt	氟	246
faahn	瓣	303		faht	怫	144		fāt	緋	353
faai	快	141		faht	罰	364		fāt	靐	500
faai	筷	343		fài	揮	183		fāt	忽	142
faai	塊	81		fài	煇	285		fāt	淴	261
faai	傀	22		fài	暉	208		fāt	惚	150
faai	噲	72		fài	輝	447		fāt	囫	74
fàan	番	307		fài	徽	140		fāt	笏	341
fàan	幡	125		fài	麾	508		fāt	紱	353

fāt	炊	238	fó	顆	491	fù	桴	223
fāt	窟	338	fo	貨	433	fù	孵	103
fāt	歘	510	fo	課	423	fù	呼	57
fáu	缶	363	fòhng	防	477	fù	枯	218
fáu	否	54	fòhng	妨	93	fù	骷	500
fáu	剖	38	fòhng	房	164	fù	敷	198
fàuh	涪	258	fok	縛	359	fù	呼	57
fàuh	浮	256	fok	鑊	322	fù	跗	440
fàuh	蜉	403	fok	攉	195	fù	剕	37
fauh	阜	476	fok	霍	484	fù	戲	163
fauh	埠	79	fok	藿	399	fù	膚	377
fè	啡	62	fòng	方	200	fù	夫	87
fèi	妃	92	fòng	坊	76	fù	伕	11
fèi	飛	493	fòng	芳	385	fù	趺	440
fèi	非	486	fòng	枋	217	fù	麩	507
fèi	菲	390	fòng	肪	372	fú	父	289
fèi	緋	357	fòng	肓	372	fú	斧	200
fèi	扉	164	fòng	慌	154	fú	釜	465
fèi	蜚	403	fòng	荒	388	fú	苦	386
fèi	霏	485	fòng	謊	426	fú	甫	305
féi	匪	44	fóng	仿	10	fú	脯	375
féi	悱	149	fóng	彷	136	fú	撫	189
féi	菲	390	fóng	昉	203	fú	虎	400
féi	斐	198	fóng	紡	353	fú	唬	63
féi	痱	310	fóng	訪	418	fú	琥	300
féi	誹	423	fóng	舫	382	fú	拊	170
féi	翡	367	fóng	髣	500	fú	府	127
féi	蜚	403	fóng	恍	145	fú	俯	17
fèih	肥	372	fóng	晃	205	fú	腑	376
fèih	淝	260	fóng	幌	124	fú	傅	22
feih	狒	294	fong	放	196	fu	咐	58
feih	翡	367	fong	況	33	fu	戽	163
fò	科	333	fong	況	33	fu	庫	128
fò	蝌	403	fong	況	252	fu	褲	413
fò	窠	339	fong	眖	434	fu	袴	413
fó	火	279	fù	孚	101	fu	富	107
fó	伙	11	fù	俘	17	fu	副	39
fó	棵	227	fù	莩	389	fu	賦	436
fó	夥	87	fù	桴	220	fùh	乎	4

fùh	夫	87	fùi	喹	66				
fùh	扶	166	fùi	魁	502	gà	加	40
fùh	芙	384	fúi	洧	256	gà	伽	12
fùh	苻	386	fúi	賄	434	gà	茄	387
fùh	符	342	fui	喙	65	gà	枷	218
fùh	鳧	504	fui	悔	147	gà	笳	342
fúh	婦	97	fui	晦	206	gà	痂	310
fuh	父	289	fui	誨	423	gà	迦	451
fuh	仆	8	fūk	幅	124	gà	袈	410
fuh	訃	417	fūk	福	331	gà	家	106
fuh	赴	438	fūk	蝠	404	gà	傢	22
fuh	付	9	fūk	輻	447	gà	嘎	67
fuh	附	477	fūk	腹	377	gà	嘉	69
fuh	咐	58	fūk	複	412	gà	葭	392
fuh	駙	497	fūk	蝮	404	gá	斝	199
fuh	輔	446	fūk	馥	496	gá	假	21
fuh	賻	437	fūk	覆	414	gá	賈	435
fuh	傅	22	fùn	寬	109	gá	檟	235
fuh	負	432	fùn	懽	161	ga	架	217
fuh	腐	376	fùn	歡	239	ga	咖	57
fuhk	伏	11	fùn	讙	429	ga	价	10
fuhk	洑	255	fún	款	238	ga	駕	497
fuhk	茯	387	fún	鹽	317	ga	假	21
fuhk	袱	410	fùng	丰	3	ga	價	25
fuhk	宓	104	fùng	封	109	ga	嫁	98
fuhk	復	139	fùng	風	492	ga	稼	336
fuhk	服	212	fùng	楓	228	gàai	佳	14
fùhng	馮	496	fùng	瘋	311	gàai	街	408
fùhng	逢	453	fùng	豐	430	gàai	皆	314
fùhng	蓬	394	fùng	灃	278	gàai	偕	21
fùhng	縫	360	fùng	酆	461	gàai	楷	229
fuhng	奉	89	fùng	烽	282	gàai	階	480
fuhng	鳳	504	fùng	峯	116	gáai	蒯	393
fuhng	縫	360	fùng	蜂	402	gáai	解	416
fùi	悝	147	fùng	鋒	468	gaai	戒	161
fùi	灰	279	fúng	俸	18	gaai	誡	422
fùi	恢	146	fúng	唪	63	gaai	界	306
fùi	詼	421	fung	諷	425	gaai	屆	112
fùi	奎	89	fut	闊	475	gaai	解	416

gaai	廨	130	gaap	甲	306	gahp	蛤	402
gaai	懈	159	gaap	岬	115	gaht	疙	309
gaai	介	8	gaap	胛	373	gài	雞	483
gaai	价	10	gaap	鉀	466	gài	笄	342
gaai	玠	111	gaap	夾	88	gái	偈	21
gaai	芥	384	gaap	莢	389	gai	計	417
gaai	疥	309	gaap	裌	411	gai	繼	362
gaak	亿	9	gaap	頰	490	gai	髻	501
gaak	革	487	gaap	鋏	468	gai	薊	397
gaak	鬲	502	gaat	戛	162	gàm	今	8
gaak	隔	480	gaat	恝	147	gàm	衿	409
gaak	嗝	67	gàau	交	7	gàm	金	465
gaak	膈	377	gàau	郊	460	gàm	禁	331
gaak	格	221	gàau	蛟	402	gàm	甘	304
gaak	胳	375	gàau	跤	441	gàm	泔	253
gaak	骼	500	gàau	鮫	503	gàm	柑	219
gàam	緘	358	gàau	膠	377	gàm	疳	309
gàam	監	317	gàau	膠	448	gám	錦	469
gám	減	263	gáau	佼	15	gám	敢	197
gaam	淦	261	gáau	姣	95	gám	感	153
gaam	橄	234	gáau	狡	294	gam	淦	261
gaam	尷	111	gáau	皎	315	gam	噤	71
gaam	鑑	472	gáau	絞	354	gam	禁	331
gàan	奸	91	gáau	餃	494	gam	灨	279
gàan	姦	95	gáau	鉸	467	gam	贛	438
gàan	菅	389	gáau	搞	186	gàn	巾	121
gàan	間	474	gáau	攪	195	gàn	斤	199
gàan	艱	383	gaau	校	221	gàn	根	221
gáan	柬	220	gaau	窖	338	gàn	跟	440
gáan	揀	181	gaau	滘	267	gàn	勄	416
gáan	鹼	327	gaau	酵	463	gàn	筋	343
gáan	繭	362	gaau	敎	196	gán	緊	357
gáan	簡	347	gaau	覺	416	gán	僅	24
gáan	鐧	472	gaau	斠	199	gán	槿	232
gaan	諫	425	gaau	較	446	gán	殣	242
gaan	間	474	gàh	嘎	67	gán	瑾	302
gaan	澗	272	gahm	撖	188	gán	謹	427
gaan	鐧	472	gahn	近	450	gán	饉	495
gàang	耕	369	gahn	殣	242	gán	覲	415

gan	艮	383	gau	救	196	gêi	庪	127
gan	靳	487	gau	谷	57	gêi	幾	127
gàng	更	210	gau	夠	86	gei	既	202
gàng	浭	257	gau	够	86	gei	寄	107
gàng	梗	349	gau	究	337	gei	記	418
gàng	庚	127	gau	垢	78	gei	覬	415
gàng	賡	435	gau	詬	421	geih	洎	254
gáng	耿	369	gau	疚	309	geih	忌	140
gáng	埂	78	gau	廏	129	geih	伎	11
gáng	梗	224	gau	搆	186	geih	技	167
gáng	哽	61	gau	構	231	geih	妓	92
gáng	綆	355	gau	媾	99	geih	芰	384
gáng	骾	500	gau	遘	456	géng	頸	491
gáng	鯁	500	gau	彀	134	geng	鏡	471
gáng	亙	6	gau	枢	220	gèui	車	445
gang	更	210	gauh	枢	220	gèui	居	111
gāng	羹	366	gauh	舊	381	gèui	据	176
gāp	急	145	gèi	奇	88	gèui	琚	300
gap	閣	474	gèi	犄	292	gèui	裾	412
gap	鴿	505	gèi	畸	308	géui	炬	281
gāt	吉	53	gèi	几	34	géui	柜	218
gāt	佶	15	gèi	卣	5	géui	矩	323
gāt	桔	223	gèi	基	79	géui	筥	343
gāt	詰	421	gèi	箕	344	géui	枸	218
gāt	訖	417	gèi	姬	96	géui	舉	381
gàu	鳩	504	gèi	肌	372	géui	欅	237
gàu	溝	266	gèi	飢	493	géui	踽	442
gáu	九	4	gèi	幾	127	geui	鉅	120
gáu	久	3	gèi	嘰	70	geui	句	50
gáu	玖	298	gèi	璣	302	geui	瞿	322
gáu	苟	386	gèi	機	234	geui	倨	20
gáu	狗	294	gèi	磯	328	geui	据	176
gáu	枸	218	gèi	畿	308	geui	踞	441
gáu	笱	342	gèi	譏	427	geui	鋸	468
gáu	糾	351	gèi	饑	495	geui	屨	114
gáu	赳	438	gèi	羈	365	geui	據	191
gáu	韭	488	géi	己	121	geuih	巨	120
gau	灸	279	gêi	杞	215	geuih	苣	386
			gêi	紀	351	geuih	炬	281

geuih	詎	419	gìn	犍	293	gíu	矯	323
geuih	具	30	gín	謇	426	gíu	轎	448
geuih	颶	492	gín	蹇	443	giu	叫	51
geuih	懼	160	gin	見	415	giu	徼	140
geuih	遽	458	gin	建	131	giuh	嶠	118
geuk	腳	376	gin	健	245	giuh	轎	448
gèung	羌	365	gin	腱	376	giuh	撬	189
gèung	姜	94	gìng	京	7	gò	哥	60
gèung	僵	25	gìng	涇	257	gò	歌	239
gèung	薑	397	gìng	兢	29	go	個	19
gèung	殭	243	gìng	經	355	gòi	陔	478
gèung	彊	308	gìng	荆	389	gòi	賅	434
gèung	礓	328	gìng	莖	389	gòi	該	421
gèung	繮	362	gìng	矜	323	gói	改	195
gihk	極	228	gìng	瓊	303	goi	蓋	394
gihm	儉	26	gìng	驚	499	gok	各	52
gihn	件	10	gìng	景	207	gok	鉻	467
gihn	健	21	gìng	憬	158	gok	角	416
gihn	鍵	470	gìng	竟	340	gok	珏	298
gihng	勁	41	gíng	境	82	gok	閣	474
gihng	痙	310	gíng	到	38	gok	攔	193
gihng	競	341	gíng	儆	25	gok	覺	416
giht	桀	222	gíng	警	428	gòn	干	125
giht	傑	23	ging	敬	197	gòn	杆	214
giht	偈	21	ging	涇	257	gòn	肝	372
gīk	革	487	ging	徑	137	gòn	竿	341
gīk	亟	6	ging	逕	452	gòn	乾	5
gīk	激	275	gip	劫	41	gón	桿	225
gīk	殛	242	git	拮	172	gón	稈	334
gīk	棘	226	git	結	354	gón	趕	439
gīk	擊	192	git	頡	490	gón	揯	191
gīk	戟	162	git	絜	354	gón	扞	165
gìm	兼	31	git	潔	271	gon	幹	126
gím	撿	192	git	撷	193	gon	榦	230
gím	檢	235	gìu	澆	273	gòng	亢	7
gím	瞼	322	gìu	嬌	100	gòng	江	248
gim	劍	40	gìu	驕	499	gòng	扛	165
gìn	肩	372	gíu	徼	140	gòng	肛	372
gìn	堅	80	gíu	繳	362	gòng	缸	363

gòng	罡	364
gòng	岡	115
gòng	剛	38
gòng	崗	117
gòng	綱	356
góng	港	265
góng	講	426
gong	洚	258
gong	降	478
gong	絳	355
gong	鋼	469
gong	槓	231
gòu	羔	365
gòu	高	500
gòu	篙	345
gòu	皋	315
gòu	睪	320
gòu	糕	349
gòu	膏	377
góu	杲	216
góu	槁	230
góu	稿	336
góu	縞	359
gou	告	55
gou	誥	423
got	葛	392
got	轕	448
got	割	39
gù	沽	252
gù	怙	143
gù	咕	58
gù	姑	94
gù	菇	389
gù	辜	449
gù	鴣	505
gù	呱	56
gù	孤	101
gù	菰	390
gù	觚	416
gú	凸	34
gú	古	50
gú	估	11
gú	罟	364
gú	牯	292
gú	詁	419
gú	賈	435
gú	股	372
gú	羖	365
gú	鼓	510
gú	臌	379
gú	瞽	322
gú	蠱	407
gu	估	11
gu	故	196
gu	固	75
gu	痼	311
gu	錮	469
gu	雇	482
gu	僱	25
gu	顧	491
guhk	局	112
guhk	侷	16
guhk	跼	441
guhng	共	30
gúi	獪	297
gūk	梏	223
gūk	谷	430
gūk	鵠	505
gūk	掬	180
gūk	菊	389
gūk	鞠	488
gūk	麴	508
gūk	穀	230
gūk	縠	336
gūk	轂	448
gùn	觀	416
gùn	莞	389
gùn	官	105
gùn	倌	19
gùn	棺	227
gùn	冠	31
gún	莞	389
gún	脘	375
gún	瞼	322
gún	琯	300
gún	管	343
gún	館	495
gun	觀	416
gun	冠	31
gun	貫	433
gun	灌	278
gun	罐	363
gun	盥	317
gùng	工	120
gùng	功	40
gùng	攻	195
gùng	紅	351
gùng	公	30
gùng	蚣	401
gùng	弓	132
gùng	芎	384
gùng	躬	445
gùng	供	15
gùng	龔	512
gùng	宮	105
gùng	恭	147
gúng	拱	172
gúng	鞏	487
gung	供	15
gung	貢	432
gung	贛	438
gung	灨	279
gyùn	蠲	407
gyùn	涓	258
gyùn	捐	175
gyùn	悁	148
gyùn	娟	96

gyùn	鵑	505	gwài	鮭	503	gwán	鯀	503
gyún	卷	47	gwài	飯	315	gwan	棍	225
gyún	捲	177	gwài	歸	241	gwàng	觥	416
gyun	芬	37	gwài	龜	512	gwàng	薨	397
gyun	狷	294	gwái	鬼	502	gwàng	轟	448
gyun	絹	355	gwái	佹	15	gwāt	骨	499
gyun	卷	47	gwái	詭	421	gwāt	滑	265
gyun	眷	319	gwái	宄	103	gwāt	榾	230
gyuhn	倦	20	gwái	軌	445	gwāt	鶻	506
gyuhn	圈	75	gwái	庋	127	gwāt	汩	248
gwà	瓜	303	gwái	晷	207	gwāt	橘	234
gwà	呱	56	gwái	簋	346	gwat	括	172
gwá	寡	108	gwái	癸	101	gwīk	洫	256
gwa	卦	46	gwai	癸	314	gwīk	郤	460
gwa	掛	179	gwai	貴	433	gwīk	隙	480
gwa	褂	412	gwai	瞶	322	gwīk	虩	400
gwa	罣	364	gwai	桂	222	gwīk	闃	475
gwa	詿	421	gwai	瑰	302	gwìng	扃	164
gwàai	乖	4	gwai	鱖	504	gwíng	迥	451
gwáai	拐	170	gwaih	炅	280	gwíng	烱	281
gwáai	枴	218	gwaih	柜	218	gwíng	炯	282
gwáai	蒯	393	gwaih	悸	149	gwíng	泂	251
gwaai	怪	144	gwaih	簣	347	gwíng	扃	164
gwaak	摑	186	gwaih	匱	44	gwíng	炅	280
gwàan	矜	323	gwaih	櫃	236	gwíng	憬	158
gwàan	綸	356	gwaih	跪	441	gwò	戈	161
gwàan	關	476	gwaih	餽	495	gwò	渦	264
gwàan	鰥	503	gwàn	君	53	gwó	果	217
gwaan	慣	155	gwàn	均	77	gwó	菓	390
gwaan	摜	186	gwàn	軍	445	gwó	裹	412
gwaan	擐	192	gwàn	昆	203	gwo	過	455
gwaat	刮	37	gwàn	焜	283	gwō	撾	192
gwaat	颳	492	gwàn	錕	469	gwok	國	75
gwahn	郡	460	gwàn	鯤	503	gwok	幗	124
gwaht	掘	179	gwàn	鈞	466	gwok	郭	460
gwaht	倔	19	gwán	緄	357	gwok	椁	228
gwaht	崛	117	gwán	輥	447	gwok	槨	228
gwài	圭	76	gwán	袞	409	gwok	廓	129
gwài	閨	475	gwán	滾	268	gwòng	光	28

gwòng	胱	374	haaih	械	225	hah	夏	86
gwòng	桄	222	haaih	駭	497	hah	廈	129
gwóng	廣	130	haaih	解	416	hah	暇	208
gwóng	獷	297	haaih	廨	130	hàhm	含	54
gwóng	誆	422	haaih	邂	458	hàhm	唅	62
			haak	客	105	hàhm	酣	462
hà	哈	60	haak	嚇	72	háhm	頷	490
hà	蝦	404	hāak	克	28	háhm	頜	490
hàahm	唅	62	hāak	赫	438	hahm	撼	190
hàahm	函	35	háam	餡	495	hahm	憾	159
hàahm	涵	259	haam	喊	64	hahm	嵌	117
hàahm	咸	59	hàan	慳	155	hàhn	痕	310
hàahm	鹹	507	hàang	夯	88	hahn	恨	146
hàahm	銜	467	hàang	坑	77	hàhng	恆	145
háahm	菡	390	hàang	吭	54	hàhng	行	407
háahm	餡	495	haap	呷	57	hàhng	桁	222
háahm	檻	236	haap	挾	175	hàhng	衡	408
haahm	陷	479	haap	招	178	hàhng	蘅	399
hàahn	閑	474	hàau	尻	111	hahng	杏	214
hàahn	閒	474	hàau	嘐	69	hahng	荇	388
hàahn	嫻	100	hàau	敲	197	hahng	幸	126
hàahn	癇	313	hàau	烤	282	hahng	倖	19
haahn	限	478	hàau	哮	60	hahng	悻	149
haahp	狎	294	hàau	酵	463	hahp	匣	44
haahp	柙	219	hàau	猇	295	hahp	合	52
haahp	狹	295	háau	巧	120	hahp	盒	316
haahp	篋	345	háau	考	368	hahp	閤	474
hàai	咳	59	háau	拷	173	hahp	盍	316
hàai	揩	182	háau	烤	282	hahp	溘	266
hàaih	鞋	487	haau	孝	101	hahp	俠	17
hàaih	諧	425	haauh	傚	23	hahp	峽	116
hàaih	孩	103	haauh	效	196	hahp	瞌	321
hàaih	骸	500	haauh	校	221	hahp	磕	328
háaih	懈	159	hàh	蛤	402	hahp	闔	476
háaih	澥	274	hàh	遐	455	haht	劾	41
háaih	蟹	406	hàh	瑕	301	haht	核	221
haaih	嗐	67	hàh	霞	485	haht	閡	474
haaih	瀣	278	háh	哈	60	haht	礉	234
			hah	下	1	haht	黠	509

haht	瞎	321	hàng	鏗	471	hei	汽	249
haht	轄	448	háng	肯	372	hei	氣	246
haht	齂	415	háng	啃	63	hei	器	71
hàih	兮	30	hap	嗑	68	hei	棄	228
hàih	奚	90	hāp	洽	255	hei	憩	158
hàih	徯	139	hāp	恰	146	hei	戲	163
hàih	蹊	443	hāt	乞	4	hek	吃	52
hàih	谿	430	háu	口	50	hek	喫	52
hàih	縣	510	hau	叫	55	hèu	靴	487
haih	系	351	hàuh	侯	16	hèui	吁	52
haih	係	16	hàuh	喉	64	hèui	訏	418
haih	禊	331	hàuh	猴	296	hèui	虛	400
haih	繫	362	háuh	厚	48	hèui	墟	83
hāk	可	51	hauh	后	53	hèui	噓	70
hāk	克	28	hauh	逅	452	hèui	歔	239
hāk	剋	38	hauh	後	137	héui	呴	205
hāk	黑	508	hauh	候	19	héui	許	418
hāk	刻	37	hèi	義	366	héui	栩	221
hàm	憨	158	hèi	犧	293	héui	詡	420
hàm	堪	80	hèi	曦	210	heui	去	48
hàm	戡	163	hèi	熹	286	hèung	香	496
hàm	嘁	72	hèi	僖	25	hèung	鄉	461
hàm	龕	512	hèi	嬉	100	héung	享	7
hám	坎	77	hèi	嘻	70	héung	晌	206
hám	砍	324	hèi	禧	332	héung	餉	494
hám	歁	238	hèi	希	122	héung	響	489
ham	勘	41	hèi	晞	61	héung	饗	495
ham	墈	82	hèi	烯	282	heung	向	53
ham	磡	328	hèi	稀	334	heung	曏	209
ham	瞰	322	hèi	欷	238	heung	嚮	72
ham	矙	322	hèi	晞	206	hihp	協	45
hán	很	137	hèi	嘿	71	hihp	叶	52
hán	狠	294	hèi	欺	238	hìm	謙	426
hán	墾	83	hèi	熙	285	hím	險	481
hán	懇	159	héi	屺	114	him	欠	237
hán	齦	511	héi	起	438	him	茨	384
hàng	亨	7	héi	豈	420	him	歉	239
hàng	哼	61	héi	喜	65	him	慊	154
hàng	莖	389	hei	炁	280	hìn	祆	330

hìn	愆	153	hìu	撬	234	hòhng	沆	249
hìn	掀	177	hìu	曉	444	hòhng	吭	54
hìn	牽	292	hìu	驍	499	hòhng	杭	215
hìn	軒	445	hìu	梟	224	hòhng	航	382
hìn	搴	186	hìu	囂	73	hòhng	骯	499
hìn	褰	413	híu	曉	209	hòhng	降	478
hìn	騫	498	hiu	撬	189	hohng	桁	222
hín	愆	153	hiu	竅	339	hohng	巷	121
hín	蜆	403	hò	呵	57	hohng	項	489
hín	遣	456	hò	苛	385	hòi	開	474
hín	譴	428	hò	訶	419	hói	海	256
hín	繾	362	hó	可	51	hói	嗨	67
hín	顯	492	hó	坷	78	hói	剴	39
hìn	絳	360	hòh	何	13	hói	愷	154
hin	憲	158	hòh	河	251	hói	凱	34
hin	獻	297	hòh	荷	388	hói	闓	476
hìng	兄	27	hoh	荷	388	hói	鎧	470
hìng	氫	246	hoh	賀	434	hòih	骸	500
hìng	脛	375	hohk	貉	431	hoih	亥	7
hìng	輕	446	hohk	鶴	506	hoih	氣	246
hìng	興	381	hohk	學	103	hoih	害	106
hìng	卿	47	hòhn	汗	247	hok	売	243
hìng	馨	496	hòhn	犴	293	hok	殼	243
hìng	夐	86	hòhn	軒	511	hòhn	豻	293
híng	興	381	hòhn	邯	459	hohn	扞	165
híng	慶	156	hòhn	韓	488	hòn	看	318
híng	磬	328	hòhn	寒	107	hón	侃	14
híng	馨	363	hòhn	旱	203	hón	刊	36
hip	叶	52	hóhn	捍	176	hón	罕	363
hip	怯	144	hóhn	悍	148	hon	看	318
hip	挾	175	hohn	汗	247	hon	漢	270
hip	愜	152	hohn	捍	176	hon	嘆	209
hip	慊	154	hohn	焊	282	hōn	刊	36
hip	歉	239	hohn	豻	511	hòng	匡	44
hip	協	45	hohn	翰	367	hòng	框	222
hip	脅	374	hohn	瀚	277	hòng	眶	319
hit	歇	238	hòhng	行	407	hòng	腔	376
hìu	枵	218				hòng	康	128
hìu	僥	25				hòng	糠	350

hóng	嵻	156	hùhng	鴻	505	hyūn	褖	332
hong	烘	281	hùhng	鱟	508	hyut	血	407
hot	曷	210	huhng	泓	248			
hot	渴	265	huhng	閧	501	jà	咋	56
hot	喝	65	huk	槲	232	jà	吒	53
hot	褐	413	hūk	哭	60	jà	咱	59
hòu	嚆	72	hùng	烘	281	jà	挓	172
hòu	蒿	394	hùng	凶	34	jà	抓	167
hòu	薅	397	hùng	兇	28	jà	查	220
hóu	好	91	hùng	恟	145	jà	渣	264
hou	好	91	hùng	空	337	jà	嗏	66
hou	犒	293	hùng	崆	116	jà	揸	183
hòuh	毫	245	hùng	倥	20	jà	楂	228
hòuh	皋	68	hùng	詾	419	jà	撾	192
hòuh	號	400	hùng	匈	43	ja	乍	4
hòuh	豪	431	hùng	洶	255	ja	吒	58
hòuh	蠔	406	hùng	胸	374	ja	咋	56
hòuh	壕	84	húng	孔	101	ja	柞	219
hòuh	嚎	72	húng	哄	59	ja	炸	281
hòuh	濠	275	húng	倥	20	ja	痄	310
houh	昊	203	húng	恐	146	ja	詐	419
houh	浩	256	hung	泓	248	ja	蚱	401
houh	暭	315	hung	哄	59	ja	搾	185
houh	皓	315	hung	控	179	ja	榨	230
houh	犒	293	hyùn	烜	281	ja	喋	285
houh	鎬	471	hyùn	煖	285	jaahk	翟	367
houh	耗	369	hyùn	諼	424	jaahk	宅	104
houh	號	400	hyùn	捲	227	jaahk	擇	191
houh	顥	492	hyùn	圈	75	jaahk	澤	274
houh	灝	279	hyùn	喧	66	jaahk	摘	186
huhk	鵠	505	hyùn	暄	207	jaahk	蹢	443
huhk	酷	463	hyùn	萱	391	jaahk	謫	427
huhk	斛	199	hyùn	嬛	101	jaahk	擲	193
hùhng	訌	417	hyùn	燻	84	jaahk	躑	444
hùhng	虹	401	hyún	犬	293	jaahk	磔	328
hùhng	紅	351	hyun	券	37	jáahm	晰	321
hùhng	洪	256	hyun	綣	356	jaahm	站	340
hùhng	熊	285	hyun	絢	354	jaahm	暫	208
hùhng	雄	481	hyun	勸	42	jaahn	綻	357

jàng	掙	179	jauh	胄	31	jeuhng	匠	44
jàng	崝	117	jauh	胃	373	jeuhng	象	431
jàng	猙	295	jauh	袖	410	jeuhng	像	24
jàng	箏	344	jauh	就	111	jeuhng	橡	234
jàng	睜	319	jauh	僦	25	jèui	佳	481
jàng	錚	469	jauh	紂	351	jèui	堆	80
jang	諍	424	jauh	驚	506	jèui	椎	227
jāp	汁	247	jauh	驟	499	jèui	睢	482
jāp	執	79	jauh	簉	346	jèui	騅	498
jāt	質	436	jè	嗟	66	jèui	錐	469
jāt	驚	498	jè	嘛	69	jèui	追	451
jàu	舟	382	jè	遮	457	jèui	狙	294
jàu	周	56	jé	姐	94	jèui	苴	386
jàu	喌	62	jé	者	368	jèui	蛆	401
jàu	週	454	jé	赭	438	jèui	疽	309
jàu	睭	435	je	柘	219	jèui	沮	251
jàu	州	119	je	借	20	jéui	咀	57
jàu	洲	255	je	這	453	jéui	嘴	70
jàu	湫	264	je	藉	397	jéui	龃	511
jàu	揪	183	je	蔗	395	jeui	惴	152
jàu	啾	64	je	鷓	506	jeui	最	211
jàu	諏	424	jeh	謝	427	jeui	沮	251
jàu	鄒	461	jeh	榭	230	jeui	醉	463
jàu	謅	426	jehk	蓆	394	jeui	贅	437
jàu	騶	498	jehng	鄭	461	jeui	蕞	396
jáu	走	438	jek	炙	280	jeui	綴	356
jáu	肘	372	jek	摭	187	jeuih	序	127
jáu	帚	122	jek	隻	481	jeuih	敍	196
jáu	酒	462	jek	跖	440	jeuih	漵	270
jau	咒	56	jek	脊	375	jeuih	隊	83
jau	晝	206	jek	瘠	312	jeuih	嶼	119
jau	奏	89	jéng	井	6	jeuih	懟	160
jau	揍	183	jeuhk	着	319	jeuih	縋	359
jau	呪	56	jeuhk	嚼	73	jeuih	聚	370
jau	縐	359	jeuhn	盡	316	jeuih	罪	364
jau	皺	315	jeuhn	燼	288	jeuk	鵲	504
jau	愀	155	jeuhng	丈	1	jeuk	芍	384
jauh	宙	106	jeuhng	仗	9	jeuk	妁	91
jauh	岫	115	jeuhng	杖	215	jeuk	酌	462

jeuk	灼	279	jèung	嶂	405	jì		資	434
jeuk	著	391	jèung	張	133	jì		貲	434
jeuk	桌	222	jèung	將	110	jì		知	323
jeuk	焯	283	jèung	漿	270	jì		蜘	403
jeuk	着	319	jèung	長	473	jì		茲	387
jeuk	斫	200	jéung	掌	180	jì		滋	268
jeuk	雀	481	jéung	漲	270	jì		咨	58
jeuk	繳	362	jéung	奬	90	jì		姿	95
jeuk	爵	289	jéung	獎	231	jì		諮	425
jèun	屯	114	jéung	蔣	395	jì		脂	374
jèun	肫	372	jeung	悵	149	jì		髭	501
jèun	榛	230	jeung	帳	123	jì		淄	259
jèun	蓁	394	jeung	脹	375	jì		菑	390
jèun	臻	380	jeung	賬	436	jì		緇	357
jèun	諄	423	jeung	漲	270	jì		錙	469
jèun	津	256	jeung	嶂	118	jì		輜	447
jèun	樽	234	jeung	幛	125	jí		子	101
jèun	遵	457	jeung	障	480	jí		仔	9
jéun	准	33	jeung	瘴	312	jí		阯	77
jéun	隼	481	jeung	將	110	jí		籽	369
jéun	準	266	jeung	醬	464	jí		止	239
jéun	儘	26	jēut	卒	45	jí		址	77
jeun	晉	206	jēut	捽	177	jí		芷	385
jeun	搢	184	jēut	怵	144	jí		祉	329
jeun	縉	359	jēut	詘	420	jí		趾	440
jeun	俊	16	jēut	黜	509	jí		旨	202
jeun	浚	256	jì	之	3	jí		指	173
jeun	峻	116	jì	芝	384	jí		只	51
jeun	竣	340	jì	支	195	jí		枳	218
jeun	畯	307	jì	吱	55	jí		呮	58
jeun	駿	498	jì	枝	217	jí		姊	93
jeun	雋	482	jì	肢	372	jí		秭	334
jeun	進	454	jì	孜	102	jí		祇	329
jeun	濬	276	jì	孳	103	jí		紙	352
jèung	章	340	jì	卮	46	jí		訾	420
jèung	漳	270	jì	梔	225	jí		紫	354
jèung	彰	136	jì	氏	245	jí		徵	139
jèung	樟	232	jì	祇	330	jí		滓	509
jèung	璋	302	jì	質	436	jí		梓	224

jí	滓	268	jih	耜	369	jīk	職	371
jí	籽	348	jihk	夕	86	jīk	稷	336
ji	知	323	jihk	汐	247	jìm	尖	111
ji	智	207	jihk	矽	324	jìm	占	46
ji	志	141	jihk	席	123	jìm	沾	252
ji	痣	311	jihk	湜	264	jìm	粘	349
ji	誌	422	jihk	寂	106	jìm	霑	485
ji	忮	142	jihk	直	317	jìm	詹	421
ji	恣	147	jihk	值	20	jìm	瞻	322
ji	至	380	jihk	殖	242	jìm	譫	428
ji	致	380	jihk	植	227	jìm	臢	379
ji	輊	446	jihk	藉	397	jìm	漸	270
ji	緻	358	jihk	籍	347	jìm	佔	13
ji	識	428	jihm	漸	270	jìm	僭	25
ji	置	364	jihn	賤	436	jìn	戔	162
ji	質	436	jihng	淸	33	jìn	箋	344
ji	漬	270	jihng	阱	477	jìn	牋	291
ji	懥	159	jihng	淨	261	jìn	湔	263
ji	摯	188	jihng	靖	486	jìn	煎	283
jih	巳	121	jihng	靜	486	jìn	氈	245
jih	祀	329	jihng	靚	486	jìn	邅	458
jih	字	101	jiht	捷	177	jìn	氊	366
jih	牸	292	jiht	婕	97	jín	展	113
jih	自	380	jiht	睫	320	jín	碾	327
jih	豸	431	jiht	截	163	jín	攆	186
jih	雉	482	jik	蹟	443	jín	輾	447
jih	麑	134	jīk	炙	280	jín	剪	39
jih	眦	318	jīk	陟	478	jín	翦	367
jih	治	252	jīk	即	47	jín	戩	163
jih	俟	17	jīk	唧	65	jín	闡	476
jih	涘	258	jīk	鯽	503	jín	戰	163
jih	寺	109	jīk	迹	451	jín	餞	494
jih	痔	310	jīk	嘖	69	jín	薦	397
jih	伺	12	jīk	幘	124	jin	箭	344
jih	笥	342	jīk	漬	270	jin	顫	492
jih	飼	493	jīk	積	336	jìng	正	240
jih	嗣	68	jīk	磧	328	jìng	怔	145
jih	稚	335	jīk	績	360	jìng	征	136
jih	食	493	jīk	織	361	jìng	晶	207

Reading	字	No.
juhk	俗	17
juhk	逐	452
juhk	族	201
juhk	嗾	68
juhk	鏃	471
juhk	濁	275
juhk	躅	444
juhk	鐲	472
juhk	妯	93
juhk	軸	446
juhk	舳	382
juhk	續	362
juhng	仲	10
juhng	重	465
juhng	訟	418
juhng	頌	489
juhng	誦	423
jūk	足	439
jūk	浞	258
jūk	捉	175
jūk	祝	330
jūk	竺	341
jūk	竹	341
jūk	筑	343
jūk	築	345
jūk	粥	349
jūk	燭	288
jūk	觸	416
jūk	屬	114
jūk	囑	73
jūk	矚	322
jùng	中	3
jùng	忠	141
jùng	盅	315
jùng	忪	143
jùng	終	353
jùng	舂	380
jùng	縱	360
jùng	蹤	443
jùng	宗	104
jùng	棕	226
jùng	綜	356
jùng	糉	501
jùng	鍾	470
jùng	鐘	472
júng	總	360
júng	種	335
júng	腫	376
júng	踵	442
júng	糉	349
jung	中	3
jung	衆	407
jung	綜	356
jung	縱	360
jung	種	335
jyù	朱	213
jyù	侏	15
jyù	洙	255
jyù	姝	94
jyù	株	221
jyù	珠	299
jyù	茱	387
jyù	誅	421
jyù	硃	325
jyù	蛛	402
jyù	銖	467
jyù	諸	424
jyù	猪	295
jyù	豬	295
jyù	豬	431
jyù	瀦	277
jyù	櫫	236
jyú	煮	283
jyú	渚	263
jyú	主	1
jyú	拄	169
jyu	注	254
jyu	炷	281
jyu	註	419
jyu	蛀	401
jyu	駐	497
jyu	著	391
jyu	鑄	472
jyuh	住	13
jyuh	筯	344
jyuh	箸	344
jyuhn	傳	23
jyuht	絕	354
jyùn	尚	109
jyùn	耑	369
jyùn	耑	110
jyùn	專	109
jyùn	磚	328
jyùn	鐫	472
jyùn	鑽	473
jyún	傳	23
jyún	撙	189
jyún	轉	448
jyún	囀	73
jyún	轉	448
jyun	纘	363
jyun	鑽	473
jyun	纂	362
jyut	梲	225
jyut	嗄	69
jyut	拙	171
jyut	茁	386
jyut	咄	57
jyut	紬	353
jyut	掇	178
jyut	惙	151
jyut	啜	62
jyut	綴	356
jyut	輟	447
jyut	裰	412
kà	咖	57

ká	卡	46	kāt	咳	59	kei	驥	499
ka	喀	64	kāt	欪	238	kèih	祁	329
kā	卡	46	kàu	句	50	kèih	圻	77
káai	楷	229	kàu	摳	187	kèih	祈	329
káai	鍇	470	kàu	鳩	504	kèih	旂	201
káai	捆	175	kàu	溝	266	kèih	岐	114
kaau	銬	467	kàu	篝	345	kèih	歧	240
kaau	靠	486	kau	叩	51	kèih	跂	440
kàhm	芩	384	kau	扣	165	kèih	奇	88
kàhm	琴	301	kau	媾	99	kèih	琦	300
kàhm	禽	332	kau	構	231	kèih	其	30
kàhm	噙	71	kau	購	437	kèih	淇	259
kàhm	擒	190	kau	寇	107	kèih	冀	31
kàhm	檎	235	kau	蔻	395	kèih	祺	331
káhm	妗	92	kau	臼	380	kèih	琪	300
kàhn	芹	385	kau	柏	223	kèih	旗	201
kàhn	勤	42	kàuh	仇	8	kèih	棋	225
kàhn	懃	159	kàuh	虬	401	kèih	期	212
kahp	及	49	kàuh	求	247	kèih	蜞	403
kài	溪	267	kàuh	毬	245	kèih	麒	507
kài	秙	117	kàuh	逑	452	kèih	其	391
kài	稽	336	kàuh	球	299	kèih	耆	368
kài	谿	430	kàuh	裘	411	kèih	鰭	503
kái	啟	62	káuh	臼	380	kèih	蘄	399
kái	啓	62	káuh	舅	380	kèih	綦	356
kái	启	62	kèh	伽	12	kèih	祇	329
kái	棨	227	kèh	茄	387	kéih	企	10
kái	稽	336	kèh	瘸	312	kéih	跂	440
kai	契	89	kèh	騎	498	keuhk	噱	72
kàm	衾	409	kehk	屐	113	kèuhng	強	134
kàm	衿	409	kehk	劇	40	kèuhng	强	134
kàm	襟	413	kèi	歧	238	kéuhng	襁	413
kāp	汲	248	kèi	猗	292	kéuhng	鏹	471
kāp	岌	114	kèi	崎	116	kèui	俱	18
kāp	吸	55	kèi	畸	308	kèui	袪	330
kāp	笈	341	kèi	敬	195	kèui	袪	410
kāp	級	352	kei	亟	6	kèui	拘	171
kāp	給	354	kei	暨	209	kèui	駒	497
kāp	歙	239	kei	冀	31	kèui	區	44

kèui	崛	118	kiu	竅	339	kúi	創	40
kèui	軀	445	kìuh	喬	66	kúi	澮	274
kèui	驅	499	kìuh	僑	24	kúi	檜	235
kèuih	劬	41	kìuh	嶠	118	kúi	繪	361
kèuih	渠	263	kìuh	橋	234	kúi	潰	272
kèuih	瞿	322	kìuh	蕎	396	kúi	憒	157
kèuih	衢	408	kìuh	翹	367	kúi	職	371
kèuih	癯	313	kòhng	狂	293	kūk	曲	210
kéuih	佢	12	koi	丐	2	kūk	麴	508
kéuih	拒	168	koi	慨	155	kut	括	172
kéuih	距	440	koi	溉	269	kut	豁	430
keuk	卻	47	koi	概	231	kyùhn	惓	151
kìhm	拑	169	koi	愾	154	kyùhn	蜷	403
kìhm	鉗	466	koi	鈣	466	kyùhn	鬈	501
kìhm	箝	344	koi	蓋	394	kyùhn	拳	172
kìhm	黔	509	kok	恪	146	kyùhn	權	237
kìhn	乾	5	kok	涸	259	kyùhn	顴	492
kìhn	掮	180	kok	摧	184	kyut	孑	101
kìhn	虔	400	kok	榷	231	kyut	決	32
kìhng	擎	190	kok	郝	460	kyut	決	249
kìhng	檠	235	kok	确	325	kyut	抉	167
kìhng	棻	284	kok	確	327	kyut	訣	418
kìhng	鯨	503	kok	慤	156	kyut	缺	363
kìhng	瓊	303	kok	堅	84	kyut	厥	48
kìng	傾	24	kóng	慷	156	kyut	撅	188
kíng	頃	489	kong	亢	7	kyut	蕨	396
kit	孑	101	kong	伉	10	kyut	獗	296
kit	訐	417	kong	抗	168	kyut	蹶	444
kit	詰	421	kong	炕	280	kyut	譎	428
kit	頡	490	kong	擴	193	kyut	關	476
kit	擷	193	kong	礦	328	kyut	闋	476
kit	挈	174	kù	箍	344	kwà	夸	88
kit	鍥	470	kùhng	邛	459	kwà	挎	173
kit	揭	183	kùhng	蛩	402	kwà	垮	78
kit	楬	229	kùhug	筇	342	kwà	姱	95
kit	碣	327	kùhng	穹	337	kwà	誇	421
kit	竭	340	kùhng	窮	339	kwà	跨	440
kit	羯	366	kúi	會	211	kwá	褂	412
kit	蠍	406	kúi	儈	26	kwa	胯	374

kwáaih	攞	191	kwán	壺	85	làahn	攔	194
kwáang	筐	343	kwán	悃	147	làahn	欄	237
kwàang	逛	453	kwán	捆	175	làahn	爛	199
kwàang	眶	319	kwan	困	74	làahn	蘭	399
kwàang	框	222	kwan	睏	319	láahn	懶	160
kwaang	逛	453	kwan	窘	338	laahn	爤	289
kwàhn	裙	411	kwàng	框	222	láahng	冷	33
kwàhn	羣	366	kwàng	眶	319	laahp	垃	78
kwàhn	麕	507	kwòhng	狂	293	laahp	臘	379
kwài	盔	316	kwok	擴	193	laahp	蠟	406
kwài	規	415	kwong	廓	461	laaht	剌	38
kwài	窺	339	kwong	壙	84	laaht	辣	449
kwài	蛙	404	kwong	曠	210	làai	拉	170
kwài	虧	400	kwong	礦	328	laai	癩	313
kwài	巋	119	kwúi	晦	434	laaih	賴	436
kwai	愧	154	kwúi	膾	378	laaih	瀨	278
kwàih	畦	307	kwut	聒	370	laaih	籟	348
kwàih	哇	66	kwut	括	172	laaih	落	392
kwàih	馗	496	là	啦	63	laaih	酹	463
kwàih	逵	454	là	喇	65	laak	仂	8
kwàih	揆	181	là	嘞	69	laam	欖	237
kwàih	暌	208	la	喇	65	laat	瘌	312
kwàih	睽	320	la	罅	363	làauh	撈	188
kwàih	葵	392	làahm	嵐	118	lahk	肋	372
kwàih	夔	86	làahm	藍	398	lahk	勒	41
kwáih	傀	154	làahm	籃	347	lahk	泐	250
kwáih	攜	190	làahm	襤	413	làhm	林	217
kwáih	媿	154	làahm	婪	97	làhm	淋	259
kwáih	揆	181	láahm	覽	416	làhm	琳	300
kwàn	困	75	láahm	攬	195	làhm	霖	485
kwàn	坤	77	láahm	欖	195	làhm	婪	97
kwàn	堃	80	láahm	欖	237	làhm	臨	379
kwàn	昆	203	laahm	濫	276	làhm	廩	130
kwàn	焜	283	laahm	檻	236	láhm	凜	34
kwàn	崑	116	laahm	纜	363	láhm	懍	159
kwàn	琨	300	laahm	艦	383	láhm	檁	235
kwán	捃	175	làahn	闌	476	lahp	立	340
kwán	閫	475	làahn	讕	429	làih	犁	292
kwán	菌	390	làahn	瀾	278	làih	黎	508

leuhng	輷	447	leuih	濾	277	lìhng	苓	385
leuht	率	298	leuih	類	491	lìhng	囹	74
leuht	栗	220	léun	卵	47	lìhng	羚	365
leuht	慄	154	lì	哩	60	lìhng	蛉	402
leuht	溧	267	lihk	力	40	lìhng	聆	370
leuht	律	137	lihk	歷	240	lìhng	鈴	466
lèuih	雷	484	lihk	曆	209	lìhng	零	483
lèuih	擂	191	lihk	瀝	277	lìhng	翎	366
lèuih	鐳	472	lihk	靂	486	lìhng	齡	511
lèuih	累	353	lihk	鬲	502	lìhng	凌	33
lèuih	嫘	100	lihk	酈	461	lìhng	淩	261
lèuih	縲	360	lìhm	帘	122	lìhng	陵	479
lèuih	騾	498	lìhm	奩	90	lìhng	棱	227
lèuih	壘	84	lìhm	匲	90	lìhng	菱	390
lèuih	纍	362	lìhm	簾	347	lìhng	綾	357
lèuih	蠡	363	lìhm	廉	129	lìhng	稜	397
lèuih	閭	475	lìhm	鐮	472	lìhng	鯪	503
lèuih	櫚	236	lìhm	濂	275	lìhng	靈	486
lèuih	驢	499	líhm	瀲	278	líhng	領	490
lèuih	贏	366	líhm	斂	198	líhng	嶺	119
léuih	呂	56	líhm	臉	378	lihng	令	9
léuih	侶	16	líhm	殮	243	lihng	另	51
léuih	鋁	468	líhm	董	447	lihng	靚	486
léuih	裏	411	lihm	斂	198	lihng	愣	153
léuih	磊	327	lihm	撿	193	lihp	獵	297
léuih	蕾	396	lìhn	連	454	liht	列	36
léuih	儡	27	lìhn	漣	269	liht	冽	33
léuih	壘	84	lìhn	蓮	394	liht	洌	254
léuih	旅	201	lìhn	鏈	471	liht	烈	281
léuih	膂	377	lìhn	憐	157	liht	裂	410
léuih	褸	413	líhn	撚	193	liht	捩	176
léuih	縷	360	líhn	揀	181	lìk	嚦	72
léuih	屢	113	líhn	煉	283	lìk	櫪	236
leuih	淰	251	líhn	練	358	lìk	靂	486
leuih	戾	164	líhn	鍊	470	lìk	礫	329
leuih	唳	62	líhn	棟	229	lìk	櫟	236
leuih	淚	260	lìhng	伶	12	lìm	令	9
leuih	累	353	lìhng	泠	253	ling	拎	170
leuih	慮	156	lìhng	玲	298	liu	撂	187

粵拼	字	頁
lìuh	僚	25
lìuh	潦	272
lìuh	獠	297
lìuh	撩	189
lìuh	寮	109
lìuh	嘹	70
lìuh	遼	458
lìuh	燎	287
lìuh	瞭	321
lìuh	繚	361
lìuh	療	312
lìuh	鐐	472
lìuh	鷯	506
lìuh	寥	108
lìuh	聊	370
líuh	了	5
líuh	瞭	321
liuh	料	199
liuh	廖	129
lò	囉	73
ló	裸	412
lo	咯	58
lòh	羅	365
lòh	玀	298
lòh	囉	73
lòh	欏	237
lòh	蘿	400
lòh	籮	348
lòh	邏	459
lòh	鑼	473
lòh	螺	405
lòh	騾	498
lohk	雒	482
lohk	絡	354
lohk	落	392
lohk	駱	497
lohk	樂	232
lohk	濼	277
lòhng	郎	460
lòhng	廊	129
lòhng	啷	64
lòhng	榔	230
lòhng	蜋	405
lòhng	狼	295
lòhng	琅	300
lòhng	鋃	468
lóhng	朗	212
lóhng	烺	282
lohng	浪	256
lohng	晾	207
lòih	耒	369
lòih	誄	421
lòih	來	14
lòih	淶	262
lòih	徠	138
lòih	睞	319
lòih	萊	391
lok	洛	255
lok	咯	58
lok	烙	282
lok	酪	462
lok	犖	293
lòu	嚕	72
lóu	佬	15
lòuh	牢	291
lòuh	勞	42
lòuh	嘮	70
lòuh	撈	188
lòuh	磅	312
lòuh	盧	317
lòuh	瀘	277
lòuh	廬	130
lòuh	爐	288
lòuh	櫨	236
lòuh	臚	379
lòuh	蘆	399
lòuh	顱	492
lòuh	轤	449
lòuh	鑪	383
lòuh	驢	499
lòuh	鱸	504
lòuh	醪	464
lòuh	髏	500
lóuh	老	368
lóuh	姥	94
lóuh	潦	272
lóuh	鹵	507
lóuh	滷	269
lóuh	魯	503
lóuh	櫓	236
lóuh	虜	400
lóuh	擄	190
louh	路	441
louh	潞	273
louh	璐	302
louh	賂	434
louh	露	485
louh	鷺	506
louh	潦	273
luhk	六	30
luhk	陸	479
luhk	淥	261
luhk	氯	246
luhk	祿	331
luhk	綠	357
luhk	錄	469
luhk	鹿	507
luhk	漉	271
luhk	戮	163
lùhng	龍	512
lùhng	瀧	278
lùhng	瓏	303
lùhng	嚨	72
lùhng	曨	210
lùhng	朧	212
lùhng	櫳	237
lùhng	蘢	399

lùhng	朧	322	mà	孃	101	màh	蟆	405
lùhng	礱	329	màahn	謾	427	máh	馬	496
lùhng	籠	348	màahn	鰻	504	máh	瑪	302
lùhng	聾	371	màahn	彎	407	máh	碼	327
lùhng	隆	479	máahn	晚	206	máh	螞	405
lùhng	窿	339	maahn	曼	211	mah	禡	332
lùhng	癃	312	maahn	漫	270	mah	罵	364
lúhng	儱	27	maahn	慢	155	mah	螞	405
lúhng	壟	84	maahn	幔	124	mahk	麥	507
lúhng	攏	194	maahn	蔓	395	mahk	陌	477
lúhng	隴	481	maahn	縵	360	mahk	脈	374
lúhng	籠	348	maahn	謾	427	mahk	墨	83
luhng	弄	132	maahn	饅	495	mahk	默	509
lūk	碌	326	maahn	萬	391	mahk	驀	498
lūk	簏	346	màahng	盲	317	màhn	文	198
lūk	麓	507	máahng	錳	470	màhn	旻	203
lūk	轆	448	máahng	猛	295	màhn	紋	351
lyùhn	聯	370	máahng	蜢	403	màhn	民	246
lyùhn	孿	103	maahng	孟	101	màhn	氓	246
lyùhn	欒	119	màaih	埋	78	màhn	岷	115
lyùhn	攣	195	màaih	霾	486	màhn	聞	370
lyùhn	孌	279	máaih	買	433	máhn	抆	167
lyùhn	鑾	473	maaih	賣	436	máhn	泯	254
lyùhn	灤	237	maaih	邁	458	máhn	抿	170
lyùhn	鸞	506	maak	擘	192	máhn	憫	153
lyúhn	戀	161	māau	貓	432	máhn	吻	55
lyúhn	變	101	màauh	矛	322	máhn	刎	36
lyúhn	臠	379	màauh	茅	387	máhn	驚	504
lyuhn	亂	5	màauh	蝥	404	máhn	黽	510
lyuht	捋	175	màauh	蟊	405	máhn	脗	55
lyuht	埒	79	màauh	錨	470	máhn	閩	475
lyún	戀	161	máauh	牡	291	máhn	憫	158
lyut	劣	40	máauh	卯	46	máhn	敏	196
lyut	酹	463	máauh	昂	205	máhn	澠	274
			maauh	貌	432	máhn	汶	249
m̀	唔	61	màh	麻	508	mahn	紊	351
mà	嗎	67	màh	嘛	69	mahn	問	63
mà	媽	99	màh	蘪	395	mahn	璺	303
mà	螞	405	màh	麻	311	màhng	萌	391

màhng	盟	316	mèih	微	139	mihn	麪	508
maht	勿	43	mèih	徽	509	mìhng	明	204
maht	物	292	mèih	薇	397	mìhng	名	53
maht	宓	104	mèih	徵	140	mìhng	銘	467
maht	密	106	mèih	麋	350	mìhng	溟	266
maht	蜜	403	mèih	麋	360	mìhng	暝	208
maht	袜	410	mèih	麋	507	mìhng	瞑	321
maht	襪	413	mèih	彌	278	mìhng	螟	405
maht	謐	426	mèih	獼	297	mìhng	鳴	504
mài	咪	58	méih	美	365	míhng	皿	315
màih	迷	451	méih	鎂	470	míhng	冥	32
màih	謎	426	méih	尾	112	míhng	茗	387
máih	米	348	méih	娓	96	míhng	酩	462
máih	眯	319	méih	弭	133	míhng	銘	467
máih	弭	133	méih	枚	196	mihng	命	57
maih	袂	409	méih	靡	487	miht	蔑	395
màn	炆	280	meih	未	213	miht	篾	346
màn	蚊	401	meih	味	56	miht	蠛	407
māt	乜	4	meih	寐	107	miht	滅	268
màuh	牟	291	meih	魅	502	mìu	喵	64
màuh	眸	319	meih	媚	98	mìuh	苗	385
màuh	謀	425	m̀h	唔	61	mìuh	描	181
màuh	繆	361	mihk	糸	350	mìuh	瞄	320
máuh	某	219	mihk	汨	248	míuh	杳	216
máuh	泖	253	mihk	覓	415	míuh	浼	258
máuh	畝	307	mihk	冪	32	míuh	森	263
mauh	茂	386	mìhn	棉	225	míuh	窈	338
mauh	袤	410	mìhn	綿	357	míuh	淼	265
mauh	貿	434	mìhn	眠	319	míuh	杪	215
mauh	繆	361	míhn	丏	2	míuh	秒	333
mauh	謬	427	míhn	沔	250	míuh	眇	318
mauh	懋	159	míhn	免	28	míuh	緲	358
mé	乜	4	míhn	勉	41	míuh	藐	398
mèi	乜	4	míhn	娩	96	míuh	邈	458
mèi	眯	319	míhn	晃	31	miuh	妙	92
mèih	眉	318	míhn	湎	263	miuh	廟	130
mèih	嵋	117	míhn	腼	377	miuh	繆	361
mèih	湄	265	mihn	緬	358	mò	麽	508
mèih	楣	229	mihn	面	487	mò	摩	188

mò	魔	502	mòuh	嘸	70	mùhn	門	473
mó	摸	187	mòuh	無	396	mùhn	們	19
mó	模	233	mòuh	巫	120	mùhn	捫	176
mòh	磨	328	mòuh	誣	422	mùhn	瞞	321
mòh	礳	399	mòuh	摸	187	mùhn	蹣	443
mohk	莫	389	mòuh	模	233	múhn	滿	269
mohk	漠	271	mòuh	摹	188	muhn	悶	151
mohk	寞	107	mòuh	謨	427	muhn	燜	287
mohk	膜	377	móuh	冇	31	muhn	懣	159
mohk	幕	124	móuh	母	244	mùhng	蒙	393
mohk	瘼	312	móuh	侮	15	mùhng	濛	276
mòhng	亡	6	móuh	姆	93	mùhng	檬	125
mòhng	忙	141	móuh	姥	94	mùhng	矇	210
mòhng	邙	459	móuh	拇	170	mùhng	朦	212
mòhng	忘	141	móuh	武	240	mùhng	曚	322
mòhng	芒	384	móuh	憮	158	mùhng	礞	328
mòhng	茫	387	móuh	廡	130	mùhng	朦	383
mòhng	硭	325	móuh	舞	382	múhng	懵	160
mòhng	氓	246	mouh	戊	161	muhng	夢	87
mòhng	妄	92	mouh	耄	368	muht	末	213
mòhng	莽	389	mouh	冒	31	muht	沫	251
móhng	漭	272	mouh	帽	124	muht	茉	387
móhng	蟒	406	mouh	瑁	301	muht	袜	410
móhng	罔	364	mouh	募	42	muht	沒	250
móhng	惘	150	mouh	墓	82	muht	歿	241
móhng	網	356	mouh	暮	208	mùih	枚	217
móhng	魍	502	mouh	慕	156	mùih	玫	298
mohng	望	212	mouh	務	42	mùih	媒	98
mōk	剝	38	mouh	霧	485	mùih	煤	284
mòng	杧	215	mouh	婺	98	mùih	梅	223
mòng	芒	215	mouh	鶩	498	mùih	莓	389
mòng	芒	384	mouh	騖	506	mùih	霉	484
mòuh	毛	245	muhk	木	213	múih	每	244
mòuh	氄	245	muhk	沐	249	múih	浼	258
mòuh	髦	500	muhk	目	317	muih	妹	93
mòuh	母	244	muhk	苜	386	muih	昧	205
mòuh	无	202	muhk	睦	320	mùng	檬	235
mòuh	無	283	muhk	牧	291	múng	懵	160
mòuh	嘸	130	muhk	穆	336	mut	沫	251

mut	抹	169	nāp	凹	35	nìhng	濘	275
mut	秣	334	nāp	粒	348	nihng	擰	192
			nàu	孬	101	nihng	濘	275
nàahm	男	306	náu	呦	142	nihng	佞	13
nàahm	囡	74	náu	妞	92	nihp	捻	177
nàahm	南	46	náu	扭	166	nihp	涅	256
nàahm	喃	64	náu	犯	293	nihp	揑	175
nàahm	楠	229	náu	紐	352	nihp	聶	371
náahm	腩	376	náu	鈕	466	nihp	躡	444
nàahn	難	483	náu	朽	213	nīk	匿	44
náahn	板	438	nauh	糅	349	nīk	暱	209
naahn	難	483	nē	呢	56	nīk	慝	156
naahp	吶	55	nèih	尼	112	nīk	搦	185
naahp	訥	418	nèih	呢	56	nīk	溺	267
naahp	衲	409	nèih	妮	93	nīk	惄	151
naahp	納	352	nèih	怩	144	nìm	拈	170
naahp	鈉	466	nèih	禰	332	nìm	粘	349
naaht	捺	177	nèih	彌	134	nìm	黏	508
náaih	乃	3	nèih	瀰	278	ním	捻	177
náaih	奶	91	néih	你	11	nín	撚	189
náaih	嬭	91	néih	您	149	nīp	鎳	471
náaih	氖	246	neih	泥	253	níuh	鳥	504
náaih	蒳	510	neih	餌	494	níuh	裊	411
náaih	迺	131	neih	膩	378	níuh	嬈	101
nàauh	撓	189	nèuhng	娘	96	níuh	嫋	99
nàauh	橈	234	nèuhng	孃	101	níuh	孬	101
naauh	淖	260	néuih	餒	494	niuh	尿	112
naauh	鬧	501	néuih	女	91	niuh	溺	267
nàh	拿	174	nìhm	黏	508	nòh	按	175
nàh	哪	61	nihm	廿	131	nòh	挪	174
nàh	娜	96	nihm	念	142	nóh	娜	96
náh	那	459	nihm	唸	63	noh	懦	160
náh	哪	61	nìhn	年	126	noh	糯	350
náh	稔	335	nîhn	碾	327	nohk	偌	21
náhm	稔	335	nìhng	寧	108	nohk	喏	63
nàhng	能	374	nìhng	擰	192	nohk	諾	425
nàih	坭	78	nìhng	嚀	72	nòhng	囊	73
nàih	泥	253	nìhng	嬣	297	nòhng	瓤	303
nán	撚	189	nìhng	檸	236	nóhng	曩	210

nóhng	攘	195
noih	內	29
noih	奈	89
noih	耐	368
noih	餒	494
nòuh	奴	91
nòuh	孥	103
nòuh	駑	497
nóuh	努	40
nóuh	弩	133
nóuh	惱	151
nóuh	瑙	301
nóuh	腦	375
nouh	怒	144
nuhk	忸	141
nùhng	農	450
nùhng	儂	26
nùhng	濃	275
nùhng	穠	337
nùhng	膿	378
nyúhn	暖	208
nyúhn	煖	285
nyuhn	嫩	100
ńg	嗯	67
ngà	丫	3
ngà	啞	62
ngà	枒	217
ngà	鴉	505
ngá	啞	62
nga	亞	6
nga	婭	98
ngaahk	逆	452
ngaahk	額	491
ngàahm	岩	115
ngàahm	巖	119
ngàahm	癌	313
ngàahn	顏	491
ngáahn	眼	319
ngaahn	雁	481
ngaahn	贋	437
ngaahng	硬	325
ngaaht	仡	9
ngàai	呅	58
ngàai	唉	61
ngàai	埃	78
ngàai	挨	174
ngaai	隘	480
ngàaih	崖	117
ngàaih	涯	258
ngàaih	捱	177
ngàaih	睚	319
ngaaih	艾	383
ngaaih	刈	36
ngāak	扼	166
ngāak	偓	22
ngāak	握	182
ngāak	幄	124
ngaan	晏	205
ngaap	鴨	505
ngaat	押	169
ngaat	恝	147
ngaat	遏	455
ngaat	揠	182
ngaat	閼	475
ngaat	壓	84
ngáau	拗	171
ngaau	凹	35
ngaau	拗	171
ngàauh	爻	290
ngàauh	肴	373
ngàauh	淆	259
ngàauh	殽	244
ngáauh	咬	58
ngaauh	樂	232
ngàh	牙	291
ngàh	枒	217
ngàh	芽	385
ngàh	椏	228
ngàh	衙	408
ngàh	碼	332
ngáh	瓦	303
ngáh	瓩	304
ngáh	雅	481
ngah	迓	450
ngah	訝	418
ngàhn	垠	78
ngàhn	銀	467
ngàhn	鄞	461
ngàhn	齦	511
ngaht	仡	9
ngaht	兀	27
ngaht	杌	214
ngaht	屹	114
ngaht	迄	450
ngaht	矻	324
ngaht	訖	417
ngaht	齧	511
ngái	矮	323
ngai	曀	209
ngai	翳	367
ngàih	危	47
ngàih	倪	20
ngàih	霓	485
ngàih	嵬	118
ngàih	巍	119
ngáih	蟻	406
ngáih	隗	480
ngaih	羿	366
ngaih	睨	320
ngaih	詣	420
ngaih	毅	244
ngaih	僞	24
ngaih	魏	502
ngaih	藝	398
ngaih	囈	73
ngāk	厄	48
ngāk	呃	56

ngāk	阨	477	ngh	悟	292	ngoi	暖	209
ngāk	渥	264	ngh	寤	108	ngòih	呆	56
ngāk	喔	65	ngò	阿	477	ngoih	外	86
ngāk	齷	511	ngò	屙	113	ngoih	礙	328
ngám	闇	475	ngò	疴	309	ngok	惡	151
ngam	暗	208	ngò	喔	65	ngok	噁	71
ngàn	夵	88	ngó	婀	96	ngòn	盦	316
ngàng	鶯	506	ngòh	俄	16	ngòn	胺	374
ngàu	區	44	ngòh	峨	116	ngòn	鞍	487
ngàu	漚	271	ngòh	哦	60	ngon	按	173
ngàu	歐	239	ngòh	娥	96	ngon	案	222
ngàu	甌	304	ngòh	蛾	402	ngòu	嗷	69
ngàu	謳	427	ngòh	鵝	505	ngòuh	嗷	69
ngàu	鷗	506	ngòh	訛	418	ngòuh	鰲	405
ngàu	勾	43	ngóh	我	162	ngòuh	熬	286
ngàu	鉤	467	ngoh	餓	494	ngòuh	遨	457
ngáu	嘔	69	ngoh	臥	379	ngòuh	聱	370
ngáu	毆	244	ngohk	岳	115	ngòuh	鼇	510
ngau	漚	271	ngohk	愕	152	ngòuh	翱	367
ngàuh	牛	290	ngohk	鄂	491	ngouh	傲	23
ngáuh	偶	22	ngohk	萼	392	ngouh	遨	457
ngáuh	耦	369	ngohk	腭	377	ngūk	屋	112
ngáuh	藕	398	ngohk	諤	425	ngūk	渥	264
ngȟh	吾	55	ngohk	顎	460			
ngȟh	唔	61	ngohk	樂	232	ò	柯	219
ngȟh	梧	224	ngohk	噩	71	ò	疴	309
ngȟh	顒	510	ngohk	鱷	504	ò	軻	446
ngȟh	吳	54	ngohk	嶽	119	o	啊	61
ngȟh	蜈	403	ngohn	奸	293	òh	哦	60
ngh	午	45	ngohn	岸	115	òi	欸	238
ngh	仵	10	ngòhng	昂	203	ói	藹	399
ngh	忤	141	ngohng	戇	161	ói	靄	486
ngȟh	五	6	ngòi	哀	59	oi	嬡	100
ngȟh	伍	11	ngòi	唉	61	òn	安	104
ngh	迕	450	ngòi	埃	78	on	案	222
ngh	惧	148	ngói	藹	399	on	摁	186
ngh	誤	422	ngói	噯	72	òng	航	499
ngh	悟	148	ngói	靄	486	òu	噢	71
ngh	晤	206	ngoi	愛	153	òu	鏖	471

óu	媼	99	paau	砲	325	pei	屁	112
óu	襖	413	paau	豹	431	pei	媲	99
ou	奧	90	paau	豹	439	pei	譬	428
ou	澳	274	pàauh	咆	57	pei	劈	100
ou	懊	159	pàauh	刨	37	pèih	皮	315
			pàauh	庖	127	pèih	陂	477
pà	趴	439	pàauh	匏	43	pèih	疲	309
pà	葩	392	pàh	扒	165	pèih	脾	375
pa	怕	143	pàh	杷	216	pèih	裨	412
pàahng	彭	135	pàh	爬	289	pèih	埤	79
pàahng	澎	273	pàh	耙	369	pèih	鼙	510
pàahng	膨	378	pàh	琶	301	pèih	毗	245
pàahng	蟛	406	pàhn	瀕	277	pèih	枇	216
pàahng	棚	226	pàhn	貧	432	pèih	琵	301
pàahng	鵬	505	pàhn	頻	491	pèih	貔	432
pàahng	硼	326	pàhn	蘋	399	péih	被	410
páahng	棒	226	pàhn	顰	492	péih	婢	97
paai	湃	265	pàhn	嬪	101	pek	劈	40
paai	派	255	páhn	牝	291	pìhn	便	16
pàaih	俳	18	pàhng	朋	212	pìhn	胼	376
pàaih	牌	290	pàhng	硼	326	pìhn	駢	498
pàaih	排	178	pàhng	憑	157	pìhn	蹁	442
paak	拍	170	pài	批	166	pìhn	諞	425
paak	泊	252	páih	睥	320	pìhng	平	126
paak	柏	219	pan	噴	71	pìhng	坪	78
paak	珀	299	pāt	匹	44	pìhng	枰	218
paak	帕	122	pāt	疋	308	pìhng	萍	391
paak	魄	502	páu	剖	38	pìhng	評	420
pàan	扳	166	pàuh	捊	178	pìhng	屏	113
pàan	攀	194	pàuh	抔	167	pìhng	瓶	304
paan	盼	318	pèi	丕	2	pìhng	泙	259
pàang	烹	282	pèi	呸	56	pìhng	駢	498
pàang	澎	273	pèi	帔	122	pìhng	蘋	399
pàang	髟	304	pèi	披	169	pīk	辟	449
pàau	拋	168	pèi	砒	324	pīk	僻	25
pàau	泡	253	péi	否	54	pīk	擗	191
pàau	疱	310	péi	庀	127	pīk	劈	40
páau	跑	440	péi	仳	10	pīk	澼	275
paau	炮	280	péi	鄙	461	pīk	癖	313

pīk 霹 485
pīk 闢 476
pìn 扁 164
pìn 偏 21
pìn 篇 345
pìn 編 358
pìn 翩 367
pín 片 290
pin 片 290
pin 徧 139
pin 遍 455
pin 騙 498
pìng 姘 97
pìng 拼 177
pìng 拚 171
pìng 砰 324
pìng 怦 143
pìng 抨 169
pìng 俜 17
pìng 娉 96
ping 聘 370
pit 撇 188
pit 瞥 321
pìu 漂 269
pìu 摽 187
pìu 飄 492
piu 票 331
piu 漂 269
piu 驃 499
pìuh 嫖 99
pìuh 縹 360
pìuh 瓢 303
píuh 剽 39
píuh 瞟 321
píuh 鰾 504
píuh 莩 389
píuh 殍 242
pó 叵 52
pó 笸 342
pó 頗 489
po 破 324
pòh 婆 97
pòh 鄱 461
pòhng 彷 136
pòhng 旁 201
pòhng 傍 22
pòhng 徬 139
pòhng 滂 267
pòhng 膀 377
pòhng 螃 404
pòhng 逄 451
pòhng 龐 131
póhng 蚌 401
póhng 謗 426
pok 撲 190
pok 樸 233
pok 噗 71
pok 璞 302
pok 朴 213
pok 粕 348
pong 謗 426
póng 嗙 68
pòu 鋪 468
póu 普 206
póu 譜 428
póu 圃 75
póu 浦 256
póu 脯 375
póu 溥 266
pou 舖 381
pou 鋪 468
pòuh 匍 43
pòuh 蒲 393
pòuh 葡 392
pòuh 泡 253
pòuh 菩 390
pòuh 袍 410
póuh 抱 168
pùhn 盆 315
pùhn 湓 263
pùhn 槃 231
pùhn 磐 327
pùhn 盤 317
pùhn 蟠 406
pùhng 蓬 394
pùhng 篷 346
pùi 坯 78
pùi 胚 373
pui 佩 14
pui 珮 299
pui 沛 250
pui 霈 484
pui 配 462
pùih 培 79
pùih 陪 478
pùih 賠 435
pùih 徘 138
pùih 裴 412
púih 倍 19
púih 蓓 394
pūk 仆 8
pùn 番 307
pùn 潘 272
pun 判 36
pun 拚 171
pun 泮 254
pun 拌 170
púng 捧 176
pung 碰 326
put 潑 271

sà 卅 45
sà 啥 63
sà 沙 250
sà 砂 324
sà 莎 388
sà 痧 311
sà 裟 412

sà	紗	352	saan	傘	23	sahp	拾	174
sà	鯊	503	saan	篡	345	saht	實	108
sá	耍	368	saan	潸	263	sài	西	414
sá	洒	255	sáang	省	318	sài	恓	147
sá	灑	255	saap	圾	77	sài	茜	387
sá	灑	279	saap	颯	492	sài	犀	292
sa	嗄	67	saap	歃	239	sài	樨	233
sàah	卅	45	saap	霎	484	sài	篩	345
sàahn	孱	103	saap	澀	273	sài	嘶	70
sàahn	潺	273	saat	利	37	sái	洗	255
sáai	舐	381	saat	殺	243	sái	枲	218
sáai	蒽	393	saat	鍛	471	sái	駛	497
sáai	徙	138	saat	煞	284	sai	世	2
sáai	屣	113	saat	撒	189	sai	細	353
sáai	壐	303	saat	薩	397	sai	婿	98
saai	曬	210	sàau	梢	224	sai	壻	85
saak	索	353	sàau	筲	343	sai	勢	42
sàam	三	1	sàau	艄	383	saih	噬	71
sàam	杉	214	sàau	鞘	487	saih	澨	274
sàam	衫	409	sáau	稍	335	saih	逝	453
sàam	參	49	saau	哨	60	saih	誓	422
sàam	芟	384	saau	潲	272	sāk	塞	82
sàan	山	114	sàhm	忱	142	sàm	心	140
sàan	舢	382	sàhm	涔	258	sàm	芯	384
sàan	芟	384	sàhm	岑	115	sàm	深	262
sàan	拴	172	sáhm	諶	425	sàm	琛	300
sàan	栓	221	sahm	甚	304	sàm	森	227
sàan	删	36	sahm	什	8	sàm	參	49
sàan	姍	94	sàhn	辰	449	sám	沈	250
sàan	珊	299	sàhn	宸	106	sám	審	108
sàan	栅	220	sàhn	晨	206	sám	嬸	101
sàan	跚	440	sàhn	蜃	403	sám	潘	277
sàan	閂	474	sàhn	臣	379	sám	譖	429
sàan	潛	272	sàhn	神	330	sám	諗	424
sáan	散	197	sáhn	蜃	403	sam	沁	249
saan	汕	247	sahn	慎	154	sam	滲	269
saan	疝	309	sahn	腎	376	sàn	申	306
saan	訕	417	sahp	十	44	sàn	伸	12
saan	散	197	sahp	什	8	sàn	呻	57

sàn	砷	325	sáu	艘	383	sei	泗	253
sàn	紳	353	sáu	颼	492	sek	錫	469
sàn	身	445	sáu	喉	68	sèuhn	淳	262
sàn	辛	449	sáu	撒	193	sèuhn	醇	463
sàn	莘	389	sáu	藪	398	sèuhn	鶉	506
sàn	鋅	468	sau	宿	107	sèuhn	唇	61
sàn	新	200	sau	狩	294	sèuhn	馴	496
sàn	薪	397	sau	秀	333	seuhn	純	352
sàn	甡	305	sau	銹	468	seuhn	順	489
sàn	娠	96	sau	繡	361	seuhn	徇	137
sàn	燊	287	sau	瘦	312	sèuhng	常	123
sàng	生	304	sau	嗽	68	sèuhng	徜	138
sàng	牲	292	sau	漱	270	sèuhng	嫦	100
sàng	笙	341	sau	獸	297	sèuhng	裳	412
sang	搑	193	sàuh	仇	8	sèuhng	償	26
sāng	甥	305	sàuh	愁	153	sèuhng	嘗	69
sāp	濕	275	sauh	受	50	séuhng	上	1
sāp	澀	273	sauh	授	178	seuhng	上	1
sāt	失	88	sauh	綬	356	seuhng	向	111
sāt	室	105	sauh	售	62	seuht	尤	213
sāt	虱	401	sauh	壽	85	seuht	述	451
sāt	瑟	301	sè	些	6	seuht	術	408
sāt	膝	377	sè	賒	435	sèui	胥	374
sàu	收	195	sé	舍	381	sèui	湑	264
sàu	嗖	66	sé	捨	176	sèui	諝	425
sàu	溲	266	sé	寫	108	sèui	需	484
sàu	廋	129	se	舍	381	sèui	須	489
sàu	颼	383	se	卸	47	sèui	衰	409
sàu	修	18	se	赦	438	sèui	荽	388
sàu	脩	375	se	瀉	277	sèui	綏	355
sàu	羞	365	sèh	佘	13	sèui	睢	320
sàu	饈	495	sèh	蛇	402	sèui	雖	482
sáu	手	164	séh	社	329	séui	水	247
sáu	守	104	seh	射	109	séui	糔	349
sáu	首	496	seh	麝	507	seui	碎	326
sáu	蒐	393	sehk	石	323	seui	帨	123
sáu	叟	50	sehk	碩	327	seui	稅	334
sáu	搜	183	séi	死	241	seui	蛻	402
sáu	嗖	320	sei	四	74	seui	說	423

seui	帥	123	séun	榫	230	sì	斯	200
seui	歲	240	seun	凶	74	sì	撕	189
sèuih	垂	78	seun	汛	247	sì	廝	130
sèuih	陲	479	seun	迅	450	sì	澌	273
sèuih	誰	423	seun	訊	417	sì	私	333
séuih	悴	149	seun	信	17	sì	施	201
séuih	墅	82	seun	巽	121	sì	絲	355
séuih	髓	500	seun	舜	382	sì	師	123
seuih	淬	261	seun	瞬	321	sì	獅	296
seuih	萃	391	seun	遜	456	sì	蓍	394
seuih	瘁	311	sèung	商	63	sí	死	241
seuih	粹	349	sèung	相	318	sí	史	52
seuih	誶	423	sèung	湘	264	sí	使	14
seuih	崇	330	sèung	廂	129	sí	屎	113
seuih	睡	320	sèung	箱	345	si	四	74
seuih	瑞	301	sèung	霜	485	si	泗	253
seuih	穗	337	sèung	孀	101	si	駟	497
seuih	絮	355	sèung	襄	413	si	使	14
seuih	遂	455	sèung	鑲	473	si	肆	371
seuih	邃	458	sèung	傷	23	si	嗜	68
seuih	隧	480	sèung	殤	242	si	試	420
seuih	燧	287	sèung	觴	416	si	弒	132
seuih	彗	134	sèung	雙	482	si	諡	426
seuih	槵	231	sèung	瀧	278	sī	詩	420
seuk	杓	215	séung	想	152	sìh	時	206
seuk	削	38	séung	賞	435	sìh	鰣	503
seuk	爍	288	seung	相	318	sìh	匙	43
seuk	鑠	473	sēut	戌	161	síh	市	122
sèun	逡	453	sēut	卹	47	sih	氏	245
sèun	徇	137	sēut	恤	146	sih	士	85
sèun	洵	255	sēut	帥	123	sih	仕	9
sèun	峋	115	sēut	率	298	sih	示	329
sèun	恂	145	sēut	捽	186	sih	視	415
sèun	郇	460	sēut	蟀	405	sih	峙	115
sèun	珣	299	sì	司	52	sih	侍	15
sèun	殉	242	sì	尸	111	sih	是	205
sèun	荀	388	sì	屍	113	sih	事	5
sèun	詢	420	sì	思	144	sih	豉	430
séun	筍	342	sì	偲	22	sihk	食	493

sihk	蝕	404	siht	蝕	404	sín	跣	441
sihm	嬋	100	sik	錫	469	sín	鮮	503
sihm	禪	332	sik	刺	37	sín	蘚	399
sihm	簷	347	sīk	式	132	sín	癬	313
sihm	蟬	406	sīk	拭	172	sín	燹	288
sihm	蟾	406	sīk	軾	446	sin	腺	377
sihm	潭	274	sīk	息	147	sin	線	357
sihm	瞻	437	sīk	媳	98	sin	扇	164
sihn	單	66	sīk	螅	404	sin	倩	20
sihn	潭	274	sīk	熄	285	sin	煽	285
síhn	鱔	504	sīk	晰	315	sin	搧	185
sihn	茜	387	sīk	昔	204	sin	霰	485
sihn	倩	20	sīk	惜	150	sìng	升	45
sihn	單	66	sīk	腊	375	sìng	昇	203
sihn	撣	190	sīk	色	383	sìng	陞	478
sihn	禪	332	sīk	悉	148	sìng	星	204
sihn	瞻	437	sīk	蟋	405	sìng	猩	296
sihn	嬗	101	sīk	淅	259	sìng	惺	152
sihn	擅	191	sīk	析	217	sìng	腥	376
sihn	羨	366	sīk	晰	207	sìng	勝	42
sihn	善	64	sīk	奭	91	sìng	聲	370
sihn	鄯	461	sīk	蜥	403	síng	省	318
sihn	膳	378	sīk	薔	67	síng	醒	463
sihn	蟮	406	sīk	穡	337	sing	姓	94
sihn	繕	361	sīk	飾	494	sing	性	144
sihng	成	162	sīk	適	457	sing	聖	370
sìhng	城	78	sīk	螢	405	sing	勝	42
sìhng	晟	206	sīk	識	428	sip	涉	258
sìhng	盛	316	sīk	釋	464	sip	攝	194
sìhng	誠	422	sīk	瀉	273	sip	慴	161
sìhng	丞	2	sīk	骰	499	sip	歃	239
sìhng	承	168	sím	陝	478	sit	舌	381
sìhng	乘	4	sím	閃	474	sit	屑	113
sìhng	澠	274	sìn	先	28	sit	泄	252
sìhng	繩	361	sìn	仙	9	sit	契	89
sìhng	乘	4	sìn	鮮	503	sit	楔	229
sìhng	剩	39	sìn	僊	24	sit	洩	256
sìhng	盛	316	sìn	躚	444	sit	綫	354
siht	舌	381	sín	冼	33	sit	漢	264

sit	薛	397	sò	簑	394	sou	掃	177
sit	孽	288	só	所	164	sou	數	198
sit	褻	413	só	瑣	301	sou	臊	378
sit	竊	339	só	嗩	67	sōu	穌	336
sìu	宵	106	só	鎖	470	sōu	甦	305
sìu	消	257	sòh	傻	24	suhk	孰	103
sìu	逍	452	sòi	腮	376	suhk	塾	82
sìu	硝	325	sòi	鰓	503	suhk	熟	286
sìu	銷	468	sok	索	353	suhk	蜀	402
sìu	絹	355	sok	朔	212	suhk	屬	114
sìu	霄	484	sok	搠	186	suhk	淑	260
sìu	燒	287	sok	嗍	68	suhk	贖	437
sìu	蕭	396	sok	槊	230	sùhng	崇	116
sìu	簫	346	sok	數	198	sūk	夙	86
sìu	瀟	278	sòng	喪	66	sūk	叔	49
síu	小	110	sòng	桑	223	sūk	倏	20
síu	少	111	sóng	嗓	67	sūk	粟	349
síu	筱	343	sóng	爽	290	sūk	宿	107
síu	少	111	song	喪	66	sūk	蓿	395
siu	笑	341	sòu	酥	462	sūk	縮	360
siu	霰	485	sòu	蘇	399	sūk	肅	371
siu	嘯	70	sòu	嗽	73	sùng	忪	143
sìuh	韶	489	sòu	搔	184	sùng	崧	117
sìuh	兆	28	sòu	騷	498	sùng	淞	260
sìuh	劭	41	sòu	臊	378	sùng	鬆	501
sìuh	邵	47	sòu	鬚	501	sùng	嵩	118
sìuh	邵	459	sòu	繰	362	sùng	從	138
sìuh	紹	353	sòu	繅	361	súng	悚	148
sìuh	肇	371	sòu	甦	305	súng	竦	340
sò	唆	61	sóu	嫂	98	súng	慫	156
sò	梭	225	sóu	數	198	súng	聳	371
sò	梳	225	sou	訴	419	sung	宋	104
sò	蔬	395	sou	素	352	sung	送	452
sò	疏	308	sou	漱	270	syù	抒	167
sò	娑	96	sou	愫	154	syù	紓	352
sò	莎	388	sou	嗉	67	syù	舒	381
sò	挲	174	sou	塑	81	syù	姝	95
sò	桫	223	sou	溯	267	syù	書	211
sò	嗦	67	sou	愬	155	syù	樞	232

syù	樗	232	syut	雪	483	taan	歎	239
syù	輸	447	syut	說	423	taan	褪	413
syù	攄	193				taap	拓	170
syú	暑	207	tà	他	9	taap	嗒	67
syú	黍	508	tà	她	91	taap	塔	81
syú	鼠	510	tà	牠	104	taap	搨	185
syu	戌	161	tà	祂	291	taap	榻	230
syu	恕	146	tà	它	104	taap	塌	81
syu	庶	128	tàhm	覃	413	taap	遢	456
syùh	殳	243	tàhm	譚	428	taap	褟	413
syùh	殊	242	tàhm	談	424	taat	撻	190
syùh	薯	397	tàhm	痰	311	taat	闥	476
syúh	曙	209	tàhm	潭	272	tàhng	疼	309
syuh	豎	430	tàhm	曇	209	tàhng	膯	426
syuh	澍	274	tàhm	壜	85	tàhng	臘	405
syuh	樹	233	tàahn	彈	134	tàhng	滕	268
syùhn	船	382	tàahn	壇	84	tàhng	螣	359
syùhn	旋	201	tàahn	檀	234	tàhng	騰	498
syùhn	漩	270	taai	太	87	tàhng	藤	398
syùhn	璇	302	taai	汰	248	tài	梯	225
syúhn	吮	54	taai	泰	254	tài	銻	468
syúhn	雋	482	taai	貸	434	tái	睇	319
syuhn	篆	345	taai	態	155	tái	體	500
syùn	孫	103	tàam	貪	433	tai	剃	38
syùn	猻	296	táam	毯	245	tai	涕	258
syùn	蓀	394	taam	探	179	tai	替	211
syùn	宣	105	tàan	坍	77	tai	薙	397
syùn	渲	265	tàan	癱	314	tai	雁	113
syùn	揎	181	tàan	灘	279	tai	嚏	72
syùn	悛	148	tàan	攤	194	tàih	啼	64
syùn	痠	311	táan	癱	314	tàih	醍	463
syùn	酸	463	táan	靼	487	tàih	緹	358
syùn	殏	493	táan	疸	309	tàih	褆	332
syún	損	184	táan	袒	410	tàih	堤	81
syún	選	457	táan	坦	77	tàih	提	181
syún	蠲	407	táan	姐	93	tàih	題	491
syun	渲	265	táan	忐	141	tàih	稊	335
syun	算	344	taan	炭	281	tàih	蹄	442
syun	蒜	393	taan	碳	327	táih	娣	96

táih	綈	355	tìhng	婷	98	tìuh	苕	385
tàn	飩	493	tìhng	廷	131	tìuh	迢	450
tàn	暾	209	tìhng	梃	224	tìuh	笤	342
tàn	吞	54	tìhng	庭	128	tìuh	調	423
tan	褪	413	tìhng	蜓	403	tìuh	髫	500
tàu	偸	22	tìhng	霆	484	tìuh	鰷	511
tau	透	452	tìhng	鋌	468	tìuh	條	224
tàuh	投	167	tìhng	町	306	tíuh	窕	338
tàuh	骰	499	tíhng	挺	174	tò	拖	171
tàuh	頭	490	tìhng	艇	383	to	唾	62
téhng	艇	383	tìk	剔	38	tòh	佗	13
tek	踢	442	tìk	惕	150	tòh	沱	251
tèng	廳	131	tìk	裼	412	tòh	陀	477
teu	唞	62	tìk	忐	141	tòh	柁	218
téuhn	盾	317	tìk	忑	141	tòh	跎	440
tèui	推	180	tìk	倜	20	tòh	舵	382
téui	腿	377	tìk	俶	18	tòh	駝	497
teui	蛻	402	tìk	趯	156	tòh	鴕	505
teui	退	452	tìk	逖	453	tòh	馱	496
teui	褪	413	tìm	添	263	tóh	妥	93
tèuih	頹	491	tím	忝	141	tóh	橢	234
tèun	湍	263	tím	舔	381	tòhng	幢	125
tìhm	恬	146	tìn	天	87	tòhng	唐	61
tìhm	湉	265	tín	腆	375	tòhng	搪	185
tìhm	甜	304	tín	靦	415	tòhng	鄌	461
tíhm	餂	494	tín	靦	487	tòhng	塘	81
tíhm	殄	241	tìng	汀	247	tòhng	糖	350
tíhm	簟	347	tìng	廳	131	tòhng	堂	80
tìhn	田	305	ting	聽	371	tòhng	棠	226
tìhn	佃	12	tip	帖	122	tòhng	螳	405
tìhn	畋	306	tip	貼	434	tòhng	膛	377
tìhn	鈿	466	tit	鐵	472	tòi	苔	385
tìhn	滇	268	tiu	佻	15	tòi	胎	373
tìhn	塡	82	tiu	挑	173	tói	怠	144
tìhn	闐	476	tiu	桃	331	tói	枱	235
tíhn	殄	241	tiu	脁	375	tòih	苔	385
tìhng	亭	7	tiu	朓	319	tòih	台	51
tìhng	停	21	tiu	跳	441	tòih	抬	172
tìhng	渟	263	tiu	糶	350	tòih	枱	220

waahn	患	149	wáhn	允	27	wai	尉	110
waahn	澴	271	wáhn	狁	293	wai	蔚	395
waahn	宦	106	wáhn	愠	154	wai	慰	156
waahn	篆	431	wáhn	隕	480	wai	穢	337
wàahng	橫	233	wáhn	殞	242	wàih	惟	150
waahng	橫	233	wáhn	韻	489	wàih	帷	123
waaht	滑	265	wáhn	蘊	398	wàih	濰	276
waaht	猾	296	wahn	混	262	wàih	唯	62
wàai	歪	240	wahn	渾	265	wàih	維	356
wàaih	淮	261	wahn	鄆	460	wàih	韋	488
wàaih	槐	231	wahn	惲	151	wàih	幃	124
wàaih	懷	160	wahn	運	455	wàih	違	456
waaih	壞	85	wahn	諢	425	wàih	闈	475
wàan	彎	134	wahn	溷	267	wàih	遺	457
wàan	灣	279	wàhng	宏	104	wàih	爲	289
wáan	綰	356	wàhng	弘	133	wàih	桅	222
waat	挖	173	wàhng	泓	253	wàih	隗	480
waat	斡	199	waht	核	221	wàih	圍	75
wàh	華	390	waht	鶻	506	wàih	韋	488
wàh	嘩	71	waht	鷸	506	wàih	韙	488
wáh	踝	441	waht	聿	371	wáih	偉	21
wah	話	421	wài	委	94	wáih	煒	284
wah	畫	307	wài	逶	454	wáih	瑋	301
wah	華	390	wài	萎	391	wáih	諉	425
wah	樺	233	wài	威	95	wáih	緯	358
wàhn	勻	43	wái	卉	45	waih	惠	151
wàhn	昀	203	wái	猥	296	waih	蕙	396
wàhn	筠	343	wái	喟	66	waih	蟪	406
wàhn	云	6	wái	唯	62	waih	位	13
wàhn	云	483	wái	委	94	waih	恚	147
wàhn	雲	483	wái	萎	391	waih	爲	289
wàhn	芸	385	wái	瘘	311	waih	慧	156
wàhn	耘	369	wái	諉	424	waih	彙	134
wàhn	紜	352	wái	毀	244	waih	遺	457
wàhn	魂	502	wái	燬	288	waih	衛	408
wàhn	暈	207	wái	譭	428	waih	胃	373
wàhn	渾	265	wai	畏	306	waih	渭	265
wàhn	餛	494	wai	喂	64	waih	猬	296
wáhn	尹	112	wai	餵	495	waih	蝟	404

waih	謂	426	wòh	禾	333	wu	惡	151
wàn	溫	266	wòh	和	57	wùh	胡	373
wàn	氳	246	woh	和	57	wùh	湖	264
wàn	瘟	312	woh	禍	331	wùh	猢	296
wán	搵	184	wohk	獲	297	wùh	瑚	301
wán	穩	337	wohk	穫	337	wùh	葫	392
wan	揾	184	wohk	鑊	472	wùh	蝴	404
wan	愠	154	wòhng	王	298	wùh	糊	349
wan	縕	359	wòhng	皇	315	wùh	醐	463
wan	醞	463	wòhng	凰	34	wùh	餬	495
wan	輼	488	wòhng	隍	480	wùh	鬍	501
wāt	屈	112	wòhng	惶	152	wùh	狐	294
wāt	尉	110	wòhng	湟	264	wùh	弧	133
wāt	熨	286	wòhng	徨	139	wùh	壺	85
wāt	蔚	395	wòhng	煌	283	wuh	互	6
wāt	嗢	67	wòhng	遑	455	wuh	怙	143
wāt	詘	420	wòhng	篁	345	wuh	芋	383
wāt	喬	323	wòhng	蝗	404	wuh	戶	163
wāt	鬱	501	wòhng	黃	508	wuh	扈	164
wihk	域	79	wòhng	潢	272	wuh	滬	268
wihk	棫	227	wòhng	璜	302	wuh	護	428
wihk	蜮	403	wòhng	磺	328	wuh	瓠	303
wìhng	扔	165	wòhng	簧	346	wùhn	垣	78
wìhng	榮	230	wóhng	往	136	wùhn	桓	223
wìhng	嶸	118	wohng	旺	203	wùhn	爰	289
wíhng	永	247	wòng	汪	248	wùhn	援	183
wihng	泳	254	wóng	枉	216	wùhn	媛	98
wihng	詠	419	wù	圬	76	wùhn	緩	358
wihng	穎	336	wù	汙	247	wúhn	莞	389
wihng	潁	271	wù	烏	281	wúhn	皖	315
wò	倭	20	wù	鄔	461	wúhn	澣	275
wò	渦	264	wù	嗚	68	wuhn	玩	298
wò	娲	98	wù	鎢	471	wuhn	奐	89
wò	窩	339	wù	於	200	wuhn	渙	263
wò	萵	392	wù	惡	151	wuhn	換	182
wò	鍋	470	wú	祜	330	wuhn	喚	65
wò	蝸	404	wú	塢	82	wuhn	煥	284
wò	窠	339	wú	搗	186	wuhn	瘓	311
wo	涴	263	wú	滸	269	wuhn	緩	358

wuht	活	255	yàhn	仁	8	yam	蔭	395
wùi	偎	21	yàhn	寅	107	yàn	因	74
wùi	猥	296	yàhn	夤	87	yàn	姻	95
wùi	隈	479	yàhn	引	132	yàn	恩	147
wùi	煨	284	yàhn	蚓	401	yàn	婣	95
wúi	會	211	yàhn	忍	141	yàn	茵	387
wùih	回	74	yahn	癮	313	yàn	氤	246
wùih	洄	254	yahn	刃	35	yàn	絪	354
wùih	徊	137	yahn	仞	9	yàn	殷	243
wùih	廻	131	yahn	紉	351	yàn	慇	154
wùih	迴	451	yahn	軔	446	yàn	湮	264
wùih	蛔	402	yahn	韌	488	yàn	禋	331
wuih	會	211	yahn	釁	464	yàn	甄	304
wuih	燴	288	yahn	孕	101	yàn	忻	141
wuih	匯	44	yahn	胤	374	yàn	昕	204
wuih	滙	268	yahp	入	29	yàn	欣	237
wuih	彙	134	yaht	日	202	yán	忍	141
wún	剜	38	yaht	佚	13	yán	隱	481
wún	悗	150	yaht	泆	251	yan	印	47
wún	浣	256	yaht	軼	446	yan	釁	464
wún	豌	430	yaht	佾	14	yāp	泣	253
wún	碗	326	yaht	腋	375	yāp	邑	459
wún	腕	376	yaht	逸	454	yāp	挹	175
			yaht	溢	266	yāp	悒	148
yáh	也	5	yaht	鎰	471	yāp	浥	256
yah	廿	131	yaih	曳	210	yāp	揖	182
yàhm	壬	85	yaih	拽	173	yāp	熠	286
yàhm	任	10	yaih	跩	441	yāt	一	1
yàhm	妊	92	yàm	音	488	yāt	壹	85
yàhm	淫	261	yàm	愔	153	yàu	丘	2
yàhm	霪	485	yàm	歆	239	yàu	邱	459
yàhm	吟	54	yàm	喑	65	yàu	蚯	401
yáhm	荏	388	yàm	欽	238	yàu	憂	157
yáhm	袵	411	yàm	陰	479	yàu	優	27
yahm	任	10	yàm	歁	118	yàu	休	11
yahm	恁	146	yàm	鑫	473	yàu	庥	128
yahm	賃	434	yám	飲	493	yàu	貅	431
yahm	飪	493	yám	飲	493	yàu	髹	501
yàhn	人	8	yam	廕	129	yàu	幽	127

yáu	朽	213	yauh	柚	219	yèuhng	楊	228
yáu	柚	219	yauh	釉	464	yèuhng	煬	285
yáu	糅	349	yauh	鼬	510	yéuhng	仰	10
yáu	黝	509	yèh	耶	369	yéuhng	癢	313
yau	幼	126	yèh	揶	181	yéuhng	嚷	72
yàuh	尤	111	yèh	爺	290	yéuhng	氧	246
yàuh	攸	195	yèh	椰	228	yéuhng	養	494
yàuh	由	305	yèh	玡	298	yeuhng	羕	147
yàuh	油	251	yéh	嗻	63	yeuhng	漾	270
yàuh	鈾	467	yéh	惹	151	yeuhng	樣	233
yàuh	柔	219	yéh	冶	32	yeuhng	攘	194
yàuh	揉	181	yéh	野	465	yeuhng	壤	85
yàuh	蹂	442	yeh	偌	21	yeuhng	讓	429
yàuh	郵	460	yeh	夜	86	yeuhng	釀	464
yàuh	縣	361	yeuhk	曰	210	yéuih	蕊	396
yàuh	悠	149	yeuhk	弱	133	yeuih	汭	248
yàuh	游	265	yeuhk	虐	400	yeuih	枘	217
yàuh	遊	455	yeuhk	瘧	311	yeuih	蚋	401
yàuh	蝣	404	yeuhk	謔	426	yeuih	裔	411
yàuh	疣	309	yeuhk	龠	512	yeuih	銳	468
yàuh	魷	503	yeuhk	瀹	278	yeuih	睿	320
yàuh	銪	462	yeuhk	鑰	473	yeuk	約	351
yàuh	猷	296	yeuhk	若	386	yèung	央	88
yàuh	猶	295	yeuhk	葯	392	yèung	決	254
yáuh	友	49	yeuhk	藥	398	yèung	殃	241
yáuh	有	211	yeuhk	躍	444	yèung	秧	334
yáuh	酉	461	yeuhn	閏	474	yèung	鴦	505
yáuh	羑	365	yeuhn	潤	272	yéung	怏	143
yáuh	卣	46	yèuhng	羊	365	yéung	炜	281
yáuh	莠	389	yèuhng	佯	14	yeung	快	143
yáuh	誘	422	yèuhng	徉	137	yì	衣	408
yáuh	牖	291	yèuhng	洋	254	yì	依	15
yauh	又	49	yèuhng	烊	281	yì	銥	467
yauh	右	52	yèuhng	陽	479	yì	伊	11
yauh	佑	13	yèuhng	瘍	311	yì	咿	59
yauh	祐	330	yèuhng	颺	492	yì	椅	227
yauh	侑	16	yèuhng	穰	337	yì	漪	270
yauh	宥	105	yèuhng	禳	332	yì	噫	71
yauh	囿	75	yèuhng	揚	182	yì	禕	332

yì	醫	464	yíh	坺	385	yìhm	嫌	99
yí	倚	19	yíh	巳	121	yìhm	閻	475
yí	椅	227	yíh	耳	369	yìhm	嚴	73
yí	漪	270	yíh	矣	323	yìhm	簷	347
yí	綺	357	yíh	迤	451	yìhm	鹽	507
yí	旖	201	yíh	議	428	yìhm	冉	31
yi	衣	408	yíh	擬	193	yìhm	苒	386
yi	意	153	yíh	爾	290	yìhm	琰	301
yi	薏	397	yíh	邇	458	yìhm	染	219
yi	殪	243	yìh	二	5	yìhm	儼	27
yi	懿	161	yìh	弍	132	yìhm	焱	283
yìh	沂	249	yìh	貳	433	yìhm	焰	283
yìh	圯	76	yìh	易	204	yìhm	燄	287
yìh	兒	27	yìh	誼	423	yìhm	驗	499
yìh	迤	451	yìh	異	307	yìhm	艷	430
yìh	儀	26	yìh	義	366	yìhm	灩	279
yìh	蛇	401	yìh	肆	371	yìhm	彥	135
yìh	疑	308	yihk	亦	7	yìhm	諺	426
yìh	皚	315	yihk	弈	132	yìhn	言	417
yìh	而	368	yihk	奕	89	yìhn	焉	282
yìh	彝	135	yihk	弋	132	yìhn	賢	436
yìh	洏	256	yihk	逆	452	yìhn	妍	94
yìh	頤	490	yihk	役	136	yìhn	研	325
yìh	宜	105	yihk	疫	309	yìhn	延	131
yìh	誼	423	yihk	翌	367	yìhn	涎	258
yìh	洟	256	yihk	翊	367	yìhn	筵	343
yìh	姨	95	yihk	翼	367	yìhn	弦	133
yìh	咦	58	yihk	易	204	yìhn	舷	382
yìh	夷	88	yihk	場	79	yìhn	然	283
yìh	痍	310	yihk	蜴	403	yìhn	燃	286
yìh	胰	374	yihk	液	259	yìhn	衍	408
yìh	移	334	yihk	掖	178	yìhn	巘	119
yìh	簃	346	yihk	腋	375	yìhn	現	300
yìh	迻	452	yihk	懌	159	yìhn	莧	389
yìh	怡	143	yihk	斁	198	yìhn	峴	116
yìh	詒	419	yihk	譯	428	yìhn	唁	61
yìh	貽	433	yihk	繹	362	yìhn	彥	135
yìh	飴	493	yihk	驛	499	yìhn	諺	426
yíh	以	10	yìhm	炎	280	yìhn	讞	429

yìhng	仍	8	yīk	抑	168	yin	嘅	72
yìhng	扔	165	yīk	益	316	yìng	英	386
yìhng	盈	316	yīk	嗌	67	yìng	瑛	301
yìhng	楹	229	yīk	閱	501	yìng	應	159
yìhng	刑	37	yīk	億	26	yìng	膺	378
yìhng	邢	135	yīk	憶	158	yìng	鷹	506
yìhng	形	135	yīk	臆	378	yìng	嬰	101
yìhng	型	79	yìm	奄	88	yìng	攖	194
yìhng	硎	326	yìm	淹	262	yìng	櫻	237
yìhng	垄	81	yìm	腌	375	yìng	嚶	73
yìhng	瑩	302	yìm	閹	475	yìng	瓔	303
yìhng	瀅	277	yìm	醃	463	yìng	纓	363
yìhng	熒	268	yìm	愍	160	yìng	鸚	506
yìhng	焚	286	yìm	奄	88	yìng	癭	313
yìhng	營	288	yìm	掩	180	yìng	映	204
yìhng	螢	405	yìm	弇	132	yíng	影	136
yìhng	縈	359	yìm	偃	21	yìng	應	159
yìhng	瀅	278	yìm	魘	502	yip	醫	487
yìhng	邢	459	yìm	俺	18	yit	咽	59
yìhng	贏	100	yìm	厭	48	yit	噎	70
yìhng	瀛	278	yìm	饜	496	yit	謁	426
yìhng	贏	437	yìn	烟	281	yìu	夭	86
yìhng	迎	450	yìn	咽	59	yìu	要	413
yìhng	陘	478	yìn	胭	374	yìu	腰	376
yìhng	凝	34	yìn	焉	282	yìu	吆	53
yìhng	蠅	406	yìn	煙	285	yìu	徼	140
yíhng	郢	460	yìn	菸	390	yìu	夭	87
yìhng	認	422	yìn	燕	287	yìu	要	414
yìhng	媵	99	yìn	殷	243	yìu	邀	458
yihp	頁	489	yìn	關	475	yíu	妖	92
yihp	葉	392	yìn	嫣	99	yíu	祅	241
yihp	燁	287	yín	兗	29	yíu	窅	380
yihp	曄	209	yín	硯	325	yíu	繞	361
yihp	業	229	yín	偃	21	yíu	窈	338
yihp	鄴	461	yín	堰	81	yíu	鳶	504
yihp	孽	103	yín	鍵	245	yíu	擾	193
yiht	臬	380	yín	演	271	yíu	要	414
yiht	熱	286	yin	宴	106	yiuh	堯	80
yiht	嚙	511	yin	燕	287	yiuh	嬈	100

yìuh	嶢	118	yùh	峿	119	yúh	瘐	311
yìuh	蟯	406	yùh	歟	239	yuh	與	381
yìuh	饒	495	yùh	輿	448	yuh	瘉	312
yìuh	姚	94	yùh	如	91	yuh	喻	66
yìuh	搖	184	yùh	茹	388	yuh	諭	424
yìuh	徭	139	yùh	娛	96	yuh	癒	313
yìuh	瑤	302	yùh	予	5	yuh	峪	116
yìuh	遙	456	yùh	余	13	yuh	裕	411
yìuh	謠	427	yùh	禺	332	yuh	御	138
yìuh	繇	361	yùh	愚	153	yuh	寓	107
yìuh	窰	339	yùh	嵎	118	yuh	淤	255
yíuh	舀	209	yùh	魚	502	yuh	語	422
yìuh	曜	380	yùh	漁	269	yuh	預	489
yìuh	耀	368	yùh	盂	315	yuh	豫	431
yò	唷	63	yùh	隅	479	yuh	遇	455
yò	喲	64	yùh	餘	494	yuh	馭	496
yù	竿	341	yùh	虞	400	yuh	譽	428
yù	于	6	yùh	舁	380	yuh	禦	332
yù	迂	450	yùh	臾	380	yuh	籲	348
yù	紆	351	yùh	萸	392	yuhk	谷	430
yù	於	200	yùh	諛	424	yuhk	浴	257
yù	瘀	311	yùh	腴	376	yuhk	欲	238
yù	傴	23	yùh	儒	26	yuhk	慾	157
yù	嫗	99	yùh	孺	103	yuhk	玉	298
yù	淤	261	yùh	嚅	72	yuhk	鈺	467
yú	淤	261	yùh	濡	275	yuhk	肉	371
yu	煦	284	yùh	愈	153	yuhk	育	373
yu	酗	462	yúh	予	5	yuhk	獄	296
yùh	俞	29	yúh	宇	104	yuhk	鷸	502
yùh	逾	263	yúh	汝	247	yuhk	辱	450
yùh	愉	152	yúh	雨	483	yuhk	溽	267
yùh	揄	181	yúh	羽	366	yuhk	褥	413
yùh	榆	229	yúh	乳	5	yuhk	縟	359
yùh	覦	415	yúh	與	381	yuhk	蓐	394
yùh	瑜	301	yúh	語	422	yùhn	丸	1
yùh	逾	454	yúh	圉	75	yùhn	紈	351
yùh	踰	442	yúh	齬	511	yùhn	爰	289
yùh	與	381	yúh	禹	332	yùhn	媛	98
yùh			yúh	庾	129	yùhn	湲	264

yùhn	玄	298	yùhng	庸	128	yún	畹	307
yùhn	炫	280	yùhng	傭	23	yun	怨	145
yùhn	眩	319	yùhng	慵	156	yùng	喁	68
yùhn	沿	252	yùhng	墉	82	yùng	邕	459
yùhn	原	48	yùhng	勇	41	yùng	雍	482
yùhn	源	266	yuhng	用	305	yùng	壅	84
yùhn	員	60	yuht	乙	4	yùng	饔	495
yùhn	圓	76	yuht	月	211	yùng	翁	366
yùhn	元	27	yuht	曰	210	yùng	臃	313
yùhn	完	104	yuht	穴	337	yúng	冗	31
yùhn	沅	249	yuht	悅	148	yúng	宂	104
yùhn	芫	384	yuht	說	423	yúng	絨	354
yùhn	浣	282	yuht	越	439	yúng	佣	14
yùhn	袁	409	yuht	閱	475	yúng	甬	305
yùhn	猿	296	yuht	粵	349	yúng	俑	17
yùhn	轅	448	yūk	沃	249	yúng	涌	258
yùhn	緣	358	yūk	昱	205	yúng	蛹	402
yùhn	園	75	yūk	煜	284	yúng	慂	155
yùhn	圜	75	yūk	旭	202	yúng	湧	264
yùhn	鉛	466	yūk	或	135	yúng	踴	442
yùhn	懸	160	yūk	郁	459	yúng	擁	191
yúhn	遠	456	yūk	勖	41	yúng	壅	84
yúhn	軟	446	yūk	陳	481	yúng	朧	379
yuhn	炫	280	yūk	毓	244	yúng	澚	267
yuhn	眩	319	yūk	燠	288			
yuhn	衒	408	yùn	冤	107			
yuhn	愿	154	yùn	冤	32			
yuhn	願	491	yùn	蜿	404			
yuhn	媛	98	yùn	鴛	505			
yuhn	縣	359	yùn	淵	262			
yùhng	戎	161	yùn	鳶	504			
yùhng	容	106	yún	丸	1			
yùhng	溶	267	yún	鴛	505			
yùhng	熔	286	yún	阮	477			
yùhng	榕	230	yún	宛	105			
yùhng	蓉	394	yún	院	478			
yùhng	喁	64	yún	惋	150			
yùhng	茸	387	yún	婉	97			
yùhng	融	404	yún	苑	385			

、部

丸 yùhn, yún (Md wán)
① a pellet ② a small ball ③ a pill

丹 dàan (Md dān)
① cinnabar ② red, scarlet ③ a sophisticated decoction

丹麥 Dàan mahk
Denmark

丹青 dàan chìng
painting

主 jyú (Md zhǔ)
① the master; leader; chief; host ② Lord; Jesus Christ ③ to officiated at; to preside over, to take charge of

主人 jyú yàhn
host, master

主任 jyú yahm
head of office; the person in charge; director

乓 bām (Md pāng)
the sound of bām; used for the sound

一部

一 yāt (Md yī)
① one; a; an; first; uniform ② unit; union; uniformity ③ to unify; to unite ④ once

一半 yāt bun
a half

一份 yāt fahn
a part; portion or share

七 chāt (Md qī)
the number seven

七折 chāt jit
thirty percent discount

七十二行 chāt sahp yih hòhng
all the professions and avocations

丁 dìng (Md dīng)
① the fourth of the 10 "Celestial Stems,"(天干)② population ③ a chinese family name

丁香花 dìng hèung fā
lilac

丁寧 dìng nìhng
to give repeated injunctions

三 sàam (Md sān)
three; third; thrice

三等 sàam dáng
three grades or classes; the third grade; the third class; inferior

三位一體 sàam waih yāt tái
the Trinity; three-in-one

上 seuhng, séuhng (Md shàng)
① above; upper; high; superior; excellent; previous; before ② top; summit; on ③ up; upward ④ to ascend; to go to court; to mount; to board

上部 seuhng bouh
the upper portion

上馬 séuhng máh
to mount a horse

丈 jeuhng (Md zhàng)
① a unit in Chinese lineal measurement slightly longer than 10 feet ② an elder; a senior

丈夫 jeuhng fù
husband

丈母娘 jeuhng móuh nèuhng
mother-in-law (the mother of one's wife)

下 hah (Md xià)
① to descend; to put down; to lay ② to begin ③ below; under; inferior; low; next

下來 **hah lòih**
to come down

下午 **hah ńgh**
afternoon

丐 **koi** (Md **gài**)
① to beg for alms ② a beggar
③ to give

丐頭 **koi tàuh**
the leader of the beggars

丐養 **koi yéuhng**
to adopt a child or children

丏 **míhn** (Md **miǎn**)
① curtain to ward off arrows
② hidden

不 **bāt** (Md **bù**)
no; not; negative

不必 **bāt bīt**
not necessary

不及格 **bāt kahp gaak**
to fail to pass (examinations);
disqualified

丑 **cháu** (Md **chǒu**)
① the second of the twelve
"terrestrial branches"(地支)② the
period from 1 to 3 a.m. ③ a clown
④ a Chinese family name

丑時 **cháu sìh**
the period from 1 to 3 a.m.

丑角 **cháu gok**
comedian in chinese opera;
clown

且 **ché** (Md **qiě**)
moreover; now; still; further

且慢 **ché maahn**
Hold it! Not so fast!

且說 **ché syut**
Let us now talk about (usually
used at the beginning of a
narrative) moreover

丕 **pèi** (Md **pī**)
① great; distinguished; vast ② in

observance of (a ruling, etc.)

丕顯 **pèi hín**
great and distinguished

丕業 **pèi yihp**
great career (esp. referring to
the throne)

世 (丗) **sai** (Md **shì**)
① a generation ② a person's life
span ③ an age ④ the world

世界 **sai gaai**
the world

世人 **sai yàhn**
people of the world, (in the
Bible) men or man

丘 **yàu** (Md **qiū**)
① a hillock or mound ② big; elder
③ empty ④ name of Confucius

丘八 **yàu baat**
an anagram for "soldier" (often
used in contemptuous sense)

丘陵 **yàu lìhng**
mound; craggy terrains

丙 **bíng** (Md **bǐng**)
① the third of the ten "Celestial
Stems" (天干) ② another name
for fire ③ tail of a fish ④ a
chinese family name

丙等 **bíng dáng**
(in grading) roughly equivalent
to the "C" grade

丞 **sìhng** (Md **chéng**)
① to aid, to assist ② a deputy or
assistant to an official

丞相 **sìhng seung**
prime minister

丟 **dìu** (Md **diū**)
to lose; to get rid of; to reject

丟下 **dìu hah**
to throw down; to lay aside

丟臉 **dìu líhm**
to lose face

並 (幷，竝) bihng

(Md bìng)
① and; also; at the same time ② on the same level with; even; equal ③ entirely; completely

並且 bihng ché
moreover; furthermore and; in addition; to boot

並非 bihng fèi
by no means

｜部

丫 ngà (Md yā)
something that branches or forks upward

丫枝 ngà jì
a forked branch

丫頭 ngà tàuh
(in old China) a slave girl; a bought maid; a maid (in morden) a small girl

中 jùng (Md zhōng)
① the middle; among; within; between; heart ② China or Chinese; Sino-

中心 jùng sām
center; central point; persons holding important positions

中國 Jùng gwok
China, the Middle Kingdom; Cathay

中 jung (Md zhòng)
① to hit (the target); to attain (a goal) ② used together with past particle to form the passive tense

中的 jung dìk
to hit the bull's eye; to hit the right point

中計 jung gai
to walk into a trap; to be trapped

丰 fùng (Md fēng)
① good-looking; buxom ②

appearance and carriage of a person

丰采 fùng chói
good looking; dashing appearance

丰韻 fùng wáhn
charming appearance or carriage; graceful poise

串 chyun (Md chuàn)
① to string together; to league ② a string of coins

串通 chyun tùng
to collude or to conspire

串珠 chyun jyù
a string of pearls or beads; reference book; marginal references

丿部

乃 (迺、廼) náaih

(Md nǎi)
① to be ② but; however; and also moreover ③ that; those; your

乃是 náaih sih
but; which is

乃父 náaih fuh
your father

久 gáu (Md jiǔ)
① long; lasting ② for a long time

久別 gáu biht
long separated; long separation

久候 gáu hauh
to wait for a long time

之 jì (Md zhī)
① to go to; to arrive at ② zizag; winding ③ an expletive ④ third person objective case; it; this; that; these; those

之前 jì chìhn
before this

之外 jì ngoih
besides this; in addition

乍 ja (Md zhà)
① at first; for the first time
② suddenly; unexpectedly abruptly; inadvertently

乍見 ja gin
to meet for the first time; to see suddenly; to happen to see

乍冷乍熱 ja láahng ja yiht
now cold, now hot (referring to changeable weather)

乎 fùh (Md hū)
① at; in; from; than ② an interrogative particle ③ an exclamatory particle

乏 faht (Md fá)
① without; in want of; deficient; etc. ② empty; exhausted; tired; etc. ③ poor; poverty-stricken

乏力 faht lihk
to feel exhausted; to lack strength or vitality

乏味 faht meih
monotonous; dull; insipid ; tasteless

乒 bìng (Md pīng)
used for the sound

乒乓 bìng bām
ping-pong (used for the sound)

乒乓球 bìng bām kàuh
table-tennis

乖 gwàai (Md guāi)
① to turn the back on to oppose; to contradict ② perverse; obstinate; untoward; sulky; cunning; artful; crafty wily; strange; odd

乖巧 gwàai háau
clever; ingenious

乖乖 gwàai gwàai
obedient; an endearing name for children

乘 sìhng, sihng (Md chéng, shèng)
① to ride; to mount ② to avail oneself of ③ to multiply ④ a team of four horses; a set of four arrows ⑤ Buddhist teaching ⑥ historical records ⑦ an ancient carriage

乘客 sìhng haak
passengers

乘數 sìhng sou
multiplicator; multiplier

乙部

乙 yuht (Md yǐ)
① the second of the ten "Celestial Stems" (天干) ② one ③ an ancient Chinese family name

乙種 yuht júng
Category B

乙等 yuht dáng
B grade

乜 mé, māt (Md miē)
① to glance side ways ② a very rare chinese family name

乜斜 mé chèh
to glance sideways

九 gáu (Md jiǔ)
① nine; ninth ② to collect

九月 gáu yuht
September; the ninth moon of the lunar calendar; nine months

九州 Gáu jàu
Kyushu, an island of Japan

乞 hāt (Md qī)
to ask for alms; to beg; to entreat; to pray humbly

乞丐 hāt koi
beggar

乞憐 hāt lìhn
to beg for pity and charity

也 **yáh** (Md **yě**)
① and; also; besides ② still ③ even ④ an expletive in chinese writing

也門 **Yáh mùhn**
Yemen

也許 **yáh héui**
perhaps; probably

卣 **gèi** (Md **jī**)
to divine; to resolve doubts by an application to spiritual being

乳 **yúh** (Md **rǔ**)
① milk; breasts; the nipple ② the young of animals, birds etc. ③ to give birth ④ to triturate

乳名 **yúh mìhng**
pet name given to children

乳燕 **yúh yin**
young swallows

乾 **kìhn** (Md **qián**)
heaven; male; a father; a sovereign; first of the diagrams

乾坤 **kìhn kwàn**
male and female; heaven and earth

乾宅 **kìhn jaahk**
the bride groom's family

乾 **gòn** (Md **gān**)
① clean; diligent ② dry; dried; exhausted

乾杯 **gòn bùi**
to toast; bottoms up

乾洗 **gòn sái**
dry cleaning

亂 (乱) **lyuhn** (Md **luàn**)
① chaos; anarchy; distraction; confusion ② rebellion; revolt; insurrection ③ confused; perplexed; agitated; disarrange; raveled ④ out of order; to throw into disorder; to confound

亂世 **lyuhn sai**
times of anarchy and disorder

亂說 **lyuhn syut**
to say what should not be said; to lie

丿部

了 **líuh** (Md **liǎo**)
① finished; concluded ② intelligent ③ entirely; wholly ④ to understand; to complete; to finish

了事 **líuh sih**
to finish up a matter

了解 **líuh gáai**
to understand or comprehend

了 **líuh** (Md **le**)
an expletive in the Chinese language

予 **yùh, yúh** (Md **yú, yǔ**)
① me ② to give

予等 **yùh dáng**
we; us

予取予求 **yúh chéui yúh kàuh**
to make repeated demands of somebody

事 **sih** (Md **shì**)
① an affair; a matter; an undertaking; business ② a job; an occupation; a task ③ a service; duties; functions ④ a subject ⑤ to serve; to attend

事情 **sih chìhng**
matter; business; circumstances

事實 **sih saht**
fact; truth; reality

二部

二 **yih** (Md **èr**)
two; second; twice

二月 **yih yuht**
February; the second moon of the lunar calendar; two months

二等 **yih dáng**
economy class (said trains; ocean liners etc.); second grade

于 **yù** (Md **yú**)
① a particle in literary use in; at; by ② (a verb in literary use) to go or proceed; to take ③ a Chinese family name

于歸 **yù gwài**
to enter into matrimony (said of a girl)

于思 **yù sì**
long and thick beard (after days without shaving)

云 **wàhn** (Md **yún**)
to say; to speak

云云 **wàhn wàhn**
so and so; and so forth; and so on

互 **wuh** (Md **hù**)
each other; mutually; reciprocally

互相 **wuh sèung**
mutually; reciprocally each other; one another

互助 **wuh joh**
to help each other; mutual help

五 **ńgh** (Md **wǔ**)
five; fifth

五福 **ńgh fūk**
the five blessings - longevity, wealth, health, love of virtue, natural death

五金 **ńgh gām**
the five metals - gold, silver; copper; iron; tin; metals in general; hardware

井 **jéng** (Md **jǐng**)
a well

井底蛙 **jéng dái wà**
(literally) a frog in a well - a person of very limited outlook and experience

井井有條 **jéng jéng yáuh tìuh**
systematic (in handling things); orderly; methodical

互 (亘) **gáng** (Md **gèn**)
① to extend (over space or time) ② a Chinese family name

亘古未有 **gáng gú meih yáuh**
There has been nothing like it since time immemorial unprecedented

些 **sè** (Md **xiē**)
a small quantity or number; a little; a few; some

些少 **sè síu**
a little; a little bit

些微 **sè mèih**
very little; slightly

亞 (亚) **nga, a** (Md **yà**)
① second (in excellence) ② Asia

亞當 **Nga dòng**
Adam

亞洲 **Nga jàu**
Asia

亟 **gīk, kei** (Md **jí, qì**)
urgent; pressing

亟欲 **gīk yuhk**
very anxious to do something

亟需 **gīk sèui**
urgently needed

一部

亡 **mòhng** (Md **wáng**)
① to lose; to perish; to flee ② lost; dead; ruined; the late (applicable only to deceased blood relatives or friends)

亡命 **mòhng mihng**
to go into exile; to escape (from justice) to a place far away from home

亡國 **mòhng gwok**
conquered country; fall of nation

尢 **kong, gòng (Md kàng)**
① proud ② indomitable ③ excessive

尢旱 **kong hóhn**
drought

尢直 **kong jihk**
righteous(ness)

交 **gàau (Md jiāo)**
① to submit; to hand in or over ② to meet ③ to exchange ④ to intersect

交點 **gàau dím**
point of intersection

交代 **gàau doih**
to hand over responsibility; to give an explanation or excuse

亥 **hoih (Md hài)**
① the last of the twelve "Terrestrial Branches" ② the hour between 9 and 10 p.m.

亥豕 **hoih chí**
error in handwriting or typographical error due to confusion of similar words

亦 **yihk (Md yì)**
also; too; likewise; as well

亦步亦趨 **yihk bouh yihk chèui**
to follow the example of another person at each move; slavish inmitation

亨 **hàng (Md hēng)**
to go through smoothly

亨利 **Hàng leih**
transliteration of Henry

亨通 **hàng tùng**
to go well; to proceed smoothly

享 **héung (Md xiǎng)**
① to enjoy; to receive ② to offer ③ to entertain

享受 **héung sauh**
to enjoy; to indulge oneself in (some pleasant pursuit)

享福 **héung fūk**
to enjoy happiness and prosperity; to have blessing

京 **gìng (Md jīng)**
① capital (of a country) metropolis ② great

京城 **gìng sìhng**
the capital (of the country)

京戲 **gìng hei**
Peking opera

亭 **tìhng (Md tíng)**
① booth, pavilion, garden house or rest house ② slim and erect ③ exactly during

亭子 **tìhng jí**
a pavilion

亭長 **tìhng jéung**
village constable (of the Chin and Han Dynasties)

亮 **leuhng (Md liàng)**
① bright; lustrous; brilliant; luminous; radiant; clear ② to display; to understand

亮光 **leuhng gwòng**
bright light; flash

亮話 **leuhng wah**
frank remarks; outspoken speech

亳 **tok, bok (Md bó)**
the seat of government during the Shang Dynasty, located in todays'

Shang Chiu County, Ho-nan Province

人部

人 **yàhn** (Md **rén**)
human being; person; people

人民 **yàhn màhn**
people (as opposed to the ruler or the government)

人生 **yàhn sàng**
human life; life

什 **sahp, jaahp, sahm** (Md **shí, shén**)
① sundry; miscellaneious ② ten ③ what (used either in question or as an exclamation); how

什物 **jaahp maht**
miscellaneous goods; sundry items

什麼 **sahm mō**
what?

仁 **yàhn** (Md **rén**)
① benevolence; humanity; mercy; kindness; charity ② kernel

仁慈 **yàhn chìh**
benevolence; magnanimity; charity; humanity; kindness; love)

仁兄 **yàhn hìng**
dear elder brother (a designation for a friend of the same standing as oneself)

仂 **laak** (Md **lè**)
a fraction (of number)

仂語 **laak yúh**
phrase

仃 **dìng** (Md **dīng**)
lonely; solitary

仄 **jāk** (Md **zè**)
① oblique ② of the three tones other the even tone (in ancient Chinese phonology)

仄聲 **jāk sìng**
oblique tone (any of the three tones other than the even tone, i.e. rising tone, going tone and entering tone)

仆 **fuh, pūk** (Md **pū**)
to fall; to prostrate

仇 **sàuh, chàuh, kàuh** (Md **chóu, qíu**)
① foe; enemy; rival; adversary ② hatred; enmity; antagonism; hostility; feud ③ to hate ④ a Chinese family name

仇人 **sàuh yàhn**
enemy; foe; rival; opponent; adversary; antagonist

今 **gàm** (Md **jīn**)
① present; recent; modern ② now; currently; presently; nowadays

今天 **gàm tìn**
today

今宵 **gàm sìu**
tonight

介 **gaai** (Md **jiè**)
① shelled aquatic animal ② to lie between ③ upright (of character) ④ great and honorable

介紹 **gaai siuh**
to introduce (a person to another)

介入 **gaai yahp**
to get involved; to interfere with

仍 **yìhng** (Md **réng**)
still; yet

仍舊 **yìhng gauh**
still; yet

仍是 **yìhng sih**
still is (what it used to be); still was (what it had been)

仔 **jí, jái** (Md **zǐ, zǎi**)
① careful ② young animal ③ one who tends cattle

仔細 **jí sai**
careful; punctilious; minute

仔女 **jái néui**
children (sons and daughters)

仕 **sih** (Md **shì**)
① an official ② to enter government service; to serve the government

仕女 **sih néuih**
men and women; painting portraying beautiful women

仕途 **sih tòuh**
career in government service; political career

仟 **chìn** (Md **qiān**)
① leader of one thousand men ② thousand (same as 千)

他 **tà** (Md **tā**)
① he; him ② other; another ③ future

他們 **tà mùhn**
they; them

他日 **tà yaht**
another day; some other day; some other time; some time in the future

仗 **jeuhng** (Md **zhàng**)
① weaponry ② to lean upon; to rely upon; to depend on

仗恃 **jeuhng chíh**
rely upon

仗義 **jeuhng yih**
with justice; righteous

仙（僊） **sìn** (Md **xiān**)
① a god; an immortal; a fairy ② divine

仙女 **sìn néui**
a fairy; a woman of divine beauty

仙遊 **sìn yàuh**
to die (a euphemistic expression)

付 **fuh** (Md **fù**)
to pay (money); to deliver (goods); to consign

付款 **fuh fún**
to make payments; to shell out

付郵 **fuh yàuh**
to post (a letter) or to mail (a parcel)

仞 **yahn** (Md **rèn**)
① a measure of length (approximately eight feet) ② to measure depth

仡 **ngaht, gaak** (Md **yì, gē**)
① gallant; valiant ② stately; majestice ③ name of a Chinese race

代 **doih** (Md **dài**)
① generation; dynasty; era ② to be a substitute or an equivalent

代表 **doih bíu**
to represent; representative

代理 **doih léih**
agent; to serve as agent of; to act as deputy of

令 **lihng** (Md **lìng**)
① a directive; an order ② to order ③ to cause something to happen ④ nice; good; excellent

令妹 **lihng múi**
your younger sister (used in formal speech)

令箭 **lihng jin**
an arrow used as a taken of authority (by field commanders in old China)

令 **lìm** (Md **lǐng**)
a ream (of paper)

仝 **tùhng** (Md **tóng**)
① the same as 同 ② a Chinese family name

以 **yíh** (Md **yǐ**)
by means of; because of

以內 **yíh noih**
within

以後 **yíh hauh**
after (a given point, or period of time); afterward

仰 **yéuhng** (Md **yǎng**)
① to look up ② to adore, admire or revere ③ to lean or rely upon ④ to swallow

仰望 **yéuhng mohng**
to hope; to rely upon (someone for support, help, etc.)

仰慕 **yéuhng mouh**
to adore; to regard with admiration

仲 **juhng** (Md **zhòng**)
① in the middle; between two entities ② the second

仲夏 **juhng hah**
the second of the summer months (i.e. the fifth moon); mid-summer

仲裁 **juhng chòih**
to arbitrate, arbitration

仳 **péi** (Md **pǐ**)
to part company

仳離 **péi lèih**
to part (from one's spouse); to divorce

忤 **nǵh** (Md **wǔ**)
opposing; wrong

忤作 **nǵh jók**
coroner

件 **gihn** (Md **jiàn**)
an auxiliary noun applied to things, clothes, etc.

件數 **gihn sou**
number of things, items suits, etc.

件件 **gihn gihn**
all (of the things or items in question)

价 **gaai, ga** (Md **jiè, jià**)
① servant ② simple form of " 價 "

任 **yahm, yàhm** (Md **rèn, rén**)
① duty; post; office ② to let (one act at will); to bear (a burden); to employ (one for a job) ③ a Chinese family name

任命 **yahm mihng**
to appoint (someone to an office); appointment

任意 **yahm yi**
arbitrary; at will

仿 (倣) **fóng** (Md **fǎng**)
① to imitate; to copy

仿古 **fóng gú**
to imitate the ancient style

仿效 **fóng haauh**
to imitate; to copy; to follow the example of

份 **fahn** (Md **fèn**)
① a share; a part ② a copy of (newspaper, document, etc.)

企 **kéih** (Md **qǐ**)
① on tiptoe ② to hope; to long; to expect

企圖 **kéih tòuh**
to intend; to play; to scheme; to attempt; an intention; a plan; a scheme

企業 **kéih yihp**
business enterprise

伉 **kong** (Md **kàng**)
spouse

伉儷 **kong laih**
  married couple (in formal speech)

伊 **yì** (Md **yī**)
① he; she ② a Chinese family name

伊人 **yì yàhn**
  that man (in poetry or song)

伊朗 **Yì lóhng**
  Iran

伍 **ńgh** (Md **wǔ**)
① military unit of five soldiers (in the Chou Dynasty) ② a Chinese family name ③ to associate (with a person) ④ five

伍長 **ńgh jéung**
  leader of a military unit of five soldiers (in former times)

伎 **geih** (Md **jì**)
talent; ability; skill

伎倆 **geih léuhng**
  skill; dexterity; craft

伕 **fù** (Md **fū**)
labourer

伏 **fuhk** (Md **fú**)
① to prostrate; to yield ② to hide; to lie in ambush

伏兵 **fuhk bìng**
  an ambush

伏罪 **fuhk jeuih**
  to admit guilt; to be executed

伐 **faht** (Md **fǎ**)
① to cut (wood) ② to subjugate (rebels, bandits, etc.)

伐木 **faht muhk**
  to fell trees

伐罪 **faht jeuih**
  to punish the guilty

休 **yàu** (Md **xiū**)
① to rest; to stop; to cease; to pause ② happiness; joy

休息 **yàu sīk**
  to rest from work; to take a rest

休假 **yàu ga**
  a holiday; to have a holiday

伙(夥) **fó** (Md **huǒ**)
① companion; colleague ② household goods

伙計 **fó gai**
  shop clerk

伙食 **fó sihk**
  meals

伯 **baak** (Md **bó**)
① father's elder brother ② a rank of nobility - count

伯父 **baak fuh**
  uncle (father's elder brother)

伯爵 **baak jeuk**
  a rank of nobility - count

估 **gú, gù, gu** (Md **gū, gù**)
① to estimate; to calculate; to evaluate ② to sell

估計 **gú gai**
  to estimate

估衣舖 **gu yì póu**
  second-hand clothes store

你 **néih** (Md **nǐ**)
you (singular)

你們 **néih mùhn**
  you (plural)

你好嗎？ **Néih hóu ma?**
  How are you?

伴 **buhn** (Md **bàn**)
① companion ② to accompany

伴侶 **buhn léuih**
  companion; pal; buddy; chum

伴娘 **buhn nèuhng**
  bride's maid

伶 **lìhng** (Md **líng**)

① drama performer; actor; actress ② lonely; solitary ③ clever; intelligent

伶人 **lìhng yàhn**

theatrical performer; actor; actress

伶俐 **lìhng leih**

clever; intelligent; cute; sharp; bright; smart

伸 **sàn** (Md **shēn**)

① to stretch; to extend; to straighten ② to report

伸手 **sàn sáu**

to reach out, hold out, or stretch out one's hand

伸訴 **sàn sou**

to present a complain; to air a grievance

伺 **jih** (Md **sì, cì**)

① to spy; to reconnoiter; to watch ② to serve

伺機 **jih gèi**

to wait for a favorable moment or chance

伺候 **jih hauh**

to wait; or attend upon; to serve

似 **chíh** (Md **sì, shì**)

① to resemble; to seem ② like; as if

似乎 **chíh fùh**

it seems or appears that; it seems appears or looks as if or as though

似的 **chíh dìk**

to give the impression that

伽 **kèh, gà** (Md **qié, jiā**)

(the character is not used alone)

伽藍 **kèh làahm**

Buddhist temple; a Buddhist deity (sangharama or Sanghagara)

伽利略 **Gà leih leuhk**

Galileo, 1564-1642, Italian physicist, astronomer and mathematician

佃 **dihn, tìhn** (Md **diàn, tián**)

① tenant farmer ② to tenant a farm ③ hunting

佃農 **dihn nùhng**

a tenant farmer or sharecroper

佃作 **tìhn jok**

to phough the land

但 **daahn** (Md **dàn**)

① but; however; yet ② only; merely

但是 **daahn sih**

but; however; yet

但丁 **Daahn dìng**

Dante, 1265-1321, Italian poet

佢 **kéuih** (Md **qú**)

he; him; she; her

佇 (佇、竚) **chyúh** (Md **zhū**)

① to stand (for a long time) ② to hope; to expect

佇立 **chyúh lahp**

to stand still; to stand motionless

佇候 **chyúh hauh**

to stand and wait

佈 (布) **bou** (Md **bù**)

① to announce; to declare ② to arrange

佈告 **bou gou**

a bulletin; to make public announcement

佈置 **bou ji**

to make arrangement; to arrange (furniture); to decorate (a living room, convention hall, etc.)

位 **waih** (Md **wèi**)
position; rank; location

位置 **waih ji**
position (in space); location; position (in an organization)

位於 **waih yù**
situated at; located at

低 **dài** (Md **dī**)
① low ② to lower

低頭 **dài tàuh**
to bow; to lower the head in shame

低音 **dài yām**
low-pitch sound; contralto (female); bass (male)

住 **jyuh** (Md **zhù**)
① to dwell; to inhabit; to live ② to stop ③ firm; fast; fixed

住宅 **jyuh jaahk**
residence; dwelling; house

住手 **jyuh sáu**
stop! to stop an action; to halt; to hold

佐 **jo** (Md **zuǒ, zuò**)
to assist; to aid; to second

佐證 **jo jing**
the evidence

佐膳 **jo sihn**
side dishes (as distinct from the staple food)

佑 **yauh** (Md **yòu**)
to help; to aid; to protect

佑助 **yauh joh**
to help; to aid; to assist

佔(占) **jim** (Md **zhàn**)
to seize; to usurp; to occupy; to take by force

佔領 **jim líhng**
to occupy (a foreign territory)

佔先 **jim sìn**
to lead (in a game or contest)

何 **hòh** (Md **hé**)
① what; how; where; why ② a Chinese family name

何必 **hòh bīt**
why should; why must; why is it necessary

何處 **hòh chyu**
where; in what place

佘 **sèh** (Md **shé**)
a Chinese family name

余 **yùh** (Md **yú**)
① a Chinese family name ② I; me (in formal speech)

佚 **yaht** (Md **yì**)
① idleness; comfort ② to err ③ a Chinese family name

佗 **tòh** (Md **tuó**)
① a load ② he ③ a Chinese family name

佛 **faht** (Md **fó**)
① Buddha ② of Buddhism

佛教 **faht gaau**
Buddhism

佛寺 **faht jí**
Buddhist temple

作 **jok** (Md **zuò, zuō, zuó**)
① to do; to make; to write; to compose; to act the part of ② the works (of a writer etc.)

作品 **jok bán**
the works (of a writers, artist, etc.)

作用 **jok yuhng**
function; uses; effect

佞 **nihng** (Md **nìng**)
① eloquent; persuasive; gifted with a glib tongue ② obsequious; fawning ③ to believe (in superstition)

佞人 **nihng yàhn**
an obsequious person who

flatters others by his glib tongue in order to gain favors

佟 **dùng** (Md **tóng**)

a Chinese family name

佣 **yúng** (Md **yòng**)

commission

佣金 **yúng gàm**
　commission

佩 **pui** (Md **pèi**)

① to wear; something worn on a girdle or clothing ② to admire ③ to be grateful

佩服 **pui fuhk**
　to admire; to respect

佩帶 **pui daai**
　to wear

佯 **yèuhng, chèuhng** (Md **yáng**)

① to pretend; to feign ② false; deceitful; feigning

佯狂 **yèuhng kwòhng**
　to feign madness, feigned madness

佯作不知 **yèuhng jok bāt jì**
　to pretend not knowing

使 **sí, si** (Md **shǐ**)

① to use; to employ ② to make; to act ③ to send as diplomatic personnel; displomatic envoys ④ emissary

使用 **sí yuhng, sái yuhng**
　to use; to employ

使者 **si jé**
　an envoy; an emissary

佳 **gàai** (Md **jiā**)

① beautiful; good ② auspicious; distinguished

佳人 **gàai yàhn**
　a beauty

佳節 **gàai jit**
　a festival; a carnival

佾 **yaht** (Md **yì**)

a row or file of dancers especially referring to those in ancient dances sacrifices or other rites

佾生 **yaht sàng**
　young boy dancers at court or temple on ceremonial occasions

佾舞 **yaht móuh**
　rows of ceremorial dancers; a dance now performed esp. on confucius' birthday at the sage's shrine

侃 **hón** (Md **kǎn**)

① straightforward; frank; bold ② amiable; pleasant ③ with confidence and composure

侃侃而談 **hón hón yìh tàahm**
　to talk with confidence and composure

來 (来) **lòih** (Md **lái**)

① to come; coming ② future; hence ③ (used after a number) a little more than; odd ④ a Chinese family name ⑤ return

來回 **lòih wùih**
　coming and going

來年 **lòih nìhn**
　the next year; the years to come

侈 **chí** (Md **chǐ**)

① wasteful, luxurious; lavish; extravagant ② to exaggerate; bragging ③ evil doings ④ excessive

侈靡 **chí méih**
　extravagante and excesses

侈論 **chí leuhn**
　exaggerated talk; to speak boastingly

例 **laih** (Md **lì**)

① a regulation, a custom;

something with which to compare ② a precedent ③ an example

例如 laih yùh
for example

例外 laih ngoih
exceptions

侍 sih (Md shì)
① to serve; to wait upon ② to accompany one's elder or superior ③ a designation for oneself when addressing an elder or a senior

侍者 sih jé
attendants, waiters, etc; Buddhist monks as attendants or servants to Buddha

侍奉 sih fuhng
to serve; to attend on

佬 lóu (Md lǎo)
① fellows ② a vulgar person; a hill-billy

侏 jyù (Md zhū)
① short ② a pigmy or dwarf

侏儒 jyù yùh
a dwarf

佻 tìu (Md tiāo)
① frivolous; impudent ② to steal; stealthily; to act in a furtive manner ③ to delay; dilatory; slow ④ to provoke

佻薄 tìu bohk
frivolous; not dignified

佼 gáau (Md jiǎo)
beautiful; handsome; attractive; outstanding; charming

佼佼 gáau gáau
stunningly beautiful; remarkable

侑 yauh (Md yòu)
① to help ② to urge to eat or drink ③ to repay other's kindness

侘 cha (Md chà)
① to boast ② disappointed; irresolute

侘傺 cha jai
disappointed

供 gùng, gung (Md gōng, gòng)
① to supply; to contribute to ② to give a statement or an account of a criminal act; to give evidence ③ to offer in worship

供給 gùng kāp
to supply; to equip; to provide

供奉 gung fuhng
to provide for one's elders; to offer sacrifices in worshipping

依 yì (Md yī)
① to depend on; to lean to ② to follow, to comply with; to obey ③ to be tolerant to; to forgive

依賴 yì laaih
to depend on

依照 yì jiu
in accordance with; in compliance with

傀 gwái (Md guǐ)
① strange; mysterious ② accidentally

佶 gāt (Md jí)
strong

佰 baak (Md bǎi)
hundred

侮 móuh (Md wǔ)
① to insult; to ridicule ② to disgrace; to illtreat; to humiliate

侮辱 móuh yuhk
to insult; to humiliate

侮慢 móuh maahn
to be rude

侯 hàuh (Md hóu)
① (in old China) the second of the five grades of nobility; a marquis ② the target in archery ③ a Chinese family name

侯門 hàuh mùhn
the marquis door (noble family)

侵 chàm (Md qīn)
① to raid; to aggress ② to encroach upon ③ to proceed gradually ④ a year of famine or disaster

侵犯 chàm faahn
(in law) to encroach upon other's right; to invade

侵略 chàm leuhk
aggression; encroachment

侶 léuih (Md lǔ)
① a companion; a mate ② to associate with

偏 guhk (Md jú)
narrow; cramped; confined

偏促 guhk chūk
cramped; confined; fidgeting; restless

便 bihn, pìhn (Md biàn, pián)
① expedient; convenient; handy ② fitting; appropriate ③ then, in that case ④ cheap; inexpensive ⑤ excrement and urine

便飯 bihn faahn
an ordinary meal

便宜 pìhn yìh
cheap; inexpensive

係 (系) haih (Md xì)
① to bind ② relationship; consequences ③ to be

係數 haih sou
(in math.) coefficient

促 chūk (Md cù)
① close; crowded ② to urge; to hurry

促進 chūk jeun
to urge to proceed; to press forward; to promote; promotion

促成 chūk sìhng
to help to materialize

俄 ngòh (Md é)
① suddenly; sudden; momentarily ② Russia

俄頃 ngòh kíng
shortly afterward; soon

俄國 Ngòh gwok
Russia

俎 jó (Md zǔ)
① a painted wooden stand used in offering rites ② a chopping board ③ a small table or stand ④ a Chinese family name

俎豆 jó dauh
two kinds of utensils used in ancient rituals

俎上肉 jó seuhng yuhk
(literally) meet on a chopping board — a helpless victim

俏 chiu (Md qiào)
① like; similar ② pretty and cute; winsome ③ (commodities) enjoying brisk sale a higher prices ④ (said of stock) bullish

俏皮 chiu pèih
pretty and cute; winsome; sarcastic

俊 jeun (Md jùn)
① talented; capable; superior; refined ② handsome; good-looking ③ big; huge

俊美 jeun méih
good-looking; handsome

俊偉 jeun wáih
superior and great

俐 **leih** (Md **lì**)
① facile; easy and quick ② sharp; clever ③ in order; tidy; neat

俚 **léih** (Md **lǐ**)
① vulgar; rustic unpolished ② meaning; purpose ③ small town or village; a trible

俚語 **léih yúh**
slang; rustic expression vulgar expressions

俚歌 **léih gō**
folk songs; country songs

俑 **yúng** (Md **yǒng**)
(in old China) wooden figures of men and women buried with the dead

俗 **juhk** (Md **sú**)
① customs or customary; common ② vulgar; unrefined ③ lay (as distinguished from clerical) wordly ④ tasteless; trite

俗語 **juhk wá**
common saying

俗人 **juhk yàhn**
a layman as opposed to the clergy; an ordinary person

俘 **fù** (Md **fú**)
① to take prisoner; prisoners of war ② to capture (booty, etc.) from the enemy

俘虜 **fù lóuh**
to take prisoner; prisoners of the war

俘獲 **fù wohk**
to capture (weapons; documents; etc. from the enemy)

俟 **jih** (Md **sì**)
① to wait for ② until; as soon as

俟機 **jih gèi**
to wait for the opportunity

保 **bóu** (Md **bǎo**)
① to guard; guardian; to protect ② to be responsible; to guarantee; to insure ③ a waiter or tender ④ to care for

保留 **bóu làuh**
to preserve; to reserve; with reservation

保護 **bóu wuh**
to protect; to guard; protection

俠(侠) **hahp** (Md **xiá**)
① a person dedicated to helping the poor and weak ② chivalry ③ a Chinese family name

俠義 **hahp yih**
chivalry

俠客 **hahp haak**
a person dedicated to the cause of justic, fairness, etc. by fighting for the poor and the oppressed

信 **seun** (Md **xìn**)
① honesty; good faith ② believing ③ to believe or trust ④ envoy, emissary, etc. ⑤ news ⑥ a letter ⑦ credentials; evidence; a pledge or token ⑧ to let (others do what they choose); free; easy; aimless ⑨ a Chinese family name

信封 **seun fùng**
an envelope

信徒 **seun tòuh**
a believer (of a religion)

俜 **pìng** (Md **pīng**)
lonely

俯 **fú** (Md **fǔ**)
① to face down; to come down; to bow down; to stop ② to condescend; to deign

俯首 **fú sáu**
to bend (or lower) one's head (usually refer to submission or admission of a wrong doing

俯允 **fú wáhn**
to grant (your) gracious permission

併 (并) bing (Md bìng)
① on a level with; even; equal ② all; entire ③ together

併吞 bing tàn
to swallow up entirely

併發症 bing faat jing
(in medicine) a complication

修 sàu (Md xiū)
① to repair; to adorn ② long; slender ③ to prune; to cut; to sharpen ④ to study

修女 sàu néui
a Catholic nun

修理 sàu léih
to repair; repair

俱 kèui (Md jù)
① altogether; all ② to accompany; accompanying ③ a Chinese family name

俱備 kèui beih
all made ready; all complete

俱樂部 kèui lohk bouh
a club (as a country club; golf club)

俳 pàaih (Md pái)
① a variety show; a vaudeville ② insincere; not serious ③ to walk to and fro

俳諧 pàaih hàaih
funny talks

俳優 pàaih yàu
a variety show; a player in such a show

俵 bíu (Md biào)
① to give to ② to scatter

俵分 bíu fàn
to give (things) to other people

俵散 bíu saan
to scatter

俶 chūk, tīk (Md chù, tì)
① to begin; a beginning ② to arrange the baggage for travel ③ not bound by convention

俶裝 chūk jòng
to arrange the baggage

俶儻 tīk tóng
to behave merrily and freely, regardless of conventions

俸 fúng (Md fèng)
emolument; salary from the government

俸祿 fúng luhk
emolument; government salary or pay

俺 yim (Md ǎn)
the personal pronoun, used especially in Shantung Province

俾 béi (Md bǐ)
① to cause, to enable ② that; so that

俾倪 béi ngàih
to glance sideways

俾能 béi nàhng
to enable

倀 (伥) chèung, chàahng (Md chāng)
① (in mythology) a ghost controlled by the tiger ② wild; rash

倆 (俩) léuhng (Md liǎ, liǎng)
① two; a pair; a couple ② craft; ability

倆人 léuhng yàhn
two persons, usually referring to a couple in love

倆月 léuhng yuht
a couple of months

倉 (仓) chòng (Md cāng)
① a granary ② a cabin, as in the ship ③ green ④ a Chinese family name

倉庫 **chòng fu**
a warehouse; a godown

倉促 **chòng chūk**
in a hurry

倌 **gùn** (Md **guān**)
① assistant in a wineshop ② a euphemism for a prostitute ③ the groom

個 (个) **go** (Md **gè, gě**)
① a numerary adjunct ② piece ③ one ④ roughly ⑤ an adjunct to an indefinite pronoun, as this, that

個人 **go yàhn**
the individual as contrasted with the group; personal; personality

個把 **go bá**
a few; one or two

倍 **púih** (Md **bèi**)
① double; to double ② (jointed to a numeral) — times; -fold ③ to rebel; to go against; to repudiate (an agreement etc.)

倍數 **púih sou**
a multiple

倍加 **púih gà**
to double

們 (们) **mùhn** (Md **men**)
an adjunct to a pronoun or noun to indicate plurality (usually of persons)

倒 **dóu, dou** (Md **dǎo, dào**)
① to fall over; to lie down ② to pour out; to empty ③ on the contrary; but; and yet; nevertheless ④ to inverse; to place upside down

倒閉 **dóu bai**
to close down shop; to go bankrupt or insolvent

倒退 **dou teui**
to retreat; to retrospect; to review

倔 **gwaht** (Md **juè, juè**)
intransigent; tough; hard

倔強 **gwaht géuhng**
intransigent; intransigence; obstinate; stubborn

倔起 **gwaht héi**
to rise suddenly (said of a nation)

倖 **hahng** (Md **xìng**)
① good fortune; fortunate ② good luck; lucky ③ to dole on; to spoil

倖進 **hahng jeun**
to attain (a position, etc.) by luck

倖臣 **hahng sàhn**
a favorite courtier

倘 **tóng** (Md **tǎng**)
if; supposing; in the event of

倘若 **tóng yeuhk**
if; supposing; in the event of

候 **hauh** (Md **hòu**)
① to wait ② a period ③ situation; condition ④ to pay (bills) ⑤ to greet; to inquire after

候補 **hauh bóu**
waiting to fill a vacancy, such as an alternate member of a committee, etc.

候選人 **hauh syún yàhn**
a candidate (esp. in election)

倚 **yí** (Md **yǐ**)
① to rely on; to depend on ② to lean toward

倚靠 **yí kaau**
to rely on; to trust to; support

倚傍 **yí bohng**
to pattern after; to emulate

倜 **tīk** (Md **tì**)
① to raise high ② unrestrained; unoccupied

倜儻 **tīk tóng**
elegant in a casual way; free and easy of manner

借 **je** (Md **jiè**)
① to borrow ② to avail of ③ to make a pretext of ④ if; supposing

借貸 **je taai**
to ask for a loan; to borrow

借問 **je mahn**
will you please tell me?

值 **jihk** (Md **zhí**)
① prices of commodities; value; cost; to cost ② at the time of ③ to meet; to happen

值錢 **jihk chín**
valuable; expensive

值日 **jihk yaht**
to be on duty for the day

倡 **cheung, chèung** (Md **chàng**)
① to lead; to introduce ② a prostitute ③ wild and unrestrained

倡導 **cheung douh**
to lead; to advocate; to promote

倡優 **chèung yàu**
a prostitute; an actress; a musician; an entertainer

悾 **húng, hùng** (Md **kǒng**)
① pressing; urgent ② poverty - stricken; distress

悾傯 **hùng chùng**
pressing; urgent

倨 **geui** (Md **jù**)
① haughty; rude ② slightly bent

倨傲 **geui ngouh**
haughty; rude

倩 **sihn, sin** (Md **qiàn**)
① pretty dimples of smiling woman ② handsome ③ a son-in-law ④ to ask somebody to do something for oneself; to solicit the service of a ghost-writer, etc.

倩影 **sihn yíng**
beautiful image of a woman

倩人代筆 **sihn yàhn doih bāt**
to ask someone to do something for oneself

倪 **ngàih** (Md **ní**)
① young and weak ② a division ③ a beginning ④ limit or bound ⑤ a Chinese family name

倫 **lèuhn** (Md **lún**)
① normal relationships among people ② comparision ③ classification ④ order ⑤ regular; ordinary ⑥ to choose; choice

倫理 **lèuhn léih**
moral principles; ethics

倫敦 **Lèuhn dēun**
London

倬 **cheuk** (Md **zhuō**)
① obvious ② big; large

倭 **wò** (Md **wō**)
name of a human race; an old name for Japan

倭寇 **wò kau**
(in ancient usage) the dwarf-pirates; the Japs

倦 **gyuhn** (Md **juàn**)
tired; weary

倦怠 **gyuhn tóih**
to be tired; worn out

倦勤 **gyuhn kàhn**
wanting to resign from a high position

倏(儵) **sūk** (Md **shū**)
hastily; suddenly

倏忽 **sūk fāt**
all of a sudden; very suddenly

倏瞬 **sūk seun**
a brief glimpse time, for a brief glimpse

偃 **yím, yín** (Md **yǎn**)
① to cease; to be at rest; to stop ② to lie on one's back ③ an embankment ④ a Chinese family name

偃臥 **yím ngoh**
to lie (or sleep) on one's back

偃旗息鼓 **yím kèih sīk gú**
to stop fighting; to stop the fanfare

假 **gá, ga** (Md **jiǎ, jià**)
① false; not real ② supposing; if, to avail of ③ to borrow ④ a Chinese family name ⑤ holiday

假冒 **gá mouh**
to counterfeit; to assume the identity of somebody else

假日 **ga yaht**
holiday

偈 **giht, gái** (Md **jié, jì**)
① brave; martial ② hasty; scudding ③ to chat

偉 (伟) **wáih** (Md **wěi**)
① extraordinary; great; big ② a Chinese family name

偉大 **wáih daaih**
great; extraordinary

偉人 **wáih yàhn**
a great man

偌 **yeh, nohk** (Md **ruò**)
so (used as an adverb to modify an adjective)

偌大 **yeh daaih, nohk daaih**
so big; so old

偎 **wùi** (Md **wēi**)
to cuddle; to embrace; to fondle

偎倚 **wùi yí**
to cuddle or curl up

偎傍 **wùi bohng**
to stay close together

偏 **pīn** (Md **piān**)
① biased; not fair; prejudiced; partial ② leaning; inclined to one side ③ an auxiliary verb indicating a sense of contrariness or determination

偏心 **pīn sàm**
bias

偏見 **pīn gin**
prejudice; bias

偕 **gàai** (Md **xié, jiē**)
① to accompany ② together

偕老 **gàai lóuh**
to grow old together as man and wife (usually used in blessing or greeting to newly-weds)

做 **jouh** (Md **zuò**)
① to work; to make; to do ② to act as; to pretend; to be ③ to give (a party, reception, etc.) ④ to enter (a profession)

做工 **jouh gùng**
to work

做飯 **jouh faahn**
to prepare food; to prepare a meal

停 **tìhng** (Md **tíng**)
① to stop ② to suspend; to delay ③ percentage

停止 **tìhng jí**
to stop; to cease

停車場 **tìhng chè chèuhng**
a parking lot; car park

健 **gihn** (Md **jiàn**)
① healthy; strong ② vigorous; capable ③ fond of; inclined to; liable to

健康 **gihn hòng**
　health; healthy

健忘 **gihn mòhng**
　forgetful; liable to forget

偲 **sì** (Md **sī**)
mutual encouragement

側(侧)**jāk** (Md **cè, zhāi**)
　① the side; sideway ② slant; to
　slant; to incline towards ③ low
　and narrow-minded; prejudiced;
　perverted ④ crooked

側面 **jāk mihn**
　the side; flank

側門 **jāk mùhn**
　a side-door

偵(侦)**jìng** (Md **zhēn,
zhēng**)
　① to detect; to spy; to scout; to
　reconnoiter ② scout; a spy; a
　detective

偵探 **jìng taam**
　detective; an investigator; a
　private eye; to investigate; to
　survey and examine

偵察 **jìng chaat**
　reconnaissance; to reconnoiter

偶 **ngáuh** (Md **ǒu**)
　① an idol; an image ② coinciden-
　tally; accidentally; occasionally
　③ not to be taken for granted ④
　an even number ⑤ a mate; to
　mate ⑥ one's company; fellows;
　buddies

偶然 **ngáuh yìhn**
　unexpectedly; accidentally; by
　chance

偶像 **ngáuh jeuhng**
　an idol; an image

偷 **tàu** (Md **tōu**)
　① to steal; to filch ② to do
　something without others'
　knowledge; stealthily; sur-
　reptitiously ③ to while away time

without purpose ④ to have
ex-marital activity

偷盜 **tàu douh**
　to steal; stealing; burglary

偷懶 **tàu láahn**
　to loaf on a job; lazy

偓 **ngāak** (Md **wō**)
　① narrow mindedness ② a
　Chinese family name

偬(傯)**chùng**
(Md **zǒng**)
　① urgent; having no leisure; busy
　② to be in straits (financial etc.)

偬偬 **chùng chùng**
　in a hurry

傢 **gà** (Md **jiā**)
furniture; a tool or tools

傢具 **gà geuih**
　furniture

傢伙 **gà fó**
　(in a comical sense) character;
　jerk; son of the gun

傀 **faai** (Md **kuǐ**)
　① a puppet ② great; gigantic;
　wonderful

傀儡 **faai léuih**
　a puppet

傀儡戲 **faai léuih hei**
　puppet show

傅 **fuh, fú** (Md **fù**)
　① a teacher; to teach ② to go
　together with; to add to; to be
　attached with or to ③ a Chinese
　family name

傍(旁)**pòhng, bohng**
(Md **báng, bàng**)
　① beside; by the side; near; close
　② near; approaching ③ to depend
　on

傍晚 **pòhng máahn**
　twilight

傍友 **bohng yáu**
one who depends on another or others (as a follower or disciple)

傑(杰)**giht** (Md **jié**)
① outstanding; remarkable extraordinary ② a hero

傑出 **giht chēut**
outstanding; eminent; extraordinary

傑作 **giht jok**
a masterpiece

傖(伧)**chòng**
(Md **cāng**)
① vulgar; cheap; lowly (persons) ② confused; disorderly

傖父 **chòng fuh**
a vulgar person

傘(伞)**saan** (Md **sǎn**)
① an umbrella ② a paratroopers

傘兵 **saan bìng**
paratroopers

傘骨 **saan gwāt**
the ribs of an umbrella

備(备、俻)**beih**
(Md **bèi**)
① a sense of completeness; perfection ② to prepare; to provide; to be ready

備考 **beih háau**
for reference; appendix for reference

備忘錄 **beih mòhng lúk**
memorandum

傚 **haauh** (Md **xiào**)
to model after; to imitate, to emulate

傚尤 **haauh yàuh**
emulation (of a bad example)

催 **chèui** (Md **cuī**)
to hasten; to urge; to press

催促 **chèui chūk**
to hasten; to urge; to press

催眠 **chèui mìhn**
to hypnotize; to mesmerize

傭(佣)**yùhng**
(Md **yōng**)
① to hire ② a servant; a domestic help

傭工 **yùhng gūng**
to hire laborers; hired laborers or servants

傭兵 **yùhng bìng**
mercenaries

傲 **ngouh** (Md **ào**)
proud; haughty; overbearing; rude

傲慢 **ngouh maahn**
haughty and overbearing

傲世 **ngouh sai**
to look down upon the world

傳(传)**chyùhn, jyuhn, jyún** (Md **chuán, zhuàn**)
① to pass (a ball, an order, learning, etc.) ② to propagate; to desseminate; to issue; to proclaim ③ to summon ④ to preach ⑤ to infect ⑥ a biography

傳道 **chyùhn douh**
to preach

傳記 **jyuhn gei**
a biography

傴(伛)**yù** (Md **yǔ**)
hunchbacked

傴僂 **yù làuh**
hunchbacked; an attitude of reverence

傷(伤)**sèung**
(Md **shāng**)
① a cut, wound or injury ② grief; to grieve; distressed ③ to impede; impediment ④ to hurt (feelings) ⑤ to make sick

傷風 **sèung fùng**
　to catch cold

傷心 **sèung sàm**
　deeply hurt; to break one's
　heart; very sad

債(债) **jaai** (Md **zhài**)
a debt; an obligation

債主 **jaai jyú**
　the creditor

債務 **jaai mouh**
　debt or obligation

傺 **chai, jai** (Md **chì**)
① to hinder ② to be disappointed

傻(傻) **sòh** (Md **shǎ**)
① stupid; foolish; dumb ② naive
③ stunned; stupefied; terrified

傻瓜 **sòh gwā**
　a fool

傻笑 **sòh siu**
　gigging; to laugh for no con-
　ceivable reason

傾(倾) **kìng** (Md **qīng**)
① to slant; slanting ② to
collapse; to fall flat; to upset; to
subvert ③ to pour out ④ to
exhaust (one's wealth, etc.) ⑤ to
admire; to be fascinated or
intrigued

傾向 **kìng heung**
　to be inclinded to; to side with;
　tendency; trend

傾聽 **kìng ting**
　to listen carefully; to be all
　ears for

僂(偻) **làuh** (Md **lǚ**)
① hunchback; deformed ② bent
③ a Chinese family name

僅(仅) **gán** (Md **jǐn, jìn**)
① only ② barely enough;
scarcely; almost

僅僅 **gán gán**
　only; hardly enough; barely

僅有 **gán yáuh**
　to have only . . . ; there are only

僉(佥) **chìm** (Md **qiān**)
all; the whole

傔 **sìn** (Md **xiān**)
same as 仙

像(像) **jeuhng** (Md **xiàng**)
① image; potrait ② to resemble;
resemblance ③ like, as, "A person
like him is not dependable"

像是 **jeuhng sih**
　(it) looks like . . . ; it seems

像話 **jeuhng wah**
　to appeal to reason, logic,
　accepted practice, etc.

僑(侨) **kìuh** (Md **qiáo**)
to sojourn, sojourn

僑民 **kìuh màhn**
　persons who reside in a
　country other than their own;
　alien residents

僑胞 **kìuh bàau**
　overseas Chinese

僞(伪、偽) **ngaih** (Md **wěi, wèi**)
① false; counterfeit ② simulated;
artificial ③ illegal; not legally
constituted

僞造 **ngaih jouh**
　counterfeit; fogery

僞君子 **ngaih gwàn jí**
　a hypocrite

僕(仆) **buhk** (Md **pú**)
① a servant ② a modest term
referring to oneself ③ (in old
China) a driver a charioteer

僕人 **buhk yàhn**
　a servant

僕歐 **buhk ngāu**
　a boy or waiter (esp. in a

restaurant, cabaret)

僚 liuh (Md liáo)
① a companion; a friend ② a colleague or associate; subordinates

僚屬 liuh suhk
subordinates

僖 hèi (Md xī)
① joy; joyful ② a Chinese family name

僭 chim, jim (Md jiàn)
to assume; to usurp

僭越 chim yuht
to assume (title, powers, etc.)

僥(傲、儌) hiu
(Md jiǎo)
luck; lucky

僥倖 hiu hahng
luck; chance

僦 jauh (Md jiù)
to rent; to hire

僦居 jauh gèui
to rent (a house)

僧 jàng (Md sēng)
① a Buddhist priest ② a Chinese family name

僧人 jàng yàhn
a Buddhist priest

僧寺 jàng jí
a Buddhist temple

僮 tùhng, jong (Md tóng, zhuàng)
① a servant ② a boy ③ a Chinese family name

僮僕 tùhng buhk
servants

僮族 Jong juhk
name of a small tribe in southern China

僱 gu (Md gù)
to hire; to engage; to employ

僱主 gu jyú
employer

僱員 gu yùhn
employee

儆 gíng (Md jǐng)
① to be on guard; to get ready (for attack, etc.) ② to warn; to caution

儆戒 gíng gaai
to warn; to caution; warning; caution

儆儆 gíng gíng
uneasy; wary

僵 gèung (Md jiāng)
① to lie flat ② to be inactive; stiff, rigid ③ to be in a stalemate; deadlocked

僵持 gèung chìh
in a stalemate; deadlocked

僵硬 gèung ngaahng
rigid; stiff

價(价) ga (Md jià, jie)
price; cost; value

價錢 ga chìhn
prices

價值 ga jihk
value

僻 pīk (Md pì)
① biased; low; mean ② not easily accessible; out of the way; secluded ③ not common; not ordinary; ambiguous; nebulous

僻壤 pīk yeuhng
an out-of-the-way village, town, etc.

僻靜 pīk jihng
out of the way; secluded

僨 fáhn (Md fèn)
to ruin; to destroy

僨事 fáhn sih
to destroy a plan

儀(仪)**yìh** (Md **yí**)
① appearance; deportment; manner ② ceremonies; rites ③ a rule; regulation form or standard ④ customs ⑤ instruments; apparatus ⑥ a Chinese family name

儀表 **yìh bíu**
appearance and deportment; a rule; a model

儀器 **yìh hei**
(lab, medical, etc.) instruments apparatus

儂(侬) **nùhng** (Md **nóng**)
① (in old usage) I; me ② (in present-day Shanghai dialect) you ③ (in Ningpo, Chekiang, dialect) he, she ④ a Chinese family name

億(亿)**yīk** (Md **yì**)
① a hundred million ② safe ③ (according to) estimates

億兆 **yīk siuh**
astronomical in number; countless; numberless; the people; the masses

儈(侩) **kúi** (Md **kuài**)
a middle man; a go between; a brooker

儉(俭) **gihm** (Md **jiǎn**)
① frugal; economical ② meager ③ a poor harvest

儉約 **gihm yeuk**
thrifty and temperate

儉用 **gihm yuhng**
to be careful with one's spending; frugal; thrifty

儋 **dàam** (Md **dān**)
① to shoulder or bear a burden ② a load of two piculs (esp. of rice or grains)

儒 **yùh** (Md **rú**)
① the learned; scholars collectively ② Confucian; confucianism ③ weak; shrinking from hardship

儒家 **yùh gā**
scholars following Confucian thoughts; Confucianists

儒雅 **yùh ngáh**
scholarly and refined; elegant; (with) style

儐(傧) **ban** (Md **bīn**)
① to entertain guests ② to arrange; to set in order; to guide

儐相 **ban seung**
best man of a bride-groom; bride's maid

儔(俦)**chàuh** (Md **chóu**)
a companion or companions; party or company

儕(侪)**chàaih** (Md **chái**)
① a class; a company ② an adjunct to show plurality ③ to match (as man and wife)

儕輩 **chàaih bui**
persons (esp. friends or companions) of the same generation

儘(尽)**jéun** (Md **jǐn**)
① the utmost; the extreme ② to let (him do it)

儘量 **jéun leuhng**
as (much, soon, strong, etc.) as possible

儘管 **jéun gún**
even if; no matter; despite . . . ; inspite of . . .

償(偿) **sèuhng** (Md **cháng**)
① to repay; to compensate; to make restitution ② to fulfill (a

wish) ③ to offset

償還 sèuhng wàahn
to repay (what one owes)

償願 sèuhng yuhn
to fulfill one's wish; to get what one desires

儡 léuih (Md lěi)
① a puppet ② sickly and thin ③ dilapidated

優(优) yàu (Md yōu)
① good; excellent ② abundant; plenty ③ players (as in an opera) ④ victory; winning ⑤ soft ⑥ to seduce ⑦ a Chinese family name

優良 yàu lèuhng
fine; good

優伶 yàu lìhng
professional actors

儲(储)chyúh (Md chǔ)
① to save; to store; savings ② deputy; an alternate ③ a Chinese family name

儲蓄 chyúh chūk
to save (esp. money); savings

儲君 chyúh gwàn
the crwon prince

儱 lúhng (Md lǒng)
same as 籠

儷(俪) laih (Md lì)
a pair; a couple

儷影 laih yíng
the heart-warming sight of a couple in love

儻 tóng (Md tǎng)
① same as 倘 ② unexpectedly

儼 yíhm (Md yǎn)
① majestic; respectable ② (to act, talk, appear) as if; like

儼然 yíhm yìhn
dignified-looking (sometimes with a sarcastic connotation);

neat-looking (house, etc.)

儿部

兀 ngaht (Md wù)
① to cut off the feet ② high and flat on the top ③ this ④ ignorant-looking

兀立 ngaht lahp
to stand rigidly without motion

兀鷹 ngaht yīng
vulture (Gypes fulvus)

允 wáhn (Md yǔn)
① to allow; to consent; to grant ② appropriate; proper ③ sincere; loyal; faithful

允許 wáhn héui
to assent; to grant; permission; consent

允准 wáhn jéun
to approve; to grant; to consent

元 yùhn (Md yuán)
① the beginning; the first; original ② the head ③ the eldest; chief; big ④ a coin; a dollar ⑤ (in Chinese astrology) 60 years ⑥ the Yuan Dynasty (1277 - 1367) ⑦ a Chinese family name

元旦 yùhn daan
New Year's Day

元首 yùhn sáu
the chief of the state; the king; the president; etc.; the beginning

兄 hìng (Md xiōng)
① an elder brother ② a term used in addressing a senior of the same generation to show respect

兄弟 hìng daih
a kid brother; brothers; a designation for juniors' of the same generation among one's relatives; I (a modest term)

兄長 **hìng jéung**
an elder brother

兆 **siuh** (Md **zhào**)
① a sign (in fortune telling) ② an omen ③ a trillion ④ to begin; beginning ⑤ a Chinese family name

兆民 **siuh màhn**
the people; the masses

兇 **hùng** (Md **xiōng**)
① fierce; violent; cruel ② truculent; inhuman

兇猛 **hùng máahng**
fierce; violent

兇手 **hùng sáu**
the murderer; the killer

充 **chùng** (Md **chōng**)
① to fill; to be full of ② to take; to cheat; to pretend ③ a Chinese family name

充足 **chùng jūk**
plenty; abundance; sufficient plentiful abundant; suficience

充公 **chùng gùng**
to confiscate

先 **sìn** (Md **xiān**)
① before ② first; foremost ③ in front ④ the late; deceased ⑤ one's fore bears ⑥ a Chinese family name

先生 **sìn sàang**
teacher; mister; sir; husband

先夫 **sìn fù**
my late husband

光 **gwòng** (Md **guāng**)
① light; brightness; light rays ② glossy ③ glory; glorious; to glorify ④ to exhaust ⑤ alone ⑥ bare; to bare; naked ⑦ a Chinese family name

光明 **gwòng mìhng**
bright; brightness

光線 **gwòng sin**
ray of light

克 **hāk, hāak** (Md **kè**)
① to be able to ② to win; to overcome; to conquer ③ love of superiority ④ gram

克服 **hāk fuhk**
to overcome (difficulties, etc.)

克勤克儉 **hāk kàhn hāk gihm**
diligent and frugal

兌 **deui** (Md **duì**)
① to exchange; to barter ② to transfer liquid from one vessel to another

兌換 **deui wuhn**
to exchange (currencies)

兌現 **deui yihn**
to redeem; to convert (paper money) into hard money; to cash (a check, etc.); to fulfill (a promise)

免 **míhn** (Md **miǎn**)
① to avoid; to escape; to evade ② to forego; to spare; to excuse; to exempt ③ to dismiss (from office)

免費 **míhn fai**
free of charge; gratuitous; gratis

免役 **míhn yihk**
exemption from military-service

兒 (儿) **yìh** (Md **ér**)
① a child (esp. male) ② referring to oneself when addressing parents ③ a particle used after many nouns, pronouns, adjectives, adverbs and verbs

兒童 **yìh tùhng**
children

兒子 **yìh jí**
son or sons

兔(兔) tou (Md tù)

① a hare; a rabbit ② a young boy kept for sexual perversion

兔子 tou jí

a hare; a rabbit; a homo; a young boy kept for sexual perversion

兔唇 tou sèuhn

harelip, or cleft lip

兗 yín (Md yǎn)

(in ancient China) one of the Nine Division of the Empire under Yu the Great including parts of Shantung and Hopeh provinces

兜 dàu (Md dōu)

① a head-covering; a helmet ② an overall ③ to solicit ④ a small pocket in clothes

兜風 dàu fùng

to go joy-riding

兜售 dàu sauh

to peddle

兢 gìng (Md jīng)

to fear; to dread; apprehensive; cautions

兢兢業業 gìng gìng yihp yihp

with caution and fear

入部

入 yahp (Md rù)

① to enter ② to arrive at; to reach ③ to put in ④ receipt; income ⑤ to get out of sight; to disappear ⑥ to get (inside, picked, elected, etc.)

入口 yahp háu

an entrance; import (commodities, etc.)

入教 yahp gaau

to become a follower or believer of a religion

內 noih (Md nèi)

① inside; within; inner; interior; domestic ② wife ③ the palace of an emperor

內部 noih bouh

the interior; the internal part

內容 noih yùhng

contents; the meaning, theme, etc. of a literary or artistic work

全 chyùhn (Md quán)

① perfect ② complete; whole; total; intact; totally ③ to keep ④ absolute; absolutely ⑤ a Chinese family name

全部 chyùhn bouh

the whole; completely; fully

全球 chyùhn kàuh

around the globe; the globe; the world

兩(两) léuhng (Md liǎng)

① two; a pair; a couple ② a tael ③ a two-wheel cart ④ (in old China) a piece of cloth, etc. of about 44 feet ⑤ (in old China) a group of 25 soldiers

兩邊 léuhng bìn

both sides; two sides

兩用 léuhng yuhng

serving two purposes (said of an instrument, a gadget, etc.) (said of a cost) reversible

俞 yùh (Md yú)

① to answer in the affirmative ② to make a boat by hollowing the log ③ a Chinese family name

俞允 yùh wáhn

to accede to a request

八部

八 baat (Md bā)

eight

八月 **baat yuht**
August; the eighth moon of the lunar calendar; eight months

八成 **baat sìhng**
(literally) eighty per cent — nearly; almost; very likely

公 **gùng** (Md **gōng**)
① unselfish; unbiased; fair ② public; sharing with others; open to all ③ the first of old China's five grades of nobility; an old chinese official rank ④ grandfather; father of one's husband ⑤ a respectful salutation ⑥ the male (of animals) ⑦ official duties ⑧ a Chinese family name·

公平 **gùng pìhng**
fair; unbiased; just

公民 **gùng màhn**
citizens

六 **luhk** (Md **lìu**)
six

六十 **luhk sahp**
sixty

六月 **luhk yuht**
June; the six moon of the lunar calendar; six months

兮 **hàih** (Md **xī**)
① an adjunct with no independent meaning, roughly equivalent to "Oh" or "Ah" in English ② a particle of pause used in ancient poetry and still used in eulogise

共 **guhng** (Md **gòng**)
① common; same; all; collectively ② to share; to work together ③ an abbreviation of the word "Commission" or "Communist"

共同 **guhng tùhng**
common; shared by all; to cooperate in (an undertaking, etc.)

共產黨 **Guhng cháan tóng**
the Communist Party

兵 **bìng** (Md **bīng**)
① arms, weapons ② a soldier; a serviceman military ③ to strike; to attack ④ a piece in Chinese Chess - a pawn

兵士 **bìng sih**
a soldier; a foot-soldier

兵役 **bìng yihk**
compulsory military service

其 **kèih** (Md **qí**)
① a pronoun — he; she; it; they; his; her; its; their ② this; that; the ③ an adverb denoting time or used to introduce a question ④ a conjunction

其他 **kèih tà**
and the others; the rest; miscellaneous

其實 **kèih saht**
in fact; as a matter of fact; actually

具 **geuih** (Md **jù**)
① an appliance; implement, utensil, tool etc. ② talent; capability ③ equipment ④ complete; all; the whole ⑤ to prepare, draw up or write out ⑥ a Chinese family name

具備 **geuih beih**
all complete; all ready; to have (qualification or advantage)

具體 **geuih tái**
concrete (measures, results, etc.) as opposed to abstract

典 **dín** (Md **diǎn**)
① a rule; a statue; a law; a canon ② a tale or story ③ to pawn; to mortgage ④ to take charge of ⑤ a Chinese family name

典禮 **dín láih**
ceremony; rite

典當 **dín dong**
to pawn; a pawn shop

兼 **gìm** (Md **jiān**)
① to unite in one; to connect ②
and; also; together with both;
equally

兼任 **gìm yahm**
to serve concurrently as (a
secretary, etc.); to have a side
job

兼顧 **gìm gu**
to look after both sides; to
take care of the needs, etc. of
both parties

冀 **kei** (Md **jì**)
① to hope ② another name for
Hopeh Province ③ a Chinese
family name

冂部

冇 **móuh** (Md **mǎo**)
do not have; an equivalent for
"没有 muht yáuh"

冉(丹) **yíhm** (Md **rǎn**)
① gradually; to proceed gradually
② tender; weak ③ the outer edge
of a turtle's shell ④ a Chinese
family name

冉冉 **yíhm yíhm**
gradually; imperceptibly

冉冉上升 **yíhm yíhm
seuhng sìng**
to rise gradually

册(冊) **chaak** (Md **cè**)
① (in old China) a register; a
book or books in general ② a list;
statistical tables; to record;
records ③ an order to confer
nobility title

册封 **chaak fùng**
(in old China) to confer titles
of nobility on the emperor's
wives or princes

册子 **chaak jí**
a book; a pamphlet

再 **joi** (Md **zài**)
① again; repeated ② still; further; then ③ never again

再見 **joi gin**
Goodbye; See you again

再版 **joi báan**
second printing or edition (of
a book or film)

胄 **jauh** (Md **zhòu**)
① descendants; posterity ②
eldest

冒 **mouh** (Md **mào**)
① in cautions; imprudent; rash ②
to risk; to brave; to be exposed
to (hardship) ③ to put forth; to
issue forth; to go up (as fire,
smoke, etc.) ④ a Chinese family
name

冒險 **mouh hím**
to take risks; to brave dangers

冒火 **mouh fó**
to blow one's top; to become
angry

冕 **míhn** (Md **miǎn**)
① a ceremonial cap for high
ministers in old China ② a crown

冖部

冗(宂) **yúng** (Md **rǒng**)
① redundant; superfluous; ②
disorderly

冗長 **yúng chèuhng**
redundant; superfluous; super-
numerary; (of a writing)
verbose

冗員 **yúng yùhn**
superfluous members of a staff
or organization

冠 **gùn, gun** (Md **guān,
guàn**)
① to wear a cap ② the comb or
crest of a bird ③ a Chinese family
name ④ at 20 when a young man

is capped ⑤ first-rate

冠冕堂皇 gùn míhn tòhng wòhng
elegant and stately; officially or publicly

冠軍 gun gwàn
a champion; an outstanding person

冥 míhng (Md míng)
① dark; obscure; dim ② stupidity ③ far and high ④ deep; profound ⑤ the unseen world ⑥ night ⑦ a Chinese family name

冥想 míhng séung
deep meditation

冥王星 Míhng wòhng sìng
the planet Pluto

冢 chúng (Md zhǒng)
① a high grave; a peak; a summit ③ the eldest ④ great; supreme; prime (all referring to official ranks) as supreme councilor, prime minister, etc.)

冤 (寃) yùn (Md yuān)
① oppression; injustics; a greivance; a wrong ② feud; animosity; enmity ③ to cheat; to lie ④ to spend money recklessly to waste money ⑤ to make false accusation

冤鬼 yùn gwái
a wronged soul; ghost of a person who died of injustics

冤仇 yùn sàuh
feud; enmity; animus

幂 (冪) mihk (Md mì)
① to cover with cloth; cloth thus used; a veil ② power (in mathematics)

冫部

冬 dùng (Md dōng)
① winter ② (in lunar calendar) the period from the 10th to the 12th moon

冬至 dùng ji
the winter solstice

冬菇 dùng gù
mushroom

冰 (氷) bìng (Md bīng)
① ice; icicles ② cold; frost

冰淇淋 bìng kèih làhm
ice cream

冰人 bìng yàhn
a match-maker

決 (决) kyut (Md jué)
① to decide; to conclude; to judge ② to burst; to break ③ certain; sure

決定 kyut dihng
to determine; to decide; a decision

決算 kyut syun
final financial statement

沖 (冲) chùng (Md chōng)
① to wash away; to wash with running water ② to soar; to rise rapidly or shoot up ③ to pour water (to powder solid, etc.) to make beverage, etc.; to infuse ④ empty; void ⑤ to dash against; to clash with ⑥ young ⑦ to neutralize; to make void

沖茶 chùng chàh
to make tea

沖洗 chùng sái
to wash with running water; (in photography) to develop or process negatives

冶 yéh (Md yě)
① to smelt; to fuse metals ② to seduce; to fascinate

冶金學 yéh gàm hohk
metallurgy

冶遊 yéh yàuh
to frequent brothels

冷 **láahng** (Md **lěng**)
① cold ② (said of business, farming, etc.) off-season; in leisure-spell ③ a Chinese family name

冷淡 **láahng daahm**
cold (expression); indifferent (attitude)

冷靜 **láahng jihng**
clear (mind, thinking, etc.) calm or composed; secluded or quiet (place, etc.)

況 (況) **fong**
(Md **kuàng**)
① moreover; in addition; not to mention ② to compare; comparative ③ situation; circumstances ④ to visit; to call at ⑤ a Chinese family name

況且 **fong ché**
moreover; besides; furthermore

況味 **fong meih**
situation; condition; circumstances

冽 **liht** (Md **liè**)
crystal-clear

冼 **sín** (Md **xiǎn**)
a Chinese family name

准 **jéun** (Md **zhǔn**)
① to approve; to permit; to allow; to grant; to authorize ② in accordance with ③ equivalent

准許 **jéun héui**
to approve; to permit; to allow; approval; permission

准將 **jéun jeung**
a brigadier general

凊 **jihng** (Md **jìng**)
cold; cool; chilly

凋 **dìu** (Md **diāo**)
① withered; faded ② exhausted; emaciated

凋謝 **dìu jeh**
fallen-as blossoms; faded; withered

凋零 **dìu lìhng**
withered; lonely; deserted

凍 (冻) **dung** (Md **dòng**)
① to freeze ② cold; icy

凍結 **dung git**
to freeze (an account, asset, etc.)

凍僵 **dung gèung**
benumbed with cold; to be frozen stiff

凌 **lìhng** (Md **líng**)
① ice; pure; virtuous ② to insult; to maltreat; to throw one's weight around ③ to rise; to ride ④ to intrude; to traverse ⑤ a Chinese family name

凌辱 **lìhng yuhk**
to insult; to maltreat; to disgrace; to assult (a woman); to put to shame

凌亂 **lìhng lyuhn**
in total disorder or disarray messy; disheveled; untidy

凄 (淒) **chài** (Md **qī**)
① cloudy and rainy ② cold and chilly ③ sorrow; sorrowful; miserable; desolate

凄涼 **chài lèuhng**
desolate and sorrowful; lonely; lonesome

凄慘 **chài cháam**
heart-rending; heart-breaking

涼 (凉) **lèuhng**
(Md **liáng**)
① cool; chilly; cold ② thin; deficient ③ name of one of the 16 states during East Tsin ④ a Chinese family name

涼茶 **lèuhng chàh**
cold tea; (in chinese medicine)
a concoction drink of many
herbal ingredients to drive off
the "heat" in human body

涼鞋 **lèuhng hàaih**
sandals; summer shoes

湊 (湊) **chau (Md còu)**
① to put together ② to raise
(fund)

湊巧 **chau háau**
by chance; by coincidence

湊合 **chau hahp**
to manage to collect or gather
together; to make do with
what is available

凜 (凛) **láhm (Md lǐn)**
① cold; break; desolate ② to be
apprehensive; to shiver with cold
or fear ③ imposing; awe-inspiring

凜列 **láhm liht**
very cold; cold to the marrow

凜若冰霜 **láhm yeuhk bìng sèung**
(said of a woman) to be cold
as ice

凝 **yìhng (Md níng)**
① to freeze ② to congeal; to
coagulate ③ to form; to take
shape ④ to concentrate; to
cohere

凝固 **yìhng gu**
to congeal; to solidify (said of
liquid)

凝聚 **yìhng jeuih**
to concentrate; to curdle

几部

几 **gèi (Md jī)**
① a small table; a bench ② a
simplified form of the character
"幾"

几案 **gèi ngon**
a large long table

凡 (凣) **fàahn (Md fán)**
① common; ordinary; dull ②
worldly; mortal; earthly ③
generally; every; whenever;
wherever

凡人 **fàahn yàhn**
an ordinary person; one of the
masses; a layman; a mortal

凡例 **fàahn laih**
introduction of a book

凰 **wòhng (Md huáng)**
the femal phoenix, a legendary
bird in chinese mythology

凱 (凯) **hói (Md kǎi)**
① peaceful; joyful ② balmy;
soothing; tender ③ a victory-
triumphant return of an army

凱旋 **hói syùhn**
triumphant return of an army;
to return on triumph

凱歌 **hói gō**
song of victory or triumph

凳 (櫈) **dang (Md dèng)**
a stool; a bench

凳子 **dang jí**
a stool; a bench

凵部

凶 **hùng (Md xiōng)**
① evil ② famine ③ unlucky;
unfortunate ④ fear; fearsome ⑤
very; excessive; excess

凶兆 **hùng siuh**
a bad omen

凶年 **hùng nìhn**
a year of famine; a year of
misfortune

凸 **daht, gú (Md tū)**
① protuberant; jutting; convex ②
to protrude

凸面 **daht mín**
convex

凸鏡 **daht geng**
convex mirror

凹 **nāp, wà, ngaau**
(Md **āo**)
① indented; an indention; a hollow ② concave

凹面 **nāp mín**
concave

凹陷 **nāp hahm**
a hollow or depression (said of place)

出 **chēut** (Md **chū**)
① to go out; to come out ② to produce; to reproduce ③ to happen or to occur; to incur ④ to put forth; to bud; to burst (into flame, etc.) ⑤ to divorce (a wife, etc.); to chase away; to banish ⑥ to expand; to pay out ⑦ to escape; to leave (one's home, etc.) ⑧ to appear; to overtake ⑨ to take an office ⑩ to vent (one's anger, etc.)

出版 **chēut báan**
to publish

出品 **chēut bán**
products (of a certain company etc.)

函(圅) **hàahm**
(Md **hán**)
① a letter; correspondence ② armor ③ to contain; to envelop ④ a sheath, as for sword or knife

函件 **hàahm gín**
letters; correspondence

函購 **hàahm kau**
to purchase by mail order

刀部

刀 **dōu** (Md **dāo**)
① a knife; a blade; a sword ② knife-shaped coins of ancient China

刀片 **dōu pín**
a razor blade

刀叉 **dōu chā**
knives and forks (used in Western meals)

刁 **dìu** (Md **diāo**)
① low cunning; crafty; wicked; artful; knavish ② a Chinese family name

刁難 **dìu naahn**
to (deliberately) make things difficult for others

刁詐 **diu ja**
knavish; crafty

刃(刄) **yahn** (Md **rèn**)
① the blade or edge of a knife ② to kill

刄兒 **yahn yìh**
the edge or blade of a knife

分 **fàn, fahn** (Md **fēn, fèn**)
① to devide; to part; to share; to distribute; to distinguish ② one minute; one cent; one hundredth of a tael; a centimeter ③ located seperately; branch ④ a role or part (played by a person in life) ⑤ a part or portion (of a whole); component

分別 **fàn biht**
to depart (from a person); to distinguish or tell apart; seperately; to separate

分量 **fahn leuhng**
amount; weight or impact (said of statements)

切 **chit, chai** (Md **qiē, qiè**)
① to cut; to mince; to slice; to carve ② to be in close contact ③ all; as a whole

切開 **chit hòi**
to cut open

切磋 **chit chò**
to improve oneself through discussions with another

刈 **ngaaih** (Md **yì**)
to mow; to reap

刈草機 **ngaaih chòu gèi**
lawn mower; mowing machine; mower

刊 **hón, hōn** (Md **kān**)
① to hew; to cut; to engrave ② a publication; to publish

刊登 **hón dàng**
(for a writer) to publish (an article in a periodical); (for a periodical) to carry (an article)

刊物 **hón maht**
a periodical; a publication)

刎 **máhn** (Md **wěn**)
to cut the throat

刎頸之交 **máhn géng jì gàau**
ties between friends willing to sacrifice even life for each other; profound mutual devotion between friends

划 **wà** (Md **huá**)
① an oar ② to oar; to row

划船 **wà syùhn**
to row a boat

划子 **wà jí**
a small boat

列 **liht** (Md **liè**)
① to arrange in a line; to enumerate; to display ② arranged in a line; numerous ③ a line; a series ④ a Chinese family name

列入 **liht yahp**
to be included in; to be incorporated in

列島 **liht dóu**
chain of islands; archipelago

利 **leih** (Md **lì**)
① profit; benefit; advantage; gain ② sharp ③ to benefit; to serve

利潤 **leih yeuhn**
profit; gain; net profit

利用 **leih yuhng**
to utilize; to make use of; to take advantage of; to avail oneself of

初 **chò** (Md **chū**)
① first ② new; original ③ junior ④ early; initial

初次 **chò chi**
the first time or occasion

初學 **chò hohk**
in the beginning stage of an effort to learn (a subject); a beginner

刪 (刪) **sàan** (Md **shān**)
to delete; to take out; to erase

刪改 **sàan gói**
to remove superfluities and correct errors (in a writing); to revise

刪除 **sàan chèuih**
to delete; expunge; strike out; erase; or remove (superfluities from a writing)

判 **pun** (Md **pàn**)
to judge; to conclude

判別 **pun biht**
to distinguish; to tell apart

判決 **pun kyut**
verdict; sentense

別 **biht** (Md **bié, biè**)
① to part ② to distinguish; to differ ③ other; seperate; different ④ do not (in imperative expressions)

別名 **biht mìhng**
an alias; a second name

別離 **biht lèih**
parting; seperation

刨 **pàauh** (Md **páo, bào**)
to dig; to excavate

刨地 **pàauh deih**
to dig the ground

刨子 **pàauh jí**
a plane

刮 **gwaat** (Md **guā**)
to pare; to shave; to scrape

刮破 **gwaat po**
to cut or hurt (the face, etc.)
in shaving

刮臉 **gwaat líhm**
to shave (the face)

到 **dou** (Md **dào**)
① to reach; to arrive ② a Chinese
family name

到達 **dou daaht**
to reach or to arrive

到底 **dou dái**
after all; in the long run; at
lenght; in the end; finally; to
reach the extremity

刑(刑)**yìhng** (Md **xíng**)
penalty; punishment

刑罰 **yìhng faht**
penalty; punishment

刑法 **yìhng faat**
criminal law; criminal code;
penal law

剁(剁)**dó** (Md **duò**)
to chop; to mince; to hash

剁肉 **dó yuhk**
to mince or hash meat

剁碎 **dó seui**
to mince; to hash

刳 **fù** (Md **kū**)
to gouge; to scoop; to hollow

制 **jai** (Md **zhì**)
① to establish; to institute ② to
force; to prevail; to overpower ③
a system ④ used before the

signature in letter writing to
indicate the writer in mourning

制度 **jai douh**
a system; an institution

制止 **jai jí**
to stop by force

刷 **chaat** (Md **shuā,
shuà**)
to brush; to scrub; to clean

刷洗 **chaat sái**
to scrub

刷牙 **chaat ngàh**
to brush the teeth

刺 **chi, sik** (Md **cì, cī**)
① to pierce; to stab; to irritate;
to hurt ② a thorn ③ to
assassinate

刺激 **chi gīk**
to stimulate; to provoke; to
excite; to irritate; stimulus

刺刀 **chi dōu**
a bayonet

刻 **hāk** (Md **kè**)
① to carve; to engrave; to cut ②
a quarter (of an hour) ③ cruel;
heartless; unfeeling

刻刀 **hāk dōu**
a chisel

刻字 **hāk jih**
to engrave words (on stone,
blocks, etc.)

券 **hyun, gyun**
(Md **quàn**)
① a ticket ② a certificate ③ a
bond

刹 **saat** (Md **chà, shā**)
① a (buddhist) temple, shrine,
monastry or abbey ② to stop (a
car or engine)

刹那 **saat náh**
ksana; a moment; an instant;
a twinkling

利車 **saat chè**
  to stop a car (in a sudden)

則(则)**jāk (Md zé)**
① a law; a rule ② a particle indicating consequence or result (usually used after a supposition) ③ a numerary particle used before news reports, advertisement, etc.

剃(鬀)**tai (Md tì)**
to shave

剃刀 **tai dōu**
  a razor

剃頭 **tai tàuh**
  to shave the head

剄(刭)**gíng (Md jǐng)**
to cut the throat

削 **seuk (Md xuē, xiāo)**
to cut; to pare; to trim; to shave

削減 **seuk gáam**
  to curtail; to cut down; to slash

削髮 **seuk faat**
  to shave the head (so as to become a Buddhist nun or monk)

剋(尅)**hāk (Md kēi)**
to overcome; to limit

尅扣 **hāk kau**
  to withhold (military supplies, etc.) for personal gain

尅星 **hāk sìng**
  (literaly) a malignant star; a person who always bars another person from success; an unbeatable rival; a jinx

剌 **¹laaht (Md là)**
to go against; to contradict

前 **chìhn (Md qián)**
① front; forward ② previous; former; preceding; past ③ future ④ to advance; to proceed; to progress; to precede

前天 **chìhn tìn**
  day before yesterday

前途 **chìhn tòuh**
  the prospect; promise (in the sense of an indication of a successful prospect or future)

剔 **tīk (Md tī)**
① to seperate bones from meat ② to pick out inferior materials

剔除 **tīk chèuih**
  to eliminate (undisirable materials)

剔牙 **tīk ngàh**
  to pick the teeth

剖 **páu, fáu (Md pōu)**
① to cut, rip or tear open ② to explain; to analyze

剖開 **páu hòi**
  to cut or rip open

剖白 **páu baahk**
  to dispel suspicion by explanation

剛(刚)**gòng (Md gāng)**
① tough; unyielding; inflexible; hard ② just now

剛才 **gòng chòih**
  just a moment ago; a very short while ago

剛強 **gòng kèuhng**
  tough and strong; indomitable; fortitudinous

剜 **wún (Md wān)**
to scoop out; to gouge out

宛空心思 **wún hùng sàm sì**
  to exhaust one's wits or ingenuity

剝(剥)**mōk, bōk (Md bō, bāo)**
① to strip ② to skin; to denude; to make bare; to peel

剝開 **mōk hòi**
　　to strip

剝奪 **mōk dyuht**
　　(bōk dyuht)
　　to deprive or strip one of
　　(rights, property, etc.)

剮(剐) **wá** (Md **guǎ**)
　　① cut to pieces (a form of capital
　　punishment in ancient times);
　　dismember ② cut; slit

副 **fu** (Md **fù**)
　　① to assist; to supplement ②
　　secondary (in importance)

副本 **fu bún**
　　a duplicate copy; a copy

副主席 **fu jyú jihk**
　　vice chairman

剪 **jín** (Md **jiǎn**)
　　to cut or clip with scissors; to
　　shear

剪刀 **jín dōu**
　　scissors; shears

剪綵 **jín chói**
　　to cut the ribbon (to
　　inaugurate a building, etc.)

剴(剀) **hói** (Md **kǎi**)
　　to sharpen a knife

剴切 **hói chit**
　　(said of statements) clearly

割 **got** (Md **gē**)
　　to cut; to sever; to divide

割斷 **got tyúhn**
　　to cut off; to sever by cutting

割愛 **got ngoi**
　　to give up what one treasures;
　　to give up something
　　reluctantly

創(创) **chong, chòng**
　　(Md **chuàng, chāung**)
　　① to start; to begin; to initiate;
　　to create ② original; unprece-
　　dented ③ a wound

創辦 **chong baahn**
　　to start (a business publica-
　　tion, etc.) to found (a school,
　　a club, etc.)

創傷 **chòng sèung**
　　a wound; a cut

剩(賸) **sihng**
　　(Md **shèng**)
　　to remain; left over; in excess;
　　residue; remainder; surplus

剩下 **sihng hah**
　　left over; remainder

剩餘 **sihng yùh**
　　the excess; the surplus; the
　　balance

剿(勦) **jíu** (Md **jiǎo**)
　　to exterminate; to stamp out; to
　　destroy; to put down

剿滅 **jíu miht**
　　to exterminate or destroy

剿匪 **jíu féi**
　　to launch attacks against the
　　bandits

剷 **cháan** (Md **chǎn**)
　　① a shovel ② to shovel

剷平 **cháan pìhng**
　　to level to the ground, to level

剷除 **cháan chèuih**
　　to root out

剽 **píuh** (Md **piāo**)
　　① to plunder; to rob; to steal ②
　　agile

剽掠 **píuh leuhk**
　　to plunder; to rob

剽竊 **píuh sit**
　　to steal; to puloin; to plagiarize

劃(划) **waahk** (Md **huà, huá**)
　　① to unify ② to lay boundaries
　　③ to plan or to design ④ to set
　　aside ⑤ to cut

劃分 **waahk fàn**
　　to devide and delimit.

劃開 **waahk hòi**
　　to cut open; to slash open

劇(剧) **kehk** (Md **jù**)
　　① drama ② intense; strenuous

劇本 **kehk bún**
　　a play; a scenario

劇烈 **kehk liht**
　　strenuous; intense; hard; fierce

劈 **pek, pīk** (Md **pǐ, pī**)
　　① to cleave; to split; to rive; to
　　rend ② a wedge

劈開 **pīk hòi**
　　to split open; not to say the
　　fact that . . . ; cleavage (in
　　mining)

劈柴 **pek chàaih**
　　to split or chop firewood

劉(刘) **làuh** (Md **liú**)
　　① a Chinese family name ② to
　　kill

劉邦 **Làuh bòng**
　　Liu Pang, founder of the Han
　　Dynasty whose reign lasted
　　from 206 to 194 B.C.

劊(刽) **kúi** (Md **guì**)
　　to amputate; to cut off

劊子手 **kúi jí sáu**
　　an executioner; a hatchetman

劍(剑、劒) **gim**
(Md **jiàn**)
sword

劍客 **gim haak**
　　a swordman; a fencing master

劍蘭 **gim làahn**
　　gladiolus

劑(剂) **jài** (Md **jì**)
　　① a dose (of medicine) ②
prepared medicines or drugs ③ to
prepare (medicines and drugs)

力部

力 **lihk** (Md **lì**)
　　① stength; force; power; vigor;
might ② vigorously; earnestly;
energetically

力氣 **lihk hei**
　　physical strength or power

力量 **lihk leuhng**
　　strength; force; power

功 **gùng** (Md **gōng**)
　　① merit; achievement ②
usefulness; effectiveness ③
effort ④ function ⑤ (in physics)
work

功勞 **gùng lòuh**
　　merit; credit; meritoriours
deeds; contributions

功課 **gùng fo**
　　school work; homework

加 **gà** (Md **jiā**)
　　to add; to increase; to augment

加價 **gà ga**
　　to raise or hike the price

加入 **gà yahp**
　　to join (a group); to add into

劣 **lyut** (Md **liè**)
　　① inferior; mean ② minor (in
mathmatics)

劣點 **lyut dím**
　　a defect; a demerit

劣貨 **lyut fo**
　　goods of poor quality;
substandard goods

助 **joh** (Md **zhù**)
　　to help; to aid; to assist

助手 **joh sáu**
　　an assistant

助教 **joh gaau**
　　a teaching assistant

努 **nóuh** (Md **nǔ**)
　　to exert

努力 **nóuh lihk**
to make efforts; to strive; to endeavour; to work hard

努嘴 **nóuh jéui**
to move lips; to purse up lips (to show displeasure)

劫(刧、刼) **gip**
(Md **jié**)
① to rob; to plunder ② suffering; disaster

劫掠 **gip leuhk**
to plunder; to rob; to pillage

劫數 **gip sou**
ill luck; all fortune

劬 **kèuih** (Md **qú**)
labor; toil

劬勞 **kèuih lòuh**
toil (especially said of one's own mother)

劭 **siuh** (Md **shào**)
① to encourage; to urge ② beautiful; graceful

劾 **haht** (Md **hé**)
to accuse; to charge

劾狀 **haht johng**
a list of charges (against a public official)

勁(劤) **gihng** (Md **jìn, jìng**)
① strong; tough ② vigor; energy; strength interest

勁風 **gihng fùng**
gale; blast

勁兒 **gihng yìh**
vigor; energy; strength interest; enthusiasm

勃 **buht** (Md **bó**)
sudden; quick

勃發 **buht faat**
to break out; to begin suddenly

勃起 **buht héi**
to have an erection; erection

勇 **yúhng** (Md **yǒng**)
brave; courageous; bold valiant; intrepid; fearless; gallant; heroic

勇氣 **yúhng hei**
courage; bravery; valor; prowess; gallantry heroism; fearlessness

勇猛 **yúhng máahng**
intrepid; fierce

勉 **míhn** (Md **miǎn**)
to urge; to encourage; to compel; to force; to make effort

勉勵 **míhn laih**
to encourage; to urge; to rouse to action

勉強 **míhn géuhng**
reluctantly; in a forced manner

勒 **lahk** (Md **lè, lēi**)
① to force ② to engrave; to carve ③ to stop

勒令 **lahk lihng**
to compel by an order or injunction; to order

勒馬 **lahk máh**
to stop a horse from going ahead

勖(勗) **yūk** (Md **xù**)
to encourage

勖勉 **yūk míhn**
to encourage; to prompt

勘 **ham** (Md **kān**)
to investigate; to compare; to collate; to examine; to check

勘察 **ham chaat**
to investigate; to review; to examine

勘誤 **ham ngh**
to collate; to correct errors

務 (务) **mouh** (Md **wù**)
① to attend to; to strive after ②
duty; business ③ must;
necessary

務必 **mouh bīt**
must; by all means

務農 **mouh nùhng**
engage in farming

動 (动、働) **duhng**
(Md **dòng**)
to move

動筆 **duhng bāt**
to start writing

動脈 **duhng mahk**
an artery

勝 (胜) **sing, sìng**
(Md **shèng, shēng**)
① to win; to excel; to triumph ②
a place of natural beauty ③ to be
competent enough

勝敗 **sing baaih**
victory and defeat; outcome
(of a contest)

勝任 **sìng yahm**
to be adequate for and happy
with a job

勞 (劳) **lòuh** (Md **láo**)
① to labor; to toil; to work; to
trouble; to worry; to bother; to
tire ② a Chinese family name

勞動 **lòuh duhng**
to labor (physically); to toil; to
sweat; to trouble (a person
with a request)

勞工 **lòuh gùng**
laborers; workers

勢 (势) **sai** (Md **shì**)
power; force; influence; tendency

勢力 **sai lihk**
power; influence

勢利 **sai leih**
power and wealth; snobbish

募 **mouh** (Md **mù**)
① to recruit or enlist (personnel)
② to raise (funds)

募捐 **mouh gyùn**
to solicit or collect
contributions

募兵 **mouh bìng**
to recruit or enlist soldiers; to
raise troops

勤 **kàhn** (Md **qín**)
diligent; industrious; sedulous

勤勞 **kàhn lòuh**
to toil or labor sedulously

勤學 **kàhn hohk**
to study diligently

勳 (勋) **fàn** (Md **xūn**)
merit; honor

勳章 **fàn jēung**
a medal of honor; a decoration

勳爵 **fàn jeuk**
a rank conferred in recognition
of merits

勵 (励) **laih** (Md **lì**)
to incite; to encourage; to rouse
(to action)

勵行 **laih hàhng**
to enforce or practise with
determination

勵志 **laih ji**
to purse a goal with
determination

勸 (劝) **hyun** (Md **quàn**)
to exhort; to urge; to advise

勸告 **hyun gou**
to advise; to counsel

勸阻 **hyun jó**
to dissuade

勹部

勺 **cheuk** (Md **sháo**)
a ladle; a spoon; a spoonful

勺子 **cheuk jí**
a ladle; a spoon

勻 **wàhn** (Md **yún**)
uniform; even

勻稱 **wàhn ching**
symmetrical; balanced even;
harmonious

勾 **ngàu** (Md **gōu, gòu**)
① to mark; to put a check; mark
on ② to cancel ③ to hook; to
join; to connect; to entice ④ a
hook ⑤ to manage ⑥ business;
affair

勾結 **ngàu git**
to collude or collaborate
collusion or collaboration

勾當 **ngàu dong**
an underhand job; a slot; an
intrigue

勿 **maht** (Md **wù**)
do not; not; never; negative
marker in formal speech

勿念 **maht nihm**
do not worry

勿失 **maht sāt**
do not let (a chance, etc.) slip
away

包 **bàau** (Md **bāo**)
① to wrap; to include; to contain;
to surround ② to guarantee; to
contract ③ a parcel; a package;
a bundle

包括 **bàau kwut**
to include; to comprise

包裹 **bàau gwó**
to wrap up; a parcel; a bundle;
a package

匈 **hùng** (Md **xiōng**)
① the breast; the bosom; the
thorax ② to clamor

匈奴 **Hùng nòuh**
the Huns

匈牙利 **Hùng ngàh leih**
Hungary

匍 **pòuh** (Md **pú**)
to crawl; to creep; to lie prostrate

匍匐 **pòuh baahk**
to crawl; to creep

匐 **baahk** (Md **fú**)
to lie prostrate; to crawl; to creep

匏 **pàauh** (Md **páo**)
① a gourd; a bottle gourd; a
calabash ② a kind of wind instrument originally made of a gourd

匏瓜 **pàauh gwā**
a gourd; a bottle gourd; a
calabash

匕部

匕 **béi, beih** (Md **bǐ**)
① a ladle; a spoon ② an
arrow-head

匕首 **béi sáu**
a daggar; a stiletto

化 **fa** (Md **huà**)
① to change; to influence ②
short for "chemistry"

化石 **fa sehk**
a fossil

化學 **fa hohk**
chemistry

北 **bāk** (Md **běi**)
north; northern; northerly

北京 **Bāk gìng**
Peking

北極 **Bāk gihk**
the North Pole

匙 **chìh, sìh** (Md **chí, shi**)
① spoon ② key

匚部

帀(帀) jaap (Md zā)
to make a revolution round; to encompass

帀月 jaap yuht
a whole month

匠 jeuhng (Md jiàng)
a craftsman; an artisan

匠人 jeuhng yàhn
carpenters, masons, bricklayers, etc.

匠心 jeuhng sàm
inventiveness; ingenuity originality

匡 hòng (Md kuāng)
to rectify; to correct; to deliver

匡復 hòng fuhk
to restore national prestige or prosperity

匡正 hòng jing
to rectify; to correct; to reform

匣 hahp (Md xiá)
a case; a small box

匣子 hahp jí
a case; a small box

匪 féi (Md fěi)
① bandits; rebels; insurgents ② not

匪徒 féi tòuh
bandits; brigands; robbers

匪解 féi haaih
do not idle or relax

匯(汇、滙) wuih (Md huì)
① to remit money ② to converge

匯款 wuih fún
a remittance; to remit money

匯率 wuih leuht
exchange rate (between currencies)

匱(匮) gwaih (Md kuì)
① to lack ② a chest or cabinet

匱乏 gwaih faht
to lack; to be short of

匸部

匹 pāt (Md pǐ)
① a bolt (of cloth) ② to match ③ common ④ a numerary particle for horse

匹配 pāt pui
to match

匹夫之勇 pāt fù jì yúhng
fool hardiness

匾 bín (Md biǎn)
a (wooden) tablet

匾額 bín ngáak
a (wooden) tablet

匿 nīk (Md nì)
to hide; to conceal

匿名信 nīk mìhng seun
an anonymous letter

匿笑 nīk siu
to laugh in secret

區(区) kèui, ngàu (Md qū, ōu)
① to distinguish; to discriminate ② a district; an area; a zone ③ a border ④ little; few ⑤ a Chinese family name

區別 kèui biht
to discriminate; to distinguish

區域 kèui wihk
a district; an area

十部

十 sahp (Md shí)
① ten; the tenth ② complete; completely; perfect; perfectly; extremely

十分 sahp fàn
complete; completely; one

hundred per cent; very; 10 points

十誡 **sahp gaai**
(in the Bible) the ten commandments

千 **chìn** (Md **qiān**)
① thousand ② many; numerous ③ a Chinese family name

千金 **chìn gām**
a courteous expression referring to another's daughter; a thousand pieces of gold

千萬 **chìn maahn**
a huge amount; an expression used to emphasize an injunction or advice

卅 **sà, sàah** (Md **sà**)
thirty; 30th (of a month)

升 **sìng** (Md **shēng**)
① to rise; to raise; to advance; to ascend; to promote ② a unit of volume measurement (esp. for grains) ③ a Chinese family name

升天 **sìng tìn**
to ascend to heaven-to die; (in christianity) the Ascension

升學 **sìng hohk**
to enter a higher school; to advance to a higher school

午 **ngh** (Md **wǔ**)
① noon; high noon ② (in old chinese time measurement) 11 a.m. to 1 p.m. ③ seventh of the Twelve Terrestrial Branches (地支) ④ a Chinese family name

午飯 **ngh faahn**
lunch

午睡 **ngh seuih**
an afternoon nap; a siesta

半 **bun** (Md **bàn**)
half; to halve; to divide

半票 **bun piu**
a half-fare ticket; half-price ticket

半球 **bun kàuh**
a hemisphere

卉 **wái** (Md **huì**)
① a general term for plants ② myriads of

花卉 **fà wái**
flowering plants

卑 **bèi** (Md **bēi**)
① low; debased; depraved; vile; base ② inferior ③ a modest expression referring to oneself

卑下 **bèi hah**
base; mean; humble

卑鄙 **bèi péi**
(said of a person's character) mean; depraved; crooked; base; (said of a person's social position) low; inferior

卒 **jēut** (Md **zú, cù**)
① a servant; an underling; a lackey ② a soldier ③ suddenly; unexpectedly ④ at last; after all ⑤ to complete; to finish ⑥ dead; to die

卒子 **jēut jí**
a soldier

卒業 **jēut yihp**
to graduate; to complete study (at an institution)

卓 **cheuk** (Md **zhuō**)
① lofty; high; eminent ② profound; brilliant ③ (to stand) upright; erect ④ a Chinese family name

卓見 **cheuk gin**
a brilliant idea or view

卓越 **cheuk yuht**
excellence; remarkable; outstanding; foremost

協 (协) **hip, hihp** (Md **xié**)
① to agree; agreement ② to be united; to bring into harmony; to

coordinate ③ to assist; to aid; to help

协定 hip dihng
an agreement (usually between nations)

協助 hip joh
to assist; to help mutually

南 nàahm (Md nán)
① south; southward ② a type of ancient music played in the south of China ③ a Chinese family name

南方 nàahm fòng
the south

南京 Nàahm gìng
Nanking

博 bok (Md bó)
① wide; extensive; ample ② broadly; knowledgeable; learned; erudite well-read ③ to barter for; to exchange ④ to gamble; to play games ⑤ a Chinese family name

博士 bok sih
a doctorate; a doctorate degree; a official rank; initiated in Chin and conperved upon scholars of profound learning

博物館 bok maht gún
a museum

卜部

卜 būk (Md bǔ)
① to divine; to foretell; to prophesy; to anticipate ② to choose; to select ③ a Chinese family name

卜卦 būk gwa
to divine by the Eight Diagrams

卜居 būk gèui
to choose a residence

卞 bihn (Md biàn)
① hurriedly; rash ② excitable ③

a Chinese family name

卞急 bihn gāp
testy; irascible

占 jìm (Md zhān)
① to divine ② to observe

占卜 jìm būk
to divine

卡 ká, kā (Md qiǎ, kǎ)
① a card; as a visiting card; cardboard ② an abbreviation for calorie ③ a guardhouse ④ a customs barrier; a road-block; a check point ⑤ to be squeezed in between

卡通 kā tūng
a cartoon (esp. a cartoon movie)

卡車 kā chè
a truck

卣 yáuh (Md yǒu)
(in ancient China) a container for wine; a chinese chalice

卦 gwa (Md guà)
① to divine; a divination ② one of the Eight Diagrams of the book of changes

八卦 baat gwa
the eight diagrams, consisting of an arrangement of single divided lines in eight groups of three lines each as specified in the Book of Change

卩部

卮(巵) jì (Md zhī)
a container for holding wine; a cup; a goblet with handles

漏卮 lauh jì
leaky wine; leakage of interest

卯 máauh (Md mǎo)
① the fourth of the 12 Terrestrial Branches ② the period from 5 to 7 a.m. ③ a roll call

卯時 **máauh sìh**
the period from 5 to 7 a.m.

印 **yan** (Md **yìn**)
① a seal; a stamp; a chop ② to print; to stamp; to imprint ③ an imprint; a mark ④ a Chinese family name

印度 **Yan douh**
India

印刷 **yan chaat**
to print

危 **ngàih** (Md **wēi**)
① danger; dangerous; precarious; perilous ② to fear; to be upset ③ lofty; high ④ just; honest; upright straightforward ⑤ a Chinese family name

危險 **ngàih hím**
danger; dangerous; unsafe

危害 **ngàih hoih**
to endanger; to harm

卵 **Léun** (Md **luǎn**)
① an egg; an ovum ② fish roe ③ the testicles

卵子 **léun jí**
testes; testicles

卵巢 **léun chàauh**
ovaries

邵 **siuh** (Md **shào**)
good; nice

卹 (恤) **sēut** (Md **xù**)
① pity; to pity ② sympathy; commiseration to sympathize

卹金 **sēut gām**
compensation, pension

卹養 **sēut yéuhng**
to raise (orphants etc.) to aid in the sustenance (of the sick, old, etc.)

卷 **gyun, gyún** (Md **juàn, juǎn, juán**)
① a book or painting which can be easily folded or rolled up ② a division of a book ③ a test paper ④ filed documents; files ⑤ curly; to curl

卷軸 **gyun juhk**
a book; books

卷曲 **gyún kūk**
to curl up; to roll up

卸 **se** (Md **xiè**)
① promptly; immediately; now ② then; accordingly ③ even if - indicating supposition or sequence office

卸貨 **se fo**
to unload cargoes

卸任 **se yahm**
to quit a public office

即 (即) **jīk** (Md **jí**)
① promptly; immediately; now ② then; accordingly ③ even if - indicating supposition or sequence

即刻 **jīk hāak**
immediately; promptly; now

即使 **jīk sí**
even if

卻 (却) **keuk** (Md **què**)
① still; but; yet; etc. ② to refuse to accept ③ to retreat; to withdraw

卻是 **keuk sih**
the fact is; nevertheless; in fact

卻步 **keuk bouh**
to retreat or withdraw for fear or disgust

卿 (卿) **hìng** (Md **qīng**)
① (in old China) a salutation of an emperor to his ministers ② used in addressing one's wife- Honey, Darling, Dear, etc. ③ (in old China) a nobleman; a high official rank ④ a Chinese family name

卿卿我我 **hìng hìng ngóh ngóh**
to be very much in love

厂部

厄 **ngāk** (Md **è**)
① in difficulty; distressed ②
impeded; cramped

厄運 **ngāk wahn**
bad luck

厄難 **ngāk naahn**
distress; difficultly; hardships

厚 **háuh** (Md **hòu**)
① thick; thickness; height ②
deep friendship ③ to treat kindly,
generous ④ substantial ⑤ kind;
considerate; virtuous

厚待 **háuh doih**
to treat kindly and generously

厚薄 **háuh bohk**
thickness

原 **yùhn** (Md **yuán**)
① the source; the origin; the
beginning; originally ② a steppe;
a vast plain; a field ③ a graveyard
④ a Chinese family name

原子 **yùhn jí**
an atom

原來 **yùhn lòih**
originally or formerly

厝 **chou** (Md **cuò**)
① to place; to place a coffin in a
temporary shelter pending burial
at a permanent site ② a grave
stone ③ to cut or engrave

厝火積薪 **chou fó jīk sàn**
(literally) to place fire near
piles of fagots — in imminent
danger

厥 **kyut** (Md **jué**)
① to faint ② the; this; that ③ a
personal pronoun

厥後 **kyut hauh**
after this; afterwards

厥功甚偉 **kyut gùng sahm wáih**
to have made great contributions to the successful conclusion of a task

厭(厌) **yim** (Md **yàn**)
① to dislike; to detest; to reject;
to hate ② to be wearied with; to
be repugnant ③ satiated; bored

厭惡 **yim wu**
to loath; to dislike; to detest

厭倦 **yim gyuhn**
to be tired of

厲(厉) **laih** (Md **lì**)
① a coarse whetstone ② harsh;
violent; severe; stern; serious ③
to persuade; to advise; to
encourage ④ bad; evil ⑤ a
Chinese family name ⑥ an
epidemic ⑦ to oppress;
oppressive; cruel

厲害 **laih hoih**
fierceness; very

厲鬼 **laih gwái**
a fierce ghost; a malicious
spirit

厶部

去 **heui** (Md **qù**)
① to go away ② to get rid of; to
remove ③ to be . . . apart ④ past;
gone ⑤ an auxiliary verb ⑥
fourth of the four tones in
Chinese phonetics ⑦ (in Chinese
Opera) to play the part of

去年 **heui nìhn**
last year; the year past

去留 **heui làuh**
to go or stay

參(参) **chàam** (Md **cān**)
① to take part in; to intervene;
to get involved in ② to visit; to
interview; to call on ③ to

impeach; to censure ④ to recommend ⑤ to counsel; to collate; to compare

參加 chàam gà
to attend; to participate in

參觀 chàam gùn
to visit, inspect or tour (a place, a plant, etc.); to watch or witness (a military exercise, etc.)

參 sàm (Md shēn)
ginseng

人參 yàhn sàm
ginseng

參商 sàm sèung
animosity between two brother

參 chàm (Md cēn)

參差 chàm chì
(of) irregular, different, varied sizes

參 sàam (Md sàn)
a formal form of the Chinese character "三" — those — used in accounting to prevent fraud

又 部

又 yauh (Md yòu)
① also; again; in addition to; and ② moreover; furthermore ③ and (used in mixed fraction such as one and three fourths)

又及 yauh kahp
P.S. (postscript)

又問 yauh mahn
to ask again

叉 chà (Md chā, chá, chǎ)
① to interlace fingers; to cross arms ② to thrust; to pierce; to stab ③ a prong; a fork (used in catching fish, etc.) ④ to push

another's neck with one's hand

叉路 chà louh
the fork of a road

叉枝 chà jì
a forked branch

及 kahp (Md jí)
① to reach; to attain; to come up to ② and; as well as ③ just at the moment ④ as long as ⑤ or ⑥ such as ⑦ to continue; to proceed

及時 kahp sìh
in time; on time; at the right time; seasonable

及格 kahp gaak
to pass an examination; to be qualify

友 yáuh (Md yǒu)
① a friend; friendly; friendship ② fraternity; fraternal spirit or love ③ to befriend

友善 yáuh sihn
friendly

友誼 yáuh yìh
friendship

反 fáan (Md fǎn)
① reverse; opposite; contrary ② to return (something); to turn back; to retreat ③ to introspect ④ to rebel; rebellion; to revolt ⑤ to infer

反比 fáan béi
(in math) inverse ratio

反叛 fáan buhn
to rebel; rebellion; to revolt; treason

叔 sūk (Md shū)
① younger brothers of one's father; paternal uncles ② younger brothers of one's husband ③ a general designation for members of one's father's generation who are younger than one's father ④ decline ⑤ a Chinese family name

叔父 **sūk fuh**
 a younger brother of one's father

叔伯 **sūk baak**
 paternal uncles

取 **chéui** (Md **qǔ**)
 ① to take; to receive; to fetch; to obtain; to take hold of ② to select; to choose ③ to summon; to recall ④ to marry

取代 **chéui doih**
 to replace; to substitute

取消 **chéui sìu**
 to cancel; to nullify

受 **sauh** (Md **shòu**)
 ① to receive; to accept; to get ② to take; to stand; to suffer; to tolerate to endure ③ to be pleasant to (the ears, etc.) ④ preceding a verb to form a passive voice

受傷 **sauh sèung**
 to be injured; to get hurt; to be wounded

受洗 **sauh sái**
 to be baptized

叛 **buhn** (Md **pàn**)
 to rebel; to revolt

叛徒 **buhn tòuh**
 a rebel; an insurgent, a turncoat

叛國 **buhn gwok**
 to commit high treason; sedition

叟 **sáu** (Md **sǒu**)
 an elder; a senior; an old man; the old

老叟 **lóuh sáu**
 an old man

叢 (藂、丛) **chùhng** (Md **cóng**)
 ① to crowd together; to meet in large numbers ② a shrub (plant); thicket ③ a hideout or den (for robbers; etc.) ④ a Chinese family name

叢林 **chùhng làhm**
 a dense wood; a Buddhist monastery

叢書 **chùhng syù**
 a collection of books by an author or on a subject; a library series

口部

口 **háu** (Md **kǒu**)
 ① a mouth; an opening ② a (person); a certain article (as a cistern; a big jar, etc.) ③ the edge or blade of a knife; a (sword) ④ a gate (esp. in the Great Wall or city walls) ⑤ a crack

口才 **háu chòih**
 eloquence

口吃 **háu hek**
 to stammer; to stutter; stuttering

叨 **dòu, tòu** (Md **dāo, tāo**)
 ① talkative; garrulous; chatterbox ② to be favored with; to receive

叨叨 **dòu dòu**
 garrulous; chatterbox; to nag

叨光 **tòu gwòng**
 thanks (for a favor done)

古 **gú** (Md **gǔ**)
 ① ancient; antiquated; old ② not following current customs or practices ③ a Chinese family name

古代 **gú doih**
 ancient time

古人 **gú yàhn**
 ancient people

句 **geui, kàu** (Md **jù, gōu**)
 ① a sentence ② name of an ancient country; name of an

ancient emperor

句子 **geui jí**
a sentence

句踐 **Kàu chíhn**
Kou Chien — king of Yueh during the Peirod of Warring States

另 **lihng** (Md **lìng**)
① another; separate; extra in addition; besides ② to separate; separation (as of a couple); to divide; to cut up

另外 **lihng ngoih**
besides; another; other; in addition; additionally

另議 **lihng yíh**
to be discussed or negotiated separately

叩 **kau** (Md **kòu**)
① to knock ② to ask ③ to kowtow

叩問 **kau mahn**
to ask

叩頭 **kau tàuh**
to kow tow — to kneel and touch the ground with the forehead to show great deference, practised in old China as the highest form of salutation

只 **jí** (Md **zhǐ**)
① only; merely ② but; yet ③ the simple form for '隻' jek

只有 **jí yáuh**
to have only; to have to do (or be)

只管 **jí gún**
(do anything) as you wish, please don't hesitate to; to be responsible for . . . only

叫(呌) **giu** (Md **jiào**)
① to be called or known as ② to cry; the cry of a bird or animal ③ to shout; to scream; a shout or scream ④ to call; to summon ⑤ to cause; to permit

叫菜 **giu choi**
to order food (in a restaurant

叫醒 **giu síng**
to waken

召 **jiuh** (Md **zhào**)
① to summon; to call up ② to cause; to entail

召集 **jiuh jaahp**
to convene (a meeting, etc.) to summon (a council); to call to arms

召見 **jiuh gin**
to summon a subordinate; to be summoned by a superior

叭 **bā** (Md **bā**)
a trumpet

喇叭 **la bā**
a trumpet

叮 **dìng** (Md **dīng**)
① the chimes of a bell ② to exhort or enjoin repeatedly ③ to sting; as a mosquito

叮噹 **dìng dòng**
ding dong, used for the sound

叮囑 **dìng jūk**
to enjoin and urge repeatedly

可 **hó, hāk** (Md **kě, kè**)
① may; can; might; able ② around; estimated at ③ an auxiliary ④ but; however ⑤ a Chinese family name

可以 **hó yíh**
can; may; yes, (you) can (or may); okay, That will do

可汗 **Hāk hohn**
Khan

台(臺) **tòih** (Md **tái**)
① a raised platform ② eminent; exalted

台灣 **Tòih wāan**
Taiwan, or Formosa

台端 **tòih dyùn**
you (can honorific in addressing one's equal)

叱 **chīk (Md chì)**
to scold; to revile

叱罵 **chīk mah**
to scold; to revile; to raid at

叱喝 **chīk hot**
to shout or bawl angrily

史 **sí (Md shǐ)**
① history; chronicle; annals ② a Chinese family name

史實 **sí saht**
historical facts

史書 **sí syù**
a book of history; an annal; a history book

右 **yauh (Md yòu)**
① right (as opposed to left) ② west ③ to assist; to aid ④ to emphasize

右手 **yauh sáu**
the right hand, the right hand side

右傾 **yauh kìng**
right-leaning; conservative

叵 **pó (Md pǒ)**
unable, improbable

叵測 **pó chāk**
unfathomable; unpredictable

叵耐 **pó noih**
it is an unfortunate fact that

叶 **hihp, hip (Md xié)**
to harmonize; to rime (rhyme)

叶韻 **hihp wáhn**
to rime (rhyme), to put into rime

司 **sì (Md sī)**
① to have charge of; to preside over ② a (governmental) department

司法 **sì faat**
judicature; judiciary; judicial

司儀 **sì yìh**
master of ceremonies; M.C.; emcee

叼 **dìu (Md diāo)**
to hold in the mouth

合 **hahp (Md hé, gě)**
① to combine; to unite; to gather; to collect ② to close; to shut

合作 **hahp jok**
to cooperate; to collaborate; cooperation

合約 **hahp yeuk**
contract; agreement

吁 **hèui (Md xū)**
a sigh

吁吁 **hèui hèui**
the sound of panting

吃（喫）**hek (Md chī)**
to eat; to sustain

吃力 **hek lihk**
tired; exhausted; tiring or exhausting (work)

吃香 **hek hèung**
to be welcome or valued everywhere; popular; in great demand

各 **gok (Md gè)**
① each; every ② all

各位 **gok wái**
ladies and gentlemen, gentlemen, or ladies (used in addressing a gathering)

各有千秋 **gok yáuh chìn chàu**
each shows a unique quality. Each has a unique style.

吉 **gāt** (Md **jí**)
good; lucky; auspicious propitious; favorable

吉祥 **gāt chèuhng**
favorable, propitious; auspicious

吉卜賽 **Gāt būk choi**
the Gipsies or the Gypsies

吋 **chyun** (Md **cùn**)
an inch

吆 **yìu** (Md **yāo**)
to shout; to cry

吆喝 **yìu hot**
to shout; to cry; to hawk

同 **tùhng** (Md **tóng**)
① same; equal; identical; similar; common ② to share; to agree ③ together

同學 **tùhng hohk**
a fellow student; a schoolmate

同時 **tùhng sìh**
at the same time; simultaneously

名 **mìhng** (Md **míng**)
① name; designation; title; rank; position; honor; fame; renown; reputation ② famous; noted; distinguished; renowned; valuable; precious; noble; rare; great

名單 **mìhng dāan**
a name list; a roster; a roll

名片 **mìhng pín**
a calling card; a visiting card

后 **hauh** (Md **hòu**)
① empress ② god of the earth ③ same as 後 — after; behind

后土 **hauh tóu**
the earth

后冠 **hauh gùn**
tiara

吏 **leih** (Md **lì**)
a civil officer

吏部 **leih bouh**
the department of civil personnel (in ancient times)

吐 **tou** (Md **tǔ, tù**)
① to spit; to utter ② to vomit; to throw up; to spew

吐痰 **tou tàahm**
to spit phlegm; to spit

吐沫 **tou muht**
saliva

向 **heung** (Md **xiàng**)
① to turn; to face ② direction; trend ③ until now ④ a Chinese family name

向來 **heung lòih**
hitherto; heretofore; until now

向隅 **heung yuh**
to miss the opportunity (of seeing a great show getting a handsome gift, buying a new product, etc.)

吒 **jà** (Md **zhā**)
① to shout with anger ② to smack in eating

君 **gwàn** (Md **jūn**)
① a sovereign; a monarch; a king; a lord ② you (used in addressing a male in formal speech)

君主 **gwàn jyú**
a sovereign; a monarch; a ruler

君子 **gwàn jí**
a perfect or true gentleman; a man of virtuous

吝 **leuhn** (Md **lìn**)
stingy; niggardly; parsimonious

吝惜 **leuhn sīk**
to hold stingily on to; to be stingy about

吝嗇 **leuhn sīk**
stingy; miserly; niggardly

parsimonious

吞 **tàn** (Md **tūn**)
to swallow; to engulf; to gulp

吞併 **tàn bing**
to annex (foreign territory); to take possession of (another's property)

吞服 **tàn fuhk**
to swallow or take (medicine)

吟(唫) **yàhm** (Md **yín**)
to chant; to sing; to recite; to moan; to sigh

吟詠 **yàhm wihng**
to chant or intone (a verse)

吟味 **yàhm meih**
to enjoy or appreciate (a poem, etc.)

否 **fáu, péi** (Md **fǒu, pǐ**)
① no; not ② negative ③ evil; bad; undesirable

否認 **fáu yihng**
to deny; reject; repudiate; disown; disclaim; or gainsay (a statement, report, etc.) denial; rejection

否極泰來 **péi gihk taai lòih**
Adversity, after reaching its extremity; is followed by felicity

吩 **fàn** (Md **fēn**)
to instruct or direct (someone to do something)

吩咐 **fàn fu**
to instruct or direct (someome to do something; instruction or direction (to do something)

吠 **faih** (Md **fèi**)
to bark (said of a dog)

吠影吠聲 **faih yíng faih sìng**
to bark at shadows and sounds; to raise an uproar over an unconfirmed rumor

含 **hàhm** (Md **hán**)
① to hold in the mouth; to contain; to include ② to bear

含淚 **hàhm leuih**
with tears in the eyes

含蓄 **hàhm chūk**
with concealed or implied deep meanings

吭 **hòhng, hàang** (Md **háng, kēng**)
① throat ② utter a sound or a word

吭聲 **hòhng sìng**
utter a sound or a word

吮 **syúhn** (Md **shǔn**)
to suck; to lick

吮墨 **syúhn mahk**
to be deep in thought while writing

吸吮 **kāp syúhn**
to suck

呈 **chìhng** (Md **chéng**)
① to submit, present, or hand in (to a superior) ② to show, manifest, expose, etc. ③ a petition or appeal

呈交 **chìhng gàau**
to handle or submit (to a higher authority)

呈祥 **chìhng cheùhng**
(the appearance of something or phenomenon which is interpreted as) a sign of auspice

吳 **ǹgh** (Md **wú**)
① name of a state in the Three-Kingdom period ② name of state in the Warring States period ③ a Chinese family name

吳國 **Ǹgh gwok**
the state of Wu in the Three Kingdom period and the Warring States period

吳下阿蒙 Ǹgh hah a mùhng
an ignorant person

吵 **cháau** (Md **chǎo, chāo**)
① to quarrel; to wrangle; to dispute; to row ② to disturb; to annoy

吵架 **cháau ga**
to quarrel; to brawl; to argue; to row; to wrangle

吵鬧 **cháau naauh**
to quarrel noisily; to brawl; noisy

吶 **naahp** (Md **nà**)
① to shout ② to speak hesitatingly

吶吶 **naahp naahp**
to speak haltingly

吶喊 **naahp haam**
to give a war whoop; to shout in battle

吸 **kāp** (Md **xī**)
to absorb; to imbibe; to suck in; to attract; to draw; to inhale

吸收 **kāp sàu**
to absorb; to take in; to recruit or enlist

吸煙 **kāp yīn**
to smoke; smoking

吹 **chèui** (Md **chuī**)
① to blow; to puff ② to brag or boast; to praise in exaggerated words

吹笛 **chèui dehk**
to play a flute

吹牛 **chèui ngàuh**
to brag; to boast

吻(脗) **máhn** (Md **wěn**)
① the lip ② the tone of one's speech ③ to kiss; a kiss

吻別 **máhn biht**
to kiss someone good-bye

吻合 **máhn hahp**
(of two things) to agree, correspond, match, or tally

吼 **hau** (Md **hǒu**)
(of beast) to roar or howl

獅子吼 **sì jí hau**
the howls of a shrew; the preaching of Buddha that shakes the world-like lion's roars

吱(嗞) **jì** (Md **zhī**)
squeaky cries of an animal

吱喳 **jì jà**
chatter (made by birds or animals)

吱吱 **jì jì**
(to cry) in a squeak; squeaking sound (made by insects)

吾 **ǹgh** (Md **wú**)
① I, me, or us (in literary usage) ② my, our

吾愛 **ǹgh ngoi**
my love; my darling

吾等 **ǹgh dáng**
we; us

告 **gou** (Md **gào**)
to tell; to inform; to report; to accuse

告假 **gou ga**
to ask for leave of absence

告示 **gou sih**
to make known; to announce, to proclaim; to give notice; an offical notice, announcement, or proclamation

呀 **à, a** (Md **yā, ya**)
① a creaking sound ② to gape (as in surprise) ③ a particle used after a phrase for emphasis, expressing surprise, etc.

呀然一聲 **à yìhn yāt sìng**
(of a door) to fling open with a creaking sound

大家快來呀！**Daaih gā faai lòih a!**
please, come quickly!

呂 **léuih** (Md **lǔ**)
① a Chinese family name ② one of the five musical notes in ancient China
呂宋 **Léuih sung**
Luzon

呃 **ngāk** (Md **è**)
to hiccup or hiccough
打呃 **dá ngāk**
to hiccup

呆 **ngòih, dāai** (Md **ái, dāi**)
dull; dull-minded; stupid; unintelligent
呆板 **ngòih báan**
boring; dull; monotonous; unvarying
書呆(獃)子 **syù dāai jí**
a studious idiot; a pedant

呎 **chek** (Md **chǐ**)
the foot (in English measure)
呎磅 **chek bohng**
foot pound

吧 **bah, bā** (Md **ba, bā**)
① a particle used after an imperative sentence ② a transliteration for English "bar"
好吧！**hóu bah!**
all right!
吧女 **bā néui**
a bar girl

呢 **nèih, nē** (Md **ní, ne**)
① woolen fabric ② a murmur ③ Interrogative or emphatic particle used after a sentence
呢喃 **nèih nàahm**
the chirp of a swallow; to murmur

呢絨 **nèih yúng**
a general term for woolen materials

呸 **pèi** (Md **pēi**)
snort of contempt

咋 **jaak, ja, jà** (Md **zhà, zǎ, zhā**)
① to bite; to gnaw ② a loud noise
咋舌 **jaak siht**
to bite the tongue

咒(呪) **jau** (Md **zhòu**)
① to curse; to swear ② chants by Buddhist monks or Taoist priests to exorcize ghosts
咒語 **jau yúh**
curse; imprecations; exorcism
咒罵 **jau mah**
to swear at; to curse; to call (a person) names

周 **jàu** (Md **zhōu**)
① the Chou Dynasty ② circumference; one round ③ complete; universal; all around; everywhere ④ to aid; to provide for ⑤ a Chinese family name
周年 **jàu nìhn**
anniversary; a full year
周全 **jàu chyùhn**
to aid; to help; complete with all that is desired

呱 **gwà, gù** (Md **guā, gū**)
the cries of an infant
呱呱墮地 **gwà gwà doh deih**
(of a baby) to come into this world; to raise the first cry of life

味 **meih** (Md **wèi**)
① taste; flavor; smell; odor ② delicacy·a dainty
味道 **meih douh**
a taste; a flavor; a smell; an

odor

味精 **meih jīng**
flavor essence; gourmet powder; mono-sodium glutamate

呵 **hò** (Md **hē**)
① to scold in a loud voice ② to yawn

呵斥 **hò chīk**
to scold in a loud voice; to thunder against

呵欠 **hò him**
to yawn and to stretch

呷 **haap** (Md **xiā**)
to sip

呷茶 **haap chàh**
to sip tea

呻 **sàn** (Md **shēn**)
to groan; to moan; to drone

呻吟 **sàn yàhm**
to groan; to moan

呼 **fù** (Md **hū**)
① to call; to cry ② to exhale

呼吸 **fù kāp**
to breathe; to inhale and exhale; breathing inhalation and exhalation

呼喊 **fù haam**
to yell; to shout

命 **mihng** (Md **mìng**)
① life ② fate; destiny; lot ③ order; command

命令 **mihng lihng**
command; order; injunction; direction; directive; to order; to command; to direct; to instruct

命運 **mihng wahn**
fate; destiny; lot

咀 **jéui** (Md **jǔ, zuǐ**)
① to chew; to masticate ②

simplified form for ˝嘴˝

咀嚼 **jéui jeuk**
to chew; to masticate; to dwell on (a word, sentense, passage, etc;) in order to fully appriciate or understand its meaning

咄 **jyut** (Md **duō**)
a bizarre cry; an angry cry

咄咄迫人 **jyut jyut bīk yàhn**
to overwhehn with awe or fear; to browbeat; overbearing

咄咄怪事 **jyut jyut gwaai sih**
What a queer story! What a strange-phenomenon!

咆 **pàauh** (Md **páo**)
to roar

咆哮 **pàauh hàau**
to roar (said of a lion, tiger, etc.); to bluster (said of winds, waves, etc.); to rage (said of a person)

和 **wòh, woh** (Md **hé, hè, huó, huò**)
① harmony; peace ② peaceful; harmonious; mild; gentle ③ sum or aggregate ④ of Japan ⑤ and ⑥ to match; to harmonize ⑦ to knead; to make dough; to mix

和平 **wòh pìhng**
peace; peaceful

和韻 **woh wáhn**
to adapt rhymes to a given sound; to rhyme

咎 **gau** (Md **jiù**)
fault; guilt; blame; disaster

咎由自取 **gau yàuh jih chéui**
have only oneself to blame

咖 **ga, kà** (Md **gā, kā**)
a form used in transliteration

咖啡 **ga fē (kà fē)**
coffee

咖哩 **ga lēi**
curry

吩 **fu, fuh (Md fu)**
to instruct or direct (someone to
do something)

吩咐 **fàn fu**
to instruct or direct (someone
to do something; instruction
or direction (to do something)

咕 **gù (Md gū)**
to murmur

咕咚 **gù dùng**
the sound of impact caused by
a falling object; a thumping
sound

咕嚕 **gù lóuh**
mumbled sound or indistinct
utterance; the rumbling sound
in the belly

呷 **jaahp (Md zā)**
to take in food with the tongue;
to suck

呷嘴 **jaahp jéui**
to click the tongue (to express
admiration or envy)

咚 **dùng (Md dōng)**
sound of impact caused by a
falling object

哎 **ngàai (Md āi)**
(an interjection of surprise mixed
with regret) What a surprise!
What a pity

哎呀! **ngàai a!**
What a surprise! oh! oh!

哎喲 **ngàai yò**
What a pity

咤 **ja (Md zhà)**
to shout with anger

叱咤 **chīk ja**
to shout with anger

咦 **yìh (Md yí)**
an interjection of surprise

咨 **jì (Md zī)**
① to inquire; to consult ② a very
formal official communication
(between offices of equal rank)

咨詢 **jì sèun**
to inquire; to consult

咨文 **jì màhn**
a very formal official communication between offices of
equal rank

咪 **mài (Md mī)**
① a meow (meou, miaow, miaou)
② smiling

咪咪叫 **mài mài giu**
to meow (meou, miaow, miaou)

笑咪咪 **siu mài mài**
smiling

咫 **jí (Md zhǐ)**
the foot measure of the Chou
Dynasty (divided into eight
inches)

咫尺天涯 **jí chek tìn
ngàaih**
so near and yet so far

咬 **ngáauh (Md yǎo)**
to bite; to gnaw

咬牙切齒 **ngáauh ngàh
chit chí**
to gnash the teeth (in anger or
hatred)

咬耳朵 **ngáauh yíh déu**
to whisper into anothcr's ear

咯 **lok, lo (Md kǎ, lo)**
① to cough ② a phrase-final
particle

咯血 **lok hyut**
to cough up blood

好咯! **hóu lo!**
That's fine

咧 **lè, lé, lèh** (Md **liě, lié, lie**)
① to stretch (the mouth) horizontally ② to babble ③ a sentence final particle

咧着嘴 **lé jeuhk jéui**
　　to grin

咧咧 **lè lè**
　　baby's crying sound; to babble

咱 **jà** (Md **zán, zá**)
I, me (in Northern China dialect)

咱們 **jà mùhn**
　　(inclusive) we; you and I

咳 **kāt, hàai** (Md **ké, hāi**)
① to cough ② an interjection of regret or remorse

咳嗽 **kāt sau**
　　to cough

咳！ **hàai!**
　　an interjection of regret or remorse

咸 **hàahm** (Md **xián**)
together; all; completely; wholly

咸信 **hàahm seun**
　　generally believed that

咸陽 **Hàahm yèuhng**
　　Hsienyang, capital of Chin Dynasty, in northwest Shensi Province

咽 **yìn, yit** (Md **yān, yè**)
① the throat; the larynx. the pharynx; the gullet ② to swallow; to gulp down

咽喉 **yìn hàuh**
　　the larynx; the throat; a narrow, throat-like passage of strategic importance

咽下去 **yit hah heui**
　　to swallow; to gulp down

咿 **yì** (Md **yī**)
a form used to represent sound

咿啞學語 **yì ngà hohk yúh**
　　(of a baby) to begin, to babble, prattle, or lisp

哀 **ngòi** (Md **āi**)
① to grieve; to mourn; to lament; to pity; to sympathize; to commiserate ② sad; sorrowful; lamentable; pitiful

哀悼 **ngòi douh**
　　to mourn; grieve over or lament (one's death)

哀求 **ngòi kàuh**
　　to entreat, implore, beg or appeal pathetically

哇 **wà** (Md **wā, wa**)
① to vomit ② the sound of whinning or crying by a child ③ a phrase-final particle

哇哇大哭 **wà wà daaih hūk**
　　(of a child) to cry very loudly

品 **bán** (Md **pǐn**)
① personality; character ② an article; a commodity ③ rank or grade in government service in former times ④ to appraise; to rate; to grade

品茗 **bán míhng**
　　to drink tea (with critical appreciation of its taste and quality)

品格 **bán gaak**
　　one's moral character

哂 **chán** (Md **shěn**)
to give a sneering smile

哂納 **chán naahp**
　　Please accept (my small gift)

哄 **hung, húng** (Md **hōng, hǒng**)
① (of a group of people) to make a roaring noise ② to beguile; to cheat; to defraud

哄動 **hung duhng**
　　to create a sensation; to excite

(the public)

哄騙 **húng pin**
　　to defraud; to cheat; to
　　swindle; to take in

哆 **dò** (Md **duō**)
　to shiver; to tremble

哆嗦 **dò sok**
　　to shiver with cold or tremble
　　with fear

哈 **hà, háh** (Md **hā, hǎ, hà**)
　① a form used in transliteration
　② sound of hearty laughter

哈哈大笑 **hà hà daaih siu**
　　to roar with laughter; to laugh
　　heartily

哈巴狗 **háh bā gáu;
　　hà bā gáu**
　　a Pekingese or Pekinese (dog)

哉 **jòi** (Md **zāi**)
　phrase-final particle expressing
　surprise, admiration, grief, doubt,
　etc. (a literal form)

員(员) **yùhn** (Md **yuán**)
　① member (of a organization etc.)
　② outer limit (of land, space, etc.)

員工 **yùhn gùng**
　　employees (collectively)

員外 **yùhn ngói**
　　salutation for a rich man in
　　ancient China; an official title
　　in ancient China

哥 **gò** (Md **gē**)
　an elder brother

哥哥 **gò gò**
　　an elder brother

哥倫布 **Gò lèuhn bou**
　　Christopher Columbus,
　　1451-1506, discover of
　　America

哦 **ngòh, òh** (Md **ó, ò, é**)
　① to recite (verses, etc.) ② (an

interjection) oh; ah

吟哦 **yàhm ngòh**
　　to chant or intone (a verse)

哦！ **òh**
　　oh!

哨 **saau** (Md **shào**)
　① a whistle ② to patrol ③ an
　outpost; a guard station

哨兵 **saau bìng**
　　a sentinel or sentry

哨子 **saau jí**
　　a whistle

哩 **lì, léih** (Md **lī, lǐ**)
　① to speak indistinctly ② a mile

哩哩囉囉 **lì lì lò lò**
　　to speak indistinctly; to utter
　　inarticulate words

哭 **hūk** (Md **kū**)
　to weep; to cry; to sob; to wail;
　to whimper

哭泣 **hūk yāp**
　　to sob; to weep

哭哭啼啼 **hūk hūk tàih
　　tàih**
　　to whimper; to blubber

哮 **hàau** (Md **xiāo**)
　① to roar; to howl ② to pant; to
　gasp; to breathe with difficulty

哮喘 **hàau chyún**
　　asthma

哲 **jit** (Md **zhé**)
　① a sage; a thinker; a philosopher
　② wise; sagacious

哲學 **jit hohk**
　　philosophy (as a field of
　　intellectual pursuit)

哲人 **jit yàhn**
　　a wise man

哺 **bouh** (Md **bǔ**)
　to chew (before swallowing); to
　feed (a baby, etc.)

哺乳 **bouh yúh**
to give suck to

哺乳類 **bouh yúh leuih**
mammals; Mammalia

哼 **hàng (Md hēng)**
① to hum (a melody) ② to groam; to moan ③ the grant of disapproval or contempt

哼哈 **hàng hà**
to hum and haw

哼哼 **hàng hàng**
to groan or moan continually

哽 **gáng (Md gěng)**
to choke

哽塞 **gáng sāk**
to choke

哽咽 **gàng yit**
to be choked with sobs; to sob (with catches and breaks in the voice)

唁 **yihn (Md yàn)**
to condole with or express sympathy for (the bereaved)

唁電 **yihn dihn**
a condolatory telegram

唁信 **yihn seun**
a condolatory letter

唆 **sò (Md suō)**
to instigate; to incite

唆使 **sò sí**
to instigate; to insite

唉 **ngàai, ngòi (Md āi, ài)**
(an interjection of regret or disgust) alas!

唉聲嘆氣 **ngàai sìng taan hei**
to give deploring interjections and sighs

唏 **hèi (Md xī)**
to weep or sob with sorrow; to greive

唏嘘 **hèi hèui**
to sob

唐 **tòhng (Md táng)**
① the Tang Dynasty ② a Chinese family name ③ abrupt; rude; preposterous; impossible

唐代 **tòhng doih**
the Tang Dynasty (618-907 A.D.)

唐突 **tòhng daht**
abrupt; rude; brusque blunt; to be rude or impertinent

唔 **ǹgh, m̀(h) (Md ú)**
① sound of reading ② not (in Cantonese)

唔好 **m̀ hóu**
not good

呷唔 **yì ǹgh**
sound of reading

哪 **náh, nàh (Md nǎ, něi, na, né)**
(an interrogative particle) where; how ② phrase final particle

哪怕 **náh pa**
even if

哪個 **náh go?**
which one? who is it?

唇(脣) **sèuhn (Md chún)**
the lips; the labia

唇膏 **sèuhn gōu**
lipstick

唇齒相依 **sèuhn chí sèung yì**
mutually dependant like the lips and teeth

啊 **à, á (Md ā, ǎ, à, a, á)**

啊哈 **à hà**
aha (an exclamation to show irony or mockery)

啊唷 **à yò**
"a yo" (the sound uttered when

suddenly get hurt)

售 sauh (Md shòu)
to sell

售票處 sauh piu chyu
ticket office; box office

售貨員 sauh fo yùhn
a shop clerk; a sale clerk; a
salesman; a salesgirl

唯 wàih, wái (Md wéi, wěi)
① yes ② the only one

唯一 wàih yāt
the only one; the only kind,
etc.

唯唯否否 wái wái fáu fáu
yes or no; to have no independant opinion; to echo others

唱 cheung (Md chàng)
to sing; to chant

唱片 cheung pín
a (phonograph) record

唱歌 cheung gō
to sing songs; to sing

唳 leuih (Md lì)
the cry of a crane, wild goose, etc.

風聲鶴唳 fùng sìng hohk
leuih
to sense danger everywhere
very scared and jittery; to be
afraid of one's own shadow

啤 bè (Md pí)
a character used in transliteration

啤酒 bè jáu
beer

啟 (启、啓) kái (Md qǐ)
① to open ② to begin ③ to
explain ④ to inform ⑤ a letter

啟示 kái sih
a revelation

啟發 kái faat
to prompt mental development
(of another); to teach; to
instruct

啜 jyut (Md chuò, chuài)
① to drink ② to cry in a subdued
manner; to sob

啜泣 jyut yāp
to sob

啜茗 jyut míhng
to drink tea

啣 hàhm, hàahm (Md xián)
the Vulgar form of '銜' ① a bridle
② to hold in the mouth

啞 (唖) ngá, ngà (Md yǎ, yā)
① dumb; mute ② the cries of a
crow; the sound of laughter ③ a
phrase-final particle

啞巴 ngá bā
a deaf-mute (person)

咿啞 yì ngà
the cries of a crow

唾 to, teu, tou (Md tuò)
① saliva ② to spit

唾沫 to muht
saliva; spittle

唾罵 to mah
to spit on and to revile

啡 fè (Md fēi)
a form used in transliterating

咖啡 ga fè
coffee

嗎啡 mà fè
morphine

啁 jàu (Md zhōu, zhāo)
the twittering or chirping of a bird

啁啾 jàu jàu
to twitter; to chirp

商 **sèung** (Md **shāng**)
① commerce; trade; business ②
merchant; trader; business-man
③ to discuss; to exchange views;
to confer ④ the quotient (in
arithmatic) ⑤ the Shang Dynasty
(c. 1800-1400 B.C.)

商品 **sèung bán**
a commodity; a ware; mer-
chandise; goods

商店 **sèung dim**
a shop; a store

啄 **deuk** (Md **zhuó**)
(of a bird) to peck

啄木鳥 **deuk muhk níuh**
a woodpecker

啄食 **deuk sihk**
to eat by pecking

問 (问) **mahn** (Md **wèn**)
to ask; to inquire; to investigate

問答 **mahn daap**
questions and answers; a
dialogue; a conversation

問題 **mahn tàih**
a problem; a question

唪 **fúng** (Md **fěng**)
to chant; to recile

唪經 **fúng gìng**
to chant liturgies

啐 **cheui** (Md **cuì**)
① to taste; to sip ② to spit

啐一口痰 **cheui yāt háu**
tàahm
to spit phlegm

啃 **háng** (Md **kěn**)
to bite; to gnaw

啃骨頭 **háng gwāt tàuh**
to pick out the residual meat
on the bones with teeth

啃書本 **háng syù bún**
to study very hard

唷 **yò** (Md **yō**)
an exclamation expressing
suprise or pain

啦 **là** (Md **la**)
a phrase-final particle

啦啦隊 **là là déui**
cheer squad

啥 **sà** (Md **shà**)
what; which; who; why

啥人 **sà yàhn**
(in Shanghai dialect) who are
you? who is it? who is there?

啥事體 **sà sih tái**
(in Shanghai dialect) what's
the matter?

啕 (咷) **tòuh** (Md **táo**)
to wail; to weep

號啕大哭 **hòuh tòuh daaih**
hūk
bitter weeping and wailing

啖 (啗、噉) **daahm**
(Md **dàn**)
(a literary expression) to eat; to
feed)

唬 **fú** (Md **hǔ**)
① to intimidate; to scare ② the
roar of a tiger

唬人 **fú yàhn**
to intimidate people; to
assume an intimidating air

唸 **nihm** (Md **niàn**)
to read; to chant; to recite

唸書 **nihm syù**
to read a book

唸唸有詞 **nihm nihm yáuh**
chìh
to mumble to oneself

喏 **yéh, nohk** (Md **rě,**
nuò)
① an address or greeting of

respect when meeting a superior, etc. ② same as 諾 to respond or answer; to yes. to promise

唱喏 **cheung yéh**
an address or greeting of respect when meeting a superior, etc.

喵 **mìu** (Md **miāo**)
the mew of the cat

啻 **chi** (Md **chì**)
only; merely

不啻 **bāt chi**
not only; not merely

啼 **tàih** (Md **tí**)
to cry (said especially of birds)

啼哭 **tàih hūk**
to cry; to weep and wail; to whimper; to whine

啼笑皆非 **tàih siu gàai fèi**
between tears and laughter; unable to cry or to laugh

啾 **jàu** (Md **jiū**)
① the chirping of birds or insects ② the wailing of infants

啾啾 **jàu jàu**
the chirp of insects

啷 **lòhng** (Md **lāng**)
a loud resonant metallic sound, see '噹'

喀 **ka** (Md **kā**)
a character used for transliterating

喀拉蚩 **Ka làai chì**
Karach, a port city of Pakistan

喀什米爾 **Ka jaahp máih yíh**
Kashmir

喁 **yùhng** (Md **yóng**)
① harmony or unison of sounds ② the state of a fish putting its mouth above the water surface

喁喁 **yùhng yùhng**
the state of people showing unanimous respect for their leader

善 **sihn** (Md **shàn**)
① good; virtuous; goodness; virtue; good deed benevolent action ② to be good at; to be skilled in; to be apt to ③ to remedy; to relieve

善心 **sihn sàm**
kindness; compassionate heart

善終 **sihn jùng**
to die a natural death

喲(哟) **yò** (Md **yō, yo**)
another form of the character '唷'

喂 **wai** (Md **wèi**)
(an interjection for calling another's attention) hello; please; if you please; I say

喃 **nàahm** (Md **nán**)
① the cries of a swallow ② to murmur; to mumble

喃喃自語 **nàahm nàahm jih yúh**
to murmur to oneself

喉 **hàuh** (Md **hóu**)
the throat; the gullet; guttural

喉嚨 **hàuh lùhng**
the throat; the gullet; the windpipe; esophagus

喉音 **hàuh yàm**
(in phonetics) glottals; gutteral sound

喊 **haam** (Md **hǎn**)
to call aloud; to shout; to scream; to cry; a loud call or cry; a shout or scream

喊救 **haam gau**
to call for help; to cry for help

喊苦 **haam fú**
to complain about hardships loudly; to cry out one's grievances

喋 dihp (Md diè)
to nag; to chatter; to prattle; to babble; to be very talkative

喋喋不休 **dihp dihp bāt yàu**
to keep talking; to chatter without stopping

喋血 **dihp hyut**
blood flowing

喇 là, la (Md lǎ)
① a character used for its sound ② a horn; a trumpet; a bugle ③ a Lama

喇叭 **la bā**
a horn; a trumpet; a bugle

喇嘛 **Là màh**
a Lama (priest of Lamaism)

喎（㖞）wà (Md wāi)
a wry mouth

喑 yàm (Md yīn)
① to lose one's voice — dumb or mute ② to keep silent — to talk nothing

喑啞 **yàm ngá**
dumb; unable to talk

喑聾 **yàm lùhng**
deaf mute; a deaf mute

喔 ngò, ngāk (Md ō, wō)
① an exclamation ② the crowing of a cock; the cackling of fowls

喔唷 **ngò yò**
an exclamation to indicate understanding

喔喔 **ngāk ngāk**
the crowing of a cock; the cockly of fowls

喘 chyún (Md chuǎn)
to pant; to gasp; to breathe hard

喘氣 **chyún hei**
to pant; to gasp; to breathe hard

喘息 **chyún sīk**
to take breath; or rest (after strenuous exercise; asthma

喙 fui (Md huì)
a beak; a bill; a snout

喙長三尺 **fui chèuhng sàam chek**
(literally) to have a beak three feet long — fond of exposing other's secrets; fond of fault-finding

喚 wuhn (Md huàn)
to call; to summon; to arouse

喚起 **wuhn héi**
to arouse to action

喚醒 **wuhn síng**
to arouse; to awaken; to call up

喜 héi (Md xǐ)
① a joyful thing; joy; delight ② to like; to love; to be fond of ③ joyful; happy; delightful; pleasant; auspicious

喜歡 **héi fùn**
to like; to be fond of; to love; to be pleased with

喜劇 **héi kehk**
a comedy

喝 hot (Md hē, hè)
① to drink ② to shout; to call out aloud

喝酒 **hot jáu**
to drink (alcoholic beverages)

喝彩 **hot chói**
to shout "bravo!" to applaud

唧 jīk (Md jī)
① a pump ② the buzzing sound

唧筒 **jīk túng**
a pump

唧唧 **jīk jīk**
　the buzz (as of cicadas)

喟 **wái** (Md **kuì**)
　to sigh heavily
　喟然長嘆 **wái yìhn chèuhng taan**
　　with a heavily sigh

喧 **hyūn** (Md **xuān**)
　① to talk noisily; to clamor ②
　noise; hubbud; uproar; noisy
　喧鬧 **hyūn naauh**
　　noise from a crowd; hubbub;
　　noisy
　喧天 **hyūn tìn**
　　to fill the air with noise

喻 **yuh** (Md **yù**)
　① to liken; to compare; to use a
　figure of speech; to parable ② to
　know; to be acquainted with ③
　to instruct; to explain
　比喻 **béi yuh**
　　to parable; a parable
　家喻戶曉 **gà yuh wuh híu**
　　to be known by everybody or
　　family

喪 (丧、裘) **song, sòng** (Md **sàng, sāng**)
　① to lose; to be deprived of ② of
　death; funeral ③ to mourn
　喪命 **song mihng**
　　to lose one's life; to die
　喪禮 **sòng láih**
　　funeral rites

喫 another form of "吃" see "口"
　radical

喬 (乔) **kiùh** (Md **qiáo**)
　① tall ② to disguise; to pretend
　③ a Chinese family name
　喬木 **kiùh muhk**
　　a tall tree; a large tree

喬裝 **kiùh jòng**
　to disguise oneself

單 **dàan, sìhn, sìhn** (Md **dān, shàn, chán**)
　① single; individual; sole; only;
　solitary; simple ② of an odd
　number ③ a slip of paper; a list
　④ a Chinese family name ⑤ chief
　of the Huns (a common term
　during the Han Dynasty)
　單眼 **dàan ngáahn**
　　(zoology) single eye
　單于 **sìhn yù**
　　the chieftain of the Huns (a
　　common term during the Han
　　Dynasty)

喹 **kwàih, fùi** (Md **kuí**)
　quinoline
　喹林 **kwàih làhm**
　　quinoline

喆 **jit** (Md **zhé**)
　another form of "哲" mostly used
　in a name

喱 **lèi** (Md **lí**)
　a character used in transliteration
　see "咖喱" in "咖"

喳 **jà** (Md **zhā**)
　sound of chattering
　喳喳 **jà jà**
　　chattering sound

嗖 **sàu** (Md **sōu**)
　① the laughing expression ② the
　sound one makes to drive away
　birds
　嗖嗖 **sàu sàu**
　　with laughter; laughingly

嗟 **jè** (Md **jiē**)
　an exclamation expressing grief
　or regret
　嗟嘆 **jè taan**
　　to sigh with grief or regret; to

lament; to deplore

嗟來之食 jē loih jì jih (sihk)
meal offered from pity mixed with contempt; favor done without courtesy

隔 gaak (Md gé)
to hiccup or hiccough; to belch

嗝兒 gaak yìh
a hiccup or hiccough; a belch

嗄 sa, á (Md shà, á)
① (of voice) hoarse ② (interjection) what?

嗒 taap (Md tà)
depressed; dejected; despondent; in low spirits

嗒然 taap yìhn
looking dejected or despondent

嗒喪 taap song
in low spirits; depressed dejected; despondent

㗋 wāt (Md wèn)
to laugh

嗅 chau (Md xiù)
to smell; to scent

嗅覺 chau gok
the sense of smell; alfactories

嗅鹽 chau yìhm
smelling salts

嗐 haaih (Md hài)
an exclamation of surprise or regret

嗨 hói (Md hāi)
heave ho; yo-heave-ho; yo-ho

嗆(嗆)chèung
(Md qiàng, qiǎng)
① to peck ② stupid; foolish ③ to cough because of a temporary blackade of the nasal passage which sometimes happens during

eating or drinking water; to initate the throat or nose (of smoke, smell, etc.)

嗇(嗇)sīk (Md sè)
stingy; parsimonious; miserly

嗇己奉公 sīk géi fuhng gùng
to save money for public welfare by being parsimonious in one's personal spending

吝嗇 leuhn sīk
miserly; stingy

嗉 sou (Md sù)
crop (of a bird)

嗉囊 sou nòhng
crop (of a bird)

嗉子 sou jí
a small pot which holds wine

嗦 sò (Md suō)
to shiver; to tremble see "哆嗦" in "哆"

嗩 só (Md suǒ)
a trumpet-like wind instrument

嗩吶 só naahp
a trumpet-like wind instrument

嗌 yīk (Md yì)
the larynx; the throat

嗯 ńg (Md ńg, ňg, ǹg)
the nasal sound used· when responding to a call

嗎(吗)mà (Md ma, má, mǎ)
① phrase-final particle used in yes-no questions ② a character used in transliterating

嗎啡 mà fè
morphine

嗓 sóng (Md sǎng)
the throat (as the source of one's

voice); one's voice

嗓子 **sóng jí**
throat; vocal cord

嗓音 **sóng yàm**
one's voice

嗔 **chàn** (Md **chēn**)
to be angry; to take offense; to fly
into a temper

嗔怒 **chàn nouh**
to get angry; to be engaged; to
be offended to get or fly into
a temper

嗔怪 **chàn gwaai**
to rebuke; to scold; to
reproach; to blame

嗚 (呜) **wù** (Md **wū**)
① to weep; to sob ② Alas!

嗚呼 **wù fù**
Alas; to die

嗚咽 **wù yit**
to sob; to weep

嗜 **si** (Md **shì**)
to delight in; to be fond of; to
relish; to like

嗜好 **si hou**
one's liking, hobby, or
weakness for something

嗜酒 **si jáu**
given to drinking

嗣 **jih** (Md **sì**)
① to inherit; to succeed to ② to
continue; to follow

嗣位 **jih waih**
to succeed to the throne

嗣後 **jih hauh**
thereafter; thenceforth; thence
forward; from that time on;
after that) afterward

嗡 **yùng** (Md **wēng**)
the hum or buzz of insects

嗡嗡叫 **yùng yùng giu**
to hum or buzz (said of

insects)

嗍 **sok** (Md **suō**)
to suck

嗤 **chì** (Md **chī**)
to laugh or chuckle sneeringly

嗤笑 **chì siu**
to laugh or chuckle sneeringly

嗤之以鼻 **chì jì yíh beih**
to pooh-pooh

嗑 **hap** (Md **kè**)
to bite; to eat; to chew

嗑瓜子兒 **hap gwà jí yìh**
to crack melon seeds

嗥 (嘷) **hòuh** (Md **háo**)
the roaring of wild beasts; to
howl; to wail; to bawl

嗥啕 **hòuh tòuh**
to wail; to bawl

嗁
same as "啼" see "口" radical

嗙 **póng** (Md **pǎng**)
to boast; to speak figuratively

嗙喻 **póng yuh**
sound of singing

嗶 (哔) **bāt** (Md **bì**)
a character used in transliterating

嗶嘰 **bāt gèi**
serge (a fabrice)

嗽 **sau** (Md **sòu**)
to cough; to clear the throat

咳嗽 **kāt sau**
cough; to cough

嗾 **sáu, juhk** (Md **sǒu**)
① to give vocal signals to a dog
② to instigate; to incite; to spur
on; to urge on

嗾使 **sáu sí**
to instigate; to incite; to spur
on; to urge on

嗷 **ngòuh, ngòu** (Md **áo**)
cry of hunger

嗷嗷待哺 **ngòuh ngòu doih bouh**
crying with hunger; waiting to be fed with cries of hunger

嘈 **chòuh** (Md **cáo**)
noisy; clamorous

嘈雜 **chòuh jaahp**
noisy and confused; full of confused noises; clamorous

嘉 **gà** (Md **jiā**)
① to praise; to commend; to admire ② good; fine; excellent

嘉賓 **gà bàn**
honored guest; respected guest

嘉獎 **gà jéung**
to commend or praise (as an encouragement)

嘍 (喽) **làu, làuh** (Md **lou, lóu**)
① a bandit's lackey or follower ② a phrase-final particle

嘍囉 **làuh lòh**
a bandit's lackey or follower

嘀 (啲) **dihk** (Md **dí**)
① to whisper; talk in whispers ② have misgivings about something; have something on one's mind

嘀咕 **dihk gù**
have something on one's mind

嘞 **là** (Md **lei**)
a phrase-final particle

嘐 **hàau** (Md **jiāo**)
to boast

嘐啁 **hàau jàu**
verbose

嘔 (呕) **ngáu** (Md **ǒu**)
① to vomit; to throw up; to

disgorge ② to annoy

嘔吐 **ngáu tou**
to vomit; to throw up; to disgorge

嘔氣 **ngáu hei**
to be angry but refrain from showing it; to feel annoyed or irritated

嘖 (啧) **jaak, jīk** (Md **zé**)
① an interjection of approval or admiration ② to argue; to dispute

嘖嘖 **jaak jaak**
used for the sound to indicate approval or admiration; cries of a bird

嘖有煩言 **jaak yáuh fàahn yìhn**
there are noisy arguments among the people; there are complaints from everybody

嘗 (尝) **sèuhng** (Md **cháng**)
to taste; to try; to test; to experience

嘗試 **sèuhng si**
to try; a try

嘗新 **sèuhng sàn**
to taste a new delicacy

嘛 **jè** (Md **zhè**)
to screen; loquacious

嘛 **màh** (Md **ma**)
an interrogative particle indicating a reason is obvious

嘎 **gà, gàh** (Md **gā, gá**)
sound of laughter

嘣 **bàng** (Md **bēng**)
sound of thumping (heartbeating, etc.); bang bang (sound of firecrackers)

嘬 **jyut** (Md **zuō**)
to suck

喼奶 **jyut náaih**
　　to suck the milk

嘮 (嘮)**lòuh** (Md **lào**)
　loquacious; garrulous; voluble

嘮叨 **lòuh tòu**
　　to nag; to din; to chatter
　　incessantly

嘰 (叽)**gèi** (Md **jī**)
　to talk indistinctly in a low voice

嘰咕 **gèi gù**
　　to grumble; to mumble or
　　mutter compliants

嘰哩咕嚕 **gèi lèi gù lòu**
　　to talk in an indistinct manner
　　(of bowels) to give forth a roll-
　　ing sound

噓 **hèui** (Md **xū, shī**)
　① to warm with exhaled air ② to
　speak well of (another) ③ a deep
　sigh ④ to hiss

噓氣 **hèui hei**
　　to send out breath from the
　　mouth; to blow

噓聲 **hèui sìng**
　　hissing sound uttered to show
　　hatred or disapproval; catcalls

嘲 **jàau** (Md **cháo, zhāo**)
　to ridicule; to jeer; to sneer; to
　scoff; to mock; to deride

嘲罵 **jàau mah**
　　to jeer and abuse

嘲笑 **jàau siu**
　　to laugh at; to jeer at; to sneer
　　at; to deride; to ridicule; to
　　scoff; to gibe

嘶 **sài** (Md **sī**)
　① the neighing of a horse ② (of
　voice) hoarse

嘶啞 **sài ngá**
　　hoarse-voiced; hoarse

嘸 **mòuh** (Md **ḿ**)
　① an expletive ② (in Soochow

and Shanghai dialect) same as 無

嘸啥稀奇 **mòuh sè hèi kèih**
　　nothing strange; nothing to be
　　proud of

嘹 **liùh** (Md **liáo**)
　(of voice) resonant

嘹亮 **liùh leuhng**
　　loud and clear; resonant

嘻 **hèi** (Md **xī**)
　① (in literary text) an interjection
　of grief or surprise ② laughing
　happily

嘻笑 **hèi siu**
　　to giggle; to titter

嘻皮笑臉 **hèi pèih siu
níhm**
　　laughing in a frolicsome
　　manner; showing a frolicsome
　　expression

嘴 **jéui** (Md **zuǐ**)
　mouth; bill or beak (of a bird);
　snout; nozzle

嘴巴 **jéui bā**
　　the mouth; (colloquial); the
　　cheeks

嘴唇 **jéui sèuhn**
　　the lips

噍 **jiu** (Md **jiào**)
　① to chew; to eat ② the human
　race

噍噍 **jiu jiu**
　　(of birds) chirping

噍類 **jiu leuih**
　　the human kind

噎 **yit** (Md **yē**)
　to be choked with food

噎住 **yit jyuh**
　　to be choked with food

嘯 (啸)**siu** (Md **xiào**)
　① to whistle ② to howl; to cry
　or shout in a sustained voice

嘯傲 **siu ngouh**
to talk and behave freely
without regard for decorum

噚 (𡬈) **chàhm**
(Md **xún**)
a unit for measuring the depth of
water (6 feet or 1.828 meters)

嘩 (譁、譁) **wà, wàh**
(Md **huá, huā**)
① noisy and confused ② the
sound of a massive object falling
to pieces

喧嘩 **hyùn wà**
noisy (especially from a brawl-
ing crowd); uproar turmoil

嘩啦一聲 **wàh là yāt sìng**
with a thunderous noise

嘿 **hèi** (Md **hēi**)
an interjection

噙 **kàhm** (Md **qín**)
to hold in the mouth; to hold back

噗 **pok** (Md **pū**)
puff

噗嗤 **pok chì**
tittle; snigger

噁 **ngok** (Md **ě**)
to vomit

噁心 **ngok sàm**
to vomit; to make a person feel
sick

噴 (喷) **pan** (Md **pēn,
pèn**)
to spurt; to blow out; to puff out

噴嚏 **pan tai**
to sneeze

噴射機 **pan seh gèi**
a jet airplane

噢 **òu** (Md **ō**)
same as '喔'

噤 **gam** (Md **jìn**)
to keep the mouth shut; to shut
up

噤若寒蟬 **gam yeuhk hòhn
sìhm**
(literally) as silent as a winter
cicada — to say or reveal
nothing (especially out of fear)

器 (器) **hei** (Md **qì**)
① instrument; implement;
utensil; tool; apparatus ②
magnanimity ③ talent; ability④
to think highly of (a person)

器具 **hei geuih**
tool; instrument; apparatus;
implement; utensil

器量 **hei leuhng**
the capacity for magnanimity;
tolerance

噩 **ngohk** (Md **è**)
startling; awesome; dreadful;
alarming; grave; serious

噩夢 **ngohk muhng**
a nightmare

噩耗 **ngohk houh**
shocking news (usually news
of a person's death)

噪 **chou** (Md **zào**)
① to be noisy ② (of birds),
insects, etc.) to cry loudly

噪聒 **chou kut**
noisy

噪音 **chou yàm**
impleasant noise; din

噫 **yì** (Md **yī**)
interjection of sorrow or regret (in
literary texts)

噬 **saih** (Md **shì**)
to bite; to snap at; to gnaw

噬臍莫及 **saih chìh mohk
kahp**
too late to regret

噱 **keuhk** (Md **jué, xuế**))
loud laughterer

噱頭 **keuhk tàuh; cheuk tàuh**
(in Shanghai dialect) a promotional gimmick

噲 (哙) **faai** (Md **kuài**)
to swallow

噸 (吨) **dèun** (Md **dūn**)
ton (unit of weight)

噸位 **dēun wái**
tonnage (of a ship)

噯 (嗳) **ngói** (Md **ǎi, ài**)
an interjection

噹 (当) **dòng** (Md **dāng**)
a loud, resonant metallic sound

噹啷 **dòng lòhng**
clanking sound

噷 **hàm** (Md **hm**)
an interjection

嚎 **hòuh** (Md **háo**)
to cry loudly

嚎啕大哭 **hòuh tòuh daaih hūk**
to cry loudly with abandon

嚅 **yùh** (Md **rú**)
to talk indistinctly and falteringly

嚅囁 **yùh jip**
to falter in one's speech

嚆 **hòu** (Md **hāo**)
to give forth sound; to sound

嚆矢 **hòu chí**
an arrow flying with a hum; harbinger; prelude; herald

嚀 (咛) **nìhng** (Md **níng**)
to enjoy; to instruct

叮嚀 **dìng nìhng**
to exhort or enjoin repeatedly

嚇 (吓) **haak** (Md **xià, hè**)
① to intimidate; to threaten ② sound of laughter

嚇詐 **haak ja**
to take (money, etc.) by threats and deceit

嚇阻力量 **haak jó lihk leuhng**
deterrent force

嚏 **tai** (Md **tì**)
to sneeze

嚏噴 **tai pan**
to sneeze

嚕 **lòu** (Md **lū**)
① verbose; wordy ② indistinct speech sound

嚕嚦 **lòu sòu**
to talk incessantly and tediously

嚮 (向) **heung** (Md **xiàng**)
① to guide; to direct; to lead ② to lean toward; to be inclined toward

嚮導 **heung douh**
a guide

嚮往 **heung wóhng**
to aspire; to long

嚦 (呖) **lìk** (Md **lì**)
sounds of plitting or cracking; a crash

嚥 **yin** (Md **yàn**)
to swallow; to gulp

嚥氣 **yin hei**
to breathe one's last; to die

嚨 (咙) **lùhng** (Md **lóng**)
the throat

喉嚨 **hàuh lùhng**
the throat

嚴（严）**yìhm** (Md **yán**)
① stern; strict; severe; grim; inclement; forbidding; inexorable; relentless; rigorous; rigid; austere; grave; solemn; awe-inspiring ② father ③ a Chinese family name

嚴格 **yìhm gaak**
strict; stringent

嚴冬 **yìhm dùng**
severe winter; very cold winter

嚶（嚶）**yìng** (Md **yīng**)
the cry of a bird

嚷 **yéuhng** (Md **rǎng, rāng**)
to shout; to cry; to call out loudly

囁 **jip** (Md **niè**)
to move the mouth (when speaking); to falter in speech

囁嚅 **jip yùh**
to speak haltingly

嚼 **jeuhk, jiuh** (Md **jiáo, jiào, jué**)
① to chew; to masticate ② to be glib

嚼蠟 **jeuhk laahp**
as tasteless as chewing wax; dry; uninteresting

嚼舌 **jeuhk siht**
glib-tongue

囀（啭）**jyún** (Md **zhuàn**)
① to warble; to twitter; to chirp ② pleasing to ear

囂（嚣）**hìu** (Md **xiāo**)
① to be noisy ② to be haughty or proud

囂張 **hìu jèung**
haughty; bossy; to push people around

囂俄 **Hìu ngòh**
Victor Hugo, 1802-1885, French writer

囈（吣、讛）**ngaih** (Md **yì**)
to talk in sleep

囈語 **ngaih yúh**
to talk while asleep; somniloquy

囉（啰）**lò, lòh** (Md **luō, luó**)
to chatter

囉唆 **lò sò**
vexingly verbose or wordy

囊 **nòhng** (Md **nāng, náng**)
a bag; a sack

囊中物 **nòhng jùng maht**
a thing which is already in one's bag; a thing very easy to get

囊括 **nòhng kut**
to encompass; to include; to embrace; to comprise; to pocket or win all (the medals in a sports meeting)

囌 **sòu** (Md **sū**)
① verbose; wordy ② indistinct speech sound

嚕囌 **lòu sòu**
to talk indistinctly and tediously

囑（嘱）**jūk** (Md **zhǔ**)
to ask another to do something; to instruct; to enjoin; to direct; to entrust; to charge

囑咐 **jūk fu**
to charge (a person) with a task; to instruct or bid (a person to do something)

囑託 **jūk tok**
to entrust (a person with a

task); to request (a person with a task); to request (a person to do something)

口部

囚 **chàuh** (Md **qíu**)
① a prisoner ② to imprison

囚犯 **chàuh fáan**
a prisoner; a convict; a jail bird

囚禁 **chàuh gam**
to imprison; to jail; to confine; to detain; to shut up in prison

四 **sei, si** (Md **sì**)
① four; fourth ② all around

四月 **sei yuht**
April; the fourth moon of the lunar calendar; four months

四季 **sei gwai**
the four seasons

囡 **nàahm** (Md **nān**)
little child

囟 **seun** (Md **xìn**)
another form of '顖' see '頁' radical

因 **yàn** (Md **yīn**)
① cause; reason; because of ② in accordance with; according to ③ to follow (a practice, convention, etc.)

因數 **yàn sou**
(in mathematics) factor

因素 **yàn sou**
factors

回（囘、囬）**wùih** (Md **huí**)
① to return; to reply; to repay; to bring back; ② number of times ③ chapters in a novel ④ of Mohammedanism

回答 **wùih daap**
to reply; to answer; to respond; reply; answer

回教 **wùih gaau**
Mohammedanism; Islam

囤 **tyùhn, deuhn** (Md **tún, dùn**)
① to store up; to hoard; to stockpile ② a container which is made of bamboo skin

囤積居奇 **tyùhn jīk gèui kèih**
to store up goods in the hope of selling them at higher prices later

困 **kwan** (Md **kùn**)
① difficult; hard ② poor ③ tired; weary; fatigued ④ to trouble; to worry; to harass

困難 **kwan nàahn**
difficult; hard; difficulty; hardship

困倦 **kwan gyuhn**
weary; tired

囱 **chùng, chèung** (Md **cōng**)
① a chimney; a flue ② a window (same as '窗')

烟囱 **yìn chùng**
a chimney

囫 **fāt** (Md **hú**)
entire; whole

囫圇吞 **fāt lèuhn tàn**
to swallow food without chewing

囫圇吞棗 **fāt lèahn tàn jóu**
(literally) to swallow a date intact — to accept a fact without understanding or analyzing

囹 **lìhng** (Md **líng**)
a prison; a jail

囹圄 **lìhng yúh**
a prison; a jail

囷 **kwàn** (Md **qūn**)
a granary

固 **gu** (Md **gù**)
① firm; sturdy; secure; solid; hard; strong ② obstinate; stubborn ③ sure; certain

固定 **gu dihng**
to fix; to make immovable; fixed unfluctuating; firm; stationary; not movable

固執 **gu jāp**
obstinate; stubborn; opinionated; obstinacy; stubbornness

囿 **yauh** (Md **yòu**)
① an enclosure for keeping animals; menagerie ② to confine; to limit; to enclose

囿於一隅 **yauh yù yāt yuh**
confined to a corner; unable to see widely enough

囿於成見 **yauh yù sìhng gin**
bound by prejudice; biased

圃 **póu, bóu** (Md **pǔ**)
① a vegetable garden; an orchard; a plantation ② a planter

花圃 **fā póu**
a flower garden; a flower farm

圄 **yúh** (Md **yǔ**)
a prison; a jail

囹圄 **lìhng yúh**
a prison; a jail

國（国）**gwok** (Md **guó**)
① a country; a nation; a kingdom; a state ② national; governmental ③ Chinese

國民 **gwok màhn**
a citizen; the people

國籍 **gwok jihk**
nationality

圈 **hyùn, gyuhn**
(Md **quān, juàn, juān**)
① a circle; a ring; a range; to draw circles ② to encircle; to confine ③ an enclosure or pen for keeping livestock

圈子 **hyùn jí**
a circle

羊圈 **yèuhng gyuhn**
sheepfold; sheepcot

圇 **lèuhn** (Md **lún**)
entire; whole
see '囫' character

圍（围）**wàih** (Md **wéi**)
① to surround; to enclose; to encircle; to hem in ② surrounding; environment ③ the circumference of a circle formed by a person's arms

圍牆 **wàih chèuhng**
an enclosing wall; a fence

圍攻 **wàih gùng**
to attack from all sides; to besiege; to beleaguer

園（园）**yùhn** (Md **yuán**)
a garden; a park; an orchard; a plantation

園丁 **yùhn dīng**
a gardener

園主 **yùhn jyú**
owner of a park or a garden

圓（圆）**yùhn** (Md **yuán**)
① round; circular ② complete; to complete ③ satisfactory ④ a monetary unit

圓形 **yùhn yìhng**
round; spherical; circular

圓滿 **yùhn múhn**
satisfactory; complete; rounded out

圖（图）**tòuh** (Md **tú**)
① a picture; a map; a portrait; a

chart; a diagram ② to plan; to scheme; to conspire; to desire ③ a Chinese family name

圖畫 **tòuh wá**
　　a drawing; a picture

圖書館 **tòuh syù gún**
　　a library

團（团）**tyùhn** (Md **tuán**)

① a sphere ② a mass; a lump ③ a group; a party; a mission; an organization a society ④ (in infantry) a regiment of three battalions of foot-soldiers

團體 **tyùhn tái**
　　a group; party or mission

團圓 **tyùhn yùhn**
　　a union or reunion (esp. of a family)

圜 **wàahn, yùhn** (Md **huán, yuán**)

① to surround; surrounding ② same as '圓'

土部

土 **tóu** (Md **tǔ**)

① earth; soil ② land; ground; territory ③ local; native ④ opium ⑤ an abbreviation for Turkey

土地 **tóu deih**
　　land; the God of the earth

土頭土腦 **tóu tàuh tóu nóuh**
　　rustic; hill billy; unsophisticated

在 **joih** (Md **zài**)

① at; in; on; up to ② to stay (in a position); to rest with; to consist in ③ to be alive; living; to be present ④ used to indicate a progressive tense

在家 **joih gà**
　　to be at home

在場 **joih chèuhng**
　　to be present (when an incident or accident (occurred)

圳 **jan** (Md **zhèn**)

a drain by the field (usually used as the name of place)

深圳 **Sàm jan**
　　Sham Chun (a place near Lo Hu the border of Hong Kong)

圬（杇）**wù** (Md **wū**)

① a trowel used for plastering ② to plaster

圭 **gwài** (Md **guī**)

a jade tablet with a square base and pointed top used in official ceremonies in ancient China

圭臬 **gwài yiht, gwài nihp**
　　an ancient time piece; a principle for one to look up to

圭亞那 **Gwài nga nàh**
　　Guiana

圯 **yìh** (Md **yí**)

a bridge; a bank

地 **deih** (Md **dì, de**)

① the earth ② land; soil; ground ③ region; territory; belt; place; locality ④ position; place; situation ⑤ an adjunct after a word (usually adjective) to form an adverbial phrase

地方 **deih fòng**
　　locality; a place ; local; locally

地平線 **deih pìhng sin**
　　the horizon

坊 **fòng** (Md **fāng, fáng**)

① a community; a sub-division of a city; a neighborhood ② a workshop of a trade ③ an arch-like memorial building

坊間 **fòng gàan**
　　on the market (especially referring to the book shops)

坊肆 **fòng si**
shops

圻 **kèih** (Md **qí**)
① the bank (of a stream) ② a boundary

址 (阯) **jí** (Md **zhǐ**)
land on which to build a house; a foundation; a location

地址 **deih jí**
address of a place; location

均 **gwàn** (Md **jūn**)
① equal; equally; even; level ② all; also; too ③ a potter's wheel ④ an ancient musical instrument

均等 **gwàn dáng**
equality

均勻 **gwàn wàhn**
even (blending, etc.); uniform

坂 (阪、岅) **báan**
(Md **bǎn**)
a slope; a hillside

坍 **tàan** (Md **tān**)
sliding of earth (as in a land slide); to fall into ruins; to collapse

坍方 **tàan fòng**
land slide

坍塌 **tàan taap**
to collapse; to cave in

坎 **hám** (Md **kǎn**)
① a pit; a hole; a depression ② one of the eight Diagrams in the book of changes ③ a sound of percussion ④ a snare; or danger; a crisis

坎坷 **hám hó**
unlucky; bad luck; ruggedness of the road

坎穽 **hám jehng**
a snare; a trap

坑 **hàang** (Md **kēng**)
① a pit; a hole; a gully ② to bury

alive ③ to entrap; to injure; to harm

坑道 **hàang douh**
a tunnel; an underground passage

坑殺 **hàang saat**
to bury alive

坐 **joh** (Md **zuò**)
① to sit; a seat ② to ride (on a bus, train, etc.) ③ to kneel ④ to reach; to arrive at; to be placed at ⑤ to get (profit, etc.) without work

坐標 **joh bìu**
co-ordinates

坐墊 **joh jin**
seat cushion

圾 **saap** (Md **jī**)
garbage; refuse; wastes

垃圾 **laahp saap**
garbage; refuse; wastes

坡 **bò** (Md **pō**)
a slope; a bank; a hillside

坡度 **bò douh**
the degree of steepness of a slope

坤 (堃) **kwàn** (Md **kūn**)
① one of the Eight Diagrams — earth ② compliance; obediance ③ female; feminine

坤宅 **kwàn jaahk**
the home of the bride

坦 **táan** (Md **tǎn**)
① wide and smooth; level ② self-possessed; composed calm; peaceful ③ a son-in-law

坦白 **táan baahk**
frank; honest; to tell the truth

坦途 **táan tòuh**
a level road; a smooth ride (ahead)

坭 **nàih** (Md **ní**)
the same as '泥'

坯 (坏) **pùi** (Md **pī**)
① a hillock or mound ② unburt bricks or tiles

坷 **hó** (Md **kē, kě**)
bad luck; unfortunate; rugged (road, etc.); uneven

坎坷 **hám hó**
unlucky; bad luck; ruggedness of the road

坼 **chaak** (Md **chè**)
① to crack ② to chap; to tear; to rip open

坳 (圳) **aau** (Md **ào**)
a hollow in the ground; a cavity

垂 **sèuih** (Md **chuí**)
① to hang down; to let fall ② to hand down ③ nearly; almost ④ to condescend

垂釣 **sèuih diu**
to fish with a hook and line

垂青 **sèuih chìng**
to give preferential treatment; to bestow favor

垃 **laahp** (Md **lā**)
garbage; refuse and wastes

垃圾 **laahp saap**
garbage

垃圾桶 **laahp saap túng**
a dust bin

坪 **pìhng** (Md **píng**)
① a level piece of ground ② (in Japanese measurement) an area of 6 feet square)

草坪 **chóu pìhng**
lawn; meadow; pasture

垠 **ngàhn** (Md **yín**)
① the bank (of a stream) ② a boundary

垢 **gau** (Md **gòu**)
① dirt; filth; stains ② shame; disgrace ③ unclean

垢膩 **gau neih**
dirt and grease on human skin; skin excrement and dirt

垢穢 **gau wai**
dirty

垣 **wùhn** (Md **yuán**)
wall, space enclosed by a constellation

垤 **diht** (Md **diè**)
mound; ant-hill

垮 **kwà** (Md **kuǎ**)
to topple; to collapse; to fall (out of power); collapse or fall

垮臺 **kwà tòih**
the fall (of a government, administration, organization, project, person, etc.)

埋 **màaih** (Md **mái, mán**)
to bury; to secrete; to lie in wait

埋葬 **màaih jong**
to bury (a corpse)

埋怨 **màaih yun**
to blame; to grumble; to complain

城 **sìhng** (Md **chéng**)
① a city; a town ② the walls of a city; to surround a city with wall

城門 **sìhng mùhn**
the gate of city wall

城市 **sìhng síh**
a city or town

埂 **gáng** (Md **gěng**)
① a pit; a cave ② an irrigation ditch

埃 **ngòi, ngàai** (Md **āi**)
① fine dust ② Egypt

埃及 **Ngòi (Ngàai) kahp**
Egypt

塵埃 **chàhn ngòi**
fine dust

堨 **lyuht (Md liè)**
a dike; embankment

埔 **bou (Md pǔ, bù)**
① a plain; an arena ② a port; a mart

大埔 **Daaih bou**
Tai Po

培 **pùih (Md péi)**
① to bank up with earth ② to nourish; to strengthen; to cultivate

培育 **pùih yuhk**
to cultivate and grow; to raise; to nourish

培養 **pùih yéuhng**
to cultivate by banking up; to grow (plants); to raise (kids); to cultivate (one's mind, etc.), to invigorate

型 **yìhng (Md xíng)**
① an earthern mold for casting ② a model; a pattern; a standard ③ a statute; a law ④ a style; a fashion; a type

新型 **sàn yìhng**
new style; new fashion

模型 **mòuh yìhng**
a miniature; a model

域 **wihk (Md yù)**
① a frontier; a boundary ② a region; a country ③ to live; to stay

區域 **kèui wihk**
a region

域外 **wihk ngoih**
beyond the frontier; a foreign country

埠 **fauh, bouh (Md bù)**
① a harbor; a port ② a mart on the bank of a river or seacoast

埠頭 **bouh tàuh**
a pier; water margin

商埠 **sèung fauh**
a commercial port

埤 **pèih (Md pí)**
① a low wall; a parapet ② an increase; increasingly to add to ③ low-lying

埤汙 **pèih wù**
mean (said of one's personality)

執 (执) **jāp (Md zhí)**
① to hold; to grasp; to seize ② to detain; to arrest ③ to maintain or uphold (a principle); to hold on stubbornly to ④ to shut (gossipers, etc.) up ⑤ a Chinese family name

執行 **jāp hàhng**
to execute (an order)

執迷不悟 **jāp màih bāt ngh**
to adhere stubbornly to errors; to hold on to wrong beliefs obstinately

場 **yihk (Md yì)**
boarder; boundary

疆場 **gèung yihk**
the boarder

基 **gèi (Md jī)**
① a foundation or base; fundamental ② an origin; a basis; a root ③ on the basis of; according to; on the strength of ④ the base of a chemical compound

基督 **Gèi dūk**
Jesus Christ

基本 **gèi bún**
root; foundation or base; fundamental

堂 **tòhng** (Md **táng**)
① a hall; an office; a reception room ② a meeting place; a court of justice ③ a salutation for another's mother ④ an open level place on the hill ⑤ relatives born of the same grandfather ⑥ venerable; grave; imposing; dignified ⑦ a set, as, a set of porcelains ⑧ a team or a group, as a team of drummers

堂堂正正 **tòhng tòhng jing jing**
dignified and imposing

堂兄弟 **tòhng hìng daih**
male first cousins on the father's side

大會堂 **Daaih wuih tòhng**
City Hall

堅 (坚) **gìn** (Md **jiān**)
① strong and durable ② solid; firm ③ to dedicate to; to devote to ④ calm; steady; stable; determined ⑤ close; intimate ⑥ armor; etc. ⑦ the strongest position or point of enemy troops ⑧ a Chinese family name

堅定 **gìn dihng**
determined; firm of purpose

堅硬 **gìn ngaahng**
hard and solid

堆 **dèui, jèui** (Md **duī, zuī**)
① to heap up; to pile ② a heap; a pile; a mass ③ a crowd

堆積 **dèui jīk**
to store up; to pile; to amass

堆砌 **dèui chai**
to lay (bricks, etc.); to pile up; (in composition) allusions, corny expressions, etc. senselessly heaped together

塾 **kwàn** (Md **kūn**)
the same as '坤'

堵 **dóu** (Md **dǔ**)
① to stop; to block up; to shut off; to guard ② a wall ③ a Chinese family name

堵塞 **dóu sāk**
to stop up; to gag; blocked

堵牆 **dóu chèuhng**
a wall surrounding a house

報 (报) **bou** (Md **bào**)
① to repay; to recompense; to requite ② a reward; a retribution ③ to report; to announce; a report ④ a newspaper

報告 **bou gou**
to report; a report

報名 **bou mìhng (méng)**
to enroll; to enlist; to enter one's name (as in an examination, competition, etc.)

堪 **hàm** (Md **kān**)
① to sustain; to bear; to stand ② fit for; worthy of; adequate for

堪虞 **hàm yùh**
precarious, distressing, dangerous, etc.

堪輿 **hàm yùh**
one who practices geomancy as a profession

堯 (尧) **yìuh** (Md **yáo**)
① name of a legendary sage king in ancient China whose reign is said to have extended from 2357 to 2255 B.C. ② high; eminent; lofty ③ a Chinese family name

堯舜 **Yìuh Seun**
Yao and Shun, two of the most celebrated sage kings in ancient China

堡 **bóu** (Md **bǎo, bǔ, pù**)
① a walled village; a town ② a pretty military station; a fort

堡壘 **bóu léuih**
a fortress; a bastion

堰 **yín** (Md **yàn**)
a bank of earth; an embankment; a dike; a levee

場(场、塲)**chèuhng**
(Md **cháng, chǎng**)
① an area of level ground; an open space ② an act of a play; an act of an opera ③ an arena for drill; a place; a playground ④ a site or place for a special purpose; as examination, meeting etc.

場合 **chèuhng hahp**
occasion; situation; condition

場所 **chèuhng só**
a location; a place; a theatre; a playground

堤(隄)**tàih** (Md **tí, dī**)
a dike, levee or embankment

堤岸 **tàih ngohn**
a dike, levee or embankment

堤邊 **tàih bìn**
the side of a dike; by the side of a levee

塊(块)**faai** (Md **kuài**)
① a lump of earth; a lump ② a piece of (land, bread, etc.) ③ alone; to be all by oneself

塊根 **faai gàn**
bulb root

一塊兒 **yāt faai yìh**
together

塌 **taap** (Md **tā**)
① to sink; to cave in; to fall in ruins; to collapse ② a little house ③ to bang down

塌陷 **taap hahm**
to sink

塌鼻 **taap beih**
a flat nose; a snubby nose

塋(茔)**yìhng** (Md **yíng**)
a grave; a tomb

塋地 **yìhng deih**
a grave; a tomb

塑 **sou** (Md **sù**)
① to mold in clay ② plastics

塑膠 **sou gàau**
plastics

塑像 **sou jeuhng**
to make an idol; image or statue; a statue

塚 same as '冢' see 冖 radical
a high tomb, a mound; a grave

塔 **taap** (Md **tǎ**)
a pagoda; a tower; a spire; a lighthouse; a tall building with a pointed top

塔頂 **taap díng**
the top of a pagoda or tower, etc.

塔斯社 **Taap sì séh**
Tass, the official Soviet news agency

塗(涂)**tòuh** (Md **tú**)
① to smear; to daub; to spread (oinment on a wound, etc.) ② to paint ③ to erase; to blot out; to efface; to obliterate ④ mud; mire ⑤ same as 途 — way; road

塗抹 **tòuh mut**
to erase; to obliterate; to scribble

塗改 **tòuh gói**
to erase and change the wording of an article, etc, to alter

塘 **tòhng** (Md **táng**)
① an embankment; a bund; a bank; a dike ② a square pool; a pond; a tank

池塘 **chìh tòhng**
a pond

水塘 **séui tòhng**
a reservoir

塞 sāk, choi (Md sāi, sè, sài)

① to block; to stop up ② to stuff; to satiate; to fill ③ to seal; a cork or stopper; to cork ④ strategic points along the frontiers

塞車 **sāk chè**
traffic jam

塞外 **choi ngoih**
beyond the borders; beyond the frontiers (esp. northern frontiers of China)

塡 tìhn (Md tián)

① to fill up; to fill in ② sound of drum-beat

塡表 **tìhn bíu**
to fill a blank; to fill a form

塡字遊戲 **tìhn jih yàuh hei**
cross-word puzzle

塢(坞、陽) wú (Md wù)

① a low wall around a village for defense; an entrenchment ② a structure which slants to a lower center on all sides — as a shipyard

船塢 **syùhn wú**
a dockyard

塵(尘) chàhn (Md chén)

① dust; dirt ② trace; trail ③ this world; ways of the world ④ vice; sensual pleasures ⑤ (in Taoism) a life-time

塵土 **chàhn tóu**
dust

塵世 **chàhn sai**
this mortal life; this world

墓 mouh (Md mù)

a grave; a tomb

墓碑 **mouh bèi**
a tomb stone

墓地 **mouh deih**
the site of a grave or tomb; a cemetery

塹(壍) chim (Md qiàn)

① the moat around a city ② a pit; a hole or cavity in the ground

塾 suhk (Md shú)

① an anti-room or vestibule ② a family school; a village school

塾師 **suhk sì**
tutor of a family or village school

私塾 **sì suhk**
a family school; a village school

墅 séuih (Md shù)

a villa; country house; a summer place

別墅 **biht séuih**
a villa; a country house; a resort

境 gíng (Md jìng)

① a boundary; a frontier; a region; a place ② a state; a situation; a circumstances ③ (in scholastic pursuit, etc.) a plateau

境遇 **gíng yuh**
one's financial or business condition

境況 **gíng fong**
situation; condition

墈 ham (Md kàn)

a dangerous bank; a ledge; a cliff; a step

墉(陽) yùhng (Md yōng)

a fortified wall; a wall

墊 dìn, dihn, dim (Md diàn)

① to advance (money); to pay for another ② a cushion; a bed-mat;

to cushion; to prop up; to make good ③ to sink into; to be over-whelmed

墊付 **dihn fuh**
to pay for another temporarily

墊子 **din jí**
cushion; mat

墀 **chìh** (Md **chí**)
a porch; a courtyard

墜(坠) **jeuih** (Md **zhuì**)
to fall down; to sink; the fall (of a person, state, etc.)

墜地 **jeuih deih**
to fall down; failure; to come to this world

墜子 **jeuih jí**
earrings; pendant ear-drops; a pendent or pendents attached to a bigger object as ornaments

墟 **hèui** (Md **xū**)
① a high mound ② an ancient town; a ghost town ③ wild, waste land ④ a periodical market-place where goods are bartered ⑤ ruins; destruction

墟里 **hèui léih**
a small village

廢墟 **fai hèui**
a wild, waste land

增 **jàng** (Md **zēng**)
to add to; to increase; to enlarge

增加 **jàng gà**
to add to; to increase; increase

增長 **jàng jéung**
increases and advances

墨 **mahk** (Md **mò**)
① black; dark; a black dye ② a Chinese ink-stick; calligraphy ③ language; letters ④ statutes; institutions ⑤ to be greedy; to covet; corrupt ⑥ tatooing one of the five punishments in ancient

China ⑦ name of one of the great philosophers in the warring states period

墨汁 **mahk jàp**
the Chinese dark ink; ink

墨子 **Mahk jí**
Mo Ti 墨翟 or Mocius, one of the greatest philosophers of the Warring States period, who preached love without distinction

墩 **dèun** (Md **dūn**)
a mound; a heap

墮(堕) **doh** (Md **duò**)
① to fall; to sink; to let fall ② to indulge in evil days ③ lazy; idle

墮胎 **doh tòi**
abortion; to abort

墮落 **doh lohk**
to indulge in evil ways; to sink in moral standard; degenerate; degeneracy; the fall (of a nation, family, etc.)

墳 (坟) **fàhn** (Md **fén**)
① a grave; a mound ② big; large; great

墳墓 **fàhn mouh**
a grave

墳場 **fàhn chèuhng**
a place of burial; a cemetery; a grave yard

壁 **bīk** (Md **bì**)
① a partition-wall; the walls of a room ② a camp; a military breast-work ③ a cliff

壁報 **bīk bou**
a wallpaper; a wall poster; a wall newspaper; bulletins

壁爐 **bīk lòuh**
fireplace

墾(垦) **hán** (Md **kěn**)
to open new land for farming, etc.; to reclaim land

墾荒 **hán fòng**
　　to open up barren lands for farming

墾殖 **hán jihk**
　　to reclaim land and live on it

壅 **yùng, yúng** (Md **yōng**)
① to stop; to block up ② to bank up roots of plants ③ to obstruct; to impede (flow, etc.)

壅塞 **yúng sāk**
　　to block up, obstruct, impede, the flow of (a severage pipe, etc.)

壅蔽 **yúng bai**
　　to conceal; to block up; to cover

壇(坛) **tàahn** (Md **tán**)
① a platform for sacrificial rites; an altar ② an arena; a hall for important meetings and ceremonies in ancient China

神壇 **sàhn tàahn**
　　an altar

天壇 **Tìn tàahn**
　　the Altar of heaven at Peking — where the emperors used to worship

壓(压) **ngaat** (Md **yā**)
① to press; to oppress; to pressure; to repres ② to crush ③ to close in; to press near (said of enemy troops, etc.) ④ to hold (a document, etc.) without taking action ⑤ a way of making a stroke in Chinese calligraphy ⑥ to surpass others (in ability, etc.)

壓力 **ngaat lihk**
　　pressure

壓抑 **ngaat yīk**
　　to curb; to repress; to suppress (one's emotions, etc.)

壎(埙) **hyùn** (Md **xūn**)
an ancient Chinese wind instrument, made of porcelain and shaped like an egg

壎篪 **hyùn fú**
　　two musical instruments played together harmoniously; signifying love between brothers

壑 **kok** (Md **hè**)
① a gully; a pool ② a narrow ravine at the foot of a hill

壑溝 **kok kàu**
　　a ditch; a narrow strip of water; a moat around a city wall

壕 **hòuh** (Md **háo**)
the ditch around a city wall; a moat

壕溝 **hòuh kàu**
　　a trench (in warfare); a ditch

壙 **kwong** (Md **kuàng**)
① a vault; a tomb ② a field; an open space ③ to leave vacant or idle

壙穴 **kwong yuht**
　　the vault of a tomb

壘(垒) **léuih, lèuih** (Md **lěi**)
① a military wall; a rampart ② to pile up; a pile; to repeat; repeatedly ③ base (on a baseball diamond) ④ a Chinese family name

壘球 **lèuih kàuh**
　　baseball

堡壘 **bóu léuih**
　　a fortress; a bastion

壟(垄、壠) **lúhng** (Md **lǒng**)
① a grave; a mound of earth ② a high place in a field

壟斷 **lúhng dyuhn**
　　monopoly; to monopolize

壜(坛、罎) **tàahm**
(Md tán)
earthen-ware jar or jug for wine

壞(坏) **waaih**
(Md huài)
① broken down; decaying; rotten; out of order; useless ② bad; poor (scores, marks, etc.) ③ vicious; mean; evil (persons, etc.)

壞人 **waaih yàhn**
　a bad guy; an evil person

壞處 **waaih chyu**
　bad points; shortcomings; defects

壤 **yeuhng (Md rǎng)**
① loose soil; earth ② a region; a place; a land ③ rich; abundant ④ a Chinese family name

壤界 **yeuhng gaai**
　boundary of a piece of land

土壤 **tóu yeuhng**
　loose soil; earth

壩(坝) **ba (Md bà)**
an embankment; a dike; a levee; a dam

壩工 **ba gùng**
　dam construction work

士部

士 **sih (Md shì)**
① a scholar; a man of learning; a gentleman ② an official rank in ancient China; an officer ③ a soldier ④ men ⑤ name of a chessman in Chinese chess ⑥ a Chinese family name

士兵 **sih bìng**
　soldiers; enlisted men

士敏土 **sih máhn tóu**
　cement

壬 **yàhm (Md rén)**
① the ninth of the Ten Celestial Stems ② artful and crafty ③ great ④ pregnant

壬人 **yàhm yàhn**
　an artful person

壯(壮) **jong**
(Md zhuàng)
① big; great ② strong; vigorous; flourishing ③ portly; stout ④ prime of one's life ⑤ another name for the eighth moon of the lunar calender

壯士 **jong sih**
　a brave man; a man of stout heart; a hero

壯健 **jong gihn**
　healthy and strong

壳 same as '殼' see '殳' radical

壺(壶) **wùh (Md hú)**
① a pot; a jug; a wine-vessel ② any potbellied container with a small opening ③ a Chinese family name

壺中物 **wùh jùng maht**
　wine; liquor; drinks

茶壺 **chàh wùh**
　tea-pot

壹 **yàt (Md yī)**
an elaborate form of "一" (one) used mostly in accounting and esp. in checks to prevent forgery or alterations

壻(婿) same as '婿' see '女' radical

壼(壸) **kwán (Md kǔn)**
a lane, passage way or corridor in a palace

壼範 **kwán faahn**
　a paragon of feminine virtues

壽(寿) **sauh**
(Md shòu)
① life span of a person ② old age; long life; longevity ③ birthday ④ to die in old age ⑤ to present

another with gold, silk, etc. ⑥ to toast another ⑦ a Chinese family name

壽命 **sauh mihng**
life span of a person

壽辰 **sauh sàhn**
birthday

夊部

夏 **hah** (Md **xià**)
① summer ② big; spacious; a big house; a mansion ③ Cathay, the ancient name of China ④ a dynasty in Chinese history (2205 — 1782 B.C.) ⑤ a Chinese family name

夏季 **hah gwai**
the summer season

夏威夷 **Hah wài yìh**
Hawaii

夐(敻)**hing** (Md **xiòng**)
① to seek; to aim high ② pre-eminent; superior

夐古 **hing gú**
a long, long time ago; in ancient times

夐絕 **hing jyuht**
peerless; second to none

夔 **kwàih** (Md **kuí**)
① a monster; a strange or grotesque monster ② name of a court musician in the reign of Emperor Shun (2255 B.C.) ③ name of a feudal state in the Chou Dynasty ④ a Chinese family name

夕部

夕 **jihk** (Md **xī**)
① dusk; evening; night ② slant; oblique; not properly oriented ③ to meet in the evening

夕陽 **jihk yèuhng**
the setting sun

除夕 **chèuih jihk**
(Lunar) New Year's Eve

外 **ngoih** (Md **wài**)
① out; outside ② foreign; alien ③ diplomatic; diplomacy ④ without; beyond ⑤ a term referring to one's husband ⑥ a role in Chinese opera for old man ⑦ to alienate; to treat as outsiders

外表 **ngoih bíu**
outward appearance

外國 **ngoih gwok**
a foreign country

夙 **sūk** (Md **sù**)
① early morning; daytime ② old or original (desires, etc.)

夙願 **sūk yuhn**
an old wish

夙夜 **sūk yeh**
day and night

多 **dò** (Md **duō**)
① many; much; too much ② more than; over ③ to praise ④ only ⑤ a Chinese family name

多謝 **dò jeh**
Many thanks; Thank you very much

多疑 **dò yìh**
suspicious

夜(亱)**yeh** (Md **yè**)
① night; dark; darkness ② night trip; night travelling

夜晚 **yeh máahn**
night; in the night

夜校 **yeh haauh**
a night school

夠(够)**gau** (Md **gòu**)
① enough; satiated; more than enough; too much ② bored ③ fully; quite

夠朋友 **gau pàhng yáuh**
a person whose friendship is worth having; a true friend; a friend in need

足夠 **jūk gau**
be enough; be sufficient

夢(梦) **muhng**
(Md **mèng**)
① a dream; to dream; to see visions ② stupid; wishful-thinking; wishful ③ a Chinese family name

夢想 **muhng séung**
a daydream; day dreaming vain hope

夢遊病 **muhng yàuh behng**
somnambulism

夤 **yàhn** (Md **yín**)
① to advance ② to respect ③ a distant place; remote

夤夜 **yàhn yeh**
deep in the night

夤緣 **yàhn yùhn**
to rise or climb on somebody's coattail

夥 **fó** (Md **huǒ**)
① many; much; plenty; lots of ② a partner; a company; an assistant ③ a waiter; a clerk

夥伴 **fó buhn**
a companion; a partner; a business associate

夥計 **fó gai**
a waiter; a clerk

大部

大 **daaih** (Md **dà, dài**)
① big; large; great; tall; high; vast; extensive; spacious ② much; very; highly; extremely ③ the eldest; the highest in the rank; senior; noble ④ full-grown; adult ⑤ (referring to date only) before; after ⑥ to make large; to make great ⑦ a Chinese family name

大亨 **daaih hàng**
big shot; VIP; tycoon; magnate

大夫 **daaih fù**
a physician or doctor; (in old and ancient China) high officials of state

天 **tìn** (Md **tiān**)
① the sky; the heaven; the vault of heaven; the void; the firmament ② Nature; God; where God or Gods live ③ natural; not artificial ④ day ⑤ season of the year; climate weather ⑥ husband ⑦ something indispensable; necessity

天線 **tìn sin**
antenna (for radio, TV, etc.)

天眞 **tìn jàn**
naive; naivety

太 **taai** (Md **tài**)
① very big or large ② much; too; excessive; excessively ③ a term of respect, used in titles ④ a Chinese family name

太空 **taai hùng**
space; the great void

太子 **taai jí**
the crown prince

夫 **fù, fùh** (Md **fū, fú**)
① a man; a male adult ② those eligible for military service ③ a master ④ husband ⑤ a demonstrative pronoun that in most cases ⑥ a final particle; a particle

夫妻 **fù chài**
husband and wife; a couple

夫子 **fù jí**
a title of respect for the eldest; a master; a teacher

夭 **yìu** (Md **yāo**)
① to die young ② to suppress; to repress ③ young; fresh-looking; tender

夭折 **yìu jit**
to die young; an early death

夭亡 **yìu mòhng**
to die young

失 **sāt** (Md **shī**)
① to slip; to neglect; to miss; to err ② to lose ③ an omission; a mistake

失敗 **sāt baaih**
to fail; a failure; a defeat

失明 **sāt mìhng**
to lose one's eyesight; to become blind; blind

央 **yēung** (Md **yāng**)
① the center; central; middle ② the finish or conclusion ; to finish ③ to request; to entreat

中央 **jùng yēung**
the center; central; middle

央求 **yēung kàuh**
to beg; to entreat; to implore

夯 **hàang** (Md **hāng, bèn**)
① to raise with force; a heavy load; burden ② (in levee construction) to fill cracks and leakage with earth

夷 **yìh** (Md **yí**)
① (in ancient China) barbarians in the east; foreign tribes or foreigners ② at ease; peaceful; pleased ③ to level; to make level; even or smooth ④ to eliminate; to exterminate; to kill; to execute; to injure ⑤ grades; classes ⑥ common; usual; ordinary ⑦ great; big ⑧ a Chinese family name

夷狄 **yìh dihk**
barbarian tribes in the east and north of ancient China

夷為平地 **yìh wàih pìhng deih**
to level (a town, etc.) to the ground (a threat used by an invading army in demanding the surrender of the defenders)

夸 **kwà** (Md **kuā**)
① big; large ② to brag; to talk big ③ good-looking, pleasant ④ lavish; luxurious ⑤ a Chinese family name

夾 **gaap** (Md **jiā, jiá, gā**)
① to be wedged between; to be sandwiched; to insert between ② to squeeze; to press ③ pincers; to pick up or hold something with pincers or chopsticks ④ of two or more layers; lined (garments, etc.) ⑤ a folder to keep sheets of paper, etc. ⑥ to carry secretly ⑦ to mix; to contaminate

夾子 **gaap jí**
folders for keeping documents, papers, pictures, etc.; clips

夾雜 **gaap jaahp**
mixed up

奀 **ngàn** (Md **ēn**)
thin (skinny) and small

奄 **yìm, yím** (Md **yǎn, yàn**)
① to soak; to bathe; to drown ② to remain ③ to castrate; a castrated man ④ to cover; to surround ⑤ suddenly; abruptly; rapidly

奄奄一息 **yìm yìm yāt sīk**
dying; barely breathing

奄忽 **yím fāt**
suddenly; adruptly; rapidly

奇 **kèih, gèi** (Md **qí, jī**)
① strange; uncanny; occult; rare ② wonderful ③ to feel strange about; to wonder ④ odd (number)

奇妙 **kèih miuh**
wonderful; rare; too good to be true

奇數 **gèi souh**
odd number

奈 **noih** (Md **nài**)
① what; how; but ② to bear; to endure

奈何 **noih hòh**
what to do now? what can we (or I) do now? what then?; to cope with; to deal with

奈良 **Noih lèuhng**
Nara, ancient Japanese capital

奉 **fuhng** (Md **fèng**)
① to receive with respect ② an expression of respect ③ to offer; to serve; to wait on ④ to admire; to love and respect ⑤ pay; salary ⑥ a Chinese family name

奉命 **fuhng mihng**
to receive orders from above; (to do something) as ordered

奉上 **fuhng séuhng**
may I present

奎 **fùi** (Md **kuí**)
① between the buttocks the stride made by a man ② one of the twenty-eight constellations which ancient Chinese astrologers believed to control the literary trends of the world ③ a Chinese family name

奎寧 **fùi nìhng**
quinine

奔 **bàn** (Md **bēn, bèn**)
① to move quickly; to run; to hurry ② to run for one's life; to be defeated ③ to elope

奔放 **bàn fong**
(said of a horse) galloping; (said of a writing or emotional manifestation) expressive and unrestrianed; moving and forceful

奔跑 **bàn páau**
to run in great hurry

奏 **jau** (Md **zòu**)
① to report to the throne ② to play (music or musical instruments) ③ to move; to advance

奏章 **jau jēung**
a written report or statement to the emperor; a memorial

奏樂 **jau ngohk**
to play music (in solemn ceremonies)

奐 **wuhn** (Md **huàn**)
① leisurely ② brilliant; colorful; gay; lively ③ excellent; elegant ④ numerous; many ⑤ a Chinese family name

奕 **yihk** (Md **yì**)
① great; grand; abundant ② gorgeous; elegant; good-looking ③ worried; unsettled; anxious ④ in good order; in sequence

奕奕 **yihk yihk**
grand and graceful; gorgeous; anxious; unsettled

契 **kai, sit** (Md **qì, xiè**)
① a contract; an agreement; a bond ② a diving instrument in ancient China ③ compatible; harmonious in thought and aspirations ④ to adopt; to dedicate to ⑤ to be separated from ⑥ to cut; to carve; to notch

契約 **kai yeuk**
a written contract or agreement

契闊 **kai fut**
to be seperated from one another

奘 **johng** (Md **zhuǎng, zàng**)
large; stout; thick; powerful

玄奘 **Yùhn johng**
Hsuan Tsang, 596-664, a Buddhist monk in the Tang Dynasty, who toured India for more than ten years and

brought back 600-odd Buddish scriptures 75 of which he and his disciples translated into Chinese

套 tou (Md tào)
① a case; an envelope; a wrapper; an overall ② a trap; a snare; a harness; a noose ③ to encase ④ to trap or trick a person (into telling the truth) ⑤ to harness; to wear or slip on (a sweater, etc.) ⑥ to pattern or model after; a set pattern ⑦ a suit (of clothing); a set (of tableware, etc.)

套口供 tou háu gùng
to trap a suspect into admitting his guilt

套房 tou fóng
a suite (of rooms)

奚 hàih (Md xī)
① why? how? what? which? ② a servant ③ name of a Tartar tribe in ancient China ④ a Chinese family name

奚落 hàih lohk
to laugh at; to make a fool of

奚如 hàih yùh
How about it?

奠 dihn (Md diàn)
① to settle; to lay (foundation, etc.); to secure; to consolidate ② to offer libations

奠定 dihn dihng
to lay foundation and consolidate it; to settle

奠儀 dihn yìh
money presented to the bereaved family in place of offerings

奢 chè (Md shē)
① extravagant; wasteful; lavish ② excesses; excessive; excessively ③ to exaggerate; to brag

奢侈 chè chí
luxury; waste; wasteful; prodigal!

奢望 chè mohng
to entertain hopes beyond one's ability to realize; a wild hope; a fancy

奧 ou (Md ào)
① mysterious; obscure; profound (learning) ② secret cabin or corner of a house or palace ③ Austria

奧秘 ou bei
deep, profound and mysterious; subtle; subtety

奧國 Ou gwok
Austria

奪(夺) dyuht (Md duó)
① to take by force; to rob ② to snatch; to grasp; to carry away (the first prize, etc.) ③ to settle; to decide

奪標 dyuht bīu
to win the first prize, as in a race or contest

奪取 dyuht chéui
to take by force; to wrest from

獎(奖) jéung (Md jiǎng)
① to encourage; to exhort ② to praise; to commend ③ to cite or give a prize or reward (for a merit, etc.) ④ a prize or reward

獎狀 jéung johng
a citation of meritorious service, etc.

獎勵 jéung laih
to encourage by rewards

奩(衺、匲) lìhm (Md lián)
a toilet case; a dressing case

妝奩 jòng lìhm
lady's dressing case; the

bride's trousseau

頳 **sīk** (Md **shī**)
① red ② angry ③ a Chinese family name

奮(奋) **fáhn** (Md **fèn**)
① to rise in force; to arouse; to exert with force ② (said of a bird) to take wing ③ to advance, promote or invigorate (a cause, etc.)

奮勇 **fáhn yúhng**
courageously; bravely (esp. in fighting enemy troops)

奮鬥 **fáhn dau**
struggle; to struggle; to strive; to fight for

女部

女 **néuih** (Md **nǔ**)
① a woman; a female; a daughter; a girl; a maiden ② feminine ③ name of one of the 28 constallations ④ to marry a girl

女紅 **néuih hùhng; néuih gùng**
needle work

女權 **néuih kyùhn**
women's rights

奴 **nòuh** (Md **nú**)
① a slave; a servant ② a self-derogatory expression used by a girl to refer to herself in former times ③ a despicable yes-man

奴僕 **nòuh buhk**
slaves; servants; lackeys

奴役 **nòuh yihk**
to enslave

奶(嬭) **náaih** (Md **nǎi**)
① the breasts of a woman ② milk; to feed with milk; breast-feeding ③ a term of respect for women; grandma

奶媽 **náaih mā**
a wet nurse

奶油 **náaih yàuh**
butter

奸 **gàan** (Md **jiān**)
① false ② selfish ③ disloyal ④ crafty; wicked; villainous; cunning ⑤ adultery; fornication; licentiousness

奸細 **gàan sai**
a spy (from the enemy side); a stool pigeon

奸詐 **gàan ja**
crafty; low cunning

她 **tà** (Md **tā**)
she

妁 **jeuk** (Md **shuò**)
a matchmaker; a go-between

媒妁 **mùih jeuk**
a matchmaker

好 **hóu, hou** (Md **hǎo, hào**)
① good; nice; fine; excellent ② pleasing (looks, taste, etc.) easy (to deal with) ③ to finish (dressing, eating, etc.) ④ very; much ⑤ can; so that ⑥ All right! Wonderful! Bravo! ⑦ an exclamatory expression ⑧ to love to; to like to; to be fond of ⑨ to be addicted to ⑩ what one likes or prefers

好消息 **hóu sìu sīk**
good news

好奇心 **hou kèih sàm**
curiosity

如 **yùh** (Md **rú**)
① like; as ② if; as if; supposing ③ as good as; equal to ④ to follow (advice); to listen to ⑤ to go to; to arrive at ⑥ should; ought to ⑦ on or in (time)

如果 **yùh gwó**
if; supposing

如常 **yùh sèuhng**
as usual; like always

妃 **fēi** (Md **fēi**)
① a wife; a spouse ② concubine of a king or an emperor ③ wife or spouse of a crown prince

妃子 **fēi jí**
a king's or emperor's concubine; ladies-in-waiting

妃嬪 **fēi ban**
concubines or wives of a king or emperor

妄 **móhng** (Md **wàng**)
① absurd; untrue; false ② ignorant; stupid; wild; fanciful ③ reckless

妄念 **móhng nihm**
an idea or disire one is not supposed to have; a fancy

妄爲 **móhng wàih**
to act without principle or wildly; untoward behaviour; reckless acts

妓 **geih** (Md **jì**)
① a prostitute ② (in old China) a songstress

妓女 **geih néuih**
a prostitute; a whore

妓院 **geih yún**
a brothel

妊（姙）**yàhm** (Md **rèn**)
pregnant

妊娠 **yàhm sàn**
to be pregnant

妊婦 **yàhm fúh**
a pregnant woman

妒（妬）**dou** (Md **dù**)
jealous; envious; jealousy; envy

妒忌 **dou geih**
jealousy

妒恨 **dou hahn**
to be very jealous; bitter jealousy; hate born of jealousy

妖 **yíu** (Md **yāo**)
① weird; unaccountable; supernatural ② a monster; monstrous; a goblin; a phantom; a ghost

妖怪 **yíu gwaai**
a monster or demon; a circe; a siren

妖冶 **yíu yéh**
seductive charms; seductive; (with) heavy make-up; meretricious

妗 **káhm** (Md **jìn**)
① aunt (mother-side) ② wife of one's wife's younger brother

妗母 **káhm móuh**
aunt (mother-side)

妝（妆、粧）**jòng**
(Md **zhuāng**)
① to doll up; to adorn oneself; a woman's make-up ② jewels, etc. for adornment ③ to disguise; to pretend

妝臺 **jòng tòih**
a lady's dressing

妝奩 **jòng lìhm**
lady's dressing case; the bride's trousseau

妞 **náu** (Md **nīu**)
a girl; a little girl

妞兒 **náu yìh**
girl

妙 **miuh** (Md **miào**)
① wonderful; excellent; ingenious ② intriguing; very interesting; nerve-tickling ③ subtle

妙不可言 **miuh bāt hó yìhn**
too subtle to be described; ingenious beyond description

妙哉妙哉！**miuh jòi miuh jòi**
Wonderful! Bravo!

姓 béi (Md bǐ)
one's deceased mother

先妣 sìn béi
my deceased mother

妥 tóh (Md tuǒ)
① firm; safe; secure ②
appropriate; satisfactory ③
ready; set

妥當 tóh dong
appropriate; secure; ready

妥協 tóh hip
amity; a compromise; recon-
ciliation; appeasement (in
international relations)

妨 fòhng (Md fáng,
fāng)
① to hinder; to impede; to
obstruct; to interfere with ② to
undermine; to harm; to damage

妨礙 fòhng ngoih
to hinder; a hindrance; to
impede; to interfere with

妨害自由 fòhng hoih jih
yàuh
offense against personal
freedom

姊 jí (Md zǐ)
one's elder sister or sisters

姊妹 jí muih
sisters

姊夫 jí fù
husband of one's elder sister

似 chíh (Md sì)
① wife of one's husband's elder
brother ② (in ancient China) the
elder of twins ③ a Chinese family
name

妲 táan, daat (Md dā)
concubine of Chou Hsin, the last
ruler of the Shang Dynasty

妲己 Táan géi
concubine of Chou Hsin

(紂王辛), the last ruler of
Shang Dynasty noted for his
cruelty and orgies

妮 nèih (Md nī)
① a maid ② a little girl; little
darling

妮子 nèih jí
a girl

妯 juhk (Md zhóu)
sisters-in-law; wives of brothers

妯娌 juhk léih
sisters-in-law (a reference
among wives of brothers)

妹 muih (Md mèi)
a younger sister

妹妹 muih muih
a younger sister

妹夫 muih fù
husband of a younger sister

妻 chài (Md qī)
one's formal or legal wife

妻子 chài jí
one's wife; one's wife and
children

妻室 chài sāt
one's formal or legal wife

妾 chip (Md qiè)
① a concubine ② (in old China)
a polite term used by a woman to
refer to herself when speaking to
her husband

妾侍 chip sih
a concubine

姆 móuh (Md mǔ)
a governess; a woman tutor; a
matron

媬姆 bóu móuh
a governess; a woman tutor; a
matron

始 chí (Md shǐ)
① the beginning; the start; the

first ② to start; to begin; to be the first ③ only then; so that ③ a Chinese family name

始祖 **chí jóu**
the founder; the first ancestor

始料未及 **chí liuh meih kahp**
unexpected

姍 **sàan (Md shān)**
① to ridicule; to laugh at ② to walk slowly-like a woman

姍姍來遲 **sàan sàan lòih chìh**
to walk or proceed slowly (and keep others waiting); to be late in reaching the destination

姐 **jé (Md jiě)**
① one's elder sister or sisters ② a general term for women, usually young

姐姐 **jé jé**
elder sister

姐夫 **jé fù**
husband of one's elder sister

姓 **sing (Md xìng)**
① one's family name ② a clan; a family; people

姓名 **sing mìhng**
full name of a person

姓氏 **sing sih**
the surname; the family name

姑 **gù (Md gū)**
① sisters of one's father ② mother of one's husband ③ sisters of one's husband ④ a general term for unmarried woman ⑤ for the time being; meanwhile ⑥ Let us

姑媽 **gù mā**
elder sisters of one's father

姑且 **gù ché**
for the time being; in the meantime; to let be

委 **wái, wài (Md wěi, wēi)**
① to depute; to deputize ② to send; to put in charge of; to commission ③ to give up; to abandon ④ to be frustrated, weakened or tired ⑤ really; truly; indeed ⑥ a grievance; a wrong ⑦ to stoop or lower oneself (in order to avoid an open conflict, etc.) ⑧ a Chinese family name

委託 **wái tok**
to commission; to entrust to

委蛇 **wài yìh**
in a carefree manner

妍 **yìhn (Md yán)**
① beautiful; pretty; good-looking; cute; attractive charming ② seductive; coquettish

妍麗 **yìhn laih**
beautiful; attractive; charming; beauty; charms

妍媸 **yìhn chì**
the beautiful and the ugly

姚 **yìuh (Md yáo)**
① handsome; elegant; good-looking ② a Chinese family name

姜 **gèung (Md jiāng)**
a Chinese family name

姜太公 **Gèung taai gùng**
Chiang Tse-ya who helped Wu Wang (武王) found the Chou Dynasty

姝 **jyù, syù (Md shū)**
a beautiful girl

姥 **lóuh, móuh (Md lǎo, mǔ)**
① maternal grandmother ② a midwife ③ an old woman

姥姥 **lóuh lóuh**
maternal grandmother; a midwife

姦 **gàan** (Md **jiān**)
① adultery; debauchery; licentiousness ② to debauch; to ravish; to attack (a woman) sexually ③ a crook

姦淫 **gàan yàhm**
fornication; adultery; debauchery; lewdness; to seduce; to rape

姦污 **gàan wù**
to seduce and rape

姨 **yìh** (Md **yí**)
① sisters of one's wife ② sisters of one's mother ③ a concubine

姨媽 **yìh mā**
married elder sisters of one's mother

姨太太 **yìh taai táai**
a concubine

姪（侄）**jaht** (Md **zhí**)
① children of one's brother-nephews or nieces ② I, me (when speaking to a family friend of father's generation)

姪女 **jaht néui**
a niece-daughter of one's brother

姪婦 **jaht fúh**
wife of one's nephew

姱 **kwà** (Md **kuā**)
pretty; good-looking; fascinating; elegant

姹（奼）**cha** (Md **chà**)
① young (girl) ② charming; attractive; seductive ③ to boast; to talk big; to lie

姹紫嫣紅 **cha jí yìn hùhng**
(said of flowers) beautiful and luxuriant, (said of party, etc.) colorful; star-studded

姻（婣）**yàn** (Md **yīn**)
① families of the married couple ② relations or connections through marriage

姻緣 **yàn yùhn**
the invisible bond that makes a man and a woman husband and wife

姻親 **yàn chàn**
relatives through marriage

姿 **jì** (Md **zī**)
① manner; air; carriage poise; bearing ② beauty; looks

姿勢 **jì sai**
carriage; department; bearing; posture; (in photography) a pose

姿色 **jì sīk**
looks (of a woman); (female) beauty

威 **wài** (Md **wēi**)
① dignity; majesty; severity; authority; imposing; majestic; dignified ② severe; stern ③ awe; awe-inspiring ④ a Chinese family name

威脅 **wài hip**
to threaten; to intimidate; threat; intimidation

威風 **wài fùng**
awe-inspiring; imposing

姣 **gáau** (Md **jiāo**)
① handsome; pretty; good-looking ② coquettish

姣好 **gáau hóu**
good-looking; pretty; pleasant (looks)

娃 **wà** (Md **wá**)
① a beautiful woman ② a baby

娃娃 **wà wà**
a baby; a young child

娃娃魚 **wà wà yùh**
a species of fish in Kwangsi and Kweichow that utters cries like a baby

娓 **méih** (Md **wěi**)
① complying; subservient ② beautiful; attractive pleasant

娓娓動聽 **méih méih duhng ting**
persuasive (account, narration, etc.)

娉 **pìng** (Md **pīng**)
good-looking; elegant; graceful; charming

娉婷 **pìng tìhng**
buxom and elegant; graceful and charming

娌 **léih** (Md **lǐ**)
a brother's wife; a sister-in-law

妯娌 **juhk léih**
sister-in-law (a reference among wives of brothers)

娑 **sò** (Md **suō**)
to dance; to gambol; to frisk; to saunter

婆娑 **pòh sò**
to make dancing motion; sauntering

娘(孃) **nèuhng**
(Md **niáng**)
① mother ② girls or women (collectively)

娘家 **nèuhng gà**
the wife's family

娘娘 **nèuhng nèuhng**
the queen; goddess

娛 **yùh** (Md **yú**)
to amuse; to give pleasure to; to entertain amusement; entertainment; pleasure

娛樂 **yùh lohk**
amusement; entertainment to amuse; to entertain

娛樂場 **yùk lohk chèuhng**
entertainment establishment

娜 **nóh** (Md **nà, nuó**)
tender, slender and graceful; well poised

婀娜多姿 **ngó nóh dò jì**
graceful; well-poised

姬 **gèi** (Md **jī**)
① a handsome girl; a charming girl ② a concubine ③ a Chinese family name

姬妾 **gèi chip**
a charming concubine; concubines; collectively

娠 **sàn, jan** (Md **shēn**)
pregnant

妊娠 **yàhm sàn**
to be pregnant

娟 **gyùn** (Md **juān**)
pretty; good-looking; graceful; attractive

娟秀 **gyùn sau**
good-looking; pretty; cute

娣 **daih, táih** (Md **dì**)
① a younger sister ② wife of a younger brother of one's husband

娥 **ngòh** (Md **é**)
① good; beautiful ② a common name for a girl ③ a Chinese family name

娥眉 **ngòh mèih**
(literally) beautiful eyebrows — a beautiful girl; a girl

娩 **míhn** (Md **miǎn**)
① to give birth to a child ② complaisant; agreeable

分娩 **fàn míhn**
to give birth to a child

婀 **ngó** (Md **ē**)
① graceful; elegant ② a Chinese family name

婀娜多姿 **ngó nóh dò jì**
graceful; well-poised

婆 pòh (Md pó)
① an old woman ② mother of one's husband ③ one's grandmother

婆婆 pòh pòh
mother of one's husband; a term of respect for an old lady

婆娑 pòh sò
to make dancing motion; sauntering

姘 pìng (Md pīn)
to make love without a formal wedding; illicit intercourse

姘頭 pìng tàuh
a lover; a paramour

姘居 pìng gèui
to live together without a formal wedding

娶 chéui (Md qǔ)
to take a wife

娶親 chéui chàn or
娶妻 chéui chài
(said of a man) to get married; to take a wife

婁(娄)làuh (Md lóu)
① one of the 28 constellations ② to tether (oxes) ③ to wear ④ to trail along ⑤ a Chinese family name

婉 yún (Md wǎn)
① amiable; genial; agreeable; pleasant; gently; genially; amicably ② good-looking; beautiful

婉轉 yún jyún
(to persuade or state something) gently; suavely-without hurting another's feeling

婉謝 yún jeh
to decline (an invitation a present, etc.) with great gentleness and courtesy

婦(妇)fúh (Md fù)
① a woman; a female; a matron ② wife of one's son ③ a wife ④ a married woman

婦女節 Fúh néuih jit
Women's day on March 8

婦孺 fúh yùh
women and children

婕 jiht (Md jié)
① an official title for women in the Han Dynasty (206 B.C. — 220 A.D.) ② handsome

婕妤 jiht yùh
an official title conferred upon an accomplished imperial concubine during the Han Dynasty

婚 fàn (Md hūn)
① a wedding; to wed ② marriage

婚姻 fàn yàn
marriage

婚禮 fàn láih
wedding ceremony

婪 làahm (Md lán)
covetous; greedy; avarice

貪婪 tàam làahm
greedy

婢 péih (Md bì)
① a maidservant; a female slave ② (in old China) a humble term used by a girl to refer to herself

婢女 péih néuih
a maid servant

奴婢 nòuh péih
(in old China) a humble term used by a girl to refer to herself

娼 chèung (Md chāng)
a prostitute; a whore

娼妓 chèung geih
a prostitute

娼婦 chèung fúh
a whore; a prostitute; a slut

婭(娅) nga (Md yà)
a mutual address between one's sons-in-law

婊 bíu (Md biǎo)
a prostitute

婊子 bíu jí
a prostitute

婊子養的 bíu jí yéuhng dīk
you s.o.b.! Bastard!

婷 tìhng (Md tíng)
pretty; attractive; graceful

婷婷 tìhng tìhng
attractive and well poised; graceful

婺 mouh (Md wù)
① beautiful; charming ② name of a star

媒 mùih (Md méi)
① a marriage go-between a matchmaker ② a medium

媒介 mùih gaai
a go-between; a medium

媒人 mùih yàhn
a marriage go-between; a matchmaker

媛 yuhn, yùhn, wùhn (Md yuàn, yuán)
① a beautiful woman; a beauty ② (in southern dialects) a young lady; a miss

令媛 lihng yùhn
your honorable daughter

媚 meih (Md mèi)
① to fawn on; to flatter; to please ② to love; to coax ③ attractive; fascinating; seductive

媚態 meih taai
seductive appearance or gestures of a girl; fawning manner; obsequiousness

媚世 meih sai
to fawn on others; to please the world

媧(娲) wò (Md wā)
the mythical sister and successor of Fu Hsi (伏羲), the legendary emperor (2852 − 2738 B.C.)

女媧 Néuih wò
the mythical sister and successor of Fu Hsi (伏羲), the legendary emperor (2852 − 2738 B.C.)

婿(壻) sai (Md xù)
① son-in-law ② a reference to one's husband

女婿 néuih sai
son-in-law

夫婿 fù sai
a reference to one's husband

嫁 ga (Md jià)
① (said of a woman) to get married; to marry a man ② to marry off a daughter ③ to impute (blame, crime, etc.) to another

嫁娶 ga chéui
marriage

嫁禍 ga woh
to impute blames, crime, punishment, etc. (to another person)

媳 sīk (Md xí)
a daughter-in-law

媳婦 sīk fúh
a daughter-in-law; wife (colloquial)

嫂 sóu (Md sǎo)
wife of one's elder brother

嫂夫人 sóu fù yàhn
(a polite expression to a friend) your wife

嫂子 sóu jí
wife of an elder brother

媵 yihng (Md yìng)
① a maid who accompanies a bride to her new home ② a concubine ③ to present as a gift

媵婢 yihng péih
a maid who accompanies a bride to her new home

媸 chì (Md chī)
ugly; and ugly woman

媽 (妈) mà (Md mā)
① mother ② a woman-servant (when used immediatly after her family name)

媽媽 mà mà
mama; mother

媽祖 Mà jóu
Matsu, Goddess of the sea, worshiped by most fishermen in Fukien and Taiwan Provinces

媾 gau, kau (Md gòu)
① to marry; to wed ② to negotiate peace; amity ③ to couple; to copulate

媾和 gau wòh
to negotiate peace

嫉 jaht (Md jí)
① jealous; envious; jealousy ② to hate; to detest

嫉妒 jaht dou
jealous; to envy; jealousy

嫉惡如仇 jaht ngok yùh sàuh
not to compromise with evil deeds or evil persons; to view good and evil on black and white basis

嫋 same as '裊' see '衣' radical

媲 béi, pei (Md pì)
to pair; to match

媲美 béi méih
a pair

嫌 yìhm (Md xián)
① to detest; to dislike ② to suspect; suspicion; a suspect ③ to complain; to reject; to object

嫌棄 yìhm hei
to reject; to give up in disgust

嫌疑 yìhm yìh
suspicion; suspected

媼 óu (Md ǎo)
① an old woman ② (in old China) a general term for old woman ③ the Goddess of earth

媿 same as '愧' see '心' radical

嫠 lèih (Md lí)
a widow

嫠婦 lèih fúh
a widow

嫖 (闞) pìuh (Md piáo)
to patronize whorehouses

嫖客 pìuh haak
a patron of brothel

嫖妓 pìuh geih
to visit prostitutes

嫗 (妪) yú (Md yú)
an old woman

嫡 dīk (Md dí)
① the legal wife as opposed to a concubine ② sons born of the legal wife of a man

嫡子 dīk jí
sons born of the legal wife of a man

嫡系 dīk haih
the legal or official branch of the family tree-children begotten by the legal wife of a man

嫣 yìn (Md yān)
captivating; charming; lovely; facinating

嫣紅 **yìn hùhng**
bright red; rich crimson

嫣然一笑 **yìn yìhn yāt siu**
a captivating smile

嫦 **sèuhng** (Md **cháng**)
(see below)

嫦娥 **Sèuhng ngòh**
(in Chinese legend) Chang-O, who ascended the moon after secretly eating her husband's immortallty pill)

嫩 **nyuhn** (Md **nèn**)
① tender; delicate ② young; immature ③ (of color) light; yellowish

嫩葉 **nyuhn yihp**
young leaf; tender leaf

嫩芽 **nyuhn ngàh**
a tender shoot

嫘 **lèuih** (Md **léi**)
(see below)

嫘祖 **Lèuih jóu**
(in Chinese legend) Lei-Zu, concubine of Huangti, who invented raising silk-warm

嬉 **hèi** (Md **xī**)
to have fun; to sport; to play; to frolic

嬉戲 **hèi hei**
to frolic; to play; to sport; to have fun; to make merry; to gambol; to romp

嫻（嫺）**hàahn**
(Md **xián**)
① refined; gracious ② skillful; skilled

嫻雅 **hàahn ngáh**
polished; cultured; refined

嫻習 **hàahn jaahp**
skilled in; adept at

嬈（娆）**yìuh** (Md **ráo, rǎo**)
charming; beautiful

嬌嬈 **gìu yìuh**
charming; beautiful

嬋（婵）**sìhm** (Md **chán**)
graceful, lady-like, attractive, beautiful or pretty

嬋娟 **sìhm gyùn**
graceful, lady-like, attractive, beautiful or pretty

嬌（娇）**gìu** (Md **jiāo**)
① tender; delicate; lovely; beautiful ② spoiled; pampered; coddled

嬌媚 **gìu meih**
beautiful; handsome

嬌妻 **gìu chài**
a beloved wife

嬡（嫒）**oi** (Md **ài**)
daughter (a complimentary term referring to the daughter of the person one is speaking to)

令嬡 **lihng oi**
your honorable daughter

嬴 **yìhng** (Md **yíng**)
① to win ② to have surplus ③ a Chinese family name

嬴土 **yìhng tóu**
fertile land

嬴秦 **Yìhng chèuhn**
the state of Chin during the Warring States period

嬖 **pei** (Md **bì**)
① to enjoy the favor of a powerful person (said of people of mean birth) ② a minion

嬖人 **pei yàhn**
a favorite of the ruler

嬖倖 **pei hahng**
to be favored by the ruler (said of concubines and sycophants)

嬗 **sihn** (Md **shàn**)
to change; to be replaced

嬙（嫱）**chèuhng**
(Md **qiáng**)
a court lady

嬙媛 **chèuhng yùhn**
ladies-in-waiting

嬛 **hyùn** (Md **xuān**)
① lonely; solitary ② fickle;
frivolous

嬛薄 **hyùn bohk**
frivolous

嫋 **níuh** (Md **niǎo**)
same as '裊' see '衣' radical

嬪（嫔）**ban, pàhn**
(Md **pín**)
① a court lady ② be married to
(said of a woman)

嬪從 **ban chùhng**
ladies-in-waiting

嬰（婴）**yìng** (Md **yīng**)
an infant; a baby; a sucking

嬰孩 **yìng hàaih**
a baby; an infant

嬲 **níuh, nàu** (Md **niǎo**)
① to dally with; to flirt with ②
be angry

孃 **mà** (Md **mā**)
a wet nurse

孃孃 **mà mà**
a wet nurse

嬸（婶）**sám** (Md **shěn**)
① aunt (wife of father's younger
brother) ② sister-in-law (wife of
husband's younger brother)

嬸母 **sám móuh**
aunt (wife of father's younger
brother)

孀 **sèung** (Md **shuāng**)
a widow

孀婦 **sèung fúh**
a widow

孀居 **sèung gèui**
to remain in widowhood; to
live as a widow

孃 **nèuhng** (Md **niáng**)
same as '娘' see '女' radical

孌（娈）**lyúhn** (Md **luán**)
① beautiful; handsome ②
obedient; docile

孌童 **lyúhn tùhng**
a catamite

子部

子 **jí** (Md **zǐ**)
① child; son; offspring ② seed;
egg; fruit ③ the first of the twelve
Celestial Stems (天干) ④ a rank
of nobility equivalent to viscount
⑤ a designation used in speaking of or to a man in former times
(somewhat similar to 'mister')

子女 **jí néuih**
sons and daughters; children
(as opposed to parents)

子宮 **jí gùng**
the womb; the uterus

孑 **kit** (Md **jié**)
① larvae of mosquitoes ②
solitary; unaccompanied lonely

孑孓 **kit kyut**
larvae of mosquitoes

孑然一身 **kit yìhn yāt sàn**
alone; living without
companions

孓 **kyut** (Md **júe**)
larvae of mosquitoes

孔 **húng** (Md **kǒng**)
① a hole; an orifice; an opening;
an aperture ② a Chinese family

name ③ of, or having to do with, Confucius or Confucianism ④ urgent; badly

孔夫子 Húng fù jí
Confucius

孔雀 húng jeuk
the peacock

孕 yahn (Md yùn)
to be pregnant; to conceive

孕育 yahn yuhk
to let develop (as in the womb); to nourish; to foster; to nurture

孕婦 yahn fúh
a pregnant woman

字 jih (Md zì)
① word; character; letter; logograph ② to betroth a girl ③ a name or style one assumes upon reaching manhood in former times

字母 jih móuh
an alphabet; a letter (of an alphabet)

字典 jih dín
a dictionary; a lexicon; a thesaurus

存 chyùhn (Md cún)
① to live; to exist; to survive; to remain ② to keep; to deposit

存在 chyùhn joih
to exist; to be present

存款 chyùhn fún
money put in a bank; deposit; to make a deposit

孚 fù (Md fú)
① confidence; trust ② to spread widely

孛 buht, buih (Md bó)
a comet

孛孛 buht buht
radiant

孛星 buht sìng
a comet

孜 jì (Md zī)
never wearying; unweariedly diligent

孜孜不倦 jì jì bāt gyuhn
to work with diligence and without fatigue

孝 haau (Md xiào)
of, or having to do with, filial piety or devotion

孝順 haau seuhn
to show filial piety or devotion for (one's parents)

孝服 haau fuhk
mourning dress worn by bereaved children

孟 maahng (Md mèng)
① a Chinese family name ② the eldest of brothers; the first of the months of a season ③ rude; rough ④ of, or having to do with, Mencius

孟浪 maahng lohng
rude; rough

孟買 Maahng máaih
Bombay, India

季 gwai (Md jì)
① a season; a quarter of a year ② the last (of the months of a season) ③ the youngest (of brothers)

季節 gwai jit
a season

季軍 gwai gwàn
the second runner-up in a contest; the third prize winner

孤 gù (Md gū)
① solitary; lone; lonely; friendless; helpless; unaided ② fatherless; orphaned ③ (of disposition) essentric ④ negligent in an obligation

孤獨 **gù duhk**
solitary; friendless

孤兒 **gù yìh**
an orphan

孥 **nòuh** (Md **nú**)
one's children

妻孥 **chài nòuh**
wife and children

孩 **hàaih** (Md **hái**)
① a child; an infant; a baby ② young; small

孩子 **hàaih jí**
a child

孩提 **hàaih tàih**
a child that still has to be carried in arms; an infant

孫 (孙) **syùn** (Md **sūn**)
① grandchild; descendent ② a Chinese family name

孫女 **syùn néui**
a grand daughter

孫中山 **Syùn jùng sàan**
Dr. Sun Yat-san, father of the Republic of China

孰 **suhk** (Md **shú**)
(in literary texts) who; whom; what; which

孰若 **suhk yeuhk**
what better than

孱 **sàahn** (Md **chán**)
weak; feeble; frail

孱弱 **sàahn yeuhk**
feeble; weak; ill

孳 **jì** (Md **zī**)
① to bear or beget in large numbers ② to work with sustained diligence

孳生 **jì sàng**
to grow and multiply

孳息 **jì sīk**
to grow; interest (from money)

孵 **fù** (Md **fū**)
① to hatch (eggs); to incubate ② to emerge from eggs or spawn

孵化 **fù fa**
to emerge from eggs; to spawn

孵卵 **fù léun**
to hatch eggs; to incubate

學 (学、斈) **hohk**
(Md **xué**)
① to learn; to study; to imitate ② of, or having to do with learning; academic

學生 **hohk sāang**
a student; a pupil

學派 **hohk paai**
a school (of thought)

孺 **yùh** (Md **rú**)
a young child; an infant

孺子 **yùh jí**
a child

孺慕 **yùh mouh**
to adore as a child adores its parents; to love and respect very much

孽 (孼) **yihp** (Md **niè**)
① son of a concubine ② a monster ③ sin; evil

孽種 **yihp júng**
a child born of adultery; a bastard

孽黨 **yihp dóng**
members of a traitorous party, band, etc.

孿 (孪) **lyùhn** (Md **luán**)
twin

孿生 **lyùhn sāng**
born as twins

宀部

宄 **gwái** (Md **guǐ**)
a treacherous fellow; a traitor; a

thief

它 (牠) **tà** (Md **tā**)
it; that; this

冗 **yúng** (Md **rǒng**)
same as '冗' see '宀' radical

宅 **jaahk** (Md **zhái**)
a dwelling; a residence; a house

宅心 **jaahk sàm**
intention

宅眷 **jaahk gyun**
one's dependents

宇 **yúh** (Md **yǔ**)
① a house; a roof ② look; appearance; countenance ③ space

宇宙 **yúh jauh**
the universe

宇內 **yúh noih**
in the country; in the world

守 **sáu** (Md **shǒu**)
① to guard; to protect; to defend; to watch ② to wait ③ to keep ④ to stick to; to maintain

守約 **sáu yeuk**
to keep a promise; to honor a pledge

守法 **sáu faat**
to abide by the law

安 **òn** (Md **ān**)
① peaceful; quiet; calm; safe; secure; stable ② to quiet; to stabilize; to pacify; to console ③ to put; to place; to arrange ④ to be content with ⑤ how, why ⑥ a Chinese family name

安排 **òn pàaih**
to arrange; to make arrangement for

安眠藥 **òn mìhn yeuhk**
sleeping pills; hypnotics; soporifics

宋 **sung** (Md **sòng**)
① the Sung Dynasty (960 – 1279 A.D.); of, or having to do with, the Sung Dynasty ② a Chinese family name ③ a state in the Warring States period

宋朝 **sung chìuh**
the Sung Dynasty (960 – 1279 A.D.)

宋詞 **sung chìh**
poetry of the Sung Dynasty (characterized by lines of irregular length)

宏 **wàhng** (Md **hóng**)
great; vast; wide; ample

宏大 **wàhng daaih**
great; grand; vast; immense

宏願 **wàhng yuhn**
an ambition; an ambitious plan

完 **yùhn** (Md **wán**)
① to finish; to complete; to bring to a conclusion; to settle ② whole; complete; perfect; intact

完美 **yùhn méih**
perfect; very satisfactory

完畢 **yùhn bāt**
finished; completed

宕 **dohng** (Md **dàng**)
① a quarry man ② to delay; to procrastinate ③ to loiter; to loaf

宕戶 **dohng wuh**
a quarryman

宓 **maht, fuhk** (Md **mì**)
① quiet; silent; still ② a Chinese family name

宗 **jùng** (Md **zōng**)
① ancestor; clan ② sect; religion ③ to believe in ④ a Chinese family name

宗教 **jùng gaau**
religion

宗旨 **jùng jí**
　purport; purpose; aim;
　objective

官 **gùn** (Md **guān**)
　① a government official ② of, or
　having to do with the government
　or the state ③ an organ (in
　biology) ④ a Chinese family name

官話 **gùn wá**
　the language of official dom;
　Mandarin

官邸 **gùn dái**
　official residence

宙 **jauh** (Md **zhòu**)
infinite time; time without beginning or end; eternity

宙合 **jauh hahp**
　all embracing, or all
　encompassing

宇宙 **yúh jauh**
　universe

定 **dihng** (Md **dìng**)
　to decide; to fix; to settle;
definite; fixed; stable;
unalterable; irreversible; final

定律 **dihng leuht**
　law (in science)

定義 **dihng yih**
　a definition

宛 **yún** (Md **wǎn**)
　① as if; as though ② crook;
roundabout

宛延 **yún yìhn**
　long and winding (roads, lines,
　etc.)

宛如 **yún yùh**
　as if; as though; like

宜 **yìh** (Md **yí**)
　① right; fitting; proper; good ②
should; ought to; had better ③
matter ④ to fit; to suit; to put in
order

宜室宜家 **yìh sāt yìh gà**
　to make a harmonious and
　orderly home (used as a con-
　gradulatory message on
　wedding)

適宜 **sīk yìh**
　be suitable

宣 **syùn** (Md **xuān**)
　① to announce; to declare; to
propagate; to circulate ② a
Chinese family name

宣佈 **syùn bou**
　to announce

宣傳 **syùn chyùhn**
　to publicize; to promote;
　(sales) propaganda; promotion
　(of sales)

客 **haak** (Md **kè**)
　① guest; stranger; alien; foreigner
　② spectator; audience;
customers ③ foreign; strange;
alien; nonnative ④ an advanturer

客戶 **haak wuh**
　client

客觀 **haak gùn**
　objective (as oppose to subjec-
　tive); not biased

宥 **yauh** (Md **yòu**)
to forgive; to pardon; to be lenient

宥罪 **yauh jeuih**
　to forgive an offense

原宥 **yùhn yauh**
　to forgive

室 **sāt** (Md **shì**)
　① a room; a house; a home ② a
wife

室內 **sāt noih**
　indoor (as opposed to out
　door)

室女 **sāt néuih**
　an unmarried girl; a virgin

宦 **waahn** (Md **huàn**)
① a government official; the government service ② castrated

宦官 **waahn gùn**
a eunuch

宦海浮沉 **waahn hói fàuh chàhm**
the ups and downs in officialdom

宮 **gùng** (Md **gōng**)
① palace ② castration

宮殿 **gùng dihn**
a palace

宮娥 **gùng ngòh**
court ladies; ladies-in-waiting

宰 **jói** (Md **zǎi**)
① to preside; to govern; to rule ② to slaughter; to butcher; to kill

宰相 **jói seung**
prime minister (in former times)

宰殺 **jói saat**
to slaughter; to butcher; to kill

宴(醼) **yin** (Md **yàn**)
① to entertain; to feast ② leisurely; comfort; ease

宴會 **yin wuih**
a banquet; a dinner party; a feast

宴客 **yin haak**
to entertain guests at a banquet

害 **hoih** (Md **hài**)
① to injure; to harm; to damage; to destroy; to kill; damage; injury; harm; detriment ② a vital point

害處 **hoih chyu**
harms; detriments; disadvantages; shortcomings

害怕 **hoih pa**
to be afraid of; to be scared of; to fear

宵 **sìu** (Md **xiāo**)
night; dark; evening

宵夜 **sìu yé**
a snack before going to bed

宵禁 **sìu gam**
curfew (enforced at night for public order)

容 **yùhng** (Md **róng**)
① face; expression; countenance ② to contain; to hold; to accept; to tolerate; to allow; to permit; to forgive; to pardon

容貌 **yùhng maauh**
look; countenance; features

容許 **yùhng héui**
to allow; to permit

家 **gà** (Md **jiā, jie**)
① home; house; household; family; of a household; at home; domestic ② specialist (in any branch of art or science)

家庭 **gà tìhng**
a home; a household

家長 **gà jéung**
head of a family or household

宸 **sàhn** (Md **chén**)
① abode of the emperor ② a large mansion

宸遊 **sàhn yàuh**
emperor on tour

密 **maht** (Md **mì**)
① dense; close; intimate; tight; thick ② secret; confidential; hidden

密件 **maht gín**
confidential or secret documents

密雲 **maht wàhn**
dense clouds

寂 **jihk** (Md **jì**)
① death of a Buddhist monk or nun ② quiet; still; serene;

peaceful; desolate

寂寞 jihk mohk
lonely; lonesome

寂靜 jihk jihng
quiet; still

宿 sūk, sau (Md sù, xiǔ, xiù)

① to stay overnight; to lodge; to sojourn ② long-harbored; long-cherished; old ③ of the former life; inborn; innate; destined ④ night ⑤ a constellation; an asterism

宿舍 sūk se
dormitory; living quarters

星宿 sìng sau
stars or planets in heaven

寄 gei (Md jì)

① to send; to transmit; to mail ② to entrust; to consign; to commit; to deposit

寄信 gei seun
to send or mail a letter

寄生 gei sàng
parasitism; to be a parasite (on); to be parastic(on)

寅 yàhn (Md yín)

① the third of the twelve terrestrial branches (地支) ② a fellow officer; a colleague ③ horary sign (for the period from 3 to 5 a.m.)

寅月 yàhn yuht
the first moon of the lunar calender

寅夜 yàhn yeh
3 to 5 a.m.

寇 kau (Md kòu)

① bandits; enemy ② to invade; to pillage; to plunder ③ a Chinese family name

寇仇 kau chàuh
an enemy; a foe

倭寇 wò kau
(in ancient usage) the dwarf-pirates; the Japs

冤 yùn (Md yuān)

same as '冤' see '冖' radical

富 fu (Md fù)

① rich; wealthy; affluent; abundant; plentiful ② a Chinese family name

富貴 fu gwai
wealthy and high position

富庶 fu syu
(of a land) plentiful and populous

寐 meih (Md mèi)

a sound sleep; a deep sleep; to doze; to drowse; to sleep

夢寐 muhng meih
the state of sleep and dreaming; very eagerly; visionary; vague

寒 hòhn (Md hán)

① cold; chilly; wintry ② poor

寒假 hòhn ga
winter vacation

寒酸 hòhn syùn
poverty; poverty-stricken condition (especially referring to face-loving intellectuals); unpresentable (dress, gifts, etc.)

寓(庽)yuh (Md yù)

① to live temporarily; to sojourn; to dwell ② to consign

寓所 yuh só
one's residence or dwelling

寓言 yuh yìhn
a fable; an allegory

寞 mohk (Md mò)

still; silent; quiet; lonely

寂寞 jihk mohk
lonely; lonesome

察 **chaat** (Md **chá**)
to examine; to observe; to
investigate; to survey; to study;
to scrutinize

察看 **chaat hon**
to observe; to watch

察勘 **chaat ham**
to survey; to examine

寡 **gwá** (Md **guǎ**)
① widowed; surviving the spouse
② lonely; alone; solitary ③ little;
few; rate

寡婦 **gwá fúh**
a widow

寡歡 **gwá fùn**
unhappy

寢(寑)**chám** (Md **qǐn**)
① to sleep; to rest ② a tomb ③
a residence

寢室 **chám sāt**
a bedroom

寢食不安 **chám sihk bāt
ngòn**
restless due to deep worries

寤 **ngh** (Md **wù**)
to awake from a sound sleep

寤寐 **ngh meih**
between sleep and wakeful-
ness

寤生 **ngh sàng**
to give birth to a baby while
asleep

實(实)**saht** (Md **shí**)
① fruit; real; true; actual; honest;
faithful; sincere ② practical ③
concrete; substantial; solid;
tangible ④ fact; reality; truth;
actuality

實際 **saht jai**
actual situation; actuality

實現 **saht yihn**
to realize (a plan, a dream, etc.)
(of a dream, etc.) to come true

寥 **lìuh** (Md **liáo**)
① few; not many ② deserted;
desolate; empty

寥落 **lìuh lohk**
sparse

寥寥無幾 **lìuh lìuh mòuh
géi**
not many; few

寧(宁、甯)**nìhng**
(Md **níng, nìng**)
① peace; repose; serenity; tranquility ② would rather; had
rather; would sooner

寧可 **nìhng hó**
would rather

寧靜 **nìhng jihng**
quiet; tranquil; serene; placid;
calm

寨 **jaaih** (Md **zhài**)
a stockade

寨主 **jaaih jyú**
leader (used by bandits in
speaking of their leader)

審(审)**sám**
(Md **shěn**)
① to examine; to review; to
investigate ② to know; to
discern; to appreciate ③ cautions; judicious; careful

審判 **sám pun**
to try (a case or person in a law
court); a trial

審核 **sám haht**
to examine and consider

寫(写)**sé** (Md **xiě**)
① to write; to sketch; to draw;
to represent ② unrestrained

寫字間 **sé jih gāan**
an office room

寫生 **sé sāng**
to draw; or paint from nature;
to sketch

宀部

寬（宽）**fùn** (Md **kuān**)

① board; wide; spacious; vast ② magnanimous; lenient; general; tolerant; liberal; forgiveness; ample; indulgent ③ to loosen; to widen

寬闊 **fùn fut**
roomy; wide; spacious

寬恕 **fùn syu**
to forgive; to pardon; forgiveness; pardon

寮 **lìuh** (Md **liáo**)

① a fellow officer or official; a colleague ② a hut; a cottage

寮國 **Lìuh gwok**
Laos

寰 **wàahn** (Md **huán**)

a large domain; a vast space

寰內 **wàahn noih**
the domain of the empire

寰宇 **wàahn yúh**
the world

寵（宠）**chúng** (Md **chǒng**)

① a concubine ② to favor; to dote on; to patronize ③ favor or love (especially of the emperor)

寵愛 **chúng ngoi**
to favor or patronize; to dote on

寵壞 **chúng waaih**
to spoil (a child)

寶（宝、寳）**bóu** (Md **bǎo**)

① treasure ② precious; valuable ③ respectable; honorable

寶貴 **bóu gwai**
valuable; precious

寶藏 **bóu johng**
a treasury; a treasure house; a collection of treasures

寸部

寸 **chyun** (Md **cùn**)

① a measure of length (equal to about 1/10 foot) ② as small as an inch; small; tiny; little

寸進 **chyun jeun**
a little progress; to advance by inches

寸土必爭 **chyun tóu bīt jàng**
even an inch of land has to be fought for

寺 **jih** (Md **sì**)

a temple; a monastery; a shrine; a mosque

寺觀 **jih gun**
temples and monasteries

寺院 **jih yún**
temples

封 **fùng** (Md **fēng**)

① a numerary adjunct for letters ② to install as a feudal lord or a nobleman ③ to seal; to block; to close completely ④ covering; wrapper; envelope

封閉 **fùng baih**
to seal; to close completely

封面 **fùng mihn, fùng mín**
cover (of a book)

射 **seh** (Md **shè**)

① to shoot; to eject; to spurt; to squirt; to issue forth ② archery (listed by confucius as one of six arts required of a scholar)

射擊 **seh gīk**
to shoot; shooting; marks manship

射箭 **seh jin**
to shoot an arrow; archery

專（专、耑）**jyùn** (Md **zhuān**)

① to concentrate; to focus; to

monopolize; to specialize ②
exclusive; special

專門 **jyùn mùhn**
a specialty; a special field;
exclusively

專利 **jyùn leih**
monopoly; a patent

將 (将) **jèung, jeung**
(Md **jiāng, jiàng**)
① going to or about to (used with
a verb expressing future action)
② used with a noun functioning
as a direct object ③ to manage;
to adapt; to conform; to nourish
④ a general; an admiral; a military
leader of high rank ⑤ to lead
(soldiers)

將來 **jèung lòih**
the future; the days to come

將近 **jèung gahn**
approximately

將官 **jeung gùn**
a general officer

將士 **jeung sih**
officers and men

尉 **wai, wāt** (Md **wèi, yù**)
① a company-grade military
officer ② (in former times) a
grade of military official ③ in
尉遲 (wāt chìh) a double family
name

上尉 **seuhng wai**
(in navy) lieutenant (s.g.); (in
army, marine and air force)
captain

尉遲 **wāt chìh**
a double family name

尊 **jyùn** (Md **zūn**)
to honor; to respect; to venerate;
to revere; to esteem; honored;
honorable; esteemed; respectable; noble

尊重 **jyùn juhng**
to venerate; to hold in
reverence; to honor; to
respect; to esteem; to uphold

尊嚴 **jyùn yìhm**
dignity; respectability; honor

尋 (寻) **chàhm**
(Md **xún, xín**)
① a measure of length in former
times (roughly equivalent to eight
feet) ② to seek; to search; to
inquire ③ to beg; to entreat

尋求 **chàhm kàuh**
to seek; to try to get

尋錢的 **chàhm chìn dīk**
a beggar

對 (对) **deui** (Md **duì**)
① right, correct or proper ②
parallel or opposing ③ a pair; a
couple ④ to check or ascertain;
to oppose or face ⑤ to; as to;
with regard to

對比 **deui béi**
contrast; correlation

對面 **deui mihn**
on the opposite side; right in
front

導 (导) **douh** (Md **dǎo**)
to guide; to lead; to instruct; to
conduct; to direct

導演 **douh yín**
director (of a dramatic
performance)

導遊 **douh yàuh**
a tourist guide

小部

小 **síu** (Md **xiǎo**)
① small; little; tiny ② minor;
young ③ humble; mean; junior;
lowly ④ light; slight; unimportant; trivial; pretty; moderate

小販 **síu fáan**
stall keepers; hawkers;

peddlers

小姐 **síu jé**
a young (unmarried) lady

少 **síu, siu** (Md **shǎo, shào**)
① small or little (in number, quantity or duration) ② missing; absent; wanting; lost ③ to be sparing in; to refrain from ④ young; youthful; junior; juvenile

少數 **síu sou**
a few; a small number (of); minority

少年 **siu nìhn**
a boy; a juvenile; a youth

尖 **jìm** (Md **jiān**)
sharp; acute; pointed; keen

尖銳 **jìm yeuih**
sharp; acute; keen

尖端 **jìm dyùn**
a pointed end or head

尚 **seuhng** (Md **shàng**)
① yet; still ② to up hold; to honor; to esteem ③ a Chinese family name

尚佳 **seuhng gàai**
passable; not too bad

尚武 **seuhng móuh**
militaristic

尤部

尤 (尢) **yàuh** (Md **yóu**)
① to feel bitter against; to reproach; to blame ② a mistake; an error ③ especially or particularly ④ outstanding or special ⑤ a Chinese family name

尤人 **yàuh yàhn**
to blame others

尤物 **yàuh maht**
an uncommon person; a rare personage; a woman of extraordinary beauty; a rare

beauty

尬 **gaai** (Md **gà**)
embarrassed of; ill at ease

尷尬 **gaam gaai**
embarrassing; embarrassed

就 **jauh** (Md **jiù**)
① to receive ② to undergo ③ to assume ④ to follow ⑤ to come or go to ⑥ forthwith; right away ⑦ exactly; precisely ⑧ namely

就職 **jauh jīk**
to be sworn into office; to be sworn in; to be inaugurated

就業 **jauh yihp**
to get employment; to get a job

尷 (尲、尲) **gaam** (Md **gān**)
embarrassing; embarrassed

尷尬 **gaam gaai**
embarrassing; embarrassed

尸部

尸 **sì** (Md **shī**)
① a corpse ② to preside; to direct

尸諫 **sì gaan**
to admonish (one's master, lord, etc.) at the cost of one's own life

尸位素餐 **sì wai sou chàan**
to neglect the duties of an office while taking the pay

尺 **chek, ché** (Md **chī, chě**)
① a foot ruler ② a unit in Chinese linear measurement slightly longer than a foot same as in 尺 ③ a note in old Chinese musical scale

尺寸 **chek chyun**
size (of a garment)

尺碼 **chek máh**
dimensions (of an object); specification (about size, quality, etc.)

尹 **wáhn** (Md **yǐn**)
① to govern; to rule ② a Chinese family name

尻 **hàau** (Md **kāo**)
the sacrum

尼 **nèih** (Md **ní**)
a nun

尼姑 **nèih gū**
a nun

尼龍 **nèih lùhng**
nylon

尾 **méih** (Md **wěi, yǐ**)
① the tail; the rear; the stern (of a ship); rear; back ② last; final ③ remaining

尾巴 **méih bā**
a tail; a follower (in derogatory sense)

尾隨 **méih chèuih**
to follow close behind; to tail; to shadow

尿 **niuh** (Md **niào, suī**)
urine; to urinate

尿道 **niuh douh**
urethra; urinary canal

尿酸 **niuh syùn**
uric acid

屁 **pei** (Md **pì**)
① a fart ② the hip

屁股 **pei gú**
the hip; the buttocks; the rump

屁滾尿流 **pei gwán niuh làuh**
to be frightened out of one's wits

局 **guhk** (Md **jú**)
① an office; a bureau ② situation; state of affairs

局部 **guhk bouh**
having to do only with a part; partial; local

局限 **guhk haahn**
to limit; to confine; limited; confined

居 **gèui** (Md **jū**)
① to dwell; to reside; to inhabit; to occupy; an abode; a dwelling ② a Chinese family name

居民 **gèui màhn**
resident or inhabitant

居然 **gèui yìhn**
incredibly; to my surprise to my disbelief

屈 **wāt** (Md **qū**)
① to bend; to flex ② to humilate; to humble ③ a Chinese family name

屈曲 **wāt kūk**
crooked; winding

屈服 **wāt fuhk**
to succumb, yield or submit (to power, threat, etc.); to give in

屆 (届) **gaai** (Md **jiè**)
① numerary adjunct for periodic terms or events ② (of an appointed date) to arrive ③ (of a term) to expire

屆滿 **gaai múhn**
(of a term) to expire

屆時 **gaai sìh**
at the appointed time (in the future)

屋 **ngūk** (Md **wū**)
a house; a room; a shelter

屋宇 **ngūk yúh**
houses in general

屋簷 **ngūk sìhm**
the eaves

屍 **sì** (Md **shī**)
a corpse; a carcass

屍體 **sì tái**
a corpse; remains

屍首 **sì sáu**
a corpse; remains

屎 **sí** (Md **shǐ**)
excrement

屎尿 **sí niuh**
excrement and urine; body waste

屎坑 **sí hàang**
a lavatory

展 **jín** (Md **zhǎn**)
① to open ② to stretch; to extend ③ to unfold; to unroll ④ to expand; to dilate ⑤ to prolong ⑥ to visit

展覽 **jín láahm**
to exhibit; to display; to put on display

展期 **jín kèih**
to be postponed; to put off; to extend the deadline or time limit

屐 **kehk** (Md **jī**)
wooden shoes, clogs; pattens

屐齒 **kehk chí**
teeth of clogs or pattens

屑 **sit** (Md **xiè**)
① chips; crumbs; bits; odds and ends; trifles ② to care; to mind

木屑 **muhk sit**
crumbs of wood

屑意 **sit yi**
to care; to mind

屏 **pìhng, bíng** (Md **píng, bǐng**)
① a shield; a screen; to shield; to screen; to guard ② to reject; to dicard; to dismiss

屏風 **pìhng fūng**
a screen

屏棄 **bíng hei**
to reject; to dicard

屜（屉）**tai** (Md **tì**)
a drawer

屜子 **tai jí**
a drawer

抽屜 **chàu tai**
a drawer

屙 **ngò** (Md **ē**)
to discharge

屙肚 **ngò tóuh**
diarrhea

屙尿 **ngò niuh**
to move bowels

屠 **tòuh** (Md **tú**)
① to slaughter; to butcher; to massacre ② a Chinese family name

屠夫 **tòuh fū**
a butcher

屠殺 **tòuh saat**
to massacre; wholesale slaughter; a massacre

屢（屡）**léuih** (Md **lǚ**)
frequently; repeatedly; often; time after time; time and again; again and again

屢次 **léuih chi**
repeatedly; frequently; time and again; again and again; time after time

屢敗屢戰 **léuih baaih léuih jin**
to fight repeatedly in spite of repeated setbacks

屣 **sáai** (Md **xǐ**)
shoes; sandals

層 (层) **chàhng**
(Md **céng**)

a layer; a stratum; a story (of a building)

層次 **chàhng chi**
　order (of importance or priority)

層雲 **chàhng wàhn**
　stratus

履 **léih** (Md **lǔ**)

① shoes ② to step on; to tread on; to walk upon; to follow

履約 **léih yeuk**
　to keep or fulfill an agreement; to keep a promise or pledge

履歷表 **léih lihk bíu**
　a biographic sketch (used in applying for a position); curriculum vital)

屨 (屦) **geui** (Md **jù**)

sandals; shoes made of coarse material

屬 (属) **suhk, jūk**
(Md **shǔ, zhǔ**)

① a category; a class; a kind ② to belong to; to be subordinate to; to be governed by ③ to compose (a piece of writing) ④ to instruct; to direct

屬於 **suhk yù**
　to belong to

屬文 **jūk màhn**
　to compose a piece of writing

屮 部

屯 **tyùhn, jèun** (Md **tún, zhūn**)

① to station (an army) ② to stockpile

屯兵 **tyùhn bìng**
　to station troops

屯田 **tyùhn tìhn**
　to station an army in the countryside and make it engage in farming

山 部

山 **sàan** (Md **shān**)
mountain; hill; peak

山峯 **sàan fùng**
　mountain top

山河 **sàan hòh**
　mountains and rivers (as physical aspect of a country)

屹 **ngaht** (Md **yì**)
(of a mountain, building, etc.) to rise high; to stand erect or majestically

屹立 **ngaht lahp**
　to stand erect; to stand magnificently (like a mountain)

屹然 **ngaht yìhn**
　erect and firm (like a mountain)

屺 **héi** (Md **qǐ**)
a bare (or bald) mountain or hill

岌 **kāp** (Md **jí**)
① (of a peak) rising high above others ② perilous; hazardous

岌岌可危 **kāp kāp hó ngàih**
　in a very critical situation; to hang by a thread

岔 **cha** (Md **chà**)
to branch; to diverge; branching point

岔口 **cha háu**
　fork (in a road)

岔子 **cha jí**
　trouble (in the course of an activity)

岐 **kèih** (Md **qí**)
to diverge; to branch

岐山 **Kèih sàan**
　Mt. Chi (between Shansi and

Shensi)

岐黃之術 **kèih wòhng jì seuht**
Chinese herbal medical science

岑 **sàhm (Md cén)**
① a relatively high, pointed hill ② silent; still; quiet ③ a Chinese family name

岑寂 **sàhm jihk**
quiet; still; silent

岑樓 **sàhm làuh**
a mountain-like, lofty and tapering building

岡(冈) **gòng (Md gàng)**
ridge (of a hill or mountain)

岡巒起伏 **gòng lyùhn héi fuhk**
full of mountain ridges

岩(巖) **ngàahm (Md yán)**
① a large rock ② a mountain

岩石 **ngàahm sehk**
a rock; a crag

岩洞 **ngàahm duhng**
cavern; cave; grotto

岫 **jauh (Md xiù)**
① a cavern; a cave ② a mountain peak

岬 **gaap (Md jiǎ)**
a cape; a promontory; a headland; a point

岬碣 **gaap hot**
continuous

岱 **doih (Md dài)**
Mt. Tai (in Shantung Province, one of the five Sacred Mountains)

岱宗 **Doih jùng**
Mt. Tai (泰山) in Shantung Province, one of five Sacred Mountain)

岳 **ngohk (Md yuè)**
① a great mountain ② a high mountain; wife's parents ③ a Chinese family name

岳父 **ngohk fuh**
father-in-law (wife's father)

岳飛 **Ngohk fèi**
Yueh Fei (1103 — 1141), hero of the Sung Dynasty

岷 **màhn (Md mín)**
① the Min River (in Szechwan) ② Mt. Min (in Szechwan)

岷江 **Màhn gòng**
the Min River (in Szechwan)

岷山 **Màhn sàan**
Mt. Min (in Szechwan)

岸 **ngohn (Md àn)**
① shore; bank; beach; coast ② majestic; proud

岸然 **ngohn yìhn**
solemn and dignified look

岸巾 **ngohn gàn**
to wear a head covering in a neglectful manner so as to expose the forehead

峒 **duhng, tùhng (Md dòng, tóng)**
① name of a mountain in Kansu Province ② name of a tribe in Kwangsi and Kweichow

峒丁 **tùhng dìng**
soldiers from the Tung tribe

峒人 **tùhng yàhn**
the people of the Tung tribe

峙 **sih (Md zhì, shì)**
to stand erect like a mountain

對峙 **deui sih**
to confront each other (often implying a stalemate)

峋 **sèun (Md xún)**
irregular stretch of mountains

嶙峋 **lèuhn sèun**
(of mountains) rugged; (of a person) upright

峨（峩）**ngòh** (Md **é**)
lofty

峨眉 **Ngòh mèih**
Mt. Omei (a Buddhist resort in Szechwan)

峨峨 **ngòh ngòh**
looking majestic

峭（陗）**chiu** (Md **qiào**)
① steep; precipitous ② harsh; sharp; stern; unkind

峭壁 **chiu bik**
a precipice; a cliff; steep; precipice

峭急 **chiu gāp**
impatient; quick-tempered

峴（岘）**yihn** (Md **xiàn**)
① a mountain in Hupeh Province ② a steep hill

峴港 **Yihn góng**
Danang; American military base in South Vietnam during the war against Viet Cong

峯（峰）**fùng** (Md **fēng**)
a peak; a summit; a hump

峯巒 **fùng lyùhn**
peaks and ridges

島（岛）**dóu** (Md **dǎo**)
island; isle

島嶼 **dóu jeuih**
island; isle

島國 **dóu gwok**
an island nation

峻 **jeun** (Md **jùn**)
① high; lofty; steep ② severe; harsh; rigorous; uncompromishing

峻法 **jeun faat**
severe, harsh or rigorous law

峻嶺 **jeun líhng**
a lofty range (of mountains)

峽（峡）**hahp** (Md **xiá**)
① a gorge; straits ② an isthmus ③ narrow

峽谷 **hahp gūk**
a dale; a gorge; a valley; a canyon

峪 **yuh** (Md **yù**)
① a valley; a ravine ② Chiayu 嘉峪 (a city in Kansu Province) where the Great Wall terminates

嘉峪關 **Gà yuh gwàan**
The Chiayu Fortress in Kansu which marks the western end of the Great Wall

崇 **sùhng** (Md **chóng**)
① to honor; to respect; to revere; to adore; to worship; to venerate; to esteem; to uphold ② high; lofty; noble; dignified; exalted

崇拜 **sùhng baai**
to worship; to idolize; to adore; to lionize

崇高 **sùhng gòu**
lofty; upright

崆 **hùng** (Md **kōng**)
name of mountain

崆峒山 **Hùng duhng sàan**
Mt. Kangdong (in Kansu Province)

崎 **kèi** (Md **qí**)
rugged; uneven; rough; jagged

崎嶇 **kèi kèui**
(of terrain) uneven; rolling; rough; rugged

崑 **kwàn** (Md **kūn**)
① the Kunlun Mountain ② Kunshan, name of a country and mountain in Kiangsu)

崑曲 **Kwàn kūk**
name of a class of tunes

originating in Kunshan, Kiangsu

崑崙山 **Kwàn lèuhn sàan**
the Kunlun Mountains (between Tibet and Siu Kiang, extending to Central China)

崖（崕、厓）**ngàaih** (Md **yá, yái**)
① a cliff; a precipice; brink; verge ② precipitous; high and steep; forbidding

崖岸 **ngàaih ngohn**
haughty

崖略 **ngàaih leuhk**
an outline

崗（岗）**gòng** (Md **gǎng, gāng**)
the place where a sentry is posted; post; position

崗位 **gòng waih**
one's post; one's duty

崗警 **gòng gíng**
a policeman who performs his duties at a fixed post

崙（岺）**lèuhn** (Md **lún**)
the Kunlun Mountains

崛 **gwaht** (Md **juế**)
to rise abruptly

崛起 **gwaht héi**
to rise abruptly

崛崎 **gwaht kèi**
steep

崢（峥）**jàng** (Md **zhēng**)
① lofty; noble; distinguished ② steep; perilous; dangerous ③ harsh; severe; rigorous

崢嶸 **jàng wìhng**
lofty; steep; dangerous; rigorous; sharp; distinguished; outstanding (said of a person)

崔 **chèui** (Md **cuī**)
① a Chinese family name ② high and steep

崔嵬 **chèui ngàih**
a rocky height or peak

崔巍 **chèui ngàih**
(of mountains) lofty and steep

崩 **bàng** (Md **bēng**)
① to collapse; to disintegrate; to fall ② to die (said of an emperor)

崩潰 **bàng kwúi**
to collapse; to break down; to fall to pieces; to cave in

崩裂 **bàng liht**
to crack up

崧 **sùng** (Md **sōng**)
see '嵩' character

嵇 **kài** (Md **jī**)
① a Chinese family name ② name of a mountain in Honan

嵇山 **Kài sàan**
name of a mountain in Honan

嵇康 **Kài hòng**
Chi Kang, a man of letters of the Wei Dynasty, one of the Seven Wise Men of the Bamboo Grove

崽 **jói** (Md **zǎi**)
(西崽) Chinese servant of a foreigner (derogatory term)

崽子 **jói jí**
son of a bitch; s.o.b.

嵋 **mèih** (Md **méi**)
Mt. Omei, a Buddhist resort in Szechwan

峨嵋 **Ngòh mèih**
Mt. Omei (a Buddhist resort in Szechwan)

嵌 **hahm** (Md **qiàn**)
to inlay; to set in

嵌工 **hahm gùng**
the handicraftmanship displayed in a piece of jewelry inlaid with gold or stones

嵌金 **hahm gàm**
to inlay with gold

嵎 **yùh** (Md **yú**)
a strategic point in the mountains

嵐(岚) **làahm** (Md **lán**)
mountain vapor; mist

嵐氣 **làahm hei**
mountain vapor; mist

嵩(崧) **sùng** (Md **sōng**)
① lofty ② Sungshan, the highest and central peak of the Five Sacred Mountains, situated in Honan

嵩壽 **sùng sauh**
longevity; to live as long as Sungshan

嵩呼 **sùng fù**
to shout "Long live the Emperor!"

嵬 **ngàih** (Md **wéi**)
(of a mountain) high and uneven

嵬然 **ngàih yìhn**
lofty

嵯 **chò** (Md **cuó**)
(of mountains) high and irregular or rugged

嵯峨 **chò ngòh**
(of mountains) high and irregular

嶇(岖) **kèui** (Md **qū**)
rugged; uneven; irregular

崎嶇 **kèi kèui**
(of terrain) uneven; rolling; rough; rugged

嶂 **jeung** (Md **zhàng**)
a mountain barrier

嶄(崭) **jáam, jaam**
(Md **zhǎn**)
① (of a mountain) high and pointed ② novel; new

嶄新 **jaam sàn**
brand new

嶄然 **jáam yìhn**
(of a mountain) high and pointed; completely changed

嶒 **chàhng** (Md **céng**)
steep; lofty

嶓 **bò** (Md **bō**)
name of a mountain in Shensi

嶓冢 **bò chúng**
name of a mountain in Shensi

嶠(峤) **giuh, kiuh**
(Md **jiào, qiáo**)
a high pointed mountain

嶙 **lèuhn** (Md **lín**)
(of mountains) rugged

嶙嶙 **lèuhn lèuhn**
(of terrain) rolling and rugged

嶙峋 **lèuhn sèun**
(of mountains) rugged; (of a person) upright

嶢(峣) **yìuh** (Md **yáo**)
(of mountains) high or tall

嶔 **yàm** (Md **qīn**)
(of a mountain) lofty

嶔崎磊落 **yàm kèi léuih lohk**
(of a person) honest and upright

嶸(嵘) **wìhng**
(Md **róng**)
lofty; prominent; majectic

崢嶸 **jàng wìhng**
lofty; steep; dangerous; rigorous; sharp; distinguished; outstanding (said of a person)

嶺 (岭) **líhng** (Md **lǐng**)
ridge of a mountain; a mountain range; a mountain; a mountain peak

嶺表 **líhng bíu**
the front or southern side of the Five Ridges (i.e. Kwangtung)

嶺南 **Líhng nàahm**
area south of the Five Ridges (i.e. Kwangtung)

嶼 (屿) **jeuih, yùh**
(Md **yǔ, xù**)
an islet; an island

島嶼 **dóu jeuih**
an island

大嶼山 **Daaih yùh sàan**
Lantau Island (an Outlying Island west of Hong Kong)

嶽 **ngohk** (Md **yuè**)
a high mountain; a peak; a lofty summit

嶽峙 **ngohk sih**
(of one's character or bearing) as noble as a lofty peak

巉 **chàahm** (Md **chán**)
precipitous

巉巖 **chàahm ngàahm**
a crag

歸 (岿) **kwài** (Md **kuī**)
① grand and secure; stately and lasting ② rows after rows of small hills

歸然獨存 **kwài yìhn duhk chyùhn**
to remain secure majestically while all others have crumbled into decay

巍 **ngàih** (Md **wēi**)
lofty; majestic

巍然 **ngàih yìhn**
lofty and massive

巍峨 **ngàih ngòh**
lofty; majestic

巒 (峦) **lyùhn** (Md **luán**)
a pointed hill

巔 **dìn** (Md **diān**)
① mountain top; peak; summit ② treetop

巔峯 **dìn fùng**
highest point; summit; climax; zenith; peak

巔峯狀態 **dìn fùng johng taai**
in peak condition (said of athletes, artists)

巖 (岩) **ngàahm**
(Md **yán**)
① a rock; a crag ② a cave

巖石 **ngàahm sehk**
a rock; a crag

巖穴 **ngàahm yuht**
a cave or cavern

巘 **yíhn** (Md **yǎn**)
a peak; a mountain

《《部

川 **chyùn** (Md **chuān**)
① a river; a stream; a water way ② a flow; a constant flow ③ (in cooking) to boil with water ④ Szechwan Province

川流不息 **chyùn làuh bāt sīk**
(said of traffic, people, etc.) a constant flow; an incessant flow; continuous

川貝 **chyùn bui**
fritillaria produced in Szechwan Province

州 **jàu** (Md **zhōu**)
① an administrative district in ancient China roughly equivalent to a province today; a region with 2,500 families ② (in old China) a county ③ a state (in the U.S.A.)

④ a place surrounded by water; an islet; a sand bar ⑤ a Chinese family name

州長 **jàu jéung**
governor of a state (in the U.S.A.); governor of a zhōu

州城 **jàu sìhng**
a town within a zhōu

巡 (廵)**chèuhn**
(Md **xún**)
① to patrol; to inspect ② to cruise; to go on circuit ② a round (of drinks) ③ a policeman; a cop

巡捕 **chèuhn bouh**
a policeman

巡行 **chèuhn hàhng**
to make rounds of inspection

巢 **chàauh** (Md **cháo**)
① a living quarter in a tree; a bird's nest ② a haunt; a den; a hideout (for bandits, etc.) ③ a Chinese family name

巢居 **chàauh gèui**
to live in trees (before the house was introduced

巢穴 **chàauh yuht**
a den; a lair; a haunt; a hideout

工部

工 **gùng** (Md **gōng**)
① labor; a laborer ② a shift; time used in doing a piece of work ③ work; a worker; a day's work; a job ④ an engineering or building project; a defense work ⑤ fine; delicate ⑥ to be skilled in

工會 **gùng wúi**
a labor union

工具 **gùng geuih**
tools; implements; equipment

左 **jó** (Md **zuǒ**)
① left side; east side ② improper; depraved ③ supporting (documents, evidence, etc.); to

assist ④ to be demoted; to decend ⑤ inconvenience; inconvenient ⑥ erroneous; unduly stubborn ⑦ a Chinese family name

左轉 **jó jyun**
to turn left

左手 **jó sáu**
left hand; left side

巧 **háau** (Md **qiǎo**)
① clever; ingenious; artful; skillful; witty ② a clever feat; a stunt ③ pretty; cute ④ coincidence; coincidental; coincidentally; opportune

巧妙 **háau miuh**
ingenuity; ingenious; skillful; clever

巧合 **háau hahp**
a coincidence

巨 (鉅)**geuih** (Md **jù**)
① great; big ② chief ③ very ④ a Chinese family name

巨著 **geuih jyu**
a great book; a monumental literary work

巨額 **geuih ngáak**
a great deal of; a tremendous amount of; a huge sum of

巫 **mòuh** (Md **wū**)
① a wizard or witch; sorcery; witch craft; etc. ② a Chinese family name

巫婆 **mòuh pòh**
a witch

巫術 **mòuh seuht**
sorcery; voodoo

差 **chàai, chà, chì**
(Md **chāi, chà, chī**)
① a massenger; an errand man to dispatch; to send (a person) ③ one's duty or job; one's official business or assignment ④ to error; to mistake; errors or

mistakes ⑤ to differ; discrepancy ⑥ nearly; almost; approximately ⑦ uneven; irregular

差人 **chàai yàhn**
servants of an official; office boys; an official messenger

差事 **chàai sih**
a job

差別 **chà biht**
discrepancy; difference; distinction

參差 **chàam chì**
uneven

己部

己 **géi** (Md **jǐ**)
① self; one's own; oneself ② the sixth of the ten Celestial Stems (天干)

己任 **géi yahm**
one's duty; responsibility or obligation

自己 **jih géi**
oneself

已 **yíh** (Md **yǐ**)
① stop; to stop; to come to an end; finished ② already ③ used to indicate the past ④ excessive; very; much ⑤ a final particle to add emphasis

已經 **yíh gìng**
already; some time ago

已往 **yíh wóhng**
before; in the past

巳 (巳) **jih** (Md **sì**)
① the sixth of the twelve Terrestrial Branches (地支) ② 9 to 11 a.m. ③ a Chinese family name

巳牌 **jih pàaih**
9 to 11 a.m.

巴 **bà** (Md **bā**)
① name of an ancient state which occupied today's eastern Szechwan ② a crust formed as a result of heart or dryness ③ to expect; to hope for anxiously ④ used to with part of human body; hand; cheeks ⑤ a final particle implying closeness or adhesion ⑥ a Chinese family name

巴黎 **Bà làih**
Paris

巴結 **bà git**
to curry favor; to toady; to flatter; to try hard to please; to exert oneself for advancement

巷 **hohng** (Md **xiàng, hàng**)
a lane; an alley

巷口 **hohng háu**
either end of a lane; entrance to a lane

巷議 **hohng yíh**
local rumous or gossips; the comments among the men in the street

巽 **seun** (Md **xùn**)
① subservient; submissive; mild; bland; insinuating ② the fifth of the Eight Diagrams

巽他羣島 **Seun tà kwàhn dóu**
the Sunda Islands including Sumatra, Java, Bali, Lombok, Sumbawa and Flores

巾部

巾 **gàn** (Md **jìn**)
① a napkin, kerchief or towel ② a headgear; articles for dressing the hair

巾幗 **gàn gwok**
female; woman; womankind; women's decorative articles

毛巾 **mòuh gàn**
towel

市 **síh** (Md **shì**)
① a market-place; a market; a place for bartering goods ② a city; municipal ③ to buy or sell ④ a Chinese family name

市民 **síh màhn**
the residents of a city

市場 **síh chèuhng**
(domestic or world) market; a marketplace

布 **bou** (Md **bù**)
① cloth; textiles ② to declare; announce or proclaim ③ to display; to distribute or disseminate; to spread out ④ a Chinese family name

布疋 **bou pāt**
piece goods

布甸 **bou dīn**
pudding

帆 **fàahn** (Md **fān**)
① a sail (of a boat); a boat ② canvas; sail-cloth

帆船 **fàahn syùhn**
a sailboat

帆布 **fàahn bou**
canvas

希 **hèi** (Md **xī**)
① rare; strange; precious ② to hope; to expect; to wish; to desire; to long ③ to come to a stop gradually ④ to become silent ⑤ very; much ⑥ a Chinese family name

希望 **hèi mohng**
hope; wish; expectations; to hope; to desire; to look forward to

希罕 **hèi hón**
rare; uncommon; to care; to value; to hold as precious

帔 **pèi** (Md **pèi**)
a cape (usually worn by women)

帑 **tóng** (Md **tǎng**)
a treasury; public fund or money

帑藏 **tóng johng**
a treasury; public fund

公帑 **gùng tóng**
public fund

帕 **paak** (Md **pà**)
① a turban; a handkerchief; a veil ② a wrapper; to wrap and bind

帕米爾 **Paak máih yíh**
the Pamirs, known as the "roof of the world"

手帕 **sáu paak**
handkerchief

帖 **tip** (Md **tiè, tiě, tiē**)
① an invitation card ② a lable; a placard; a document ③ a copybook (of calligraphy) ④ a medical prescription ⑤ submissive or obedient ⑥ settled; decided

請帖 **chéng tip**
invitation card

帖服 **tip fuhk**
submissive and subservient

帘 **lìhm** (Md **lián**)
① a flag sign of a wine-house or tavern ② a door or window screen

帘子 **lìhm jí**
a screen for door or window

酒帘 **jáu lìhm**
a bar; a wine-house

帙 **diht** (Md **zhì**)
a book wrapper or casing

帚 (箒) **jáu, jáau** (Md **zhǒu**)
a broom; a besom

帚星 **jáau sìng**
a comet; a jinx

掃帚 **sou jáu**
broom

帛 **baahk** (Md **bó**)
① silk; fabrics; collectively ②
wealth; property ③ a Chinese
family name

布帛 **bou baahk**
cloth; materials

帛書 **baahk syù**
a letter written on silk (before
paper was invented)

帥 (帅) **seui, sēut**
(Md **shuài**)
① to command; to lead; the commanding gerneral; commander-in
chief ② to follow or comply (with
instruction or orders) ③ (slang)
dashing; smart-looking

帥令 **seui lihng**
orders of the commander-in
chief

元帥 **yùhn seui**
field marshal; five-star general;
the commander in chief

帝 **dai** (Md **dì**)
① the emperor; a ruler ② a god;
a deified being ③ Heaven (as a
divine being) ④ imperial

帝國 **dai gwok**
an empire; a monarchy

帝王 **dai wòhng**
the emperor; the king; the
throne

帨 **seui** (Md **xuèi**)
a kerchief; a handkerchief

席 **jihk** (Md **xí**)
① a mat ② a feast ③ a seat; to
take a seat ④ to rely on ⑤ (very
rare) a sail ⑥ a Chinese family
name

席地而坐 **jihk deih yìh joh**
to sit on the ground

主席 **jyú jihk**
chairman

師 (师) **sì** (Md **shī**)
① a division in the Chinese army;
an army ② a master; a teacher;
a tutor; to teach ③ to pattern or
model after another ④ a
specialist (esp. of medicine,
painting, music, divining, etc.) ⑤
a local administrative chief ⑥ a
Chinese family name

師父 **sì fú**
tutors, masters, teachers, collectively; a respectful term of
address for monks, nuns, etc.

師範大學 **sì faahn daaih
hohk**
a normal university

帳 (帐) **jeung**
(Md **zhàng**)
① a canopy above the bed ② a
tent ③ a curtain or screen; a
mosquito-net ④ a scroll (sent as
a gift for wedding, birthday party,
funeral, etc.) ⑤ same as 賬

帳幕 **jeung mohk**
a tent

帳子 **jeung jí**
a mosquito-net

帶 (带) **daai** (Md **dài**)
① a girdle; a sash or scarf; a belt;
a band; a ribbon; a string; a tie ②
to wear (a smile, sword, etc.) ③
to bear; to take or bring along ④
to lead (the way, troops, etc.); to
head (an army, etc.) ⑤ a climate
zone

帶笑 **daai siu**
smilingly; carrying a smile

帶領 **daai líhng**
to lead (an army, a party, etc.)

常 **sèuhng** (Md **cháng**)
① common; ordinary; normal ②
long; lasting; permanent (job,

etc.) ③ often; frequent; frequently; regular; regularly ④ ordinarily; usually; on ordinary occasions ⑤ a rule; a principle ⑥ a Chinese family name

常用 **sèuhng yuhng**
to use often; used often

常人 **sèuhng yàhn**
ordinary people

帷 **wàih** (Md **wéi**)
a curtain; a screen; a tent

帷幔 **wàih maahn**
screens, cloth partition

帷幄 **wàih ngāak**
a military tent

幅 **fūk** (Md **fú**)
① the breath of cloth or paper; a piece (of cloth) ② a border ③ a numerary adjunct for pictures, scrolls, etc.

幅度 **fūk douh**
(said of stocks, commodity prices, etc.) rate of rise or fall

幅員 **fūk yùhn**
(literally) breath and circumference — territory (of a country)

帽 **mouh** (Md **mào**)
① a hat; headwear ② a cap (of fountain-pen, screw, etc.)

帽子 **mouh jí**
a hat or cap

帽纓 **mouh yìng**
a throat-band to hold the hat

幀 (幀) **jing** (Md **zhèng**)
① a numerary adjunct for (paintings, pictures, photos, etc.) ② one of a pair — as of scrolls

幃 (幃) **wàih** (Md **wéi**)
① a curtain ② a perfume-bag ③ women's apartments

幄 **ngāak** (Md **wò**)
a big tent

帷幄 **wàih ngāak**
a military tent

幌 **fóng** (Md **huǎng**)
a curtain; a cloth screen; a strip of cloth

幌子 **fóng jí**
a flag-sign for a wine-shop or a store; a front (esp. a gaudy front); something to dazzle or cheat another with, as boats or swash buckling ways

幔 **maahn** (Md **màn**)
a curtain; a screen; a tent

幔子 **maahn jí**
a curtain; a cloth screen

幔亭 **maahn tìhng**
a tent pavilion

幕 **mohk** (Md **mù**)
① a curtain; a screen; a tent ② an advisor; staffs; private secretaries

幕僚 **mohk lìuh**
staffs; secretaries; advisors

幕後新聞 **mohk hauh sàn màhn**
behind-the-screens news; inside story

幗 (幗) **gwok** (Md **guó**)
a woman's headdress

巾幗英雄 **gàn gwok yìng hùhng**
a heroine

幘 (幘) **jīk** (Md **zé**)
a turban; a headdress

巾幘 **gàn jīk**
a head-wrapper; a hair-dressing article of linen, silk, etc.

幛 **jeung** (Md **zhàng**)
a scroll of silk or cloth mounted or embroidered with appropriate wording sent as a gift for wedding, funeral, etc.
幛子 **jeung jí**
(same as above)

幣 (币) **baih** (Md **bì**)
① currency; money; a legal tender ② a present; an offering
幣值 **baih jihk**
the purchasing power of a currency
幣制 **baih jai**
currency system

幟 (帜) **chi** (Md **zhì**)
a flag; a pennant; a pennon
旗幟 **kèih chi**
flags, pennants, streamers, etc.

幡 (旛) **fàan** (Md **fān**)
① a flag; a pennant; a pennon; a streamer ② sudden; suddenly
幡幟 **fàan chi**
flags, pennants, streamers, collectively
幡然 **fàan yìhn**
suddenly; to come to a sudden realization

幢 **tòhng, chòhng** (Md **zhuàng, chuáng**)
① a curtain for a carriage ② a numerary adjunct for buildings of more than one story ③ flags, penants, streamers, etc. ④ flickering; waving
幢幢 **tòhng tòhng**
shadowy
幢隊 **chòhng deuih**
pennants or standards leading troops in march

幞 (襆) **buhk** (Md **fú**)
a turban; a headdress; a scarf
幞頭 **buhk tàuh**
a turban; headdress; a scarf

幬 (帱) **chàuh, douh** (Md **chóu, dào**)
① a curtain; a canopy ② a covering; a canopy; to cover

幫 (帮) **bòng** (Md **bāng**)
① to help; to assist ② a gang; a group; a class; a fleet ③ the sides of a shoe or gutter
幫助 **bòng joh**
to help; to assist; help or assistance
幫會 **bòng wúi**
secret societies

幪 **mùhng** (Md **méng**)
a cover; a screen; to cover
幪幪 **mùhng mùhng**
lush or luxuriant (growth of vegetation)

幮 **chyùh** (Md **chú**)
bed-screen or mosquito-net that looks like a small cabinet

干部

干 **gòn** (Md **gān**)
① to offend; to oppose; to invade ② to harry; to jam (radio broadcasts, etc.); to interfere; to intervene; intervention ③ to concern; to involve ④ to seek; to beseech ⑤ the bank (of a river, etc.) ⑥ a sheild ⑦ (how) many or much ⑧ a stem; the Celestial Stems ⑨ a Chinese family name
干涉 **gòn sip**
to interfere; interference; intervention
干戈 **gòn gwò**
(literally) shields and weapons — warfare; armed conflicts

平 **pìhng** (Md **píng**)
① level; even ② equal; equity; equality ③ peaceful; satisfactory; amity ④ to conquer; to quell (a revolt); to calm down ⑤ to control; to regulate ⑥ (said of prices) to go back to normal after sharp rises ⑦ short for Peiping ⑧ a Chinese family name

平等 **pìhng dáng**
equality; equal; name of a country in Honan Province

平均 **pìhng gwàn**
the average; even (distribution, etc.)

年(秊) **nìhn** (Md **nián**)
① a year ② one's age ③ a Chinese family name

年齡 **nìhn lìhng**
the age of a person

年輕 **nìhn hìng**
young; youthful

并 **bing, bìng** (Md **bìng, bīng**)
① on a level with; even; equal ② and; also; or; at the same time; together with ③ Pingchow; one of the ancient Chinese administrative divisions, consisting of parts of today's Hopei, Shanshi, etc.

并日而食 **bing yaht yìh sihk**
to eat on alternate days

幸 **hahng** (Md **xìng**)
① well-being and happiness ② fortunately; luckily; thanks to ③ to feel happy about; to favor ④ an imperial tour or progress ⑤ a Chinese family name

幸福 **hahng fūk**
happiness and well-being

幸運 **hahng wahn**
good fortune; good luck; lucky

幹(干) **gon** (Md **gàn**)
① the trunk (of a tree or of human) body ② the main part of anything ③ capabilities; talents; capable; skillful ④ to do; to attend to business; to manage ⑤ (slang) to eliminate or kill

幹部 **gon bouh**
a cadre; a hardcore member of any organization

幹勁 **gon gihng**
enthusiasm; eagerness in doing things

幺部

幺(么) **yìu** (Md **yāo**)
① tiny; small ② the youngest son or daughter of a family ③ one on dice; one ④ lone; alone ⑤ a Chinese family name

幺兒 **yìu yìh**
the youngest son

幺麼 **yìu mō**
tiny; diminutive; minute

幻 **waahn** (Md **huàn**)
illusion; hallucination magic; fantasy; illusory; unreal; deceptive; changeable

幻燈 **waahn dāng**
a magic lantern

幻想 **waahn séung**
to day dream; to be lost in reverie; day-dream; reverie; fantasy; illusion; vision

幼 **yau** (Md **yòu**)
① young; delicate; tender; immature ② to take care of the young

幼兒 **yau yìh**
infant; baby

幼稚園 **yau jih yùhn**
a kindergarten

幽 **yàu** (Md **yōu**)
① hidden; secret; dark; gloomy; obscure; melancholy; ghostly ② lonely; solitary; secluded ③ quiet; tranquil ④ deep; profound

幽谷 **yàu gūk**
a deep valley

幽默 **yàu mahk**
humorous; humor

幾(几) **géi, gèi** (Md **jǐ, ji**)
① how many; how much ② a few; several; some ③ which; when ④ small; minute; tiny; slight ⑤ nearly; almost ⑥ an omen; a portent

幾何 **géi hòh**
how much; geometry

幾乎 **gèi fùh**
almost; nearly

广部

庀 **péi** (Md **pǐ**)
to prepare

庄(莊) **jōng** (Md **zhuāng**)
① farmhouse ② market place ③ banker (in gambling games)

床 **chòhng** (Md **chuáng**)
same as '牀' see '爿' radical

庇 **bei** (Md **bì**)
to hide; to conceal; to harbor; to protect

庇護 **bei wuh**
to give protection to; to harbor; Chinese transliteration for Pius

庇佑 **bei yauh**
(of a god) to give divine assistance to a mortal

庋 **gwái, géi** (Md **guǐ**)
① a cupboard; a closet ② to put into the proper place; to put away

庋置 **géi ji**
to put into the proper place; to put away

庋藏 **gwái chòhng**
to put away for safe keeping

序 **jeuih** (Md **xù**)
① a preface; a forword; an introduction ② sequence of things; order

序曲 **jeuih kūk**
prelude

序幕 **jeuih mohk**
the prologue; the curtain raiser

底 **dái** (Md **dǐ, de**)
underside; base; bottom; end; basis; foundation

底下 **dái hah**
the underside; the downward position

底蘊 **dái wáhn**
reality beneath the surface

府 **fú** (Md **fǔ**)
① mansion ② a govenment agency ③ an administrative destrict in former times; a prefecture ④ a treasury; an archives

府第 **fú daih**
a mansion

府帑 **fú tóng**
money in the treasury

庖 **pàauh** (Md **páo**)
the kitchen; the cusine

庖丁 **pàauh dìng**
a cook

庖廚 **pàauh chèuih**
kitchen

庚 **gàng** (Md **gēng**)
① the seventh of the Ten Celestial Stems ② age (of a person)

貴庚 **gwai gàng?**
What's your honorable age?

庚帖 **gàng tip**
a card containing the horoscopes of a betrothed couple

店 **dim** (Md **diàn**)
a commercial establishment; a shop; a store; an inn; a hotel

店舖 **dim pou**
a store; a shop

店主 **dim jyú**
proprietor (of a store or shop)

度 **douh, dohk** (Md **dù, duó**)
① instrument for measuring length ② degree; killowatt-hour ③ (number of) times ④ a system ⑤ manner; bearing ⑥ to pass ⑦ consider

度數 **douh sou**
reading (of a barometer, thermometer, water meter, etc.)

度支 **dohk jì**
finance

庠 **chèuhng** (Md **xiáng**)
a school during the Chou Dynasty

庠序 **chèuhng jeuih**
school

庠生 **chèuhng sàng**
student of a prefectural or country school in former times

庥 **yàu** (Md **xiū**)
to shelter; to shade; to protect

座 **joh** (Md **zuò**)
a seat; a stand

座位 **joh wái**
a seat

座談會 **joh tàahm wúi**
a discussion meeting; a symposium; a panel discussion

庫(库) **fu** (Md **kù**)
① storeroom; storehouse; warehouse ② treasury

庫房 **fu fòhng**
a storeroom; a storehouse; a warehouse

庫收 **fu sàu**
receipts of the treasury

庭 **tìhng** (Md **tíng**)
① a hail; a yard ② the imperial court ③ court of justice

庭院 **tìhng yún**
a yard; a garden

庭上 **tìhng seuhng**
in court (of justice); at (imperial) court

庵(菴) **ām** (Md **ān**)
① a hut; a cottage ② a small temple; a nunnery

庵堂 **ām tòhng**
a nunnery; a convent

庵主 **ām jyú**
superior (of a convent or monastery)

庶 **syu** (Md **shù**)
① deviant ② numerous; various ③ general; common ④ almost; nearly

庶母 **syu móuh**
father's concubine

庶務 **syu mouh**
general affairs

康 **hòng** (Md **kāng**)
① healthy ② peaceful ③ abundant ④ easy ⑤ a Chinese family name

康復 **hòng fuhk**
recovery (from illness)

康寧 **hòng nìhng**
healthy and undisturbed

庸 **yùhng** (Md **yōng**)
① mediocre; common; stupid ②

to employ ③ to require ④ to reward ⑤ interrogative (how)

庸才 **yùhng chòih**
man of mediocre ability

庸俗 **yùhng juhk**
Vulgar; unrefined; unpolished

庾 **yúh** (Md **yǔ**)
① a stock of grain ② an ancient measure of capacity ③ a Chinese family name

庾信 **Yúh seun**
Yee Hsin (513 – 581 A.D.), pre Tang man of letters

廁(厕) **chi** (Md **cè**)
① toilet; lavatory; latrine; etc. ② to mingle with; to be a member of

廁所 **chi só**
water closet; toilet; lavatory; restroom; latrine; men's room; women's room

廁身社會 **chi sàn séh wúi**
to be a member of society

廂(厢) **sèung** (Md **xiāng**)
① wing (of a building); side room ② the vicinity or outskirts of a city

廂房 **sèung fòhng**
a side room

西廂 **sài sèung**
the west wing (of a building)

廊 **lòhng** (Md **láng**)
portico; corridor; hallway

廊下 **lòhng hah**
corridor; portico; hallway

廊廟 **lòhng miuh**
the court (of a monarch)

廋 **sàu** (Md **sōu**)
① to conceal; to hide ② to search

廋語 **sàu yúh**
a riddle; a puzzle; an enigma; a cryptogram

廋疏 **sàu sò**
to search

廈(厦) **hah** (Md **shà, xià**)
a tall building; an edifice

廈門 **Hah mùhn**
Amoy (port city in Fukien Province)

大廈 **daaih hah**
a tall building; a mansion

廉 **lìhm** (Md **lián**)
① incorrupt; clean; honest; upright ② inexpensive; cheap ③ to examine; to inspect

廉潔 **lìhm git**
incorrupt; incorruptible; honest

廉政公署 **Lìhm jing gùng chyúh**
I.C.A.C. (Independant commission against corruption)

廖 **liuh** (Md **liào**)
a Chinese family name

廐 **gau** (Md **jiù**)
a stable

廐肥 **gau fèih**
animal refuse used as fertilizer

廐卒 **gau jèut**
a groom

廓 **gwok** (Md **kuò**)
open; wide; empty

廓落 **gwok lohk**
wide; open

廓土 **gwok tóu**
an open ground

廕 **yam** (Md **yìn**)
to shelter; to harbor; to protect

廕庇 **yam bei**
to protect; to shelter; to harbor

廕監 **yam gaam**
off spring of distinguished officials admitted to the Imperial Academy in recognition of the latter's contribution

廣 (广) **gwóng**
(Md **guǎng**)
① wide; broad; spacious; extensive ② to stretch; to extend ③ Kwantung or Kwangsi

廣播 **gwóng bo**
to broadcast; to telecast a broadcast; a telecast

廣東 **Gwóng dùng**
Kwang Tung Province

廚 (厨) **chèuih, chyùh**
(Md **chú**)
① kitchen ② closet; chest; wardrobe; cupboard

廚房 **chèuih fóng**
kitchen

廚櫃 **chèuih gwaih**
closet; chest; cupboard

廝 (厮) **sì** (Md **sī**)
① a servant; a person who performs mean labor ② each other; together

廝守 **sì sáu**
to wait upon each others; to take care of each other

小廝 **síu sì**
boy (of a hotel); office boy

廟 (庙) **miuh** (Md **miào**)
a temple; a shrine

廟宇 **miuh yúh**
a temple; a shrine

廟祝 **miuh jūk**
a person whose duty (it) is to keep incense burning at a temple

廠 (厂、厰) **chóng**
(Md **chǎng**)
factory; plant; workshop

廠商 **chóng sèung**
manufacturers and business firms

廠房 **chóng fòhng**
a factory building

廡 (庑) **móuh, mòuh**
(Md **wǔ**)
① a corridor; a hallway ② (of vegetation) dense or luxuriant

廢 (废) **fai** (Md **fèi**)
① to give up; to abandon; to discontinue; to abolish; to reject ② useless; disabled

廢紙 **fai jí**
waste paper

廢掉 **fai diuh**
to abolish; to abrogate

廛 **chìhn** (Md **chán**)
① living space for one family in ancient times ② a store; a shop

廛肆 **chìhn si**
a store; a shop

廨 **gaai, haaih** (Md **xiè**)
a public office; a government building

廨宇 **gaai yúh**
government office building

廩 (廪) **láhm** (Md **lǐn**)
① a granary ② to supply (food stuff) ③ to stockpile

廩倉 **láhm chòng**
a public granary

廩生 **láhm sāng**
scholars who live on government grants during the Ming and Ching Dynasties

廬 (庐) **lòuh** (Md **lú**)
① a thatched cottage ② Mt. Lu

(in Kiangsi)

廬舍 **lòuh se**
a cottage; a hut

廬山 **Lòuh sàan**
Mt. Lu, a famous summer resort (in Kiangsi)

龐（龐、庞）**pòhng** (Md **páng**)
① disorderly; confused ② huge ③ face ④ a Chinese family name

龐雜 **pòhng jaahp**
disorderly; confused

龐然大物 **pòhng yìhn daaih maht**
a huge object; a manmoth animal

廳（廳、厅）**tìng, tèng** (Md **tīng**)
① central room ② a government agency

廳堂 **tèng tòhng**
central room of a house; hall

廳長 **tèng jéung**
director of a department under a provincial government

廴部

延 **yìhn** (Md **yán**)
① to extend; to spread; to length ② to prolong; to delay; to defer; to postpone ③ to invite ④ to procrastinate

延長 **yìhn chèuhng**
to lengthen; to extend; to prolong

延聘 **yìhn ping**
to invite the service of

廷 **tìhng** (Md **tíng**)
the imperial court; the court

廷議 **tìhng yíh**
discussion at imperial court; court discussion; court meeting

廷試 **tìhng si**
the imperial examination (the last step in the periodic civil service examinations in former times)

建 **gin** (Md **jiàn**)
① to establish; to build; to construct ② to bring up; to propose; to suggest

建立 **gin lahp**
to establish; to set up; to build; to found

建設 **gin chit**
to construct; to build; to develop; construction; development

廼 **náaih** (Md **nǎi**)
the same as '乃' see '丿' radical

廻 **wùih** (Md **huí**)
the same as '迴' see '辵' radical

廾部

廿 **yah, nihm** (Md **niàn**)
twenty

廿八 **yah baat**
twenty eight

廿四史 **Yah sei sí (nihm sei sí)**
the Twenty-four Books of History, or the Twenty-four Dynastic Histories (up to the Ming Dynasty, authorized during the Ching Dynasty)

弁 **bihn** (Md **biàn**)
① a conical cap worn on ceremonious occassions in ancient times ② low-ranking military officers ③ a Chinese family name

弁言 **bihn yìhn**
a preface; a forward; an introductory remark

弁髦 **bihn mòuh**
useless things; to slight; to

underestimate; to despise

弄 **luhng** (Md **nàng lōng**)

① to play with; to sport with; to make fun of; to mock ② to handle; to do; to perform

弄瓦 **luhng ngáh**
to give birth to a daughter

弄錯 **luhng cho**
to make a mistake; to commit an error

弇 **yìm** (Md **yǎn**)

① a narrow-necked container ② to cover ③ profound

弈 **yihk** (Md **yì**)

the "go" game

弈棋 **yihk kèih**
the "go" game

弈具 **yihk geuih**
the black and white stones and the chessboard for the "go" game

弊 **baih** (Md **bì**)

① bad; undesirable; harmful; ② dishonest; improper ③ exhausted; tired; worn out

弊病 **baih behng**
corrupt practises

弊政 **baih jing**
misrule; maladministration

弋部

弋 **yihk** (Md **yì**)

① to catch; to take ② to shoot with arrow and bow

弋取 **yihk chéui**
to catch

弋獵 **yihk lihp**
to hunt

式(貳) **yih** (Md **èr**)

the same as "二"; two

式 **sīk** (Md **shì**)

① style; form; mode; pattern; fashion; type ② system ③ ceremony

式樣 **sīk yeuhng**
a type; a model; a mode; a style

式微 **sīk mèih**
decline (of a nation, a dynasty, family, etc.)

弑 **si** (Md **shì**)

to kill or murder one's superior, senior, etc.

弑君 **si gwàn**
regicide; to commit regicide

弑逆 **si yihk**
one who commits particle or regicide

弓部

弓 **gùng** (Md **gōng**)

① a bow ② bent; arching; arched ③ a measure of length (equal to five chinese feet)

弓箭 **gùng jin**
bow and arrow

弓背 **gùng bui**
to bend the back like a bow; back arched like a bow

引 **yáhn** (Md **yǐn**)

① to pull; to attract ② to guide ③ to introduce ④ to quote ⑤ to retire ⑥ a unit in weight measurement

引導 **yáhn douh**
to guide; to lead; to direct

引起 **yáhn héi**
to cause; to give rise; to trigger

弔(吊) **diu** (Md **diào**)

① to condole; to mourn; to console ② to hang; to suspend; suspended

弔唁 **diu yihn**
  to mourn in sympathy; to console

弔起 **diu héi**
  to hang up; to lift by crane

弗 **fāt** (Md **fú**)
not

弗克 **fāt hāk**
  unable

弗如 **fāt yùh**
  not as good as; not equal to; worse than; inferior to

弘 **wàhng** (Md **hóng**)
great; magnanimous; capacious

弘大 **wàhng daaih**
  great; immense

弘揚 **wàhng yèuhng**
  to propagate

弛 **chìh** (Md **chí**)
to unstring; to relax; to neglect

弛緩 **chìh wùhn**
  to relax; to be idle

弛廢 **chìh fai**
  to neglect

弟 **daih** (Md **dì**)
① a younger brother ② a junior

弟兄 **daih hìng**
  brothers; soldiers

弟子 **daih jí**
  diciple; pupil; student; youngsters

弧 **wùh** (Md **hú**)
① a wooden bow ② a segment of a circle

弧度 **wùh douh**
  circular measure

弧角 **wùh gok**
  spherical angle

弦 (絃) **yìhn** (Md **xián**)
① string (of a bow, a musical instrument, etc.) ② chord of an arc ③ the first or last quarter of a lunar month

弦線 **yìhn sin**
  string (of a musical instrument)

弦月 **yìhn yuht**
  a crescent moon

弩 **nóuh** (Md **nǔ**)
a bow; a cross bow

弩弓 **nóuh gùng**
  a bow; a cross bow

弩手 **nóuh sáu**
  an archer; a crossbowman

弭 **méih, máih** (Md **mǐ**)
① to stop; to end; to eliminate ② end of a bow

弭災 **méih jòi**
  to end disaster

弭患 **méih waahn**
  to eliminate trouble

弱 **yeuhk** (Md **ruò**)
① weak; fragile; feeble; tender; delicate; infirm ② young

弱點 **yeuhk dím**
  a weak point; weakness; vulnerability

弱冠 **yeuhk gun**
  a twenty-year-old man (who has just undergone the capping ceremony); a youth; a youngster

張 (张) **jèung** (Md **zhāng**)
① to open; to stretch; to extend; to display ② a sheet (of paper); a leaf (of a book) ③ a Chinese family name

張開 **jèung hòi**
　　to stretch open; to open

張望 **jèung mohng**
　　to look around; to look about

強 (强、彊) **kèuhng, kéuhng** (Md **qiáng, qiǎng, jiàng**)

① strong; powerful; vigorous ②
better ③ violent ④ force ⑤
inflexible; obstinate; stubborn

強大 **kèuhng daaih**
　　powerful and strong

強記 **kéuhng gei**
　　to force oneself to memorize

弼 **baht** (Md **bì**)

① device for regulating bows;
bow regulator ② to correct ③ to
assist; to aid

弼教 **baht gaau**
　　to assist in education

彀 **gau** (Md **gòu**)

① to draw a bow to the full ② a
rule ③ sufficient ④ the same as
'夠'

彆 **biht** (Md **biè**)

awkward

彆扭 **biht náu**
　　awkward; refractory; an
　　awkward situation

彈 (弹) **daahn, tàahn** (Md **dàn, tán**)

① a pellet ② to rebound ③ to
play (a string instrument sounded
by snapping action) ④ to
impeach; to put down

彈弓 **daahn gùng**
　　a sling shot; a catapult

彈劾 **tàahn haht**
　　to impeach

彌 (弥) **nèih** (Md **mí**)

to fill; to complete

彌補 **nèih bóu**
　　to stop or fill up (a gap); to
　　make up for or offset (a loss,
　　shortcoming, etc.); to
　　supplement

彌撒 **nèih saat**
　　a (Catholic) mass

彎 (弯) **wàan** (Md **wān**)

to bend; to curve

彎曲 **wàan kūk**
　　bent; curved

彎兒 **wàan yìh**
　　a curve; a bend

⇒部

彗 (篲) **seuih** (Md **huì, sui**)

① a broom ② a comet

彗星 **seuih sìng**
　　a comet

彗掃 **seuih sou**
　　to sweep with a broom

彘 **jih** (Md **zhì**)

a hog; a pig; a swine

彘肩 **jih gìn**
　　the shoulder of a hog

彙 **waih, wuih** (Md **huì**)

① a category; a class; a series;
to categorize; to classify ② to
collect (materials, data, etc.)

彙編 **wuih pìn**
　　to edit (assembled reports,
　　data, etc.)

彙集 **waih jaahp**
　　to collect (materials, data,
　　etc.)

彝 (彝) **yìh** (Md **yí**)
① vessel for wine, a goblet ② laws or regulations ③ regular; constant ④ vessels or items used in ceremonies at temples; etc. such as bells, tripods; chalice, etc.

彝器 **yìh hei**
vessels or items used in ceremonies at temples, etc.

彝訓 **yìh fan**
regular exhortations

彡 部

彤 **tùhng** (Md **tóng**)
① red; vermilion ② name of an ancient state

彤雲 **tùhng wàhn**
red clouds

彤闈 **tùhng wàih**
imperial palace

形 **yìhng** (Md **xíng**)
① form; shape; appearance; figure ② complexion; manner ③ terrain; contour ④ expression; description; to describe ⑤ in comparison ⑥ to show; to manifest

形狀 **yìhng johng**
appearance, form or shape of a thing

形容 **yìhng yùhng**
to describe; appearance; form; shape

彥 **yihn, yihm** (Md **yàn**)
① outstanding; handsome; elegant; refined; learned; accomplished ② an erudite scholar

彥士 **yihn sih**
a refined and accomplished scholar

彥會 **yihn wuih**
a gathering of distinguished personalities

彧 **yūk** (Md **yù**)
refined; learned and accomplished

彫 **dìu** (Md **diāo**)
same as '雕' see '隹' radical

彩 **chói** (Md **cǎi**)
① colors; variegated colors ② make up in various chinese operas ③ special feats or stunts in chinese operas ④ ornamental; brilliant; gay ⑤ stakes in a gambling game; prize money

彩票 **chói piu**
a lottery ticket; a raffle ticket

彩色 **chói sīk**
color (film, picture, photography, etc.)

彪 **bìu** (Md **biāo**)
① a tiger cub ② stripes or streaks on the skin or a tiger ③ tall and big; shining and brilliant; outstanding ④ a Chinese family name

彪形 **bìu yìhng**
tall and big

彪炳 **bìu bíng**
brilliant and shining (achievement, example, etc.)

彬 **bàn** (Md **bīn**)
① intelligent, refined and gentle ② a Chinese family name

彬彬 **bàn bàn**
refined; gentle and elegant

彬蔚 **bàn waih**
extremely erudite and refined

彭 **pàahng** (Md **péng**)
① a Chinese family name ② big ③ longevity ④ proud

彭年 **pàahng nìhn**
an advanced age

彭亨 **pàahng hàng**
　　pot-bellied; proud and smug

彰 **jèung** (Md **zhāng**)
　　① ornamental; colorful ② evi-
　　dent; obvious ③ to manifest; to
　　make known; to display

彰明 **jèung mìhng**
　　to manifest; to clarify; to
　　expound; name of a country in
　　Szechwan

彰彰 **jèung jèung**
　　famous; well-known; evident

影 **yíng** (Md **yǐng**)
　　① a shadow; an image; a reflec-
　　tion ② to copy and imitate ③ to
　　hide; to conceal ④ a sundial

影片 **yíng pín**
　　a motion picture; movies; the
　　film of a motion picture

影響 **yíng héung**
　　influence; impact; effect; to
　　affect; to influence

彳部

彳 **chīk** (Md **chì**)
　　① short steps or paces; a step
　　taken with the left foot ② a
　　phonetic sign for "ch"

彳亍 **chīk chūk**
　　to walk (with left and right
　　feet)

彷 **fóng, pòhng**
(Md **fǎng, páng**)
　　① like; resembling; similar to ②
　　hesitating; unsettled

彷彿 **fóng fāt**
　　like; resembling; similar to

彷徨 **pòhng wòhng**
　　undecided; agitated

役 **yihk** (Md **yì**)
　　① to guard the frontier; military
　　service ② to work on official
　　duties; to dispatch ③ a servant;

to do; to undertake

役夫 **yihk fù**
　　a laborer; a servant

役於人 **yihk yù yàhn**
　　to serve others

彼 **béi** (Md **bǐ**)
　　① that; those ② the other;
　　another ③ there

彼此 **béi chí**
　　you and me; both parties; that
　　and this; each other

彼等 **béi dáng**
　　those people

彿 **fāt** (Md **fú**)
　　like; similar to; as if

彷彿 **fóng fāt**
　　like; resembling; similar to

往 **wóhng** (Md **wǎng,
wàng**)
　　① to go toward; to depart ②
　　formerly; past; by gone; gone

往昔 **wóhng sīk**
　　in the past; in ancient time

往返 **wóhng fáan**
　　to come and go; to arrive and
　　depart; to make a round-trip

征 **jìng** (Md **zhēng**)
　　① to journey far away ② to
　　attack; to reduce to submission;
　　to conquer ③ to levy taxes; to
　　collect taxes ④ a Chinese family
　　name

征服 **jìng fuhk**
　　to conquer; a conquest

征收 **jìng sàu**
　　to levy and collect (taxes)

徂 **chòuh** (Md **cú**)
　　① to go to; to go ahead; to
　　advance ② the preposition "to"
　　③ to die ④ past

徂落 **chòuh lohk**
　　to pass away; to die

徂暑 **chòuh syú**
the hottest days of summer

待 **doih** (Md **dài, dāi**)
① to treat; to entertain ② to wait; to wait for ③ until

待發 **doih faat**
ready to depart

待人接物 **doih yàhn jip maht**
the way one treats people; one's personality

徇 **sèun, seuhn** (Md **xùn**)
① pervading ② to profit

徇私 **sèun sì**
to profit oneself; favoritism; nepotism

徇情 **sèun chìhng**
favoritism; to let personal feelings influence one's decision

很 **hán** (Md **hěn**)
① very; quite ② fierce; cruel ③ disobedient; intractable; quarrelsome; truculent

很好 **hán hóu**
very good; very nice

律 **leuht** (Md **lù**)
① a law; a rule; a regulation; a statute ② to bind by law; to control or restrain; to descipline ③ a series of standard bamboo tuning pitch-pipes used in ancient music ④ a form in Chinese poetry — a stanza of eight lines

律師 **leuht sī**
a lawyer; a barrister; a polite expression for Buddhist monks

律例 **leuht laih**
laws or statutes and precedents

後(后) **hauh**
(Md **hòu**)
① behind; the back of ② after

wards; to come after ③ descendants; posterity ④ an auxiliary to indicate "then" or afterwards ⑤ a Chinese family name

後門 **hauh mùhn**
the back door; the rear gate (of a city wall)

後輩 **hauh buih**
juniors; inferiors; descendants; posterity

徉 **yèuhng** (Md **yáng**)
① to stray; to roam; unsettled ② hesitating

徜徉 **sèuhng yèuhng**
lingering or loitering

徊 **wùih** (Md **huái**)
① hesitating; irresolute; indecisive ② to move to and fro; to walk around

徘徊 **pùih wùih**
to linger; to walk to and fro; to move around without purpose; hesitating; irresolute

徐 **chèuih** (Md **xú**)
① slow; calm; composed ② name of a state in ancient China occupying part of today's Anhuei Province ③ a Chinese family name

徐緩 **chèuih wùhn**
slowly or unhurriedly

徐州 **Chèuih jàu**
Hsuchow a city in Kiangsu Province famous for its strategic position; one of the nine ancient Chinese political divisions

徑(径) **ging** (Md **jìng**)
① a narrow path; a byway ② diameter ③ to decide and proceed (to do something, etc.) without getting orders, etc.; direct; straight ④ already? — implying a sense of surprise

徑路 **ging louh**
　　a byway; a narrow path

徑庭 **ging tìhng**
　　quite different; poles apart

徒 **tòuh** (Md **tú**)
① disciple; followers; pupils; apprentics ② a crowd; a gang; a group of people ③ to go on foot ④ a punishment; banishment ⑤ only; merely; in vain ⑥ empty; as empty — handed

徒步 **tòuh bouh**
　　to go on foot

徒弟 **tòuh daih**
　　an apprentice; a diciple; a pupil

徘 **pùih** (Md **pái**)
① hesitating; irresolute; indecisive ② to walk to and fro; to move around

徘徊 **pùih wùih**
　　to linger; to walk to and fro; to move; around without purpose; hesitating; irresolute

得 **dāk** (Md **dé, děi, de**)
① to get; to obtain; to acquire; to gain; to attain; to effect ② complacent ③ agreement; harmony ④ can; may; able to ⑤ must; should; ought to ⑥ an adverbial expletive such as in 覺得, 想得要命　, etc.

得到 **dāk dou**
　　to succeed in getting or obtaining

得用功 **dāk yuhng gùng**
　　must be more studious

徙 **sáai** (Md **xǐ**)
　　to move one's abode; to immigrate; to shift; to be exiled

徙移 **sáai yìh**
　　to move; (said of birds, fish, etc.) to migrate

徙居 **sáai gèui**
　　to move one's abode; to immigrate

徜 **sèuhng** (Md **cháng**)
　　going to and fro; lingering; loitering

徜徉 **sèuhng yèuhng**
　　lingering or loitering

徠 (徕) **lòih** (Md **lái**)
the ancient version of 來 ; to come; to induce (customers) to come; to encourage to come to buy

招徠 **jìu lòih**
　　to induce customer to come to buy

從 (从) **chùhng, sùng** (Md **cóng, cōng**)
① from; by; whence; through ② to undertake; to manage; to dedicate oneself to; to attend to ③ to follow; to yield; to listen to; to comply with; to obey ④ a follower; an attendant; a servant ⑥ secondary; relation other than one's direct blood relatives ⑦ an accessory ⑧ vice or deputy ⑨ lax; easy ⑩ plentiful; abundant ⑪ to urge; to persuade strongly

從來 **chùhng lòih**
　　from the beginning (used only in negative expression)

從犯 **chùhng faahn**
　　an accessory

從容 **sùng yùhng**
　　unhurried; naturally; calm; composed

御 **yuh** (Md **yù**)
① a drive; a chariot or carriage ② a driver; an attendant ③ to control; to manage; to superintend; to tame (a shrew) ④ imperial ⑤ to wait on; to set before; as food; to offer or present to ⑥ a Chinese family name

御駕 **yuh ga**
the imperial carriage; the emperor

御人 **yuh yàhn**
a driver (of horse-drawn carriage)

復(复)**fuhk** (Md **fù**)
① to return; to come back ② to answer; to reply ③ to repeat; again; repeatedly ④ to return to normal or original state ⑤ a Chinese family name

復活 **fuhk wuht**
resurrection

復興 **fuhk hìng**
a revival; a return to prosperity

偏 **pin** (Md **biàn**)
same as '遍', see '辶' radical

徨 **wòhng** (Md **huáng**)
① agitated; alarmed ② irresolute

徨徨 **wòhng wòhng**
alarmed and anxious; agitated and indecisive

彷徨 **pòhng wòhng**
undecided; agitated

循 **chèuhn** (Md **xún**)
① to follow; to comply with ② to postpone; to procrastinate ③ in orderly fashion ④ law-abiding; good ⑤ (obsolete) to touch; to inspect

循環 **chèuhn wàahn**
to move in a circle; to come round in; order; circulation; rotation

循例 **chèuhn laih**
in accordance with precedents, common practices or former examples

微 **mèih** (Md **wēi**)
① small; minute; diminutive; trifling; little ② low; mean; humble ③ a polite expression for "I, my, me" ④ weak; sickly; feeble ⑤ subtle; intricate; hidden; concealed; obscure

微笑 **mèih siu**
to smile; a smile

微雨 **mèih yúh**
light rain; a drizzle

徬 **pòhng** (Md **páng**)
same as '彷', see '彳' radical

徯 **hàih** (Md **xī**)
① to wait for; to expect ② a narrow path; a short cut; a snap course

徯待 **hàih doih**
to expect; to look forward to

徯徑 **hàih ging**
a narrow path; a short cut; a snap course

傜(徭)**yìuh** (Md **yáo**)
compulsory labor service

傜役 **yìuh yihk**
compulsory labor service

傜賦 **yìuh fu**
compulsory labor and land tax

德 **dāk** (Md **dé**)
① morality; decency; virtues ② favors; appreciation of such; to repay kindness ③ behavior; conduct ④ Germany; German

德行 **dāk hahng**
morality and conduct; (colloquial) manners or appearance; mannerisms

德國 **Dāk gwok**
Germany

徵 **jìng, jí** (Md **zhēng, zhǐ**)
① to summon ② to levy or raise (taxes) ③ to call to arms ④ to ask; to inquire; to solicit ⑤ to request; to seek for ⑥ to prove; evidence; verification ⑦ a Chinese family name ⑧ one of

the five musical notes in chinese scale

徵兵 **jìng bìng**
to draft able-bodied male citizens for military service

徵求 **jìng kàuh**
to seek; to solicit (answers, etc.) to want (a clerk, etc.)

徹 (彻) **chit** (Md **chè**)
① penetrating; discerning ② to remove ③ a tax in tithe ④ to manage; to cultivate (farm) ⑤ to destroy ⑥ to deprive; to take away

徹底 **chit dái**
to get to the bottom of; (said of a stream, etc.) to be able to see the bottom; thorough; exhaustive

徹夜 **chit yeh**
all through the night; from dusk to dawn

徼 **gíu, gíu, yìu** (Md **jiǎo, jiào**)
① to be lucky; fortunate ② to pray for ③ to shade; to hide ④ frontiers or bounderies ⑤ to take an inspection trip

徼倖 **gíu hahng**
lucky; beyond one's expectations (said of happy events)

徼福 **gíu fūk**
to pray for blessing

徽 **fài** (Md **huī**)
① good and beautiful; honorable ② stops on a lute ③ a streamer; flag, pennant, etc., a flag-sign ④ an emblem; a badge ⑤ Anhwei or Huichow

徽章 **fài jèung**
a badge

徽號 **fài houh**
a flat with emblem; a high-sounding title

心部

心 **sàm** (Md **xīn**)
① the heart; the core ② the mind ③ the conscience; the moral nature ④ intention; idea; ambition; design ⑤ (usually used as a suffix) the middle, center or inside ⑥ one of the 28 constellations

心中 **sàm jùng**
in one's heart or mind

心理 **sàm léih**
mentality thought and idea; psychology; mental

必 **bīt** (Md **bì**)
① most certainly; must; necessarily ② an emphatic particle

必定 **bīt dihng**
most certainly; must

必要 **bīt yiu**
necessary; necessity; need

忉 **dòu, tòu** (Md **dāo**)
grieved; distressed

忉怛 **dòu daat**
grieved; distressed

忉忉 **dòu dòu (tòu tòu)**
distressed; worried

忌 **geih** (Md **jì**)
① jealours; to envy ② to fear; a fear (usually superstitious); a shun ③ to prohibit or proscribe (usually for superstitious purposes) ④ death anniversary of one's parents or grand-parents

忌憚 **geih daahn**
fears that keep a person from committing irregularities; to dread

忌辰 **geih sàhn**
death anniversaries of one's parents, etc.; (in ancient China) death anniversary of

the emperor or empress of the reigning dynasty

忖 chyún (Md cǔn)

to surmise; to consider; to presume; to suppose

忖度 chyún dohk

to suppose; to consider; to pressure; to gauge what's on another's mind

忖量 chyún lèuhng

to consider; to suppose; to gauge what's on another's mine; to reflect

忙 mòhng (Md máng)

① busy; short of time ② hurried; in haste

忙亂 mòhng lyuhn

busy and flurried

忙中有錯 mòhng jùng yáuh cho

Haste makes waste. Errors are likely to occur in haste

忍 yán, yáhn (Md rěn)

① to endure; to bear; to tolerate ② to suffer; to stand (an insult, etc.) ③ merciless; truculence ④ to forbear; to repress

忍耐 yán noih

patience; forbearance; patient; to preserve; to persist

忍受 yán sauh

to endure; to bear; to suffer

忐 táan (Md tǎn)

① timid; apprehensive ② indecisive; vacillating

忐忑 táan tīk

indecisive; vacillating; apprehensive

忑 tīk (Md tè)

nervous; apprehensive; indecisive

忐忑 táan tīk

indecisive; vacillating; apprehensive

志 ji (Md zhì)

① will; purpose; determination ② desire; ambition; interest ③ annals; records

志向 ji heung

purpose; ambition

志願 ji yuhn

to volunteer; voluntary; free choice

忘 mòhng (Md wàng)

① to forget ② to omit; to miss (a line, etc.) ③ to neglect; to overlook

忘記 mòhng gei

to fail to remember; to forget; to have forgotten

忘憂草 mòhng yàu chóu

day lily — Hemerocalis flora

忒 tīk (Md tè, tuī)

① excessive; too; very ② to change ③ to err

忒殺 tīk saat

excessive; too much

忒甚 tīk sahm

much; too much

忠 jùng (Md zhōng)

① faithful; loyal; sincere; patriotic; loyalty; sincerity ② devoted; honest (advice, etc.)

忠實 jùng saht

loyal and faithful; reliable or truthful (reports, etc.)

忠言 jùng yìhn

sincere advice

怅(懺)chùng (Md chāng)

worried; anxious; uneasy

怅怔 chùng jìng

feeling anxious and unsettled

怅怅 chùng chùng

worried and sad

忤 **nǵh** (Md **wǔ**)
① recalcitrant; stubbornly defiant; disobedient ② a blunder; a mistake; wrong

忤逆 **nǵh yihk**
recalcitrant; stubborn defiance; disobedient to one's parents (a crime in former time)

忤物 **nǵh maht**
to disagree with others; to be at odds with others

快 **faai** (Md **kuài**)
① quickly; fast; hasty; soon; prompt ② sharp (blades, etc.) keen ③ pleasant; happy; to make happy or pleasurable ④ (in old China) criminal police ⑤ honest; straightforward

快樂 **faai lohk**
happy; joy

快捷 **faai jiht**
speedy; fast; nimble

忭 **bihn** (Md **biàn**)
overjoyed; pleased; delighted

忭賀 **bihn hoh**
to congratulate with joy; to celebrate

忭頌 **bihn juhng**
to be pleased to offer best wishes

忮 **ji** (Md **zhì**)
jealous; jealousy

忮求 **ji kàuh**
jealous and greedy

忮心 **ji sàm**
jealousy

忱 **sàhm** (Md **chén**)
sincere; sincerity

忱悃 **sàhm kwán**
genuine feelings; sincere sentiments

忱辭 **sàhm chìh**
words uttered with all sincerity; words from the bottom of one's heart

忸 **náu, nuhk** (Md **niǔ**)
① to be accustomed to; to be inclined to (evils, etc.) ② bashful; ashamed

忸怩 **náu nèih**
ashamed; bashful

忻 **yàn** (Md **xīn**)
happy; joy; delight

忻忻 **yàn bihn**
great joy; overjoyed

忝 **tím** (Md **tiǎn**)
① ashamed; to disgrace ② a depreciatory expression referring to oneself

忝任 **tím yahm**
to have served (in an office); I have served as . . .

忝辱家門 **tím yuhk gà mùhn**
to disgrace one's family

念 **nihm** (Md **niàn**)
① to think of; to remember (someone) ② to read out aloud; to chant; to intone; to mumble ③ twenty

念經 **nihm gìng**
to chant or intone (Buddhist) scriptures

念頭 **nihm tàuh**
an idea; a thought; a hunch

忽 **fāt** (Md **hū**)
① suddenly; abruptly; unexpectedly ② to disregard; to be careless or indifferent; to neglect ③ (in math.) 0.00001; minute ④ one millionth of a tael

忽然 **fāt yìhn**
suddenly; unexpectedly

忽略 **fāt leuhk**
to overlook; to neglect; an oversight

忿 **fáhn** (Md **fèn**)
① anger; indignation; fury ② complaining; hatred; grudge; bitterness

忿怒 **fáhn nouh**
indignation; wrath; fury; angry; furious; indignant

忿怨 **fáhn yun**
to harbor a grudge; animus

忪 **sùng, jùng** (Md **sōng, zhōng**)
agitated; frightened

惺忪 **sìng sùng**
wavering; indecisive

怍 **johk** (Md **zhò**)
① to be ashamed ② to change color; to blush

怍色 **johk sīk**
ashamed; to blush; to color

怍意 **johk yi**
to feel ashamed; to be ashamed

怖 **bou** (Md **bù**)
① terrified; frightened ② to frighten; to threaten

怖慄 **bou leuht**
trembling with fear

恐怖 **húng bou**
terror; horror; fear

怏 **yéung, yeung** (Md **yàng**)
discontented; disheartened; dispirited

怏然 **yéung yìhn**
disheartened; dispirited

怏怏 **yéung yéung**
discontented; disperited; sad

怕 **pa** (Md **pà**)
① to fear; to dread; afraid; scared or frighten; apprehensive ② maybe; perhaps ③ a Chinese family name

怕羞 **pa sàu**
shy; bashful

怕老婆 **pa lóuh pòh**
hen-pecked

怙 **wuh, gù** (Md **hù**)
① to rely on; to presume on; things or persons that one relies on ② one's father

怙富 **wuh fu**
to presume on one's wealth

失怙 **sāt gù**
to lose one's father; to be orphaned

怛 **daat** (Md **dá**)
① grieved; distressed ② surprised; shocked; alarmed ③ (obsolete) striving and toiling

怛怛 **daat daat**
toiling and striving

怛傷 **daat sèung**
distressed; grieved

怡 **yìh** (Md **yí**)
① harmony; on good terms ② pleasure; joy; jubilation ③ a Chinese family name

怡神 **yìh sàhn**
to inspire peace and harmony in one's mind

怡顏 **yìh ngàahn**
a pleasant look or expression; to be cheerful

怦 **pìng** (Md **pēng**)
eager; anxious; impulsive

怦怦 **pìng pìng**
eager and anxious (to do something); to become excited

怦然 **pìng yìhn**
with a sudden shock

性 **sing** (Md **xìng**)
① nature; natural property; disposition; temper ② a quality or property ③ sex

性命 **sing mihng**
a person's life

性別 **sing biht**
sex of a person — male or female

怩 **nèih** (Md **ní**)
shy and bashful; socially timid; to blush; to look embarrassed

忸怩 **náu nèih**
ashamed; bashful

怯 **hip** (Md **qiè**)
① lacking in courage; cowardly ② nervous; socially timid; fright, as stage fright

怯懦 **hip noh**
cowardice

怯場 **hip chèuhng**
stage-fright

怪(恠) **gwaai** (Md **guài**)
① strange; queer; monstrous; peculiar ② ghost; a goblin; an apparition; a monster ③ uncanny; weird ④ very (interesting, tired, etc.) ⑤ to blame

怪癖 **gwaai pīk**
strange hobbies; eccentric behavior; eccentricity

怪異 **gwaai yih**
strange; wild (talks, account, etc.) weird; uncanny

怫 **faht, fai** (Md **fú, fèi**)
① depressed and discontented ② angry; annoyed; indignant

怫鬱 **faht wāt**
depressed and discontented

怫恚 **fai waih**
angry; indignant

怵 **jēut** (Md **chù**)
① sacred; afraid; timorous ② to entice; to induce ③ to coere; to intimidate

怵惕 **jēut tīk**
sacred and cautious

怵然 **jēut yìhn**
sacred; to look frightened

怎 **jám** (Md **zěn**)
why? how? what?

怎樣 **jám yeuhng**
how? in what way? what?

怎敢 **jám gám**
how can one dare? don't dare?

怒 **nouh** (Md **nù**)
① anger; rage; angry; furious ② to put forth in vigor (as plants, etc.); to sprout; forceful and vigorous

怒氣 **nouh hei**
anger; wrath

怒目相視 **nouh muhk sèung sih**
to give each other the black looks

思 **sì** (Md **sī**)
① to think; to contemplate; to consider ② to remember; to recall; memory; remembrance ③ to mourn; to grieve ④ to admire; to pine for ⑤ a final particle to sound off an expression

思想 **sì séung**
to think; thinking; thought; ideas; mentally; ideological inclination; ideology

思念 **sì nihm**
to remember (old days, friends, etc.); to recall

怠 **tóih, doi** (Md **dài**)
① idle; remiss; lax; negligent ② to treat coldly

怠惰 **tóih doh**
idle and lazy

怠慢 **tóih maahn**
to neglect a visitor or guest (often used as a polite expression); to treat coldly

急 **gāp** (Md **jí**)
① quick; quickly; with expedition ② urgent; hurried; hasty ③ anxious; very eager; worried

急忙 **gāp mòhng**
quickly; urgently; hastily

急症 **gāp jing**
(in medicine) an emergency case

怔 **jìng** (Md **zhēng**)
terrified; scared; nervous

怔忪 **jìng jùng**
scared and nervous

怔忡 **jìng chùng**
(in Chinese medicine) a disease resembling neurosis with such common symptoms as palpitation of the heart, melancholia and aptness to get tired

怨 **yun** (Md **yuàn**)
① ill-will; hatred; enmity; animus; resentment ② to complaint; to blame (others); to impute ③ to harbor; to store up

怨恨 **yun hahn**
ill-will; enmity; animus

埋怨 **màaih yun**
to complain; to blame

怱(匆、悤) **chùng** (Md **cōng**)
hasty; hastily; in haste

怱忙 **chùng mòhng**
haste; in haste; hastily

怱怱 **chùng chùng**
hurriedly; suddenly and imperceptibly (said of the passage of time)

恆(恒) **hàhng** (Md **héng**)
① constant; regular; persevering ② lasting; continually ③ a Chinese family name

恆心 **hàhng sàm**
perseverance

恆產 **hàhng cháan**
immovable property — real estate

恂 **sèun** (Md **xún**)
① to trust; to have faith in ② sincere ③ careful ④ suddenly ⑤ afraid; scared

恂實 **sèun saht**
sincerely honest

恂恂 **sèun sèun**
faithfully; trustingly; courteously

恃 **chíh** (Md **shì**)
to rely on; to depend on; to presume upon

恃勢 **chíh sai**
to presume on one's position or influence

恃才傲物 **chíh chòih ngou maht**
to be arrogant because of one's talents or ability

恟 **hùng** (Md **xiōng**)
① afraid; frightened ② noisy

恟懼 **hùng geuih**
afraid; frightened

恟恟 **hùng hùng**
tumultuous

恍 **fóng** (Md **huǎng**)
absent-minded; unconscious

恍忽 **fóng fāt**
absent-minded; unconscious

恍然大悟 **fóng yìhn daaih ngh**
to come to understand suddenly

恢 **fùi** (Md **huī**)
① great; immense; enormous; vast; extensive ② to recover; to restore; to regain

恢復 **fùi fuhk**
to restore; to regain; to recover from illness

恢恢 **fùi fùi**
spacious

恤 (卹、賉) **sēut** (Md **xù**)
① to relieve; to help ② to sympathize; to be considerate

恤貧 **sēut pàhn**
to give relief to the poor

恤金 **sēut gàm**
relief payment

恨 **hahn** (Md **hèn**)
① to resent; to hate ② to regret

恨不得 **hahn bāt dāk**
to wish that one could (do something which is not proper to do)

恨海 **hahn hói**
deep hatred

恪 **kok** (Md **kè**)
respectful; reverent; to respect; respectfully

恪守 **kok sáu**
to observe (rules) strictly

恪遵 **kok jèun**
to obey or follow (orders) rules, etc.) with respect

恫 **duhng, tùng** (Md **dòng**)
① to threaten, intimidate, or scare loudly ② pain

恫喝 **duhng hot**
to threaten, imtimidate or scare loudly; to browbeat; to bully

恫矜 **tùng gìng**
hardship; illess

恬 **tìhm** (Md **tián**)
quiet; peaceful; undisturbed

恬靜 **tìhm jihng**
undisturbed; having peace of mind

恬逸 **tìhm yaht**
free from worry or disturbance; peaceful and leisurely

恰 **hāp** (Md **qià**)
proper; appropriate; suitable

恰當 **hāp dong**
appropriate; fitting; apt; apposite

恰巧 **hāp háau**
coinciding luckily; by coincidence

恁 **yahm** (Md **nèn**)
① this; such; that ② how; what

恁地 **yahm deih**
in this way; to such extent; how

恁般 **yahm bùn**
to such extent

恐 **húng** (Md **kǒng**)
to fear

恐佈 **húng bou**
terror; horror; fear

恐龍 **húng lùhng**
a dinosaur

恕 **syu** (Md **shù**)
to forgive; to excuse

恕罪 **syu jeuih**
to forgive a fault

恕道 **syu douh**
the principle of forgiveness; magnanimity

恙 **yeuhng** (Md **yàng**)
① disease ② worry

恙蟲 **yeuhng chùhng**
chigger or jigger; red bug

抱恙 **póuh yeuhng**
to be ill; to be sick

恚 **waih** (Md **hùi**)
rage; anger

恚怒 **waih nouh**
to be enraged; to be indignant;
to be furious

恚怨 **waih yun**
to resent bitterly

恝 **ngaat, gaat** (Md **jiá**)
indifferent; unworried; carefree

恝置 **ngaat ji**
to disregard; to neglect

恣 **ji, chi** (Md **zì**)
to throw off restraints; to
dissipate; to debauch

恣肆 **chi si**
licentious; headless of all
restraints; willful

恣情 **chi chìhng**
to abandon oneself to passion

恥(耻) **chi** (Md **chǐ**)
shame; disgrace; humiliation; to
feel ashamed

恥笑 **chi siu**
to laugh at; to ridicule

恥辱 **chi yuhk**
shame; disgrace; humiliation

恓 **sài** (Md **xī**)
frightened and worried

恓惶 **sài wòhng**
frightened and worried

恩 **yàn** (Md **ēn**)
favor; grace; kindness;
benevolence; affection; mercy;
charity

恩惠 **yàn waih**
a kind act; kindness; charity;
bounty

恩義 **yàn yih**
spiritual debt; gratitude

恭 **gùng** (Md **gōng**)
respectful; reverent; deferential

恭喜 **gùng héi**
Congratulations!

恭候 **gùng hauh**
to wait-respectfully

息 **sīk** (Md **xī**)
① a breath ② news; tidings ③ to
stop; to end ④ interest (on
money) ⑤ a son

息怒 **sīk nouh**
to let one's anger cool off;
(Please) be not angry

消息 **siu sīk**
news; informations

悔 **fui** (Md **huǐ**)
to regret; to repent

悔改 **fui gói**
to repend of (a sin); to be
repentant of

悔氣 **fui hei**
bad luck

悃 **kwán** (Md **kǔn**)
honest; sincere

悃誠 **kwán sìhng**
sincere

悃款 **kwán fún**
single-minded; sincere

悝 **fùi** (Md **kuī**)
① sad; grieved; worried ② to
ridicule

悄 **chiu** (Md **qiǎo, qiāo**)
quiet

悄然 **chiu yìhn**
quietly

悄語 **chiu yúh**
　　to talk in a low voice; to speak
　　softly; to whisper

悅 **yuht** (Md **yuè**)
　to delight; to gratify; to please;
　delighted; pleased; gratified;
　happy

悅目 **yuht muhk**
　　pleasant to the eye; having a
　　pleasant appearance; beautiful

悅耳 **yuht yíh**
　　pleasant to the ear; musical

悌 **daih** (Md **tì**)
　to show brotherly love

悌睦 **daih muhk**
　　to live at peace as brothers

悌友 **daih yáuh**
　　to be kind to friends; to show
　　brotherly love for friends

悍 **hóhn** (Md **hàn**)
　① violent; fierce; cruel ② brave;
　audacious ③ stubborn

悍婦 **hóhn fúh**
　　a shrew; a virago; a termagant

悍戾 **hóhn leuih**
　　cruel; atrocious

悒 **yāp** (Md **yì**)
　troubled in mind; unhappy

悒悒 **yāp yāp**
　　sad; grieved; worried; depress-
　　ed; unhappy

悒鬱 **yāp wāt**
　　malancholy; disconsolate;
　　unhappy

悖 **buih** (Md **bèi**)
　to go against; to go counter to;
　to revolt against; contrary to

悖理 **buih léih**
　　absurd;　　unreasonable;
　　irrational

悖亂 **buih lyuhn**
　　revolt; rebellion; sedition

悚 **súng** (Md **sǒng**)
　fearful; terrified; frightened

悚慄 **súng leuht**
　　to tremble with fear; frighten-
　　ed; terrified

悚然 **súng yìhn**
　　in terror; fear-stricken

悛 **syùn** (Md **quān**)
　to repent; to reform

悛改 **syùn gói**
　　to reform oneself; to repent of
　　one's sin

悛悍 **syùn yihk**
　　to reform oneself; to repent of
　　one's sin

悞 **ngh** (Md **wù**)
　same as '誤', see '言' radical

悟 **ngh** (Md **wù**)
　to become aware of; to realize; to
　awake to; to comprehend

悟道 **ngh douh**
　　(in Buddhism) to awake to
　　Truth

悟性 **ngh sing**
　　capacity for understanding;
　　understanding

悁 **gyùn** (Md **juān**)
　indignant; angry

悁悁 **gyùn gyùn**
　　sad; unhappy

悁忿 **gyùn fáhn**
　　angry; enraged; indignant

悉 **sīk** (Md **xī**)
　① to know ② all; whole; total;
　entire

悉力 **sīk lihk**
　　with all one's strength; with
　　might and main

悉數 **sīk sou**
　　the entire sum (of money)

悠 **yàuh** (Md **yōu**)
① far; long; vast; extensive ②
sad; pensive; meditative ③
gentle; slow; soft

悠久 **yàuh gáu**
long in time

悠閒 **yàuh hàahn**
leisurely; unrestrained;
unhurried

患 **waahn** (Md **huàn**)
① suffering; adversity; tribula-
tion; distress; trouble; worry ②
to be troubled by; to be worried
about

患難 **waahn naahn**
suffering; distress; adversity

患病 **waahn behng**
to get sick; to fall ill

您 **néih** (Md **nín**)
a deferential form of "你"; a
respectful form for "you"

悵(怅) **jeung**
(Md **chàng**)
disappointed; frustrated;
dissatisfied

悵然 **jeung yìhn**
disappointedly

悵望 **jeung mohng**
to long pensively or wistfully

悱 **féi** (Md **fěi**)
① inarticulate; unable to give
vent to one's emotion ②
sorrowful

悱憤 **féi fáhn**
sadness kept to oneself

悱惻 **féi chāk**
affected by sorrow, sorrowful

悴(顇) **séuih** (Md **cuì**)
① haggard; worn-out; tired out ②
worried; sad

悴賤 **séuih jihn**
needly and lowly

憔悴 **chìuh séuih**
to have a worn look; to look
haggard; to suffer distress,
worries, etc.

悸 **gwaih** (Md **jì**)
① palpitation of the heart ② fear

悸慄 **gwaih leuht**
to tremble with fear

悻 **hahng** (Md **xìng**)
angry; indignant; enraged

悻悻 **hahng hahng**
angry; enraged

悻直 **hahng jihk**
blunt; bluff; brusque

悼 **douh** (Md **dào**)
to mourn (for or ever); to lament;
to regret; to grieve

悼亡 **douh mòhng**
to be bereaved of one's wife

悼念 **douh nihm**
to remember (the deseased)
with sorrow

悽 **chài** (Md **qī**)
① grieved; sorrowful; suffering;
afflicted ② tragic; pathetic;
pitiful; grievous

悽涼 **chài lèuhng**
dreary; desolate

悽慘 **chài cháam**
tragic; heart-rending

情 **chìhng** (Md **qíng**)
① feeling; emotion; sentiment ②
fact; detail; situation; condition
③ love; affection ④ nature;
reason

情況 **chìhng fong**
situation; state of affairs;
circumstances

情緒 **chìhng séuih**
emotion; feeling; mood

惆 **chàuh** (Md **chóu**)
regretful; rueful

惆悵 **chàuh jeung**
rueful; regretful

惆然 **chàuh yìhn**
regretful; wistful

惇 **dèun** (Md **dūn**)
sincere; kind; generous

惇惇 **dèun dèun**
kind; generous; sincere

惇誨 **dèun fui**
to teach kindly

惋 **yún, wún** (Md **wǎn**)
① to regret ② to be alarmed

惋惜 **yún sīk**
to feel sorry for (a loss, etc.);
to regret

惋嘆 **wún taan**
to regret; to deplore

惕 **tīk** (Md **tì**)
① cautious; careful; prudent ②
afraid ③ anxious

惕惕 **tīk tīk**
apprehensive; fearful

惕厲 **tīk laih**
to exercise caution and
dicipline

惘 **móhng** (Md **wǎng**)
dejected; frustrated; discouraged

惘然 **móhng yìhn**
in a daze; at a loss; stupefied

惚 **fāt** (Md **hū**)
absent-minded; entranced

恍惚 **fóng fāt**
absent-minded; unconscious

惛 **fàn** (Md **hūn**)
① confused ② senile

惛惛 **fàn fàn**
confused in mind; absorbed;
carried away; entranced

惛憊 **fàn beih**
muddle-headed

惜 **sīk** (Md **xī**)
to pity; to regret; to grudge

惜別 **sīk biht**
reluctant to part company; to
say good-bye

惜玉憐香 **sīk yuhk lìhn hèung**
to be tender to the fair sex

惟 **wàih** (Md **wéi**)
① to think; to mediate ② only;
alone ③ but; however

惟獨 **wàih duhk**
only; alone

惟物 **wàih maht**
materialistic

惦 **dim** (Md **diàn**)
to remember; to bear in mind; to
miss

惦念 **dim nihn**
to feel or regret the absence or
loss of; to miss (a friend or
beloved one)

惦記 **dim gei**
to feel concern about someone
far away

惝 **chóng, tóng** (Md **tǎng**)
dispirited; disheartened; discouraged

惝然 **tóng yìhn**
crestfallen; dispirited;
discouraged; disheartened;
dejected

悲 **bèi** (Md **bēi**)
① sad; sorrowful; mournful;
woeful; rueful; doleful ② to
lament; to deplore; to mourn; to
pity; to sympathize

悲哀 **bèi ngòi**
mournful; woeful

悲觀 **bēi gūn**
passimistic

悶 (闷) **muhn** (Md **mèn, mēn**)
① (of weather, rooms, etc.) oppressive or suffocating; ② stuffy melancholy; depressed

悶氣 **muhn hei**
oppressive air (due to poor ventilation)

悶悶不樂 **muhn muhn bāt lohk**
unhappy

愵 **nīk** (Md **nì**)
pensive; worried

惓 **kyùhn** (Md **quán**)
sincere; candid

惓惓 **kyùhn kyùhn**
sincere; candid

惑 **waahk** (Md **huò**)
① to confuse; to delude; to beguile; to mislead; to misguide ② to doubt; to suspect

惑衆 **waahk jung**
to delude or confuse the people

惑亂 **waahk lyuhn**
to delude or confuse

惠 **waih** (Md **huì**)
① to benefit; to profit; to favor ② kind; benevolent; gracious; gentle

惠存 **waih chyùhn**
to be so kind as to keep (my gift); to condescend to accept

惠臨 **waih làhm**
to favor with one's presence

惡 (恶) **ngok, wu, wù** (Md **è, wù, ě, wū**)
① bad; evil; wicked; vice; wickedness ② to disgust; to sicken; to nauseate ③ to hate; to detest; to dislike; to abhor; to loathe ④ how; where ⑤ O; oh; ah

惡夢 **ngok muhng**
nightmare

惡嫌 **wu yìhm**
to hate; to detest; to abhor; to loathe

惙 **jyut** (Md **chuò**)
melancholy; doleful; mournful; gloomy

惙惙 **jyut jyut**
melancholy; gloomy

惙怛 **jyut daat**
mournful; doleful; rueful

惲 (恽) **wahn** (Md **yùn**)
① to plan; to consider; to deliberate ② a Chinese family name

惲謀 **wahn màuh**
to scheme; to plan

惲議 **wahn yíh**
to discuss; to deliberate

惰 **doh** (Md **duò**)
lazy; idle

惰性 **doh sing**
inertia

惰懈 **doh haaih**
to be negligent or neglectful

惹 **yéh** (Md **rě**)
to provoke; to rouse; to induce; to bring upon oneself; to incur

惹事 **yéh sih**
to create trouble

惹起 **yéh héi**
to incite; to provoke

惱 (恼) **nóuh** (Md **nǎo**)
① to anger; to annoy; to irritate; to vex; to trouble ② angered; offended; vexed; annoyed

惱怒 **nóuh nouh**
angry; indignant; irritated; anger; indignation; rage

惱羞成怒 **nóuh sàu sìhng nouh**
　to be moved to anger by the feeling of shame

惴 **chyún, jeui (Md zhuì)**
worried; afraid; anxious; apprehensive

惴惴 **chyún chyún**
　timorous; afraid; fearful, apprehensive; to feel uneasy or apprehensive

惴慄 **chyún leuht**
　to tremble from fear; to shudder

愎 **bīk (Md bì)**
perverse; self-willed; obstinate; stubborn

愎諫 **bīk gaan**
　deaf to remonstrances

剛愎自用 **gòng bīk jih yuhng**
　stubborn; obstinate; not yielding to reason or advice

惶 **wòhng (Md huáng)**
① afraid; fearful; apprehensive ② anxious; uneasy; hurried ③ flurried; hurried

惶恐 **wòhng húng**
　apprehensive; fearful; afraid

惶惑 **wòhng waahk**
　anxious; uneasy; ill at ease; apprehensive

惺 **sìng (Md xīng)**
① clever; intelligent; wise ② wavering; indecisive

惺惺 **sìng sìng**
　intelligent; clever; wakeful; alert

惺忪 **sìng sùng**
　wavering; indecisive

惻 (恻) **chāk (Md cè)**
to feel anguish

惻然 **chāk yìhn**
　sadly; sorrowfully

惻隱之心 **chāk yán jì sàm**
　natural compassion; innate mercy

愀 **chíu (Md qiǎo)**
① anxious looking ② to show sudden change of expression

愀愴 **chíu chong**
　rueful; doleful; sad

愀然 **chíu yìhn**
　showing a sudden change of expression; turning; pale or red suddenly; anxious looking

愉 **yùh (Md yú)**
happy; contented; pleased

愉快 **yùh faai**
　happy; pleased; delighted

愉悅 **yùh yuht**
　joyful; glad; happy

愕 **ngohk (Md è)**
startled; astonished; amazed

愕然 **ngohk yìhn**
　astonished; flabbergasted; dumbfounded

愕顧 **ngohk gu**
　to look in amazement

愜 (慊、㥦) **hip (Md qiè)**
cheerful; satisfied; content

愜意 **hip yi**
　satisfied; contented

愜當 **hip dong**
　proper; appropriate

想 **séung (Md xiǎng)**
① to think; to consider ② to hope; to expect ③ to plan

想念 **séung nihm**
　to give thought to (a person); to miss (something or someone)

想像力 **séung jeuhng lihk**
imagination

愁 **sàuh** (Md **chóu**)
① sad; distressed; worried; unhappy; melancholy ② depressing; saddening; gloomy ③ to worry about; to be anxious about

愁悶 **sàuh muhn**
unhappy; distressed; distressful; worried

愁容滿面 **sàuh yùhng múhn mihn**
to wear a sad look; to look distressed

愆 **hìn, hín** (Md **qiān**)
a fault; a mistake; a misdemeanor

愆過 **hìn gwo**
a fault; a mistake

愆滯 **hìn jaih**
behind time or schedule

愈 (瘉) **yuh** (Md **yù**)
① to recover (from illness) ② to a greater degree; even more

愈多愈好 **yuh dò yuh hóu**
the more the better

痊愈 **chyùhn yuh**
to have been cured; to have recovered from illness

憫 (憫) **máhn** (Md **mǐn**)
to pity; to commiserate (same as '憫')

意 **yi** (Md **yì**)
① thought; idea; sentiment ② intention; inclination ③ expectation ④ meaning

意見 **yi gin**
opinion; view; idea; proposals

意向 **yi heung**
intention; inclination

愚 **yùh** (Md **yú**)
① stupid; foolish; silly; unwise;

unintelligent ② to fool; to cheat; to deceive

愚昧 **yùh muih**
stupid; ignorant

愚弄 **yùh luhng**
to make a fool of somebody

愛 (爱) **ngoi** (Md **ài**)
① to love; to like; to be fond of; to be kind to ② love; affection; kindness; benevolence

愛國 **ngoi gwok**
patriotic

愛慕 **ngoi mouh**
to adore; adoration

愔 **yàm** (Md **yīn**)
peaceful; composed; serene

愔愔 **yàm yàm**
peaceful; composed; serene

愣 **lihng** (Md **lèng**)
① dumbfounded; agape with horror; stupefied ② reckless, irresponsible; rash; rude ③ outspoken

愣頭愣腦 **lihng tàuh lihng nóuh**
rash; reckless; stupid-looking; stupid; in a stupor

愣住了 **lihng jyuh líuh**
to become speechless because of astonishment, an unexpected question, etc., to be taken aback

感 **gám** (Md **gǎn**)
① to feel; to perceive; to respond to ② to affect, move or touch ③ feeling; sensation; emotion

感激 **gám gìk**
to feel grateful; to be moved; touched or affected

感冒 **gám mouh**
a cold; to catch a cold

愧(媿) **kwáih, kwai**
(Md **kuì**)
ashamed; shameful; abashed; embarrassed; to suffer pains of conscience

愧色 **kwáih sīk**
　expression of shame

慚愧 **chàahm kwáih**
　ashamed

愴(怆) **chong**
(Md **chuàng**)
broken-hearted; sad; sorrowful

愴然 **chong yìhn**
　broken-hearted; in anguish of sorrow

愴惻 **chong chāk**
　sad; grieved; sorrowful

愫 **sou** (Md **sù**)
sincerity; honestly

情愫 **chìhng sou**
　innermost feeling

愠(慍) **wáhn, wan**
(Md **yùn**)
angry; indignant; displeased; irritated; vexed

愠怒 **wáhn nouh**
　angry; irritated; displeased

愠色 **wáhn sīk**
　a displeased look; an angry-appearance

愷(恺) **hói** (Md **kǎi**)
joyful; contented; good; kind; gentle

愷悌 **hói daih**
　happy and easy-going

愷樂 **hói ngohk**
　tune or music in celeberation of victory

慎 **sahn** (Md **shèn**)
cautious; careful; scrupulous; prudent

慎重其事 **sahn juhng kèih sih**
　to take careful precautions; to do something in a serious manner

慎獨 **sahn duhk**
　to exercise caution about one's personal life

愾(忾) **koi** (Md **kài**)
enmity; hatred; anger; wrath

愾憤 **koi fáhn**
　angry; to show wrath

慄 **leuht** (Md **lì**)
to shudder; to tremble

慄慄 **leuht leuht**
　timorous; fearful; terrified; frightful

懍慄 **láhm leuht**
　trembling with awe

慊 **him, hip** (Md **qiàn, qiè**)
① to resent ② contented; satisfied gratified; pleased

慊慊 **him him**
　resentful

不慊意 **bāt hip yi**
　dissatisfied; discontented

慌 **fòng** (Md **huāng**)
to lose self-possession; to lose head; panicky

慌亂 **fòng lyuhn**
　hurry and confusion

慌張 **fòng jèung**
　lacking self-possession; nervous and excited

愿 **yuhn** (Md **yuàn**)
sincere; honest; faithful; virtuous

慇 **yàn** (Md **yīn**)
① mournful; sorrowful ② regardful; respectful

慇勤 **yàn kàhn**
polite; courteous; civil

慇慇 **yàn yàn**
mournful; sorrowful; sad

慈 **chìh** (Md **cí**)
① kind; benevolent; benignant; benign; charitable; loving; food; merciful ② of one's mother; maternal

慈悲 **chìh bèi**
mercy; clemency

慈善 **chìh sihn**
charity; philanthropy; humanitarianism

態 (态) **taai** (Md **tài**)
① attitude; bearing; manner; carriage; deportment ② situation; condition; circumstances ③ (in physics) state of matter

態度 **taai douh**
attitude; manner

態勢 **taai sai**
(military) situation

慆 **jau** (Md **zhòu**)
stubborn; not easy to be convinced

慂 (恿) **yúng** (Md **yǒng**)
to persuade; urge

慫慂 **súng yúng**
to instigate; to incite; to egg on

愬 **sou** (Md **sù**)
same as "訴", see '言' radical

慘 (惨) **cháam** (Md **cǎn**)
① sorrowful; sad; miserable; tragic ② cruel; merciless; brutal ③ dark; gloomy; dull

慘酷 **cháam huhk**
cruel and sadistic

慘劇 **cháam kehk**
tragic event; tragedy

慨 **koi** (Md **kǎi**)
① to sigh emotionally ② generous; magnanimous

慨歎 **koi taan**
to deplore or lament with sighs

慨憤 **koi fáhn**
indignant; angry

慟 (恸) **duhng**
(Md **tòng**)
extreme grief

慟哭 **duhng hūk**
to weep bitterly

慢 **maahn** (Md **màn**)
① slow; sluggish; leisurely ② negligent ③ haughty; rude; disrespectful

慢動作 **maahn duhng jok**
slow motion

慢待 **maahn doih**
to treat (a guest) rudely or discourteously (often used in a polite conversation)

慣 (惯) **gwaan**
(Md **guàn**)
① habitual; customary; usual ② to spoil (a child) ③ accustomed to; used to; experienced in

慣例 **gwaan laih**
usual practice; established practice; custom

慣性 **gwaan sing**
inertia

慳 (悭) **hàan** (Md **qiān**)
stingy; niggardly; parsimonious; close

慳吝 **hàan leuhn**
stingy; niggardly; miserly; parsiminious

慳囊 **hàan lòhng**
(literally) a money-bag which is closed after money is put in — a miser; a niggard

慚(惭、慙)**chàahm**
(Md **cán**)
ashamed; mortified; humiliated

慚愧 **chàahm kwáih**
ashamed

慚色 **chàahm sīk**
shamed-faced look

慵 **yùhng** (Md **yōng**)
indolent; lazy; idle

慵惰 **yùhng doh**
lazy; indolent; idle; inactive

慵困 **yùhng kwan**
tired and indolent

慥 **chou, jouh** (Md **zào**)
sincere; kind-hearted

慥慥 **chou chou**
sincere and honest

慷(忼)**hóng, kóng**
(Md **kāng**)
① ardent; impassioned ②
generous; liberal; magnanimous;
unselfish

慷慨 **hóng koi**
generous; unselfish; liberal;
heroic; ardent

慷慨激昂 **hóng koi gīk
ngòhng**
(of speech or conduct) impassioned; arousing

慕 **mouh** (Md **mù**)
① to yearn for; to long for ② to
adore; to admire

慕效 **mouh haauh**
to imitate in admiration

羨慕 **sihn mouh**
to admire; to adore

慝 **nīk, tīk** (Md **tè**)
evil idea; evil; vice

慧 **waih** (Md **huì**)
intelligent; bright; wise

慧眼 **waih ngáahn**
discerning eyes; insight

智慧 **ji waih**
intelligence; wisdom

慫(慫)**súng** (Md **sǒng**)
to instigate; to incite

慫慂 **súng yúng**
to instigate; to incite; to egg
on

慮(慮)**leuih** (Md **lù**)
① to consider; to take into
account ② to worry about;
anxious about

慮及 **leuih kahp**
to have anticipated; to have
taken into account

憂慮 **yàu leuih**
worried; anxious; apprehensive; to worry; worries; anxiety

慪(怄)**au** (Md **òu**)
① to irritate; to exasperate ②
same as " 嘔 " (to disgust)

慪氣 **au hei**
to become exasperated

慪人 **au yàhn**
exasperating; to anger

慰 **wai** (Md **wèi**)
to console; to comfort; to soothe;
to assuage; to relieve

慰問 **wai mahn**
to show sympathy by making
inquiries

慰唁 **wai yihn**
to console with (the bereaved)

慤(愨、殼)**kok**
(Md **què**)
honest; prudent

慶(庆)**hing** (Md **qìng**)
① festivity; blessing; felicity; joy
② to celebrate; to congratulate;
to rejoice

慶祝 **hing jūk**
to celeberate; celebration

慶功宴 **hing gùng yin**
dinner party in celeberation of triumph; a celeberation party

慼(慽)**chīk** (Md **qī**)
① mournful; woeful ② ashamed

慼慼 **chīk chīk**
sorrowful; sad; rueful

慼憂 **chīk yāu**
sad and depressed

慾 **yuhk** (Md **yù**)
desire; appetite; passion; lust; greed

慾望 **yuhk mohng**
desire; longing; aspiration; craving; urge

慾火 **yuhk fó**
passion; fire of lust

憂(忧)**yàu** (Md **yōu**)
① sad; pensive; mournful; grieved ② to worry about; concerned over; anxious; apprehensive

憂懼 **yàu geuih**
anxious and fearful

憂鬱 **yàu wāt**
melancholy; depressed; dejected; cheerless; despondent

憋 **bit** (Md **biē**)
to suppress inner feeling with efforts

憋氣 **bit hei**
to suffer breathing obstruction; to suppress resentment, grudge, etc.

憋悶 **bit muhn**
melancholy; depressed

憑(凭、馮)**pàhng**
(Md **píng**)
① to lean upon; to rely on; to depend upon ② to be based on ③ basis; proof; evidence

憑據 **pàhng geui**
basis (for belief or supposition); ground; reason; proof; evidence

憑藉 **pàhng jihk**
by means of; on the strength of; to rely on; something on which one relies

憎 **jàng** (Md **zēng**)
to hate; to loathe; to abhor; to abominate; to detest

憎恨 **jàng hahn**
to hate; to hold a grudge against

憎惡 **jàng wu**
to hate; to loathe; to destest; to abhor; to hate evil

憐(怜)**lìhn** (Md **lián**)
① to pity; to commiserate ② to feel tender regard for

憐憫 **lìhn máhn**
to pity; to commiserate

可憐 **hó lìhn**
to pity; pitiful

憒(愦)**kúi** (Md **kuì**)
muddle-headed; confused in mind

憒亂 **kúi lyuhn**
confused in mind; at a loss; dazed

憒憒 **kúi kúi**
confused; muddle-headed

憔 **chìuh** (Md **qiáo**)
emaciated; haggard; worn

憔悴 **chìuh séuih**
to have a worn look; to look haggard; to suffer-distress; worries; etc.

憔慮 **chìuh leuih**
impatient and anxious

憧 **tùhng, chùng**
(Md **chōng**)
① indecisive; irresolute ② to

yearn; to aspire

憧憬 **tùhng gíng**
to imagine something or a place with yearning or longing

憧憧 **tùhng tùhng**
indecisive; irresolute; wavering

憚(惮) **daahn** (Md **dàn**)
to fear; to shirk

憚改 **daahn gói**
reluctant to correct for fear of difficulty or trouble; afraid to reform

忌憚 **geih daahn**
fears that keep a person from committing irregularities; to dread

憫 **máhn** (Md **mǐn**)
to pity; to commiserate; to feel concerned over

憫惻 **máhn chāk**
to pity

憐憫 **lìhn máhn**
to pity; to commiserate

憬 **gíng, gwíng** (Md **jǐng**)
to realize; to come to understand; to awake

憬悟 **gíng ngh**
to become awake of; to realize; to come to understand

憬然 **gíng yìhn**
aware; knowing

憮(怃) **móuh** (Md **wǔ**)
regretful; disappointed

憮然 **móuh yìhn**
regretfully; disappointedly

憊(惫) **baaih, beih** (Md **bèi**)
tired; exhausted; weary

憊倦 **baaih gyuhn**
tired; exhausted; weary; fatigued

憊累 **baaih leuih**
tired; weary; exhausted

憨 **hàm** (Md **hān**)
silly; stupid; foolish

憨態 **hàm taai**
a silly appearance

憨笑 **hàm siu**
to giggle; to titter

憝 **deuih** (Md **duì**)
① wicked or vicious persons ② to hate

憲(宪) **hin** (Md **xiàn**)
① law; code; statute; ordinance; constitution ② intelligent ③ a reference to superiors

憲法 **hin faat**
constitution (of a national government)

憲章 **hin jèung**
a charter

憩 **hei** (Md **qì**)
to rest; to repose

憩息 **hei sīk**
to pause for rest; to rest; to take a rest

憤(愤) **fáhn** (Md **fèn**)
to resent; indignant; angry

憤怒 **fáhn nouh**
anger; wrath; indignation; rage

憤激 **fáhn gīk**
vehemence; excitement; fury

憶(忆) **yīk** (Md **yì**)
to remember; to bear in mind; to recall; to recollect

憶起 **yīk héi**
to call to mind; to remember; to recall

記憶 **gei yīk**
to remember; memory or recollection

憾 **hahm** (Md **hàn**)
regret; remorse; dissatisfaction

憾事 **hahm sih**
a regretable thing; a matter for regret

憾怨 **hahm yun**
chagrin

懂 **dúng** (Md **dǒng**)
to understand; to comprehend; to know

懂事 **dúng sih**
familiar with human affairs

懂得 **dúng dāk**
to understand; to comprehend; to know

懈 **háaih, gaai** (Md **xiè**)
negligent; remiss; relaxed; inattentive

懈怠 **háaih tóih**
to neglect; to goldbrick; negligent

懈弛 **háaih chìh**
to relax; to slow down

懊 **ou** (Md **ào**)
regretful; remorseful; resentful

懊惱 **ou nóuh**
to take it to heart; to feel remorseful and angry

懊悔 **ou fui**
regretful; remorseful

懌 (怿) **yihk** (Md **yì**)
delighted; pleased; happy; glad

懌悅 **yihk yuht**
delighted; pleased; happy; glad

懍 (懔) **láhm** (Md **lǐn**)
filled with awe; awe-struck; inspiring awe; aweful

懍然 **láhm yìhn**
awe-struck; awe-stricken; filled with awe

懍懍 **láhm láhm**
awe-struck; awe-stricken; inspiring awe; dignified

懃 **kàhn** (Md **qín**)
cordial; hearty

懃懃懇懇 **kàhn kàhn hán hán**
cordial and sincere

慇懃 **yàn kàhn**
polite; courteous; civil

懇 (恳) **hán** (Md **kén**)
cordial; sincere; earnest

懇切 **hán chit**
very sincere

懇求 **hán kàuh**
to entreat; to beseech; to implore; to plead

應 (应) **yìng, ying**
(Md **yīng, yìng**)
① should; ought to ② to respond to; to answer; to react to ③ to deal with; to cope with ④ to assent to ⑤ a Chinese family name

應該 **yìng gòi**
ought to; should

應付 **yìng fuh**
to deal with; to cope with; to handle

懋 **mauh** (Md **mào**)
① grand; majestic; great ② trade ③ to encourage

懋績 **mauh jīk**
great achievements or contributions

懋賞 **mauh séung**
to reward in order to encourage

懣 (懑) **muhn** (Md **mèn**)
resentful; sullen; sulky

懥 **ji, chi** (Md **zhì**)
enraged; indignant; angry

懕(恹、懨)**yìm**
(Md **yān**)
① sickly; in poor health ②
peaceful; content

懕懕 **yìm yìm**
sickly; in poor health; peaceful;
content

懦 **noh** (Md **nuò**)
timid; cowardly; weak

懦夫 **noh fū**
a coward

懦弱 **noh yeuhk**
timid and weak

懟(怼)**deuih, jeuih**
(Md **duì**)
to resent; to hate

怨懟 **yun deuih**
ill-will; hatred; grudge

懲(惩)**chìhng**
(Md **chéng**)
to punish; to chastise; to reprimand; to reprove; to warn

懲罰 **chìhng faht**
to punish; to chastise; to
penalize

懲戒 **chìhng gaai**
to reprimand; to discipline; to
punish

懷(怀)**wàaih**
(Md **huái**)
① bosom; breast ② to hold; to
embrace; to entertain; to harbor
③ to think of; to recollect ④ a
Chinese family name

懷念 **wàaih nihm**
to have sweet memory of; to
remember with longing or
nostalgia

懷抱 **wàaih póuh**
embrace; hug; in arms; to
embrace; to hug; the ideas one
entertains; ambition

懵 **múng, múhng**
(Md **měng**)
① ignorant ② muddle-head;
confused

懵然 **múng yìhn**
ignorant

懵懂 **múng dúng**
to have a confused mind;
muddle-headed

懶(懒、嬾)**láahn**
(Md **lǎn**)
lazy; indolent; idle; inactive;
listless; reluctant; disinclined

懶惰 **láahn doh**
lazy; idle; indolent; slothful;
inactive

懶洋洋 **láahn yèuhng**
yèuhng
indolent

懸(悬)**yùhn** (Md **xuán**)
① to hang or be hanged or hung;
to suspend or be suspended ② to
be in suspension; to be in a
suspense; unsettled; unsolved ③
unfounded; without a basis;
unsupported

懸掛 **yùhn gwa**
to hang (decorations)

懸案 **yùhn ngon**
an unsettled case; an outstanding issue (between nations)

懺(忏)**chaam**
(Md **chàn**)
to confess one's sin; to repent

懺悔 **chaam fui**
to repent one's sin

懺悔錄 **Chaam fui luhk**
Confessions

懼(惧)**geuih** (Md **jù**)
to fear; to dread; to be afraid of

懼怕 **geuih pa**
to fear; to dread; afraid of

懼內 **geuih noih**
henpecked

懾（攝、慴）**sip, jip**
(Md **shè**)
fearful; awe-struck

懾服 **sip fuhk**
to yield from fear

懽 **fūn** (Md **huān**)
① happy; glad; joyous ② same as
" 歡 ", see radical " 欠 "

懿 **yi** (Md **yì**)
① virtuous; fine; good ② having
to do with womanly virtue;
modest; chaste

懿德 **yi dāk**
fine virtue

懿望 **yi mohng**
good reputation

戀（恋）**lyún, lyúhn**
(Md **liàn**)
① to love (one of the other sex)
② to feel a persistent attachment
(for a thing)

戀愛 **lyún ngoi**
tender passions; amour;
romantic attachment; love

戀棧 **lyún jaahn**
reluctant to give up a position
(particularly a public post) one
is holding

戇（戆）**ngohng, jong**
(Md **zhuàng, gàng**)
simple-minded

戇直 **ngohng jihk**
simple and upright

戈部

戈 **gwò** (Md **gē**)
a spear; a lance; a javelin

戈戟 **gwò gīk**
spears; lances

戈壁 **Gwò bīk**
Manchurian for "desert"

戊 **mouh** (Md **wù**)
the fifth of the ten celestial stems

戊夜 **mouh yeh**
the pre-dawn hours

戊戌政變 **Mouh sēut jing
bin**
the Coup of Wu Hsu Year
(1898), in which Kang Yiu-wei
(康有為) and other pro-
gressives tried in vain to
introduce political reform in
China

戌 **sēut** (Md **xū**)
the eleventh of the terrestrial
branches

戌時 **sēut sìh**
7-9 p.m.

戌月 **sēut yuht**
the ninth month of the lunar
year

戍 **syu** (Md **shù**)
to guard; to defend

戍邊 **syu bìn**
to guard the border or the
frontier

戍役 **syu yihk**
garrison duty or military
service as a punishment in
former time

戎 **yùhng** (Md **róng**)
① war; fighting; arms; troops ②
barbarians to the west

戎裝 **yùhng jòng**
military dress; military uniform

戎馬之間 **yùhng máh jì
gàan**
among war horses; on the
fighting line

戒 **gaai** (Md **jiè**)
① to warn; to admonish; to
caution ② to guard against; to

abstain from; to refrain

戒備 **gaai beih**
on guard (against enemy attacks natural disasters, etc.)

戒煙 **gaai yīn**
to give up smoking; to abstain from smoking

成 **sìhng** (Md **chéng**)
① completed; accomplished; finished; fixed; settled; to accomplish; to succeed; to complete ② to achieve ③ to become; to constitute ④ acceptable; all right ⑤ one tenth

成本 **sìhng bún**
(in commerce) cost

成功 **sìhng gùng**
to succeed; success

我 **ngóh** (Md **wǒ**)
I; me; my; we; our; us

我國 **ngóh gwok**
our country

我儕 **ngóh chàaih**
we; us

戔 **jìn** (Md **jiān**)
small; little; tiny

戔戔 **jìn jìn**
tiny; small

戕 **chèuhng** (Md **qiāng**)
to slay

戕害 **chèuhng hoih**
to slay

戕賊 **chèuhng chaahk**
to injure; to destroy

或 **waahk** (Md **huò**)
① a certain; some ② perhaps; probably; maybe ③ or

或者 **waahk jé**
or

或然率 **waahk yìhn leuht**
probability (in mathematics)

戚 **chīk** (Md **qī**)
① relatives by marriage ② sad; mournful; woeful ③ a battle-ax ④ a Chinese family name

戚誼 **chīk yìh**
the ties between relatives

親戚 **chān chīk**
relatives

戛(戛) **aat, gaat** (Md **jiá**)
① a lance ② inharmonious; discordent; different ③ to tap

戛戛 **aat aat**
difficult

戛然而止 **aat yìhn yìh jí**
stop suddenly

戟(戟) **gīk** (Md **jǐ**)
a two-pronged spear or lance

戟指 **gīk jí**
to point at another and scold him

戟門 **gīk mùhn**
door of a noble family

戢 **chāp** (Md **jí**)
to put away or store up; to fold; to cease

戢兵 **chāp bìng**
to cease hostilities

戢翼 **chāp yihk**
to fold the wings (said of a bird); (figurativly) to retire

戥 **dahng, dang** (Md **děng**)
a small steelyard for weighing gold, jewels, etc.

戥盤 **dahng pùhn**
weighing scale of a small steelyard

戥星 **dahng sìng**
sliding weight on a small steelyard

戡 **hàm** (Md **kān**)
① to subdue; to suppress; to put down ② to kill; to slay

戡亂 **hàm lyuhn**
to suppress a rebellion

戡定 **hàm dihng**
to put down or suppress (a rebellion); to subdue (barbarian tribes)

殲(殲) **jín** (Md **jiǎn**)
① to exterminate ② blessing

截 **jiht** (Md **jié**)
① to cut; to section; to truncate ② a slice; a division; a section ③ to detain; to withhold ④ to stop; to close; to end; to intercept

截斷 **jiht tyúhn**
to disrupt; to cut off

截止 **jiht jí**
to close (application, registration, etc.) upon reaching the deadline

戧(戗) **cheung**
(Md **qiāng, qiàng**)
to support

戧金 **cheung gàm**
gold jewelries

戧柱 **cheung chyúh**
a side support (for a falling house, etc.)

戮 **luhk** (Md **lù**)
① to massacre; to slay; to oppress ② to unite or join

戮力 **luhk lihk**
to join force; to cooperate

戮民 **luhk màhn**
to oppress the people

戰(战) **jin** (Md **zhàn**)
① war; warfare; fighting; battle ② to contest; to fight; to contend ③ to shudder; to shiver; to tremble

戰艦 **jin laahm**
warship

戰爭 **jin jàng**
war

戲(戏、戱) **hei, fù**
(Md **xī, hū**)
① to play; to toy; to sport ② to jest; to have fun; to make fun ③ a drama; a play ④ a game ⑤ alas; oh; o; ah

戲劇 **hei kehk**
drama

於戲 **wù fù**
alas; oh

戴 **daai** (Md **dài**)
① to wear on the head, the nose, the ear or the hand ② to support; to sustain; to bear ③ a Chinese family name

戴高帽 **daai gòu móu**
to receive flattery or compliment; to flatter

戴眼鏡 **daai ngáahn geng**
to wear eye-glasses or spectacles

戳 **cheuk** (Md **chuō**)
① to jab; to poke; to pierce ② a chop; a stamp; a seal

戳子 **cheuk jí**
a stamp; a seal; a chop

戶部

戶 **wuh** (Md **hù**)
① a door ② a household; a family

戶外 **wuh ngoih**
outdoor

戶口 **wuh háu**
an account; households

戽 **fu** (Md **hù**)
a pail; a bucket

戽斗 **fu dáu**
a device operated by manual

labor to draw water for irrigation of the farms

戽水 **fu séui**
to draw water for farm irrigation by the above device

戾 **leuih** (Md **lì**)
① perverse; recalcitrant; irregular; abnormal ② criminal; atrocious

戾氣 **leuih hei**
perversity; disharmony; irregularity

戾愆 **leuih yín**
sin; crime; guilt

所(所) **só** (Md **suǒ**)
① a place; a location; a position ② a building; an office ③ that which

所得 **só dāk**
income; what one gets or receives

所以 **só yíh**
therefore; so; consequently

房 **fòhng** (Md **fáng**)
① a house; a building ② a room; a chamber ③ a wife; a concubine ④ a Chinese family name

房地產 **fòhng deih cháan**
real estates

房事 **fòhng sih**
sexual act; love-making

扁 **bín, pín** (Md **biǎn, piān**)
① flat ② a tablet ③ small

扁平 **bín pìhng**
thin and flat

扁舟 **pìn jàu**
a small boat

扃 **gwìng, gwìng** (Md **jiōng**)
a bolt; to bolt (doors)

扃門 **gwìng mùhn**
to bolt (doors)

扃鍵 **gwìng gihn**
to lock

扇 **sin** (Md **shàn**)
① a fan ② a numerary auxiliary for door or gate leaves ③ to fan; to instigate, to incite

扇子 **sin jí**
a fan

扇風 **sin fùng**
to fan the air

扈 **wuh** (Md **hù**)
① to follow as escort or retinue ② insolent; impertinent

扈駕 **wuh ga**
to escort the emperor in travel

扈從 **wuh chùhng**
escort or retinue of the emperor when he travels

扉 **fèi** (Md **fēi**)
a door leaf

扉頁 **fèi yihp**
flying leaf of a book

柴扉 **chàaih fèi**
a door of brushwood-poor family

手部

手 **sáu** (Md **shǒu**)
① hand; of the hand; having to do with the hand ② a skilled person; a person ③ action ④ personally

手帕 **sáu paak**
a handkerchief

手續 **sáu juhk**
procedures; red-tape; formalities

才 **chòih** (Md **cái**)
① natural ability; gift; talent; mental faculty ② a gifted person; a brilliant man

才能 **chòih nàhng**
talent; ability; gift

才子 **chòih jí**
a talented person; a man of talent; a brilliant man; a genius

扎 **jaat** (Md **zhā, zhá, zā**)
① pierce ② to struggle; to strive

扎實 **jaat saht**
solid; firm

掙扎 **jàng jaat**
to struggle; to strive

扒 **pàh** (Md **bā, pá**)
① to scratch; to claw; to strip ② to climb; to scale

扒手 **pàh sáu**
a pickpocket

扒住 **pàh jyuh**
to hold on to

打 **dá, dā** (Md **dǎ, dá**)
① to beat; to strike; to hit; to smash; to dash; to attack; to invade; to fight ② to make, do, get, fetch, play, buy, etc. (depending on the object) ③ from; to; toward ④ a dozen

打架 **dá ga**
to have a brawl; a row or a fight

一打 **yāt dā**
one dozen

扔 **yìhng, wìhng**
(Md **rēng**)
to throw; to hurl

扔掉 **yìhng diuh**
to throw away; to cast away

扔下 **yìhng hah**
to throw down; to leave behind

扛 **gòng** (Md **káng, gāng**)
to lift (especially when only a single person is involved)

扛夫 **gòng fù**
a porter

扛在肩上 **gòng joih gìn seuhng**
to carry on the shoulder; to shoulder

托 **tok** (Md **tuō**)
① to hold; or lift; on the palm ② to entrust; to charge; consign; to rely

托賴 **tok laaih**
to rely upon or be indebted to (a phrase usually used to show one's modesty)

托兒所 **tok yìh só**
a public nursery

扣(釦) **kau** (Md **kòu**)
① to tap; to strike; to rap ② to fasten; to button; to buckle ③ to detain; to confine ④ to deduct; to discount ⑤ a button; a hook; a buckle ⑥ to impound; to withhold

扣除 **kau chèuih**
to deduct

扣留 **kau làuh**
to detain; to confine; to keep in custody; to impound

扞 **hohn, gón** (Md **hàn**)
① to resist; to oppose; to obstruct ② to defend; to guard; to withstand

扞衛 **hohn waih**
to defend; to guard

扞拒 **hohn kéuih**
to withstand; to resist; to oppose

扦 **chìn** (Md **qiān**)
① to pierce; to penetrate; to pick ② a pick

扦手 **chìn sáu**
a customs examiner or searcher

扦脚 **chìn geuk**
to trim toe nails; chiropody

扠 **chā** (Md **chā**)

harpoon

扠腰 **chā yìu**
　　to stand with arms akimbo

扳 **pàan** (Md **bān**)

to pull

扳開 **pàan hòi**
　　to pull open

扳機 **pàan gèi**
　　a trigger

扭 **náu** (Md **niǔ**)

① to wrench; to twist; to turn;
to wring ② to seize; to grasp

扭斷 **náu tyúhn**
　　to dislocate (the bones) by
　　twisting or wrenching

扭轉 **náu jyun**
　　to wring; to wrench; to twist;
　　to turn (the tide of a war or
　　contest) for the better

扮 **baan, baahn**
(Md **bàn**)

to dress up; to disguise

扮演 **baahn yín**
　　to play or act

打扮 **dá baan**
　　to make up (said of a woman,
　　an actor or actress); to dress
　　up; dressed like

扯（撦）**ché** (Md **chě**)

① to tear ② to pull; to drag; to
haul ③ to talk nonsense; to lie;
to prevaricate; to digress

扯破 **ché po**
　　to tear to pieces or shreds

扯謊 **ché fòng**
　　to tell a lie; to lie

抃 **bihn** (Md **biàn**)

to clap hands; to cheer

抃舞 **bihn móuh**
　　to cheer and dance; to make

merry

抃手 **bihn sáu**
　　to clap hands

扶 **fùh** (Md **fú**)

① to support; to prop up; to aid;
to help; to shield; to shelter; to
harbor; to protect ② to lean upon

扶助 **fùh joh**
　　to aid; to help; to assist; to
　　support

扶梯 **fùh tài**
　　a flight of stairs with a handrail
　　or balustrade; a staircase

批 **pài** (Md **pī**)

① to comment; to judge; to
criticize ② a whole batch (of
things or people); a large quantity
or number ③ to slap

批評 **pài pìhng**
　　to criticize; criticism;
　　comment

批發 **pài faat**
　　wholesale

扼 **āak, ngāak** (Md **è**)

① to repress; to restrain; to
control ② to clutch; to grasp; to
choke ③ to hold and defend (a
city, etc.)

扼守 **āak sáu**
　　to hold and defend (a strategic
　　position)

扼要 **āak yiu**
　　to hold and strategic position;
　　main point of statement or
　　article; in summary

找 **jáau** (Md **zhǎo**)

① to seek; to look for; to search
for ② to return (change)

找換 **jáau wuhn**
　　to give change for money of
　　larger denominations

找尋 **jáau chàhm**
　　to search for; to look for

技 **geih** (Md **jì**)
skill; ingenuity; dexterity; special ability

技能 **geih nàhng**
skill

技術 **geih seuht**
techniques; technology; skill

抄 **chàau** (Md **chāo**)
① to copy; to transcribe; to plagiarize ② to seize; to confiscate; to take; to search

抄本 **chàau bún**
a handwritten copy

抄集 **chàau jaahp**
to collect by copying

抆 **máhn** (Md **wěn**)
to wipe

抆淚 **máhn leuih**
to wipe tears away

抆拭 **máhn sīk**
to wipe away

抉 **kyut** (Md **jué**)
① to choose; to pick; to select ② to gouge; to dig

抉剔 **kyut tīk**
to pick out; to choose

抉摘 **kyut jaahk**
to choose; to select; to pick out

把 **bá** (Md **bǎ, bà**)
① handle; a hold ② to hold; to take ③ to guard; to watch over; to keep under surveillance ④ a bundle; a grasp; a handful ⑤ around; about; approximately; more or less ⑥ sworn ⑦ (rare) to give

把手 **bá sáu**
a handle; to hold hand

把持 **bá chìh**
to monopolize; dominate or control

抒 **syù** (Md **shū**)
① to give expression to; to express ② to relieve; to ease; to lighten

抒情 **syù chìhng**
to express one's feelings

抒念 **syù nihm**
to be relieved of thoughts or emotions burdening one's mind

抓 **jáau, jà** (Md **zhuā**)
① to scratch ② to grasp; to seize; to take; to snatch; to clutch; to catch ③ to arrest

抓癢 **jáau yéung**
to scratch an itchy part

抓取 **jáau chéui**
to take by grasping or gripping

抔 **pàuh** (Md **póu**)
to scoop up with both hands

抔土 **pàuh tóu**
a double handful of earth; a grave

抔飲 **pàuh yám**
to drink out of the hands

投 **tàuh** (Md **tóu**)
① to throw; to pitch ② to present as gift; to deliver (mail, etc.) to send (letter, script, etc.) ③ to lodge; to stay ④ to head (west, etc.) ⑤ agreeable; harmonious; to fit in with ⑥ to join; to submit to ⑦ to project

投票 **tàuh piu**
to cast vote; to ballot

投資 **tàuh jì**
to invest; investment

抖 **dáu** (Md **dǒu**)
① to tremble ② to shake; to rouse; to jerk ③ (colloquial) to make good; to become well-to-do

抖翻 **dáu fàan**
to turn up; to expose

抖擻精神 **dáu sáu jìng sàhn**
> to pull oneself together or to muster one's energies (for an important task ahead)

抗 kong (Md **kàng**)
① to resist; to oppose ② to reject; to refute; to rebuke ③ high and virtuous ④ to raise; to set up ⑤ to hide; to conceal; to screen; to secrete ⑥ a Chinese family name

抗議 **kong yíh**
> to protest; a protest

抗拒 **kong kéuih**
> to resist; to oppose

折 jit (Md **zhé, shé, zhē**)
① to break; to snap ② to bend; to humble; to bow down ③ to decide a course; to judge ④ to sell; barter or exchange ⑤ a discount in price ⑥ to fold ⑦ to tear into halves; to distroy ⑧ to submit to; to be willing ⑨ a Chinese family name ⑩ to lose money; to fail in business

折頭 **jit tàuh**
> a discount rate

折耗 **jit houh**
> to lose money

抑 yīk (Md **yì**)
① to press down; to repress ② to restrain; to force to (do, perform, etc.) ③ to bend or bow, as head ④ or; or if; still; else; either; then ⑤ but; an opening particle of an expression ⑥ an exclamatory, roughly equivalent to "oh" or "alas"

抑制 **yīk jai**
> to repress; to restrain

抑或 **yīk waahk**
> besides; moreover; or

承 sìhng (Md **chéng**)
① to receive; to inherit; to succeed; (another in a task, etc.) ② to undertake; to make it one's responsibility ③ by (order of) ④ to continue; to carry on; as a theme ⑤ to hold; to contain; to support ⑥ to confess ⑦ obliged; with thanks ⑧ to please; to flatter

承認 **sìhng yihng**
> to confess; to admit; to recognize (a nation, a new regime, etc.)

承繼 **sìhng gai**
> to inherit; to continue an unfinished task left by a predecessor; to adopt; to take an heir

拒 kéuih (Md **jù**)
① to defend; to ward off ② to refuse; to reject; to resist; to oppose

拒絕 **kéuih jyuht**
> to refuse; to reject; a refusal

拒捕 **kéuih bouh**
> to resist arrest

抱 póuh (Md **bào**)
① to embrace; to enfold; to hold in the arms ② to harbor; to cherish; to bosom ③ aspiration; ambition

抱怨 **póuh yun**
> to complain; to blame (another)

抱病 **póuh behng**
> indisposed; sick or ill

拋 (抛) pàau (Md **pāo**)
① to throw; to cast; to throw away ② to abandon; to reject; to give up

拋棄 **pàau hei**
> to abandon; to throw away; to give up

拋物線 **pàau maht sin**
> a parabola

抨 **pìng** (Md **pēng**)
① to impeach; to censure ② to attack or to assail by words

抨擊 **pìng gīk**
to attack or assail by words

抨劾 **pìng haht**
to impeach; to censure

拑 **kìhm** (Md **qián**)
to hold; to grasp

拑釘子 **kìhm dèng jí**
to pull out a nail

拑口 **kìhm háu**
to hold the tongue

披 **pèi** (Md **pī**)
① to open (a book, scroll, etc.) to unroll ② to spread out; to disperse ③ to thumb through or read casually ④ to throw on (a garment, etc.); to wear untidily

披露 **pèi louh**
to reveal; to make known

披閱 **pèi yuht**
to read

押 **aat, ngaat** (Md **yā**)
① to mortgage; to pledge; to obtain loans against security ② to detain or imprison (temporarily) ③ to pawn; a pawn shop ④ to prohibit; to hold at hand; to keep ⑤ to sign; a signature

押當 **aat dong**
to pawn; a pawn shop

押送 **aat sung**
to send (goods or criminals) to another place under escort or guard

抵(牴) **dái** (Md **dǐ**)
① to resist; to oppose ② to off-set ③ to substitute; to give as an equivalent ④ to offer as collateral ⑤ to arrive at; to reach (a place) ⑥ to go against; to offend (law and regulation)

抵抗 **dái kong**
to resist; to oppose; to fight against (an enemy, etc.); resistance

抵押 **dái aat**
to mortgage

抹 **mut** (Md **mǒ, mò, mā**)
① to wipe; to rub; to mop ② to smear ③ to obliterate; to blot out

抹掉 **mut diuh**
to wipe out; to obliterate; to blot out; to erase

抹煞 **mut saat**
to fail to mention (one's merits, achievements, etc.) purposely; to withhold recognition for; do not give credit to

抽 **chàu** (Md **chōu**)
① to draw out; to pull out or open; to take out ② to sprout; to put forth shoots ③ to rid; to take away ④ to whip; to lash ⑤ to smoke (cigarettes, etc.)

抽獎 **chàu jéung**
to draw a lottery or raffle

抽象 **chàu jeuhng**
abstract (as opposed to concrete)

拂 **fāt** (Md **fú**)
① to brush; to shake ② to dust; a duster ③ to oppose; to expel; to drive away

拂曉 **fāt híu**
daybreak; dawn

拂袖而去 **fāt jauh yìh heui**
to leave in displeasure or anger

拄 **jyú** (Md **zhǔ**)
① a post; a prop ② to lean on (a stick, etc.) ③ to ridicule; to make sarcastic remarks

拄杖 **jyú jeuhng**
a crutch, staff or stick

拆 **chaak** (Md **chāi, cā**)
① to split; to break or rip open
② to tear down (a house, etc.) to destroy to dismantle ③ to analyse; to scrutinize

拆開 **chaak hòi**
to take apart; to dismantle (machinery, etc.) to part from each other; to open (a package, letter, etc.)

拆息 **chaak sīk**
short-term interest

拇 **móuh** (Md **mǔ**)
① the thumb ② the big toe

拇指 **móuh jí**
the thumb

拇趾 **móuh jí**
the big toe

拈 **nìm** (Md **niān**)
① to take or hold with fingers ②
to draw lots

拈弄 **nìm luhng**
to finger and play

拈花惹草 **nìm fà yéh chóu**
to fool around with women; to play casanova; lewd and prurient

拉 **làai** (Md **lā, lá**)
① to pull; to drag; to hold; to seize; to draw (a bow) ② to discharge (esp. stool, urine, etc.) ③ to lengthen; to elongate

拉平 **làai pìhng**
to even up; to end up in a draw

拉丁 **Làai dìng**
Latin

拊 **fú** (Md **fǔ**)
① to touch with hand lightly or tenderly; to pat ② to slap; to tap ③ the handle of a vessel or utensil

拊心 **fú sàm**
to slap one's chest — an expression of distress or indignation

拌 **buhn, pun** (Md **bàn**)
① to mix ② to abandon

拌勻 **buhn wàhn**
to mix evenly

拍 **paak** (Md **pāi**)
① to strike with the hand; to slap; to clap; to pat; to swat ② the beat of a piece of music ③ to fawn; to flatter

拍手 **paak sáu**
to clap hands

拎 **lìng** (Md **līng**)
to haul; to take

拎他一把 **lìng tà yāt bá**
to lend a helping hand; give him a hand

抿 **máhn** (Md **mǐn**)
① to smooth (hair); to stroke; to caress ② to purse up (lips) to contract

抿嘴笑 **máhn jéui siu**
to smile with mouth closed

抿頭 **máhn tàuh**
to smooth one's hair

拐 **gwáai** (Md **guǎi**)
① to kidnap; to abduct ② to turn or change direction (in walking, driving, etc.) ③ to swindle

拐帶 **gwáai daai**
to abduct; to kidnap

拐彎 **gwáai wāan**
to turn the corner; at the corner

拓 **tok, taap** (Md **tuò, tà**)
① to expand; to aggrandize; to open up (new frontier, etc.) ② to push with hand ③ to copy characters from an ancient tablet or tomb by rubbing over a paper placed on its surface

拓殖 **tok jihk**
　to open up new land for settlement

拓本 **taap bún**
　stone rubbings

拔 **baht** (Md **bá**)
　① to pull out; to uproot ② to promote (another to a higher position, etc.) ③ outstanding; remarkable ④ to attack and take (a city)

拔取 **baht chéui**
　to take or capture (a city, etc.)

拔除 **baht chèuih**
　to uproot; to eradicate

拖 **tò** (Md **tuō**)
　① to drag along, after or out ② to procrastinate; to delay ③ to involve; to implicate

拖累 **tò leuih**
　to involve or implicate; to suffer because of other's fault

拖欠 **tò him**
　to owe and delay payment for a long time

拗(抝) **ngáau, ngaau** (Md **ǎo, ào, niù**)
obstinate;　stubborn;　unmanageable; recalcitrant

拗斷 **ngáau tyúhn**
　to break by twisting

拗口 **ngaau háu**
　to twist the tongue; tongue twisting

拘 **kèui** (Md **jū**)
　① to detain; to arrest ② to be restricted by cares, worries, convention, etc. ③ confined; not free; restricted; restrained

拘捕 **kèui bouh**
　to detain or arrest (a suspect)

拘束 **kèui chūk**
　to restrain; restrained; timid

and awkward; to feel not at home

拙 **jyut** (Md **zhuō**)
　① stupid; crude; poor (works, etc.); slow and clumsy ② a conventional term referring to oneself

拙荊 **jyut gìng**
　my stupid wife (used in polite conversation)

拙劣 **jyut lyut**
　clumsy and inferior

拚 **pun, pìng** (Md **pàn, pīn**)
　① to go all-out for ② at the risk of; to disregard ③ to reject

拚命 **pun mihng**
　to go all-out (for a cause) even at the risk of one's life; to risk one's life

拚財 **pun chòih**
　to make rush speculations

招 **jìu** (Md **zhāo**)
　① to beckon with hand; to summon ② to ask for (an insult, etc.); to invite (disaster, etc.) ③ to raise (an army, capital, etc.); to recruit ④ to confess; to admit ⑤ a poster; a notice; a signboard ⑥ to cause; to effect; to incite ⑦ to entice; to induce ⑧ to welcome; to receive ⑨ (rare) a target; a bull's-eye ⑩ a Chinese family name

招募 **jìu mouh**
　to enlist troops (usually mercenaries); to solicit (investment, capital)

招待 **jìu doih**
　to receive; to welcome; reception

拜 **baai** (Md **bài**)
　① to do obeisance; to salute; to pay respects to ② to appoint (as a government official); an

appointment ③ to visit; to call on or at ④ a Chinese family name

拜訪 **baai fóng**
　　to visit; to call on

拜神 **baai sàhn**
　　to worship god

担(擔)**dàam, daam** (Md **dān, dàn**)

① to shoulder; to take upon oneself ② a load; a burden

担保 **dàam bóu**
　　to guarantee; to pledge; a guaranty or guarantee; a pledge

担子 **daam jí**
　　a load or burden upon the shoulder

抬(擡)**tòih** (Md **tái**)

to lift; to raise

抬舉 **tòih géui**
　　to do a good turn or favor; a good turn or favor

抬槓 **tòih gong**
　　to argue

拳 **kyùhn** (Md **quán**)

① a fist ② sparring feats; various forms of boxing

拳頭 **kyùhn tàuh**
　　a fist

拳師 **kyùhn sī**
　　an expert in the art of boxing; a boxing master

括 **kwut, gwat** (Md **kuò, guā**)

① to include; to embrace ② to seek; to search for ③ to restrain; to tie (hair, etc.)

括號 **kwut houh**
　　(in mathematics) sign of aggregation

包括 **bàau kwut**
　　to include; including

拭 **sīk** (Md **shì**)

① to wipe; to rub (eyes, etc.) ②

to dust; to clean

拭拂 **sīk fāt**
　　to wipe; to dust and clean

拭目以待 **sīk muhk yíh doih**
　　to wipe or rub the eyes and take a good look at what is going to happen; to wait for the result anxiously

拮 **git** (Md **jié**)

laboring hard; occupied

拮据 **git gèui**
　　financial strait; trouble or difficulty

拱 **gúng** (Md **gǒng**)

① to hold hands before the breast as when making a bow; to salute ② to encircle with the hands ③ (in architecture) arched (door, window, etc.) ④ to raise up (in the middle)

拱手 **gúng sáu**
　　to fold one's hands in a bow (usually in greeting or saying farewell)

拱門 **gúng mùhn**
　　an arched door or doorway

拯 **chíng** (Md **zhěng**)

① to save; to deliver ② to raise; to lift up

拯救 **chíng gau**
　　to save; to rescue; to deliver; deliverance (in the Bible)

拯恤 **chíng sēut**
　　to save and help (the refugees, poor, etc.)

挓 **jà** (Md **zhā**)

stiff and erect

挓挲 **jà sà**
　　bristling; stiff and erect

拴 **sàan** (Md **shuān**)

① to tie up; to fasten ② to drive a wedge between two parties

拴縛 **sàan bok**
　　to tie up (with rope or chain, etc.)

拴馬 **sàan máh**
　　to tie up a horse

拶 **jaat** (Md **zā, zǎn**)
a torture device in old China consisting of several contractible wooden sticks, in between which the fingers of a suspect are placed and pressed to extort confessions

拶子 **jaat jí**
　　an old chinese torture device (see above)

拶指 **jaat jí**
　　to press the fingers with the device described above

拷 **háau** (Md **kǎo**)
to flog, whip, torture, etc. (in order to get a confession, etc.)

拷貝 **háau bui**
　　a copy

拷打 **háau dá**
　　to flog or whip; to torture

持 **chìh** (Md **chí**)
① to hold; to grasp ② to maintain; to support; to keep; to uphold ③ a tie or stalement

持久 **chìh gáu**
　　to last for a long time; lasting; durable

持續 **chìh juhk**
　　continuous;　incessant; uninterrupted

指 **jí** (Md **zhǐ**)
① the finger ② to point; to direct ③ to indicate; to refer to; to mean ④ the number of people ⑤ intentions ⑥ the main theme ⑦ to hope ⑧ to depend on

指導 **jí douh**
　　to direct; to guide; to supervise; direction or guidance

指示 **jí sih**
　　to instruct; an instruction; to show; to indicate

挎 **kwà** (Md **kuà**)
① carry on the arm ② carry over one's shoulder or at one side

挑 **tìu** (Md **tiāo, tiǎo**)
① to carry things with a pole on one's shoulder; to shoulder ② to select; to choose; to pick ③ to pick by pitchfork

挑夫 **tìu fù**
　　a collie; a bearer; a porter

挑剔 **tìu tīk**
　　to be very particular in making selection; to be over punctilious in making a choice; to find fault with somebody or something

按 **ngon** (Md **àn**)
① to place the hand on; to press, control, etc. with hand ② to examine ③ to stop; to halt; to repress ④ to impeach; to censure ⑤ according to; in (good order); as ⑥ to follow (a map, river, etc.)

按照 **ngon jiu**
　　according to; in accordance with; in conformity with

按摩 **ngon mō**
　　to massage; massage

挖 **waat** (Md **wā**)
① to scoop out; to dig out ② to engrave with knife; to cut or gouge

挖掘 **waat gwaht**
　　to dig; to excavate

挖苦 **waat fú**
　　to ridicule; to make sarcastic remarks

拽 **yaih** (Md **zhuài, zhuāi**)
① to pull; to drag ② to trail; to

drag after

拾 sahp (Md shí)

① to pick up; to collect ② a formal form of the figure "ten" used to prevent fraud in a document or check ③ to go up; to ascend

拾起 sahp héi
to pick up

拾級而上 sahp kāp yìh séuhng
to go up by a flight of steps

挈 kit (Md qiè)

① to help; to assist; to lead ② to rise above; to raise

挈領 kit líhng
to present the main points; to make a summary or a synopsis

挈眷 kit gyun
to travel with one's dependents

拿 (拏) nàh (Md ná)

① to hold in hand; to grasp; to take ② to arrest; to apprehand ③ to use; to employ (a method, device, etc.) ④ (now rare) to be confined or restrained

拿去 nàh heui
Take it! to take away

拿手 nàh sáu
to be particularly good or dexterous at; one's special skill or ability

挪 nòh (Md nuó)

to move; to shift; to transfer

挪用 nòh yuhng
to use money for a purpose not originally intened

挪動 nòh duhng
to move

挺 tíhng (Md tǐng)

① to stand upright; rigidly; rigid ② to pull up ③ unyielding; unbending; tough ④ outstanding; remarkable; eminent; prominent ⑤ to thrust forward (as one's breast)

挺直 tíhng jihk
straight and upright

挺好 tíhng hóu
very good

挨 ngàai (Md āi)

① (to stay) near; next to; close to; to lean to ② to suffer (hunger, beating, etc.); to be beaten ③ to wait; to delay ④ according to order; in good order ⑤ (now rare) to rub; to scratch

挨近 ngàai gahn
near to; to be close to

挨次 ngàai chi
in order; according to order

挫 cho (Md cuò)

① to break; to damage ② to damp; to dent ③ to humiliate; to treat harshly

挫折 cho jit
set back; defeat; failure

挫辱 cho yuhk
to humiliate; to put to shame

振 jan (Md zhèn)

① to arouse to action; to raise ② to pull up; to save; to relieve ③ to shake; to flap as wings ④ to restore order

振動 jan duhng
(in physics) vibration; to vibrate

振興 jan hìng
to promote (industrial endeavor, etc.); to prosper

挲 (挱) sò (Md suō, sha, sa)

to touch; to feel with hands

摩挲 mò sò
to caress, touch, rub, etc. with

the hand; to smooth out creases with the hand

挹 **yāp** (Md **yì**)
① to decant liquids, esp. wine ② to retreat ③ to make place for another

挹注 **yāp jyu**
to supplement; to draw from one to make up the deficits in the other

挹酌 **yāp jeuk**
to pour out wine

挼 **nòh** (Md **ruó, ruá**)
① to crumple (paper into a ball, etc.) ② to stroke; to fondle; to grope for

挼搓 **nòh chō**
to crumple

挼挱 **nòh sò**
to stroke; to fondle; to grope for

挾(挟)**hip, haap**
(Md **xié, jiā**)
① to clasp or hold under the arm ② to embrace; to bosom ③ to presume upon (one's influence, advantage, etc.) ④ to extort; to blackmail to hold (a crown prince, etc.) as hostage

挾嫌 **hip yìhm**
to bear grudge

挾持 **hip chìh**
to blackmail to hold (a crown prince, etc.) as hostage

捃 **kwán** (Md **jùn**)
to pick up; to gather; to collect

捃摭 **kwán jek**
to collect (samples, specimens, etc.)

捃拾 **kwán sahp**
to collect; to gather; to pick up

捆(綑)**kwán** (Md **kǔn**)
① to bind; to tie up ② a bundle

捆綁 **kwán bóng**
to bind; binding (of evil habits; influence; etc.)

捆住 **kwán jyuh**
to tie up

捉 **jūk** (Md **zhuō**)
① to seize; to grasp ② to apprehend; to arrest

捉拿 **jūk nàh**
to apprehend; to arrest

捉賊 **jūk chaahk**
to catch thieves

捋 **lyuht** (Md **luō, lǔ**)
① to pluck; to gather in the fingers ② to pull ③ to squeeze with hand ④ to stroke (one's beard, etc.)

捋虎鬚 **lyuht fú sòu**
(literally) to pluck the tiger's whiskers — to offend the powerful

捋汗 **lyuht hohn**
to be very much embarrassed

捏(揑)**nihp** (Md **niē**)
① to knead; to pinch; to squeeze or press with fingers ② to mold (mud, etc.) ③ to fabricate; to trump up; to slander

捏造 **nihp jouh**
to fabricate (evidence, etc.) to trump up (charges, etc.)

捏詞 **nihp chìh**
lies; slanders

捐 **gyùn** (Md **juān**)
① a tax, duty, charge or due ② to donate; to contribute; to subscribe ③ to buy or purchase (an official rank) ④ to give up (one's life for a cause, etc.); to reject

捐錢 **gyùn chín**
to donate money

捐軀 **gyùn kèui**
to die for one's country or duty

捕 **bouh** (Md **bǔ**)
① to arrest; to apprehend; to catch; to seize ② a policeman (in foreign settlements or concession in old China)

捕捉 **bouh jūk**
to chase or hunt down (a criminal, etc.) to arrest

捕快 **bouh faai**
constables or policemen (in old China)

捌 **baat** (Md **bā**)
an elaborate form of eight — used in checks or accounts to prevent fraud

捍 **hohn, hóhn** (Md **hàn**)
to defend; to guard; to ward off

捍衛 **hohn waih**
to defend (a nation's territory, etc.)

捍禦 **hohn yuh**
to ward off; to guard against

挽 **wáahn** (Md **wǎn**)
① to draw (a bow, etc.); to pull ② to restore ③ to seize ④ to roll up (sleeves, etc.)

挽留 **wáahn làuh**
to request to stay

挽手 **wáahn sáu**
to hold hands; hand in hand

捧 **púng** (Md **pěng**)
① to hold something in both hands; to offer respectfully ② to flatter; to treat as a VIP ③ to support, cheer or render assistance by one's presence

捧腹 **púng fūk**
to hold one's sides with laughter

捧場 **púng chèuhng**
to render support or

assistance, by one's presence, endorsement, etc.

据 **gèui, geui** (Md **jū**)
① sames as 據 (geui), according to ② same as 倨 (gèui), arrogant, haughty ③ used in 拮据 , stiff joints in the hand used most often to describe financial stringency

捨 **sé** (Md **shě**)
① to reject; to give up; to abandon; to relinquish; to renounce; to part with; to forsake; to let go ② to give alms; to give to charity

捨得 **sé dāk**
to be willing to part with (a person, thing, etc.)

捨棄 **sé hei**
to give up or renounce; to relinquish

捩 **liht** (Md **liè**)
① to twist with hands; to turn ② to rip or tear apart

轉捩點 **jyún liht dím**
turning point

捫 (扪) **mùhn** (Md **mén**)
① to feel or touch with hands; to hold ② to search (in one's pocket, etc.)

捫心自問 **mùhn sàm jih mahn**
to examine oneself; introspection

捫舌 **mùhn siht**
to hold the tongue with fingers so that one cannot talk; to hold one's tongue

捭 **báai** (Md **bǎi**)
① to open; to spread out ② to strike with both hands

縱橫捭闔 **jùng wàahng báai hahp**
suave and ingenious persuasion

拼 **pìng** (Md **pīn**)
① to join together; to incorporate; to put together to make a whole ② to spell (a word) ③ to risk; to take chance

拼音 **pìng yàm**
to spell phonetically; to pronounce a word by enunciating the phonetic signs

拼合 **pìng hahp**
to join together

捱 **ngàaih** (Md **ái**)
① to suffer; to endure ② to procrastinate; to put off ③ to rub (shoulders) ④ to draw near; to come close to

捱苦 **ngàaih fú**
to endure hardship

捱不住 **ngàaih bāt jyuh**
cannot endure any more

捲 **gyún** (Md **juǎn**)
① to roll up, to gather; a roll, as egg-rolls ② to curl (hair, etc.); curly (hair)

捲髮 **gyún faat**
to curl hair (at a hair-dresser's etc.); curly hair

捲起 **gyún héi**
to roll up (sleeves, screen, etc.); to cause (an incident, trouble)

捷(捷) **jiht** (Md **jié**)
① to win; to triumph; the prizes of a victory ② swift; quick; rapid ③ a Chinese family name

捷徑 **jiht gìng**
a short cut; a snap course

捷報 **jiht bou**
report of success in examination; war bulletin announcing a victory

捺 **naaht** (Md **nà**)
① to press hard with hands, to press down ② a downstroke slanting toward the right in Chinese calligraphy ③ to repress ④ to stitch

捺攔 **naaht gok**
to delay something intentionally

捺印 **naaht yan**
to press one's thumb-print on a document, etc., in place of signature or chop; a seal or chop

捻 **ním, nihp** (Md **niǎn**)
to pinch or knead with the fingers

捻花 **ním fā**
to pluck flowers

捻手捻脚 **ním sáu ním geuk**
stealthily or clandestinely; to pussyfoot

捽 **jēut, chyut** (Md **zuó**)
① to hold with hands; to seize; to grasp ② to go against; to contradict

捽頸 **jēut géng**
to seize by the throat

捽住頭髮 **jēut jyuh tàuh faat**
to grasp by the hair

掀 **hìn** (Md **xiān**)
① to lift with the hands; to raise up ② to stir; to stir up; to cause to rise

掀動 **hìn duhng**
to raise; to stir up; to instigate

掀起 **hìn héi**
to stir up (a movement, etc.)

掃(扫) **sou** (Md **sǎo, sào**)
① to sweep with broom; to clear away; to clean ② to wipe out; to weed out; to exterminate; to mop up ③ sweepingly, totally ④ to paint (eyebrow, etc.); to doll up ⑤

to cast a quick side-glance ⑥ a broom

掃地 **sou deih**
to sweep the floor; to soil (said of reputation)

掃帚 **sou jáau**
a broom

搶 (抢) **lèuhn** (Md **lūn, lún**)

① to select; to choose ② to turn or spin with hands or arms; to swing

搶元 **lèuhn yùhn**
to come out first in examinations

搶刀 **lèuhn dòu**
to swing a knife (at somebody)

掂 **dìm** (Md **diān**)

to estimate the weight of something by weighing it with hands

掂算 **dìm syun**
to consider; to ponder; to estimate; to weigh

掂對 **dìm deui**
to weigh and consider (situation, atternatives, etc.)

掇 **jyut** (Md **duō**)

① to collect; to gather ② to plagiarize; to pirate ③ to select; to pluck

掇拾 **jyut sahp**
to collect; to select

掇採 **jyut chói**
to gather; to select; to pluck

授 **sauh** (Md **shòu**)

① to give; to hand over to; to confer (a degree, prize, etc.) ② to teach; to tutor ③ to give up (life, etc.)

授課 **sauh fo**
to teach; to tutor

授權 **sauh kyùhn**
to authorize; to delegate powers

掉 **diuh** (Md **diào**)

① to turn; to move; to shake; to wag (tail, etc.) ② to fall ③ to change; to substitute

掉換 **diuh wuhn**
to change; to exchange; to invert; to substitute

掉下來 **diuh hah lòih**
to fall down

掊 **pàuh** (Md **pǒu**)

① to strike; to cut; to break ② to exact; to collect (taxes)

掊擊 **pàuh gīk**
to strike; to break

掊斂 **pàuh líhm**
to exact high taxes from people

掐 **haap** (Md **qiā**)

① to dig the nail into ② to pluck; to cut with finger-nails to nip; to pinch ③ to hold; to grasp

掐斷 **haap tyúhn**
to break; to nip

掐住 **haap jyuh**
to seize; to grasp; to hold

排 **pàaih** (Md **pái, pǎi**)

① a row; a line; a rank; to fall in line ② (in military) a platoon ③ to push; to clear out ④ to reject; to expel

排隊 **pàaih déui**
to fall in line or formation; to line up; to stand in a queue

排長 **pàaih jéung**
a platoon leader

掖 **yihk** (Md **yè, yē**)

① to support another; to extend a helping hand ② armpits ③ side; by the side ④ side-apartments in the palace ⑤ to conceal; to hide (something) ⑥ to fold; to roll up (part of one's clothing)

掖門 yihk mùhn
a small side-door of the palace

掖掖蓋蓋 yihk yihk koi koi
steathily; clandestinely afraid that others may discover the things one's trying to hide

掘 gwaht (Md juĕ)
to dig; to excavate; to make a hole or cave

掘金 gwaht gām
to dig for gold; golddigging

掘穿 gwaht chyùn
to dig through

掙(挣) jàng (Md zhèng, zhēng)
① to make efforts; to strive ② to get free from ③ to struggle (for one's life etc.) ④ to earn (money etc.)

掙脫 jàng tyut
to break away with force; shake off

掙錢 jàng chìn
to earn money

掛(挂) gwa (Md guà)
① to hang up; to suspend; suspense ② to worry; to think of, anxious ③ with one's name registered or listed; recorded

掛念 gwa nihm
to think of; to be anxious about; to worry about; to be on one's mind

掛號信 gwa houh seun
a registered letter

掠 leuhk (Md luè)
① to take by force; to rob; to plunder ② to brush; to pass lightly on the side ③ to whip; to flog ④ a long stroke to the left in Chinese calligraphy

掠取 leuhk chéui
to take by force; to rob

掠過 leuhk gwo
to sideswipe; to fly past; (of airplanes) to buzz

採 chói (Md cǎi)
① to pluck; (flowers, etc.); to gather; to collect ② to select; to pick ③ (now rare) to drag ④ (now rare) to beckon; to take notice of

採訪 chói fóng
to cover (a news item or story)

採集 chói jaahp
to gather (samples, etc.); to collect

探 taam (Md tàn)
① to find; to search; to locate; to prospect; to feel (in a pocket or bag) ② to watch; to spy; a spy; a detective; to investigate; a secret agent ③ to try; to venture; to tempt ④ to stick out ⑤ to explore ⑥ to visit; to inquire about

探病 taam behng
to visit the sick

探究 taam gau
to investigate; to probe

接 jip (Md jiē)
① to receive; to accept; to take with the hand ② to welcome ③ to join; to connect; to graft; to make contract with ④ to succeed to

接待 jip doih
to receive (a guest); reception

接合 jip hahp
to connect; to assemble

控 hung (Md kòng)
① to accuse; to charge; to use ② to control; control ③ to draw (a bow) ④ (now rare) to throw; to hit

控告 hung gou
to sue somebody in court; to

accuse

控制 **hung jai**
to control; control

措 **chou** (Md **cuò**)
① to place ② to collect; to arrange; to manage ③ to abondon; to renounce ④ to make preparation for an undertaking

措施 **chou sì**
a (political, financial, etc.) measure

措手不及 **chou sáu bāt kahp**
to be caught unawares or unprepared; to be taken by surprise

推 **tèui** (Md **tuī**)
① to push ② to look into; to find out; to ponder; to infer; to deduce ③ to shirk (responsibility; etc.); to refuse ④ to elect; to recommend; to praise; to esteem ⑤ to move along; to change in succession (as seasons) ⑥ to extend; to enlarge

推動 **tèui duhng**
to push (a sales project, etc.); to land impetus to (a movement, etc.)

推辭 **tèui chìh**
to decline (an offer; invitation, etc.) to reject

掩(揜) **yím** (Md **yǎn**)
① to cover; to conceal; to cover up; to shut

掩蔽 **yím bai**
to cover; to conceal; to take cover

掩飾 **yím sīk**
to cover (a lie, error; etc.) to conceal (the truth, etc.)

捐 **kìhn** (Md **qián**)
to bear load on the shoulder

捐客 **kìhn haak**
a broker

掬 **gūk** (Md **jū**)
to hold in both hands

掬水 **gūk séui**
to scoop up water with the hands

掌 **jéung** (Md **zhǎng**)
① palm of the hand; sole of the foot; paw of an animal ② to slap with hand ③ to have charge of; to supervise; to control ④ a Chinese family name

掌管 **jéung gún**
to take charge of; to supervise; to manage

掌故 **jéung gu**
historical anecdotes or records; national legends; national institutions

掣 **jai** (Md **chè**)
① to pull; to drag ② to hinder; to snatch away

掣肘 **jai jáau**
to impede another from doing work

掣電 **jai dihn**
at the twinkle of an eye; as fast as lightning

掏(搯) **tòuh** (Md **tāo**)
to take out; to pull out; to dredge

掏腰包 **tòuh yìu bāau**
to spend one's own money; to shell out

掏井 **tòuh jéng**
to dredge a well

拽(抻) **chán** (Md **chēn**)
① to lengthen and extenuate — as in making noodles ② to drag out

拽麵 **chán mihn**
to make noodles by lengthening and extenuating dough

拵練 **chán lihn**
to embarras someone by making him solve a difficult problem or answer a tough question

捶(搥) **chèuih**
(Md **chuí**)
to beat; to thrash

捶鍊 **chèuih lihn**
to submit to strict disciplinary training

捶平 **chèuih pìhng**
to flatten by pounding

揶 **yèh** (Md **yé**)
to jeer at; to ridicule; to play joke on

揶揄 **yèh yùh**
to ridicule; to jeer at; to play joke on

揀(拣) **gáan** (Md **jiǎn**)
① to select; to choose; to pick ② to pick up (something another has left behind, etc.)

揀選 **gáan syún**
to choose; to select; to pick

揀別 **gáan biht**
to distinguish; to tell one thing from another

揄 **yùh** (Md **yú**)
① to draw out; to scoop out (grain from a mortar) ② to praise; to show the merits of ③ to hang

揄揚 **yùh yèuhng**
to praise

揄袂 **yùh maih**
to walk with hands hanging motionless in sleeves

揆 **kwàih, kwáih**
(Md **kuí**)
① to survey and weigh; to consider; to investigate; to estimate ② premier; prime minister

揆測 **kwàih chāk**
to culculate or guess; to estimate

英揆 **Yīng kwàih**
the Prime minister of England

揉 **yàuh** (Md **róu**)
① to rub ② to crumble by hand ③ to massage ④ to subdue; to make smooth or peaceful ⑤ mixed-up; confused

揉合 **yàuh hahp**
to combine; to blend; to merge; to incorporate

揉雜 **yàuh jaahp**
mixed up

揎 **syùn** (Md **xuān**)
① to pull up the sleeves and show the arms ② to fight with bare hands

揎拳捋袖 **syùn kyùhn lyuht jauh**
to pull up the sleeves — to get ready to work or fight

描 **mìuh** (Md **miáo**)
① to trace; to draw; to sketch ② to describe; to depict

描寫 **mìuh sé**
to describe; to depict; to portray

描繪 **mìuh kwúi**
to paint; to sketch; to depict; to describe

提 **tàih** (Md **tí, dī**)
① to lift by hand; to pull up; to raise; to arouse ② to cause to rise or happen ③ to mention; to bring forward; to suggest; to table (a motion, etc.) ④ to obtain; to make dilivery ⑤ to manage; to control ⑥ a Chinese family name

提包 **tàih bāau**
a hang bag

提醒 **tàih síng**
to remind

插 chaap (Md chā)
① to insert; to stick into ② to plant ③ to take part in

插頭 chaap tàuh
a plug

插手 chaap sáu
to take part in; to meddle

揖 yāp (Md yī)
① to bow with hands folding in front ② to yield politely; to defer to

揖拜 yāp baai
to make a bow with the hands folding in front (usually during greeting or parting

揖謝 yāp jeh
to bow in thanks

揚(扬、敭) yèuhng (Md yáng)
① to raise ② to praise; to acclaim ③ to display; to expose; to make evident ④ high or raised (voice, cry, etc.) ⑤ to scatter; to spread ⑥ to stir; to get excited ⑦ a Chinese family name

揚棄 yèuhng hei
to discard; to renounce

揚聲 yèuhng sìng
to raise one's voice; to boast prestige

換 wuhn (Md huàn)
① to exchange; to change ② to alter; to substitute

換錢 wuhn chín
to change money (into small changes); to convert one currency to another; to barter goods for money

換言之 wuhn yìhn jì
in other words

揠 ngaat (Md yà)
to pull up or out

揠苗助長 ngaat mìuh joh jéung
(literally) to pull up the seedling hoping to make it grow faster — a stupid and self-defeating effort

握 ngāak (Md wò)
① to hold fast; to grasp; to grip ② a handful

握筆 ngāak bāt
to hold a pen

握別 ngāak biht
to part; to shake hands in parting; to say good-bye

揣 chyún (Md chuǎi, chuāi, chuài)
① to measure; to weigh; to estimate ② to try; to probe (for possibilities); to put out a feeler

揣測 chyún chāk
to conjecture; to fathom; to speculate; to make an intelligent guess

揣摩 chyún mō
to study; to learn; to ponder; to examine; to assume; to speculate; to guess

揩 hàai (Md kāi)
to wipe; to scrub; to rub; to dust; to clean

揩面 hàai mihn
to wipe the face

揩油 hàai yáu
to make some (usually small) outside gain not included in a deal; to report a purchase at blown-up price (so that one gets the difference); (said of a male) to caress or touch a woman without her knowledge or when she is unable or inconvenient to offer resistence

揪 **jàu** (Md **jiū**)
to clutch; to grasp with hand

揪扭 **jàu náu**
to seize by hand; to grapple

揪住 **jàu jyuh**
to seize or grasp (somebody) with force

揭 **kit** (Md **jiē**)
① to lift up or off; to raise high ② to unveil uncover or unearth; to expose ③ to announce; to publicize ④ a Chinese family name

揭曉 **kit híu**
to make public; to announce

揭幕 **kit mohk**
to raise curtain (of a meeting, exhibition, etc.)

揮(挥) **fài** (Md **huī**)
① to wield (a sword, pen, etc.); to move; to shake ② to direct (troops) ③ to wipe away (sweat, tears, etc.) ④ to scatter; to sprinkle ⑤ to squander (money, etc.) ⑥ to swing

揮兵 **fài bìng**
to march troops to war

揮手 **fài sáu**
to wave one's hand (in greeting or bidding farewell)

援 **wùhn** (Md **yuán**)
① to lead ② to take hold of ③ to aid; to help; reinforcement; to rescue ④ to invoke (a law, precedence, etc.)

援助 **wùhn joh**
to aid; aid; to help

援救 **wùhn gau**
to rescue; to come to the aid of

揸(攎、戲) **jà** (Md **zhā**)
to pick up with fingers

揍 **jau** (Md **zòu**)
① to beat; to slug (somebody); to hit hard ② to break (a glass, etc.)

揍人 **jau yàhn**
to slug a person

揍一頓 **jau yāt deuhn**
to give a sound beating

揹 **bui** (Md **bēi**)
to carry on the back; to shoulder (a load; responsibility, etc.)

揹包袱 **bui bàau fuhk**
to carry a fordel on the back; to carry a burden

揹黑鍋 **bui hāk wō**
to be made the scapegoat for somebody; to take blame for somebody

搜 **sáu** (Md **sōu**)
① to search; to seek ② to inquire into; to investigate

搜查 **sáu chàh**
to search (a house, a person, etc.)

搜集 **sáu jaahp**
to seek and gather; to collect (rare stamps, books, data, evidence against a suspect, etc.)

搥(捶) **chèuih** (Md **chuí**)
to pound; to beat; to strike with a stick or fist

搥打 **chèuih dá**
to pound with fist; to beat

搥鼓 **chèuih gú**
to beat a drum

搓 **chò** (Md **cuō**)
① to rub hands; to rub between the hands ② to twist (a thread, etc.) between the hands

搓弄 **chò luhng**
to rub

搓麻將 **chò màh jeung**
to play mahjong

損 (损)**syún** (Md **sǔn**)
① to damage; to injure; to destroy ② to lose; loss ③ to reduce ④ weak; emaciated ⑤ to ridicules; to jeer at ⑥ wicked and mean; cruel ⑦ (in chinese medicine) a long-term emaciation

損失 **syún sāt**
losses; casualties

損害 **syún hoih**
to cause damage or loss; to injure; damages or losses

推 **kok** (Md **què**)
① to knock; to strike ② to discuss; to negotiate; to consult

推商 **kok sèung**
to consult; to discuss; consultation; discussion

捵 **chí, chàai** (Md **chuāi**)
① to conceal something in the bosom ② to knead (dough)

捵麭 **chí mihn**
to knead dough

捵在懷裏**chí joih wàaih léuih**
to carry or hold in the bosom

搵 **wan, wán** (Md **wèn**)
① to wipe off (tears) ② to press with fingers

搵鈴 **wan lìhng**
to press the bell

搊 **chàu** (Md **chōu**)
① to pluck stringed instruments with fingers ② to tighten ③ to hold and support

搏 **bok** (Md **bó**)
① to grasp; to seize; to spring upon ② to catch; to arrest ③ to strike; to box; to engage in a hand-to-hand combat

搏擊 **bok gīk**
to strike; to fight with hands

搏鬥 **bok dau**
to box; to engage in hand-to-hand combat

搔 **sòu** (Md **sāo**)
① to scratch lightly ② to irritate; to annoy

搔首 **sòu sáu**
to scatch one's head in perplexity, etc.

搔擾 **sòu yíu**
to annoy; to harass; to cause disturbances

搗(捣、擣)**dóu**
(Md **dǎo**)
① to thresh (grains); to hull or unhusk ② to beat; to pound ③ to attack ④ to sabotage

搗亂 **dóu lyuhn**
to cause disturbance; to sabotage; to make trouble

搗碎 **dóu seui**
to pound to pieces

搖 **yìuh** (Md **yáo**)
① to shake (the head, etc.); to toss ② to wave (flags; etc.); to sway, wobble ③ to scull; to row (a boat, etc.) ④ to agitate; to incite; to annoy

搖動 **yìuh duhng**
to shake; to rattle

搖籃 **yìuh làahm**
a cradle

搢 **jeun** (Md **jìn**)
① to stick into ② to shake

搢紳 **jeun sàn**
the gentry; the official class

搢笏 **jeun fāt**
to stick the official tablet into the girdle

搦 **nĭk** (Md **nuò**)

① to hold; to seize ② to challenge ③ to incite ④ to suppress

搦管 **nĭk gún**
to hold a pen to write

搦戰 **nĭk jin**
to challenge to battle

搧 **sin** (Md **shān**)

① to fan ② to stir up; to incite ③ to slap on the face

搧風 **sin fùng**
to fan

搧動 **sin duhng**
to stir up; to incite; to agitate

搨 **taap** (Md **tà**)

① to take rubbing of an inscription on stone, etc. ② to make an exact copy with paper and writing brush

搨本 **taap bún**
a rubbing

搨碑 **taap bèi**
to take a rubbing of an inscription on a stone tablet

搪 **tóng, tòhng**
(Md **táng**)

to ward off; to parry; to keep out (rain, wind, cold, etc.)

搪塞 **tóng sāk**
to perform a task perfunctorily or for form's sake

搪瓷 **tóng chìh**
enamel; enamel ware

搬 **bùn** (Md **bān**)

to move; to transport

搬家 **bùn gà**
to move from one dwelling to another; to change residence

搬運 **bùn wahn**
to move; to transport

搭 **daap** (Md **dā**)

① to attach to; to join together; to add to; to mix with ② to raise; to build (a shed, etc.); to pitch (a tent, etc.) ③ to take (a passage on bus, train, boat, etc.) ④ to help; to rescue ⑤ a short garment; a cover

搭客 **daap haak**
passengers (of bus train, boat, plane, etc.); to take passengers

搭擋 **daap dong**
a partner

搶 (抢) **chéung**
(Md **qiǎng**)

① to take by force; to snatch; to rob ② to try to beat others in speed of performance; to do something in haste, as in emergency ③ to oppose; to ruffle

搶掠 **chéung leuhk**
to rob; to loot; to plunder; robbery; looting

搶先 **chéung sìn**
to rush ahead; to try to be the first; to try to beat others in performing something

榨 (榨) **ja** (Md **zhà**)

to press (for juice or oil); to extract

榨油 **ja yàuh**
to press (soybean, peanut, etc.) for oil

榨果汁 **ja gwó jāp**
to press or squeeze fruit for juice

搽 **chàh** (Md **chá**)

to rub on (ointment, etc.); to smear; to anoint; to paint

搽粉 **chàh fán**
to powder (the face)

搽藥 **chàh yeuhk**
to rub on some external medicine, ointment, etc.

搴 **hìn** (Md **qiān**)
to pull or pluck up

搴旗斬將 **hìn kèih jáam jeung**
(literally) to pull up the enemy flag and kill the opposing general — to defeat the enemy decisively

搐 **chūk** (Md **chù, chōu**)
spasm; cramp; convulsions; to shake involuntarily

抽搐 **chàu chūk**
to shake involuntarily

搞 **gáau** (Md **gǎo**)
to stir up; to cause trouble; to do mischief

搞鬼 **gáau gwái**
(said of a person) to cause trouble or pull legs in secret

搞清楚 **gáau chìng chó**
to make clear; to clarify (a matter, etc.)

摁 **on** (Md **èn**)
① to press (a door-bell, etc.) ② to delay or hold

搠 **sok** (Md **shuò**)
① to thrust (at one's enemy) ② to smear; to daub

搌 **jín** (Md **zhǎn**)
① to bind ② to wipe; to mop

搌布 **jín bou**
mopping cloth

搗 (捂) **wú** (Md **wǔ**)
① to cover; to conceal; to hide ② to put into an air-tight container (in cooking)

搗蓋 **wú koi**
to cover up; to hide; to disguise; to masquerade

搗不住 **wú bāt jyuh**
cannot be covered or concealed

搆 (構) **gau** (Md **gòu**)
① to pull; to drag ② to reach ③ to implicate ④ to make (war, peace, etc.); to bring (disaster, grudge, etc.); to incur (animosity, etc.)

搆兵 **gau bìng**
to be at war or on the warpath

搆和 **gau wòh**
to make negotiate for peace

摘 **jaahk** (Md **zhāi**)
① to take off (one's hat, etc.); to pluck; to pick ② to choose; to select ③ to jot down (notes) ④ to expose; to unevil (a conspiracy, etc.)

摘要 **jaahk yiu**
to make an epitome; an epitome

摘花 **jaahk fā**
to pluck flowers

摑 (掴) **gwaak**
(Md **guāi, guó**)
to slap another on his face; to box

摔 **sēut** (Md **shuāi**)
① to throw to the ground ② to get rid of; to shake off (a tail, etc.) ③ to fall down

摔角 **sēut gok**
to wrestle; wrestling

摔傷 **sēut sèung**
to get hurt in a fall

摜 (掼) **gwaan**
(Md **guàn**)
① to throw on the ground ② to be accustomed or used to

摜交 **gwaan gàau**
to wrestle; wrestling

摟 (搂) **láuh** (Md **lǒu, lōu**)
① to drag; to pull ② to exact ③ to scrape (money, etc.); to collect

④ to monopolize ⑤ to hold in arms; to embrace; to hug

摟算 **láuh syun**
to calculate; to audit

摟攬 **láuh láahm**
to monopolize (a project, business)

摟抱 **láuh póuh**
to embrace

摧 **chèui** (Md **cuī**)
① to break; to smash; to destroy; to injure; to harm ② to damp; to dent ③ to cause to cease ④ to be sad and sorrowful; to grieve

摧毀 **chèui wái**
to destroy (enemy positions, heavy weapons, etc.)

摧殘 **chèui chàahn**
to destroy; to humilate

摭 **jek** (Md **zhí**)
to pick up from the ground; to take up; to collect

摭取 **jek chéui**
to pick up from the ground; to take up; to collect

摭採 **jek chói**
to collect

摳 (抠) **kàu** (Md **kōu**)
① to raise ② to feel for ③ to inquire into ④ to dig with fingers ⑤ to be stingy ⑥ to throw at

摳破 **kàu po**
to damage or injure by scrutching

摳得緊 **kàu dāk gán**
to be very stingy

摶 (抟) **tyùhn**
(Md **tuán**)
① to roll round with the hand ② to rely on ③ to take or follow (a trail, etc.)

摶飯 **tyùhn faahn**
to roll rice ball

摶風 **tyùhn fùng**
(literally) to ride on the wind — to rise very quickly

摸 **mó, mòuh** (Md **mō, mó**)
① to feel or touch lightly with finger; to caress ② to grope

摸不清 **mó bāt chìng**
do not quite understand; not quite sure

摸彩 **mó chói**
to draw lot to determine the prize winners in a raffle or lottery

摺 **jip** (Md **zhé**)
① to fold (paper, etc.); to plait ② curved and winding ③ to pull and break

摺扇 **jip sin**
a folding fan

摺痕 **jip hàhn**
a line made by a folding

摽 **piu** (Md **biào**)
① to fall; falling ② the razor of a sword ③ high; lofty ④ to throw out; to push

摽末 **piu muht**
the edge of a sword

摽梅 **piu mùih**
(said of girls) marriageable age

摒 **bing** (Md **bìng**)
① to get rid of; to expel ② to arrange in order

摒棄 **bing hei**
to abandon; to get rid of

摒除 **bing chèuih**
to get rid of; to renounce (bad habits, evil thoughts, etc.)

撂 **liu** (Md **liào**)
to put down; to lay down

撂下 **liu hah**
to put down; to lay down; to

leave behind; to be survived by

摺手 **lìu sáu**
to pocket one's hands; to have nothing to do with it, to give up

摩 **mò** (Md **mó, mā**)
① to chafe; to scour; to rub ② friction ③ to squeeze past ④ to feel with the hand; to massage ⑤ (now rare) to work and encourage each other (esp. in study)

摩登 **mò dàng**
morden; fashionable

摩擦力 **mò chaat lihk**
friction

摯(挚) **ji** (Md **zhì**)
① sincere; cordial ② a Chinese family name

摯友 **ji yáuh**
bosom friend

眞摯 **jàn ji**
sincere; cordial

摹 **mòuh** (Md **mó**)
① to copy; to make an exact copy ② to model or pattern after; to imitate

摹仿 **mòuh fóng**
to copy; to model or pattern after; to imitate; to ape

摹臨 **mòuh làhm**
(in art and calligraphy) to copy or imitate the works of ancient masters

撇 **pit** (Md **piē, piě**)
① to cast away; to throw away; to discard; to abandon ② to skim off ③ (in calligraphy) a stroke made in the lower left direction

撇開 **pit hòi**
to dismiss or exclude (from discussion or consideration); to set aside

一撇 **yāt pit**
(in calligraphy) a stroke made in the lower left direction

撳(搇、揿) **gahm**
(Md **qìn**)
to press with hand

撳鈴 **gahm lìhng**
to push a bell

撳壓 **gahm ngaat**
to press down; to push down

撥(拨) **buht** (Md **bō**)
① to dispel; to remove ② to move; to transfer ③ to distribute; to issue ④ to set aside; to set apart; to appropriate ⑤ to stir up, or arouse (disputes, etc.)

撥開 **buht hòi**
to push aside

撥欵 **buht fún**
to issue or appropriate funds; an appropriation

撅 **kyut** (Md **juē**)
① to break; to snap ② to stick up; to protrude

撅嘴 **kyut jéui**
to protrude the lips (in displeasure); to pout

撅豎小人 **kyut syuh síu yàhn**
a mean fellow

撈(捞) **làauh, lòuh, lòu** (Md **lāo**)
to pull or drag out of the water; to fish up; to salvage

撈起 **làauh héi**
to recover from water, river bed, sea bottom, etc.

撈什子 **lòuh jaahp jí**
a disgusting thing

撏(挦) **chàhm**
(Md **xián**)
to take; to pick; to pluck

撦搋 **chàhm ché**
　　to pick here and there

撐（撑）**chàang**
(Md chēng)
① to prop up; to support ② to pole or punt (a raft or a boat)

撐船 **chàang syùhn**
　　to pole or punt a boat

撐竿跳 **chàang gòn tiu**
　　pole vault

撒 **saat (Md sā, sǎ)**
① to relax; to ease ② to loosen; to unleash ③ to exhibit; to display; to show ④ to scatter; to sprinkle; to disperse

撒旦 **Saat daahn**
　　Satan

撒種 **saat júng**
　　to sow seeds

撓（挠）**nàauh (Md náo)**
① to bend; to daunt; to subjugate ② to scratch; to rub

撓折 **nàauh jit**
　　to bend and break

撓鈎 **nàauh ngàu**
　　a hook with a long handle used in fire fighting; name of an ancient weapon

撕 **sì (Md sī)**
　　to tear; to rip

撕破 **sì po**
　　to tear; to rip

撕票 **sì piu**
　　to kill a hostage

撙 **jyún (Md zǔn)**
① to comply with ② to economize

撙節 **jyún jit**
　　to follow rule and order; to restrain; to exercise self restrain; to economize

撙省 **jyún sáang**
　　to economize

撚 **nán, nín (Md niǎn)**
　　to twist with fingers; to toy with

撚鬚 **nán sòu**
　　to toy with one's beard

撚錢 **nán chín**
　　to spin a coin (for amusement, etc.)

撞 **johng (Md zhuàng)**
　　to bump

撞倒 **johng dóu**
　　to knock down by bumping

撞騙 **johng pin**
　　to swindle

撤 **chit (Md chè)**
　　to remove; to withdraw; to take back

撤兵 **chit bìng**
　　to withdraw troops

撤銷 **chit sìu**
　　to abolish; to do away with

撩 **lìuh (Md liāo, liáo)**
① to provoke; to excite; to stir up ② disorderly; confused ③ to raise

撩撥 **lìuh buht**
　　to provoke; to entice

撩亂 **lìuh lyuhn**
　　confused; disorderly

撫（抚）**fú (Md fǔ)**
① to stroke; to touch ② to soothe; to comfort; to console; to relieve ③ to bring up; to rear

撫摸 **fú mó**
　　to pass one's hand over; to feel; to stroke

撫恤 **fú sēut**
　　to relieve

撬 **hiu, giuh (Md qiào)**
　　to raise; to lift; to pry

撬門 **giuh mùhn**
to pry the door open

播 **bo** (Md **bō**)
① to sow ② to spread; to propagate ③ to move ④ to cast away; to abandon

播種 **bo júng**
to sow seeds; to sow; to seed

播音 **bo yàm**
to make broadcast

撲 (扑) **pok** (Md **pū**)
to pat; to beat; to strike; to pound; to dash; to smash

撲滅 **pok miht**
to exterminate (vermino); to extinguish (a fire)

撲滿 **pok múhn**
a savings box; a piggy bank

撮 **chyut** (Md **cuō, zuǒ**)
① a very small amount; a pinch ② to take with fingers; to pinch; to gather

撮合 **chyut hahp**
to bring (two persons or parties) together; to make a match

撮要 **chyut yiu**
to select what is important

撰 **jaan** (Md **zhuàn**)
to write; to compose

撰寫 **jaan sé**
to write or compose (usually light works)

撰述 **jaan seuht**
to write an account of (facts, happenings, etc.) to narrate

撢 (撣、撢) **daahn, sihn** (Md **dǎn, shàn**)
① to dust ② a duster

撢灰 **daahn fùi**
to brush off dust; to dust

撢子 **daahn jí**
a duster

撻 (挞) **taat** (Md **tà**)
to strike; to chastise

撻伐 **taat faht**
to send troops to punish; to launch a private expedition

撻辱 **taat yuhk**
to beat and disgrace

擒 **kàhm** (Md **qín**)
to arrest; to capture

擒拿 **kàhm nàh**
to arrest; to capture

擒住 **kàhm jyuh**
to succeed in capturing

攜 (攜、携、擕) **kwàih** (Md **xié**)
to take; to carry; to lend

攜帶 **kwàih daai**
to carry with oneself

攜眷 **kwàih gyun**
to take one's family along

擎 **kìhng** (Md **qíng**)
to lift; to support

擎起 **kìhng héi**
to lift up

擎天神 **kìhng tìn sàhn**
Atlas

撼 **hahm** (Md **hàn**)
to shake; to rock; to jolt; to joggle

撼動 **hahm duhng**
to shake; to rock

撼搖 **hahm yìuh**
to shake; to rock; to jolt; to joggle

擄 (掳) **lóuh** (Md **lǔ**)
to capture; to take captive

擄掠 **lóuh leuhk**
to plunder; to rob; to pillage

擄獲 **lóuh wohk**
to capture; to take captive

擁(拥)**yúng** (Md **yōng**)
① to hug; to embrace; to hold ② to have; to possess ③ to crowd; to throng; to clog ④ to follow; to support

擁抱 **yúng póuh**
to embrace; to hug; to hold in one's arms

擁擠 **yúng jài**
crowded; packed

擂 **lèuih** (Md **léi, lèi, lēi**)
① to grind ② to beat

擂鼓 **lèuih gú**
to beat a drum

擂臺 **lèuih tòih**
a platform for contests in martial arts

擅 **sihn** (Md **shàn**)
① unauthorized; unilateral; arbitrary ② to monopolize; to take exclusive possession

擅長 **sihn chèuhng**
to excel in; to be good at

擅作主張 **sihn jok jyú jèung**
to make a unilateral or arbitrary decision

擇(择)**jaahk** (Md **zé, zhái**)
to select; to choose; to pick out

擇偶 **jaahk ngáuh**
to select a spouse or mate

選擇 **syún jaahk**
to select; to choose; to pick out

擋(挡、攩)**dóng, dong** (Md **dǎng, dàng**)
to obstruct; to impede; to stop; to resist; to ward off

擋風 **dóng fùng**
to keep winds away; to keep off winds

擋住 **dóng jyuh**
to block; to impede; to hinder; to obstruct

擓(㧟)**kwáaih** (Md **kuǎi**)
① to scratch (lightly) ② to carry on the arm

擓破 **kwáaih po**
to break by scratching

擓籃子 **kwáaih làahm jí**
to carry a basket on the arm

操 **chòu** (Md **cāo**)
① to handle; to manage; to manipulate; to control ② to hold ③ to exercise; to drill

操縱 **chòu jung**
to manage, control or manipulate (activities, people, etc.)

操練 **chòu lihn**
to drill (in military sense)

擗 **pīk** (Md **pǐ**)
to beat the breast

擗踊 **pīk yúng**
to beat the breast and stamp the feet in great grief

據(据)**geui** (Md **jù**)
① according to; on the basis of ② to occupy; to take possession of ③ proof; evidence

據說 **geui syut**
according to hearsay; It is said that . . .

據點 **geui dím**
a base (for an operation or activity)

擀 **gón** (Md **gǎn**)
to stretch out with a rolling pin

擀麵 **gón mihn**
　to roll dough

擀麵杖 **gón mihn jeuhng**
　a rolling pin

擊(击) **gīk** (Md **jī**)
to beat; to strike; to attack

擊倒 **gīk dóu**
　to knock down; to floor

擊敗 **gīk baaih**
　to defeat; to beat; to conquer

撾(挝) **jà, gwō**
(Md **zhuā, wō**)
to beat; to strike

撾鼓 **jà gú**
　to beat a drum

老撾 **Lóuh gwō**
　Laos

擘 **maak** (Md **bò**)
① the thumb ② to split; to tear apart

擘開 **maak hòi**
　to open (hard-rinded fruit)

擘畫 **maak waahk**
　to plan; to scheme; to make arrangements for

擐 **gwaan** (Md **huàn**)
to put on; to wear

擐甲執兵 **gwaan gaap jāp bìng**
　to put on one's armor and take up arms

撿(捡) **gím** (Md **jiǎn**)
to pick up; to collect

撿起 **gím héi**
　to pick up (from the ground or floor)

撿破爛 **gím po laahn**
　to collect scrap

擔 **daam, dàam**
(Md **dàn, dān**)
same as '担', see 'hand' radical

擯(摈) **ban** (Md **bìn**)
① to expel; to reject; to oust ② an usher (same as 儐)

擯除 **ban chèuih**
　to expel; to oust; to eliminate

擯介 **ban gaai**
　a person serving to bridge the gap between the host and the guest

擠(挤) **jài** (Md **jǐ**)
to crowd; to throng; to push; to squeeze

擠滿 **jài múhn**
　to pack (a place, car, etc.) to capacity

擠提 **jài tàih**
　a run on a bank

擢 **johk** (Md **zhuó**)
to pull out; to pick out; to select

擢升 **johk sìng**
　to promote (an official, etc.)

擢用 **johk yuhng**
　to pick and promote (promising employees or subordinates)

擦 **chaat** (Md **cā**)
to wipe; to rub; to polish

擦亮 **chaat leuhng**
　to shine (shoes, utensils, etc.)

擦去 **chaat heui**
　to wipe off

擰(拧) **nihng, nìhng**
(Md **nǐng, níng**)
① to wrench ② determined; dogged; stubborn ③ to twist; to pinch

擰開 **nihng hòi**
　to wrench apart

擰眉瞪眼 **nìhng mèih dàng ngáahn**
　to look angry

擬(拟) yíh (Md nǐ)
① to plan; to intend; to propose; to decide; to determine ② to imitate

擬定 yíh dihng
to draw up or map out (a plan)

擬稿 yíh góu
to prepare manuscripts or write copies (for publication)

擱(搁) gok (Md gē, gé)
to lay; to put; to delay; to put aside; to neglect

擱置 gok ji
to shelve or pigeonhole (a plan, proposal, etc.)

擱淺 gok chín
to run aground; to get stranded

擤(揸) sang (Md xǐng)
to blow (the nose)

擤涕鼻 sang beih tai
to blow the nose

擲(掷) jaahk (Md zhì, zhī)
to throw; to cast

擲還 jaahk wàahn
to return (a thing); please return . . . to me

擲骰子 jaahk sik jí
to cast dice; to throw dice

擴(扩) kwok, kong (Md kuò)
to enlarge; to magnify; to expand

擴大 kwok daaih
to enlarge; to expand; to swell; to distend; to dilate; to magnify

擴張 kwok jèung
to stretch; to extend; to spread; to expand

擷(撷) kit, git (Md xié)
to pick; to collect; to gather

擷芳 kit fòng
to pick flowers

擷采 kit chói
to cull; to pick; to gather

擺(摆) báai (Md bǎi)
① to arrange; to display; to place; to put ② to wave; to swing; to oscillate; to wag

擺開 báai hòi
to arrange; to place for display

擺動 báai duhng
to swing; to oscillate

擻(擞) sáu (Md sòu, sǒu)
to shake; to quake

抖擻 dáu sáu
to exhaust one's means; to expose another's secrets ③ to catch cold

擾(扰) yíu (Md rǎo)
to disturb; to agitate; to harass

擾亂 yíu lyuhn
to disturb or to agitate; to harass (enemy troops)

擾攘 yíu yeuhng
disturbance

攆(撵) líhn, lihm (Md niǎn)
to expel; to oust; to drive

攆出去 líhn chēut heui
to throw (someone) away

攆走 líhn jáu
to drive (someone) away

攄(摅) syù (Md shū)
to make known; to vent

攄憤 syù fáhn
to vent one's indignation

攄陳 syù chàhn
to present (a proposal, an opinion, etc.)

攀 **pàan** (Md **pān**)
① to hold to; to climb; to hang on ② to involve

攀登 **pàan dàng**
to climb; to scale

攀談 **pàan tàahm**
to strike up a conversation; to drag another into conversation

攏(拢) **lúhng** (Md **lǒng**)
① to gather; to collect ② to lean ③ a special fingering in playing the lute

攏統 **lúhng túng**
vague; general; lacking details

攏岸 **lúhng ngohn**
to approach shore (said of a ship)

攖(撄) **yìng** (Md **yīng**)
① to offend ② to disturb; to stir up

攖其鋒 **yìng kèih fùng**
to blunt the thrust (of an attacking force)

攖人心 **yìng yàhn sàm**
to disturb peace of mind

攔(拦) **làahn** (Md **lán**)
to impede; to obstruct; to hinder; to block

攔截 **làahn jiht**
to intercept; to attack or stop on the way

攔擋 **làahn dóng**
to impede; to obstruct; to hinder; to block

攘 **yeuhng** (Md **rǎng**)
① confused; disorderly ② to take by force ③ to eliminate; to repel ④ to shake

攘除 **yeuhng chèuih**
to rid; to eliminate; to dispel

攘攘 **yeuhng yeuhng**
in a state of confusion

攙(搀) **chàam, chàahm** (Md **chān**)
① to lead (a person) by the hand ② to mix; to blend

攙扶 **chàam fùh**
to lead (a person) by the hand

攙合 **chàam hahp**
to mix; to blend; to mingle

攛(撺) **chyun** (Md **cuān**)
① to throw ② to urge; to persuade; to induce

攛弄 **chyun luhng**
to urge; to persuade; to induce

攛掇 **chyun jyut**
to urge; to persuade; to induce

攝(摄) **sip** (Md **shè**)
① to take in; to absorb; to attract ② to regulate ③ to represent

攝取 **sip chéui**
to take in; to absorb

攝影 **sip yíng**
photography

攢(攒) **jáan, chyùhn** (Md **zǎn, cuán**)
① to hoard ② to bring together; to gather; to assemble; to collect

攢錢 **jáan chìhn**
to hoard money

攢聚 **chyùhn jeuih**
to huddle together; to crowd together

攤(摊) **tàan** (Md **tān**)
① to spread; to open ② to divide equally; to apportion ③ a booth; a stand; a stall

攤開 **tàan hòi**
to spread out; to unfold

攤還 **tàan wàahn**
to repay in installments

攣(挛) **lyùhn** (Md **luán**)
① tangled; entwined ② crooked

攣縮 **lyùhn sūk**
spasm

攣弱 **lyùhn yeuhk**
crooked and weak

攥 **jaahn** (Md **zuàn**)
to grasp

攪(挢、搞) **gáau**
(Md **jiǎo**)
① to stir; to agitate; to disturb
② to do; to manage; to handle

攪拌 **gáau buhn**
to stir or churn

攪鬼 **gáau gwái**
to play underhand tricks

攫 **fok** (Md **jué**)
to seize; to take hold of; to snatch

攫奪 **fok dyuht**
to seize; to snatch

攫取 **fok chéui**
to take by force; to seize

攬(揽) **láahm** (Md **lǎn**)
① to be in full possession of; to grasp ② to make selective collection or coverage of

攬權 **láahm kyùhn**
to grasp full authority

攬筆 **láahm bāt**
to take the pen; to write

攘 **nóhng** (Md **nǎng**)
to thrust; to stab

攘子 **nóhng jí**
a daggar or bodkin

支部

支 **jì** (Md **zhī**)
① to pay; to disburse; to defray
② to support; to sustain; to prop up ③ a branch; a subdivision

支付 **jì fuh**
to pay (what is owed)

支店 **jì dim**
a branch store

攲 **kèi** (Md **qī**)
to incline; to lean; to slant

攲斜 **kèi chèh**
to slant; to incline

攲側 **kèi jāk**
to incline; to lean; to lurch

攴(攵)部

收(収) **sàu** (Md **shōu**)
① to draw together; to gather; to collect ② to receive; to accept; to take ③ to end; to come to a close ④ to retrieve; to take back

收入 **sàu yahp**
income; earnings; revenue; receipts

收回 **sàu wùih**
to recover; to retrieve; to recoup

改 **gói** (Md **gǎi**)
to change; to alter; to modify; to transform; to convert

改變 **gói bin**
to change; to alter; to modify; to transform; to convert

改良 **gói lèuhng**
to improve; to better

攸 **yàuh** (Md **yōu**)
① far; distant ② fast; fleeting ③ to concern

攸攸 **yàuh yàuh**
far; distant; deep

攸關 **yàuh gwàan**
(It) concerns (reputation, life, etc.); (It's) a matter of (reputation, life and death, etc.)

攻 **gùng** (Md **gōng**)
① to attack; to raid; to assult ②

to accuse; to charge ③ to work
at; to apply oneself to

攻打 **gùng dá**
　to attack; to raid; to invade

攻讀 **gùng duhk**
　to apply oneself diligently in
　study

放 **fong** (Md **fàng**)
　① to let go; to release; to free;
　to literate; to loosen; to relax ②
　to put; to place ③ to dissipate;
　to debauch; to indulge

放任 **fong yahm**
　to leave alone; to let (a person)
　do as he pleases; to let (a
　matter) take its own course

放映 **fong yíng**
　to project (on screen)

政 **jing** (Md **zhèng**)
　government; administration;
　management; politics

政府 **jing fú**
　government

政策 **jing chaak**
　policy

故 **gu** (Md **gù**)
　① former; past; previous; old;
　antique; ancient ② intention;
　willful ③ cause; reason ④ to die
　⑤ incident; event; matter ⑥
　therefore

故事 **gu sih**
　a story; a narrative; an account

故意 **gu yi**
　intentional; on purpose;
　intentionally

效 **haauh** (Md **xiào**)
　① to imitate; to mimic; to follow
　② effect, effectiveness, efficacy
　③ to devote ④ to offer

效能 **haauh nàhng**
　effect

效法 **haauh faat**
　to take as a model; to imitate

綏 **méih** (Md **mǐ**)
　to stabilize; to quiet; to pacify; to
　soothe

綏平 **méih pìhng**
　to succeed in putting down a
　revolt or rebellion

綏寧 **méih nìhng**
　to give peace; to pacify

敍（叙、敘）**jeuih**
（Md **xù**)
　① to tell; to narrate; to describe;
　to express; to vent; to talk about
　② to get together; to gather ③
　to rate or evaluate (as a basis for
　reward, appointment, etc.)

敍舊 **jeuih gauh**
　to talk about old days

敍述 **jeuih seuht**
　to narrate

教 **gaau** (Md **jiào, jiāo**)
　① a religion ② an order; a direc-
　tive ③ to educate; to bring up ④
　to incite; to urge; to bid; to
　instigate ⑤ to teach; to guide

教導 **gaau douh**
　to teach and guide

教堂 **gaau tòhng**
　a church; a mosque

敏 **máhn** (Md **mǐn**)
　① quick; agile; speedy; clever;
　smart ② diligent; industrious;
　earnest; eager

敏捷 **máhn jiht**
　agile; adroit

敏銳 **máhn yeuih**
　keen; sharp; sharp-witted

救 **gau** (Md **jiù**)
　to save; to relieve; to rescue; to
　deliver; to aid

救命 **gau mihng**
　　to save life; help!

救濟 **gau jai**
　　to relieve (the suffering, the poor, etc.)

敗(败)**baaih** (Md **bài**)
　① to defeat or be defeated; to thwart or be thwarted; to decline; to go down ② to spoil or be spoiled; to corrupt or to be corrupted

敗北 **baaih bāk**
　　to suffer defeat; a defeat

敗壞 **baaih waaih**
　　to corrupt or be corrupted

敕(勅、勑)**chīk** (Md **chì**)
　① an imperial order to confer title or rank on an official ② cautions

敕命 **chīk mihng**
　　an imperial order to confer title or rank on an official

敕書 **chīk syù**
　　imperial letter

敝 **baih** (Md **bì**)
　① worn-out; broken; tattered ② exhausted; tired ③ my, or our (self-depreciatory term)

敝校 **baih haauh**
　　(self-depreciatory term) my or our school

敝屣 **baih sáai**
　　worn-out shoes — useless things

散 **saan, sáan** (Md **sàn, sǎn**)
　① to scatter; to disperse; to dissipate; to break up ② to disseminate; to spread ③ loose; loosened; scattered ④ idle; leisurely ⑤ powdered medicine

散播 **saan bo**
　　to disseminate; to spread

散工 **sáan gùng**
　　odd jobs

敞 **chóng** (Md **chǎng**)
　open; uncovered; spacious; broad

敞開 **chóng hòi**
　　to open; to unfold

敞亮 **chóng leuhng**
　　spacious and bright

敢 **gám** (Md **gǎn**)
　to dare; to venture

敢言 **gám yìhn**
　　courageous enough to express one's beliefs

敢死隊 **gám séi déui**
　　a suicide squad; a death band; a commando unit given a very dangerous mission

敦 **dèun, deuih** (Md **dūn, duì**)
　① honest; sincere; candid ② to deepen or strengthen (relations, etc.) ③ a sort of container ④ to urge; to press

敦睦 **dèun muhk**
　　to have cordial and friendly ties

敦促 **dèun chūk**
　　to earnestly urge or press

敬 **ging** (Md **jìng**)
　① to respect; to revere; to honor; to esteem ② to present; to offer

敬佩 **ging pui**
　　to admire; to respect; to think highly of

敬重 **ging juhng**
　　to respect; to esteem; to revere; to have high regard for

敲 **hàau** (Md **qiāo**)
　① to rap; to tap; to beat ② to extort; to blackmail

敲打 **hàau dá**
　　to tap; to rap; to knock; to beat

敲詐 **hàau ja**
to blackmail

敵 (敌) **dihk** (Md **dí**)
① enemy; foe ② to oppose; to resist

敵人 **dihk yàhn**
enemy; foe

敵視 **dihk sih**
to regard with hostility

敷 **fù** (Md **fū**)
① to apply or spread over (a surface); to paint ② to suffice; to be enough ③ to state; to explain; to expound

敷粉 **fù fán**
to apply face powder

敷衍 **fù yín**
to act in a perfunctory manner; to deal with a person insincerely

數 (数) **sou, sóu, sok**
(Md **shù, shǔ, shuò**)
① number, ② several; a few ③ plan ④ to count; to enumerate ⑤ often; frequently

數目 **sou muhk**
number; sum

數不清 **sóu bāt chìng**
innumerable; countless

整 **jíng** (Md **zhěng**)
① orderly; systematic; neat; tidy ② whole; complete; entire; intact ③ to tidy; to set in order; to adjust; to arrange; to repair; to make ready

整理 **jíng léih**
to arrange; to put in order; to adjust; to regulate

整日 **jíng yaht**
the whole day; all day long

斁 **yihk, dou** (Md **yì, dù**)
① to dislike ② to corrupt; to spoil

斂 (敛) **líhm, lihm**
(Md **liǎn**)
① to draw together; to contract; to fold ② to collect; to gather

斂跡 **líhm jīk**
to abstain from vice; (said of undesirable elements) to be subdued; to mend ways

斂足 **líhm jūk**
to slow down one's steps — to hesitate; to advance further

斃 **baih** (Md **bì**)
to die; to fall dead; to kill

斃命 **baih mihng**
to meet violent death

斃敵 **baih dihk**
to kill enemy troops (usually followed by the number of enemy soldiers killed)

文部

文 **màhn** (Md **wén**)
① a writing; a composition; an article ② literature; culture; education ③ elegant; cultured; polished; suave; civil; polite; urbane; mild ④ civilian or civil (as opposed to military) ⑤ a former monetary unit ⑥ a Chinese family name

文章 **màhn jèung**
a writing; a composition

文化 **màhn fa**
culture; civilization

斐 **féi** (Md **fěi**)
① elegant; beautiful ② a Chinese family name

斐然 **féi yìhn**
(said of results, achievements, etc.) excellent, very satisfactory

斐斐 **féi féi**
elegant; beautiful; a Chinese family name

斑 **bàan** (Md **bān**)
① speckles; spots; mottles ②
mottled; variegated; motley

斑斑 **bàan bàan**
mottled; spotted

斑馬 **bàan máh**
a zebra

斌 **bàn** (Md **bīn**)
same as "彬", see radical "彡"

斕（斓）**làahn** (Md **lán**)
multicolored

斑斕 **bàan làahn**
gorgeous; resplendent

斗部

斗 **dáu** (Md **dǒu**)
① Chinese peck ② a large container for wine ③ one of the 28 constellations

斗篷 **dáu pùhng**
a mantle; a cape

斗膽 **dáu dáam**
great intrepidity or boldness

料 **liuh** (Md **liào**)
① to conjecture; to reckon; to estimate ② to infer; to foresee ③ to consider; to calculate ④ to manage; to handle; to care ⑤ material; stuff

料理 **liuh léih**
to manage; to dispose of; a Japanese dish; Japanese cooking

料度 **liuh dohk**
to estimate; to reckon; to infer

斛 **huhk** (Md **hú**)
a dry measure 10 or 5 times that of 斗

斜 **chèh** (Md **xié**)
inclined; sloping; slanting; leaning; oblique; diagonal

斜坡 **chèh bò**
a slope

斜陽 **chèh yèuhng**
the declining sun; the setting sun

斝 **gá** (Md **jiǎ**)
a jade wine cup

斟 **jàm** (Md **zhēn**)
① to fill a cup with (beverage); to pour (beverage) into a cup ② to consider

斟茶 **jàm chàh**
to fill a cup or glass with tea

斟酌 **jàm jeuk**
to fill a cup, or glass, with wine or liquor; to consider

斡 **waat** (Md **wò**)
to revolve; to turn; to rotate

斡旋 **waat syùhn**
to mediate; to use one's good offices or influence (in setting a dispute)

斡運 **waat wahn**
to move in a circle

斠 **gaau** (Md **jiào**)
leveling stick (used in measuring volume of grain, etc.)

斤部

斤 **gàn** (Md **jīn**)
① Chinese pound; catty ② an ax ③ discerning; keen in observation

斤兩 **gàn léung**
weight

斤斤計較 **gàn gàn gai gaau**
to be particular about every point, detail or trifle

斥 **chīk** (Md **chì**)
① to accuse; to blame; to reproach; to reprove; to censure; to scold; to condemn ② to expel; to drive off; to banish; to reject

③ to survey; to observe

斥喝 **chīk hot**
to scold

斥責 **chìk jaak**
to rebuke; to reprove; to reproach; to censure

斧 **fú** (Md **fǔ**)
① a hatchet; an ax ② to chop; to cut

斧頭 **fú tàuh**
an ax; an hatchet

斧正 **fú jing**
to correct (a composition) freely

斫 **jeuk** (Md **zhuó**)
to chop or cut (wood)

斫斬 **jeuk jáam**
to chop; to cut; to hew

斫殺 **jeuk saat**
to kill by means of hatchet, ax or sword

斬 (斩) **jáam** (Md **zhǎn**)
to cut; to kill; to behead

斬首 **jáam sáu**
discapitation; beheading

斬釘截鐵 **jáam dèng jiht tit**
to speak; or act, with determination and courage

斯 **sì** (Md **sī**)
① this; these; such ② a connecting particle ③ to tear; to rip

斯文 **sì màhn**
cultured; refined; elegant

斯事 **sì sih**
this matter

新 **sàn** (Md **xīn**)
① new; fresh; novel ② beginning; starting ③ modern; recent ④ the suffix "neo" ⑤ the Hsin Dynasty (8-22 A.D.)

新版 **sàn báan**
new edition (of a book)

新年 **sàn nìhn**
New Year

斲 **deuk** (Md **zhuó**)
to chop; to hew

斲喪 **deuk song**
to chop down completely; to waste one's vitality by dissipation

斲輪老手 **deuk lèuhn lóuh sáu**
an old hand; an experienced man

斷 (断) **dyuhn, dyun, tyún** (Md **duàn**)
① to cut apart; to sever ② to abstain from ③ to decide; to conclude ④ to break; broken

斷定 **dyuhn dihng**
to conclude; to decide

斷送 **dyuhn sung**
to lose for good

方部

方 **fòng** (Md **fāng**)
① square; rectangular ② honest; morally upright ③ a region; an area; a place ④ a prescription; a recipe; a method; a plan ⑤ direction; bearing ⑥ occultism ⑦ just now; just then ⑧ (in mathematics) root ⑨ side ⑩ a Chinese family name

方法 **fòng faat**
method

方言 **fòng yìhn**
a dialect

於 (于) **yù, wù** (Md **yú, yū, wū**)
① in; on; at; by; from ② than; then; to; with reference to ③ compared with ④ a Chinese family name ⑤ an interjection roughly equivalent to hurah, bravo, alas, etc.

於是 **yù sih**
then; so; thus; thereafter;
thereupon

於戲 **wù fù**
Alas!

施 **sì** (Md **shī**)
① to act; to do; to make ② to
bestow; to grant; to give (alms,
etc.) ③ to apply (fertilizers, etc.)
④ a Chinese family name

施洗 **sì sái**
to baptize

施捨 **sì sé**
to give to charity

旁 **pòhng** (Md **páng**)
① side (branch, door, way, etc.);
the side ② by the side of; nearly

旁邊 **pòhng bīn**
the side; by the side of; nearly;
in the vicinity of

旁觀 **pòhng gùn**
to look on; to watch from the
side line

斾 **kèih** (Md **qí**)
frag or streamer attached with
small bells; flag

旅 **léuih** (Md **lǔ**)
① a traveler; a passenger; a
lodger; to travel; to lodge ② a
multitude; people ③ disciples;
pupils; followers; subordinates ④
order; sequence; to arrange ⑤ (in
military) a brigade; troops ⑥
(now rare) a sacrifice to the
mountains ⑦ to proceed
together; to do things together

旅行 **léuih hàhng**
to travel; to go in a group from
one place to another

旅費 **léuih fai**
traveling expenses

旋 **syùhn** (Md **xuán, xuàn**)
① to return; to turn back ② to
revolve; to move in an orbit ③ a
very short while; a moment ④ to
urinate

旋轉 **syùhn jyún**
to turn round and round; to
revolve

旋律 **syùhn leuht**
melody

旌 **jìng** (Md **jīng**)
① a kind of flag, banner, standard, etc. ornamented with
feather ② to cite (one's merits,
virtues, etc.); to make manifest

旌旗 **jìng kèih**
a general name for flags and
banners

族 **juhk** (Md **zú**)
① a tribe; a clan; a family;
relatives ② a race (of people) ③
a class, a family of animals ④ (to
grow) in thicket

族人 **juhk yàhn**
fellow clansman

族譜 **juhk póu**
pedigree of a clan

旗 **kèih** (Md **qí**)
① a flag; a pennant; a banner; a
streamer ② a sign; an insignia; an
emblem ③ an administrative
division of Mongolia and Tsinghai
④ the Manchus

旗子 **kèih jí**
a flag

旗艦 **kèih laahm**
flag ship

旖 **yí** (Md **yǐ**)
① romantic; tender ② charming;
lovely; attractive; graceful ③
fluttering of flags

旖旎 **yí neíh**
(of flags) fluttering; (of scenery) enchanting

旖旎風光 **yí neíh fùng gwòng**
a romantic or charming sight

无部

无 **mòuh (Md wú)**
the ancient form of 無 , not, no, negative, without

无妄之災 **mòuh móhng jì jòi**
unexpected trouble or bad break; a disaster brought on not by oneself

旣 **gei (Md jì)**
① since (as, since he's here) ② already; defacto ③ to finish ④ a Chinese family name

旣定 **gei dihng**
already decided or fixed; (said of a rebellion, etc.) already quelled

旣然 **gei yìhn**
since (it is so, etc.); this being the case

日部

日 **yaht (Md rì)**
① the sun ② a day; daily; daytime; time of the year; the bygone days, the other day; sometime (in the future) ③ Japan; Japanese

日本 **Yaht bún**
Japan

日間 **yaht gāan**
daytime

旦 **daan (Md dàn)**
① day break; dawn ② day; morning ③ a female role in Chinese Opera

旦旦 **daan daan**
every day; daily; sincerely

旦日 **daan yaht**
tomorrow

早 **jóu (Md zǎo)**
① early; earlier; soon; beforehand; previous; premature ② morning; Good Morning! ③ ago; before

早飯 **jóu faahn**
breakfast

早年 **jóu nìhn**
years ago; in the bygone years; many years ago

旨(恉) **jí (Md zhǐ)**
① purpose; will; intention; objective ② an imperial decree ③ good; excellent; beautiful ④ tasty; pleasant to the palate; delicious

旨意 **jí yi**
will; intention; imperial decree; or God's will

旨酒 **jí jáu**
good wine

旬 **chèuhn (Md xún)**
① a period of ten days ② a period of ten years (usually used to indicate a person's age) ③ widespread, throughout ④ to tour; to inspect

旬日 **chèuhn yaht**
ten days

旬刊 **chèuhn hón (hōn)**
a ten-day periodical; a magazine issue once every ten days

旭 **yūk (Md xù)**
① brightness or radiance of daybreak ② the rising sun ③ proud smug or complacent

旭日 **yūk yaht**
the rising sun

旭旭 **yūk yūk**
proud, smug or complacent; uproarious; disappointed; unhappy

旱 **hóhn** (Md **hàn**)
① drought; dry ② (by) land route (as opposed to waterway)

旱災 **hóhn jòi**
a drought

旱天 **hóhn tìn**
dry days; dry weather; a drought

旺 **wohng** (Md **wàng**)
① prosperous; to prosper ② vigorous; prolific; productive ③ brilliant; bright or brightly (said of light burning, etc.)

旺季 **wohng gwai**
(said of business) boom season; busy season

旺盛 **wohng sihng**
prosperous; prolific; productive; high (morale)

旻 **màhn** (Md **mín**)
autumn

旻天 **màhn tìn**
autumn

旻序 **màhn jeuih**
autumn festival

昂 **ngòhng** (Md **áng**)
① to raise ② lofty and proud; bold and not easily bent; straightforward ③ high ④ expensive; costly

昂貴 **ngòhng gwai**
expensive; costly

昂首 **ngòhng sáu**
to raise one's head high

昃 **jāk** (Md **zè**)
after noon; afternoon; the sun on the western side of the sky

昆 **kwàn, gwàn** (Md **kūn**)
① an elder brother ② descendants; posterity ③ multitudes ④ insects ⑤ together; in unison

昆仲 **kwàn juhng**
brothers

昆蟲 **kwàn chùhng**
insects

昇 **sìng** (Md **shēng**)
① to ascend ② peace; peaceful ③ a Chinese family name

昇平 **sìng pìhng**
time of peace

昇降機 **sìng gong gèi**
an elevator

昉 **fóng** (Md **fǎng**)
① dawn; day break ② beginning

昊 **houh** (Md **hào**)
① summer time ② sky; heaven

昊天 **houh tìn**
summer time; sky or heaven

昊天罔極 **houh tìn móhng gihk**
as vast as the boundless heaven (said of parental love)

昌 **chèung** (Md **chāng**)
① proper; good; straight (talk) ② prosperous; robust; vigorous; to make prosperous or glorify ③ light; brightness ④ a Chinese family name

昌盛 **chèung sihng**
powerful; prosperous; abundant; glory

昌言 **chèung yìhn**
proper words or commands; straight talk

昀 **wàhn** (Md **yún**)
① day break; sunrise; dawn ② sunshine

昏 fàn (Md hūn)

① dusk; dark ② confused; muddled; mixed-up ③ unclear of sight; dizzy ④ (now rare) same as 婚 , to marry ⑤ a Chinese family name

昏迷 fàn màih
in a coma; apoplexy; unconscious; delirious; stupor

黃昏 wòhng fàn
twilight

明 mìhng (Md míng)

① light; bright; brilliant ② clear; understandable; to clarify; to understand; obvious; evident ③ intelligent; clever ④ eye sight; seeing faculty ⑤ day; daybreak; dawn ⑥ to state; to show; to assert ⑦ next (day, or year) ⑧ the Ming Dynasty (1386 – 1644 A.D.) ⑨ a Chinese family name

明天 mìhng tìn
tomorrow

明白 mìhng baahk
to understand; to know (a trick, secret, etc.); clever and bright; clear and evident; obvious

易 yih, yihk (Md yì)

① to exchange; to barter ② to change (places, job, owners, etc.) ③ easy; lenient ④ the Book of Changes ⑤ a Chinese family name

易行 yih hàhng
easy to practise; easy to do

易主 yihk jyú
to change owners or masters

昔 sīk (Md xī)

① by-gone; of old; formerly; ancient ② a night ③ the end

昔日 sīk yaht
old days; former times

昔賢 sīk yìhn
ancient sages

昕 yàn (Md xīn)

day break; dawn

昕夕從公 yàn jihk chùhng gùng
to devote to official duties day and night

星 sìng (Md zīng)

① any heavenly body that shines; stars, planets, satellites, etc. ② a spark or sparks ③ droplets; small particles of anything; very tiny ④ name of one of the 28 constellations ⑤ a movie star ⑥ by night; nocturnal ⑦ an ancient percussion musical instrument consisting of two or more brass-cup like pieces played by hitting them against one another ⑧ a Chinese family name

星宿 sìng sau
stars or planets in heaven; a person who is considered an incarnation of a star

星期 sìng kèih
week

映 yíng (Md yìng)

① to reflect; a reflection ② to project (slides, picture, etc.) ③ shining; blinding (glare, light, etc.)

映照 yíng jiu
to shine and reflect; to combine to make a pretty scene; bright and shining

反映 fáan yíng
to reflect

春 chèun (Md chūn)

① the first of the four seasons — spring ② sensuallity; lustful; lewd; pornographic ③ alive; living ④ joyful ⑤ youth ⑥ wine (esp. in the Tang Dynasty)

春天 chèun tìn
spring; spring-time

春節 **chèun jit**
the lunar new year festival;
lunar new year holidays

昧 **muih** (Md **mèi**)
① obscure; dark ② to hide ③ to
ignore (one's conscience, etc.) ④
blind; ignorant ⑤ to faint; fainting

昧良心 **muih lèuhng sàm**
to ignore one's conscience

愚昧 **yùh muih**
ignorant; stupid

昨 **jok** (Md **zuó**)
yesterday; last (night); lately; past

昨天 **jok tìn**
yesterday

昨非 **jok fèi**
past mistakes

昭 **chìu** (Md **zhāo**)
① bright; brightness; luminous
② prominent; eminent; evident
obvious ③ to make open; to
show; to display ④ a Chinese
family name

昭彰 **chìu jèung**
prominent; eminent; obvious;
evident

昭昭 **chìu chìu**
clear and evident; known to all

是 **sih** (Md **shì**)
① yes; right; positive (as contrasted to negative) ② the verb
to be (for all persons and number)
③ this, that or which

是必 **sih bìt**
must be; surely; certainly

是非 **sih fèi**
right or wrong; right and
wrong; yes and no; gossip;
scandal; discord

昱 **yūk** (Md **yù**)
sunshine; light; brightness;
shinning; dazzling

昱昱 **yūk yūk**
dazzling

昳 **diht** (Md **dié, yì**)
the setting sun

昳麗 **diht laih**
radiantly beautiful

昴 **máauh** (Md **mǎo**)
one of the 28 constellations

昴星 **máauh sìng**
the Pleiades

昶 **chóng** (Md **chǎng**)
① a long day ② comfortable and
easy

昫 **héui** (Md **shǔ**)
warmth of the rising sun

昫嫗 **héui ngàu**
to caress — as sunshine

晏 **ngaan** (Md **yàn**)
① clear (sky, sea, water, etc.) ②
late; evening ③ peaceful; quiet ④
a Chinese family name

晏晏 **ngaan ngaan**
mild and tender

晏起 **ngaan héi**
to get up late

晁 (鼂)**chiuh**
(Md **cháo**)
① an ancient form of 朝 ② a
Chinese family name

晃 **fóng** (Md **huǎng,
huàng**)
① brightness ② dazzling; glaring
③ a glimpse; to appear and
disappear very quickly ④ to
sway; to oscillate

晃朗 **fóng lóhng**
bright and brilliant

晃漾 **fóng yeuhng**
to sway; swaying

時(时) **sìh** (Md **shí**)
① a season ② an era; an epoch; an age; a period ③ time ④ hour ⑤ often; frequently ⑥ fashionable; proper and adequate ⑦ opportune (moment); opportunity ⑧ timely; seasonable ⑨ a Chinese family name

時光 **sìh gwòng**
time

時代 **sìh doih**
an era; an epoch; a period; an age; a time

晌 **héung** (Md **shǎng**)
① high noon ② a certain duration or interval of time ③ (in Northeast China dialect) a day's work

晌午 **héung ngh**
high noon

晉(晋) **jeun** (Md **jìn**)
① to advance; to increase; to flourish ② a state during the Period of Spring and Autumn, occupying parts of today's Shensi and Hopei Provinces ③ another name for Shansi Province ④ the Tsin Dynasty (265 − 420 A.D.) ⑤ a Chinese family name

晉見 **jeun gin**
to call on (a superior); to be granted and audience

晟 **sìhng** (Md **shèng**)
the brightness of the sun; light; splendor

晚 **máahn** (Md **wǎn**)
① sunset; evening; night ② late; drawing toward the end ③ junior

晚飯 **máahn faahn**
dinner; supper

晚年 **máahn nìhn**
old age

晝(昼) **jau** (Md **zhòu**)
day; day-time; daylight

晝夜 **jau yeh**
day and night

晝寢 **jau chám**
to take a nap; a siesta

晞 **hèi** (Md **xī**)
① to dry in the sun; dry ② sunshine at day-break

晞髮 **hèi faat**
to loosen the hair in order to dry it

晤 **ngh** (Md **wù**)
① to meet; to see face to face ② enlightened; wise

晤面 **ngh mihn**
to meet; to see each other

晤商 **ngh sèung**
face-to-face negotiation; to discuss in an interview

晦 **fui** (Md **huì**)
① the last day of every moon in the lunar calendar ② night; evening; dark ③ obscure; indistinguishable ④ unlucky; bad luck

晦暗 **fui ngam**
dark; gloomy

晦氣 **fui hei**
unlucky; bad luck; to encounter rough going

晨 **sàhn** (Md **chén**)
① morning; daybreak ② (said of a cock) to announce the arrival of morning

晨昏 **sàhn fàn**
morning and evening

晨雞 **sàhn gāi**
crowing of cocks at daybreak

普 **póu** (Md **pǔ**)
① universal; widespread; general; everywhere; all ② Prussia ③ a Chinese family name

普遍 **póu pin**
universal; widespread; everywhere; common

普魯士 **Póu lóuh sih**
Prussia

景 **gíng** (Md **jǐng**)
① scenery; view ② prospects; circumstances; situation ③ (in motion picture, stage-shows, etc.) setting; background scenes ④ big and strong ⑤ great ⑥ high ⑦ bright and luminous ⑧ to admire; to respect ⑨ a Chinese family name ⑩ shadow

景象 **gíng jeuhng**
appearance; conditions; outlook

景仰 **gíng yéuhng**
to admire and respect; to look up to

晰(晢) **sīk** (Md **xī**)
clear, clearly

晴 **chìhng** (Md **qíng**)
① fine (day); fair (weather); clear sky ② when the rain stops

晴天 **chìhng tìn**
a fine day; a cloudless day

晴雨表 **chìhng yúh bíu**
barometer

晶 **jìng** (Md **jīng**)
① crystal ② bright; clear; brilliant; radiant

晶瑩 **jìng yìhng**
sparkling

晶體 **jìng tái**
(in radio) crystal

晷 **gwái** (Md **guǐ**)
① shadows caused by the sun ② a sundial ③ time

晷儀 **gwái yìh**
a sundial

晷刻 **gwái hāak**
time; a short time

智 **ji** (Md **zhì**)
① talented; capable; intelligent; clever; wise; wisdom; knowledge ② prudence ③ a Chinese family name

智慧 **ji waih**
wisdom; intelligence

智利 **Ji leih**
Chile; or Chili

晾 **lohng** (Md **liàng**)
① to dry in the air; to hang in the wind to dry ② to dry in the sun

晾衣服 **lohng yì fuhk**
to hang clothes in the wind to dry; to dry clothes on laundry lines; to air clothes

晾乾 **lohng gòn**
to dry in the air; to hang in the wind to dry

暈(暉) **wàhn** (Md **yùn, yūn**)
① to faint; giddy and dizzy ② (usually used sarcastically) to do things without purpose ③ a halo; vaspors; a mist ④ dazzled; to feel faint or dizzy

暈倒 **wàhn dóu**
to faint and fall; to swoon

暈船 **wàhn syùhn**
to be sea-sick

暑 **syú** (Md **shǔ**)
① hot; heat; the heat of summer ② mid-summer

暑假 **syú ga**
summer vacation

暑熱 **syú yiht**
scorching heat; heat of summer

暄 **hyùn** (Md **xuān**)
comfortable and genial (climate); warm

暄風 **hyùn fùng**
spring breeze

暄妍 **hyùn yìhn**
warm weather and captivating scenery (in spring season)

暇 **hah** (Md **xiá**)
leisure; spare time

暇日 **hah yaht**
free days; leisure; spare time

暇時 **hah sìh**
leisure; spare time

暉(晖) **fài** (Md **huī**)
sunshine; bright; radiant

暉映 **fài yíng**
bright and brilliant

暉夜 **fài yeh**
firefly

暌 **kwàih** (Md **kuí**)
① in opposition ② to separate; to part

暌違 **kwàih wàih**
(said of friends) separated; separation

暌合 **kwàih hahp**
to meet and to part; union and separation

暖(煖) **nyúhn**
(Md **nuǎn**)
warm, genial (weather)

暖和 **nyúhn wòh**
warm

暖爐 **nyúhn lòuh**
a stove for keeping room warm in winter

暗 **ngam** (Md **àn**)
① dark; obscure ② stupid; ignorant ③ secret; clandestine; stealthy ④ hidden (meaning, drainage, system, rocks, etc.)

暗示 **ngam sìh**
to hint; to suggest; a hint; an insinuation; a suggestion

暗號 **ngam houh**
secret mark, sign, signal or password

暢(畅) **cheung**
(Md **chàng**)
① smoothly ② easily accessible ③ with gusto; to one's heart's content ④ long; expanding ⑤ luxuriant ⑥ (to state or elaborate) freely; without restraint; clear ⑦ very ⑧ a Chinese family name

暢談 **cheung tàahm**
to talk to heart's content

暢快 **cheung faai**
cheerful and exuberant; spiritually elevated

暝 **mìhng** (Md **míng**)
night, dark, obscure

暫(暂) **jaahm** (Md **zàn**)
① temporarily; for a short time; not lasting ② suddenly; abruptly

暫時 **jaahm sìh**
for the time being

暫停 **jaahm tìhng**
to stop; halt, or suspend temporarily

暮 **mouh** (Md **mù**)
① sunset; evening; dusk ② closing (year); ending; late

暮年 **mouh nìhn**
closing years of one's life; old age

暮氣 **mouh hei**
to feel dull and hopeless; despondent and emaciated; gloomy; dejection

暴 **bouh** (Md **bào**)
① violent; fierce; atrocious; cruel ② sudden

暴動 **bouh duhng**
a riot

暴力 **bouh lihk**
violence; brute force; naked force

暵 **hon** (Md **hàn**)
to expose to sunshine; to dry

暵暵 **hon hon**
exposed to scorching sunshine

暱 (昵) **nīk** (Md **nì**)
intimate; close

暱愛 **nīk ngoi**
love or affection (between opposite sexes)

暱友 **nīk yáuh**
close friend

暹 **chim** (Md **xiān**)
to rise (said of the sun)

暹羅 **Chim lòh**
Siam, old name of Thailand

暾 **tàn** (Md **tūn**)
sunrise

暾暾 **tàn tàn**
bright; glowing; blazing

曆 (历) **lihk** (Md **lì**)
① calendar ② era; age ③ to calculate; to count

曆書 **lihk syù**
an almanac

歷法 **lihk faat**
calendar (as a system)

曁 **kei** (Md **jì**)
① and ② to reach; to attain

曁南大學 **Kei nàahm daaih hohk**
the National Chinan University

曇 (昙) **tàahm** (Md **tán**)
cloudy; overcast

曇曇 **tàahm tàahm**
cloudy; overcast

曇花 **tàahm fà**
night blomming cereus

曉 (晓) **híu** (Md **xiǎo**)
① daybreak; dawn ② to tell; to explain ③ to know; to understand

曉得 **híu dāk**
to know; to be aware of

曉色 **híu sīk**
scene in the early morning

曀 **ngai** (Md **yī**)
dim; obscure

曄 (晔) **yihp** (Md **yè**)
① bright; radiant ② prosperous; thriving

曄然 **yihp yìhn**
prosperous; thriving

曌 **jiu** (Md **zhào**)
same as 照 coined by 武則天 and used as her name

曏 **heung** (Md **xiàng**)
① period of time ② once upon a time

曏者 **heung jé**
once upon a time

曖 (暧) **ngoi, ngói** (Md **ài**)
dim; indistinct; ambiguous; vague

曖昧 **ngoi muih**
ambiguous; vague; a secret impropriety

曖曖 **ngoi ngoi**
dim; obscure; dark

曙 **chyúh, syúh** (Md **shǔ**)
dawn

曙光 **chyúh gwòng**
light at dawn

曙日 **chyúh yaht**
in the morning

曜 **yiuh** (Md **yào**)
daylight; sunshine

曜靈 **yiuh lìhng**
the sun

曚 **mùhng** (Md **méng**)
dim; obscure

曚曨 **mùhng lùhng**
dim; obscure

曛 **fàn** (Md **xūn**)
twilight; dusk; sunset

曛黑 **fàn hāk**
dusky

曛黃 **fàn wòhng**
sunset; dusk

曠 **kwong** (Md **kuàng**)
① open; wide; broad; empty; unoccupied ② to neglect

曠野 **kwong yéh**
a wild plain; a prairie

曠日持久 **kwong yaht chìh gáu**
to maintain a situation for a longer time to no avail

曝 **bouh, buhk** (Md **pù**)
to expose to sunlight; to sun

曝光 **bouh gwōng**
(in photography) exposure

曝獻 **buhk hin**
to offer a humble but sincere gift or service

曦 **hèi** (Md **xī**)
sunshine; sunlight

曦光 **hèi gwōng**
sunshine; sunlight

曨(曨) **lùhng** (Md **lóng**)
① vague; dim ② bright

曩 **nóhng** (Md **nǎng**)
past; former

曩昔 **nóhng sīk**
in the past; former times

曩日 **nóhng yaht**
bygone-days

曬(晒) **saai** (Md **shài**)
to expose to sunlight; to dry in the sun

曬太陽 **saai taai yèuhng**
to be exposed to the sun; to bask in the sun

曬棚 **saai pàahng**
a drying stand or rack

曰部

曰 **yeuhk, yuht** (Md **yuē**)
to say (an archaic usage)

曲 **kūk** (Md **qū, qǔ**)
① bent; crooked; twisted; winding ② little known; obscure ③ a piece of music

曲折 **kūk jit**
bends, turns; curves; turns and twists; complications of an affair

曲調 **kūk diuh**
tune; melody

曳(抴、拽) **yaih**
(Md **yè**)
to drag

曳杖 **yaih jeuhng**
to walk with a cane

曳引機 **yaih yáhn gèi**
a tractor

更 **gàng, gang** (Md **gēng, gèng**)
① watches of the night ② night watchman ② to change; to alter; to shift ④ to experience ⑤ to alternate ⑥ more; further; to a greater degree

更新 **gàng sàn**
to renew; to renovate

更好 **gang hóu**
better; so much the better

曷 **hot** (Md **hé**)
① what ② why not

曷故 **hot gu**
why; what for

曷若 **hot yeuhk**
Wouldn't it be better to . . . ?

書(书) **syù** (Md **shū**)
① writing; book; letter ② to write

書本 **syù bún**
a book

書法 **syù faat**
calligraphy

曹 **chòuh** (Md **cáo**)
a Chinese family name

曹操 **Chòuh chòu**
Tsao Tsao (155 — 220) ruler of the Kingdom of Wei during the age of Three Kingdoms

曼 **maahn** (Md **màn**)
① delicately beautiful; graceful ② long; vast

曼延 **maahn yìhn**
to spread; to continue or extend endlessly

曼谷 **Maahn gūk**
Bangkok, capital of Thailand

曾 **jàng, chàhng** (Md **zēng, céng**)
① older or younger by three generations ② a Chinese family name ③ ever; once

曾孫 **jàng syùn**
great-grandchild; great-grand children

曾經 **chàhng gìng**
to have had the experience; to have already

替 **tai** (Md **tì**)
① to replace; to substitute ② to decay; to decline ③ to neglect

替代 **tai doih**
to substitute

替換 **tai wuhn**
to replace; to substitute

最 **jeui** (Md **zui**)
extreme; superlative

最多 **jeui dò**
the most; at most

最初 **jeui chò**
the first; the earliest; at first; in the beginning

會(会) **wuih, wúi, wúih, kúi** (Md **huì, kuài**)
① to meet ② to assemble; to gather; to converge ③ to understand; to comprehend ④ a meeting; a convention; an association; a society ⑤ a private banking cooperative ⑥ to be able ⑦ shall; will ⑧ to add; to compute

會議 **wuih yíh**
conference; meeting

會見 **wuih gin**
to meet

教會 **gaau wúi**
a church

會不會 **wúih bāt wúih**
Is it likely that . . .

會計 **kúi gai**
accounting; accountant; treasurer

月部

月 **yuht** (Md **yuè**)
① the moon ② month

月票 **yuht piu**
a monthly ticket

月台 **yuht tòih**
platform (at a railway station)

有 **yáuh** (Md **yǒu, yòu**)
to have; to be present; to exist; there is

有道理 **yáuh douh léih**
　reasonable; plausible; convincing

有空 **yáuh hùng**
　to have time (for doing something)

朋 **pàhng** (Md **péng**)
　① friend; companion ② group; clique

　朋友 **pàhng yáuh**
　　friend

　朋黨 **pàhng dóng**
　　a clique; a faction; factionalism

服 **fuhk** (Md **fú, fù**)
　① clothes; dress; garment; costume ② mouning ③ to wear (clothes) ④ to obey; to yield; to concede; to admit ⑤ to serve

　服裝 **fuhk jòng**
　　costume; dress; clothes

　服侍 **fuhk sih**
　　to wait upon; to attend on

朔 **sok** (Md **shuò**)
　① to begin ② north ③ the first day of the moon of the lunar calendar

　朔風 **sok fùng**
　　north wind

　朔日 **sok yaht**
　　the first day of each moon of the lunar calendar

朕 **jahm** (Md **zhèn**)
　① the royal "we" (used exclusively by the emperor or king to mean "I") ② omen; augury; portent; sign

　朕兆 **jahm siuh**
　　omen; portent; augury; sign

朗 **lóhng** (Md **lǎng**)
　① bright; clear ② resonant; sonorous

朗誦 **lóhng juhng**
　to recite aloud

朗月 **lóhng yuht**
　bright moon

望 **mohng** (Md **wàng**)
　① to view; to watch ② to hope; to expect ③ the 15th day of each moon of the lunar calendar

　望遠鏡 **mohng yúhn geng**
　　a telescope

　望族 **mohng juhk**
　　a respected family in a community; a family of renown

期 **kèih** (Md **qī**)
　① period; time ② designated time; time limit ③ to expect; to hope; to wait

　期間 **kèih gāan**
　　a period; a term

　期望 **kèih mohng**
　　to expect; to hope

朝 **jìu, chìuh** (Md **zhāo, cháo**)
　① morning; ② day ③ an imperial court ④ a dynasty ⑤ to go to imperial court ⑥ to face

　朝陽 **jìu yèuhng**
　　morning sun

　朝代 **chìuh doih**
　　a dynasty

朦 **mùhng** (Md **méng**)
　① state of the moon just before setting ② dim; vague; hazy

　朦朧 **mùhng lùhng**
　　appearance of the moon just before setting; dim; vague; hazy

朧（朧）**lùhng**
　(Md **lóng**)
　the moon's brightness

　朧朧 **lùhng lùhng**
　　brightness of the moon

木部

木 **muhk** (Md **mù**)
① tree ② wood; timber; lumber
③ simple; honest ④ senseless;
benumbed; dull

木材 **muhk chòih**
lumber; timber

木偶 **muhk ngáuh**
a puppet

未 **meih** (Md **wèi**)
① not yet ② not ③ the eighth of
the Twelve Terrestrial Branches
④ 2:00 – 4:00 p.m.

未必 **meih bīt**
not always; not necessarily

未來 **meih lòih**
furture; in the future

末 **muht** (Md **mò**)
① last; final ② late; recent ③
trivial; unimportant; insignificant
④ end; tip

末日 **muht yaht**
the last day

末代 **muht doih**
the last year (of a dynasty)

本 **bún** (Md **běn**)
① stem; root; origin; source;
basis; foundation ② a book; a
copy ③ capital (in business) ④
our; this; the present

本地 **bún deih**
local

本來 **bún lòih**
from the beginning; originally

札 **jaat** (Md **zhá**)
① (in ancient China) a thin
wooden tablet for writing ②
correspondence; a letter ③ (in
ancient China) a document or
instruction to a subordinate ④
(now rare) to die before one
comes of age

札記 **jaat gei**
a notebook in which one
records his comments on the
book he is reading

札幌 **Jaat fóng**
Sapporo, city in Japan

朮 **seuht** (Md **zhú**)
a plant with violet, green or red
flowers and white root, used in
herbal medicine

朮酒 **seuht jáu**
wine in which the plant 朮
has been soaked; medicinal
wine

朱 **jyù** (Md **zhū**)
① red; vermillion ② a Chinese
family name

朱古力 **jyù gù līk**
chocolate

朱門 **jyù mùhn**
rich and influential families

朴 **pok** (Md **pò, pó**)
① saltpeter ② plain; simple
(clothing, manner, etc.) ③ a kind
of oak

朴硝 **pok sìu**
saltpeter

朴忠 **pok jùng**
honest; sincere; loyal or
faithful

朵 (朵) **dó** (Md **duǒ**)
① a flower; a cluster of flowers;
a bud ② lobe of the ear

朵雲 **dó wàhn**
your esteemed letter

朵頤 **dó yìh**
the movement of the jaw in
eating – palate as, "The food
pleases my palate"

朽 **náu, yáu** (Md **xiǔ**)
① to rod; to decay; rotten;
decayed ② old and useless

朽敗 **náu baaih**
　decayed and rotten

朽木糞土 **náu muhk fan tóu**
　decayed wood and filthy soil a
　hopeless person

李 **léih** (Md **lǐ**)
　① plums ② (now rare) a judge; a
　justice ③ a Chinese family name

李樹 **léih syuh**
　the plum tree

李代桃僵 **léih doih tòuh gèung**
　to substitute this for that

杆 **gòn** (Md **gān**)
　① a wooden pole; the shaft of a
　spear ② rod; a unit of measure-
　ment which equals to 5.2 yards
　③ a wooden fence; balustrade

杆子 **gòn jí**
　a pole; a rod; a gang of bandits

欄杆 **làahn gòn**
　a railing; a balustrade; silk
　trimming for girls

杈 **chà** (Md **chā, chà**)
　① branch of a tree ② a pitch fork;
　a fish-fork ③ any fork-like object
　④ a kind of weapon in ancient
　China

杈枒 **chà ngà**
　a branching out of a tree; a
　branch

杈子 **chà jí**
　a branch of a tree

杉 **chaam, sàam** (Md **shān**)
　the various species of fir and pine

杉木 **chaam muhk**
　fir wood

杉杆子 **chaam gòn jí**
　straight and slender fir timber
　for building scaffolds and make
　shift shelters

杌 **ngaht** (Md **wù**)
　① a tree without branch; stump
　of a tree ② a square stool

杌凳 **ngaht dang**
　a square stool

杌子 **ngaht jí**
　a stool or bench

杏 **hahng** (Md **xìng**)
　① apricot ② almond-apricot
　kernels ③ apricot flower

杏子 **hahng jí**
　the apricot fruit

杏林 **hahng làhm**
　a term used in praise of a good
　and kind physician or referring
　to the medical profession in
　general

材 **chòih** (Md **cái**)
　① material — especially timber
　— for building houses, furniture,
　etc. ② material in its broadest
　sense ③ property of a substance
　④ coffin

材幹 **chòih gon**
　gift, talent or ability timber

材料 **chòih liuh**
　material — for all building
　purposes; raw materials;
　materials such as data,
　statistics, figure, information
　for writing an article, story,
　novel, etc.; ingredients of a
　preparation (food, medicine,
　etc.)

村(邨) **chyùn** (Md **cūn**)
　① a village; the country-side; a
　hamlet ② vulgar; naive; simple-
　minded ③ (now rare) to embar-
　rass ④ (now rare) to scold

村女 **chyùn néui**
　a country girl; a farmer's
　daughters

村莊 **chyùn jòng**
　a village; a formstead

杖 **jeuhng** (Md **zhàng**)
① a stick; a staff; a cane ② (an old punishment) to beat with cane; to flog ③ (now rare) a mourning staff ④ to presume on (one's connections, influence, etc.)

杖責 **jeuhng jaak**
to punish by caning; to flagellate

杖擊 **jeuhng gīk**
to hit or beat with a cane

杓 (勺) **seuk, bìu** (Md **sháo, biāo**)
① a receptacle or container, as a cup, ladle, spoon, etc.; the handle of such ② name of a constellation — the handle of the Dipper

杜 **douh** (Md **dù**)
① to plug (a hole, leak, etc.); to stop; to prevent ② to shut out; to restrict; to impede ③ the crab-apple; the russet pear ④ to fabricate; to practice forgery ⑤ a Chinese family name

杜絕 **douh jyuht**
to stop (a bad practice, etc.) for good; to cut off (relations with; irrevocable (contract, title-deed, etc.)

杜鵑 **douh gyūn**
cuckoo; goatsucker or night-jar

杞 **géi** (Md **qǐ**)
① a species of willow; a medlar tree ② Chi, name of a state in the Chow Dynasty in today's Honan Province ③ a Chinese family name

杞柳 **géi láuh**
a kind of willow

杞人憂天 **géi yàhn yàu tìn**
groundless worries or anxiety

束 **chūk** (Md **shù**)
① to bind; a bondage ② a bundle ③ to control; to restrain ④ a Chinese family name

束縛 **chūk bok**
restrains; restrictions; bandage

束手無策 **chūk sáu mòuh chaak**
no way out; powerless; at the end of the rope

杧 (芒) **mòng** (Md **máng**)
mango

杧果 **mòng gwó**
mango

杪 **míuh** (Md **miǎo**)
① a twig; the tip of a small branch ② end (of a period)

杪末 **míuh muht**
the end-point; the tip

杪冬 **míuh dùng**
end of winter (other seasons are spoken of in similar manner)

杭 **hòhng** (Md **háng**)
① Hangchow ② same as 航 — to sail; to cross a stream; to navigate ③ a Chinese family name

杭州 **Hòhng jàu**
Hangchow, captial of Chekkiang Province

杭綢 **Hòhng chàuh**
silk from Hangchow (consider the best)

杯 (盃) **bùi, būi** (Md **bēi**)
a cup; a tumber; a glass; a goblet

杯葛 **bùi got**
to boycott; a boycott

杯弓蛇影 **bùi gùng sèh yíng**
(literally) to mistake the shadow of a bow in one's cup as a snake — a false alarm

東 (东) **dùng** (Md **dōng**)
① the east; eastern ② to travel eastward ③ the host; the master; the owner ④ a Chinese family name

東方 **dùng fòng**
the east; oriental; a Chinese family name

東家 **dùng gà**
the owner of a house where one stays; the host; an owner of a company or shop

杲 **góu** (Md **gǎo**)
① bright — as the shining sun ② high

杲杲 **góu góu**
bright and scintillating

杳 **míuh** (Md **yǎo**)
① deep and expansive ② quiet; silent

杳無音信 **míuh mòuh yàm seun**
without any news (of him, etc.) for a long time

杳然 **míuh yìhn**
quiet and silent; lonely

杵 **chyúh** (Md **chǔ**)
a pestle; a baton used to pound launders

杵臼關節 **chyúh kau gwàan jit**
(in physiology) ball and socket joint

杵歌 **chyúh gō**
a tune one sings while pounding grains in a mortar with a pestle

枇 **pèih** (Md **pí**)
loquat

枇杷 **pèih pàh**
loquat

枇杷膏 **pèih pàh gōu**
condensed loquat extract (used as a medicine)

杷 **pàh** (Md **pa**)
loquat

杼 **chyúh** (Md **zhù**)
the shuttle of a loom

杼柚 **chyúh yáu**
looms

松 **chùhng** (Md **sōng**)
① pine; fir ② a Chinese family name

松樹 **chùhng syuh**
pine

松節油 **chùhng jit yàuh**
turpentine

板 **báan** (Md **bǎn**)
① a wood-board; a plank ② a plate (of tin, aluminium, etc.) a slab ③ printing blocks ④ rigid; stiff; immovable

板畫 **báan wá**
a wood cut

板起面孔 **báan héi mihn húng**
to make a long face; to look glum

枉 **wóng** (Md **wǎng**)
① to waste; useless; in vain ② crooked ③ to do or suffer wrong; aggrieved; oppression; to abuse (law) ④ (in polite language) to request another to deign or condescend to

枉法 **wóng faat**
to abuse law; to twist law to suit one's own purpose

枉然 **wóng yìhn**
useless; to no purpose; in vain

枋 fòng (Md fāng)
sandal wood

析 sīk (Md xī)
① to split; to rip or break apart; to devide; to separate ② to interpret; to explain; to analyse

析疑 sīk yìh
to explain a doubt; to clarify a doubt

分析 fàn sīk
to analyse

枕 jám, jam (Md zhěn)
① a pillow ② to use something as a pillow

枕頭 jám tàuh
a pillow

枕戈待旦 jam gwò doih daan
(literally) to use the spear as a pillow and wait for the morning — to be on the alert; ever-prepared for emergency

林 làhm (Md lín)
① a forest; a grove; a copse ② a collection of books; works literary extracts, etc. ③ many; numerous; a great body of (capable persons, etc.) ④ a Chinese family name

林木 làhm muhk
a forest; wooded land

林肯 Làhm háng
Abraham Lincoln (1809 – 1865), 16th U.S. President

枘 yeuih (Md ruì)
a wooden handle

枘鑿 yeuih johk
(literally) a square handle and a round socket — not fitting

枚 mùih (Md méi)
① the stalk; the trunk as opposed to branch ② a numerary auxiliary (used in connection with coins, fruits, stamps, bombs, etc.) ③ a gag for troops marching at night when silence means a lot ④ a Chinese family name

枚舉 mùih géui
to enumerate; to recount one by one

枝 jì (Md zhī)
① the branches of a tree; a branch; to branch off ② limbs

枝幹 jì gon
the trunk and the branches

枝頭 jì tàuh
on the branch

果 gwó (Md guǒ)
① fruit of a plant ② effect (in cause and effect) ③ surely; really; truly; exactly; if really ④ to stuff; to fill ⑤ to succeed ⑥ a Chinese family name

果汁 gwó jāp
fruit juice

果然 gwó yìhn
exactly as one expected; a kind of long-tailed monkey; having eaten enough

枒(椏、椏)ngà, ngàh (Md yā)
① the coconut tree ② the felloe of a wheel ③ disorderly growth of twigs

枒杈 ngà chà
twigs

架 ga (Md jià)
① a prop; a stand; a rack; a frame; to prop up; to support ② a framework or scaffold ③ to frame up (a charge, etc.); to fabricate

架子 ga jí
a rack; a stand; a frame; a scaffold; a skeleton

架式 ga sīk
a style (usually affected); a manner (usually assumed); a

pose

柜 **géui, gwaih** (Md **jǔ, guì**)
① a tree of the willow family ② same as 櫸, a very large tree whose beautiful fine-grained wood is good for making furniture, etc. ③ simplified form of "櫃" **gwaih**

柜柳 **géui láuh**
a tree of the willow family; same as above ②

枯 **fù** (Md **kū**)
① withered; dry ② dried wood ③ ill health; emaciated

枯燥 **fù chou**
dry; listless; languid

枯涸 **fù kok**
(usually said of wells, rivers, etc.) dry or waterless

柱 **chyúh** (Md **zhù**)
① a pillar; a post ② a cylinder ③ to support ④ to stab; to pierce

柱子 **chyúh jí**
a pillar; a post

柱石 **chyúh sehk**
pillars of a nation; key ministers of a nation

枰 **pìhng** (Md **píng**)
① a chess board ② a chess game

柿 **chíh, chí** (Md **shì**)
the persimmon

柿子 **chíh jí**
the persimmon fruit

柿餅 **chí béng**
flattened and dried persimmon

枲 **sái** (Md **xǐ**)
the male nettle-hamp

枳 **jí** (Md **zhǐ**)
① bramble ② a variety of orange with very thick skin

枳實 **jí saht**
a variety of arange with thick skin which is used in herbal medicine

枳棘 **jí gīk**
thorns; thorny; plants with many thorns

枵 **hiù** (Md **xiāo**)
empty

枵腹從公 **hiù fūk chùhng gùng**
to do one's duty even with an empty stomach

枴 **gwáai** (Md **guǎi**)
① to swindle; to decoy; to kidnap ② to turn ③ a staff for and old person; a cane

拐杖 **gwáai jeuhng**
an old person's staff

拐子 **gwáai jí**
a kidnapper

枷 **gà** (Md **jiā**)
① the cangue — worn by prisoners in former times ② a frame; a scaffold

枷鎖 **gà só**
the cangue and lock; (used figuratively) bondage; shackle

枸 **gáu, géui** (Md **gōu, gǒu, jǔ**)
medlar

枸杞 **gáu géi**
medlar

柁 **tòh** (Md **tuó, duò**)
① large tie-beams ② same as 舵 the rudder of a ship

柄 **bing, beng** (Md **bǐng, bìng**)
① the handle of something ② authority; power ③ to operate; to handle; to control

權柄 **kyùhn bing**
authority; power

刀柄 **dōu beng**
the handle of a knife

柏 **paak, baak** (Md **bǎi, bó**)
① cypress; cedar ② a Chinese family name

柏樹 **paak syuh**
the cypress; cedar

柏林 **Baak làhm**
Berlin, Germany

某 **máuh** (Md **mǒu**)
① a certain person or thing ② formerly used in place of "I"

某日 **máuh yaht**
a certain day

某某 **máuh máuh**
so-and-so; a certain person

甘 **gàm** (Md **gān**)
orange

柑子 **gàm jí**
orange (fruit)

染 **yíhm** (Md **rǎn**)
① to dye ② to get infected; to catch a disease ③ to have an affair with ④ (in Chinese painting and calligraphy) to make strokes

染色 **yíhm sīk**
to dye

染病 **yíhm bihng**
to get infected; to catch a disease

柔 **yàuh** (Md **róu**)
① soft and tender ② amiable; pliant; yielding; submissive; gentle; supple ③ new grass budding in spring

柔和 **yàuh wòh**
soft; gentle; amiable; tender

柔道 **yàuh douh**
judo

柘 **je** (Md **zhè**)
① a thorny tree about 15 feet high whose leaves can be used in place of mulberry leaves in feeding silk worms and whose bark containes a yellow dye ② sugarcane

柘黃 **je wòhng**
yellow dye made from the bark of the tree

柘絲 **je sì**
silk from worms fed on these leaves

柯 **ò** (Md **kē**)
① "Pasania cuspidata" a tall evergreen tree ② handle of an axe ③ a stalk or branch ④ a Chinese family name

柯達 **Ò daaht**
Kodak, a brand name

柯駕 **ò ga**
a respectful reference to the marriage go-between

柙 **jaahp, haahp** (Md **xiá**)
① a pen for wild beasts especially the fierce one's ② a scabbard; a case for sword

柚 **yáu, yauh** (Md **yóu, yòu**)
① pumelo or pomelo; grape-fruit ② teak

柚木 **yáu muhk**
teak wood

柚子 **yáu jí**
pumelo; pomelo; grapefruit

柝 (欜) **tok** (Md **tuò**)
a watchman's rattle

柞 **jok, ja** (Md **zuò, zhà**)
"Myroxylon racemosum", an ever green thorny tree with small leaves, fine and sturdy wood; an oak

柞蠶 **ja chàahm**
tussah silkworm

柞綢 **ja chàuh**
tussah silk fabric

柢 **dái** (Md **dǐ**)
root; foundation; base

查 **chàh, jà** (Md **chá, zhā**)
① to investigate; to check; to seek out; to look into ② (used at the beginning of an offical correspondence; It appears . . . ; It seems . . . ; It is known; It is found that . .

查出 **chàh chēut**
to find out; to discover

查考 **chàh háau**
to investigate; to examine; to ponder

柩 **gauh, gau** (Md **jiù**)
a coffin with a corpse in it

靈柩 **lìhng gauh**
a coffin containing a corpse

柬 **gáan** (Md **jiǎn**)
① a letter; an invitation or visiting card ② to select; to pick

請柬 **chíng gáan**
an invitation

柬埔寨 **Gáan póu jaaih**
Cambodia

柳 **láuh** (Md **liǔ**)
① willow tree ② name of one of the 28 Constellation ③ a Chinese family name

柳絮 **láuh seuih**
willow cot kins

柳眉 **láuh mèih**
the eye brows of a beautiful woman — like leaves of the willow

柵(栅) **chaak, sàan** (Md **zhà, shān**)
a fence of bamboo or wood; a palisade; a railing of posts; window-bars

柵門 **chaak mùhn**
a door in a palisade

柵欄兒 **sàan làahn yìh**
a fence; a palisade; a railing

柴 **chàaih** (Md **chái**)
① firewood; brushwood; faggots ② thin; emaciated ③ (now rare) fence ④ a Chinese family name

柴扉 **chàaih fèi**
a door of brushwood-poor family

柴油 **chàaih yàuh**
dissel

柒 **chāt** (Md **qī**)
another form of 七 (seven), used in writing checks, etc. to prevent fraud

柘 **tòih** (Md **tái**)
① same as 檯 — a desk or table ② an ancient unit of measure-ment

柘球 **tòih kàuh**
table tennis

枹(桴) **fù** (Md **fú**)
a drum-stick

枹鼓 **fù gú**
drum beaten on the battle-field to boast morale; a drum beaten to warn invasion of bandits in Han Dynasty

栗 **leuht** (Md **lì**)
① chestnut tree ② strong and tough; firm; durable ③ respect-ful; fearful; awe-inspiring ④ dignified; majestic ⑤ a Chinese family name

栗子 **leuht jí**
chestnuts

栗鼠 **leuht syú**
a squirrel

栓 **sàan** (Md **shuān**)
a wooden pin or peg; a stopper for a bottle, etc.

校 **haauh, gaau** (Md **xiào, jiào**)
① a school ② field-grade (officers) ③ to compare; to correct ④ to proofread ⑤ to revise (books, etc.); to collate

校服 **haauh fuhk**
school uniform

校對 **gaau deui**
to proofread; to correct proofs; a proofreader

栩 **héui** (Md **xǔ**)
① a species of oak ② glad; pleased

栩栩如生 **héui héui yùh sàng**
(said of a portrait, etc.) true-to-life; life like

株 **jyù** (Md **zhū**)
① a tree; a numerary auxiliary for counting trees or similar things ② roots that grow above ground

株連 **jyù lìhn**
to involve others in a crime one committed (especially in ancient China when friends, relatives of a person who committed treason could get such incrimination)

核 **haht, waht** (Md **hé, hú**)
① a kernel; a fruit stone; a walnut; a hard lump ② to investigate; to examine; to verify; to study ③ nuclear; nucleus

核對 **haht deui**
to verify; to check the facts

核子 **waht jí**
nucleus; nuclear

根 **gàn** (Md **gēn**)
① root of a plant ② a base; a foundation ③ the beginning, cause, or source of something ④ (in math.) the root of a number ⑤ (in chemistry) base ⑥ a piece (of string, rope, etc.); a (stick, spear, or things of slender shape) ⑦ a Chinese family name

根本 **gàn bún**
root, base or origin; foundation; basis

根由 **gàn yàuh**
the source; origin or cause of something

格 **gaak** (Md **gé**)
① to correct; to adjust or regulate ② to reach; to come or go to ③ to influence ④ to resist; to attack; to fight ⑤ to obstruct; to block ⑥ to study thoroughly; to search to the very source; to investigate ⑦ a standard; a form; a rule; a pattern ⑧ a frame; a blank; a trellis ⑨ a Chinese family name

格言 **gaak yìhn**
a proverb; a motto; an aphorism

格調 **gaak diuh**
literary or artistic style; personality; form; pattern

栽 **jòi** (Md **zāi**)
① to plant ② to care; to assist ③ to fail; to fall ④ young trees, saplings, cuttings for planting

栽種 **jòi jung**
to plant; to grow

栽倒 **jòi dóu**
to fall

桀 **giht** (Md **jié**)
① ferocious and cruel ② name of the last ruler of the Hsia Dynasty ③ same as 傑 , outstanding and brave ④ a Chinese family name

桀驁 **giht ngòuh**
tyrannical and haughty

桀黠 **giht haht**
crooked and cruel

桁 **hàhng, hohng** (Md **héng, hàng**)
① a big wooden collar (for punishing a criminal) ② a rack for hanging clothes ③ the purlius of a roof

桁楊 **hàhng yèuhng**
a cangue

桁桷 **hàhng gok**
purlius and rafters

桂 **gwai** (Md **guì**)
① cassia or cinnamon ② a short name of Kwangsi Province ③ a Chinese family name

桂花 **gwai fā**
sweet osmanthus

桂林 **Gwai làhm**
Kweilin, capital of Kwangsi Province

桃 **tòuh** (Md **táo**)
① peach ② a Chinese family name

桃花 **tòuh fā**
the peach blossom

桃色新聞 **tòuh sīk sàn màhn**
news of illicit love

桄 **gwòng** (Md **guàng, guāng**)
① cross beam ② grade

桄榔 **gwòng lòhng**
coir-palm (Arenga, saccharifera)

桅 **wàih** (Md **wéi**)
the mast of a ship

桅竿 **wàih gòn**
the mast of a boat

桌 **cheuk, jeuk** (Md **zhuō**)
① table ② dishes for guests around the table — usually consisting of 20 courses ③ a tableful of guests (10 to 12 persons at a round table)

桌子 **cheuk jí**
a table

桌球 **cheuk kàuh**
table tennis; ping pong; billiard

框 **kwàang, hòng** (Md **kuàng, kuāng**)
① door frame ② frame; framework ③ skeleton (of a lantern, etc.)

框子 **kwàang jí**
a frame; framework

門框 **mùhn kwàang**
door frame

案 **ngon, on** (Md **àn**)
① a narrow, long table; a bench or bar before a judge ② according to; on the strength of; following this precedent ③ a legal case; legal records; a legal offense ④ same as 按 — to press

案件 **ngon gihn**
a legal case; a crime

案頭 **on tàuh**
on the desk

桎 **jaht** (Md **zhì**)
① fetters; shackles; to fetter ② to suffocate

桎梏 **jaht gūk**
shackles

桐 **tùhng** (Md **tóng**)
① paulownia ② a Chinese family

name

桐油 **tùhng yàuh**
tung-oil; wood-oil obtained from the seeds of paulownia

桐棺 **tùhng gùn**
a coffin made of timber of paulownia, considered to be of very inferior quality

桑 **sòng** (Md **sāng**)
① the mulberry tree ② a Chinese family name

桑田 **sòng tìhn**
a plantation of mulberry trees

桑梓 **sòng jí**
one's native place or home-town

桔 **gāt** (Md **jié, jū**)
① a well-sweep ② an abbreviated form of 橘, orange or tangerine

桔梗 **gāt gáng**
Chinese bellflower, (Platycodon grandi florus)

桓 **wùhn** (Md **huán**)
① a tree with leaves like a willow and white bark ② a Chinese family name

盤桓 **pùhn wùhn**
to linger

栖 **chài** (Md **qī, xī**)
same as 棲, to roost; to perch; to settle; to live; to stay

栖遑 **chài wòhng**
uneasy and anxious

栖栖然 **chài chài yìhn**
bustling and excited

桕 **kau** (Md **jiù**)
the tallow tree, (sapium sebiferum)

桫 **sò** (Md **suō**)
① horse chestnut (Stewartia pseudoca mellia) ② sal (Cyathea spinulosa)

桫欏 **sò lòh**
the horse chestnut (stewartia pseudoca mellia); sal (Cyathia spinulosa)

桴 **fù** (Md **fú**)
① the ridge pole on a roof ② a drumstick ③ a raft (of wood or bamboo)

桴鼓相應 **fù gú sèung ying**
to render mutual support or assistance

桶 **túng** (Md **tǎng**)
a bucket; a tub; a pail; a barrel; a keg

桶匠 **túng jeuhng**
a cooper

桶子 **túng jí**
a bucket; a pail; a barrel

梆 **bòng** (Md **bāng**)
a watchman's rattle made of wood or bamboo

梆子 **bòng jí**
a watchman's rattle; a kind of Chinese opera originated in Shensi

梆子腔 **bòng jí hòng**
a type of Chinese opera originated in Shensi

梅(楳、槑) **mùih**
(Md **méi**)
① plums; prunes ② a Chinese family name

梅子 **mùih jí**
plums

梅毒 **mùih duhk**
sypilis

梏 **gūk** (Md **gù**)
① hand-shackles; handcuffs; manacles ② to insult; to play joke on

梏亡 **gūk mòhng**
to be fettered in mind by greed

梓 jí (Md jǐ)

① Catalpa ovata. a tall, stately tree with palm-shaped leaves and yellow flowers in summer ② one's native place or home-town ③ to make furniture; furniture ④ to carve words on woodboard; printing blocks ⑤ (now rare) a Chinese family name

梓里 jí léih

one's native place or home-town

梓器 jí hei

coffin

梗 gáng (Md gěng)

① the branch or stem of a plant ② to peck or pierce with thorn; thorny ③ outline; synopsis; summary ④ to block; to obstruct ⑤ stubborn ⑥ fierce and fearless ⑦ ailment; bane; distress ⑧ honest; stiff; straight

梗概 gáng koi

outline; summary; synopsis

梗直 gáng jihk

straight and honest; out spoken

條 (条) tiuh (Md tiáo)

① an article, section, clause, etc. of an agreement, pact, treaty, law, etc. ② in good order; (to present) one by one ③ numerary adjunct for something narrow and long, as roads, fish, ropes, dogs, snakes, etc. ④ stripes

條目 tiuh muhk

clauses or articles of an agreement, etc.; particulars or details

條列 tiuh laih

rules, regulations, or laws

梃 tihng (Md tǐng, tìng)

① a club; a cudgel; a stick; a cane ② a stalk; a branch; a stem ③ straight and strong

梃杖 tihng jeuhng

a club; a stick

梁 lèuhng (Md liáng)

① a bridge ② beams of a house ③ a ridge; a swelling ④ Liang, name of a dynasty, (502 to 556 A.D.) ⑤ a state during the Warring State period, also known as Wei ⑥ a Chinese family name

梁麗 lèuhng laih

beams on a roof; (now rare) a small boat

梁山泊 Lèuhng sàan bohk

the homebase of a gang of hero-bandits in All Men Are Brothers (水滸), a very popular fiction written by Shih Naian (施耐庵)

梧 ǹgh (Md wú)

firmiana (Firmiana platani folia)

梧桐 ǹgh tùhng

firmiana

梧州 Ǹgh jàu

Wuchow, an important city in Kwangsi Province

梟 (梟) hìu (Md xiāo)

① an owl; a legendary bird said to eat its own mother ② a smuggler of contrabands, narcotics, etc. ③ brave and unscrupulous

梟雄 hìu hùhng

an unscrupulous, brave and capable person

梟鳥 hìu níuh

an owl

梢 sàau (Md shāo)

① an owl; a legendary bird said to eat its own mother ② a smuggler of contrabands, narcotics, etc. ③ brave and unscrupulous

梢公 sàau gùng

a helmsman; a boatman

梢頭 **sàau tàuh**
the tip of a tree; the close of spring

梭 **sò** (Md **suō**)
① a weaver's shuttle ② to and fro ③ swift

梭巡 **sò chèuhn**
to patrol to and fro

梭子 **sò jí**
a weaver's shuttle

桿(杆) **gón** (Md **gǎn**)
a wooden pole, cane, stick, club

桿子 **gón jí**
a club; a stick

桿菌 **gón kwán**
bacillus; bacilli

梯 **tài** (Md **tī**)
① a ladder; steps; stairs ② something to lean or depend on

梯子 **tài jí**
a ladder or steps

梯形 **tài yìhng**
(in geometry) trapezoid

械 **haaih** (Md **xiè**)
① weapons ② implements ③ shackles; fetters ④ to arrest and put in prison

械鬥 **haaih dau**
(said of mobs or gangsters) to fight with arms or implements

械用 **haaih yuhng**
implements

棁 **jyut** (Md **zhuō**)
① a joist ② a club or cane

梳 **sò** (Md **shū**)
a comb; a coarse comb; to comb

梳頭 **sò tàuh**
to comb one's hair

梳子 **sò jí**
a comb

梵 **fàahn, faahn**
(Md **fàn**)
① clean and pure ② Sanskirt; Brahman ③ anything pertaining to Buddhism

梵文 **fàahn màhn**
the Sanskirt (written)

梵諦崗 **Fàahn dai gòng**
The Vatican

梔(栀) **jì** (Md **zhī**)
gardenia

梔子 **jì jí**
gardenia

梔子花 **jì jí fà**
cape-jasmine

梨(棃) **lèih** (Md **lí**)
① a pear ② Chinese opera

梨樹 **lèih syuh**
the pear tree

梨園 **lèih yùhn**
the operatic circle

棉 **mìhn** (Md **mián**)
cotton

棉布 **mìhn bou**
cotton cloth

棉花 **mìhn fà**
cotton

棋(棊、碁) **kèih**
(Md **qí**)
chess or other similar games

棋王 **kèih wòhng**
chess champion

棋盤 **kèih pún**
a chess-board

棍 **gwan** (Md **gùn**)
① a club; a stick; a cudgel; a truncheon

棍棒 **gwan páahng**
clubs; sticks

棍騙 **gwan pin**
　　to swindle; to cheat; to
　　wheedle

棒 **páahng (Md bàng)**
　　① a club; a stick; a truncheon ②
　　to hit with a club ③ good; strong;
　　wonderful

棒打 **páahng dá**
　　to hit with a club

棒球 **páahng kàuh**
　　baseball

棗(枣) **jóu (Md zào)**
　　① jujube; commonly called dates
　　— Zizy – plus vulgaris ② a
　　Chinese family name

棗子 **jóu jí**
　　dates

棗泥 **jóu nàih**
　　mashed dates — used as stuf-
　　fing for pastry or dumpling

棘 **gīk (Md jí)**
　　① buckthorns; thorny brambles
　　② urgent; troublesome; difficult
　　③ a Chinese family name

棘手 **gīk sáu**
　　thorny (matter); difficult to
　　handle

荊棘 **gìng gīk**
　　thorns

棚 **pàahng (Md péng)**
　　a tent; a shed; an awning; a mat
　　awning

棚子 **pàahng jí**
　　a small tent; a shed

棚匠 **pàahng jeuhng**
　　a person who erects tents or
　　mat awnings as a profession

棟 (栋) **dung (Md dòng)**
　　the main-beam of a house

棟樑 **dung lèuhng**
　　pillars and beams

棟宇 **dung yúh**
　　a house

棠 **tòhng (Md táng)**
　　the crab-apple; the wild plum

棠棣 **tòhng daih**
　　the wild plum — Prunus
　　japonica; brothers

棣 **daih (Md dì)**
　　① a mountain tree, as cherry, etc.
　　② same as 弟 , kid brother

棣華 **daih wàh**
　　brothers

棕(椶) **jùng (Md zōng)**
　　the palm tree

棕色 **jùng sīk**
　　brown, the color of palm fibers

棕櫚 **jùng lèuih**
　　the coir palm of Central China
　　— Trechycarpus excelsa

棧(栈) **jaahn**
(Md zhàn)
　　① a storehouse; a warehouse; a
　　tavern; an inn ② a road made
　　along a cliff ③ (now rare) a pen
　　or stable ④ a Chinese family
　　name

棧道 **jaahn douh**
　　a log-formed road along a
　　steep cliff

棧房 **jaahn fòhng**
　　a warehouse; a storehouse; a
　　go down; a tavern; an inn

根(枨) **chàahng**
(Md chéng)
　　① door-posts ② to touch

根撥 **chàahng buht**
　　to push aside with hand

根觸 **chàahng jūk**
　　to be sentinentally touched or
　　moved; to touch with hand

棨 **kái** (Md **qǐ**)
(in ancient China) a tally or wooden pass used by a messenger as his credential in passing through a guarded gate, check-point, etc.

棨戟 **kái gīk**
(in ancient China) a black cloth draped over a spear used to herald the arrival of an official so that people will step aside to let pass

棫 **wihk** (Md **yù**)
a thorny shrub with yellow flowers and dark fruit

棫樸 **wihk pok**
title of a poem in the Book of Poetry; a multitude of talented persons

棬 **hyùn** (Md **quān**)
a wooden bowl; crooked wood

棬樞 **hyùn syù**
(literally) a door made of wraped wood — very poor family

森 **sàm** (Md **sēn**)
① luxuriant vegetation or luxuriant growth of trees ② dark and obscure; severe ③ serene; majestic

森林 **sàm làhm**
forest

森嚴 **sàm yìhm**
stern and severe; forbidden (look); awe-inspiring

棵 **fó** (Md **kē**)
a numerary adjunct for trees

一棵樹 **yāt fó syuh**
a tree

棹(櫂) **jaauh**
(Md **zhào**)
① an oar or scull ② a boat

棱(稜) **lìhng** (Md **lěng**)
① a corner; an angle; an edge ② a square piece of wood ③ an awe-inspiring air

棱角 **lìhng gok**
an angle; a corner

棱鏡 **lìhng geng**
a prism

椅 **yí, yì** (Md **yǐ, yì**)
① a chair ② Idesia polycarpa (name of a tree)

椅子 **yí jí**
a chair

椅背 **yí bui**
the back of a chair

棺 **gùn** (Md **guān**)
a coffin (usually made of wood in China)

棺材 **gùn chòih**
a coffin

棺蓋 **gùn koi**
the lid of a coffin

棼 **fàhn** (Md **fén**)
① beams on the roof of a house ② a kind of linen ③ confused; disarrayed

植 **jihk** (Md **zhí**)
① to plant; to set up; to erect ② (now rare) to lean on ③ plants; vegetation

植物 **jihk maht**
vegetables; plants; flora

植樹 **jihk syuh**
to plant trees

椎 **jèui, chèuih** (Md **zhuī, chuí**)
① a hammer; a mallet; a bludgeon ② to beat; to hammer; to hit; to strike

椎骨 **jèui gwāt**
vertebra

椎擊 **chèuih gīk**
　　to strike with a mallet, a hammer, etc.

椒 **jiu** (Md **jiāo**)
　① pepper; other spices ② mountain-top

椒目 **jiu muhk**
　　the dark seeds of pepper fruit

椒房 **jiu fòhng**
　　the palace of the queen; private apartments of the empress

椓 **deuk** (Md **zhuó**)
　① to strike; to hammer ② (an ancient punishment) to castrate; castration

棲 **chāi** (Md **qī**)
　same as '栖'

椏 **ngàh** (Md **yā**)
　same as '枒'

椁(槨) **gwok** (Md **guǒ**)
　an outer coffin

極(极) **gihk** (Md **jí**)
　① to exhaust ② extreme; highest; topmost; farthest ③ pole, as the North and South Poles

極端 **gihk dyūn**
　　an extreme; an extreme act; extremely

極限 **gihk haahn**
　　(in mathematics) a limit

椰 **yèh** (Md **yē**)
coconut; coconut palm; coconut tree

椰子 **yèh jí**
　　coconut

椰菜 **yèh choi**
　　Savoy

棄(弃) **hei** (Md **qì**)
　① to discard; to cast aside ② to reject; to abandon; to desert ③ to forget

棄權 **hei kyùhn**
　　(in voting) to abstain; to waive a right; a waiver

棄置 **hei ji**
　　to cast aside

楮 **chyúh** (Md **chǔ**)
paper mulberry

楮幣 **chyúh baih**
　　bank note

楮墨 **chyúh mahk**
　　paper and ink

椽 **chyùhn** (Md **chuán**)
beam; rafter

椽柱 **chyùhn chyúh**
　　a pillar

椽子 **chyùhn jí**
　　a beam; a rafter

椿 **chèun** (Md **chūn**)
　① father ② cedrela sinensio

椿庭 **chèun tìhng**
　　father

椿萱 **chèun syùn**
　　parents

楂(樝) **jà** (Md **zhā**)
　① a piece of hawthorn ② a wooden raft

楂楂 **jà jà**
　　the sound of magpies crowing

楊(杨) **yèuhng** (Md **yáng**)
　① poplar ② a Chinese family name

楊柳 **yèuhng láuh**
　　willow

楊桃 **yèuhng tòuh**
　　the juicy fruit of Averrhora carambibola

楓(枫) **fùng** (Md **fēng**)
maple

楓樹 **fùng syuh**
maple

楓橋 **Fùng kìuh**
name of a bridge at Soochow,
Kiangsu Province

楚 **chó** (Md **chǔ**)
① name of a powerful feudal
state which existed 740 — 330
B.C. ② a Chinese family name

楚楚可憐 **chó chó hó lìhn**
pathetically delicate; tender
and pathetic

清楚 **chìng chó**
clear

楔 **sit** (Md **xiē**)
① wedge ② gate post

楔子 **sit jí**
wedge; preface; foreword

楔形文字 **sit yìhng màhn jih**
cuneiform

楝 **lihn** (Md **liàn**)
a kind of tree (melia japonica)

榆 **yùh** (Md **yú**)
elm

榆樹 **yùh syuh**
elm; elm tree

榆莢 **yùh gaap**
elm seeds

楠(枏、柟) **nàahm**
(Md **nán**)
an even-grained; yellowish, fine
wood used for furniture; commonly known as cedar

楠木 **nàahm muhk**
cedar

楣 **mèih** (Md **méi**)
lintel

楣式 **mèih sīk**
lintel style

楨(桢) **jìng** (Md **zhēn, zhēng**)
① sturdy wood ② posts at ends
of walls

楬 **kit** (Md **jié**)
a signpost

楫 **jip** (Md **jí**)
an oar

楫師 **jip sì**
a boatman; a ferryman

業(业) **yihp** (Md **yè**)
① work; occupation; profession;
calling; trade ② estate; property
③ already

業主 **yihp jyú**
proprietor; owner

業餘 **yihp yùh**
non-professional; amateur

楷 **káai, gàai** (Md **kǎi, jiē**)
① regular; standard ② model;
norm ③ (in calligraphy) standard
script

楷模 **káai mòuh**
model (for imitation)

楷書 **káai syù**
standard script of handwriting

楸 **chàu** (Md **qiū**)
a kind of hard wood used for
making chessboard (mallotus
japonicus)

楸枰 **chàu pìhng**
a chess board

楹 **yìhng** (Md **yíng**)
a pillar; a column

楹柱 **yìhng chyúh**
a pillar; a column

楹聯 **yìhng lyùhn**
scrolls hung on a pillar

槌 **chèuih** (Md **chuí**)
a hammer

槌鼓 **chèuih gú**
to beat a drum

槌兒 **chèuih yìh**
a hammer

榦 **gon** (Md **gàn**)
same as '幹' see '干' radical

榕 **yùhng** (Md **róng**)
banyan tree

榕樹 **Yùhng syuh**
banyan tree

榕城 **Yùhng sìhng**
another name of Foochow
(福州) noted for its banyan
tree

榔 **lòhng** (Md **láng**)
① betel palm ② betel nut

榛 **jèun** (Md **zhēn**)
hazelnut

榛子 **jèun jí**
hazelnut

榛莽 **jèun móhng**
thicket; bush

榖 **gūk** (Md **gǔ**)
a kind of tree (Broussonetia
papyrifera)

榜 **bóng** (Md **bǎng**)
publicly posted roll of successful
examinees

榜文 **bóng màhn**
the writing in a public notice

榜樣 **bóng yeuhng**
example; model

榨 **ja** (Md **zhà**)
to squeeze or press (for juice)

榨取 **ja chéui**
exploitation; to exploit; to
squeeze

榨菜 **ja choi**
preserved mustard seasoned
with salt and hot pepper

榫 **séun** (Md **sǔn**)
tenon and mortise

榫眼 **séun ngáahn**
mortise

榫頭 **séun tàuh**
tenon

榮 (荣) **wìhng**
(Md **róng**)
① glory; honor ② luxuriant; lush;
teeming ③ a Chinese family name

榮幸 **wìhng hahng**
honored; to have the honor
of ...

榮耀 **wìhng yiuh**
glory; honor; splendor

榻 **taap** (Md **tà**)
a couch; a bed

榻布 **taap bou**
a kind of coarse cloth

榻登 **taap dàng**
a rug placed on a low-legged
stool beside a bed

榾 **gwāt** (Md **gǔ**)
chopped pieces of wood

榾柮 **gwāt dēut**
chopped pieces of wood

榭 **jeh** (Md **xiè**)
pavilion; arbor; kiosk

舞榭 **móuh jeh**
place for dancing

槁 (槀) **góu** (Md **gǎo**)
withered; dead; rotten

槁骨 **góu gwāt**
bones of the deceased

槁木死灰 **góu muhk séi fùi**
(literally) rotten wood and cold
ashes — a person utterly
without vitality or ambition

榴 **làuh** (Md **líu**)
pomegranate

榴火 **làuh fó**
fiery red of pomegranate blossoms

榴彈礮 **làuh dáan paau**
howitzer

槎 **chàh** (Md **chá**)
① a raft ② to hew; to chop; to cut

槊 **sok** (Md **shuò**)
a spear; a lance

構(构) **gau, kau**
(Md **gòu**)
to frame; to form; to build; to establish; to constitute; to scheme

構造 **gau jouh**
structure; construction; organization

構圖 **gau tòuh**
composition (in drawing)

槐 **wàaih** (Md **huái**)
locust tree (Sophara japonica) similar to the ash; acacia

槐序 **wàaih jeuih**
summer

槐火 **wàaih fó**
fire made by drilling a piece of locust wood

槍(枪、鎗) **chēung**
(Md **qiāng**)
① a spear; a lance; a javelin ② a rifle; a pistol; a gun

槍械 **chēung haaih**
weapons

槍決 **chēung kyut**
to execute by shooting; to shoot to death

槓(杠) **gong** (Md **gàng**)
① a lever; a carrying pole ② to

sharpen (a knife) ③ to argue; to dispute

槓桿 **gong gòn**
a lever

槓刀 **gong dōu**
to sharpen a knife

榷 **kok** (Md **què**)
① to monopolize ② to levy monopoly

榷利 **kok leih**
to enjoy monopoly

榷茶 **kok chàh**
to levy tea taxes

槃 **pùhn** (Md **pán**)
① wooden tray ② great

槃才 **pùhn chòih**
a person of great talent

槃匜 **pùhn yìh**
basin; tray (in ancient time)

櫘 **seuih** (Md **hùi**)
small coffin

槧(椠) **chim** (Md **qiàn**)
① wooden tablet for writing ② an edition, or version, of a book ③ a letter

槧本 **chim bún**
book printed by engravings

槳(桨) **jéung**
(Md **jiǎng**)
an oar

概 **koi** (Md **gài**)
general; overall; roughly

概括 **koi kut**
to summarize; skeleton

概念 **koi nihm**
a concept; a conception; a general idea

槽 **chòuh** (Md **cáo**)
① a manger ② a trough; a flume; a chute

槿 **gán** (Md **jǐn**)
hibiscus

槭 **chīk** (Md **qī**)
a kind of maple

椿(桩)**jòng** (Md **zhuāng**)
① a stake; a post; a pile ② a numerary auxiliary for affairs or matters

樅(枞)**chùng** (Md **cōng**)
a fir; a fir tree (Abies firma)

樂 (乐)**lohk, ngohk, ngaauh** (Md **lè, yuè, yào**)
① happy; glad; joyful; joyous; cheerful; elated; content; delighted; pleased; willing ② pleasant; agreeable; enjoyable; pleasing; comfortable ③ music ④ a Chinese family name ⑤ to love; to like; to be fond of; to delight in

樂觀 **lohk gùn**
optimistic

樂隊 **ngohk déui**
a band; an orchestra

樊 **fàahn** (Md **fán**)
① bird cage ② disorderly; confused; messy ③ a Chinese family name

樊籠 **fàahn lùhng**
a cage to confine birds or wild beasts (also used figuratively)

樊然 **fàahn yìhn**
disorderly; confused; messy

樓 (楼)**làuh** (Md **lóu**)
a building of two stories or more; a tower

樓房 **làuh fòhng**
a building of two stories or more

樓梯 **làuh tài**
a staircase

槲 **huk** (Md **hú**)
a species of oak (Quercus dentata)

樑 **lèuhng** (Md **liáng**)
beams of a house; interchangable with ' 梁 '

樗 **syù** (Md **chū**)
Ailanthus altissima

樗蒲 **syù pòuh**
an ancient gambling game

樗材 **syù chòih**
a good-for-nothing (a self-reference in polite conversation)

標 (标)**bìu** (Md **biāo**)
① to show; to indicate; to mark; to symbolize ② mark; sign; symbol; indication; label ③ appearance

標點 **bìu dím**
punctuation

標題 **bìu tàih**
heading; title; headline

樞 (枢)**syù** (Md **shū**)
a hinge; a pivot

樞紐 **syù náu**
the vital point; the key; the pivot

樞密院 **syù maht yún**
privy council or cabinet, of the late Tang Dynasty and the Sung Dynasty

樟 **jèung** (Md **zhāng**)
camphor tree

樟木 **jèung muhk**
camphor tree; wood of camphor tree

樟腦 **jèung nóuh**
camphor

模 **mòuh** (Md **mó, mú**)
① model; norm ② to imitate; to copy ③ a mold; a form

模仿 **mòuh fóng**
to imitate; to copy

模樣 **mòuh yeuhng**
appearance; look

樣 (样) **yeuhng**
(Md **yàng**)
① appearance; look ② style; pattern; mode; form ③ a sort; a kind; a variety ④ a sample

樣本 **yeuhng bún**
a sample (of printed material)

樣子 **yeuhng jí**
appearance; look; style; mode; pattern; a sample; a proof sheet

橫 **wàahng, waahng**
(Md **héng, hèng**)
① horizontal; cross-wise; lateral ② east to west or vice versa ③ by the side of; sideways ④ a Chinese family name ⑤ cross-grained; perverse ⑥ presumptuous and unreasonable ⑦ unexpected; uncalled for

橫寫 **wàahng sé**
to write horizontally (as distinct from the traditional chinese way of writing from top to bottom)

橫死 **waahng séi**
an unnatural death; a violent death

橐 (橐) **tok** (Md **tuó**)
a bag or sack; a bag without bottom

橐駝 **tok tòh**
a camel; a hunchback

橐橐 **tok tok**
sound of footsteps or rattles

榍 **sài** (Md **xī**)
cassia tree

樵 **chìuh** (Md **qiáo**)
① firewood; fuel ② to gather fuel or firewood ③ a wood cutter ④ to burn ④ a tower; a lookout

樵夫 **chìuh fù**
a wood cutter

樵戶 **chìuh wuh**
a family which lives on wood-cutting or gathering firewood

樸 (朴) **pok** (Md **pǔ**)
① (said of dress, clothing, literary style, etc.) plain; simple ② the substance of things; things in the rough ③ honest, sincere; simple ④ a tree of the elm family (Aphananthe aspera)

樸素 **pok sou**
(said of dresses, etc.) simple and plain

樸實 **pok saht**
(said of dresses, style, etc.) simple; plain; honest; sincere simple in taste

樹 (树) **syuh** (Md **shù**)
① tree ② to plant ③ to erect, to establish ④ a door screen (now rare)

樹皮 **syuh pèih**
bark

樹立 **syuh lahp**
to establish (a reputation, etc.)

樺 (桦) **wah** (Md **huà**)
birch

樺科 **wah fò**
Betulaceae

樺燭 **wah jūk**
a torch or candle made by rolling the bark of birch around beeswax

樽（罇）**jèun** (Md **zūn**)
① a wine vessel; a goblet; a bottle; a wine jar ② (of vegetation) luxuriant

樽組 **jèun jó**
a goblet; a wine vessel (used in ritual)

橢（楕）**tóh** (Md **tuǒ**)
oval; oblong; elliptical

橢圓 **tóh yùhn**
ellipse

橢圓形 **tóh yùhn yìhng**
oval; elliptical

橄 **gaam** (Md **gǎn**)
olive

橄欖 **gaam láam**
olives

橄欖球 **gaam láam kàuh**
American football; rugby

橇 **hìu** (Md **qiāo**)
a sledge for transportation over mud or snow

橈（桡）**nàauh** (Md **ráo**)
① crooked or bent wood ② to fear ③ to disperse ④ to wrong or to be wrong ⑤ an oar; to row

橈骨 **nàauh gwāt**
the radius of the forearm

橈足 **nàauh jūk**
the flat limbs of a shrimp, etc. for swimming

橋（桥）**kìuh** (Md **qiáo**)
① a bridge, any bridge-like structure ② beams of a structure ③ (now rare) cross-grained ④ tall; high; elevated ⑤ a Chinese family name

橋樑 **kìuh lèuhng**
any material which forms the span of a bridge

橋牌 **kìuh páai**
bridge (game)

橘 **gwāt** (Md **jú**)
the Mandarin orange; the Chinese orange; tangerine

橘子 **gwāt jí**
Mandarin oranges

橘黃 **gwāt wòhng**
orange color

橙 **cháang, chàahng** (Md **chéng, chén**)
the orange

橙汁 **cháang jāp**
orange juice

橙黃色 **cháang wòhng sīk**
orange (color)

橡 **jeuhng** (Md **xiàng**)
the oak; the chestnut oak

橡皮 **jeuhng pèih**
rubber; eraser

橡樹 **jeuhng syuh**
oak

機（机）**gèi** (Md **jī**)
① that caused by motion; mechanics; machinery ② opportune; opportunity ③ urgent ④ tricky; cunning ⑤ short for airplane

機會 **gèi wuih**
opportunity

機警 **gèi gíng**
alert; alertness; sharp and quick-witted

檀 **tàahn** (Md **tán**)
① sandalwood ② a Chinese family name

檀島 **Tàahn dóu**
the Hawiian Islands

檀香 **tàahn hèung**
incense made of sandalwood; Santalum album

檄 **haht** (Md **xí**)
a summons to arms in ancient

times

檄文 haht màhn
a written summons to arms for a cause; a manifests listing the crimes of a tyrant

檎 kàhm (Md qín)
a small red apple

檉(柽)chìng (Md chēng)
tamarisk

檉柳 chìng láuh
tamarisk

檔(档)dóng (Md dàng)
① an abbreviation for 檔案, files ② shelves; pigeonholes ③ a wooden cross-piece, as the rung of a ladder, etc. ④ (now rare) a wooden chair

檔案 dóng ngon
official files (of government offices)

檔卷 dóng gyún
official files

檜(桧)kúi (Md quì, huì)
the Chinese juniper or cypress or juniper

檜柏 kúi paak
Chinese cypress

檜木 kúi muhk
timber of Chinese cypress or juniper

檟(槚)gá (Md jiǎ)
① an ancient version of 茶, tea ② a small evergreen shrub (Mallotus japonicus)

檠(橄)kìhng (Md qíng)
a lamp stand; bracket

檢(检)gím (Md jiǎn)
① a book label ② to collate; to arrange ③ to sort; to gather ④

to inspect; to examine; to search ⑤ a form; a pattern ⑥ to restrict; to regulate

檢查 gím chàh
to inspect; to examine; to test (a machine, etc.); (physical) check up

檢討 gím tóu
to review and discuss (past performance, etc.); to make self-examination or soul-searching

檣(檣、艢)chèuhng (Md qiáng)
the mast of a ship

檣傾楫摧 chèuhng kìng chāp chèui
a totally wrecked boat

檁(檩)láhm (Md lǐn)
a cross-beam in a house

檁子 láhm jí
purlins; cross-beam

檗 baak (Md bò)
a cork tree which can be used as medicine

黃檗 wòhng baak
the bark of a cork tree used as medicine

檬 mùng (Md méng)
① a kind of locust or acacia ② lemon

檯(台、枱)tòih, tói (Md tái)
a table

檯布 tòih bou (tói bou)
table-cloth

檯燈 tòih dāng (tói dāng)
table lamp

檳(槟)bàn (Md bīn, bīng)
the areca; the betel; the areca-

nut; the betel-nut

檳榔 bàn lòhng
betel-nut

檳榔嶼 Bàn lòhng jeuih
Penang, Malaysia

檸(柠)**nìhng (Md níng)**

lemon

檸檬 nìhng mùng
lemon

檸檬酸 nìhng mùng syùn
citric acid

檻(槛)**laahm, háahm (Md jiàn, kǎn)**

① a railing; bars as window or door bars ② a cage, pen, etc. for birds or animals ③ a door-sill; threshold

檻車 laahm gèui
a cart with a cage for animals or prisoners

門檻 mùhn laahm
a door-sill

櫃(柜)**gwaih (Md guì)**

① a cabinet; a wardrobe; a cupboard ② a shop counter

櫃面兒 gwaih mihn yìh
a shop counter

櫃子 gwaih jí
a cabinet; a sideboard

櫓(櫓、樐、艣、艪)**lóuh (Md lǔ)**

① an oar; a scull; a sweep ② (in ancient warfare) a big shield; a long spear ③ (now rare) a lookout tower on a city wall

櫚(榈)**lèuih (Md lú)**

palm; coir-palm

櫛(栉)**jit (Md zhì)**

① a comb; a comb of many fine teeth ② to comb the hair; to dress up or cut hair ③ to weed

out; to eliminate; to delete

櫛工 jit gùng
a barber; a hairdresser

櫛比 jit béi
placed closely together — like teeth of a comb; joined closely together — as houses

櫝(椟)**duhk (Md dú)**

① a closet; a wardrobe; a cabinet; a sideboard or cupboard ② a coffin ③ scabbard ④ to hide; to conceal

櫥(橱)**chyùh (Md chú)**

a closet; a cabinet; a cupboard, etc.

櫥櫃 chyùh gwaih
a closet; a cabinet; a night-table with drawers, etc.

櫥窗 chyùh chēung
a display window

櫟(栎)**līk (Md lì, yuè)**

the chestnut-leaved oak (quercus chinensis and serrota)

櫟散 līk saan
useless material

櫫(橥)**jyù (Md zhū)**

a wooden peg; a post; a stalk or stick

櫨(栌)**lòuh (Md lú)**

① the square peck-shaped box half way up a staff or mast ② name of a plant

櫨薄 lòuh bohk
the square peck-shaped box half way up a staff or mast

櫬(榇)**chan (Md chèn)**

① a coffin ② tung tree, Fermiana platanifolia

櫪(枥)**līk (Md lì)**

① a stable ② Quercus serrata ③ wooden device used to torture a criminal by pressing his fingers

櫪馬 **lìk máh**
stablehorse

櫪撕 **lìk sì**
a wooden device used to torture a criminal by pressing his fingers

櫳(栊)**lùhng (Md lóng)**
① bars across a doorway, etc. ② a pen; a cage for animals

櫳檻 **lùhng laahm**
a pen or cage for animals

櫸(榉)**géui (Md jǔ)**
a kind of elm, with fine-grained wood (Abelicea serrata)

欄 (栏)**làahn (Md lán)**
① a railing; a balustrade; a fence ② a pen for domesticated animals

欄杆 **làahn gòn**
a railing; a balustrade; silk trimming for girls

櫻 (樱)**yìng (Md yīng)**
the cherry; the cherry blossoms

櫻花 **yìng fà**
cherry blossoms

櫻桃 **yìng tòuh**
cherries

權(权)**kyùhn**
(Md **quán**)
① to weigh (the significance, etc.); to assess ② power; authority; inherent rights; influence ③ an expedient way; expediency; alternative ④ temporarily; for the time being ⑤ a Chinese family name

權柄 **kyùhn bing**
authority; power

權利 **kyùhn leih**
rights; privileges

欒(栾)**lyùhn (Md luán)**
① name of a small tree with tiny

leaves and yellow flowers (Koelrevleria paniculata) ② the two corners at the mouth of a Chinese bell ③ a Chinese family name

欏 (椤)**lòh (Md luó)**
see "桫欏" in '桫'

欖 **láam, láahm (Md lǎn)**
the olive (see '橄欖' in '橄')

欠部

欠 **him (Md qiàn)**
① to owe; to owe money ② deficient; lacking ③ not

欠債 **him jaai**
to be in debt; to owe money

欠妥 **him tóh**
not very proper or appropriate, not satisfactory or dependable

次 **chi (Md cì)**
① the next in order; secondary ② inferior; lower ③ vice or deputy (minister, etc.) ④ a place where one stops for rest on a trip; a place ⑤ to stop at a place ⑥ by; at (the feast, table, etc.) in the midst ⑦ a grade; grading; a series; an interval; a category ⑧ (in chemistry) the prefix "hypo" ⑨ a time

次日 **chi yaht**
the next day; the following day

次要 **chi yiu**
secondary; not very important

欣 **yàn (Md xīn)**
glad; gladly; joyful; joyfully; delighted; happy

欣賞 **yàn séung**
to appreciate; to enjoy; to admire

欣慰 **yàn wai**
delighted; satisfied; comforted; contented satisfaction; joy

欬 **kāt** (Md **kāi**)
① to cough ② sound of laughing

欲 **yuhk** (Md **yù**)
① to desire; to intend; to long for; to want; desire; expectation; longing ② (now rare) love; to love ③ (now rare) genial and amiable

欲罷不能 **yuhk bah bāt nàhng**
unable to stop even if one wants to

欲望 **yuhk mohng**
desires; to long for; longings

款 (欵) **fún** (Md **kuǎn**)
① sincerity; sincere; sincerely ② article, item, etc. (in a contract, treaty, etc.) ③ to entertain; to treat well ④ slowly; slow ⑤ to knock (at door) ⑥ empty (words, etc.) ⑦ fund, a sum of money

款客 **fún haak**
to entertain guests or visitors

款項 **fún hohng**
a sum of money; fund; money

欸 (誒) **cíh, òi, áai**
(Md **ê, éi, ěi, èi, ǎi**)
① the sound of answering ② sighs ③ an exclamatory indicating promise or affirmation

欸乃 **áai náaih**
the sound of rowing a boat

欷 **hēi** (Md **xī**)
to sob; to sigh

欷歔 **hēi hēui**
to sob and sigh

欽 (钦) **yàm** (Md **qīn**)
① to respect; respectful ② a term of address to monarch in ancient China — Your Majesty ③ a Chinese family name

欽佩 **yàm pui**
to admire; to respect; to agree

whole-heartedly

欽賜 **yàm chi**
granted or bestowed by the emperor (for meritorious service)

欻 **fāt, chà** (Md **hū, chuā**)
① sudden; suddenly; abrupty ② used for the sound

欻忽 **fāt fāt**
quickly; swiftly

欺 **hèi** (Md **qī**)
① to cheat; to swindle; to impose on; to take advantage of ② to disregard the dictates of one's own conscience ③ to insult; to bully

欺負 **hèi fuh**
to bully; to oppress; to insult; to ridicule

欺騙 **hèi pin**
to cheat; to swindle

歁 **hám** (Md **kǎn**)
① discontented with oneself ② sad and gloomy

歁然 **hám yìhn**
dissatisfied; discontented

歆 **kèi** (Md **qī**)
① a fierce dog ② an interjection of pleasure — Bravo! God!

歆歈盛哉 **kèi yùh sìhng jòi**
What a grand occasion! What a grand sight!

歇 **hit** (Md **xiē**)
① to rest; to sleep ② to come to an end ③ to lodge

歇嘴 **hit jéui**
to stop talking; to shut up

歇息 **hit sīk**
to take a rest; to sleep; to stay at an inn

歃 saap (Md shà)

to drink blood; to smear the mouth with blood of an animal in oath-taking

歃血 saap hyut

to smear the mouth with blood in oath-taking (an ancient practice)

歆 yàm (Md xīn)

① (said of gods, etc.) to accept offerings, etc. ② to admire; to submit to willingly ③ to move; to quicken

歆羨 yàm sihn

to admire

歆艷 yàm yihm

to envy; to admire

歉 hip, him (Md qiàn)

① deficient; insufficent; deficiency ② poor crop or harvest ③ to regret; sorry

歉意 hip yi

regrets; apology

歉收 him sàu

a bad harvest

歌 gò (Md gē)

① to sing; to chant; to praise ② a song ③ a kind of poem with rhythms and rhymes suitable for use as lyrics in songs

歌曲 gò kūk

a song; a tune; a ballad

歌手 gò sáu

a songster; a vocalist

歎 (叹、嘆) taan (Md tàn)

to sigh in wonderment or lamentation; to exclaim

歎息 taan sīk

to sigh in lamentation; to lament; to exclaim

歎服 taan fuhk

to praise and admire

歐 (欧) ngàu (Md ōu)

① Europe; European ② to vomit ③ to beat ④ to sing ⑤ (in electricity) Ohm

歐洲 Ngàu jàu

Europe

歐陽 Ngàu yèuhng

a Chinese family name

歔 hèui (Md xū)

to exhale from the nose

歔欷 hèui hèi

to sob; to sniff — as after crying; to sigh

歃 kāp, sip (Md xī, shè)

① to suck ② name of a county in Anhwei Province

歟 (欤) yùh (Md yú)

a final particle indicating doubt, surprise, exclamation etc.

歡 (欢、懽、讙) fùn (Md huān)

① pleased; joy; glad; to like ② a lover ③ active and energetic; quick ④ a Chinese family name

歡迎 fùn yìhng

to welcome; welcome

歡欣 fùn yàn

jubilation; joy

止部

止 jí (Md zhǐ)

① to stop; to desist ② to detain; to rent in; to stay ③ to prohibit; to end ④ to come to; to arrive at; to stop at ⑤ still; calm; stagnant ⑥ only

止步 jí bouh

to stop; to stand still; No admittance

止血 jí hyut

to stop bleeding or hemmorrhage

正 jing, jìng (Md zhèng, zhēng)

① the observe side; the right side ② appropriate; proper; just; unbiased; to make proper; formal; to correct ③ pure; not contaminated ④ straightforward and unbending; honest and virtuous ⑤ the person in charge; person in command; principle as against secondary ⑥ to mete out punishment for a crimminal ⑦ original (text etc.) ⑧ exactly; positively ⑨ a Chinese family name ⑩ the first in the lunar calendar

正常 jing sèuhng
normal; normally; common; commonly; usual; usually

正式 jing sīk
formal; formally; official; officially; legally or lawfully

此 chí (Md cǐ)

① this; these; such ② if so; in this case ③ here

此處 chí chyu
this place; here

此外 chí ngoih
besides; aside from this; in addition

步 bouh (Md bù)

① a pace; a step ② to walk; on foot ③ situation; degree ④ bank of a river, pond, etc. ⑤ fortune, as the national fortune ⑥ a distance of approx. 5.5 feet ⑦ a Chinese family name

步行 bouh hàhng
to walk; to march on foot

步驟 bouh jaauh
procedure, or sequence of doing something; measures or steps taken

歧 kèih (Md qí)

① a path branching out from the main road; forked road ② forked; divergent; strayed ③ anything that goes astray; wayward

歧見 kèih gin
different opinions or interpretations; conflicting ideas

歧視 kèih sih
to give different treatment to people; to act biasedly; to discriminate against; discrimination

武 móuh (Md wǔ)

① force; military; warlike ② a footprint ③ the length of half a pace ④ string of an ancient hat ⑤ a Chinese family name

武器 móuh hei
weapons

武力 móuh lihk
military might; naked power; (by) force; force of arms

歪 wàai (Md wāi)

① aslant; askew; awry ② crooked; depraved; evil ③ to lie down on one side for a brief nap ④ to shirk one's responsibility and try to involve others

歪曲 wàai kūk
to twist or confuse (things, facts, etc.) intentionally; to disort

歪心 wàai sàm
a twisted mind; a crooked mind; an evil mind

歲(岁、崴、嵗) seui (Md sùi)

① a year; age (of a person) ② harvest

歲月 seui yuht
times and seasons; time

歲入 seui yahp
annual income

歷(历) lihk (Md lì)

① to pass through; to under go;

to experience ② things or duration that have come to pass ③ through; throughout; successive ④ to last (a certain period of time)

歷史 lihk sí
history

歷險 lihk hím
to undergo or experience adventures and dangers; to have had a narrow escape

歸 (归) gwài (Md guī)
① to come back; to return (something to its owner) ② (said of a woman) to marry ③ to follow; to pledge allegiance to; to merge with ④ to belong; to attribute ⑤ a Chinese family name

歸還 gwài wàahn
to return (something to its owner); to come home

歸主 gwài jyú
to return to the Lord — conversion

歹部

歹 dáai (Md dǎi)
bad; wicked; crooked; depraved; vicious

歹徒 dáai tòuh
hoodlums; bad guys; evil fellows

歹毒 dáai duhk
vicious; viciousness; malicious; malice

死 séi, sí (Md sǐ)
① to die; to die for; dead; death ② used as an intensive or superlative; very ③ condemned (persons whose lives are numbered, as criminals on the death row) ④ inanimated; dull and stupid; insert; insensible; lifeless ⑤ obstinate or stubborn; perserving; resolute; resolutely ⑥

fixed or unchangeable (regulations, etc.)

死亡 séi mòhng
to die; death

死記 séi gei
to memorize by rote

殀 yíu (Md yāo)
① to die young or untimely ② to be wronged or aggrieved

歿 muht (Md mò)
to die; death

歿世不忘 muht sai bāt mòhng
shall never forget

歿存均感 muht chyùhn gwàn gám
Both the dead and the living shall be grateful

殃 yèung (Md yāng)
① disaster; misfortune; calamity ② the return of the spirit of the deceased

殃民 yèung màhn
to wrong and suppress the people; to bring disaster to the people

殃及池魚 yèung kahp chìh yùh
(literally) (when the city gate caught fire) the disaster even extends to the fish in the moat — to cause trouble or bring disaster to innocent people

殄 tíhn, tíhm (Md tiǎn)
① to end; to terminate ② to exterminate; to weed out; to wipe out or root out

殄滅 tíhn miht
to exterminate thoroughly; to extirpate; to commit genocide

殄墜 tíhn jeuih
to be eliminated; to come to an end (said of a dynasty, reign,

etc.)

殆 tóih, doih (Md dái)

① precarious; dangerous; perilous ② tired ③ afraid ④ about; nearly; almost ⑤ only; merely; even

殆不可能 tóih bāt hó nàhng
almost impossible

殆已無望 tóih yíh mòuh mohng
nearly hopeless

殂 chòuh (Md cú)

to die; dead; death

殂殞 chòuh wáhn
to die; death (of usually an eminent figure)

殂歿 chòuh muht
to die; to perish; death

殉 sèun (Md xùn)

① to die for a cause ② (originally) to be buried with the dead (usually said of slaves, loyal servants, concubines, etc.)

殉情 sèun chìhng
to die for love

殉職 sèun jīk
to die on one's job; to die while performing one's work

殊 syùh (Md shū)

① different; special; strange ② to distinguish; distinguished ③ extremely; very ④ really

殊榮 syùh wìhng
special honors

殊途同歸 syùh tòuh tùhng gwāi
to reach the same destination by different routes, to reach the same decision or conclusion by different means or ways

殍 píuh (Md piǎo)

① to starve to death ② a person who died from starvation

殖 jihk (Md zhí, shi)

① to grow in abundance; to prosper ② to plant ③ to fatten; to become wealthy ④ to colonize

殖民地 jihk màhn deih
a colony

殖穀 jihk gūk
to plant rice

殘 (残) chàahn (Md cán)

① to destroy; to injure; to damage; to spoil ② cruel and fierse; heartless and relentless ③ crippled; disfigured ④ remnant or residue; the little amount of something left ⑤ to kill

殘暴 chàahn bouh
cruel and heartless; cold-blooded; cruelty; ruthlessness

殘缺 chàahn kyut
incomplete

殛 gīk (Md jí)

to put to death

雷殛 lèuih gīk
to be struck by thunder (lightning)

殞 (殒) wáhn (Md yǔn)

① to die; to perish ② same as 隕 to fall

殞沒 wáhn muht
to perish; to die

殞落 wáhn lohk
to fall

殣 gán, gahn (Md jìn)

① to starve to death ② to bury

殤 (殇) sèung (Md shāng)

① to die young ② national

mourning

殫(殚) **dàan** (Md **dān**)
to use up; to exhaust

殫力 **dàan lihk**
to strive; to endeavor

殫洽 **dàan hăp**
very erudite

殪 **yi** (Md **yì**)
① to die ② to kill

殭 **gèung** (Md **jiāng**)
dead and stiff

殭屍 **gèung sì**
vampire

殭硬 **gèung ngaahng**
stiff

殮(殓) **lihm** (Md **liàn**)
to prepare a body for the coffin

殮葬 **lihm jong**
to shroud and bury

殮具 **lihm geuih**
articles for preparing the body
for the coffin

殯(殡) **ban** (Md **bìn**)
funeral; to carry to the grave; to
embalm

殯儀館 **ban yìh gún**
a funeral parlor

殯殮 **ban lihm**
funeral

殲(歼) **chìm** (Md **jiān**)
to annihilate; to exterminate; to
destroy

殲滅 **chìm miht**
to annihilate; to exterminate;
to wipe out

殲敵 **chìm dihk**
to destroy the enemy

殳部

殳 **syùh** (Md **shū**)
a kind of weapon

殳書 **syùh syù**
a style of hand writing in Chin
(秦) Dynasty (used for
inscription on weapons)

段 **dyuhn** (Md **duàn**)
① a section; a division; a part; a
paragraph ② a Chinese family
name

段落 **dyuhn lohk**
end (of a paragraph, stage,
period, etc.)

殷 **yàn, yìn** (Md **yīn,
yān**)
① abundant; flourishing; thriving;
prosperous; rich; wealthy ②
polite; courteous; civil ③ sad;
sorrowful; mournful ④ alternative
name for the later half of the
Shang Dynasty ⑤ dark red

殷勤 **yàn kàhn**
courteous; polite; civil

殷紅 **yàn hùhng**
dark red

殺(杀) **saat** (Md **shā**)
to kill; to put to death; to
slaughter

殺戮 **saat luhk**
to kill; to slay

殺害 **saat hoih**
to murder; to kill

殼(壳) **hok** (Md **ké,
qiào**)
shell (as opposed to core); husk;
covering

殼果 **hok gwó**
a nut

殼子 **hok jí**
a shell (as opposed to core)

殺 **ngàauh** (Md **xiáo**)
① confusion; disorder; mess ② same as '淆', see '水' radical

殽亂 **ngàauh lyuhn**
disorderly; confused; messy

殽核 **ngàauh haht**
beans

殿 **dihn** (Md **diàn**)
① a palace; a palace hall; a temple; a sanctuary ② the rear; the rear guard

殿宇 **dihn yúh**
a palace; a palace hall; a temple; a sanctuary

殿後 **dihn hauh**
the rear; or rear guard (of marching troops); to bring up the rear

毀 **wái** (Md **huǐ**)
① to destroy; to ruin; to damage; to injure ② to libel; to slander; to abuse; to revile; to defame

毀滅 **wái miht**
to destroy; to ruin; to demolish

毀謗 **wái póhng**
to libel; to slander; a libel or slander

毅 **ngaih** (Md **yì**)
firm; resolute; determined

毅力 **ngaih lihk**
perseverance; determination; resoluteness; indomitability; firmness

毅勇 **ngaih yúhng**
firm courage; fortitude

毆(殴) **ngáu** (Md **ōu**)
to beat; to hit

毆打 **ngáu dá**
to have a fist fight; to have fisticuffs; to beat a person with fists or clubs

毆斃 **ngáu baih**
to beat to death

毋部

毋 **mòuh** (Md **wú**)
(imperative) do not

毋忘在莒 **mòuh mòhng joih lèuih**
Do not forget national humiliation in time of peace and security

母 **móuh** (Md **mǔ**)
① mother ② female

母親 **móuh chàn**
mother

母雞 **móuh gāi**
a hen

每 **múih** (Md **měi**)
every; each

每逢 **múih fùhng**
every time or whenever (a season, festival or some specific occasion comes)

每次 **múih chi**
every time; each time

毒 **duhk** (Md **dú**)
poison; toxin; venom; harm; malice; spite; to poison; poisonous; noxious; venomous; malicious

毒藥 **duhk yeuhk**
posionous drug; poison

毒打 **duhk dá**
to beat cruelly or savagely

毓 **yūk** (Md **yù**)
① to bring up; to rear; to nurture; to nurse ② to grow

比部

比 **béi** (Md **bǐ**)
① to compare; to liken ② to complete

比例 **béi laih**
ratio; proportion

比較 **béi gaau**
　　to compare; comparative

毖 **bei** (Md **bèi**)
cautious; judicious

毗(毘) **pèih** (Md **pí**)
① to assist ② to adjoin

毗連 **pèih lìhn**
　　(of lands) to adjoin each other

毗倚 **pèih yí**
　　to depend upon; to rely upon

毛部

毛 **mòuh** (Md **máo**)
① hair; fur; feather; down ②
vegetation ③ ten cents; a dime
④ gross; untouched; unpolished
⑤ a Chinese family name

毛髮 **mòuh faat**
　　body hairs and hair

毛利 **mòuh leih**
　　gross earning; gross profit

毬 **kàuh** (Md **qíu**)
① a ball; a sphere ② same as
'球' see, '玉' radical

毬果 **kàuh gwó**
　　cone (of pine, spruce, etc.);
　　strobile

毫 **hòuh** (Md **háo**)
① fine hair ② a measure of length
③ a writing brush ④ a dime

毫髮 **hòuh faat**
　　extremely little

毫無 **hòuh mòuh**
　　not at all; not in the least

毯 **táam** (Md **tǎn**)
rug; carpet; blanket

毯子 **táam jí**
　　rug; carpet; blanket

毳 **cheui** (Md **cuì**)
fine feather or fur

毨毛 **cheui mòuh**
　　fine feather or fur

毨幕 **cheui mohk**
　　felt curtain

毽 **yín, gin** (Md **jiàn**)
a shuttlecock

毽子 **yín jí**
　　a shuttle cock

氂(犛) **mòuh** (Md **máo**)
① horse tail ② long hair; thick
hair ③ yak

氂牛 **mòuh ngàuh**
　　yak

氅 **chóng** (Md **chǎng**)
garment woven of down

氅衣 **chóng yì**
　　outer garment; coat; costume
　　of Taoist priest

氈(氊、毯) **jìn**
(Md **zhān**)
① felt ② blanket

氈子 **jìn jí**
　　felt

氈帽 **jìn móu**
　　felt cap or hat

氏部

氏 **sih, jì** (Md **shì, zhī**)
① family; clan ② a character
placed after a married woman's
maiden name ③ name of an
ancient barbarian tribe

氏族 **sih juhk**
　　a family; a clan

氏譜 **sih póu**
　　family tree; lineage; genealogy

氐 **dái, dài** (Md **dǐ, dī**)
① name of an ancient barbarian
tribe to the west ② same as '抵'

氐羌 **dài gèung**
　　ancient barbarian tribes to the

west

民 màhn (Md mín)
the people (as opposed to the government); the subject (as opposed to the ruler); the populace; the public

民航 màhn hòhng
civil aviation

民族 màhn juhk
a nation; a people

氓 màhn, mòhng (Md méng, máng)
① the people; the populace ② rascal; vagabond

流氓 làuh màhn
rascal; vagabond

气部

氖 náaih (Md nǎi)
neon

氖燈 náaih dāng
neon lamp

氛 fàn (Md fèn)
air; atmosphere; prevailing mood

氛邪 fàn chèh
evil air

氛氲 fàn wàn
spirit, or atmosphere of prosperity or propitiousness; vigorous spirit; vigorous atmosphere

氟 fāt (Md fú)
fluorine

氣 (气) hei (Md qì)
① air; gas; vapor; atmosphere ② breath ③ spirit; character ④ influence ⑤ bearing; manner ⑥ smell; odor ⑦ to be angry; to be indignant ⑧ to provoke; to goad

氣氛 hei fàn
atmosphere; mood

氣溫 hei wàn
temperature

氤 yàn (Md yīn)
spirit of harmony (between heaven and earth)

氤氳 yàn wàn
spirit of harmony (between heaven and earth); spirit of vigor or prosperity

氧 yéuhng (Md yǎng)
oxygen

氧化 yéuhng fa
to oxidize or be oxidized; oxidation

氧化物 yéuhng fa maht
an oxide

氦 hoih (Md hài)
helium

氫 (氢) hìng (Md qīng)
hydrogen

氫彈 hìng dáan
hydrogen bomb

氫氧吹管 hìng yéuhng chèui gún
oxyhydrogen blowpipe

氮 daahm (Md dàn)
nitrogen

氮肥 daahm fèih
nitrogenous fertilizers

氯 (氯) luhk (Md lù)
chlorine

氯水 luhk séui
chlorine water

氯化鈉 luhk fa naahp
sodium chloride

氳 wàn (Md yūn)
spirit or atmosphere, of harmony, prosperity or vigor

水部

水 **séui** (Md **shuǐ**)
① water; liquid; fluid; juice; sap
② a Chinese family name

水壩 **séui ba**
　a dam

水族館 **séui juhk gún**
　an aquarium

永 **wíhng** (Md **yǒng**)
long in time; everlasting; permanent

永遠 **wíhng yúhn**
　forever; eternally; perpetually

永生 **wíhng sàng**
　eternal life

汀 **tìng** (Md **tīng**)
① shore; beach ② a sand bank

汀洲 **tìng jàu**
　islet in a stream; shoal

求 **kàuh** (Md **qiú**)
to seek; to ask for; to pray for; to beg

求婚 **kàuh fàn**
　to propose (to a woman)

求助 **kàuh joh**
　to seek help

汁 **jāp** (Md **zhī**)
juice; fluid; sap

汁兒 **jāp yìh**
　juice; fluid; sap

橙汁 **cháang jāp**
　orange juice

氾 **faan** (Md **fàn**)
① to spread; to fill everywhere ② extensive; vast

氾濫 **faan laahm**
　to overflow; to spread far and wide

氾論 **faan leuhn**
　general discussion

汛 **seun** (Md **xùn**)
abundant water

汊 **cha** (Md **chà**)
a branching stream

汊港 **cha góng**
　branching point of a stream

汐 **jihk** (Md **xī**)
flow of the tide at night

汕 **saan** (Md **shàn**)
basket for catching fish

汕頭 **Saan tàuh**
　Swatow, Kwantung Province

汗 **hohn, hòhn** (Md **hàn, hán**)
① sweat; perspiration ② used in '可汗' – a khan

汗腺 **hohn sin**
　sweat gland

汗顏 **hohn ngàahn**
　to perspire from embarrassment or shame

污 (汙、汚) **wù** (Md **wū**)
① dirty; filthy ② to stain; to insult; to slander ③ corrupt

污濁 **wù juhk**
　muddy

污染 **wù yíhm**
　to stain; to taint; to smear; to contaminate; to soil

汜 **chíh** (Md **sì**)
a stream that branches and afterwards merges again

汝 **yúh** (Md **rǔ**)
thou; thee; thy

汝等 **yúh dáng**
　(plural) ye (used in addressing inferiors

江 **gòng** (Md **jiāng**)
① a large river ② the Yangtze River ③ a Chinese family name

江湖 **gòng wùh**
rivers and lakes; wandering; vagrant ③ sophisticated and shrewd ④ practicing quackery; quack

江山 **gòng sàan**
the mountains and rivers of a country — the land; the throne

池 **chìh** (Md **chí**)
pond; pool; moat

池塘 **chìh tòhng**
a pond

池中物 **chìh jùng maht**
(literally) common stuff that can be found in a pond — mediocre person

汞(錄) **hung, huhng** (Md **gǒng**)
mercury (an element)

汞粉 **hung fán**
calomel

汞氧 **hung yéuhng**
oxide of mercury

汎 **faan** (Md **fàn**)
① float ② extensive

汎舟 **faan jàu**
to row a boat; boating

汎論 **faan leuhn**
general discussion

汩 **mihk** (Md **mì**)
name of a river in Hunan Province

汩羅 **Mihk lòh**
a river in Hunan Province (where ancient poet Chu Yuan 屈原 drowned himself)

汩 **gwāt** (Md **gǔ**)
① to destroy; to ruin ② confused; disorderly ③ sound of waves

汩沒 **gwāt muht**
to sink; decline

汩汩 **gwāt gwāt**
sound of waves; panicky; in confusion

汪 **wòng** (Md **wāng**)
① deep and extensive (said of water) ② a Chinese family name

汪洋 **wòng yèuhng**
extensive body of water

汪汪 **wòng wòng**
deep and extensive (said of water); the barking of dogs; brimming with tears

汭 **yeuih** (Md **ruì**)
a bend in a stream

汰 **taai** (Md **tài**)
① excessive ② to sift; to eliminate; to remove

汰去 **taai heui**
to eliminate; to remove

汰弱留强 **taai yeuhk làuh kèuhng**
to weed out the weak and retain the strong

汲 **kāp** (Md **jí**)
to draw water or liquid

汲水 **kāp séui**
to draw water

汲引 **kāp yáhn**
to employ people of talent

汴 **bihn** (Md **biàn**)
① alternative name for Honan ② ancient name of a river in Honan

汴水 **Bihn séui**
ancient name of a river in Honan

汴梁 **Bihn lèuhng**
capital of the Northern Sung Dynasty (at what is Kaifeng 開封 today)

汶 **mahn** (Md **wèn**)
name of a river in Shangtung
汶水 **Mahn séui**
name of a river in Shantung

決 **kyut** (Md **jué**)
same as '决' see, '冫' radical

汽 **hei** (Md **qì**)
gas; steam; vapor
汽車 **hei chè**
automobile
汽油 **hei yàuh**
gasoline

汾 **fàhn** (Md **fén**)
name of a tributary of the Yellow River
汾酒 **Fàhn jáu**
Kaoliang wine made in the
汾水 area
汾水 **Fàhn séui**
name of a tributary of the Yellow River

沁 **sam** (Md **qìn**)
to soak; to seep; to percolate; to permeate
沁入 **sam yahp**
to soak into; to permeate
沁人心脾 **sam yàhn sàm pèih**
to affect people deeply

沂 **yìh** (Md **yí**)
names of four rivers originating in Shantung
沂水 **Yìh séui**
name of a country in Shantung; names of rivers

沃 **yūk** (Md **wò**)
① to irrigate ② fertile (said of lands)
沃土 **yūk tóu**
fertile land

沃野千里 **yūk yéh chìn léih**
an endless expanse of fertile land

沅 **yùhn** (Md **yuán**)
name of a river flowing through Hunan
沅江 **Yùhn gòng**
name of a river flowing through Hunan

沆 **hòhng** (Md **hàng**)
① a vast expanse of water ② mist or fog ③ flowing
沆茫 **hòhng mòhng**
expanse of water; water; water everywhere
沆瀣 **hòhng haaih**
mist; fog

沉 **chàhm** (Md **chén**)
① to sink; to be drawn deep into; to submerge ② to indulge in; to be addicted to ③ deeply; very; sound (sleep) ④ persistent and lasting; for a long time ⑤ delaying; postponement ⑥ heavy (in weighing) ⑦ latent; hidden ⑧ to straighten (one's face) ⑨ to retain (one's composure); to restrain (oneself from rashness, etc.)
沉沒 **chàhm muht**
to sink
沉睡 **chàhm seuih**
deep slumber; sound sleep

沌 **deuhn** (Md **dùn**)
turbid; unclear; chaotic

沐 **muhk** (Md **mù**)
① to shampoo; to wash; to bathe; to cleanse ② a holiday; a leave; to take a leave ③ to enrich; to receive favors; to steep in ④ a Chinese family name
沐浴 **muhk yuhk**
to bathe; to steep in or receive favors; to soak in

沐猴 **muhk hàuh**
macacus monkey

沒 **muht** (Md **méi, mò**)
① none; nothing; no ② not yet; not; negative ③ to sink; to drown; to be submerge ④ to go in hiding; obscurity or oblivion ⑤ none; exhausted ⑥ finished; eliminated ⑦ to take property away from another; to confiscate ⑧ to die; dead

沒道理 **muht douh léih**
unreasonable; not justified

沒落 **muht lohk**
to sink; the fall or decline (of an empire, etc.)

沔 **míhn** (Md **miǎn**)
① overflowing (water); a flood ② name of a river

沔水 **Míhn séui**
Mian River, or River Han, in Shansi Province

沈 **sám** (Md **shěn**)
① a Chinese family name ② same as '沉'

沈腰 **sám yìu**
slender waist (the reference is about 沈約)

沙 **sà** (Md **shā, shà**)
① sand; tiny gravel or pebbles ② land around water; beach, sand bank; a desert ③ to pick, select, sort or sift ④ (said of voice) hoarse ⑥ sandy-not glossy or smooth; granular ⑦ a kind of clay for making utensils, vessels, etc. ⑧ a Chinese family name

沙灘 **sà tàan**
a piece of sandy land around water; sand bank; a sandy beach

沙啞 **sà ngá**
hoarse voice

沓 **daahp** (Md **tà, dá**)
① repeated; reiterated; joined; connected ② crowded together; joined or connected; piled up ③ lax ④ talkative

沓雜 **daahp jaahp**
crowded and mixed

沓合 **daahp hahp**
to meet

沏 **chai** (Md **qī**)
① to infuse ② (said of water flow) rapid; turbulent

沏茶 **chai chàh**
to infuse tea; to make tea

沖 **chùng** (Md **chōng**)
same as '沖', see '氵' radical

泛 **faan** (Md **fàn**)
① to float; to drift ② not exact or precise; not practical ③ not sincere; not intimate ④ generally (speaking); as a shole; pan-, as pan-American

泛泛 **faan faan**
not close or intimate; to float

泛舟 **faan jàu**
to row a boat; boating

沛 **pui** (Md **pèi**)
① copious; abundance ② quickly; rapidly sudden ③ to fall prostrate ④ to reserve water for irrigation ⑤ tall; high; great

沛沛 **pui pui**
a great flow of water; flowing copiously

沛然 **pui yìhn**
(said of rain) copious; great or vast

泐 **lahk** (Md **lè**)
① rocks splitting ② to write letters ③ to carve ④ to condense; to coagulate

勒布 **lahk bou**
　to report by letter

勒石 **lahk sehk**
　to carve on a rock; rock splitting up

沫 **muht, mut** (Md **mò**)
① tiny bubbles on the surface of water; froth; suds ② saliva ③ (now rare) to end; to finish

沫兒 **muht yìh**
　froth; suds; tiny bubbles

沫雨 **muht yúh**
　rains that cause flood

泵 **bām** (Md **bèng**)
a pump; to pump (transliteration)

沮 **jéui, jeui** (Md **jǔ, jù**)
① to stop ② to lose; to be defeated ③ to spoil; to injure; to destroy or damage ④ damp, low-lying land; marshy

沮喪 **jéui song**
　discouraged and disappointed; crest-fallen; despondent; downcast; low-spirited

沮澤 **jeui jaahk**
　swamps; marsh

沱 **tòh** (Md **tuó**)
① waterways; rivers; streams ② name of a river ③ continuous heavy rains

沱若 **tòh yeuhk**
　(said of saliva, etc.) drooling and hanging

滂沱 **pòhng tòh**
　continuous heavy rains

泆 **yaht** (Md **yì**)
① dissipated and licentious; libertine ② flooding; overflowing

河 **hòh** (Md **hé**)
① a general name for rivers, streams, waterways ② the Yellow River in Northern China, 2,700 miles long

河畔 **hòh buhn**
　river banks; by the side of the river; riverside

河山 **hòh sàan**
　rivers and mountains — territory of a country

沴 **leuih** (Md **lì**)
miasma; foul and poisonous

沴孽 **leuih yihp**
　evil spirits

沴氣 **leuih hei**
　miasma; poisonous vapour

沸 **fai** (Md **fèi**)
① boiling (water, etc.) ② to gush; bubbling up

沸點 **fai dím**
　the boiling point

沸騰 **fai tàhng**
　boiling — when liquids turn to steam; bubbling and boiling — unrest; seething; water gushing out

泂 **gwíng** (Md **jiǎng**)
① clear and deep (said of water) ② far and wide

泂泂 **gwíng gwíng**
　clear and deep

油 **yàuh** (Md **yóu**)
① general name for oils, fats, grease, either animal or vegetable ② anything in liquid from which is inflammable, as petroleum, gasoline, etc. ③ to oil; to varnish; to paint ④ greasy ⑤ suave and urbane; polished and over-experience; slecky; sly ⑥ luxuriant; prospering; flourishing

油墨 **yàuh mahk**
　printing ink

油嘴 **yàuh jéui**
　glib-tongued; persuasive

治 jih, chìh (Md zhì)
① to administer; to control; to direct; to put in order ② to govern; to regulate; to manage ③ the seat of the local government ④ to treat (a disease); to cure ⑤ to study; to research ⑥ to punish ⑦ peaceful and orderly ⑧ a Chinese family name

治病 jih bihng
　to treat a disease or ailment

治理 jih léih
　to administer; to regulate; to manage; to govern

沼 jíu (Md zhǎo)
a lake; a pond; a pool

沼氣 jíu hei
　marsh gas

沼澤 jíu jaahk
　marsh; swamp; lakes and ponds

沽 gù (Md gū)
① to buy ② to sell ③ crude; inferior (quality) ④ (now rare) negligent

沽酒 gù jáu
　to buy wine; wine or spirits bought from stores

沽名釣譽 gù mìhng diu yuh
　to seek publicity; fish for a good reputation or fame

沾 jìm (Md zhān)
① to moisten; to wet ② to tinge; to stain; to contaminate ③ to be imbued with; to be infected with ④ to benefit from

沾染 jìm yíhm
　to become addicted to (bad habits, practice, etc.)

沾襟 jìm kàm
　to moisten sleeves with tears

沿 yùhn (Md yán, yàn)
① to follow; to go along; along ② to hand down; to continue ③ successive; continuous

沿途 yùhn tòuh
　along the way

沿革 yùhn gaak
　successive changes; vicissitudes or history (of a system, institution, etc.)

况 fong (Md kuàng)
same as '況', see '冫' radical

泄(洩) sit (Md xiè)
① to leak out; to reveal; to ejaculate ② to scatter; to disperse,; to vent ③ a Chinese family name ④ mild and easy ⑤ many; crowded ⑥ to jockey for position

泄漏 sit lauh
　to leak out (secrets, etc.)

泄泄 sit sit
　to flap wings; many (people); crowded

泅 chàuh (Md qíu)
to swim; to wade; to float

泅水 chàuh séui
　to swim

泊 bohk, paak (Md bó, pō)
① to anchor a ship ② to stay ③ tranquil and quiet ④ a lake; a body of water

泊泊 bohk bohk
　ripples (of water)

泊船 bohk syùhn (paak syùhn)
　to moor a boat

泌 bei (Md mì, bì)
① to seep out; to excrete; to secrete ② swift and easy gushing of water ③ name of a river in Honan Province

泌尿器 bei niuh hei
　uropoietic organs; urinary

organs

泌水 **Bei séui**
the Pi River in Honan Province

泓 **wàhng (Md hóng)**
① clear, deep water ② ancient name of a stream in Honan Province

泓泓 **wàhng wàhng**
very deep

泓宏 **wàhng wàhng**
very loud; roaring

泔 **gàm (Md gān)**
① water from washing rice ② a way of cooking; to boil thick ③ stale (said of food)

泔水 **gàm séui**
water from washing rice; hog-wash

泔水桶 **gàm séui túng**
a bucket for hogwash

泖 **máuh (Md mǎo)**
① still waters ② name of a river in Kiangsu Province

法 **faat (Md fǎ)**
① an institution ② law; regulation; rules statutes; legal ③ method; ways of doing things ④ to pattern or model after; to emulate ⑤ (in Buddhism) the "way" — doctrines, etc. ⑥ expert or standard (calligraphy, painting, etc.) ⑦ a Chinese family name ⑧ France; French

法律 **faat leuht**
law

法師 **faat sì**
a salutation for a Buddhist monk; a Taoist high priest

泗 **si, sei (Md sì)**
① snivel; nasal mucus ② name of a river; name of a county

泗水 **Si séui**
name of a country in Shantung; Surabaya, a seaport on Java

泠 **lìhng (Md líng)**
① clear sounds ② mild and comfortable ③ same as 伶, as 伶人 an actor ④ a Chinese family name

泠風 **lìhng fùng**
mild winds; breezes

泠冽 **lìhng liht**
clear

泡 **póuh, pàau (Md pào, pāo)**
① bubbles; suds; froth; foam ② a blister ③ to soak; to dip; to infuse (tea, etc.) ④ (slang) to fool around (especially with women)

泡沫 **póuh muht**
suds and foam

泡影 **pàau yíng**
the shadow of bubbles — unreality; pie in the sky

波 **bò (Md bō)**
① waves; breakers ② undulations; to fluctuate; fluctuations ③ to affect; to involve; to implicate; to entangle

波濤 **bò tòuh**
billows; breakers; large waves

波動 **bò duhng**
undulations; (said of prices) fluctuations

泣 **yāp (Md qì)**
to weap; to come to tears without crying

泣訴 **yāp sou**
to tell one's sorrows or grievance in tear

泣別 **yāp biht**
to part in tears

泥 **nàih, neih (Md ní, nì)**
① mud; mire; earth; soil; clay ② to plaster; to paste ③ to mix finely-ground particles ④ to be

tied down by conversation, old practices; very conservative ⑤ to compel

泥濘 **nàih nìhng**
muddy

泥古 **neih gú**
very conservative; to stick to ancient ways and thought

注 jyu (Md zhù)
① to pour (liquid) ② to direct (attention, gaze, etc.) ③ same as 註 — to anotate

注意 **jyu yi**
to pay attention to

注射 **jyu seh**
to inject, injection, to get a shot

泮 pun (Md pàn)
① (in old China) an institution of higher learning ② (now rare) to dissolve; to melt

泮宮 **pun gùng**
an institution of higher learning in ancient China

泮換 **pun wuhn**
to dissolve

泯 máhn (Md mǐn)
to destroy; to eliminate; to put an end to; to vanish

泯滅 **máhn miht**
to vanish without a trace

決 yèung (Md yāng)
① great; profound ② turbulent (said of clouds)

決決 **yèung yèung**
great; magnificent; turbulent (said of clouds)

決決大國 **yèung yèung daaih gwok**
a great country

泳 wihng (Md yǒng)
to swim under water

泳池 **wihng chìh**
a swimming pool

泳衣 **wihng yì**
a swimming suit

泉 chyùhn (Md quán)
① spring; fountain ② money (archaic)

泉水 **chyùhn séui**
spring water

泉幣 **chyùhn baih**
money, or currency (archaic terms)

泰 taai (Md tài)
① great; big ② quiet; calm; peace ③ Thailand ④ good luck ⑤ same as 太 — very; much; too; excessive

泰半 **taai bun**
more than half; the greater part; the majority

泰國 **Taai gwok**
Thailand

洎 geih (Md jì)
① until; till; up to ② soup, meat broth ③ to soak; to drench

洎乎 **geih fùh**
until; till; up to

洄 wùih (Md huí)
whirling (said of water)

洄洑 **wùih fuhk**
whirling (said of water)

洋 yèuhng (Md yáng)
① an ocean ② forign; Western; Occidental ③ imported

洋葱 **yèuhng chūng**
an onion

洋服 **yèuhng fuhk**
Western clothes; Occidental dress

洌 liht (Md liè)
clear and tranparent (said of

liquid)

清冽 **chìng liht**
clear and cold (water)

洑 **fuhk** (Md **fú, fù**)
① whirlpool; vortex ② undercurrent

洒 (灑) **sá** (Md **sǎ**)
① to pour; to sprinkle ② respectful ③ deep ④ alarmed; surprised ⑤ I, me

洒掃 **sá sou**
to sprinkle water and sweep away the dirt; to clean up

洒如 **sá yùh**
respectful; deferential

洗 **sái** (Md **xǐ**)
to wash; to rinse; to cleanse; to clean; to clear

洗滌 **sái dihk**
to wash; to cleanse; to rinse

洗手間 **sái sáu gāan**
a toilet; a water closet; a restroom; a lavatory

洙 **jyù** (Md **zhū**)
name of a river in Shangtung

洙水 **Jyù séui**
name of a river in Shangtung

洲 **jàu** (Md **zhōu**)
① an island in a river ② a continent

洲嶼 **jàu jeuih**
an island in a river

洲際 **jàu jai**
intercontinental

洳 **yuh** (Md **rù**)
damp; moist

沮洳 **jeui yuh**
damp, low-lying land

洵 **sèun** (Md **xún**)
true; real; truly; really; certainly

洵屬 **sèun suhk**
truly; certainly

洵河 **Sèun hòh**
name of a river in Shensi

洶 (㳀) **hùng**
(Md **xiōng**)
① unquiet; restless; turbulent; tumultuous ② noisy; uproarious; clamorous

洶湧 **hùng yúng**
turbulent (said of water)

洶動 **hùng duhng**
unquiet; restless; disturbed

活 **wuht** (Md **húo**)
① to live; to survive; to be alive ② to save the life of ③ active; lively; vivacious ④ movable; mobile; flexible ⑤ work

活力 **wuht lihk**
vitality; vigor

活躍 **wuht yeuhk**
active

洽 **hāp** (Md **qià**)
① to spread; to diffuse ② harmony; agreement ③ to negotiate

洽商 **hāp sèung**
to negotiate

洽辦 **hāp baahn**
to handle an assignment through negotiation

派 **paai** (Md **pài**)
① a tributary; a branch ② a division; a school (of philosophy, art, etc.) ③ a faction ④ to assign; to dispatch; to send

派遣 **paai hín**
to dispatch

派出所 **paai chēut só**
a police station

洛 **lok** (Md **luò**)
name of a river

洛陽 **Lok yeùhng**
Loyang, in Honan, capital of the Eastern Han Dynasty

洛陽花 **lok yeùhng fā**
white peony

洞 **duhng** (Md **dòng**)
① a cave; a hole ② to penetrate; to see through

洞穿 **duhng chyùn**
to pierce through

洞悉 **duhng sīk**
to see and know

洟 **yìh** (Md **yí**)
nasal mucus; snivel

洟涕 **yìh tai**
nasal mucus; snivel

津 **jèun** (Md **jīn**)
① a ferry ② juicy; tasty ③ saliva ④ short for Tientsin

津液 **jèun yihk**
saliva

津貼 **jèun tip**
an allowance; subsidy; to subsidize; to help out with money

洧 **fúi** (Md **wěi**)
name of a river in Honan

洧水 **Fúi séui**
name of a river in Honan

洪 **hùhng** (Md **hóng**)
① great; immense; magnificient ② flood; turbulent water; torrent ③ a Chinese family name

洪流 **hùhng làuh**
a torrent

洪恩 **hùhng yàn**
great kindness

洫 **gwīk** (Md **xù**)
a ditch; a moat

洏 **yìh** (Md **ér**)
① tearful ② to cook food thoroughly

洩 **sit** (Md **xiè**)
to drain; to vent; to let out; to dissipate; to leak out

洩露 **sit louh**
to disclose; to reveal; to divulge

洩忿 **sit fáhn**
to give vent to one's anger

浙(淛) **jit** (Md **zhè**)
① Chekiang ② name of a river

浙江 **Jit gòng**
Chekiang Province; name of a river in Chekiang

浚 **jeun** (Md **jùn, xùn**)
to dredge

浚泥機 **jeun nàih gèi**
a dredger

浚利 **jeun leih**
unobstructed (said of a waterway)

浜 **bòng** (Md **bāng**)
a small stream

浡 **buht** (Md **bó**)
to rise; excited

浡然 **buht yìhn**
rising; excited

浣(澣) **wún** (Md **huàn**)
to wash; to rinse

浣滌 **wún dihk**
to wash; to rinse

浣紗溪 **Wún sà kài**
name of a river in Chekiang, where the famed beauty, Hsi Shih 西施 , washed cotton yarn when she was a country girl

浥 **yāp** (Md **yì**)
wet; moist

浥潤 **yāp yeuhn**
wet; moist

浥浥 **yāp yāp**
moist; fresh

浦 **póu** (Md **pǔ**)
① shore; beach ② a Chinese family name

浦口 **Póu háu**
city opposite Nanking on the Yangtze River

浩 **houh** (Md **hào**)
① great; vast ② many; much

浩蕩 **houh dohng**
vast and restless

浩劫 **houh gip**
great disaster; catastrophy

浪 **lohng** (Md **làng**)
① wave; billow ② dissolute; disbanched; unrestrained; rash

浪費 **lohng fai**
to waste; to lavish; waste

浪漫 **lohng maahn**
dissolute; debauched; romantic

浮 **fàuh** (Md **fú**)
① to float; to waft ② to overflow; to exceed ③ empty; unsubstantial; unfounded; groundless

浮萍 **fàuh pìhng**
duckweed

浮躁 **fàuh chou**
restless; impatient

浭 **gàng** (Md **gěng**)
name of a river in Hopeh

浬 **léih** (Md **lǐ**)
nautical mile

浴 **yuhk** (Md **yù**)
to bathe

浴室 **yuhk sāt**
a bathroom

浴佛 **yuhk faht**
to bathe Budda's image (as a Buddhist rite in celeberation of Buddha's birthday)

海 **hói** (Md **hǎi**)
① sea; ocean ② a Chinese family name

海報 **hói bou**
poster

海綿 **hói mìhn**
sponge

浸 **jam** (Md **jìn**)
① to dip; to immerse; to soak; to permeate; to percolate ② gradual; gradually

浸信會 **Jam seun wúi**
the Baptist Church

浸淫 **jam yàhm**
to stain gradually; to be familiar with

浹 (浃) **jip** (Md **jiā**)
soak, penetrate, period

涅 (涅) **nihp** (Md **niè**)
① to tattoo; to blacken; to dye black ② to block up

涅槃 **nihp pùhn**
nivana

涅齒 **nihp chí**
to blacken the teeth

涇 (泾) **gìng, ging** (Md **jīng**)
name of a river in Ghensi

涇渭不分 **gìng waih bāt fàn**
unable to distinguish between the clear and the muddy; unable to distinguish between good and bad

消 **sìu** (Md **xiāo**)
① to vanish; to disappear; to die

out ② to disperse; to eliminate; to remove; to alleviate; to allay; to extinguish; to quench

消費者 **sìu fai jé**
consumer

消極 **sìu gihk**
negative; pessimistic; passive

泽 **gong** (Md **jiàng**)
flood

泽水 **gong séui**
flood water; flood

涉 **sip** (Md **shè**)
① to wade ② to experience ③ to involve; to entangle; to implicate ④ a Chinese family name

涉嫌 **sip yìhm**
to come under suspicion; to be involved (in a crime)

涉歷 **sip lihk**
one's past experience

涑 **chūk** (Md **sù**)
name of a tribuary of the Yellow River

涎 **yìhn** (Md **xián**)
saliva

涎沫 **yìhn muht**
saliva

涎涎 **yìhn yìhn**
shiny; glossy

涓 **gyùn** (Md **juān**)
small stream; rivulet; brook

涓滴 **gyùn dihk**
trickle; drip

涓流 **gyùn làuh**
small stream; rivulet; brook

涔 **sàhm** (Md **cén**)
① a puddle ② fishpond ③ tearful

涔涔 **sàhm sàhm**
rainy; distressed; dusky; shadowy; tearful

涕 **tai** (Md **tì**)
① tears ② snivel

涕淚 **tai leuih**
tears

涕泣 **tai yāp**
to weep; to cry

涘 **jih** (Md **sì**)
water's edge; water front; a bank

流 **làuh** (Md **líu**)
① to flow; to move; to wander; to stray ② a branch; a division; a class; a rank ③ unsettled; unfixed; mobile

流浪 **làuh lohng**
to wander about; to roam about; to rove

流行病 **làuh hàhng behng**
epidemic

浞 **jūk** (Md **zhuó**)
to soak

浼 **múih** (Md **měi**)
① to stain; to soil; to contaminate ② full of water ③ to entrust

涌 **yúng, chùng** (Md **yǒng**)
see '湧' in water radical

涪 **fàuh** (Md **fú**)
① name of a river in Szechwan Province ② name of an old administrative district

涪江 **Fàuh gòng**
name of a river in Szechwan Province

涯 **ngàaih** (Md **yá**)
① water's edge; waterfront; a bank; a limit ② faraway places

涯岸 **ngàaih ngohn**
the edge; the limit

涯浃 ngàaih jih
water-edge; limits

液 yihk (Md yè)
liquid; fluid; juices; secretion

液體 yihk tái
liquid

液化 yihk fa
to liquefy or be liquefied; liquefaction

涵 hàahm (Md hán)
① wet; damp and marshy ② to contain ③ to show nothing ④ lencient and broadminded

涵養 hàahm yéuhng
capability to be kind, patient, lenient, tolerant or broadminded under all circumstances without showing one's inner feelings; cherish and nourish

涵蓄 hàahm chūk
reserved (said of manners, speech, etc.)

涸 kok (Md hé)
drying up; dried up; exhausted

涸澤 kok jaahk
a dried-up lake; to dry up a lake

乾涸 gòn kok
dried-up; exhausted

涼 lèuhng (Md liáng)
same as '凉', see '冫' radical

洴 pìhng (Md bǐng)
① the sound of silk, etc. floating in the wind ② to wash; to bleach

洴澼 pìhng pīk
sound of silk flapping in the wind

涿 deuk (Md zhuō)
① to soak; drip or trickle ② old and current names of countries, rivers, mountains in various places

涿鹿 Deuk luhk
name of a county in Chahar (察哈爾); name of a mountain southeast of the county, where Haung Ti, or the Yellow Emperor, killed 蚩尤 , the enemy chieftain after a decisive battle

淀 dihn (Md diàn)
shallow water

淀河 Dihn hòh
also known as Ta Ching River in Hopeh Province

淄 jì (Md zī)
① dark color ② name of a river in Shantung Province

淄水 Jì séui
a river in Shantung Province

淅 sīk (Md xī)
① water for washing rice; to wash rice ② name of a river in Honan Province

淅米 sīk máih
to wash rice

淅瀝 sīk lìk
the plattering of sleet; the sound of raindrops; the sound of falling leaves in the wind

淆 (殽)ngàauh
(Md xiáo)
confused and disorderly

淆亂 ngàauh lyuhn
to confuse; to mislead

淆雜 ngàauh jaahp
mixed; miscellaneous

淇 kèih (Md qí)
name of a river in Honan

淇水 Kèih séui
Honan

淋 làhm (Md lín, lìn)
① to soak with water; to drip ② completely; perfectly ③

gonorrhea

淋浴 **làhm yuhk**
shower

淋巴腺 **làhm bà sin**
lymphatic glands

淌 **tóng** (Md **tǎng**)
to flow down, as tears, to drip

淌眼淚 **tóng ngáahn leuih**
to shed tears

淑 **suhk** (Md **shū**)
① good; pure; virtuous ②
beautiful or charming (women) ③
clear

淑德 **suhk dāk**
female virtues — especially
chastity

淑女 **suhk néuih**
gentlewomen; ladies; unmarried girls of respectable
reputation

凄(淒) **chài** (Md **qī**)
① cloudy and rainy ② cold and
chilly ③ sorrow; sorrowful;
miserable; desolate

凄涼 **chài lèuhng**
desolate and sorrowful; lonely;
lonesome

凄慘 **chài cháam**
heart-rending; heart-breaking

淖 **naauh** (Md **nào**)
slush; mud

淖濘 **naauh nìhng**
slushy mud

淘 **tòuh** (Md **táo**)
① to wash (esp. rice); to wash in
a sieve; to clean out ② to dredge;
to scour ③ to eliminate the
inferior (by exams. contests, etc.)

淘氣 **tòuh hei**
naughty, mischievous or
annoying (children)

淘汰 **tòuh taai**
eliminate inferior contestants,
goods etc. elimination; to
clean out; to weed out; to
scour; to wash thoroughly

淙 **chùhng** (Md **cóng**)
sound of flowing water; water
flowing

淙淙 **chùhng chùhng**
gurgling sound of flowing
water — especially a creek;
tinkling sound of metals or
gems

淚(泪) **leuih** (Md **lèi**)
tears

淚痕 **leuih hàhn**
traces of tears

淚汪汪 **leuih wòng wòng**
tearful

淝 **fèih** (Md **féi**)
name of a river in Anhwei
Province

淝水 **Fèih séui**
the Fei River in Anhwei
Province

淞 **sùng** (Md **sōng**)
name of a river in Kiangsu
Province

淞江 **Sùng gòng**
the Sung River in Kiangsu

淡 **daahm** (Md **dàn**)
① weak or thin (tea, coffee, etc.)
② tasteless; without enough salt;
insipid ③ off season — when
business is poor; dull ④ light (in
color); slight ⑤ without worldly
desires ⑥ same as 氮 —
nitrogen

淡黃 **daahm wòhng**
light yellow

淡季 **daahm gwai**
slack season or off season (for
business)

淤 **yú, yù** (Md **yū**)
① muddy sediment; mud; sediment ② stalemated; blocked; to silt up

淤塞 **yú sāk**
to silt up; to block; blocked or choked by silt

淤血 **yú hyut**
blood clot

淥 (渌) **luhk** (Md **lù**)
① clear water ② to drip; to strain ③ name of a tributary of the Hsiang River in Hunan Province ④ a Chinese family name

淥淥 **luhk luhk**
damp and wet; dripping

淥水 **Luhk séui**
name of a tributary of the Hsiang River (湘江) in Hunan Province

淦 **gaam, gam** (Md **gàn**)
① water leaking into a boat ② name of a river in Kiangsi Province

淨 (净) **jihng** (Md **jìng**)
① clean; pure; to cleanse; to purify ② empty; vain ③ a role in Chinese opera ④ completely; totally; net — as opposed to gross ⑤ only ⑥ net (income, profit, etc.)

淨利 **jihng leih**
net profit

淨化 **jihng fa**
to purify

淩 (凌) **lihng** (Md **líng**)
① to pass; to traverse; to cross ② to intrude; to insult or bully ③ a Chinese family name

淴 **fāt** (Md **hū**)
sound of flowing water

淴浴 **fāt yuhk**
(in Wu dialect) to take a bath

淪 (沦) **lèuhn** (Md **lún**)
① to sink into oblivion, ruin, etc.; to fall; engulfed or lost; submerged ② ripples; eddying water

淪落 **lèuhn lohk**
to get lost (in a foreign land, country, etc.)

淪陷 **lèuhn haahm**
(said of a territory) occupied by or lost to the enemy

淫 **yàhm** (Md **yín**)
① licentious; lewd; lascivious; libidinous; dissolute ② obscene; pornographic ③ to seduce; to debauch; to tempt; temptation ④ things related to sexual desires and behaviors

淫亂 **yàhm lyuhn**
debauchery

淫蕩 **yàhm dohng**
(said esp. of women) lewd and libidinous; lascivious and wanton; profligate

淬 (焠) **cheui, seuih**
(Md **cuì**)
① to temper iron, or steel for making swords etc. (also used figuratively) ② to dip into water; to soak; to dye

淬勉 **cheui míhn**
to persuade; to urge and advise; to arouse to action

淬勵 **cheui laih**
to arouse to action; to encourage

淮 **wàaih** (Md **huái**)
name of a river, countries, regions in various parts of China

淮南 **Wàaih nàahm**
the region south of the River Huai

淮水 **Wàaih séui**
the River Huai which begins in Honan Province, runs through

Anhwei and empties into the sea on Kiangsu coast

深 **sàm** (Md **shēn**)

① deep; depth ② profound; profundity ③ far; mysterious; abstruse ④ very; extremely ⑤ (said of color) dark

深信 **sàm seun**
to believe strongly; deep faith; firmly convinced

深色 **sàm sīk**
dark color

淳 **sèuhn** (Md **chún**)

① pure; clean; simple; sincere; honest ② a couple or pair (of chariots) ③ big; great

淳樸 **sèuhn pok**
sincere and simple (villagers, etc.)

淳厚 **sèuhn háuh**
simple and sincere

淵 (渊) **yùn** (Md **yuān**)

① deep water; a gulf; an abyss; vast ② profound; (learning); depth; profundity; erudition; extensive ③ a Chinese family name

淵博 **yùn bok**
erudite; erudition; profound and extensive (of learning)

淵源 **yùn yùhn**
the source; the origin; background; relationship

淶 (涞) **lòih** (Md **lái**)

name of a river in Shantung and Hopeh Province

淶水 **Lòih séui**
name of a river in Hopeh Province; name of a river in Shantung Province

混 **wahn** (Md **hùn, hún**)

① disorderly; confused ② to mix; mixed; to mingle or blend ③ to fool around; just to get along ④ to do things at random or without purpose ⑤ turbid; muddy; not clear

混合 **wahn hahp**
to mix together; to mingle or blend together

混濁 **wahn juhk**
turbid; muddy; not clear

清 **chìng** (Md **qīng**)

① pure; clean; clear ② brief; scarce ③ virtuous; honest ④ to arrange; to place in order ⑤ to conclude; to terminate; to repay (debts) ⑥ clear; simple and easily understandable ⑦ Ching Dynasty (1644 — 1911) ⑧ to clean

清潔 **chìng git**
clean; sanitary

清新 **chìng sàn**
refreshing (style, fashion, etc.)

淹 **yìm** (Md **yān**)

① submerge; to drown; to soak; to steep in ② to delay; to procrastinate ③ a stay; to be stranded ④ (now rare) deep; well-versed; erudite; profound ⑤ (now rare) discomfort caused by perspiration or liquids on skin

淹沒 **yìm muht**
submerged; inundated; to waste a talent as if by submerging it

淹死 **yìm séi**
drowned

淺 (浅) **chín** (Md **qiǎn**)

① shallow, superficial ② light (color)

淺薄 **chín bohk**
superficial; superficiality; shallow

淺紅 **chín hùhng**
light red

添 **tìm** (Md **tiān**)
to add to; to increase; increase;
to replenish (stock, etc.)

添置 **tìm ji**
to purchase additionally

添丁 **tìm dìng**
to beget a son

淼 **míuh** (Md **miǎo**)
(of water) extensive or over
whelming

涴 **wo** (Md **wò**)
① to wind or meander (said of a
stream) ② to stain; to soil

涮 **saan** (Md **shuàn**)
① to rinse (a container) ② to boil
in a chafing pot ③ to cheat with
lies

涮羊肉 **saan yèuhng yuhk**
mutton cooked in a chafing pot

渠 **kèuih** (Md **qú**)
① a drain; a channel; a ditch ②
great; deep ③ he; she

渠輩 **kèuih bui**
they; them

渠魁 **kèuih fùi**
enemy leader

渚 **jyú** (Md **zhǔ**)
a sand bar in river

渙 **wuhn** (Md **huàn**)
① scattered; dispersed ② name
of a river

渙然 **wuhn yìhn**
scattered; dispersed

渙散 **wuhn saan**
lacking concentration or
organization; (said of morale)
to collapse

減(减) **gáam** (Md **jiǎn**)
to decrease; to reduce; to lessen;
to diminish; to subtract; to
deduct

減輕 **gáam hìng**
to lighten; to lessen; to reduce;
to diminish

減弱 **gáam yeuhk**
to weaken; to reduce in
strength or intensity

渝 **yùh** (Md **yú**)
① to change mind ② another
name of Chungking ③ another
name of Chialing River

渟 **tìhng** (Md **tíng**)
① (of water) not flowing; still ②
(of water) clear

渡 **douh** (Md **dù**)
① to cross (a river or ocean) ②
a ferry

渡船 **douh syùhn**
a ferry boat

渡航 **douh hòhng**
to sail across a river or a sea

湊 **chau** (Md **còu**)
same as '凑', see '冫' radcial

湍 **tèun** (Md **tuān**)
rapidly flowing

湍流 **tèun làuh**
rapids

湍急 **tèun gāp**
(of water) rapid

湎 **míhn** (Md **miǎn**)
① drunk ② unaware ③ changing

湓 **pùhn** (Md **pén**)
name of a river in Kiangsi

湔 **jìn** (Md **jiān**)
to wash

湔洗 **jìn sái**
to wash

湔雪 **jìn syut**
to wipe away (disgrace etc.)

湖 **wùh** (Md **hú**)
a lake

湖北 **Wùh bāk**
Hupeh Province

湖光山色 **wùh gwòng sàan sīk**
the natural beauty of lakes and mountains

湘 **sèung** (Md **xiāng**)
① name of a river flowing through Hunan ② alternative name of Hunan

湘江 **Sèung gòng**
Hsiang River flowing through Hunan

湛 **jaam** (Md **zhàn**)
① dewy ② deep; profound ③ a Chinese family name ④ same as 沈 — to sink

湛恩 **jaam yàn**
great kindness

湛憂 **jaam yàu**
deep worry

湜 **jihk** (Md **shí**)
(of water) transparent

湧(涌) **yúng** (Md **yǒng**)
to well; to spring

湧現 **yúng yihn**
to crop up (in one's mind, etc.)

湧出 **yúng chēut**
to well out; to spring out

湫 **jàu, jíu** (Md **qiū, jiǎo**)
① name of a river in Kansu Province ② a small pond ③ damp and narrow

湫隘 **jíu ngaı**
damp and narrow place

湮 **yàn** (Md **yān**)
① to bury ② to block ③ long (in time)

湮沒 **yàn muht**
to bury or be buried

湮遠 **yàn yúhn**
very long (in time)

湑 **sèui** (Md **xū**)
luxuriant; rich

湯(汤) **tòng** (Md **tāng**)
① flowing (said of water) ② hot water ③ soup; broth ④ a Chinese family name

湯麵 **tòng mihn**
noodle with soup

湯匙 **tòng chìh**
a soup spoon; a table spoon

湲 **yùhn** (Md **yuán**)
(of water) flowing

渫 **sit** (Md **xiè**)
to remove; to eliminate

湟 **wòhng** (Md **huáng**)
① mean, dirty place ② name of a river

渣 **jà** (Md **zhā**)
dregs; less; grounds; sediment

渣滓 **jà jí**
dregs; less; grounds; sediment

渤 **buht** (Md **bó**)
(of water) swelling or rising

渤海 **Buht hói**
Pohai (a gulf of the Yellow Sea)

渥 **ngāk, ngūk** (Md **wò**)
① to dye ② great (kindness)

渥丹 **ngāk dàan**
to dye red

渥恩 **ngāk yàn**
profound benefaction; great kindness

渦(涡) **wò, gwò**
(Md **wò, guō**)
① a whirlpool; eddy ② name of

a river

渦輪機 **wò lèuhn gèi**
　turbine

渦河 **Gwò hòh**
　name of a river flowing through
　Anhwei

測(測)**chāk** (Md **cè**)
to measure; to survey

測量 **chāk lèuhng**
　geodetic survey; to survey

測驗 **chāk yihm**
　to test; to examine; a quiz or
　test

渭 **waih** (Md **wèi**)
name of a river

渭河 **Waih hòh**
　the Wei River, a tributary of
　the Yellow River

港 **góng** (Md **gǎng**)
① a harbor; a seaport ② a bay;
a gulf ③ short for Hong Kong

港灣 **góng wāan**
　a harbor; a bay; a gult

港督 **Góng dūk**
　the governor of Hong Kong

渲 **syùn, syun** (Md **xuàn**)
to color with paint

渲染 **syùn yíhm**
　to color with paint; to make
　exaggerated addition in a story
　or report; to play up

湉 **tìhm** (Md **tián**)
to flow placidly

渴 **hot** (Md **kě**)
① thirsty ② to long; to crave; to
pine

渴望 **hot mohng**
　to long for; to crave for; to
　aspire after

渴死 **hot séi**
　extremely thirsty

游 **yàuh** (Md **yóu**)
① to swim; to float; to waft; to
drift ② same as 遊 — to wander
③ a Chinese family name

游泳 **yàuh wihng**
　swim; swimming

游蕩 **yàuh dohng**
　to loaf; loafing

湃 **baai, paai** (Md **pài**)
billowy; turbulent

渺 **míuh** (Md **miǎo**)
① endlessly long or vast; far ②
tiny; infinitesimal ③ indistinct;
blurred

渺小 **míuh síu**
　very small; tiny; infinitesimal

渺茫 **míuh mòhng**
　endlessly vast; boundless;
　vague; uncertain; indistinct

渾(浑)**wahn, wàhn**
(Md **hún**)
① to blend; to merge ② chaotic;
confused; messy ③ entire;
complete

渾名 **wahn mìhng**
　nickname

渾沌 **wahn deuhn**
　chaos; confusion; mess

湄 **mèih** (Md **méi**)
shore

湄公河 **Mèih gùng hòh**
　the Mekong River

滑 **waaht, gwāt**
(Md **huá**)
① to slip; to slide; to glide ②
insincere; dishonest; cunning;
comical

滑倒 **waaht dóu**
　to slip and fall

滑稽 **gwāt kài**
　ludicrous; funny; comical;
　rediculous

溫 **wàn** (Md **wēn**)
① warm; mild; temperate; lukewarm; to warm ② to review ③ a Chinese family name

溫度 **wàn douh**
temperature

溫習 **wàn jaahp**
to review (what has been learned)

源 **yùhn** (Md **yuán**)
source; head (of a stream)

源頭 **yùhn tàuh**
head or source (of a stream)

源源不絕 **yùhn yùhn bāt jyuht**
to continue without end

溲 **sàu** (Md **sōu**)
① to urinate ② to immerse; to soak; to drench

溲溺 **sàu nīk**
to urinate

溲器 **sàu hei**
a urinal

溜 **lauh** (Md **liū, liù**)
① a rapid ② a row; a column ③ to go secretly and quietly ④ to slip; to slide

溜溜 **lauh lauh**
to take a stroll; to stroll; to ramble; murmur of flowing water

溜冰 **lauh bìng**
to skate; skating

準 **jéun** (Md **zhǔn**)
① level; even ② rule; criterion; standard; accurate; accuracy ③ to aim; to sight ④ would be (bride; son-in-law, etc.); to be ⑤ (in law) quasi

準備 **jéun beih**
to prepare; to get ready; preparation

準確 **jéun kok**
accurate; precise; exact

溘 **hahp** (Md **kè**)
sudden; abrupt; unexpected

溘然 **hahp yìhn**
suddenly; unexpectedly; all of a sudden

溘謝 **hahp jeh**
to die suddenly

溝 (沟) **kàu, gàu** (Md **gōu**)
① ditch; waterway; moat ② groove

溝渠 **kàu kèuih**
a ditch; a drain; a channel; a gutter

溝通 **kàu tùng**
to bring about unobstructed interflow of (feelings, ideas, etc.); to act as an intermediary for promotion of mutual understanding or bridging the gap of difference

溟 **mìhng** (Md **míng**)
① drizzle ② vast; boundless ③ sea

溟濛 **mìhng mùhng**
drizzle; gloomy; dim; obscure

溟溟 **mìhng mìhng**
drizzling; gloomy; dim; obscure

溢 **yaht** (Md **yì**)
① to flow over; to brim over ② excessive

溢出 **yaht chēut**
to brim over; to flow over; to overflow; to spill over

溢美 **yaht méih**
to praise excessively

溥 **póu** (Md **pǔ**)
① great; wide; vast ② universal

溥博 **póu bok**
inclusive and extensive

溥儀 **Póu yìh**
Henry Pu Yi, the last emperor of the Ching Dynasty

溧 **leuht** (Md **lì**)
name of a river flowing through Anhwei and Kiangsu

溧水 **Leuht séui**
name of a county or a river in Kiangsu

溪 **kài** (Md **xī, qī**)
a mountain stream

溪流 **kài làuh**
a mountain stream

溪谷 **kài gūk**
a valley; a dale; a canyon; a gorge

溯（泝、遡）**sou** (Md **sù**)
① to go upstream; to go against a stream ② to trace

溯源 **sou yùhn**
to trace back to the source

溯洄 **sou wùih**
to go upstream

滘 **gaau** (Md **jiào**)
used in name of places in Kwantung Province

溴 **chau** (Md **xiù**)
bromine

溴水 **chau séui**
bromine water

溴酸 **chau syùn**
bromine acid

溶 **yùhng** (Md **róng**)
① to dissolve; to melt ② having much water (said of rivers)

溶液 **yùhng yihk**
(in chemistry) solution

溶解 **yùhng gáai**
to dissolve; to melt

溷 **wahn** (Md **hùn**)
① dirty ② messy

溷濁 **wahn juhk**
dirty; muddy

溷淆 **wahn ngàauh**
messy; confused; chaotic

溺 **nīk, niuh** (Md **nī, niào**)
① to drown ② to indulge ③ to urinate (usually pronounce as 'niuh')

溺死 **nīk séi**
to be drown

溺愛 **nīk ngoi**
to lavish one's love upon (a child); to pamper

溽 **yuhk** (Md **rù**)
moist; humid

溽暑 **yuhk syú**
sweltering; sultry

滂 **pòhng** (Md **pāng**)
torrential; overwhelming

滂湃 **pòhng baai**
torrential; overwhelming; surging

滂沱 **pòhng tòh**
(of rain) torrential; surging; sweeping

滃 **yúng** (Md **wěng, wēng**)
swelling or rising (said of rivers and clouds)

滃鬱 **yúng wāt**
filled with vapor

滄（沧）**chòng** (Md **cāng**)
blue; azure; green; silvan

滄海 **chòng hói**
the blue sea

滄浪 **chòng lohng**
azure water

滅 (灭) **miht** (Md **miè**)
① to destroy; to ruin; to wipe out; to exterminate ② to put out; to extinguish

滅掉 **miht diuh**
to destroy; to ruin

滅火 **miht fó**
to extinguish a fire

滇 **tìhn, dìn** (Md **diān**)
alternative name of Yunnan

滇越鐵路 **Tìhn yuht tit louh**
a railway linking Yunnan and Vietnam

滋 **jì** (Md **zī**)
① to grow; to increase; to multiply; to nourish; to give rise to; to put forth ② moisture; juice; sap

滋長 **jì jéung**
to grow; to thrive

滋事 **jì sih**
to create trouble; to disturb peace

滓 **jí, jói** (Md **zǐ**)
dregs; less; sediment

渣滓 **jà jí**
dregs; less; grounds; sediment

滔 **tòu** (Md **tāo**)
① fluent ② to fill; to prevail

滔滔不絕 **tòu tòu bāt jyuht**
talking fluently and endlessly

滔天大罪 **tòu tìn daaih jeuih**
a great sin that fills the sky; extremely serious offense

滎 **yìhng** (Md **xíng, yíng**)
(of waves) rising

滎澤 **Yìhng jaahk**
name of an ancient lake in Honan

滎陽 **Yìhng yèuhng**
name of a county in Honan

滕 **tàhng** (Md **téng**)
name of a state during the Spring and Autumn Age

滕文公 **Tàhng màhn gùng**
name of a king of the state of 滕 during the Spring and Autumn Age

滕王閣 **Tàhng wòhng gok**
a renowned tower in Nanchang, Kiangsi, built in the Tang Dynasty

滙 **wuih** (Md **huì**)
same as '匯', see '匚' radical

漓 **lèih** (Md **lí**)
、① dripping wet ② thin

淋漓 **làhm lèih**
dripping wet; (now rare) long

滾 (滚) **gwán** (Md **gǔn**)
① to turn round and round; to roll; to rotate ② boiling

滾雪球 **gwán syut kàuh**
to roll a snow ball; to snowball

滾水 **gwán séui**
boiling water

滯 (滞) **jaih** (Md **zhì**)
in a standstill; stagnant; impeded; blocked; stationary

滯留 **jaih làuh**
to remain in a standstill

滯運 **jaih wahn**
bad fortune; adversity

滬 (沪) **wuh** (Md **hù**)
alternative name of Shanghai

滬市 **Wuh síh**
Shanghai

滌 (涤) **dihk** (Md **dí**)
① to wash; to cleanse ② to sweep

滌塵 **dihk chàhn**
to wash off dust

滌除 **dihk chèuih**
to wash off; to sweep away

滲(渗) **sam** (Md **shèn**)
to permeate; to percolate; to infiltrate; to seep; to ooze

滲透 **sam tau**
to infiltrate; to permeate; to percolate; to seep through

滲出 **sam chēut**
to seep out; to ooz out

溉 **koi** (Md **gài**)
① to water; to irrigate ② to wash

溉滌 **koi dihk**
to wash

溉田 **koi tìhn**
to irrigate fields

滴 **dihk, dīk** (Md **dī**)
① water drop ② to drip

滴下 **dihk hah**
to drip

滴血 **dīk hyut**
(in former time) to drop blood in water in a test to decide kinship

漣 **lìhn** (Md **lián**)
① ripples ② weeping

漣漪 **lìhn yí**
ripples

漣漣 **lìhn lìhn**
weeping

滷(卤、鹵) **lóuh** (Md **lǔ**)
① gravy; broth; sauce ② salty; salted

滷水 **lóuh séui**
salt brine

滷蛋 **lóuh dáan**
hard-boiled egg stewed in gravy

滸(浒) **wú** (Md **hǔ, xǔ**)
waterside; shore

水滸傳 **Séui wú jyún**
All Men Are Brothers, a popular fiction by Shih Nai-an (施耐庵)

滿(满) **múhn** (Md **mǎn**)
① full; filled ② plentiful; abundant ③ proud; haughty ④ Manchu ⑤ a Chinese family name

滿座 **múhn joh**
full-house; all the people present; all the audience; all the attendants

滿月 **múhn yuht**
full moon; (of a baby) to be one month old

漁(渔) **yùh** (Md **yú**)
① to fish ② to seek; to pursue ③ to seize; to acquire forcibly

漁民 **yùh màhn**
fishing population; fisherman

漁利 **yùh leih**
to seek profits or gains by unethical means; profiteering

漂 **piu, piu** (Md **piāo, piǎo, piào**)
① to drift; to float; to be tossed about ② pretty; handsome; nice; sleek ③ to bleach

漂泊 **piu bohk**
to drift; to wander

漂亮 **piu leuhng**
pretty; handsome; wise in worldly ways

漂白 **piu baahk**
to bleach

漆 **chāt** (Md **qī**)
① varnish tree; lacquer tree ② varnish; lacquer ③ to varnish; to lacquer; to paint ④ pitch black

漆器 **chāt hei**
lacquer ware

漆黑 **chāt hāak**
　pitch black; coal black; raven

漢(汉) **hon** (Md **hàn**)
　① of the Han Dynasty (206 B.C.
　— 219 A.D.) ② of the Chinese
　people or language ③ a man; a
　fellow ④ name of a tributary of
　the Yangtze River

漢奸 **hon gàan**
　traitor to China

漢語 **Hon yúh**
　the Chinese language

漩 **syùhn** (Md **xúan**)
　a whirlpool

漩渦 **syùhn wò**
　a whirlpool; dispute; quarrel

漪 **yì, yí** (Md **yī**)
　ripples

漪瀾 **yì làahn**
　ripples

漫 **maahn** (Md **màn**)
　① overflowing; set loose; uncon-
　trolled; uninhibited; reckless;
　wild; unsystematic aimless ② to
　spread or extend over ③ (of an
　expanse of water) vast or endless

漫畫 **maahn wá**
　cartoon; caricature

漫天 **maahn tìn**
　so vast as to cover the heaven

漬(渍) **ji, jīk** (Md **zì**)
　① to soak ② to dye

漬痕 **ji hàhn**
　a stain; a spot; a smear

漬染 **ji yíhm**
　to dye

漱 **sau, sou** (Md **shù**)
　to rinse; to gargle

漱滌 **sau dihk**
　to wash; to rinse

漱口 **sou háu**
　to rinse the mouth; to gargle

漲(涨) **jéung, jeung**
(Md **zhǎng, zhàng**)
　① to go up or rise (as prices) ②
　to swell; to expand

漲價 **jéung ga**
　to register a price hike; to raise
　price

漲潮 **jeung chiùh**
　(of the tide) to flow

漳 **jèung** (Md **zhāng**)
　① name of a river in Fukien ②
　name of a river in Honan

漳河 **Jèung hòh**
　name of a river in Honan

漳州 **Jèung jàu**
　Changchow; Fukien

漵 **jeuih** (Md **xù**)
　name of a river in Hunan

漸(渐) **jihm, jìm**
(Md **jiàn, jiān**)
　① gradually; little by little; by
　degrees ② to soak; to permeate
　③ to dye

漸漸 **jihm jihm**
　gradually; little by little

漸染 **jìm yíhm**
　to soak; to imbue

漾 **yeuhng** (Md **yàng**)
　to be tossed about lightly; to
　ripple; to overflow

漾漾 **yeuhng yeuhng**
　rippling

漾舟 **yeuhng jàu**
　to enjoy boating

漿(浆) **jèung**
(Md **jiāng**)
　thick fluid; starch; to starch

漿果 **jèung gwó**
　berry

漿糊 **jèung wùh**
　paste

潁 (颍) **wihng**
(Md **yǐng**)
name of a river and a place in Anhwei

潁川 **Wihng chyùn**
　name of a river in Anhwei

潁上 **Wihng seuhng**
　name of a county in Anhwei

漶 **waahn** (Md **huàn**)
to wear out beyond recognition

漉 **luhk** (Md **lù**)
① to remove sediment by filtering
② wet; dripping

漏 **lauh** (Md **lòu**)
① to leak; to divulge; to disclose
② to slip or omit unintentionally; to neglect; to forget

漏電 **lauh dihn**
　electric leakage

漏洞 **lauh duhng**
　a shortcoming; a loophole

演 **yín** (Md **yǎn**)
① to perform for entertainment; to act; to play ② to expound ③ to exercise; to practise ④ to evolve; to develop

演員 **yín yùhn**
　an actor or actress

演進 **yín jeun**
　to evolve; to develop

漕 **chòuh** (Md **cáo**)
to transport grain by water

漕運 **chòuh wahn**
　to transport grain to the capital by water

漕銀 **chòuh ngàhn**
　money paid to the government in place of tribute rice

漚 (沤) **ngau, ngàu**
(Md **òu, ōu**)
① to soak ② foam; bubble; froth

漚麻 **ngau màh**
　to soak (so that it can be split easily)

漠 **mohk** (Md **mò**)
① a desert ② indifferent; unconcerned ③ quiet; silent

漠漠 **mohk mohk**
　overcast; silent; quiet

漠視 **mohk sih**
　to dispise; to hold in contempt; to ignore; to take no head to; to consider unimportant; to under estimate

潛 (潜) **chìhm**
(Md **qián**)
① to hide; to conceal ② to dive ③ hidden; secret; latent

潛伏 **chìhm fuhk**
　to be in hiding; to lie hidden latent; hidden; concealed

潛水艇 **chìhm séui téhng**
　a submarine

潑 (泼) **put** (Md **pō**)
① to pour; to sprinkle ② ferocious; fierce; spiteful; villainous

潑辣 **put laaht**
　fierce; ferocious; spiteful

潑皮 **put pèih**
　ruffian; villain; villainous; bullying

潔 (洁) **git** (Md **jié**)
① clean; spotless; pure; stainless; immaculate ② to clean; to keep clean

潔白 **git baahk**
　clean and white; immaculate; spotless

潔癖 **git pīk**
　a morbid fear of getting dirty;

a neurotic aversion to dirt

潘 pùn (Md pān)
① a Chinese family name ② water in which rice has been washed

漭 móhng (Md mǎng)
vast; expansive

澗 (涧、㵎) gaan (Md jiàn)
a mountain stream

澗水 gaan séui
a mountain stream

澗流 gaan làuh
a mountain stream; stream in a valley

潤 (润) yeuhn (Md rùn)
① moist; glossy; fresh ② to moisten; to freshen; to bedew; to enrich; to benefit; to embellish

潤滑 yeuhn waaht
to lubricate; smooth

潤飾 yeuhn sīk
to add color; to embellrish; to polish a writing

潢 wòhng (Md huáng)
a lake or a pond

潢池 wòhng chìh
a pond

潦 lóuh, lìuh (Md lǎo, liǎo)
① to flood ② a puddle ③ disheartened; disappointed ④ without care

潦倒 lóuh dóu
disappointed; unhappy; down in luck

潦草 lóuh chóu
in a careless; irresponsible manner; perfunctory

潭 tàahm (Md tán)
① deep water; deep pool ② deep; profound

潭影 tàahm yíng
reflection in a deep pond

潭奧 tàahm ngou
profound; deep

潮 chìuh (Md cháo)
① the tide ② damp; moist; wet ③ (now rare) inferior in skill or fineness (of gold, silver, etc.)

潮流 chìuh làuh
tide; current; trend; tendency

潮濕 chìuh sāp
humid; damp

潯 (浔) chàhm (Md xún)
① a steep bank by the stream ② alternative name of Kiukiang (九江) in Kiangsi

潯江 Chàhm gòng
name of a river in Kwangsi

潯陽 Chàhm yèuhng
name of a river near Kiukiang

潰 (溃) kúi (Md kuì)
① a river overflowing its banks ② broken up; scattered; (in military) defeated

潰敗 kúi baaih
(in military) defeated and scattered; routed

潰瘍 kúi yèuhng
an ulcer

潲 saau (Md shào)
rain slanted by wind

潲雨 saau yúh
rain slanted by wind; to get wet by slanting rain

潸 (潜) sàan (Md shān)
tears flowing; to weep

潸然 sàan yìhn
tears falling

潸潸 sàan sàan
to weep continually

潺 **sàahn** (Md **chán**)
sound of water flowing; flowing water

潺潺 **sàahn sàahn**
gurging of water flowing; murmuring of flowing water

潺湲 **sàahn yùhn**
water flowing; tears streaming down

潼 **tùhng** (Md **tóng**)
① high and lofty ② a tributary of the Yellow River ③ a county in Shansi Province

潼關 **Tùhng gwàan**
name of a strategic point and a county in Shansi Province, a gateway between Northwest and Central China

澀 (涩) **sāp, saap**
(Md **sè**)
① rough; harsh; uneven; not smooth ② a slightly bitter taste that numbs the tongue — as some unripened fruit ③ difficult or jolting (writing reading, etc.) ④ slow of tongue

澀滯 **sāp jaih**
not smooth

澀訥 **saap naahp**
slow of tongue

澄 **chìhng, dahng**
(Md **chéng, dèng**)
① clear and still (water) ② to purify water by letting the impurities settling down to the bottom

澄清 **chìhng chìng**
to purify water letting the impurities setting down to the bottom; to quell disturbances in the world; to put into order; to set right; to clarify

瀉 **sīk, cheuk** (Md **xì**)
saline land

澎 **pàang, pàahng**
(Md **pēng, péng**)
① the roaring of colliding billows; breakers ② the Pescadores

澎湃 **pàang baai**
the roaring of billows

澎湖 **Pàahng wùh**
the Penghus or the Pescadores, in the Taiwan Straits

澆 (浇) **gìu** (Md **jiāo**)
① to water (plants, flowers, etc.); to splash with water; to sprinkle ② perifidious; faithless; ungrateful

澆花 **gìu fā**
to water flowers

澆冷水 **gìu láahng séui**
to dampen enthusiasm; to discourage

澇 (涝) **louh** (Md **lào**)
① (said of farm crops) to rot in the field due to flood ② torrent; flood

潞 **louh** (Md **lù**)
name of several rivers in northern China

澈 **chit** (Md **chè**)
① thoroughly; completely ② clear water ③ to understand

澈底 **chit dái**
thoroughly; completely; thoroughgoing

澈悟 **chit ngh**
to realize or understand completely

澌 **sì** (Md **sī**)
① to exhaust; to drain out ② sound of breaking or scattering

漸滅 **sì miht**
to vanish

漸盡 **sì jeuhn**
to exhaust; to drain out

澍 **syuh** (Md **shù**)
① seasonal rains; timely rain ②
(plants, etc.), saturated with
rain-water

澤(泽) **jaahk** (Md **zé**)
① where water gathers; a marsh
② grace; favors; kindness ③
brilliance; radiance; glossy;
smooth ④ to benefit; to enrich

澤國 **jaahk gwok**
land submerged by water; a
marsh or swamp

澤民 **jaahk màhn**
to benefit the people

澠(渑) **máhn, sìhng**
(Md **miǎn, shéng**)
① name of a river in Shangtung
② ancient name of a place in
Honan Province where the kings
of China and Chao of the Period
of Warring States held their summit conference ③ name of a river
and a county in Honan Province

澠水 **Máhn séui**
name of a river in Shantung
Province

澠河 **Máhn hòh**
name of a river in Honan
Province

澡 **jóu, chou** (Md **zǎo**)
to wash; to bathe

澡盆 **jóu pùhn**
a bathtub

澡堂 **jóu tòhng**
a bathhouse; a public bath

澧 **láih** (Md **lǐ**)
① fountain or spring ② name of
a county in Hunan Province

澨 **saih** (Md **shì**)
① waterside; water front ② name
of a river in Hupeh Province

澨水 **Saih séui**
name of a river in Hupeh
Province

澮(浍) **kúi** (Md **kuài**)
① ditches on farmland ② name
of a river in Shansi and Honan
Provinces

澮水 **Kúi séui**
name of a river in Shansi; name
of a river in Honan

澱 **dihn** (Md **diàn**)
① sediment; dregs; precipitate ②
indigo

澱粉 **dihn fán**
starch

澳 **ou** (Md **ào**)
① deep water where seagoing
vessels can moor ② name of
various places (see below)

澳門 **Ou mún**
Macao

澳洲 **Ou jàu**
Australia; Oceania

澶 **sìhn, sìhm** (Md **chán**)
① placid; calm and tranquil
(water) ② name of a river

濆(渍) **fàhn** (Md **fén**)
water front

澹 **daahm** (Md **dàn**)
quiet and tranquil

澹泊 **daahm bohk**
having no worldly desires or
ambitions

澹然 **daahm yìhn**
tranquil and calm

澥 **háaih** (Md **xiè**)
① a blocked stream to stop the
flow of water ② another name of
渤海

激 **gīk** (Md **jī**)

① to stir up; to rouse; to arouse; to urge; to excite ② sudden; great; very ③ heated (debate, battle, etc.) angry; vexed ④ abnormal; unusual; drastic ⑤ to turn back the current — as a dike

激動 **gīk duhng**
aroused; stimulated; excited; agitated

激增 **gīk jàng**
to increase sharply

濁(浊) **juhk** (Md **zhuó**)

① turbid or muddy (water) ② tumultuous, evil; corrupt (world) ③ stupid and idiotic (person) ④ name of a constellation

濁流 **juhk làuh**
a turbid stream

濁世 **juhk sai**
(in Buddhism) the human world; the tumultuous world

濂 **lìhm** (Md **lián**)

name of a river in Hunan Province

濂溪 **Lìhm kài**
the River Lien; in Hunan Province

濂溪學派 **Lìhm kài hohk paai**
the Lien Hsi branch of the Li School

濃(浓) **nùhng** (Md **nóng**)

① (said of drinks, liquids, etc.) thick, strong, heavy, concentrated ② (said of colors) deep, dark ③ dense

濃縮 **nùhng sūk**
to condense; condensed

濃霧 **nùhng mouh**
heavy fog; dense mist

𤄷 **pīk** (Md **pì**)

to wash; to launder

澣 **wúhn** (Md **huàn**)

same as '浣', see '水' radical

濟(济) **jai** (Md **jì, jǐ**)

① to relieve; to aid ② to cross a stream ③ to succeed; to be up to standard ④ to benefit; benefits ⑤ various; varied; numerous ⑥ elegant and dignified ⑦ name of various counties and a river

濟世 **jai sai**
to benefit the world

濟南 **Jai nàahm**
Tsinan, capital of Shantung Province

濕(湿、溼) **sāp** (Md **shī**)

① damp; moist; wet; humid; to get wet ② (in Chinese medicine) ailments caused by high humidity

濕度 **sāp douh**
humidity

濕潤 **sāp yeuhn**
damp; moisten

濘(泞) **nihng** (Md **nìng**)

① muddy; miry ② pasty; soft and mashy

濘淖 **nihng naauh**
muddy; miry

泥濘 **nàih nihng**
mire

濠 **hòuh** (Md **háo**)

a moat; a trench or ditch

濠溝 **hòuh kàu**
a trench

濠塹 **hòuh chim**
a moat; a canal or ditch around the city wall

濡 **yùh** (Md **rú**)

① to moisten; to immerse ② linger; to procrastinate ③ glossy; smooth ④ to tolerate; tolerance ⑤ patient; to endure

濡濕 **yùh sāp**
to soak by immersion; to make wet

濡染 **yùh yíhm**
to dye; to be imbued with

濤 (涛) **tòuh** (Md **tāo**)
a big wave; a billow; a great swelling

濤聲 **tòuh sìng**
the sound of roaring billow

波濤 **bò tòuh**
billows; great waves

濫 (滥) **laahm** (Md **làn**)
① to overflow; to flood ② to go to excess; to do things without plans; reckless ③ to practice no self-restraint; to abuse (one's power influence, etc.) ④ false; not true ⑤ superfluous words or expressions

濫交 **laahm gàau**
to befriend at random; to make friends indiscriminately

濫用 **laahm yuhng**
to spend excessively; to expend too much; to misuse; to abuse

濬 **jeun** (Md **jùn, xùn**)
① to dredge a waterway; to dig or wash (a well etc.) ② deep; profound

濬哲 **jeun jit**
profound wisdom

濮 **buhk** (Md **pú**)
① name of an ancient river in today's Honan Province ② name of an ancient barbarian tribe ③ a Chinese family name

濮上 **buhk seuhng**
a place where debauchery is prevalent

濮水 **Buhk séui**
name of an ancient stream in Honan and Hupeh

濯 **johk** (Md **zhuó**)
① to wash ② to eliminate vices ③ a Chinese family name

濯濯 **johk johk**
bright and brilliant; denuded (mountain); bare; bald

洗濯 **sái johk**
to wash

濰 (潍) **wàih** (Md **wéi**)
name of a river in Shantung Province

濰水 **Wàih séui**
the Wei River, in Shantung Province

濱 (滨) **bàn** (Md **bīn**)
① water's edge; to border on; to brink on ② same as 瀕 — near at hand; close by ③ (in military) a low, level seacoast

濱近 **bàn gahn**
close to; near to

海濱 **hói bàn**
sea-side; water front

濛 **mùhng** (Md **méng**)
misty; drizzly

濛濛 **mùhng mùhng**
misty

濛霧 **mùhng mouh**
mist; fog

瀑 **buhk** (Md **pù, bào**)
① a waterfall; a cascade; a cataract ② pouring rain which comes all of a sudden; sudden shower

瀑布 **buhk bou**
a waterfall; a cascade; cataract

濺 (溅) **chin, chíhn** (Md **jiàn, jiān**)
to splash; to sprinkle; to spray; to spill

濺泥 **chin nàih**
to splash mud

濺濺 **chin chin**
　　gurgling sound of flowing water

濼(泺) **lohk, bohk**
(Md **luò, pō**)
① name of a stream in Shantung Province ② to dock; to lay anchor

濾(滤) **leuih** (Md **lù**)
　to filter; to strain out

濾管 **leuih gún**
　　filter pipe

濾水池 **leuih séui chìh**
　　settling pond; depositing reservoir

瀆(渎) **duhk** (Md **dú**)
① a ditch ② a river ③ to desecrate; to profane; to be rude and disrespectful ④ to annoy

瀆犯 **duhk faahn**
　　to be rude and profane; to desecrate; to be sacrilegious

瀆職 **duhk jīk**
　　irregularity or misconduct in office, dereliction of duty, etc.

瀉(泻) **se** (Md **xiè**)
① to drain; water flowing down ② diarrhea; to have loose bowels

瀉出 **se chēut**
　　to leak out; to spurt out

瀉肚子 **se tóuh jí**
　　diarrhea; to have loose bowels

潘(沈) **sám** (Md **shěn**)
① juice; fluid; liquid; water ② short for Shenyang (Mukden), capital of Liaoning Province

瀋陽 **Sám yèuhng**
　　Mukden (Shenyang), capital of Liaoning Province

瀏(浏) **làuh** (Md **liú**)
① clear (water); bright and clear ② fast-blowing wind; cool wind ③ to get away secretly; to take

a French leave

瀏覽 **làuh láahm**
　　to glance over; to thumb-through; to take a casual look at (a scene)

瀏亮 **làuh leuhng**
　　bright and clear (sky, etc.)

瀅(滢) **yìhng** (Md **yíng**)
clear (water); bright and clear; glossy

瀝(沥) **lihk** (Md **lì**)
① to fall down by drops; to drip; to trickle ② remaining drops of wine ③ to strain water or liquids

瀝瀝 **lihk lihk**
　　the sound of flowing water; the sound of heaving wind

瀝血 **lihk hyut**
　　to drip blood; to take a blood oath; very loyal and sincere

瀦(潴) **jyù** (Md **zhū**)
a pool; a pond

瀕(濒) **pàhn, bān**
(Md **bīn**)
① near; close to; to border or brink on ② water's edge

瀕臨 **pàhn làhm**
　　near; on the brink of; close to

瀕海 **pàhn hói**
　　close to the sea; along the coast

瀘(泸) **lòuh** (Md **lú**)
① name of a river in Yunnan Province ② name of a river in Szechwan Province

瀘水 **Lòuh séui**
　　name of a river in Szechwan Province; name of a river in Yunnan Province

瀚 **hohn** (Md **hàn**)
vast; expansive

瀚海 **Hohn hói**
the Gobi Desert

瀚瀚 **hohn hohn**
vast and expansive

瀛 **yìhng (Md yíng)**
① the sea; the ocean ② within the lake

瀛海 **yìhng hói**
the sea; the ocean

瀛寰 **yìhng wàahn**
the globe; the world

瀟 (潇) **sìu (Md xiāo)**
① sound of beating rain and wind; roar of strong wind ② name of stream in Hunan

瀟瀟 **sìu sìu**
rushing rain and wind; roar of gust

瀟灑 **sìu sá**
(usually said of a man's manner) casual and elegant; dashing and refined

瀣 **haaih (Md xiè)**
mist; vapor

瀅 (滢) **yìhng (Md yíng)**
a tiny stream

瀅洄 **yìhng wùih**
whirling of water

瀧 (泷) **lùhng, sèung**
(Md lóng, shuāng)
① raining; rainy ② wet; soaked; imbued in ③ (water flowing) swiftly ④ (in Japanese) a waterfall ⑤ name of a river in Hunan

瀧岡 **Sèung gòng**
name of a hill in Yung Feng county (永豐縣) of Kiangsi

瀨 (濑) **laaih (Md lài)**
① water rushing by ② water flowing over shadows ③ name of stream in Kwangsi, also known as River Li ④ name of a stream in

Kiangsi

瀨水 **Laaih séui**
also known as River Li (荔江), a stream in Kwangsi; name of a stream in Kiangsu

瀹 **yeuhk (Md yuè)**
① to cook or to boil with soup ② to soak; to wash ③ to harness (a stream)

瀲 (潋) **lihm (Md liàn)**
① overflowing (water) ② the edge of a large body of water

瀲瀲 **lihm lihm**
overflowing; inundating

瀲灩 **lihm yihm**
overflowing; continuing joining

瀾 (澜) **làahn (Md lán)**
① overflowing; dripping wet; vast expanse of water ② thin rice paste ③ a great wave; a huge billow

瀾漫 **làahn maahn**
overflowing; inundating; dripping wet; wet through; sprightly; carefree

瀰 (沵) **nèih, mèih**
(Md mí)
brimming, overflowing (water)

瀰漫 **nèih maahn**
brimming, overflowing water; to permeate

灌 **gun (Md guàn)**
① to water; to pour (on, into, at); to irrigate ② to offer libation ③ shrubs

灌溉 **gun koi**
to irrigate; irrigation

灌木 **gun muhk**
shrubs

灃 (沣) **fùng (Md fēng)**
name of a river in Kwangsi Province

灃沛 **fùng pui**
brimming, overflowing; abundant; copious rain

灃水 **Fùng séui**
the Feng River, in Shensi Province

灕(漓) **lèih** (Md **lí**)
name of a river in Kwangsi Province

灑 **sá** (Md **sǎ**)
same as '洒', see '水' radical

灘(滩) **tàan** (Md **tān**)
beach; sand bank; shoal

灘船 **tàan syùhn**
small boat without an awning or cover

海灘 **hói tàan**
beach; sand bank

灝(灏) **houh** (Md **hào**)
bean soup

灞 **ba** (Md **bà**)
name of a river in Shensi

灞橋折柳 **ba kìuh jit láuh**
to part with friends; to bid farewell

灞水 **Ba séui**
name of a river near Chang-an (長安), Shensi

灣(湾) **wàan** (Md **wān**)
① bay; gulf; cove ② bend of a stream

灣子 **wàan jí**
a curve

灣流 **wàan làuh**
gulf stream

灤 **lyùhn** (Md **luán**)
name of a river in Northern China

灤河 **Lyùhn hòh**
name of a river in northern China

灨 **gam, gung** (Md **gàn**)
same as '贛', see '貝' radical

灩(滟、灔) **yihm**
(Md **yàn**)
overflowing; inundating

火部

火 **fó** (Md **huǒ**)
① fire; flames; to burn with fire ② fury; anger; (the fire of) lust or desires ③ urgency; urgent; imminent ④ (in Chinese herbal medicine) the latent "heat" in human body ⑤ (now rare) a group (of people) ⑥ a Chinese family name

火把 **fó bá**
a torch

火藥 **fó yeuhk**
gunpowder

灰 **fùi** (Md **huī**)
① ashes; dust ② lime ③ gray (color) ④ disappointed or discouraged ⑤ (now rare) to break into tiny pieces or particles

灰白 **fùi baahk**
pale; ashen

灰心 **fùi sàm**
disappointed; discouraged; disheartened

灸 **gau** (Md **jiǔ**)
(in Chinese medicine) to cauterize by burning moxa; moxa cautery; moxibustion

灸治 **gau jih**
to treat by moxa cautery or moxibustion

針灸 **jàm gau**
acupuncture and moxibustion; acupuncture and cauterization

灼 **cheuk, jeuk**
(Md **zhuó**)
① to burn; to cauterize ② bright;

clear; luminous; brilliant ③
flowers in full bloom

灼熱 **cheuk yiht**
intense heat; red-hot

灼見 **cheuk gin**
brilliant views; clear views

災(灾) **jòi** (Md **zāi**)
disaster; calamity; catastrophe

災害 **jòi hoih**
disaster; calamity; damages or
casualties caused by disasters

災民 **jòi màhn**
refugees created by disasters

灶 **jou** (Md **zào**)
same as '竈', see '穴' radical

炎 **yìhm** (Md **yán**)
① burning; hot; brilliant;
glorious; parched ② to flame; to
blaze; a flame; a blaze; to flare up

炎夏 **yìhm hah**
hot summer; summer at its
hottest

炎熱 **yìhm yiht**
very hot (weather)

炊 **chèui** (Md **chuī**)
to cook

炊事 **chèui sih**
cooking

炊烟 **chèui yìn**
smoke from kitchen fire

炒 **cháau** (Md **chǎo**)
to fry; to roast; to cook; to broil
(rice)

炒飯 **cháau faahn**
to fry rice; fried rice

炒地皮 **cháau deih pèih**
to engage in land speculation

炕 **kong** (Md **kàng**)
① dry; to dry ② hot ② a brick
bed warmed by a fire underneath
(in North China)

炕牀 **kong chòhng**
a brick bed warmed by a fire
underneath

炅 **gwíng, gwaih**
(Md **jiǒng, guì**)
① light (fire) ② a Chinese family
name

炙 **jek, jīk** (Md **zhì**)
to burn; to cauterize; to roast; to
broil; to heat

炙乾 **jek gòn**
to dry by applying heat

炙手可熱 **jek sáu hó yiht**
very influential and powerful

炆 **màn** (Md **wén**)
to stew

炁 **hei** (Md **qì**)
same as '氣', see '气' radical

炖 **dahn** (Md **dūn**)
fire burning intensely

炮 **paau, bàau** (Md **páo,
bāo, pào**)
① to refine medicinal herbs ② to
roast or bake ③ same as 砲, a
big gun, cannon, etc.

炮肉 **bàau yuhk**
roasted meat; to roast or
barbecue meat

大炮 **daaih paau**
a big gun; cannon

炫 **yùhn, yuhn**
(Md **xuàn**)
① to dazzle; to show off; to
display; to flaunt ② dazzling;
bright; shining

炫目 **yùhn muhk**
to dazzle the eyes

炫耀 **yùhn yiuh**
to flaunt; to show off; bright
and brilliant

炯（烱）gwíng
(Md jiǒng)
bright; brightness; clear

炯晃 gwíng fóng
bright

炯炯 gwíng gwíng
clear and bright (eyes, etc.);
discerning

炭 taan (Md tàn)
① charcoal ② coal ③ (in chemistry) C — carbon

炭酸 taan syùn
carbonic acid

炭爐 taan lòuh
a charcoal stove

炬 geuih, géui (Md jù)
a torch

炳 bíng (Md bǐng)
bright; luminous

炳然 bíng yìhn
bright

炳燭 bíng jūk
(to take a night trip stroll, etc.)
by the bright candle light

炷 jyu (Md zhù)
① the wick (of a candle, lamp, etc.) ② a stick (of insense, etc.) ③ to burn; to cauterize

炷香 jyu hēung
to burn insense

炸 ja (Md zhà, zhá)
① to explode; to bomb ② to get mad ③ to disperse boisterously ④ to fry in oil or fat

炸彈 ja daahn
bombs

炸雞 ja gài
to fry chicken; fried chicken

炤 jiu (Md zhào)
formerly interchangeable with
照 to shine

烏（乌）wù (Md wū)
① a crow, raven or rook ② dark color ③ how; what; when ④ Alas! ⑤ (now rare) the sun ⑥ a Chinese family name

烏鴉 wù ngà
the crow; the raven

烏托邦 Wù tok bòng
Utopia

烜 hyùn (Md xuān)
bright

烟（煙）yìn (Md yān)
simplified form of '煙', see '火' radical

烈 liht (Md liè)
① fiery; vehement; fierce; strong; violent ② honest and virtuous; just and straightforward; chaste ③ merits; achievements ④ a Chinese family name

烈風 liht fùng
strong wind

烈性 liht sing
a straight forward but violent disposition

烊 yèuhng, yéung
(Md yáng, yàng)
to smelt; to melt

烊金 yèuhng gàm
molten metal; molten metal ores

打烊 dá yéung
closed (business at night)

烘 hong, hùng
(Md hōng)
① to bake; to roast ② to dry or warm near a fire

烘乾 hong gòn
to dry beside or over a fire

烘托 hùng tok
(said of writing or painting) to make conspicious by contrast

烙 **lok** (Md **lào, luò**)
to burn; to brand; to iron

烙印 **lok yan**
to brand; a brand

烙餅 **lok béng**
a kind of thick, hard pan-cake;
the baking of such a cake

烝 **jìng** (Md **zhēng**)
① to rise — as steam ② many;
numerous ③ lewdness; insect;
etc. among the older generation
④ same as 蒸 — to steam

烝黎 **jìng làih**
the people; the masses

烝烝 **jìng jìng**
rising and flourishing; (now
rare) thick

烤 **háau, hàau** (Md **kǎo**)
① to roast; to bake; to toast ②
to warm by a fire

烤鴨 **háau ngaap**
to roast duck; roasted duck

烤焦 **háau jìu**
burned in roasting or baking

烽 **fùng** (Md **fēng**)
(in ancient China) a tall structure
(on a city wall, etc.) where fire
was made to signal enemy
invasion or presence of bandits

烽烟 **fùng yìn**
smoke used as a warning
signal

烽火台 **fùng fó tòih**
a tall structure for lighting
signal (or beacon fire)

烹 **pàang** (Md **pēng**)
① to cook; to boil; to decoct ②
(in cooking) to add bean sauce
and dressing after frying ③
(slang) to frighten (away)

烹飪 **pàang yahm**
to cook; cooking

烹調 **pàang tìuh**
to cook or prepare (food);
cooking

焉 **yìn, yìhn** (Md **yān**)
① an interrogative — how, why,
when, etc. ② a pronoun — it ③
an adverb — there ④ a conjunction — and so; so that ⑤ a final
particle indicating numerous
senses

焉得 **yìn dāk**
How can one be (or attain) . .
?

烯 **hèi** (Md **xī**)
① color of fire ② alkene

烷 **yùhn** (Md **wán**)
alkane

烷基 **yùhn gèi**
alkyl

烺 **lóhng** (Md **lǎng**)
(said of fire) bright

焊（銲）**hohn** (Md **hàn**)
to solder; to weld

焊接 **hohn jip**
to join with solder; to weld

焊錫 **hohn sek**
solder

焗 **gwíng** (Md **jiǒng**)
same as '炯', see '火' radical

焙 **buih** (Md **bèi**)
to dry or heat near a fire; to toast;
to bake

焙乾 **buih gòn**
to dry by a fire

焙爐 **buih lòuh**
an oven; a toaster

焚 **fàhn** (Md **fén**)
to burn; to set fire to

焚燒 **fàhn sìu**
to consume by fire; to burn; to

destroy by burning

焚化 fàhn fa
to cremate; to burn (offerings, etc.) for the dead; to put to fire

無 (无) mòuh (Md wú)
① negative; not; no; none ② without; destitute of; wanting; to lack; to have not ③ no matter what; not yet ④ a Chinese family name

無論 mòuh leuhn
no matter, regardless; not to mention the fact that; let alone

無辜 mòuh gù
innocent; guiltless; the innocent

焦 jìu (Md jiāo)
① scorched or burned ② smell or stench of things burned ③ worried and anxious ④ a Chinese family name

焦急 jìu gāp
very anxious; in deep anxiety

焦點 jìu dím
focus; burning point; a point of tremendous significance; a focal point

焰 yihm (Md yàn)
same as '燄', see '火' radical

焜 gwàn, kwàn (Md kūn)
bright; brilliant

然 yìhn (Md rán)
① yes; most certainly; a promise or permission ② but; still; nevertheless; on the other hand ③ really; if so; although; however ④ same as 燃 to burn

然後 yìhn hauh
then; afterwards; later

然而 yìhn yìh
however; but; nevertheless; on the other hand

焱 yihm (Md yàn)
same as 燄, flames

焯 jeuk, cheuk (Md zhuō, chāo)
same as 灼, to burn; bright and brilliant

煮 (煑) jyú (Md zhǔ)
to cook; to boil; to stew; to decoct

煮飯 jyú faahn
to cook rice; to cook meal

煮鶴焚琴 jyú hohk fàhn kàhm
to destroy something pleasant or fine by behaving rudely

煉 (炼、鍊) lihn (Md liàn)
① to smelt; to refine; to condense (milk) ② (in Chinese medicine) to keep herbs, etc. boiling for a long time

煉奶 lihn náaih
condensed milk

煉丹 lihn dàan
(in Taoism) to refine (by heating) concoction for special purposes; alchemy

煌 wòhng (Md huáng)
bright and brilliant

煌煌 wòhng wòhng
bright and scintillating (stars, etc.)

煎 jìn (Md jiān)
① to fry in fat or oil ② to decoct

煎餅 jìn béng
pancake

煎熬 jìn ngòuh
to decoct until almost dry; to put somebody in hot water; to make someone suffer

煒 (炜) **wáih** (Md **wěi**)
brilliant red; glowing

煜 **yūk** (Md **yù**)
① bright and brilliant ② flame or blaze

煞 **saat** (Md **shà**)
① a fierce god; a malignant deity ② very; much; extremely ③ to bring to an end; to conclude ④ to tighten (belt, etc.); to bind ⑤ to off-set; to reduce; to mitigate ⑥ an auxilliary particle in old usage ⑦ to brake; to stop

煞星 **saat sìng**
a malignant star — (usually said of a person) that brings war, deaths, calamities, disasters

煞車 **saat chè**
to fasten goods on a truck or cart with ropes; to apply a brake; to brake; a brake

煢 (煢、惸) **kìhng**
(Md **qióng**)
to be all alone; without friends or relatives

煢獨 **kìhng duhk**
alone; friendless and childless

煢煢 **kìhng kìhng**
desolate and alone

煥 **wuhn** (Md **huàn**)
① bright; brilliant; lustrous; luminous ② shining; vigorous and elegant (appearance)

煥發 **wuhn faat**
brilliant and huminous; scintillating; shining; radiant; vivacious

煥然一新 **wuhn yìhn yāt sàn**
brand new; renovated from top to bottom

煤 **mùih** (Md **méi**)
① coal; charcoal; coke ② carbon; soot

煤氣 **mùih hei**
gas (for lighting or heating); coal gas

煤礦 **mùih kwong**
a coal mine; a coal shaft

煦 **yu** (Md **xù**)
① warm and cozy ② favors; kindness; good graces; kind and gracious

煦沫 **yu muht**
saliva; to drool

煦日 **yu yaht**
the warm sun; a warm and fine day

煅 **dyuhn** (Md **duàn**)
same as ' 鍛 ', see ' 金 ' radical

照 **jiu** (Md **zhào**)
① to shine upon; to light or illumine; sunshine ② a certificate or license ③ according to; to pattern on or after ④ to compare, collate, survey, etc. ⑤ to photograph ⑥ to look after; to take care of ⑦ to notify or proclaim

照料 **jiu liuh**
to take care of; to look after

照相 **jiu seuhng**
to take a picture or photograph

煨 **wùi** (Md **wēi**)
to bake; to stew; to simmer; burn in ashes

煨肉 **wùi yuhk**
to stew meat

煨燼 **wùi jéun**
ashes

煩 (烦) **fàahn** (Md **fán**)
to vex; to annoy; to trouble; to worry; troublesome; annoying;

annoyance; vexation

煩悶 fàahn muhn
annoyed; vexed; depressed; downcast; bored

煩惱 fàahn nóuh
worries; cares; worried; vexed; to worry

煬（炀）yèuhng
(Md yáng)
① roaring or blazing (fire) ② to put before the fire ③ same as 烊, to smelt or melt

煲 bòu (Md bāo)
to cook; a kettle; a cooking pot

煠 ja (Md zhà, zhá)
same as '炸', see '火' radical

煖 nyúhn, hyún
(Md nuǎn)
same as '暖', see '日' radical

煙 yìn (Md yān)
① smoke; fumes ② tobacco; opium; cigarette ③ mist; vapor

煙灰 yìn fùi
cigarette ashes; cigar ashes

煙草 yìn chóu
tobacco; the tobacco plant

煇 fài (Md huī)
same as '輝', see '車' radical

熙 hèi (Md xī)
① bright and brilliant; glorious ② expansive; spacious ③ flourishing; prosperous; booming ④ peaceful and happy

熙熙 hèi hèi
peaceful and happy

熙怡 hèi yìh
amiable and cordial

熄 sīk (Md xī)
① to extinguish (a fire); to put

out (a light) ② to quash; to destroy; to obliterate

熄滅 sīk miht
to extinguish (a fire); to put out (a light); to die out

熄火器 sīk fó hei
a fire-extinguisher

煽 sin (Md shān)
① to stir up; to instigate; to fan ② flaming; blazing; to flame

煽動 sin duhng
to incite; to stir up (a strike, uprising, etc.)

煽惑 sin waahk
to incite; to rouse with words or lies

熊 hùhng (Md xióng)
① a bear ② a Chinese family name ③ shining bright

熊熊 hùhng hùhng
bright and brilliant; flaming and glorious; shining

熊貓 hùhng māau
panda; raccoon or racoon

熗（炝）cheung
(Md qiàng)
① a way of cooking in which foods (esp. bivalves and some vegetables) are eaten right after being brought to a boil ② same as 嗆, to choke — with smoke, etc.

熏 fàn (Md xūn)
① smoke; to smoke; to burn; smoked (meat, fish, etc.) ② (said of smell) to assail nostrils ③ warm; mild ④ to move or touch ⑤ same as 燻 or 薰

熏風 fàn fùng
southeast (warm) winds

熏肉 fàn yuhk
to smoke meat; smoked meat; bacon

熒(荧)**yìhng (Md yíng)**
① bright; shining; luminous ②
dazzling; glittering; sparkling ③
to doubt; to suspect

熒光 **yìhng gwòng**
another name of firefly

熒燎 **yìhng liuh**
light of fire

熔(鎔)**yùhng (Md róng)**
① to smelt; to weld or fuse
metals ② a die; a mold ③ a spear
— like weapon

熔岩 **yùhng ngàahm**
lava

熔點 **yùhng dím**
melting or fusing point

熬 **ngòuh (Md áo, āo)**
① to extract (oil, etc.) by applying
heat ② to cook; to stew or
simmer ③ to endure with
perseverance; to suffer with
patience (an ordeal etc.) to
sustain ④ to cook ⑤ to be worn
by worries, cares; discouraged or
despondent; dejected

熬煎 **ngòuh jìn**
tremendous ordeal or suffering

熬菜 **ngòuh choi**
to cook food (with water)

熟 **suhk (Md shú)**
① cooked or well-done (as
opposite to raw); prepared or
processed ② ripe (fruit); to ripen
③ very familiar; well-versed;
experienced; conversant ④
careful or painstaking (study,
survey, inspection, etc.) ⑤ deep
or sound (sleep)

熟客 **suhk haak**
an old customer or patron

熟練 **suhk lihn**
experienced or skilled
dexterous

熠 **yāp (Md yì)**
bright and brilliant; luminous

熠熠 **yāp yāp**
bright and brilliant

熨 **tong, wāt (Md yùn, yù)**
① to iron (clothes or cloth) ② to
settle (matters)

熨衣服 **tong yì fuhk**
to iron clothes

熨貼 **wāt tip**
(of matters) settled or taken
care of

熱(热)**yiht (Md rè)**
① hot; heated; burning to heat ②
earnest; ardent; zealous;
enthusiastic; passionate

熱帶 **yiht daai**
the tropics

熱忱 **yiht sàhm**
enthusiasm; sincerity

燈(灯)**dāng (Md dēng)**
a lamp; a lantern; a burner

燈泡 **dāng pāau**
an electric bulb

燈塔 **dāng taap**
a lighthouse

熹 **hèi (Md xī)**
① faint sunlight ② giving out
faint light

熹微 **hèi mèih**
faint light at dawn

燃 **yìhn (Md rán)**
to burn; to ignite; to light

燃料 **yìhn liuh**
fuel

燃燒 **yìhn sìu**
to burn; to be on fire; to be in
flames; combustion

熾 (炽) **chi** (Md **chì**)
intense; vigorous; energetic

熾熱 **chi yiht**
intense heat; intensely hot

熾茂 **chi mauh**
luxuriant; teeming; lush

燎 **liuh** (Md **liáo, liǎo**)
① to burn over a wider and wider area ② to glow; to shine ③ to singe

燎原 **liuh yùhn**
to get out of control like a prairie fire

燎髮 **liuh faat**
to singe hair — a thing that can be done very easily

燉 (炖) **deuhn; dahn** (Md **dùn**)
① to stew ② Tunhwang, Kansu

燉雞 **deuhn gāi**
stewed chicken; to stew chicken

燉熟 **deuhn suhk**
to stew until it is done

燒 (烧) **sìu** (Md **shāo**)
① to burn ② to roast ③ to boil; to heat

燒烤 **sìu háau**
to roast

燒香 **sìu hēung**
to burn joss stick in worship

燔 **fàahn** (Md **fán**)
① to roast ② to burn

燔肉 **fàahn yuhk**
roast meat for offering

燁 (烨、爗) **yihp** (Md **yè**)
blazing; splendid; glorious

燕 (鷰) **yin, yìn** (Md **yàn, yān**)
① a swallow ② comfort; ease ③ to feast; to enjoy ④ a state in what is Hopeh today during the Period of Warring States

燕子 **yin jí**
a swallow

燕京 **Yìn gìng**
ancient name of Peiping

燙 (烫) **tong** (Md **tàng**)
① to scald ② to heat ③ to wash

燙酒 **tong jáu**
to heat wine or liquor in hot water

燙傷 **tong sèung**
a burn; a scald

燜 (焖) **muhn** (Md **mèn**)
to cook with mild heat in a closed vessel; to cook en casserole

燜肉 **muhn yuhk**
meat cooked en casserole

燊 **sàn** (Md **shēn**)
vigorous

燐 **lèuhn** (Md **lín**)
same as '磷', see 石' radical

燄 **yihm** (Md **yàn**)
① flame; blaze; blazing ② glowing; brilliant

燄燄 **yihm yihm**
blazing

火燄 **fó yihm**
flame

燧 **seuih** (Md **suì**)
① flint ② beacon; torch

燧石 **seuih sehk**
flint

燧人氏 **Seuih yàhn sih**
a legendary ruler said to be the first to discover fire

營 (营) yìhng (Md yíng)
① military barracks ② a battalion ③ to manage; to administer; to handle

營利 yìhng leih
to engage in profit-making

營長 yìhng jéung
battalion commander

煜 yūk (Md yù)
① warm ② very hot; sweltering

燥 chou (Md zào)
① arid; dry; parched ② impatient; restless

燥熱 chou yiht
dry and hot

燥灼 chou cheuk
very uneasy; very anxious

燦 (灿) chaan (Md càn)
bright; brilliant; brightly; resplendent

燦爛 chaan laahn
resplendent; brilliant; glorious

煨 wái (Md huǐ)
① fire; blaze ② to destroy by fire; to burn down

燭 (烛) jūk (Md zhú)
① a candle ② to illuminate

燭光 jūk gwòng
(in physics) candle power ② candle light

燭臺 jūk tòih
candlestick; candlestand

燮 sit (Md xiè)
to blend; to harmonize

燮和 sit wòh
to harmonize

燮友 sit yáuh
gentle; good-natured

燴 (烩) wuih (Md huì)
① to put (a variety of materials) together and cook ② to serve (noodle, rice, etc.) with a topping of meat, vegetable, etc., in gravy

燼 (烬) jeuhn (Md jìn)
embers

灰燼 fùi jeuhn
embers

燹 sín (Md xiǎn)
① fires set off by troops or shells ② outdoor fire

兵燹 bìng sín
fire set off by troops

燾 (焘) douh, tòuh
(Md dào, tāo)
to illuminate extensively

燾育 douh yuhk
(of Heaven) to nurse all the things on earth

爆 baau (Md bào)
to explode; to burst; to crack; to pop

爆炸 baau ja
to explode; to blow up; explosion; blast

爆竹 baau jūk
firecracker

爍 (烁) seuk (Md shuò)
to glitter; to glisten; to sparkle

爍亮 seuk leuhng
glittering; glistening; sparkling

爍爍 seuk seuk
glittering; glistening; sparkling

爐 (炉、鑪) lòuh
(Md lú)
stove; oven; furnace; fireplace; hearth

爐灰 lòuh fùi
ashes from a stove

爐灶 lòuh jou
cooking stove; cooking range

爛(烂) **laahn** (Md **làn**)
① overripe; rotten ② cooked soft; well cooked ③ bright; brilliant ④ to scald; to burn; to scorch

爛泥 **laahn nàih**
soft mud, mire

爛賬 **laahn jeung**
uncollectabe debts

爨 **chyun** (Md **cuàn**)
① to cook ② cooking stove

爨婦 **chyun fúh**
a female cook

爨室 **chyun sāt**
kitchen

爪部

爪 **jáau** (Md **zhǎo, zhuǎ**)
nail; claw

爪牙 **jáau ngàh**
nails and teeth; retainers; lackeys; cat's-paw

爪哇 **Jáau wā**
Java, an island of Indonesia

爬 **pàh** (Md **pá**)
① to creep; to crawl; to lie face down ② to climb; to clamber ③ to scratch

爬山 **pàh sàan**
to climb mountains

爬蟲 **pàh chùhng**
a reptile

爭(争) **jàng** (Md **zhēng**)
① to contend; to struggle; to fight; to dispute; to argue; to quarrel ② same as 怎 — how; why ③ same as 諍 — to admonish; to counsel

爭辯 **jàng bihn**
to argue; to debate; to dispute

爭取 **jàng chéui**
to try to get; to strive for; to compete for

爰 **wùhn, yùhn** (Md **yuán**)
thereupon; therefore; accordingly

爰於 **yùhn yù**
Accordingly, (I took such and such an action on a certain day)

爰歷 **Wùhn lihk**
an ancient wordbook by Chao Kao 趙高　of the Chin (秦) Dynasty

爲(为、為) **wàih, waih** (Md **wéi, wèi**)
① to do; to manage; to handle ② to be ③ for; on behalf of; for the good of; for the sake of

爲善 **wàih sihn**
to do good

爲己 **waih géi**
for personal interest

爵 **jeuk** (Md **jué**)
① degree or title of nobility ② ancient wine pitcher

爵位 **jeuk waih**
degree of nobility

爵士 **Jeuk sih**
Sir (title of nobility)

父部

父 **fuh, fú** (Md **fù, fǔ**)
① father ② male elder ③ to do father's duty ④ a man; an old man

父母 **fuh móuh**
parents; father and mother

師父 **sì fú**
masters, tutors, teachers collectively; a respectful term of address for an artisan as carpenter, cook, etc.

爸 **bà** (Md **bà**)
father

爹 **dè** (Md **diē**)
father

爹爹 **dè dè**
father

爹娘 **dè nèuhng**
father and mother; parents

爺 **yèh** (Md **yé**)
grandfather (father's father)

爻部

爻 **ngàauh** (Md **yáo**)
strokes in diagrams for divination

爻象 **ngàauh jeuhng**
diagram for divination

爻辭 **ngàauh chìh**
explanation of diagrams for divination

爽 **sóng** (Md **shuǎng**)
① refreshing; bracing; crisp; agreeable; pleasant; brisk ② straightforward; frank ③ to fail; to miss; to lose

爽快 **sóng faai**
straightforward; openminded; comfortable; pleasant; refreshing

爽約 **sóng yeuk**
to fail to keep a promise

爾(尔) **yíh** (Md **ěr**)
① you; thou ② that; this; those; these; such; so ③ only

爾等 **yíh dáng**
you all

爾日 **yíh yaht**
that day

爿部

爿 **baahn** (Md **pán**)
① splited firewood ② a classifier for a store

牀(床) **chòhng**
(Md **chuáng**)
bed; couch

牀舖 **chòhng pòu**
bed and bedding

牀單 **chòhng dàan**
bed linen; bedsheet; bedclothes

牆(墙、墻) **chèuhng**
(Md **qiáng**)
wall; fence

牆壁 **chèuhng bìk**
wall (of a building)

牆角 **chèuhng gok**
corner between two walls

片部

片 **pin, pín** (Md **piàn, piān**)
① a piece; a slice; a fragment; a chip ② a photograph ③ a phonograph record

片刻 **pin hāk**
a little while; a brief space of time

唱片 **cheung pín**
a phonograph record

版 **báan** (Md **bǎn**)
① house hold register ② printing plate ③ supporting boards used in building walls

版權 **báan kyùhn**
copyright

版本 **báan bún**
edition; text

牌 **pàaih** (Md **pái**)
① bulletin board ② tablet; card; tag; label; signboard ③ trademark; brand

牌子 **pàaih jí**
bulletin board; a card; a tag; a signboard; a label; a brand (of

commodities); reputation

牌照 **pàaih jiu**
a license plate; a license

牋 **jìn** (Md **jiān**)
same as '箋', see '竹' radical

牒 **dihp** (Md **dié**)
① official documents ② certificates ③ records of family pedigree

牒籍 **dihp jihk**
documents

牒文 **dihp màhn**
official dispatches

牖 **yáuh** (Md **yǒu**)
① window ② to guide; to educate; to enlighten

牖民 **yáuh màhn**
to guide the people; to educate the people

窗牖 **chèung yáuh**
window

牘(牘) **duhk** (Md **dú**)
① writing tablet ② documents; archives; letters ③ a hollow pole used to strike the ground to mark the beat of music in ancient time

牘箋 **duhk jìn**
letters

牘尾 **duhk méih**
closing part of a letter

牙部

牙 **ngàh** (Md **yá**)
① teeth ② to bite ③ ivory articles

牙膏 **ngàh gòu**
tooth paste

牙齒 **ngàh chí**
tooth or teeth

牛部

牛 **ngàuh** (Md **niú**)
① ox; cattle; cow; bull ② a Chinese family name

牛痘 **ngàuh dauh**
cowpox; vaccinia

牛犢 **ngàuh duhk**
a calf

牝 **páhn** (Md **pìn**)
female of an animal

牝馬 **páhn máh**
a mare

牝雞 **páhn gāi**
a hen

牟 **màuh** (Md **móu, mù**)
① to seek ② to bellow ③ a Chinese family name

牟尼 **Màuh nèih**
(in Buddhism) peace

牟利 **màuh leih**
to seek profit

牡 **máauh** (Md **mǔ**)
male animal

牡馬 **máauh máh**
stallion

牡丹 **máauh dàan**
peony

牠 **tà** (Md **tā**)
same as '它', see '宀' radical

牢 **lòuh** (Md **láo**)
① a pen; a stable; a cage; a jail; a prison ② secure; stable; firm ③ worried; concerned

牢獄 **lòuh yuhk**
a jail; a prison

牢固 **lòuh gu**
secure; firm

牧 **muhk** (Md **mù**)
① to pasture; to shepherd; to govern ② a magistrate; a public

administrator

牧師 **muhk sì**
　a pastor; a preacher; a
　clergyman

牧羊 **muhk yèuhng**
　to pasture sheep; to tend
　sheep

物 **maht** (Md **wù**)
① thing; matter; being ② the
physical world; nature

物質 **maht jāt**
　matter (in physics)

物價 **maht ga**
　commodity prices

牲 **sàng** (Md **shēng**)
livestock

牲口 **sàng háu**
　livestock

牲畜 **sàng chūk**
　livestock

牴(觝) **dái** (Md **dǐ**)
to gore

牴觸 **dái jūk**
　to contradict; to conflict

牴牾 **dái ńgh**
　to contradict; to conflict

牯 **gú** (Md **gǔ**)
castrated bull; ox (in its narrow
sense)

牯牛 **gú ngàuh**
　a castrated bull; an ox (in its
　narrow sense)

牯嶺 **Gú líhng**
　Kulin, a summer resort in
　Kiangsi

牸 **jih** (Md **zì**)
animal female

特 **dahk** (Md **tè**)
① special; unique; particular;
extra-ordinary; unusual; outstanding; distinguished; exclusive ②

a bull

特技 **dahk geih**
　special　skills;　stunts;
　acrobatics

特殊 **dahk syùh**
　special; unusual; unique

牾 **ńgh** (Md **wǔ**)
① to oppose ② to gore

牽(牽) **hìn** (Md **qiān**)
① to drag; to pull; to tug; to haul
② to involve; to affect ③ to
control; to restrain

牽引 **hìn yáhn**
　to involve (in trouble); to drag
　(into trouble)

牽涉 **hìn sip**
　to involve; to affect; to
　implicate

犂(犁) **làih** (Md **lí**)
① to till; to plough ② a plough

犂田 **làih tìhn**
　to plough a field

犂庭掃穴 **làih tìhng sou
yuht**
　to annihilate the enemy

犀 **sài** (Md **xī**)
① sharp-edged and hard (armor,
weapon, etc.) ② rhinoceros

犀牛 **sài ngàuh**
　the rhinoceros

犀利 **sài leih**
　hard and sharp

犄 **kèi, gèi** (Md **jī**)
horn

犄角 **kèi gok**
　horn; a corner

犇(奔) **bàn** (Md **bēn**)
ancient variant of 奔 (to run
away; to be in a hurry)

犍 **gìn** (Md **jiān, qián**)
castrated bull; ox

犖 (荦) **lok** (Md **luò**)
① spotted ox ② of many colors

犖犖 **lok lok**
clear; evident; apparent

犖确 **lok kok**
rugged or craggy (mountains)

犒 **hou, houh** (Md **kào**)
to reward (soldiers, laborers, etc.)

犒賞 **hou séung**
to reward (one for contributions) with money or gifts

犒軍 **hou gwàn**
to cheer troops with material gifts

犛 (牦) **lèih** (Md **lí**)
① a black ox ② a yak

犛牛 **lèih ngàuh**
a yak

犢 (犊) **duhk** (Md **dú**)
a calf

犢鼻 **duhk beih**
(in Chinese herb medicine) a point susceptible to acupuncture under the kneecap

犧 (牺) **hèi** (Md **xī**)
① sacrifice (as homage to a deity) ② to give up (for the sake of something of greater value); to sacrifice

犧牲 **hèi sàng**
sacrifice (offered to a deity); to sacrifice (something valued for the sake of something else)

犧尊 **hèi jyùn**
a wooden wine cup shaped like an ox

犬部

犬 **hyún** (Md **quǎn**)
a dog; canine

犬子 **hyún jí**
my son (self-depreciatory term)

犬齒 **hyún chí**
cuspid; canine tooth

犯 **faahn** (Md **fàn**)
① to violate; to offend; to break (regulations or laws) ② to commit (crimes, mistakes, etc.) ③ to invade ④ a criminal

犯法 **faahn faat**
to violate the law; to break the law

犯人 **faahn yàhn**
a criminal; a prisoner

犴 **hòhn, ngohn**
(Md **hān, àn**)
① a prison; a jail ② a species of dog with black mouth and nose

狂 **kwòhng, kòhng**
(Md **kuáng**)
① crazy; mad; mentally deranged ② unrestrained; uninhibited; wild; violent ③ haughty

狂暴 **kwòhng bouh**
wild; fierce; furious; ferocious; brutal

狂笑 **kwòhng siu**
to give a wild laughter

狁 **wáhn** (Md **yǔn**)
name of a barbarian tribe to the north in ancient time

狃 **náu** (Md **niǔ**)
① to covet ② to be accustomed

狃於成見 **náu yù sìhng gin**
to be a slave of preconceived ideas; opinionated

狄 **dihk** (Md **dí**)

① name of a barbarian tribe to the north in ancient times ② a Chinese family name

狄更斯 **Dihk gāng sī**
Charles Dickens, 1812 – 1870

狄士尼樂園 **Dihk sih nèih lohk yùhn**
Disneyland, U.S.A.

狀 (状) **johng**
(Md **zhuàng**)
① appearance; look; shape; form ② condition; state; situation ③ written appeal

狀況 **johng fong**
situation; circumstances; condition

狀詞 **johng chìh**
the contents of an accusation

狐 **wùh** (Md **hú**)
the fox

狐狸 **wùh lèih**
fox

狐疑 **wùh yìh**
suspicious; distrustful

狎 **haahp** (Md **xiá**)
to show familiarity; intimacy, or disrespect

狎弄 **haahp luhng**
to show improper familiarity with, to be rude to; to be impolite to

狎妓 **haahp geih**
to visit a brothel

狒 **feih** (Md **fèi**)
the baboon

狒狒 **feih feih**
the baboon

狗 **gáu** (Md **gǒu**)
a dog

狗吠 **gáu faih**
the bark of a dog

狗熊 **gáu hùhng**
a bear

狙 **jèui** (Md **jū**)
① monkey; ape ② to lie in ambush

狙擊 **jèui gīk**
to launch a sneak attack; to attack by surprise

狙詐 **jèui ja**
trick; ruse; wile

狡 **gáau** (Md **jiǎo**)
cunning; crafty; sly; wily; artful; shrewd

狡猾 **gáau waaht**
cunning; crafty; sly; wily; artful

狡計 **gáau gai**
a clever scheme; a cunning plot

狠 **hán** (Md **hěn**)
① vicious; cruel; atrocious ② severely; extremely

狠毒 **hán duhk**
atrocious; cruel; brutal; malicious

狠心 **hán sàm**
heartless; pitiless; merciless; cruel

狩 **sau** (Md **shòu**)
① to hunt in winter ② imperial tour

狩獵 **sau lihp**
hunting; to hunt or trap games

狴 **baih** (Md **bì**)
① a legendary wild dog ② a prison

狴犴 **baih hòhn**
a legendary wild dog; a prison or penitentiary

狷 **gyun** (Md **juàn**)
① rash; quick-tempered; narrow-

minded ② honest and straight-forward

狷介 **gyun gaai**
honest and straightforward

狷忿 **gyun fáhn**
easily excitable

狹 (狭) **haahp** (Md **xiá**)
narrow; narrow-minded

狹窄 **haahp jaak**
narrow

狹隘 **haahp ngaai**
narrow-minded

狼 **lòhng** (Md **láng**)
① wolf ② a heartless cruel person; cruel and heartless; cunning and crafty

狼狽 **lòhng bui**
heartlessly dependent; embarrassed

狼吞虎嚥 **lòhng tàn fú yin**
to devour (food) like wolf and tiger

狽 (狈) **bui** (Md **bèi**)
a kind of wolf with shorter forelegs

狸 (貍) **lèih** (Md **lí**)
① fox ② racom dog

狸貓 **lèih māau**
a kind of wild cat

狸德 **lèih dāk**
as greedy as a fox

猜 **chàai** (Md **cāi**)
① to guess; to suspect; to doubt ② cruel and suspicious

猜不透 **chàai bāt tau**
unable to guess; unable to make out

猜想 **chàai séung**
to guess; to surmise; a guess or surmising

猜忌 **chàai geih**
to be jealous and suspicious

猖 **chèung** (Md **chāng**)
wild, mad, impudent

猖狂 **chèung kòhng**
wild; ungovernable; unrestrained

猖亂 **chèung lyuhn**
wild and disorderly

猙 (狰) **jàng** (Md **zhēng**)
fierce-looking; hideous; repulsive

猙獰 **jàng nìhng**
fierce-looking; hideous; repulsive

猛 **máahng** (Md **měng**)
① bold; brave; fierce; violent ② sudden and quick ③ severe, strict; stringent

猛烈 **máahng liht**
fierce; violent and savage

猛擊 **máahng gīk**
a furious blow; a sudden and violent attack or thust; to attack with all force

猛獸 **máahng sau**
fierce wild beasts

猇 **hàau** (Md **xiāo**)
the roars of a tiger

猶 **yàuh** (Md **yóu**)
① like; similar to ② still, yet; even; especially

猶太 **Yàuh taai**
Jews or Hebrews; Judaea; stingy; miserly

猶如 **yàuh yùh**
just like

猶預 **yàuh yuh**
hesitatingly, undecided

猪 (豬) **jyù** (Md **zhū**)
a pig

猪肉 **jyù yuhk**
pork

豬肝 **jyù gòn**
pig liver

猥|**wái, wùi** (Md **wěi**)
① vulgar; wanton; low; lewd and
licentious ② many; numerous;
varied; multitudinous

猥賤 **wái jihn**
low and vulgar

猥褻 **wái sit**
obsene; obscenity; lewd

猢 **wùh** (Md **hú**)
monkey

猢猻 **wùh syùn**
monkeys

猢猻入布袋 **wùh syùn yahp bou doih**
to submit to discipline
reluctently

猩 **sìng** (Md **xīng**)
① scarlet; red ② a yellow-haired
ape

猩紅 **sìng hùhng**
scarlet

猩紅熱 **sìng hùhng yiht**
scarlet fever

猩猩 **sìng sìng**
a yellow-haired ape, a
chimpanzee

猴 **hàuh** (Md **hóu**)
① monkey ② naughty or impish
(child)

猴戲 **hàuh hei**
a monkey (in circus, zoo)

猴子 **hàuh jí**
a monkey

猷 **yàuh** (Md **yóu**)
① a plan; a program ② like,
similar to ③ a way, a path

猬（蝟 ）**waih** (Md **wèi**)
hedgehog

猻（狲 ）**syùn** (Md **sūn**)
a monkey

猿（猨 ）**yùhn** (Md **yuán**)
an ape; a gibbon

猿猴 **yùhn hàuh**
apes and monkey

猿人 **yùhn yàhn**
anthropoid apes; gorilla

獅（狮 ）**sì** (Md **shī**)
the lion

獅子 **sì jí**
the lion

獅子頭 **sì jí tàuh**
stewed meat balls

猾 **waaht** (Md **huá**)
cunning, crafty

猾賊 **waaht chaahk**
a cunning thief

猾伯 **waaht baak**
a master in cunningness

獄（狱 ）**yuhk** (Md **yù**)
a prison; a lawsuit

獄吏 **yuhk leih**
a jailer, a warden

獄卒 **yuhk jēut**
low-ranking employees who
help run a prison; gaolers

獃（呆 ）**dàai** (Md **dāi**)
① silly, stupid, foolish ②
awkward, clumsy

獃獃地 **dàai dàai deih**
stupidly; idiotically

獃子 **dàai jí**
an idiot, a stupid person

獃頭獃腦 **dàai tàuh dàai nóuh**
looking like an idiot

獗 **kyut** (Md **juế**)
unruly; lawless and wild

獠 **liuh** (Md **liáo**)
① a primitive tribe in China ② fierce (looking)

獠面 **liuh mihn**
terrifying looks, fierce appearance

獠牙 **liuh ngàh**
buckteeth; fangs

獨(独) **duhk** (Md **dú**)
① alone, single, only ② to monopolize ③ to be old and without a son

獨立 **duhk lahp**
independence, independent

獨一無二 **duhk yāt mòuh yih**
the one and the only one; unique

獪(狯) **gúi** (Md **kuài**)
cunning; artful; crafty

獪猾 **gúi waaht**
cunning

獰 **nìhng** (Md **níng**)
fierce of appearance; awe-inspiring look

獰笑 **nìhng siu**
a frightening laugh; a grin

獰惡可怖 **nìhng ngok hó bou**
fierce and terrifying

獲 **wohk** (Md **huò**)
① able; can ② to get; to obtain

獲得 **wohk dāk**
to get; to obtain

獲利 **wohk leih**
to get or obtain profit

獲赦 **wohk se**
to be pardoned

獸 **sau** (Md **shòu**)
a beast or animal

獸皮 **sau pèih**
animal skin

獸類 **sau leuih**
animals; fauna

獸心 **sau sàm**
bestiality; beastliness

獵 **lihp** (Md **liè**)
to hunt; to chase

獵取 **lihp chéui**
to chase after; to pursue

獵食 **lihp sihk**
to hunt for food

獵人 **lihp yàhn**
a hunter

獷 **gwóng** (Md **guǎng**)
fierce and rude; uncivilized

獷敵 **gwóng dihk**
savage enemy; deadly rival

獷俗 **gwóng juhk**
uncivilized customs; barbarian ways

獺 **chaat** (Md **tǎ**)
an otter

獺祭 **chaat jai**
to write an article by heaping up quotations and allusions from a large number of books

獻 **hin** (Md **xiàn**)
① to offer; to present ② to show; to stage ③ to curry (favor, etc.)

獻花 **hin fā**
to present flowers or bonquets

獻技 **hin geih**
to perform a special skill or feat

獼 **mèih** (Md **mí**)
macacus monkey

獼猴 **mèih hàuh**
macacus monkey

猡 lòh (Md luó)
a primitive tribe

玄部

玄 yùhn (Md xuán)
① far and obscure ② deep and profound

玄妙 yùhn miuh
profound; abstruse and subtle

玄虛 yùhn hèui
empty and without substance; cunning and evil schemes

率 sēut, leuht (Md shuài, lù)
① to lead; ② to follow ③ ratio

率領 sēut líhng
to lead

率直 sēut jihk
frank; honest; straight

玉部

王 wòhng (Md wáng)
① a king; a ruler ② great; of tremendous size ③ the strongest powerful ④ a Chinese family name

王法 wòhng faat
the laws of the land

王宮 wòhng gùng
a royal palace

王朝 wòhng chìuh
a dynasty

玉 yuhk (Md yù)
① jade ② a designation of things belonging to a girl or young woman

玉帛 yuhk baahk
jade and silk

玉女 yuhk néui
a young and beautiful girl

玉潔冰清 yuhk git bìng chìng
pure and virtuous

玖 gáu (Md jiǔ)
① black jade ② an elaborate form of nine

玩 wuhn (Md wán)
① to play; to play with ② to amuse oneself with

玩弄 wuhn luhng
to fool; to seduce (a girl); to play joke with; to toy with

玩具 wuhn geuih
toys

玩世不恭 wuhn sai bāt gùng
to be a cynic; to take everything lightly

玫 mùih (Md méi)
① the rose ② another name of black mica — a sparkling red gem

玫瑰 mùih gwai
the rose; blaca-mica

玫瑰紅 mùih gwai hùhng
rose-red

玫瑰油 mùih gwai yàuh
attar of roses

珏 gok (Md juế)
two pieces of jade fastened together

玡 (琊) yèh (Md yá)
ancient name of the eastern portion of Shantung; also name of a mountain in eastern Shantung

玷 dim (Md diàn)
① a stain of a piece of jade ② to blamish; to disgrace

玷辱 dim yuhk
to disgrace

玲 lìhng (Md líng)
tinkling of jade pendants

玲玎 lìhng dīng
tinkling of jade pendants;

sound of waves poundling on rocks

玲瓏 **lìhng lùhng**
pleasing; delicate; bright; fine; regular

玳 **doih** (Md **dài**)
the tortoise shell

玳瑁 **doih mouh**
hawksbill turtle

玳瑁眼鏡 **doih mouh ngáahn geng**
hawksbill shell-rimmed glasses

玻 **bò** (Md **bō**)
glass

玻璃 **bō lēi**
glass

玻璃體 **bō lēi tái**
vitreous body

珀 **paak** (Md **pó**)
amber

珊 **sàan** (Md **shān**)
① coral ② tinkling of pendants

珊瑚 **sàan wùh**
coral

珊珊 **sàan sàan**
tinkling of pendants

珍 **jàn** (Md **zhēn**)
① valuable; rare ② treasures ③ delicacies

珍寶 **jàn bóu**
jewelry and valuables

珍惜 **jàn sīk**
to treasure; to prize; to consider as very precious

珍重 **jàn juhng**
to take good care of; to think much of

琺(瑯) **faat** (Md **fà**)
enamel; enamel-wares

琺瑯 **faat lòhng**
enamel

琺瑯質 **faat lòhng jāt**
enamel — especially referring to the hard, white glossy coating of teeth

珠 **jyù** (Md **zhū**)
① a pearl ② a bead; a drop ③ the pupil of the eye ④ a Chinese family name

珠寶 **jyù bóu**
jewelry

珠聯璧合 **jyù lyùhn bīk hahp**
an excellent match (especially referring to marriage)

班 **bàan** (Md **bān**)
① a grade ② a class; a group ③ to distribute

班門弄斧 **bàan mùhn luhng fú**
to show one's talent or skill before the expert

班級 **bàan kāp**
grade; form

班次 **bàan chi**
flight number of airplane; designated number of a scheduled train or bus

珣 **sèun** (Md **xún**)
name of a kind of jade

珮 **pui** (Md **pèi**)
jade pendant

球 **kàuh** (Md **qiú**)
a sphere; a globe; a ball

球隊 **kàuh déui**
teams for playing ball games

球類 **kàuh leuih**
kinds of balls

球賽 **kàuh choi**
a ball game

現 **yihn** (Md **xiàn**)
① to appear; to reveal ② now; present; at the moment ③ ready; available

現代 **yihn doih**
modern; the present age

現成 **yihn sìhng**
ready; ready-made at hand

現象 **yihn jeuhng**
phenomenon

現實 **yihn saht**
reality; practical

琅(瑯) **lòhng** (Md **láng**)
① a kind of stine resembling pearl ② clean and white; pure

琅璫入獄 **lòhng dòng yahp yuhk**
to be put in jail clanking with manacles

琅函 **lòhng hàahm**
a bookcase; your letter (a polite expression)

理 **léih** (Md **lǐ**)
① reason; cause; right ② law; principle; theory ③ to arrange; to repair; to cut

理論 **léih leuhn**
a theory

理想 **léih séung**
ideal; idea; thought; dream

琉 **làuh** (Md **liú**)
① a glass and bright stone ② opaque; glazed

琉璃 **làuh lèih**
opaque, a glass-like substance

琛 **sàm** (Md **chēn**)
treasures; jewelry or valuable

琚 **gèui** (Md **jū**)
a jade ornament

琢 **deuk** (Md **zhuó**)
to cut; chisel or polish jade

琢磨 **deuk mòh**
to cut and polish; to study and improve (oneself)

琢句 **deuk geui**
to write and polish phrases and sentences

琥 **fú** (Md **hǔ**)
① a jade ornament in the shape of a tiger ② amber

琥珀 **fú paak**
amber

琥珀酸 **fú paak syùn**
succinic acid

琦 **kèih** (Md **qí**)
① a kind of jade ② strange

琨 **kwàn** (Md **kūn**)
fine rocks next to jade in quality

琨庭 **kwàn tìhng**
a yard dotted with white stones

琪 **kèih** (Md **qí**)
a piece of jade; a jade-like precious stone

琪花瑤草 **kèih fà yìuh chóu**
blossoms and vegetation in fairyland

琮 **chùhng** (Md **cóng**)
an octagonal jade piece with a round hole in the center

琯 **gún** (Md **guǎn**)
① a jade tube used as an instrument in ancient times ② to polish precious metals as stones

琳 **làhm** (Md **lín**)
a fine piece of jade

琳琅(琳瑯) **làhm lòhng**
fine jades; people of outstanding talent or precious collection of books

琳琅滿目 làhm lòhng múhn muhk
a vast array of beautiful and fine things

琴(琹) kàhm (Md qín)
① a musical instrument -- stringed, as piano, violin, etc. ② a Chinese lute or guitar with five or seven strings

琴譜 kàhm póu
a score for stringed instruments

琴瑟 kàhm sāt
the lute and the harp; a married couple

琰 yíhm (Md yǎn)
the glitter of gems

琵 pèih (Md pí)
the four stringed guitar or the balloon — guitar

琵琶 pèih pàh
a balloon — guitar

琵琶別抱 pèih pàh biht póuh
to marry another husband; the remarriage of a woman

琶 pàh (Md pa)
a four-stringed guitar or a balloon-guitar

瑋 wáih (Md wěi)
① a kind of jade ② precious; rare

瑕 hàh (Md xiá)
① a spot, a flaw in a piece of jade ② an error, a fault

瑕疵 hàh chì
flaws; defects

瑕不掩瑜 hàh bāt yím yùh
the defects do not outweigh the merits

瑜 yùh (Md yú)
① a fine piece of jade ② excellent; virtues ③ yoga

瑜珈 yùh gā
yoga, a mystic and ascetic practice in Hindu philosophy

瑛 yìng (Md yīng)
sheen of jade; transparent piece of jade; crystal

瑚 wùh (Md hú)
① virtue and quality of a person ② coral

瑚璉 wùh líhn
coral

瑞 seuih (Md ruì)
① a good omen ② lucky, fortunate

瑞典 Seuih dín
Sweden

瑞士 Seuih sih
Switzerland

瑞祥 seuih chèuhng
good luck, good fortune

瑟 sāt (Md sè)
① a large horizontal musical instrument ② varied and many

瑟瑟 sāt sāt
the heaving sound of wind

瑟縮 sāt sūk
stiff and numb — as from cold; timid and trembling — as from fear

瑙 nóuh (Md nǎo)
cornelian, agate

瑁 mouh (Md mào)
① a very precious piece of jade ② tortoise shell

瑣 só (Md suǒ)
① trifles; petty ② troublesome; annoying

瑣碎 só seui
petty and varied

瑣務 só mouh
trifle matters

瑣才 **só chòih**
a person of little capability

瑤 **yìuh** (Md **yáo**)
① a precious stone ② clean; pure
③ valuable; precious

瑤琴 **yìuh kàhm**
lute studded

瑤花 **yìuh fā**
rare flowers

瑩 **yìhng** (Md **yíng**)
① brilliant and bright ② clean
and shining

瑩潔 **yìhng git**
clean and lustrous

瑩徹 **yìhng chit**
clear and transparent

瑰 **gwai** (Md **guī**)
great; extraordinary

瑰麗 **gwai laih**
fabulous beautiful

瑰異 **gwai yih**
fabulous and extraordinary
things

瑪 **máh** (Md **mǎ**)
agate, cornelian

瑪瑙 **máh nóuh**
agate, cornelian

瑾 **gán** (Md **jín**)
fine jade

璃 **lèih** (Md **li**)
glass; a glassy substance

璋 **jèung** (Md **zhāng**)
an ancient jade ornament

璇 (璿) **syùhn**
(Md **xuán**)
fine jade

璇宮 **syùhn gùng**
an exquisite rome ornamented
with fine gems

璇花 **syùhn fā**
blossoms as pure and white as
jade

璀 **chèui** (Md **cuǐ**)
the lustre or glitter of jade

璀璨 **chèui chaan**
the brilliancy aud lustre of
pearls and precious stones

璀璀 **chèui chèui**
bright and clear

璜 **wòhng** (Md **huáng**)
an ancient jade ornament, semi-
circular in shape

璞 **pok** (Md **pú**)
an unpolished or uncraved jade or
gem

璣 **gèi** (Md **jī**)
① pearls, jade which are not
quite circular ② an ancient
astronomical instrument

璘 **lèuhn** (Md **lín**)
the brilliance of jade

璐 **louh** (Md **lù**)
fine jade

璨 **chaan** (Md **càn**)
bright and brilliant; lustrous and
luminous

環 **wàahn** (Md **huán**)
① a ring or bracelet ② around;
round; to encircle

環境 **wàahn ging**
surrounding, environment

環顧四周 **wàahn gu sei jàu**
to look around

環遊世界 **wàahn yàuh sai
gaai**
to take a round-a-world tour

璧 **bīk** (Md **bì**)
a general name of all kinds of
jades

璧合 **bīk hahp**
a perfect match

璧還 **bīk wàahn**
to return a gift

璧玉 **bīk yuhk**
a round and flat piece of jade
with a circular hole in it

璽 **sáai** (Md **xǐ**)
① the seal of a king ② the formal
seal of a state

璽書 **sáai syù**
documents sealed with
personal or official seals

璺 **mahn** (Md **wèn**)
a crack in jade

瓊(琼) **kìhng**
(Md **qióng**)
① fine jade ② excellent; beautiful

瓊樓玉宇 **kìhng làuh yuhk yúh**
Palace of the moon

瓊姿 **kìhng jì**
elegant or graceful appearance

瓏 **lùhng** (Md **lóng**)
① clear and crisp ② dry; parched

瓔 **yìng** (Md **yīng**)
a necklace of precious stone

瓚 **jaan** (Md **jàn**)
an ancient jade

瓜部

瓜 **gwà** (Md **guā**)
melons; cucumbers

瓜分 **gwà fàn**
to divide and distribute

瓜田李下 **gwà tìhn léih hah**
a melon field (where one may
be suspected of stealing
melons if one ties his shoe
strings) and under a plum tree
(where one may be suspected
of stealing plums if one ar-
ranges one's hat) — a position
that invites suspicion

瓜葛 **gwà got**
melon vines — a multitude of
relatives; connected; involved

瓞 **diht** (Md **dié**)
unripe melons

瓠 **wuh** (Md **hù**)
a gourd; a calabash

瓠肥 **wuh fèih**
obese; fat

瓠落 **wuh lohk**
large but useless

瓠果 **wuh gwó**
pepo

瓢 **pìuh** (Md **piáo**)
a ladle (often made of dried
calabash or gourd)

瓢蟲 **pìuh chùhng**
lady bug; lady bird

瓣 **faahn** (Md **bàn**)
① petals of a flower ② sections
(as of oranges)

瓣香 **faahn hèung**
petal-like incense used in
worship of Buddha

瓤 **nòhng** (Md **ráng**)
pulp of a fruit; section of an
orange

瓦部

瓦 **ngáh** (Md **wǎ**)
① earthern ware; pottery ② tile

瓦房 **ngáh fòhng**
a tiled house

瓦特 **Ngáh dahk**
James Watt; Watt (in
electricity)

瓦解 **ngáh gáai**
to fall apart

瓩 **chìn ngáh** (Md **qiān wǎ**)
1000 watt

瓷 **chìh** (Md **cí**)
porcelain; china ware

瓷土 **chìh tóu**
kaolin; porcelain clay

瓷器 **chìh hei**
porcelain ware, chinaware

瓷磚 **chìh jyùn**
small porcelain tile used for wall paneling

瓶 **pìhng** (Md **píng**)
bottle; jug; vase

瓶鉢 **pìhng but**
a Buddhist monk's rice bowl

瓶裝 **pìhng jōng**
bottled

瓶塞 (兒) **pìhng sāk (yìh)**
bottle stopper or plug; a cork

甄 **yàn, jàn** (Md **zhēn**)
① to grade by examination ② to make pottery ware ③ to make clear

甄拔 **yàn baht**
to select by a competitive examination

甄別考試 **yàn biht háau si**
examination for grading abilities

甄用 **yàn yuhng**
to employ by an exam

甌 **ngàu** (Md **ōu**)
a small tray; a cup

甑 **jahng** (Md **zèng**)
earthernware for cooking

甏 **pàang** (Md **bèng**)
a container; a kind of jar

甕 **ung** (Md **wèng**)
a jar; a jug; a pot

甕中之鼈 **ung jùng jì bit (biht)**
the turtle inside a jar — something that can be caught easily

甘部

甘 **gàm** (Md **gān**)
① sweet; tasty ② willing

甘拜下風 **gàm baai hah fùng**
willing to take an inferior position

甘露 **gàm louh**
sweet dew

甘心忍受 **gàm sàm yán sauh**
willing to endure

甚 **sahm** (Md **shèn**)
to a great extent; high degree; very

甚急 **sahm gāp**
very anxious; very urgent

甚殷 **sahm yàn**
very sincerely

甚爲不解 **sahm wàih bāt gáai**
very complexing

甜 **tìhm** (Md **tián**)
sweet; pleasant

甜蜜 **tìhm maht**
sweet as honey

甜睡 **tìhm seuih**
sleeping soundly

甜言蜜語 **tìhm yìhn maht yúh**
honeyed words; flattery

生部

生 **sàng** (Md **shēng**)
① to live; life ② to be born ③ to bear ④ uncook; raw

生病 **sàng bihng**
to get sick

生命 **sàng mihng**
life

生兒育女 **sàng yìh yuhk néuih**
to give birth to children and rear them

牲 **sàn** (Md **shēn**)
① numerous; many ② crowded

產 **cháan** (Md **chǎn**)
① to bear; to lay ② to produce

產量 **cháan leuhng**
production; output

產卵 **cháan léun**
to lay eggs

產業 **cháan yihp**
properties

甥 **sāng** (Md **shēng**)
a nephew (son of a sister)

甥女 **sāng néui**
a niece (daughter of a sister)

甦(穌) **sòu** (Md **sū**)
to come back to life; to rise from the dead

甦醒 **sòu síng**
to come back to life; to revive; to come to

用部

用 **yuhng** (Md **yòng**)
① to use; to employ ② purpose ③ effect

用途 **yuhng tòuh**
a purpose; usage

用心 **yuhng sàm**
to be careful; to pay attention

用盡方法 **yuhng jeuhn fòng faat**
to exhaust one's wits

甩 **lāt** (Md **shuǎi**)
to throw away; to cast away

甩不掉 **lāt bāt diuh**
cannot get rid of; cannot shake off

甩手 **lāt sáu**
to take no heed; to ignore

甫 **fú** (Md **fǔ**)
① a man; a father (euphemism) ② then and only then

甫能 **fú nàhng**
able then and only then

甬 **yúng** (Md **yǒng**)
a measure of capacity

甬道 **yúng douh**
central path in a hall

甭 **báng** (Md **béng**)
do not have to; unnecessary

田部

田 **tìhn** (Md **tián**)
field; rice field; agricultural land

田戶 **tìhn wuh**
farmer; land tiller

田野 **tìhn yéh**
fields; cultivated lands

田園 **tìhn yùhn**
fields and gardens; rural

由 **yàuh** (Md **yáu**)
① reason, cause ② from; by; up to

由不得 **yàuh bāt dāk**
involuntarily; unable to do as one pleases

由淺入深 **yàuh chín yahp sàm**
to go from the easy to the difficult and complicated

由衷 **yàuh chùng**
from the depth of one's heart

甲 **gaap** (Md **jiǎ**)
① the first of the Ten Celestial
Stems ② armor; shell; ③ most
outstanding

甲板 **gaap báan**
deck (of a ship)

甲等 **gaap dáng**
grade A

甲於天下 **gaap yù tìn hah**
unequaled in the world

申 **sàn** (Md **shēn**)
① the ninth of the Twelve
Terrestrial branches ② to appeal
③ to explain

申報 **sàn bou**
to report to a higher
authorities

申辯 **sàn bihn**
to argue; to defend myself; to
explain one's conduct

申訴 **sàn sou**
to present one's case (in a law
court)

甸 **dihn** (Md **diàn**)
① suburbs or outskirts of the
capital ② to govern

甸服 **dihn fuhk**
areas within 500 miles of the
capital in ancient time

甸役 **dihn yihk**
hunting

男 **nàahm** (Md **nán**)
a man; a boy; a son

男子漢 **nàahm jí hon**
a manly man

男女平等 **nàahm néuih
pìhng dáng**
equal rights for both sexes

男才女貌 **nàahm chòih
néuih maauh**
the man is able and the woman
is beautiful — an ideal couple

町 **tíhng dīng** (Md **tǐng**)
boundary between agricultural
lands

畀 **béi** (Md **bì**)
to confer; to bestow

界 **gaai** (Md **jiè**)
① territory; world ② to limit

界限 **gaai haahn**
outer limit; border

界線 **gaai sin**
a boundary; borderline;
dividing line

界約 **gaai yeuk**
a frontier agreement

畋 **tìhn** (Md **tián**)
① to cultivate land ② to hunt
game

畋獵 **tìhn lihp**
hunting

畏 **wai** (Md **wèi**)
① to fear; to dread; to be afraid
of ② to respect; to reverse

畏忌 **wai geih**
to have scruples about

畏懼 **wai geuih**
to fear; to be scared

畏縮 **wai sūk**
to shrink; to recoil

畔 **buhn** (Md **pàn**)
① boundary between fields ②
waterside

畔岸 **buhn ngohn**
limit; boundary

留 **làuh** (Md **liú**)
① to remain; to stay ② to keep;
to delay ③ to leave behind

留步 **làuh bouh**
(please) don't trouble yourself
by accompany me to the door

留念 **làuh nihm**
as a souvenir

留心 làuh sàm
to pay attention; to be careful

畛 chán (Md zhěn)
① footpath between fields ②
boundary; limit

畛域 chán wihk
range; scope; boundary

畜 chūk (Md xù, chù)
to rear; to raise

畜牧 chūk muhk
animal husbandry

畜產 chūk cháan
products of animal husbandry

畜養 chūk yéuhng
to rear; to raise

畝 máuh (Md mǔ)
acre

略(畧) leuhk (Md lüè)
① approximate; rough ② slight
③ omit

略去 leuhk heui
to omit; to leave out

略有所聞 leuhk yáuh só
màhn
to have heard something

略勝一籌 leuhk sìng yāt
chàuh
slightly better

畢 bāt (Md bì)
① to complete; to finish ②
whole; total

畢生 bāt sàng
in one's whole life

畢竟 bāt gíng
after all; in the long run

畢業 bāt yihp
to graduate; to be graduated

畦 kwàih (Md qí)
a plot, piece; parcel of land

畦徑 kwàih gìng
a way, a method

畦畛 kwàih chán
scope; range; a factious spirit

異 yih (Md yì)
① different ② peculiar

異口同聲 yih háu tùhng
sìng
the same thing is said by
different mouth

異鄉 yih hèung
a strange community; away
from home

異議 yih yíh
objections

畫 wá, waahk, wah
(Md huà)
① to paint, to draw ② to mark
③ a stroke in a Chinese character

畫報 wá bou
a pictorial

畫舫 wah fóng
a pleasure boat

畫圖 waahk tòuh
to paint picture

番 fàan, pùn (Md fān,
pān)
① to take turns ② order in a
series ③ barbarian ④ name of a
county in Kwangtung

番瓜 fàan gwā
pumpkin

番茄 fàan ké
tomato

番薯 fàan syú
sweet potato

番禺 Pùn yùh
name of a county in
Kwangtung

畯 jeun (Md jùn)
① official in charge of farm lands
in ancient time ② rustic; crude

畹 yún (Md wǎn)
a measure of land equaling 30

acres

當 dòng, dong (Md dāng, dàng)
① to undertake; to accept ②
ought to; should ③ to regard as;
to consider as

當局 dòng guhk
the authorities

當然 dòng yìhn
of course; naturally

當作 dong jok
to regard as

當是 dong sih
to mistake something as . . .

畸 kèi, gèi (Md jī)
① fields with irregular boundaries ② abnormal

畸形 kèi yìhng
abnormal deformed

畸人 kèi yàhn
an odd person

畿 gèi (Md jī)
areas near the capital

畿輔 gèi fuh
areas near the capital

疇 chàuh (Md chóu)
① fields ② formerly ③ class

疇輩 chàuh bui
people of the same generation
or position

疇昔 chàuh sīk
formerly; previously; in the
past

疆 gèung (Md jiāng)
boundary; border; frontier

疆土 gèung tóu
territory

疆界 gèung gaai
borders, frontiers

疊 dihp (Md dié)
① to hold up; to pile up ② to

repeat; to duplicate

疊羅漢 dihp lòh hon
pyramid building

疊起 dihp héi
to hold up; to pile up

疊韻 dihp wáhn
two words of the same rhyme

疋部

疋 pāt (Md pǐ)
a roll or bolt of cloth

疋頭 pāt tàuh
cloth; fabrics

疋練 pāt lihn
a cascade

疏 sò (Md shū)
① thin, sparse, few ② unfamiliar;
unfriendly ③ careless; neglectful

疏防 sò fòhng
to fail to take precautions

疏忽 sò fāt
careless; to neglect

疏遠 sò yúhn
to make a stranger of

疑 yìh (Md yí)
① doubtful; to doubt ②
suspicious; to suspect

疑點 yìh dím
a doubtful point

疑難 yìh nàahn
question, problem, puzzle

**疑神疑鬼 yìh sàhn yìh
gwái**
to have unnecessary suspi-
cions

广部

疔 dìng (Md dīng)
a boil

疔毒 dìng duhk
carbuncular infection

疔瘡 **dìng chōng**
a boil

疚 **gau** (Md **jiù**)
① prolonged illness ② mental discomfort

疚懷 **gau wàaih**
ashamed

疚心 **gau sàm**
ashamed

疙 **gaht** (Md **gē**)
a wart; a pustule; a pimple

疙瘩 **gaht daap**
a wart; a pustule

疝 **saan** (Md **shàn**)
hernia

疝痛 **saan tung**
colic

疝氣 **saan hei**
hernia

疣（肬）**yàuh** (Md **yóu**)
a wart; a papule

疤 **bà** (Md **bā**)
a scar; a birthmark

疤臉 **bà níhm**
a scarred face

疤痕 **bà hàhn**
a scar

疥 **gaai** (Md **jiè**)
scabies

疥癬 **gaai sín**
scabies; the ich; ringworm

疥瘡 **gaai chōng**
sores for scabies

疫 **yihk** (Md **yì**)
an epidemic, a plague

疫症 **yihk jing**
an epidemic

疫病傳染 **yihk bihng chyùhn yíhm**
contagion

疲 **pèih** (Md **pí**)
tired; fatigued; exhausted

疲乏 **pèih faht**
weary; exhausted

疲倦 **pèih gyuhn**
weary; tired

疲於奔命 **pèih yù bàn mihng**
tired from rnning around

疳 **gàm** (Md **gān**)
a kind of infantile disease caused by digestive trouble

疳積 **gàm jīk**
an infantile disease caused by digestive trouble

疴 **ò, ngò** (Md **kē**)
sickness; disease

疸 **táan** (Md **dǎn**)
jaundice

疹 **ján, chán** (Md **zhěn**)
rashes; eruptions

疹子 **ján jí**
measles; carbuncle

疼 **tàhng** (Md **téng**)
① to ache ② to be fond of

疼愛 **tàhng ngoi**
to be fond of a child

疼痛 **tàhng tung**
to ache

疼熱 **tàhng yiht**
to suffer pain and fever

疽 **jèui** (Md **jū**)
ulcer

疾 **jaht** (Md **jí**)
① disease, suffering ② to hate ③ swift; fast

疾病 **jaht bihng**
disease

疾呼 **jaht fù**
to call out loudly

疾駛 **jaht sái**
to move swiftly

痱（痱）**féi** (Md **fèi**)
heat rashes; heat spots

痱（痱）子 **féi jí**
heat rashes; heat spots;
prickly heat

痱（痱）子粉 **féi jí fán**
talcum powder; baby powder

痂 **gà** (Md **jiā**)
scab over a sore

疵 **chì** (Md **cī**)
a defect; a flaw; a mistake

疵瑕 **chì hàh**
fault; mistake; error

疵癘 **chì laih**
disease; disaster; calamity

痄 **ja** (Md **zhà**)
scrofulous swellings and sores

痄腮 **ja sòi**
mumps

病 **bihng, behng**
(Md **bìng**)
① illness; disease ② to injure; to
harm

病倒 **bihng dóu**
to be confined in bed due to
illness

病狀 **bihng johng**
symptoms of disease

病愈 **bihng yuh**
to recover from illness; to get
well

症 **jing** (Md **zhèn**)
① disease; ailment ② symptoms
of manifestations of a disease

症候 **jing hauh**
symptoms of manifestations
of a disease

疱（炮）**pàau** (Md **pào**)
acne

痔 **jih** (Md **zhì**)
piles; hemorrhoid

痔漏 **jih lauh**
anal fistula

痔瘡 **jih chōng**
piles; hemorrhoid

痊 **chyùhn** (Md **quán**)
healed; cured

痊可 **chyùhn hó**
to have been cured, to have
recovered from illness

痊愈 **chyùhn yuh**
to have recovered from illness

痍 **yìh** (Md **yí**)
a wound; a sore

痕 **hàhn** (Md **hén**)
a scar; a mark

痕跡 **hàhn jīk**
a trace

痛 **tung** (Md **tòng**)
① painful; aching ② sorrowful;
sad

痛改前非 **tung gói chìhn
fēi**
to repent past mistakes

痛愛 **tung ngoi**
to love deeply

痛楚 **tung chó**
pain; suffering

痘 **dauh** (Md **dâu**)
smallpox

痘瘡 **dauh chōng**
smallpox

痘疤 **dauh bā**
smallpox scabs

痘苗 **dauh mìuh**
vaccine; lymph

痙 **gihng** (Md **jìng**)
spasm; convulsion

痙攣 **gihng lyùhn**
convulsion; jerk; cramp

痠 **syùn** (Md **suān**)
muscular pain

痠痛 **syùn tung**
to ache (of muscles)

痠軟 **syùn yúhn**
sore and weak

痢 **leih** (Md **lì**)
diarrhea; dysentery

痢疾 **leih jaht**
dysentery; diarrhea

痣 **ji** (Md **zhì**)
birthmarks; moles

痧 **sà** (Md **shā**)
① cholera ② measles

痹 **bei** (Md **bì**)
paralysis

痰 **tàahm** (Md **tán**)
phlegm; sputum

痰喘 **tàahm chyún**
asthma

痰涎 **tàahm yìhn**
phlegm; spittle

痲 **màh** (Md **má**)
① measles ② leprosy

痲疹 **màh ján (màh chán)**
measles

痲瘋 **màh fūng**
leprosy

痲痹 **màh bei**
paralysis; palsy

痼 **gu** (Md **gù**)
chronic disease

痼習 **gu jaahp**
deep-rooted habit

痼疾 **gu jaht**
incurable chronic disease

痼癖 **gu pīk**
an addiction

痿 **wái** (Md **wěi**)
impotent; paralysis

痿痹 **wái bei**
paralysis

瘀 **yú, yù** (Md **yū**)
hematoma

瘀膿 **yú nùhng**
pus

瘀血 **yú hyut**
hematoma

瘀傷 **yú sèung**
contusion; bruise

瘁 **seuih** (Md **cuì**)
① disease; illness ② over fatigued

瘐 **yúh** (Md **yǔ**)
a prisoner who dies in jail because of hunger and illness

瘋 **fùng** (Md **fēng**)
insane; crazy; mad; mentally deranged

瘋狂 **fùng kòhng**
crazy; mad; insane

瘋話 **fùng wah**
gibberish; jargon

瘋狗症 **fùng gáu jing**
rabies

瘍 **yèuhng** (Md **yáng**)
skin disease or infection

瘓 **wuhn** (Md **huàn**)
paralysis

瘧 **yeuhk** (Md **nüè, yào**)
malaria

瘧疾 **yeuhk jaht**
malaria

瘧蚊 **yeuhk mān**
anopheles

癩(癩)laat (Md là)
favus

癩癩 laat leih (laat lēi)
favus

癩癩頭 laat lēi tàuh
a head made bald by favus

瘉(愈)yuh (Md yù)
healed; cured

瘟 wàn (Md wēn)
epidemic; plague

瘟氣 wàn hei
pestilential vapor

瘟疫 wàn yihk
epidemic; plague; pestilence

瘤 làuh (Md liú)
a tumor; a lump

瘤胃 làuh waih
rumen

瘠 jek (Md jí)
① thin; lean ② sterile; infertile

瘠地 jek deih
sterile land

瘠瘦 jek sau
lean and weak

瘡 chōng (Md chuàng)
boil; ulcer

瘡疤 chōng bā
scar of an ulcer

瘡口 chōng háu
opening of an ulcer

瘦 sau (Md shōu)
thin; slim; lean

瘦小 sau síu
thin and small

瘦長 sau chèuhng
thin and tall

瘦弱 sau yeuhk
thin and weak

瘴 jeung (Md zhàng)
miasma

瘴屬 jeung laih
disease attributed to miasma

瘴氣 jeung hei
pestilential vapor

瘳 chàu (Md chōu)
cured; healed

瘸 kèh (Md qué)
a cripple

瘸腿 kèh téui
crippled; lame

瘸子 kèh jí
a lame man; a cripple

瘻(瘻、瘺)lauh
(Md lòu)
hunchback; humpback

瘼 mohk (Md mò)
① disease; illness ② suffering

癃 lùhng (Md lóng)
humping of the back in old age

癃疾 lùhng jaht
humping of the back in old age

療 liuh (Md liáo)
to treat; to relieve; to heal

療治 liuh jih
to treat

療養 liuh yéuhng
to recuperate

療養院 liuh yéuhng yún
sanatorium; rest home

癆 lòuh (Md láo)
tuberculosis; consumption

癆病 lòuh bihng
tuberculosis; consumption

癆傷 lòuh sèung
weakened by over-exertion

癇 **hàahn** (Md **xián**)
epilepsy

癇風 **hàahn fùng**
epilepsy

癌 **ngàahm** (Md **ái**)
cancer

癌症 **ngàahm jing**
cancer

癌腫 **ngàahm júng**
Malignant tumor; cancer

瘢 **bàan** (Md **bān**)
unhealthy marks on the skin

癘 **laih** (Md **lì**)
ulcer; pestilential vapor

癖 **pīk** (Md **pǐ**)
① chronic swelling of the spleen
② addiction; habitual inclination

癖好 **pīk hou**
habitual incliniation; addiction

癖性 **pīk sing**
propensity; habitual tendency

癒 **yuh** (Md **yù**)
healed; cured

癡(痴) **chì** (Md **chī**)
silly; idiotic; stupid; foolish

癡迷 **chì màih**
infatuated

癡肥 **chì fèih**
very fat and looking stupid

癡狂 **chì kòhng**
nonsensical; irrational

癤 **jit** (Md **jiē**)
small sore; pimple

癢 **yéuhng** (Md **yǎng**)
to itch; to tickle

癢癢 **yéuhng yéuhng**
itchy; ticklish

癥 **jìng** (Md **zhēng**)
obstructions of the bowels

癥結 **jìng git**
obstructions of the bowels; a
difficult point

癩 **laai** (Md **lài**)
① leprosy ② favus

癩頭 **laai tàuh**
favus-infected head

癩癬 **laai sín**
favus; ringworm

癩瘡 **laai chōng**
scabies

癬 **sín** (Md **xuǎn**)
ringworm; tetter

癮 **yáhn** (Md **yǐn**)
addiction

癮頭 **yáhn tàuh**
addiction

癮君子 **yáhn gwàn jí**
an opium eater; a heavy
smoker

癭 **yíng** (Md **yǐng**)
① a reddish swelling on the neck
② gnarl

癰(痈) **yùng** (Md **yōng**)
carbuncle

癰疽 **yùng jèui**
carbuncle

癰腫 **yùng júng**
abscess

癯 **kèuih** (Md **qú**)
emaciated; thin; lean

癲 **dìn** (Md **diān**)
mentally deranged; insane; mad;
crazy

癲狂 **dìn kòhng**
mentally deranged; insane;
mad; crazy

癲癇 **dìn hàahn**
epilepsy

癱 **táan, tàan** (Md **tān**)
paralysis

癱瘓 **táan wuhn**
paralysis

癱子 **táan jí**
a paralytic

癶部

癸 **gwai** (Md **guǐ**)
the last of the Ten Celestial Stems

登 **dàng** (Md **dēng**)
① to climb; to rise ② to record, to register

登報 **dàng bou**
to make an announcement in the newspaper

登記 **dàng gei**
to register; registration

登門拜訪 **dàng mùhn baai fóng**
to make a special call on another at his house!

發 **faat** (Md **fā**)
① to issue; to give forth; to send ② to begin, to start

發表 **faat bíu**
to make known; to make public

發明 **faat mìhng**
to invent, invention

發生 **faat sàng**
to happen; to occur

白部

白 **baahk** (Md **bái**)
white; clear; bright; pure

白白地 **baahk baahk deih**
in vain; to no purpose

白跑一趟 **baahk páau yāt tong**
to make a futile trip

白費心機 **baahk fai sàm gèi**
to scheme in vain; to make plans to no avail

百 **baak** (Md **bǎi**)
hundred; many

百般殷勤 **baak bùn yàn kàhn**
courtesy expressed in numerous ways

百發百中 **baak faat baak jung**
to hit the target at every shot

百折不回 **baak jit bāt wùih**
pushing forward despite repeated frustrations

皂(皁) **jouh** (Md **zào**)
black; soap

皂白 **jouh baahk**
black and white; right and wrong

皂白不分 **jouh baahk bāt fàn**
to fail to distinguish between right and wrong

的 **dīk** (Md **dì, dí, de**)
① clear; manifest ② target ③ accurate; exact

的當 **dīk dong**
accurate; proper

的確 **dīk kok**
certainly; surely

皆 **gàai** (Md **jiē**)
all; every; entire

皆大歡喜 **gàai daaih fùn héi**
everybody is satisfied

皆知 **gàai jì**
all aware

皆因 **gāai yàn**
only because; just because

皇 **wòhng (Md huáng)**
① royal; imperial ② beautiful; brilliant

皇帝 **wòhng dai**
an emperor

皇恩 **wòhng yàn**
imperial favor or kindness

皇親國戚 **wòhng chàn gwok chīk**
relatives of emperor

皈(歸) **gwāi (Md guī)**
to follow

皈依 **gwāi yì**
to be converted to (Buddhism)

皋(皐、臯) **gòu (Md gāo)**
a marsh; a swamp

皋門 **gòu mùhn**
palace gate

皋壤 **gòu waaih**
land by a marsh or swamp

皎 **gáau (Md jiǎo)**
white and clean; bright; brilliant

皎厲 **gáau laih**
proud

皎潔 **gáau git**
brightly clean

皎皎 **gáau gáau**
a very white and clean

皓(皜) **houh (Md hào)**
white and clean; bright

皓天 **houh tìn**
summer sky

皓齒 **houh chí**
white teeth

皖 **wúhn (Md wǎn)**
alternative name of Anhwei

皙 **sīk (Md xī)**
white skin

皚(皑) **yìh (Md ái)**
white and clean

皚皚 **yìh yìh**
brightly white

皥 **houh (Md hào)**
bright

皮部

皮 **pèih (Md pí)**
skin; fur; hide; leather

皮膚 **pèih fù**
skin

皮鞋 **pèih hàaih**
leather shoes

皮箱 **pèih sèung**
a suitcase

皺(皱) **jau (Md zhòu)**
wrinkle; crease; ramples

皺眉 **jau mèih**
to frown; to knit the brows

皺紋 **jau màhn**
wrinkles; folds; creases

皿部

皿 **míhng (Md mǐn)**
a shallow container

盂 **yùh (Md yú)**
a basin

盅 **jùng (Md zhōng)**
a small cup

盆 **pùhn (Md pén)**
a bowl; a basin; a tub

盆地 **pùhn deih**
(in geology) a basin

盆景 **pùhn gíng**
a potted plant

盆子 **pùhn jí**
a bowl; a basin

盈 **yìhng** (Md **yíng**)
to fill; to become full

盈虧 **yìhng kwài**
waxing and waning; profits and losses

盈餘 **yìhng yùh**
surplus; profit

益 **yīk** (Md **yì**)
① to increase; to add to ② benefit; profit

益智 **yīk jì**
to grow in intelligence or wisdom

益處 **yīk chyu**
advantage; benefit

益友 **yīk yáuh**
helpful friends; useful friends

盍(盇) **hahp** (Md **hé**)
what; why not

盎 **ngòn** (Md **àng**)
① a basin; a pot; a bowl ② abundant; plentiful

盎然 **ngòn yìhn**
abundant; rich

盎斯 **ngòn sī**
ounce

盒 **hahp** (Md **hé**)
a small box; a case

盒子 **hahp jí**
a small box; a small case

盔 **kwài** (Md **kuī**)
a helmet; a pot

盔頭 **kwài tàuh**
cap formerly worn by actors in Chinese opera

盔甲 **kwài gaap**
helmet and mail; armor

盛 **sihng, sìhng**
(Md **shèng, chéng**)
abundant; rich; flourishing; grand

盛典 **sihng dín**
a grand occasion; a big ceremony

盛況空前 **sihng fong hùng chìhn**
unprecedented in grandeur, festivity

盛大 **sihng daaih**
grand, magnificent

盜(盗) **douh** (Md **dào**)
to steal; to rob

盜取 **douh chéui**
to take unlawfully; to steal

盜賊 **douh chaahk**
thief; robber

盜亦有道 **douh yihk yáuh douh**
even robbers have a code of conducts

盟 **màhng** (Md **méng**)
a convenant; an oath; a vow

盟國 **màhng gwok**
allied powers

盟主 **màhng jyú**
leader of an alliance

盟約 **màhng yeuk**
a treaty of alliance

盞(盏) **jáan** (Md **zhǎn**)
a small shallow container; a small cap

盡(尽) **jeuhn** (Md **jìn**)
① to exhaust; to use up ② to complete; to finish ③ all; entirely

盡忠 **jeuhn jùng**
to do one's duty as a subject; to be loyal to the ruler

盡責任 **jeuhn jaak yahm**
to do one's duty

盡善盡美 **jeuhn sihn jeuhn méih**
perfectly satisfactory; perfectly good

監 **gàam** (Md **jiān**)
① to supervise; to direct to inspect ② to confine; to imprison

監犯 **gàam fáan**
a prisoner

監督 **gàam dūk**
to supervise; to superintend

監護人 **gàam wuh yàhn**
guardian

盤 (盘) **pùhn** (Md **pán**)
① a tray; a plate; a dish ② to investigate; to interrogate

盤駁 **pùhn bok**
to interrogate and refute

盤據 **pùhn geui**
to occupy and hold a place

盤算 **pùhn syun**
to make a mental calculation

盥 **gun, fún** (Md **guàn**)
to wash hands, to wash

盥洗 **gun sái**
to wash oneself

盥漱 **gun sau**
to wash the hands and rinse the mouth

盧 **lòuh** (Md **lú**)
① a cottage, a hut ② a Chinese family name

盧比 **lòuh béi**
rupee (of India)

盧森堡 **Lòuh sàm bóu**
Luxemburg, Europe

盪 **dohng**
to swing; to toss about

盪槳 **dohng jéung**
to row a boat

盪秋千 **dohng chàu chìn**
to swing on a swing

盪漾 **dohng yeuhng**
to be gently tossed about

目部

目 **muhk** (Md **mù**)
① the eye ② to look; to see

目標 **muhk bīu**
an objective; a target; a goal; an aim

目睹 **muhk dóu**
to see directly; to witness

目錄 **muhk luhk**
table of contents; a catalogue

盯 **dìng** (Md **dīng**)
to look

盲 **màahng** (Md **máng**)
blind; deluded

盲目 **màahng muhk**
blind; lacking insight or understanding

盲從 **màahng chùhng**
to follow blindly

盲腸 **màahng chéung**
cecum, the vermiform appendix

直 **jihk** (Md **zhí**)
① straight, right, just ② outspoken; frank

直達 **jihk daaht**
to go nonstop to

直隸 **jihk daih**
to be directly under the jurisdiction of

直覺 **jihk gok**
intuition

盾 **téuhn** (Md **dùn**)
a shield; a buckler

盾牌 **téuhn pàaih**
a shield

相 **sèung, seung**
(Md **xiāng, xiàng**)
① each other, one another ② to examine; to study

相處 **sèung chyúh**
to spend time together; to get along with

相識 **sèung sīk**
to know each other

相貌 **seung maauh**
facial features; countenance

盼 **paan** (Md **pàn**)
to look; to hope

盼望 **paan mohng**
to hope; to wish

盼念 **paan nihm**
to long for; to hope

省 **síng, sáang**
(Md **xǐng, shěng**)
① to examine oneself; to consider ② to understand ③ province ④ economical

省悟 **síng ngh**
to realize; to awaken to

省察 **síng chaat**
to examine

省略 **sáang leuhk**
to omit

省事 **sáang sih**
to save trouble

眇 **míuh** (Md **miǎo**)
tiny; fine; unimportant

眇小 **míuh síu**
very small; tiny

眇眇忽忽 **míuh míuh fāt fāt**
indistinct; too small to identify

眈 **dàam** (Md **dān**)
to look downward

眈眈 **dàam dàam**
looking at greedily

眉 **mèih** (Md **méi**)
① eyebrows ② the side

眉目 **mèih muhk**
general facial appearance

眉急 **mèih gāp**
very urgent

眉來眼去 **mèih lòih ngáahn heui**
converse with eyes

看 **hòn, hon** (Md **kān, kàn**)
① to see; to look at; to think ② to watch

看顧 **hon gu**
to look after

看透 **hon tau**
to see through

看中 **hon jung**
to feel satisfy with; to choose

看護 **hòn wuh**
to nurse; a nurse

肫 **deuhn** (Md **dǔn**)
to doze

肫睡 **deuhn seuih**
to doze; a nap

眨 **jáam** (Md **zhǎ**)
to wink

眨眼 **jáam ngáahn**
to wink

眨眼間 **jáam ngáahn gàan**
at the twinkling of an eye

眞 **jàn** (Md **zhēn**)
true; real; actual

眞理 **jàn léih**
truth; righteousness

眞摯 **jàn ji**
sincere; faithful

眞善美 **jàn sihn méih**
truth; goodness and beautiful

眠 **mìhn** (Md **mián**)
to sleep

眠思夢想 **mìhn sì muhng séung**
to think day and night

眩 **yùhn, yuhn** (Md **xuàn**)
to confuse; to dazzle; confused vision

眩耀 **yùhn yiuh**
dazzling; to dazzle

眩暈 **yuhn wàhn**
giddiness

眦（眥） **jih** (Md **jì**)
eye sockets

眷 **gyun** (Md **juàn**)
to regard; to care for; to love

眷念 **gyun nihm**
to think of or to remember with affection

眷顧 **gyun gu**
to care for; to concern about

眷愛 **gyun ngoi**
to love; to care for

眶 **kwàang, hòng** (Md **kuàng**)
socket of the eye; rim of the eye

眸 **màuh** (Md **móu**)
the pupil of the eye

眸子 **màuh jí**
the eyes; the pupil of the eye

眺 **tiu** (Md **tiào**)
to look far away

眺望 **tiu mohng**
to look far away

眼 **ngáahn** (Md **yǎn**)
the eye

眼淚 **ngáahn leuih**
tears

眼光 **ngáahn gwòng**
discerning ability

眼神 **ngáahn sàhn**
expressions of the eyes

眯（瞇） **máih, mèi** (Md **mī, mǐ**)
to close the eyes

瞇縫眼兒 **máih fùhng ngáahn yìh**
slit-eyed; eyes half-closed

着 **jeuhk, jeuk** (Md **zháo, zhuó**)
① right to the point ② to catch ③ to bear; to take ④ to wear; to move

着火 **jeuhk fó**
to catch fire

着急 **jeuhk gāp**
anxious; worried

着涼 **jeuhk lèuhng**
to catch cold

着陸 **jeuk luhk**
to land

睏 **kwan** (Md **kùn**)
drowsy; sleepy

睇 **tái** (Md **dì**)
to take a casual look at; to look sideways

睞 **lòih** (Md **lài**)
to look at; to squint

睛 **jìng** (Md **jīng**)
the pupil of the eye; the eye ball

睛球 **jìng kàuh**
the eyeball

睜（眳） **jàng** (Md **zhēng**)
to open the eyes

睜眼 **jàng ngáahn**
to open the eyes

睜開眼睛 **jàng hòi ngáahn jìng**
to open the eyes

睡 **seuih** (Md **shuì**)
to sleep; to rest with eyes closed

睡覺 **seuih gaau**
to sleep; to go to bed

睡意 **seuih yi**
sleepiness

睡衣 **seuih yī**
pajamas; sleeping gown

睢 **sèui** (Md **suī**)
to raise one's eyes

督 **dūk** (Md **dū**)
to oversee; to supervise

督導 **dūk douh**
to direct and supervise

督工 **dūk gūng**
to superintend workers

督促 **dūk chūk**
to urge; to press (a person to complete a task)

睦 **muhk** (Md **mù**)
friendly; amiable

睦鄰 **muhk lèuhn**
to remain on friendly terms with the neighbors

睦親 **muhk chàn**
close relatives

睥 **páih** (Md **bì**)
to look askance; scornful look

睥睨 **páih ngaih**
to look askance — an expression of despise

睨 **ngaih** (Md **nì**)
to look askance

睪 **gòu** (Md **yì, gāo**)
① smooth and glossy ② testis

睪丸 **gòu yùhn**
testis; the testicle

睫 **jiht** (Md **jié**)
eyelashes

睫毛 **jiht mòuh**
eyelashes

睬 **chói** (Md **cǎi**)
① to look; to watch ② to notice; to pay attention to

睽 **kwàih** (Md **kuí**)
① separated ② to stare at

睽離 **kwàih lèih**
long separation

睽睽 **kwàih kwàih**
to stare at

瞅（眰）**cháu** (Md **chǒu**)
to look; to see; to gaze

瞅不得 **cháu bāt dāk**
should not be seen; not worth seeing

瞅不見 **cháu bāt gin**
unable to see

瞄 **mìuh** (Md **miáo**)
to take aim; to look at attentively

瞄準 **mìuh jéun**
to aim at; to take sight

睹（覩）**dóu** (Md **dǔ**)
to see; to look at; to gaze; to observe

睹物思人 **dóu maht sì yàhn**
to think of a person as one sees the thing he has left behind

睿（叡）**yeuih** (Md **ruì**)
to understand thoroughly; keen of perception

睿智 **yeuih ji**
the divine sagacity of sages

睿哲 **yeuih jit**
superior intelligence

瞍 **sáu** (Md **sǎu**)
eyes without eyeballs

瞎 **haht** (Md **xiā**)
① blind ② reckless

瞎猜 **haht chàai**
to guess wildly

瞎說 **haht syut**
to talk nonsense

瞎眼 **haht ngáahn**
blind

瞋 **chàn** (Md **chēn**)
angry; complaining

瞋目 **chàn muhk**
angry look

瞋怒 **chàn nouh**
to be beside oneself with anger

瞌 **hahp** (Md **kē**)
to be tired and dozing off

瞌睡 **hahp seuih**
to doze off while sitting

瞑 **mìhng** (Md **míng**)
① to close the eyes ② to disturb

瞑目 **mìhng muhk**
to close the eyes; to die
without regret or in peace

瞑眩 **mìhng yuhn**
to feel dizzy and upset

瞞 **mùhn** (Md **mán**)
to hide the truth; to tell lies

瞞不了人 **mùhn bāt líuh
yàhn**
can't hide the truth from
others

瞞騙 **mùhn pin**
to deceive and lie

瞠 **chàang** (Md **chēng**)
to look straight at; to gaze at

瞠目 **chàang muhk**
to gaze at fixedly

瞠目結舌 **chàang muhk git
siht**
wide-eyed and tongue-tied;
amazed with speechless

瞷(瞷) **jáahm**
(Md **zhǎn**)
to wink

瞟 **píuh** (Md **piǎo**)
to look askance

瞟眇 **píuh míuh**
obscure and indistinct

瞟了他一眼 **píuh líuh tà
yāt ngáahn**
to give him a side glance

瞥 **pit** (Md **piē**)
to have a casual and short glance

瞥見 **pit gin**
to catch a glimpse of

瞥了一眼 **pit lúih yāt
ngáahn**
to cast a casual and brief
glance

瞬 **seun** (Md **shùn**)
wink or twinkle

瞬華 **seun wàh**
time flying away

瞬息之間 **seun sīk jì gàan**
at the twinkling of an eye

瞧 **chìuh** (Md **qiáo**)
to see; to look at

瞧不透 **chìuh bāt tau**
unable to see through

瞧不起 **chìuh bāt héi**
to look down upon

瞧一瞧 **chìuh yāt chìuh**
to take a look

瞪 **dahng** (Md **dèng**)
to stare at

瞪眼 **dahng ngáahn**
to stare at angrily; to look
straight ahead

瞭 **líuh, lìuh** (Md **liào,
liǎo**)
① sharp eyed ② clear and bright

瞭亮 **lìuh leuhng**
clear and loud

瞭解 **líuh gáai**
to understand

瞭如指掌 **lìuh yùh jí jéung**
to know or understand thoroughly

瞰 **ham** (Md **kàn**)
to watch; to spy

瞰臨 **ham làhm**
to watch from above

瞰望 **ham mohng**
to overlook; to observe from above

瞳 **tùhng** (Md **tóng**)
the pupil of the eye

瞳孔 **tùhng húng**
the pupil of the eye

瞶(瞶) **gwai** (Md **kuì**)
dim-sighted; poor vision

瞻 **jìm** (Md **zhān**)
① to look up ② to regard respectfully

瞻仰 **jìm yéuhng**
to look up respectfully

瞻望 **jìm mohng**
to look forward to a faraway place

瞽 **gú** (Md **gǔ**)
blind

瞽者 **gú jé**
the blind

瞽說 **gú syut**
shallow and unreasonable talk

瞿 **geui, kèuih** (Md **jù, qú**)
shocked; scared

瞿然 **geui yìhn**
alarmed

瞼 **gím** (Md **jiǎn**)
the eyelids

矇 **mùhng** (Md **mēng**)
blind; ignorant; stupid

矇蔽 **mùhng bai**
to hide truth from the superior

矇矓 **mùhng lùhng**
hazy; sight-blurred

矍 **fok** (Md **jué**)
① to watch in flight ② old but healthy

矍然 **fok yìhn**
looking around in fear

矓 **lùhng** (Md **lóng**)
hazy; blurred

矗 **chūk** (Md **chù**)
rising; sharply; steep

矗矗 **chūk chūk**
steep and lofty

矗立 **chūk lahp**
rising up steeply

矙 **ham** (Md **kàn**)
to watch; to spy

矚 **jūk** (Md **zhǔ**)
to watch; to oversee; gaze at carefully

矚目 **jūk muhk**
to watch with great interest

矚望 **jūk mohng**
to watch at eagerly

矛部

矛 **màauh** (Md **máo**)
a spear; a lance

矛兵 **màauh bìng**
a lancer

矛盾 **màauh téuhn**
contradiction

矛槍 **màauh chēung**
spears and javelins

矜 **gìng, gwàan** (Md **jīn, guān**)
① to feel sorry for, to be sympathetic with ② to boast

矜憐 **gìng lìhn**
to commiserate, to pity

矜誇 **gìng kwà**
to boast about one's accomplishments

矜持 **gìng chìh**
to carry oneself with dignity and reserve

喬 **wāt** (Md **yù**)
① bright and brilliant; charming ② nature bursting into life

喬皇 **wāt wòhng**
bright and beautiful

喬喬 **wāt wāt**
nature bursting into life

矢部

矢 **chí** (Md **shǐ**)
① an arrow; a dart ② to vow; to take an oath

矢口不移 **chí háu bāt yìh**
to stick to one's original statement

矢誓 **chí saih**
to take an oath

矢如雨下 **chí yùh yúh hah**
the arrows come down like a shower

矣 **yíh** (Md **yǐ**)
① a final particle denoting a perfect tense ② an auxiliary denoting determination

知 **jì, ji** (Md **zhī, zhì**)
① knowledge ② to know; to feel ③ the wise; brains

知己 **jì géi**
a close or intimate friend

知悉 **jì sīk**
to know; to learn of; to be aware of

知能 **ji nàhng**
intellectual capacity

矩 **géui** (Md **jǔ**)
① a carpenters' square ② a rule; a regulation

矩步 **géui bouh**
to behave in a gentlemanly manner

矩形 **géui yìhng**
a rectangle

短 **dyún** (Md **duǎn**)
① short ② to be deficient; faults

短期 **dyún kèih**
short term

短缺 **dyún kyut**
to fall short; deficient

短處 **dyún chyu**
faults; weak points

矮 **ngái** (Md **ǎi**)
① a short person ② short, low

矮小 **ngái síu**
short statured

矮樹 **ngái syuh**
bushes; low tree

矮屋 **ngái ngūk**
a house with a low ceiling

矯(矫) **gíu** (Md **jiǎo**)
to straighten; to correct; to rectify

矯正 **gíu jing**
to rectify; to correct

矯飾 **gíu sīk**
to pretend; affectation

石部

石 **sehk** (Md **shí**)
rocks; stone; minerals

石刻 **sehk hāk**
stone-engraving

石礦 **sehk kwong**
a quarry

石油 **sehk yàuh**
crude oil; petroleum

石 **daam** (Md **dàn**)
a dry measure for grains roughly
equivalent to 120 — 160 pounds

矽 **jihk** (Md **xī**)
silicon

矽砂 **jihk sà**
quartz sand

矽酸 **jihk syùn**
silicic acid

矻 **ngaht** (Md **kū**)
diligent and industrious; very
tired

矻矻 **ngaht ngaht**
diligent and industrious; very
tired

砉 **waahk** (Md **xū, huā**)
a splitting sound; a cracking
sound

砂 **sà** (Md **shā**)
sand; gravel

砂布 **sà bou**
sand paper

砂糖 **sà tòhng**
crude sugar

砂眼 **sà ngáahn**
trachoma

砌 **chai** (Md **qì**)
to lay; to build; to pave

砌路 **chai louh**
to build a road

砌牆 **chai chèuhng**
to build a wall

砍 **hám** (Md **kǎn**)
to chop; to hack

砍斷 **hám dyuhn**
to break apart by chopping; to
cut into two

砍頭 **hám tàuh**
to behead

砍柴 **hám chàaih**
to chop wood

砒 **pèi** (Md **pī**)
arsenic

砒霜 **pèi sèung**
an arsenic compound

砒酸 **pèi syùn**
arsenic acid

砝 **faat** (Md **fǎ**)
standard weights used in scales;
steelyard weights

砝碼 **faat máh**
standard weights used in
scales

砥 **dái** (Md **dǐ**)
a whetstone

砥柱 **dái chyúh**
an indomitable person

砥石 **dái sehk**
a fine grindstone

砰 **pìng** (Md **pēng**)
sound of crashing stones, a loud
sound

砰然 **pìng yìhn**
loud; deafening

砧 (碪) **jàm** (Md **zhēn**)
a rock with fat top on which
laundry is beaten and washed

砧板 **jàm báan**
a chopping board

砧斧 **jàm fú**
ancient weapons or instruments for killing

破 **po** (Md **pò**)
broken; to break; destroyed

破例 **po laih**
to make an exception

破壞 **po waaih**
to ruin; to destroy

破案 **po ngon**
to crack a criminal case

砷 **sàn** (Md **shēn**)
arsenic

砷化氫 **sàn fa hìng**
hydrogen arsenide

砦 **jaaih** (Md **zhài**)
a stockade; a military out post

砲(炮、礮)**paau**
(Md **pào**)
a catapult; an artillery piece

砲彈 **paau dáan**
a cannon ball

砲火 **paau fó**
gun fire; artillery

砲轟 **paau gwàng**
to bombard with artillery fire

砸 **jaap** (Md **já**)
to crash and break; to smash; to
knock

砸爛 **jaap laahn**
to crash or mash

砸碎 **jaap seui**
to break to pieces

研 **yìhn** (Md **yán**)
① to go to the very source to
study; to research ② to grind

研討 **yìhn tóu**
to study and discuss

研究 **yìhn gau**
to study and research

研碎 **yìhn seui**
to grind to pieces

硃 **jyù** (Md **zhū**)
vermilion

硃筆 **jyù bāt**
a vermilion writing brush

硃砂 **jyù sà**
cinnabar

硝 **sìu** (Md **xiāo**)
niter; saltpeter

硝基 **sìu gèi**
nitro

硝酸 **sìu syùn**
nitric acid

硫 **làuh** (Md **liú**)
sulphur

硫磺 **làuh wòhng**
sulfur; brimstone

硫酸 **làuh syùn**
sulphuric acid

硬 **ngaahng** (Md **yìng**)
hard; strong; firm

硬逼 **naahng bīk**
to compel or force

硬著頭皮 **ngaahng jeuhk
tàuh pèih**
to do something no matter
what the consequences

硬著心 **ngaahng jeuhk
sàm**
to steel one's heart

硯(硯)**yín** (Md **yàn**)
an ink-slab or ink-stone

硯臺 **yín tòih**
an ink-slab

硯友 **yín yáuh**
fellow students

硭 **mòhng** (Md **máng**)
sodium sulphate

硭硝 **mòhng sìu**
sodium sulphate

确 **kok** (Md **què**)
hard stone; barren

硼 **pàahng, pàhng** (Md **péng**)
borax

硼砂 **pàahng sà**
borax

硼酸 **pàahng syùn**
boric acid

碰 **pung** (Md **pèng**)
to hit; to touch; to meet unexpectedly

碰杯 **pung bùi**
to clink glasses

碰見 **pung gin**
to meet someone unexpectedly

碰傷 **pung seùng**
to be injured or damaged after being hit by someone

碇(椗、矴) **ding** (Md **dìng**)
an anchor

碉 **dìu** (Md **diāo**)
a stone chamber

碉堡 **dìu bóu**
a fort; a pillbox

碌 **lūk** (Md **lù**)
mediocre — busy

碌碌 **lūk lūk**
mediocre; commonplace

碌磚 **lūk jyùn**
a kind of stone roller

碎 **seui** (Md **suì**)
broken; smashed; torn

碎片 **seui pín**
fragments, chips

碎裂 **seui liht**
broken to pieces

碎務 **seui mouh**
chores

硎 **yìhng** (Md **xíng**)
a whetstone; a grindstone

碑 **bèi** (Md **bēi**)
a stone table

碑記 **bèi gei**
inscriptional record

碑誌 **bèi ji**
an inscriptional writing

碓 **deui** (Md **duì**)
a pestle

碓房 **deui fòhng**
an establishment for hulling grain

碓臼 **deui káuh**
pestle and mortar

碘 **dín** (Md **diǎn**)
iodine

碘酒 **dín jáu** or **dīn jáu**
iodine tincture

碘酸 **dín syùn**
iodic acid

碗(盌、椀) **wún** (Md **wǎn**)
a bowl

碗碟 **wún dihp**
bowls and dishes

碗櫃 **wún gwaih**
a cupboard

碗筷 **wún faai**
bowl and chopsticks

碧 **bīk** (Md **bì**)
green; emerald green; blue

碧綠 **bīk luhk**
verdant; emerald green

碧水 **bīk séui**
blue water

碧玉 **bīk yuhk**
jasper; emerald

碟 **dihp** (Md **dié**)
a dish or plate

碴 **chàh** (Md **chá**)
① chipped edge of a container ②
a broken off fragment

碣 **kit** (Md **jié**)
stonetable

碩 **sehk** (Md **shuò**)
great; eminent

碩老 **sehk lóuh**
a learned elder

碩士 **sehk sih**
a wise man; a holder of the
master's degree

碩望 **sehk mohng**
a much respected man; a man
of great fame

碳 **taan** (Md **tàn**)
carbon

碳酸 **taan syùn**
carbonic acid

碳水化合物 **taan séui fa**
hahp maht
carbohydrate

鹼 (鹼、礆、堿)
gáan (Md **jiǎn**)
lye; alkali

鹼 (鹼)性 **gáan sing**
alkalinity

鹼 (鹼)石灰 **gáan sehk fùi**
soda-lime

磋 **chò** (Md **cuō**)
to polish

磋磨 **chò mòh**
to polish; to learn through
discussions with others

磋商 **chò sèung**
to exchange views

確 (确、碻、塙)
kok (Md **què**)
sure; certain; firm

確保 **kok bóu**
to secure; to insure

確據 **kok geui**
sure proof

確信 **kok seun**
to be convinced

碼 **máh** (Md **mǎ**)
① a yard (measure of length) ②
a symbol; a code

碼頭 **máh tàuh**
a dock; a wharf

碾 **níhn** (Md **niǎn**)
① a stone roller ② to roll

碾米 **níhn máih**
to husk rice

碾米機 **níhn máih gèi**
rice husking machine

磁 **chìh** (Md **cí**)
① magnetic ② porcelain

磁鐵 **chìh tit**
a magnet

磁力 **chìh lihk**
magnetic force

磁場 **chìh chèuhng**
magnetic field

磊 **léuih** (Md **lěi**)
① heap of stones ② great;
massive

磊落 **léuih lohk**
clear; distinct; open-hearted

磊磊 **léuih léuih**
innumerable

磐 **pùhn** (Md **pán**)
massive rock

磐石 **pùhn sehk**
a massive rock

磐石之安 **pùhn sehk jì**
ngòn
as stable and as secure as a
massive

磔 **jaahk** (Md **zhé**)
to dismember a human being

磕 **hahp** (Md **kē**)
to strike; to bump
磕碰 **hahp pung**
to bump against
磕頭 **hahp tàuh**
to kowtow

磨 **mòh** (Md **mó, mò**)
to rub; to grind; to polish
磨練 **mòh lihn**
to forge, to train
磨琢 **mòh deuk**
to grind and to carve
磨擦 **mòh chaat**
to rub; friction

磧 **jīk** (Md **qì**)
gravel and sand
磧鹵 **jīk lóuh**
sandy and saline land

磬 **hing** (Md **qìng**)
a kind of musical instrument
磬竭 **hing kit**
used up; emptied

磡 **ham** (Md **kàn**)
a cliff

磚(砖、甎、塼) **jyùn**
(Md **zhuān**)
bricks

磣(硶、碜) **jám**
(Md **chěn**)
① food stuff mixed with sands ②
ugly

磺 **wòhng** (Md **huáng**)
sulfur; brimstone
磺酸 **wòhng syùn**
sulfonic acid

磯 **gèi** (Md **jī**)
rocky cliff on water's edge; water
surrounded rocks

磴 **dang** (Md **dèng**)
steps on rock
磴道 **dang douh**
rocky mountain path

磷(燐) **lèuhn** (Md **lín**)
① phosphorus ② water flowing
between stones

礁 **jiu** (Md **jiāo**)
a reef; a shoal
礁石 **jiu sehk**
a reef

礅 **dàn** (Md **dūn**)
big and rough rock

礎(础) **chó** (Md **chǔ**)
plinth

礓 **gèung** (Md **jiāng**)
a kind of mineral

礙(碍) **ngoih** (Md **ài**)
to hinder; to obstruct
礙事 **ngoih sih**
to be in the way; to be an
obstacle to work
礙眼 **ngoih ngáahn**
unpleasant to the eyes
礙手礙脚 **ngoih sáu ngoih
geuk**
to be very much in the way

礞 **mùhng** (Md **méng**)
a kind of mineral

礦 **kwong, kong**
(Md **kuāng**)
① a mineral; an ore ② mining
礦坑 **kwong hāang**
a mining shaft

礦泉 **kwong chyùhn**
mineral spring

礦業 **kwong yihp**
mining industry

礪 (砺) **laih (Md lì)**
① coarse whetstone ② to sharpen

礪石 **laih sehk**
coarse whetstone

礫 (砾) **līk (Md lì)**
pebble; gravel

礫石 **līk sehk**
gravel

礫岩 **līk ngàahm**
conglomerate (in geology)

礬 **fàahn (Md fān)**
alum

礬土 **fàahn tóu**
alumina

礬石 **fàahn sehk**
alunite

礱 **lùhng (Md lóng)**
① to grind ② a kind of mill

礴 **bohk (Md bó)**
filling all space; extensive

示部

示 **sih (Md shì)**
to show; to indicate; to demonstrate

示範 **sih faahn**
to set an example; to demonstrate

示意 **sih yi**
to indicate one's wish or intention

示威 **sih wài**
to make a show of force; to show off

祁 **kèih (Md qí)**
vigorous; thriving

祁寒酷暑 **kèih hòhn huhk syú**
severe cold and intense heat

社 **séh (Md shè)**
an association; an organization; society

社團 **séh tyùhn**
an association; a civic organization

社論 **séh leuhn**
an editorial

社交 **séh gàau**
social intercourse

祀 **jih (Md sì)**
to worship; to offer sacrifices to

祀奉 **jih fuhng**
to worship

祀事 **jih sih**
religious rites

祀祖 **jih jóu**
to worship ancestors

祉 **jí (Md zhǐ)**
happiness; blessing

祉祿 **jí luhk**
happiness and wealth

祇 **jí, kèih (Md zhǐ, qí)**
① only; merely ② god of the earth

祇得 **jí dāk**
to have to; to have no alternative

祇好 **jí hóu**
to have to; to have no choice

祇要 **jí yiu**
only if

祇悔 **kèih fui**
great regret

祈 **kèih (Md qí)**
to pray; to beg

祈禱 **kèih tóu**
　　to pray; to offer a prayer

祈求 **kèih kàuh**
　　to pray for; to appeal for

祈請 **kèih chíng**
　　to beg; to entreat

祆 **hìn** (Md **xiān**)
　① calamity due to terrestial disturbances　② bizarre

祐 **yauh** (Md **yàu**)
　divine help

祐助 **yauh joh**
　　to help

祖 **jóu** (Md **zǔ**)
　① grandfather or grandmother　② ancestor　③ founder

祖國 **jóu gwok**
　　fatherland

祖宗 **jóu jūng**
　　ancestors

祖業 **jóu yihp**
　　properties, inherited from one's ancestors

祗 **jì** (Md **zhī**)
　to respect; to reverse

祗奉 **jì fuhng**
　　to respect; to hold in great respect

祗侯 **jì hauh**
　　to wait upon respectfully

祗遵 **jì jèun**
　　to observe or follow with respect

祚 **jouh** (Md **zuò**)
　blessing; throne

祚命 **jouh mihng**
　　heavenly blessing

祛 **kèui** (Md **qū**)
　to dispel; to expel

祛祛 **kèui kèui**
　　healthy and strong

祛災 **kèui jòi**
　　to dispel disasters

祛疑 **kèui yìh**
　　to dispel doubt

祜 **wú** (Md **hù**)
　blessing

祝 **jūk** (Md **zhù**)
　① to wish happiness; to pray for happiness　② to congratulate　③ to celebrate

祝福 **jūk fūk**
　　to bless

祝賀 **jūk hoh**
　　to congratulate

祝詞 **jūk chìh**
　　congratulatory message

神 **sàhn** (Md **shén**)
　① god; spirit; soul　② appearance

神秘 **sàhn beih**
　　mysterious

神情 **sàhn chìhng**
　　facial expression

神學 **sàhn hohk**
　　theology

祟 **seuih** (Md **suì**)
　evil influence of gods or demons; to haunt

祟惑 **seuih waahk**
　　to confuse by evil influence

祠 **chìh** (Md **cí**)
　① a temple; a shrine　② the spring worship

祠堂 **chìh tòhng**
　　a shrine

祠官 **chìh gùn**
　　official in charge of the spring worship

祥 **chèuhng** (Md **xiáng**)
　auspicious; propitious

祥瑞 **chèuhng seuih**
　　good omen; auspiciousness

祥麟 chèuhng lèuhn
a legendary horselike animal resembling the unicorn, whose appearance was regarded as auspicious omen

祧 tiu (Md tiāo)
an ancestral temple

票 piu (Md piào)
bill; ticket; note

票房 piu fòhng
box office; ticket window

票價 piu ga
ticket price

票選 piu syún
to elect by casting ballots

祭 jai (Md jì)
to worship; to offer sacrifices to; to honor by a rite

祭品 jai bán
offerings; sacrifices

祭壇 jai tàahn
an altar

祭司 jai sī
officiant at a religious service; high priest

祺 kèih (Md qí)
① lucky, auspicious ② peaceful; serene

祺祥 kèih chèuhng
fortunate; lucky

祺然 kèih yìhn
peaceful

禁 gam, gàm (Md jīn, jìn)
① to forbid; to prohibit ② to endure; to bear

禁閉 gam bai
to prohibit entry into government service

禁品 gam bán
prohibited merchandise

禁例 gam laih
official prohibition

禁得住 gàm dāk jyuh
able to endure

祿 luhk (Md lù)
① happiness ② official pay

祿俸 luhk fúng
official pay

祿位 luhk waih
official salary and rank

禋 yàn (Md yīn)
① to worship with sincerity ② to offer sacrifices to the heaven

禊 haih (Md xì)
semi-annual exercise performed at water's edge in ancient time

禍 woh (Md huò)
calamity; disaster; to bring disaster upon

禍端 woh dyùn
cause of a misfortune

禍害 woh hoih
harm; injury

禍水 woh séui
a woman (who is often the source of troubles)

禎 jìng (Md zhēn)
good omen

禎祥 jìng chèuhng
good omen; lucky omen

禘 dai (Md dì)
imperial sacrifices made once every five years

禘郊 dai gàau
imperial sacrifices held in the country side

福 fūk (Md fú)
happiness; good fortune; good luck

福分 fūk fahn
share of happiness allotted by destiny

福利 **fūk leih**
welfare; good; property

福音 **fūk yàm**
good news; the gospel

禔 **tàih** (Md **tí**)
happiness; good fortune; good
luck

禕 **yì** (Md **yī**)
excellent

禡 **mah, ngàh** (Md **mà**)
sacrifice to the local deity
performed by marching troops at
a camp site

禡祭 **mah jai**
sacrifice to the local deity
performed by marching troops
at a camp site

禤 **hyūn** (Md **xuān**)
a Chinese family name

禦 (御) **yuh** (Md **yù**)
to guard against; to take precautions against

禦敵 **yuh dihk**
to guard against the enemy

禦寒 **yuh hòhn**
to protect oneself from cold;
to take precautions against
cold

禪 (禅) **sìhm, sihn**
(Md **chán, shàn**)
① to cleanse; to exorcise ② of
Buddhism ③ to abdicate (throne)

禪定 **sìhm dihng**
deep meditation (in Buddhism)

禪師 **sìhm sì**
a master; or teacher of
meditation

禪位 **sihn waih**
to abdicate the throne

禧 **hèi** (Md **xǐ**)
happiness; blessing

禮 **láih** (Md **lǐ**)
① courtesy; politeness ② rites;
ceremony

禮貌 **láih maauh**
politeness; good manner;
etiquette

禮教 **láih gaau**
ethical education

禮讓 **láih yeuhng**
to make way humbly or
modestly

禰 (祢) **nèih** (Md **mí**)
a Chinese family name

禱 **tóu** (Md **dǎo**)
to pray; to plead

禱告 **tóu gou**
a prayer; to pray

禱祀 **tóu jih**
to perform a sacrifice and pray
for happiness

禳 **yèuhng** (Md **ráng**)
① a form of sacrifice performed
for exorcism ② to exorcise

内部

禹 **yúh** (Md **yǔ**)
Yu, the legendary founder of the
Hsia Dynasty

禹貢 **Yúh gung**
China's oldest known book of
Geography

禹跡 **yúh jīk**
the area where the legendary
ruler Yu traversed

禺 **yùh** (Md **yú**)
name of a mountain in Chekiang

禽 **kàhm** (Md **qín**)
① birds; fowls ② to capture; to
catch

禽獵 **kàhm lihp**
to hunt

禽獸 **kàhm sau**
　dumb creatures

禾部

禾 **wòh** (Md **hé**)
① grains still on the stalk ② rice plant

禾苗 **wòh mìuh**
　rice seeding

禾稈 **wòh gón**
　stalk of a rice plant

禾穗 **wòh seuih**
　an ear of grain

私 **sì** (Md **sī**)
private; personal; secret

私仇 **sì sàuh**
　personal grudge

私語 **sì yúh**
　private talks; to whisper or talk in a very low voice

私運 **sì wahn**
　to smuggle

禿 **tūk** (Md **tū**)
bald; bare

禿頭 **tūk tàuh**
　bald-headed; bald

禿山 **tūk sàan**
　a bare hill

禿友 **tūk yáuh**
　a pen or writing brush

秀 **sau** (Md **xiù**)
brilliant; excellent; outstanding; fine; graceful

秀麗 **sau laih**
　elegant; beautiful

秀才 **sau chòih**
　the lowest degree conferred upon successful candidates under the former civil service examination system; fine talent

秉 **bíng** (Md **bǐng**)
① to hold in hand ② to grasp

秉國 **bíng gwok**
　to rule a nation

秉鈞 **bíng gwàn**
　to be in power

秉公辦理 **bíng gùng baahn léih**
　to act strictly according to official rules

秋 **chàu** (Md **qiū**)
① autumn; fall ② a year; time; period

秋收 **chàu sàu**
　autumn harvest

秋季 **chàu gwai**
　autumn (season)

秋高氣爽 **chàu gòu hei sóng**
　the clear and crisp autumn climate

科 **fò** (Md **kē**)
a department; a section

科目 **fò muhk**
　subjects; courses

科舉 **fò géui**
　the civil services examination system of old China

科學 **fò hohk**
　science

秒 **míuh** (Md **miǎo**)
a second of time

秒針 **míuh jām**
　the second hand (on the dial of a clock or watch)

租 **jòu** (Md **zū**)
to rent; to let

租賃 **jòu yahm**
　to rent (a house)

租戶 **jòu wuh**
　a tenant

租借 **jòu je**
to rent; lend-lease

秭 **jí** (Md **zǐ**)
one trillion

秣 **mut** (Md **mò**)
① horse feed; fodder ② to feed horse

秣馬厲兵 **mut máh laih bìng**
to feed the horse and drill the soldiers — prepare for war

秤 **ching** (Md **chèng**)
scales for measuring weights

秦 **chèuhn** (Md **qín**)
the feudal state of Chin in the Chou Dynasty, which later unified the whole country under the Chin Dynasty

秦庭之哭 **chèuhn tìhng jì hūk**
a begging in tears for assistance in desperation

秦樓楚館 **chèuhn làuh chó gún**
brothels

秧 **yèung** (Md **yāng**)
rice seeding; very young plant for transplanting

秧苗 **yèung mìuh**
rice seedings

秧田 **yèung tìhn**
water field for cultivation of rice seeding

秧歌 **yèung gō**
songs sung by farmers when transplanting rice seedings

秩 **diht** (Md **zhì**)
order; orderly

秩序 **diht jeuih**
order; arrangement

秩序大亂 **diht jeuih daaih lyuhn**
in total disorder

秩序井然 **diht jeuih jéng yìhn**
in perfect order

秘(祕) **bei** (Md **mì**)
secret; confidential

秘密 **bei maht**
secret

秘書 **bei syù**
a secretary

移 **yìh** (Md **yí**)
to move; to shift; to change

移交 **yìh gàau**
to hand over to another person or organization

移民局 **yìh màhn guhk**
the immigration office

移玉 **yìh yuhk**
May I request your company at . . .

稅 **seui** (Md **shuì**)
taxes; duty on commodities

稅單 **seui dāan**
tax form

稅吏 **seui leih**
tax collectors; tax officials

稅率 **seui léut**
tax rates; duty rates

稀 **hèi** (Md **xī**)
thin; rare; few

稀薄 **hèi bohk**
thin (of air); deluted (of liquid)

稀罕 **hèi hón**
rare; rarity

稀奇 **hèi kèih**
strange; rare

稈(秆) **gón** (Md **gǎn**)
the stalk of grain; straw

程子 **gón jí**
　the stalk of rice plant; straw

稊 **tàih** (Md **tí**)
darnels

程 **chìhng** (Md **chéng**)
　① a form; a pattern ② a degree
　③ schedule
　程度 **chìhng douh**
　　degree; extend stage; standard
　程序 **chìhng jeuih**
　　procedures; order

稍 **sáau** (Md **shāo, shào**)
　① slightly ② gradually, rather
　稍後 **sáau hauh**
　　shortly afterward
　稍候 **sáau hauh**
　　to wait for a while
　稍佳 **sáau gàai**
　　a little better; slightly better

稔 **náhm** (Md **rěn**)
　① ripening of paddy or rice ②
used to; often
　稔亂 **náhm lyuhn**
　　to accumulate evils
　稔知 **náhm jì**
　　to know well
　稔熟 **náhm suhk**
　　ripe (said of a harvest)

稗 **baaih** (Md **bǎi**)
　① darnels ② small; little
　稗販 **baaih fáan**
　　peddlers or hawkers
　稗官 **baaih gùn**
　　lower-ranking officials
　稗子 **baaih jí**
　　darnels

稚(穉) **jih** (Md **zhì**)
young and tender; small and
delicate

稚嫩 **jih nyuhn**
　tender and delicate
稚氣 **jih hei**
　innocence of a child
稚子 **jih jí**
　young children

稟(稟) **bán** (Md **bǐng**)
　① to report to a superior ② to
receive commands
　稟報 **bán bou**
　　to report to a superior
　稟明 **bán mìhng**
　　to explain to an elder or
　　superior
　稟承 **bán sìhng**
　　according to orders of a
　　superior or higher office

稠 **chàuh** (Md **chóu**)
　① dense; crowded ② a great
many
　稠密 **chàuh maht**
　　crowded; dense
　稠雲 **chàuh wàhn**
　　dense clouds
　稠叠 **chàuh dihp**
　　over-lapping

種 **jung, júng** (Md **zhòng, zhǒng**)
　① to plant; to sow ② to vaccinate
　③ seeds of grain
　種痘 **jung dauh**
　　to vaccinate (against
　　small-pox)
　種植 **jung jihk**
　　to plant; to cultivate
　種類 **júng leuih**
　　kinds; variety

稱 **chìng, ching** (Md **chēng, chèng**)
　① to tell; to claim ② fit; proper
　稱呼 **chìng fù**
　　a name by which one

addresses another

稱許 **chìng héui**
to approve and praise

稱職 **chìng jīk**
competent; suitable to the job one is doing

稻 **douh** (Md **dào**)
paddy or rice

稻米 **douh máih**
rice or paddy

稻田 **douh tìhn**
rice farm

稻草 **douh chóu**
rice straw

稷 **jīk** (Md **jì**)
panicled millet

稼 **ga** (Md **jià**)
① to farm; to plant ② grains

稼穡 **ga sīk**
planting and harvesting of grains

稼穡艱難 **ga sīk gàan nàahn**
the hardships of a farmer's life

稽 **kài, kái** (Md **jī, qǐ**)
① to investigate; to test; to inspect ② to stay; to delay

稽留 **kài làuh**
to stay

稽核 **kài haht**
to examine and audit

稽查 **kài chàh**
to investigate

稽首 **kái sáu**
to kowtow — an expression of great respect

稿 **góu** (Md **gǎo**)
① a manuscript; a sketch ② a pattern for writing

稿本 **góu bún**
manuscript or draft of a literary work

稿紙 **góu jí**
draft paper

稿酬 **góu chàuh**
fees paid to a writer on piece work basis

穀 **gūk** (Md **gú**)
① grains; corns; cereals ② lucky; happy

穀類 **gūk leuih**
grains and corns

穀場 **gūk chèuhng**
a yard for sunning or drying grains

穀倉 **gūk chōng**
a barn for storing grains

穆 **muhk** (Md **mù**)
① peaceful; sincere ② respectful; majestic

穆清 **muhk chìng**
the Heaven; peaceful and orderly

穆然 **muhk yìhn**
peaceful and respectful; meditative

穌 **sōu** (Md **sū**)
① to take; to collect ② to rise gain; to revive

積 **jīk** (Md **jī**)
to accumulate; to store up

積分 **jīk fàn**
to accumulate points

積極 **jīk gihk**
active; positive

積蓄 **jīk chūk**
savings

穎 **wihng** (Md **yíng**)
outstanding; talented remarkable

穎脫 **wihng tyut**
to distinguish oneself in performance

穎悟 **wihng ngh**
very bright; unusually
intelligent

穗 **seuih** (Md **suì**)
① fruits or grains in a cluster
grown at the tip of a stem or stalk
② ear of grain

穗狀花序 **seuih johng fà
jeuih**
the spikes (of flowers)

穗子 **seuih jí**
the ear of grain

穠(秾)**nùhng**
(Md **nóng**)
luxuriant growth of plants

穠纖合度 **nùhng chìm
hahp douh**
winsome; graceful

穠艷 **nùhng yihm**
beautiful and well filled

穡 **sīk** (Md **sè**)
① to harvest grains ② to be
thrifty

穡夫 **sīk fù**
farmer

穡事 **sīk sih**
farming

穢 **wai** (Md **huì**)
① dirty; vile ② debauchery

穢名 **wai mìhng**
a notorious reputation

穢德 **wai dāk**
debauched ways

穢物 **wai maht**
filth

穩(稳)**wán** (Md **wěn**)
stable; steady;sure; secure

穩當 **wán dong**
proper and secure

穩健 **wán gihn**
firm and steady

穩重 **wán juhng**
steady and calm

穫 **wohk** (Md **huò**)
to reap or harvest; to cut grains

穰 **yèuhng** (Md **ráng**)
① crowded; milling ② mixed up;
disturbed

穰田 **yèuhng tìhn**
to offer sacrifices to Gods

穴部

穴 **yuht** (Md **xué**)
① a cave; a hole in the ground ②
points in the human body

穴道 **yuht douh**
points in the human body; an
underground channel

穴隙 **yuht kwīk**
a hole; a crack

究 **gau** (Md **jiū**)
① to study; to examine ② finally;
in the end

究查 **gau chàh**
to examine; to investigate

究竟 **gau gíng**
the very truth; the very end

穹 **kùhng** (Md **qióng**)
① high and vast ② elevated; lofty

穹冥 **kùhng mìhng**
the sky; the heaven

穹蒼 **kùhng chòng**
the sky; firmament

穹谷 **kùhng gūk**
a deep valley

空 **hùng** (Md **kōng**)
① empty; hollow ② unreal; vain
and useless ③ spare time; blank

空閒 **hùng hàahn**
leisure; spare time

空隙 **hùng gwīk**
a vacant space; a gap

空談 **hùng tàahm**
empty talks; useless talks

穿 **chyùn (Md chuān)**
① to wear (clothes; shoes) ② to pierce through ③ to cross

穿戴 **chyùn daai**
to wear (clothes; ornaments)

穿耳 **chyùn yíh**
to pierce the ear — for wearing earings

穿越 **chyùn yuht**
to pass through, to cross (a bridge, a street)

突 **daht (Md tū)**
① sudden; unexpected ② to offend; to go against

突破 **daht po**
to break or mash

突擊 **daht gīk**
to attack suddenly

突出 **daht chēut**
outstanding; remarkable

窄 **jaak (Md zhǎi)**
narrow; contracted

窄小 **jaak síu**
tight and small

窄巷 **jaak hohng**
a narrow lane

窈 **míuh, yíu (Md yǎo)**
deep; obscure

窈冥 **míuh mìhng**
obscure; dusky

窈窕 **míuh tíuh**
quiet and modest; attractive and charming (girl)

窒 **jaht (Md zhì)**
to block; to stop up

窒息 **jaht sīk**
to asphyxiate; to suffocate

窒礙 **jaht ngoih**
to obstruct; an obstacle

窕 **tíuh (Md tiǎo)**
① slender; ② quiet and modest; charming and attractive; beautiful

窗（窻、窓） **chēung (Md chuāng)**
① a window; a sky light ② a place where one studies

窗簾 **chēung lím**
a window curtain

窗紗 **chēung sà**
gauze used to cover a window

窗友 **chēung yáuh**
fellow students; schoolmates

窖 **gaau (Md jiào)**
① a cellar; a pit ② to store things in a cellar

窖冰 **gaau bìng**
to keep ice in a cellar

窖藏 **gaau chòhng**
to store things in a cellar

窘 **kwan (Md jiǒng)**
hard-pressed; embarrassed; affited

窘步 **kwan bouh**
to walk hurriedly

窘態 **kwan taai**
an embarrased look

窘急 **kwan gāp**
affited; in great difficulty

窟 **fāt (Md kū)**
① a hole; a cave ② to dig the ground and. build underground living quarters

窟窖 **fāt gaau**
a cellar

窟居 **fāt gèui**
to live in caves

窟室 **fāt sāt**
an underground room or chamber

窠 **fò, wò** (Md **kē**)
a den; a burrow; a nest

窠臼 **fò kau**
a set pattern or rule

窠巢 **fò chàauh**
a nest

窩 (窩) **wò** (Md **wō**)
① a cave; a den; an apartment ②
to hide

窩藏 **wò chòhng**
to harbor (outlaws); to keep
(stolen goods)

窩兒 **wò yìh**
a place one occupies; a cave;
a pit

窪 (洼) **wà** (Md **wā**)
deep; a pit; a swamp

窪地 **wà deih**
marsh land; low-lying land

窪田 **wà tìhn**
a low-lying field

窮 **kùhng** (Md **qióng**)
① poor; destitute ② to exhaust

窮途 **kùhng tòuh**
extremely distressed or
difficult state

窮困 **kùhng kwan**
poverty — stricken

窮鄉僻壤 **kùhng hèung pìk
yeuhng**
out-of-the way region

窯 (窑、窰) **yìuh**
(Md **yǎo**)
① a brick furnace ② a coal shaft
③ a cave — for human dwelling

窯洞 **yìuh duhng**
a cave for human dwelling

窯坑 **yìuh hàang**
a pit formed by digging for clay
in making pottery

窺 (窥、闚) **kwài**
(Md **kuī**)
to watch or see in secret; to spy;
to peep

窺探 **kwài taam**
to spy on, to peep

窺察 **kwài chaat**
to watch; to spy

窺伺 **kwài jih**
to watch and wait

窿 **lùhng** (Md **lóng**)
a hole; a cavity

竄 **chyun, chyún**
(Md **cuàn**)
① to escape; to run away ② to
change or alter

竄伏 **chyun fuhk**
to lie low

竄匿 **chyun lìk**
to flee and hide

竄逃 **chyún tòuh**
to escape

竅 (窍) **kiu, hiu**
(Md **qiào**)
a hole; the mind's pares

竅門 **kiu mùhn**
the secret of doing something
successfully

竇 **dauh** (Md **dòu**)
a hole; a cavity; a burrow; to dig
through

竈 (灶) **jou** (Md **zào**)
① a place for cooking ② cooking
stove

竈間 **jou gàan**
the kitchen

竈君 **jou kwàn**
the god of the kitchen

竊 (窃) **sit** (Md **qiè**)
to steal; a thief

竊聽 **sit ting**
to eavesdrop; to bug

竊看 **sit hon**
to peep

竊案 **sit ngon**
a theft case

立部

立 **lahp** (Md **lì**)
① to stand ② to establish; to found

立品 **lahp bán**
to cultivate one's moral character

立志 **lahp ji**
to set an object of pursuit; to make up one's mind

立約 **lahp yeuk**
to conclude a treaty

站 **jaahm** (Md **zhàn**)
① to stand ② a station

站定 **jaahm dihng**
to stand still

站崗 **jaahm gòng**
to stand guard

站長 **jaahm jéung**
station master

竟 **gíng** (Md **jìng**)
① to come to an end; to terminate ② rather unexpectedly

竟敢 **gíng gám**
to dare somewhat to one's surprise

竟日 **gíng yaht**
the whole day; all day long

竟然 **gíng yìhn**
in a way thought to be rather unlikely

章 **jèung** (Md **zhāng**)
a piece of writing, a chapter; a system

章節 **jèung jit**
chapters and sections of a writing

章程 **jèung chìhng**
set of regulations

童 **tùhng** (Md **tóng**)
a child; a minor

童年 **tùhng nìhn**
childhood; youth

童話 **tùhng wá**
nursery stories

童叟 **tùhng sáu**
children and aged people

竣 **jeun** (Md **jùn**)
completed; accomplished

竣工 **jeun gùng**
to be completed

竣事 **jeun sih**
having been completed

竦 **súng** (Md **sŏng**)
① respectful ② awed

竦然 **súng yìhn**
fearful; scared

端 **dyùn** (Md **duān**)
① an extreme; an end ② beginning; cause

端麗 **dyùn laih**
neat and beautiful

端莊 **dyùn jòng**
dignified

端坐 **dyùn joh**
to sit properly

竭 **kit** (Md **jiě**)
to devote; to use up

竭力 **kit lihk**
to do one's utmost

竭盡 **kit jeuhn**
to devote to the full

竭誠 **kit sìhng**
whole heartedly; with all sincerity

競 (竞) **gihng** (Md **jìng**)
to complete; to vie

競選 **gihng syún**
to vie in the election

競爭 **gihng jàng**
to compete; to vie; competition

竹部

竹 **jūk** (Md **zhú**)
bamboo

竹報平安 **jūk bou pìhng ngòn**
to report in a letter home that everything is well

竹幕 **jūk mohk**
the Bamboo Curtain (in reference to Communist satellites)

竹筍 **jūk séun**
a bamboo shoot

竺 **jūk** (Md **zhú**)
① an ancient name of India ② a Chinese family name

竺經 **jūk gìng**
Buddhist scriptures

竺學 **jūk hohk**
study of Buddhism

竿 **gòn** (Md **gān**)
bamboo pole

竿頭日上 **gòn tàuh yaht séuhng**
to make constant progress in one's studies

竽 **yùh** (Md **yú**)
a kind of musical instrument with 36 reeds

笈 **kāp** (Md **jí**)
bamboo bookcase

笏 **fāt** (Md **hù**)
a tablet held by a civil official during an audience with the monarch

笑 **siu** (Md **xiào**)
to laugh; to smile; to ridicule

笑話 **siu wá**
a joke; funny story

笑容 **siu yùhng**
happy expression

笑逐顏開 **siu juhk ngàahn hòi**
to beam with smiles

笨 **bahn** (Md **bèn**)
① stupid; dull ② clumsy; awkward

笨拙 **bahn jyut**
unskilled; clumsy

笨重 **bahn juhng**
too heavy for convenient handling

笨手笨脚 **bahn sáu bahn geuk**
acting clumsily

笙 **sàng** (Md **shēng**)
a kind of Pan pipe with 13 reeds

笙歌 **sàng gō**
music and song

笙管 **sàng gún**
pipes of a Pan pipe

笛 **dehk** (Md **dí**)
flute

笛子 **dehk jí**
a flute

笞 **chì** (Md **chì**)
① a bamboo whip ② to whip; to flog

笞刑 **chì yìhng**
whipping or flogging

笞罵 **chì mah**
to whip and revile

笞辱 **chì yuhk**
to whip and insult

笠 lāp (Md **lì**)
① a bamboo hat ② a bamboo shade or covering

符 fùh (Md **fú**)
a tally carried for identification; as a warrant
- 符合 **fùh hahp** to correspond; to match
- 符號 **fùh houh** a symbol; a sign
- 符咒 **fùh jau** a charm; a spell

笥 jih (Md **sì**)
bamboo box or chest
- 笥匱囊空 **jih gwaih nòhng hùng** all the boxes and bags are empty

笪 daaht, daat (Md **dá**)
① a Chinese family name ② the measure for a place

笮 johk, jaak (Md **zuó, zé**)
① narrow; pressing boards laid across rafters ② a kind of liquor container to squeeze

第 daih (Md **dì**)
① order; sequence ② rank; grade; degree
- 第六感 **daih luhk gám** the sixth sense
- 第八藝術 **daih baat ngaih seuht** the eighth art (movie)

笱 gáu (Md **gǒu**)
fishing pole

笳 gà (Md **jiā**)
a reed leaf whistle

笤 tìuh (Md **tiáo**)
bamboo broom
- 笤帚 **tìuh jáu (tìuh jáau)** bamboo broom

笸 pó (Md **pǒ**)
container for grain

等 dáng (Md **děng**)
① rank; grade ② same; equal
- 等分 **dáng fàn (dáng fahn)** to divide into equal parts; equal in quantities
- 等級 **dáng kāp** grade; rank
- 等待 **dáng doih** to wait for

筌 chyùhn (Md **quán**)
bamboo fish trap

筇 kùhng (Md **qióng**)
a kind of bamboo (commonly used to make walking sticks)
- 筇杖 **kùhng jeuhng** a kind of bamboo stick

筍(笋) séun (Md **sǔn**)
bamboo shoot
- 筍乾 **séun gòn** bamboo shoots cooked and dried for preservation
- 筍尖 **séun jīm** the tip of tender bamboo shoot
- 筍衣 **séun yī** shell of a bamboo shoot

筆(笔) bāt (Md **bí**)
① writing brush; pen ② writer's skill
- 筆法 **bāt faat** a calligraphic style
- 筆跡 **bāt jīk** one's handwriting
- 筆順 **bāt seuhn** stroke order (for characters)

笄 gài (Md **jī**)
hairpin for fastening the hair

筓年 **gài nìhn**
　age to begin wearing the hair
　pin (of a woman)

筓冠 **gài gùn**
　(of a woman) having just
　attained maturity

筏 **faht** (Md **fá**)
　a raft

筐 **kwàang** (Md **kuāng**)
rectangular box or chest woven
from bamboo strips

筐篋 **kwàang haahp**
　a rectangular box

筐子 **kwàang jí**
　a bamboo chest

筑 **jūk** (Md **zhú**)
a kind of ancient string
instrument

筒 **túng, tùhng**
　(Md **tǒng**)
a tube; a pipe; a cylinder

筒子 **túng jí**
　a tube; a pipe

筋(觔) **gàn** (Md **jīn**)
tendons; muscles

筋斗 **gàn dáu**
　a somersault

筋骨 **gàn gwāt**
　build (of one's body); strength

筋疲力竭 **gàu pèih lihk kit**
　to be completely exhausted

答 **daap** (Md **dá, dā**)
to answer; to reply

答辯 **daap bihn**
　to speak in self-defense

答覆 **daap fūk**
　to reply to; to answer

答謝 **daap jeh**
　to convey one's thanks

策 **chaak** (Md **cè**)
① a whip (for goading horse) ②
an expasitary writing on government affairs

策馬 **chaak máh**
　to whip the horse

策略 **chaak leuhk**
　stratagem; scheme

策畫 **chaak waahk**
　to plan; to make plan

筠 **wàhn** (Md **yún, jūn**)
skin of bamboo

筥 **géui** (Md **jǔ**)
bamboo basket for holding rice

筱(篠) **síu** (Md **xiǎo**)
① little slender bamboo ② little;
small

筲 **sàau** (Md **shāo**)
a basket for washing rice

筲箕 **sàau gèi**
　a basket for washing rice

筵 **yìhn** (Md **yán**)
① a bamboo mat ② a feast; a
banquet

筵席 **yìhn jihk**
　mat for sitting on; feast;
　banquet

筷 **faai** (Md **kuài**)
chopsticks

筷子 **faai jí**
　chopsticks

管(筦) **gún** (Md **guǎn**)
① a pipe; a tube ② a key ③ to
be in charge

管理 **gún léih**
　to manage; to administer

管轄 **gún haht**
　to have control over

管絃樂 **gún yìhn ngohk**
　orchestral music; orchestra

箸(筯) **jyuh** (Md **zhù**)
① chopsticks ② tongs

箋(笺) **jìn** (Md **jiān**)
① commentary; note ② letter paper; stationery

箋牘 **jìn duhk**
letters; correspondence

箋扎 **jìn jaat**
letters

箋注 **jìn jyu**
notes and commentaries

箍 **kù** (Md **gū**)
a hoop

箍桶 **kù túng**
to fix hoops on a barrel

箍桶店 **kù túng dim**
coopery

箏(筝) **jàng** (Md **zhēng**)
① a kind of string instrument ② a kite

箚 **jaap** (Md **zhā**)
① correspondence; letters ② written instructions to a lower government agency

箚記 **jaap gei**
a notebook; to put down by items

箔 **bohk** (Md **bó**)
① foil; gilt ② curtain

箕 **gèi** (Md **jī**)
① a winnowing basket ② a dust basket

箕踞 **gèi geui**
to squat

箕帚 **gèi jáu, gèi jáau**
dustpan and broom

算(祘) **syun** (Md **suàn**)
to count; to calculate; to plan

算不清 **syun bāt chìng**
uncountable

算帳 **syun jeung**
to compute income and expense

算術 **syun seuht**
arithmetic

箠 **chèuih** (Md **chuí**)
① a whip (for goading horse) ② whipping or flogging

箠楚 **chèuih chó**
whipping or flogging as a punishment

箝(鉗) **kìhm** (Md **qián**)
tongs; pincers; tweezers

箝口 **kìhm háu**
to keep one's mouth shut

箝制 **kìhm jai**
to force; to use pressure upon

箝語 **kìhm yúh**
to restrict freedom of speech

箄 **bai** (Md **bì**)
a bamboo frame for steaming food

箭 **jin** (Md **jiàn**)
an arrow

箭靶 **jin bá**
target for archery

箭豬 **jin jyù**
the parcupine

箭如雨下 **jin yùh yúh hah**
arrows descend like a shower

節(节) **jit** (Md **jié, jiē**)
① node; joint ② passage; section ③ festival ④ rhythm

節拍 **jit paak**
beat; rhythm

節儉 **jit gihm**
to be frugal; to economize

節制 **jit jai**
to restrict; to hold down

節日 **jit yaht**
a festival

箱 **sēung** (Md **xiāng**)
a box; a chest; a trunk

箱籠 **sēung lúhng**
boxes; chests

箱根 **Sēung gàn**
Hakone; Japan

箴 **jàm** (Md **zhēn**)
① a probe; a needle ② to warn; to exhort

箴石 **jàm sehk**
stone probe

箴言 **jàm yìhn**
warning words

篁 **wòhng** (Md **huáng**)
bamboo; bamboo bush; clump of bamboos; bamboo grove

範 (范) **faahn** (Md **fàn**)
model; form; rule; example; pattern

範本 **faahn bún**
copybook; model; example

範例 **faahn laih**
example; model

範圍 **faahn wàih**
range; scope; sphere

篆 **syuhn** (Md **zhuàn**)
seal type; a seal

篆章 **syuhn jèung**
a seal; a chop

篆書 **syuhn syù**
the seal type

篆字 **syuhn jih**
characters written in a seal type

篇 **pìn** (Md **piān**)
poem; chapter; section

篇目 **pìn muhk**
titles; headings

篇幅 **pìn fūk**
length of a writing

篋 (篋) **haahp** (Md **qiè**)
a chest; a box

篋篋 **haahp haahp**
long and thin slender

篝 **kàu** (Md **gōu**)
a basket

築 (筑) **jūk** (Md **zhù**)
to build; house

築堤 **jūk tàih**
to build a dike

築路 **jūk louh**
to build roads

築城 **jūk sìhng**
to build a castle or city wall

篙 **gòu** (Md **gāo**)
pole for punting a boat

篙工 **gòu gùng**
boatman

篡 **saan** (Md **cuàn**)
to seize; to usurp

篡奪 **saan dyuht**
to seize (power; the throne)

篡位 **saan waih**
to usurp the throne

篤 (笃) **dūk** (Md **dǔ**)
deep; much; great

篤信 **dūk seun**
to have deep faith in

篤學 **dūk hohk**
to study diligently

篤愛 **dūk ngoi**
deep affection

篦 **beih** (Md **bì**)
a comb

篦櫛 **beih jit**
a fine toothed comb

篩 **sài** (Md **shāi**)
a sieve; a screen; a strainer

籟鑼 **sài lòh**
　　a small gong; to beat a gong

篩子 **sài jí**
　　a sieve; a sifter

蔌 **chūk** (Md **sù**)
　(of flowers petals) falling in great
　quantities

蔌地 **chūk deih**
　　flowing (of tears)

蔌蔌 **chūk chūk**
　　luxuriant growth; a very slight
　　sound

篷 **pùhng** (Md **péng**)
　① a covering ② a sail

篷窗 **pùhng chēung**
　　windows in a boat

篼 **dàu** (Md **dōu**)
　a mountain sedan-chair; a
　bamboo chair

篾 **miht** (Md **miè**)
　a thin and long strip of bamboo
　for making baskets

篾匠 **miht jeuhng**
　　a bamboo craftsman

篾席 **miht jehk**
　　a bamboo bed mat

簏 **lūk** (Md **lù**)
　a bamboo trunk

簏蔌 **lūk chūk**
　　hanging down

簋 **gwái** (Md **guǐ**)
　a round bamboo vessel for
　holding grains in ancient offerings
　or feast

簇 **chūk** (Md **cù**)
　a cluster; a crowd

簇聚 **chūk jeuih**
　　to cluster or crowd together

簇新 **chūk sàn**
　　brand-new

簇簇 **chūk chūk**
　　piled up; in array

簍 **láuh** (Md **lǒu**)
　a basket made by weaving
　bamboo slats

簍子 **láuh jí**
　　a basket made of bamboo

簍兒 **láuh yìh**
　　a basket; a kind of dumpling
　　with stuffing

簃 **yìh** (Md **yí**)
　a small house attached to a
　pavilion

簧 **wòhng** (Md **Huáng**)
　the metal tongue in a reed organ

簧鼓 **wòhng gú**
　　to dazzle people with suave
　　talk

簧樂器 **wòhng ngohk hei**
　　the reed instruments (in a
　　symphony orchestra)

簫 (簫) **sìu** (Md **xiāo**)
　a flute; a pipe

簫管 **sìu gún**
　　a flute; a pipe

籀 **jauh** (Md **zhòu**)
　a type of Chinese calligraphy, also
　known as the large seal

籀篆 **jauh syuhn**
　　the "large seal" type of
　　Chinese calligraphy

簞 (箪) **dàan** (Md **dān**)
　a round bamboo ware for holding
　cooked rice

簞笥 **dàan jih**
　　bamboo box

簞食壺漿 **dàan jih wùh
jèung**
　　to cheer the troups with food
　　and drink

簟 **tíhm** (Md **diàn**)
a bamboo mat

簟竹 **tíhm jūk**
a variety of giant bamboo

簡 (简) **gáan** (Md **jiǎn**)
① brief; simple ② a letter

簡陋 **gáan lauh**
simple and crude

簡化 **gáan fa**
to simplify

簡易 **gáan yih**
simple and easy

簣 **gwaih** (Md **kuì**)
a bamboo basket for carrying earth

簪 **jàam** (Md **zān**)
① a clasp for clipping the cap and hair ② a hair pin for women

簪笏 **jàam fāt**
cap-clasp and jade tablet

簪花 **jàam fā**
to wear a flower; to stick a flower on one's cap or hat

簷 **sìhm, yìhm** (Md **yán**)
① the eaves of a house ② the edge or brim of anything sloping downward

簷漏 **sìhm lauh**
water from the eaves

簷下 **sìhm hah**
under the eaves

簽 (签) **chìm** (Md **qiān**)
to sign one's name

簽名 **chìm mìhng**
to sign; to put down one's signature

簽到 **chìm dou**
to sign on an attendence book of an office

簽證 **chìm jing**
a visa; to visa

簾 (帘) **lìhm** (Md **lián**)
a loose hanging screen for door or window

簾幕 **lìhm mohk**
screen and blinds

簾政 **lìhm jing**
regency of the empress-dowager

簾子 **lìhm jí**
screen; curtain

簿 **bouh** (Md **bù**)
book; a blank book for writing exercise

簿歷 **bouh lihk**
a person's records; qualifications

簿記 **bouh gei**
book keeping

簿子 **bouh jí**
a writing pad

簸 **bo, bó** (Md **bǒ, bò**)
a winnow

簸箕 **bo gèi**
a winnow; a container for dust

籃 (篮) **làahm** (Md **lán**)
a basket

籃球 **làahm kàuh**
basket ball

籃球架 **làahm kàuh ga**
basketball back stops

籌 (筹) **chàuh**
(Md **chóu**)
① chips; tally ② to plan; to raise

籌備 **chàuh beih**
to prepare and plan

籌辦 **chàuh baahn**
to plan and sponsor

籌欵 **chàuh fún**
to raise fund

籍 **jihk** (Md **jí**)
① books; volumn ② one's native

place

籍隸 **jihk daih**
to be a native of

籍貫 **jihk gun**
one's native place or
home-town

籟 **laaih** (Md **lài**)
① a kind of flute ② unspecified
sound

籠 **lùhng, lúhng**
(Md **lóng, lǒng**)
① a cage; a basket ② a bamboo
ware for holding or covering

籠罩 **lùhng jaau**
to cover completely

籠子 **lùhng jí**
a cage; a basket

籠統 **lúhng túng**
general; indiscriminate

籤 **chìm** (Md **qiān**)
a slip of bamboo engraved with
signs to be used in gambling or
lot

籤兒 **chìm yìh**
a gambling slip of bamboo
engraved with spots to determine the winner

籬 **lèih** (Md **lí**)
bamboo fence; a hedge

籬笆 **lèih bā**
a bamboo fence

籬根 **lèih gàn**
the lower part of a fence

籮 (笭) **lòh** (Md **luó**)
a bamboo basket

籮筐 **lòh kwàang**
a large basket made of bamboo

籲 (吁) **yuh** (Md **yù**)
to request; to urge; to ask

籲求 **yuh kàuh**
to urge; to implore

籲請 **yuh chíng**
to request

米部

米 **máih** (Md **mǐ**)
① uncooked rice ② meter

米飯 **máih faahn**
cooked rice

米價 **máih ga**
the price of rice

米突 **máih daht**
a meter linear measurement

籽 **jí** (Md **zǐ**)
seeds of plant

粉 **fán** (Md **fěn**)
① powder; flour ② cosmetic

粉筆 **fán bāt**
chalk

粉飾 **fán sīk**
to white wash; to make up

粉碎 **fán seui**
to break into pieces; to mash

粒 **nāp** (Md **lì**)
① a grain ② a pill; a bead

粒粒皆辛苦 **nāp nāp gàai
sàn fú**
every (rice) grain is the product
of toiling

粕 **pok** (Md **pò**)
refuse; less; dregs

粗 (觕、麤、麁)
chòu (Md **cū**)
① thick; bulky; big ② rough;
coarse ③ rude

粗劣 **chòu lyut**
crude; inferior

粗魯 **chòu lóuh**
rude or impolite

粗心大意 **chòu sàm daaih yi**
rash and careless

粘 **jìm, nìm** (Md **zhān**)
to paste up; to attach to; to stick up

粟 **sūk** (Md **sù**)
① grains ② millet

粟帛 **sūk baahk**
grain and cloth

粟米 **sūk máih**
millet

粵 **yuht** (Md **yuè**)
Kwangtung Province; Kwangtung and Kwangsi Provinces

粵海 **Yuht hói**
the south China Sea

粵江 **Yuht gòng**
another name of Pearl River

粥 **jūk** (Md **zhōu**)
congee; rice gruel

粥少僧多 **jūk síu jàng dō**
the congee is not enough for the many monks — not enough for circulation or distribution

粱 **lèuhng** (Md **liáng**)
grain; sorghums

粱肉 **lèuhng yuhk**
(literally) grain and meat — a sumptuous meal

粲 **chaan** (Md **càn**)
① bright and clear ② splendid; beautiful

粲爛 **chaan laahn**
brilliant; shiny

粲然 **chaan yìhn**
bright and brilliant

粳 (秔、稉) **gàng** (Md **jīng**)
non-glutinous rice

粹 **seuih** (Md **cuì**)
pure; unmixed; perfect

精 **jìng** (Md **jīng**)
① refined; unmixed ② the essence

精密 **jìng maht**
minute or detailed; careful; thorough

精明 **jìng mìhng**
keen or sharp

精巧 **jìng háau**
exquisite; fine and delicate

糭 (粽) **júng** (Md **zòng**)
glutinous rice tamale — made by wrapping the rice in broad leaves of reeds and boiled for a few hours

糭子 **júng jí**
rice tamal

糅 **yáu, nauh** (Md **róu**)
to mix; mixed

糅合 **yáu hahp**
to mix together

糅雜 **yáu jaahp, nauh jaahp**
mixed; disorderly

糈 **séui** (Md **xǔ**)
foodstuffs

糊 **wùh** (Md **hù, hú, hū**)
① paste; to paste ② scorched ③ not clear; confused

糊塗 **wùh tòuh**
mixed up; confused

糊口 **wùh háu**
to make a living

糕 (餻) **gòu** (Md **gāo**)
cakes; pastry

糕餅 **gòu béng**
cakes and biscuits

糕點 **gòu dím**
cakes and pastry

糍 **chìh** (Md **cí**)
a kind of dumpling made of rice

糖 **tòhng** (Md **táng**)
sugar; candy; sweetened

糖果 **tòhng gwó**
candy; sweets

糖漿 **tòhng jèung**
syrup

糖尿病 **tòhng niuh behng**
diabetes

糙 **chou** (Md **cāo**)
① coarse or unpolished ② rough; rash

糙米 **chou máih**
unpolished rice

糜 **mèih** (Md **mí**)
① congee; rice gruel ② mashed; rotten

糜費 **mèih fai**
extravagant; to waste

糜爛 **mèih laahn**
rotten; corrupt debauchery

糜粥 **mèih jūk**
congee; porridge

糞 (粪) **fan** (Md **fèn**)
① night soil ② to fertilize the land

糞便 **fan bihn**
night soil

糞堆 **fan dèui**
a dunghill

糞土 **fan tóu**
dung and earth — something with little value; dirtied earth

糟 **jòu** (Md **zāo**)
① sediment ② to soak food items

糟蹋 **jòu daahp**
to waste

糟魚 **jòu yùh**
fish cured in distiller's grains

糠 **hòng** (Md **kāng**)
① husks of rice ② of inferior quality

糠糜 **hòng mèih**
coarse food

糠粃 **hòng béi**
rice bran

糧 **lèuhng** (Md **liáng**)
grains; provisions

糧食 **lèuhng sihk**
foodstuff; provisions

糧餉 **lèuhng héung**
army provisions

糯 (糥、稬) **noh**
(Md **nuò**)
glutinous rice

糯米 **noh máih**
glutinous rice

糯稻 **noh douh**
unhusked glutinous rice

糰 **tyùhn** (Md **tuán**)
round dumplings made from glutinous rice flour

糴 (籴) **dehk** (Md **dí**)
to buy grains

糴米 **dehk máih**
to buy rice

糶 (粜) **tiu** (Md **tiào**)
to sell grains

糶米 **tiu máih**
to sell rice

糸部

糸 **mihk** (Md **mì**)
silk

系 **haih** (Md **xì**)
① a system; a line ② lineage; generalogy

系統 **haih túng**
a system

系主任 **haih jyú yahm**
chairman of department (in college)

糾 **gáu** (Md **jiū**)
① to supervise; to inspect ② to correct; to discipline

糾紛 **gáu fàn**
dispute; quarrel

糾正 **gáu jing**
to correct; to discipline

糾纏 **gáu chìhn**
to tangle; to involve

紂 **jauh** (Md **zhōu**)
the last emperor of the Ying Dynasty

紂王 **Jauh wòhng**
the last emperor of the Ying Dynasty

約 **yeuk** (Md **yuē, yāo**)
① an agreement, a convenant; a treaty ② brief; simply

約略 **yeuk leuhk**
brief; sketchy

約會 **yeuk wuih**
an appointment; a date

約束 **yeuk chūk**
to bind or restrain

紀 **géi** (Md **jì, jǐ**)
① a historical record ② a period of 12 years ③ a century

紀念 **géi nihm**
to remember; to commemorate

紀錄 **géi luhk**
a record; to take notes

紀律 **géi leuht**
discipline; laws and regulations

紆 **yù** (Md **yǔ**)
to wind; to spiral; to twist; to bend

紆迴 **yù wùih**
winding (roads); circuitous

紆曲 **yù kūk**
twists and turns

紅 **hùhng, gùng** (Md **hóng, gōng**)
① red; vermilion ② to blush; to redden ③ work; working

紅白事 **hùhng baahk sih**
wedding and funeral

紅運當頭 **hùhng wahn dòng tàuh**
lucky star shines bright

紅女 **gùng néui**
working girl

紈 **yùhn** (Md **wán**)
processed fine and light silk

紈袴 **yùhn fu**
expensive dress of children from wealthy families

紈扇 **yùhn sin**
a round, silk fan

紉 **yahn** (Md **rèn**)
① to sew; to stitch ② to tie; to wear

紉佩 **yahn pui**
to be very grateful

紉緝 **yahn chāp**
to mend; to repair

紋 **màhn** (Md **wén**)
① stripes; lines; streaks ② ripple; print

紋理 **màhn léih**
lines; stripes; lines

紋身 **màhn sàn**
tattoo; to tattoo the body

紊 **mahn** (Md **wěn**)
confused; tangled

紊亂 **mahn lyuhn**
confused; tangled

納 **naahp** (Md **nà**)
① to receive; to take ② to offer as tribute

納悶 **naahp muhn**
to feel depressed

納福 **naahp fūk**
to have a good time; to enjoy oneself

納涼 **naahp lèuhng**
to enjoy the cool air; to enjoy the cool night

紐 **náu** (Md **niǔ**)
a knot; a tie; a cord

紐扣 **náu kau**
a button

紐約 **Náu yeuk**
New York

紓 **syù** (Md **shū**)
to relax; to slacken; to slow down

紓難 **syù naahn**
to extricate from trouble

紓憂 **syù yàu**
to remove worries

純 **sèuhn** (Md **chún**)
① pure; net ② sincere; honest

純樸 **sèuhn pok**
simple and sincere

純潔 **sèuhn git**
innocent; pure and clean

純熟 **sèuhn suhk**
proficient; very skillful; deft

紗 **sà** (Md **shā**)
① gauze; thin silk ② yarn; as cotton-yarn

紗布 **sà bou**
gauze; bandage

紗帳 **sà jeung**
a mosquito net

紗窗 **sà chēung**
window screen

紙 **jí** (Md **zhǐ**)
paper

紙板 **jí báan**
cardboard

紙幣 **jí baih**
paper money; bank notes

紙鳶 **jí yíu**
kites (of paper)

級 **kāp** (Md **jí**)
① a grade; a class ② a degree; a rank

級會 **kāp wúi**
a class meeting

級長 **kāp jéung**
a class leader; a monitor

紛 **fàn** (Md **fēn**)
① confused; disorderly ② numerous; many

紛紛 **fàn fàn**
numerous and disorderly

紛爭 **fàn jàng**
a dispute; to fight with one another

紛亂 **fàn lyuhn**
confusion

紜 **wàhn** (Md **yún**)
confusing; disorderly; busy

紜紜 **wàhn wàhn**
busy comings and goings

素 **sou** (Md **sù**)
① pure white silk ② plain; simple

素描 **sou mìuh**
a sketch (of writing or painting)

素食 **sou sihk**
vegetarian food

素聞 **sou màhn**
to have often heard

紡 **fóng** (Md **fǎng**)
to reel; to spin

紡織 **fóng jīk**
to spin and weave

紡織業 **fóng jīk yihp**
the textile industry

索 **sok, saak** (Md **suǒ**)
① a thick rope ② to search; to inquire ③ to exhaust

索性 **sok sing**
directly; to go all the way

索取 **saak chéui**
to ask for; to demand

紮 (紥) **jaat** (Md **zhā, zā**)
to bind; to tie; to fasten; to stop

紮營 **jaat yìhng**
to set up tent

紮裹 **jaat gwó**
to mend and tidy up

累 **leuih, lèuih** (Md **lěi, lèi, léi**)
① to accumulate; to pile up ② to involve; tired

累積 **leuih jīk**
accumulate

累增 **leuih jàng**
to increase progressively

累人 **leuih yàhn**
to make another tired

細 **sai** (Md **xì**)
① tiny; small; little ② fine; delicate

細胞 **sai bāau**
a cell

細心 **sai sàm**
careful; cautious

細緻 **sai ji**
fine and delicate

紱 **fāt** (Md **fú**)
ribbons; strands

紱冕 **fāt míhn**
a high ranking official

紵 **chyúh** (Md **zhù**)
ramie; linen; sackcloth

紳 **sàn** (Md **shēn**)
a gentleman; gentry

紳士 **sàn sih**
a gentleman

紳商 **sàn sèung**
gentry and merchant class

紹 **siuh** (Md **shào**)
to bring together; to connect

紹介 **siuh gaai**
to introduce; to recommend

紹述 **siuh seuht**
to continue; to follow

紼 **fāt** (Md **fú**)
a large rope; cord

絀 **jyut** (Md **chù**)
to sew; to bend; to degrade; deficient

終 **jùng** (Md **zhōng**)
① the end; to come to the end ② death; to die ③ finally; at last

終點 **jùng dím**
the terminus

終歸 **jùng gwài**
the conclusion; finally

終止 **jùng jí**
to come to the end; to stop

組 **jóu** (Md **zǔ**)
① a group; a team ② to organize; to arrange; to form

組合 **jóu hahp**
combinations; to unite

組織 **jóu jīk**
to organize; an organization

組長 **jóu jéung**
chief of a department

紫 **jí** (Md **zǐ**)
purple colour

絆 (绊) **buhn** (Md **bàn**)
① fetters; shackles ② to stumble

絆倒 **buhn dóu**
to trip over

絆脚 **buhn geuk**
fettered; hindered

絆脚石 **buhn geuk sehk**
a stumbling block

結 **git** (Md **jié, jiē**)
① to tie; to knot ② to unite; to join

結論 **git leuhn**
the conclusion

結交 **git gàau**
to associate with

結繩 **git sìhng**
to tie knot on a string for record before the invention of the written language

綫 (緬) **sit** (Md **xiè**)
① reins; ropes for leading animals ② to bind; fetters

絕 (绝) **jyuht** (Md **jué**)
① to serve; to break off ② without match ③ isolated

絕版 **jyuht báan**
out-of-print (books)

絕妙 **jyuht miuh**
extremely good; wonderful

絕望 **jyuht mohng**
hopeless; to give up hope

絞 **gáau** (Md **jiǎo**)
① to twist; to wing ② to hang

絞痛 **gáau tung**
acute or gripping pain

絞腦汁 **gáau nóuh jāp**
to cudgel one's brain

絞刑 **gáau yìhng**
death by hanging

絜 **git** (Md **xié**)
① clean ② to assess; to measure

絜矩 **git géui**
to examine oneself and think of the others so that each will get what he wants

絡 **lohk** (Md **luò, lào**)
① to wrap around ② a net; a web

絡頭 **lohk tàuh**
a halter

絡繹不絕 **lohk yihk bāt jyuht**
to come one after another

絡子 **lohk jí**
a fine thread basket

給 **kāp** (Md **gěi, jǐ**)
to give

給付 **kāp fuh**
to pay

給臉 **kāp níhm**
to save face — so as not to embarrass him

絢 **hyun** (Md **xuàn**)
bright and brilliant; adorned and stylish

絢爛 **hyun laahn**
bright and brilliant; glittering

絨 (羢、毧) **yúng** (Md **róng**)
fine wool; any kind of woolen goods

絨布 **yúng bou**
flannel; woolen or cotten piece goods with a felt-like surface felt

絨花 **yúng fā**
artificial flowers made of silk

絪 **yàn** (Md **yīn**)
misty; foggy

綑緼 **yàn wáhn**
misty; foggy

絮 **seuih** (Md **xù**)
raw coarse; old; waste woolen
goods or cotton

絮煩 **seuih fàahn**
windy; talkative; tired of

絮絮不休 **seuih seuih bāt
yàu**
to din; amoyingly talkative

統 **túng** (Md **tóng**)
① to govern; to rule ② to unify
③ wholly; totally

統領 **túng líhng**
a commanding officer

統計 **túng gai**
statistics

統治 **túng jih**
to reign; to rule

絲 **sì** (Md **sī**)
① silk ② very fine thread

絲帶 **sì daai**
silk ribbons

絲毫 **sì hòuh**
the tiniest or least bit

絲襪 **sì maht**
silk stockings; silk socks

絳 **gong** (Md **jiàng**)
red; a deep red colour

絳袍 **gong pòuh**
a red robe

絳頰 **gong gaap**
rosy cheeks

絹 **gyun** (Md **juàn**)
a kind of thick, loosely — woven
raw silk fabric

絹綢 **gyun chàuh**
a kind of silk fabric

絹扇 **gyun sin**
a fan made with silk

綃 **sìu** (Md **xiāo**)
a fabric made of unprocessed or
raw silk

綃頭 **sìu tàuh**
a silk ribbon for building the
hair

綆 **gáng** (Md **gěng**)
a rope for drawing up water (from
a well)

綆短汲深 **gáng dyún kāp
sàm**
(literally) the rope is short
while the well is deep —
unequal to the job

綈 **tàih** (Md **tí, tì**)
a glossy thick silk fabric

綈袍 **tàih pòuh**
gratitude; to remember favors
given

綁 **bóng** (Md **bǒng**)
to tie; to bind

綁票 **bóng piu**
to kidnap for ransom

綁匪 **bóng féi**
a kidnaper

綏 **sèui** (Md **suí**)
① to pacify; to appease ② to
retreat

綏撫 **sèui fú**
to pacify; to soothe

綏靖 **sèui jihng**
to restore peace and order

經 **gìng** (Md **jīng**)
① classic books; religious
scriptures ② the warp of a fabric,
longitude

經典 **gìng dín**
religious scriptures

經歷 **gìng lihk**
one's past experience

經濟 **gìng jai**
economy; economic

綜 **jùng, jung** (Md **zōng, zèng**)

to sum up; to gather; to collect; in general

綜括 **jùng kut**
to sum up

綜合 **jung hahp**
synthesis; to gather together

綢 **chàuh** (Md **chóu**)

a general name of all silk fabrics

綢繆 **chàuh màuh**
to get prepared

綢緞 **chàuh dyuhn**
a general name of silk goods

綢直 **chàuh jihk**
careful; considerate and honest

綣 **hyun** (Md **quǎn**)

to make tender love; to meet in rendezvous

綦 **kèih** (Md **qí**)

① very; exceedingly ② dark grey

綦重 **kèih juhng**
very heavy

綦嚴 **kèih yìhm**
very stringent; very severe

綬 **sauh** (Md **shǒu**)

silk ribbons; sash

綬帶 **sauh daai**
a cordon

維 **wàih** (Md **wéi**)

① to tie; to hold fast ② to maintain

維妙維肖 **wàih miuh wàih chiu**
so skillfully imitated as to be indistinguishable from the original

維護 **wàih wuh**
to safeguard; to protect

維持 **wàih chìh**
to maintain; to keep

綰 **wáan** (Md **wǎn**)

to string together; to bind up

綱 **gòng** (Md **gāng**)

① the large rope of net ② main points; outline

綱目 **gòng muhk**
the outline and detailed items

綱要 **gòng yìu**
main points; outline

網 **móhng** (Md **wǎng**)

net; network; web

網羅 **móhng lòh**
to bring together; to collect

網球 **móhng kàuh**
tennis

網魚 **móhng yùh**
to net fish

綴 **jeui, jyut** (Md **zhuì**)

① to put together; to combine ② to mend clothes

綴補 **jeui bóu**
to patch up (clothes)

綴文 **jeui màhn**
to write a composition

綵 **chói** (Md **cǎi**)

varicoloured silk; motley

綵牌樓 **chói pàaih làuh**
varicoloured celebration arch

綵球 **chói kàuh**
a ball wound up from varicoloured silk

綸 **lèuhn, gwàan** (Md **lún, guān**)

① fishing line ② green silk cord

綸音 **lèuhn yàm**
thick silken thread

綸巾 **gwàan gàn**
a kind of ancient cap resembling a ridged roof

綹 láuh (Md liǔ)
a tuft; a lock; a skein (of yarn)

綺 yí (Md qǐ)
beautiful; magnificent; fine; elegant

綺年 yí nìhn
youthful

綺麗 yí laih
beautiful; fair; magnificent

綻 jaahn (Md zhàn)
ripped seam; a crack

綻裂 jaahn liht
split; ripped

綻線 jaahn sin
to have a ripped seam

綽 cheuk (Md chuò, chāo)
① spacious; roomy ② delicate

綽號 cheuk houh
a nickname

綽綽有餘 cheuk cheuk yáuh yùh
there is enough room to spare

綽約多姿 cheuk yeuk dò jì
charmingly delicate

綑 gwán (Md gǔn)
rope

綾 lìhng (Md líng)
very fine silk cloth

綾羅錦繡 lìhng lòh gám sau
expensive clothes

綿(绵、緜) mìhn (Md mián)
① cotton ② everlasting; endless ③ weak

綿綿 mìhn mìhn
continuous; everlasting

綿力 mìhn lihk
my limited power

緊 gán (Md jǐn)
tight; firm; fast

緊急 gán gāp
urgent; critical

緊張 gán jèung
tense; nervous

緊縮 gán sūk
to retrench; to cut down

緇 jì (Md zī)
black; black silk

緇帶 jì daai
black belt

緇流 jì làuh
Buddist monks

緋 fèi (Md fēi)
scarlet; crimson

緋紅 fèi hùhng
scarlet; crimson

綠 luhk (Md lù)
green

綠林 luhk làhm
the outlaws

綠水 luhk séui
crystal clean water

綠陰 luhk yàm
shade of trees

線(线、綫) sin (Md xiàn)
line; thread; wire

線條 sin tìuh
lines; streaks

線索 sin sok
a clue; a lead

緝 chāp (Md jī, qī)
to order the arrest of; to capture

緝拿 chāp nàh
to arrest

緝私 chāp sì
to arrest smugglers

緞 **dyuhn** (Md **duàn**)
satin

緞帶 **dyuhn daai**
satin ribbon

緞子 **dyuhn jí**
satin

締 **dai** (Md **dì**)
to connect; to join

締結 **dai git**
to conclude

締約 **dai yeuk**
to conclude a treaty

緣 **yùhn** (Md **yuán**)
① cause; reason ② to go along

緣分 **yùhn fahn**
relationship by fate

緣故 **yùhn gu**
cause; reason

編 **pìn** (Md **biān**)
① to knit ② to put together; to organize

編類 **pìn leuih**
to arrange into categories

編輯 **pìn chāp**
to edit; an editor

編制 **pìn jai**
organic structure

緘 **gàam** (Md **jiān**)
① to seal; to close ② a letter

緘默 **gàam mahk**
to keep silence

緘封 **gàam fùng**
to seal

緘扎 **gàam jaat**
a letter

緩 **wuhn, wùhn**
(Md **huǎn**)
① slow; gradual ② delay; to put off

緩和 **wuhn wòh**
to moderate; calm

緩急 **wùhn gāp**
degree of urgency

緩兵之計 **wùhn bìng jì gai**
a strategy for gaining time

緬 **míhn** (Md **miǎn**)
① distant; far ② to think of something or somebody of the past

緬甸 **Míhn dihn**
Burma

緬懷 **míhn wàaih**
to think of; to remember

緯 **wáih** (Md **wěi**)
woof; parallels showing latitude on a map

緯度 **wáih douh**
degree of latitude

緯線 **wáih sin**
latitude on maps

緲 **míuh** (Md **miǎo**)
distant; far; dim

練 **lihn** (Md **liàn**)
① to train; to practice ② skill; experience

練兵 **lihn bìng**
to drill troops

練習 **lihn jaahp**
to practice

練習生 **lihn jaahp sàng**
a trainee, a student; an apprentice

緹 **tàih** (Md **tí**)
reddish yellow silk

緹騎 **tàih kèh**
cavaliers in reddish yellow

緻 **ji** (Md **zhì**)
fine; close; dense

緻密 **ji maht**
fine; close; delicate

縉 **jeun** (Md **jìn**)
red silk

縉紳 **jeun sàn**
a ranking government official

縈 **yìhng** (Md **yíng**)
to coil; to entwine; to wind around and around

縈懷 **yìhng wàaih**
to be constantly on one's mind

縈繞 **yìhng yíu**
to encircle

縈紆 **yìhng yù**
to wind around

縊 (缢) **ai** (Md **yì**)
to strangle

縊頸 **ai géng**
to hang oneself

縊殺 **ai saat**
to strangle to death

縕 **wan** (Md **yùn**)
loose hemp; old yarn

縕袍 **wan pòuh**
coarse clothing

縋 **jeuih** (Md **zhuì**)
to hang by a rope

縋登 **jeuih dàng**
to climb by a rope

縋城 **jeuih sìhng**
to climb down a city wall by a rope

縐 (绉) **jau** (Md **zhòu**)
① crepe; crape ② wrinked; crinkled

縐布 **jau bou**
crepe; crape

縐綢 **jau chàuh**
crepe silk

縐紋 **jau màhn**
wrinkles; folds

縛 **bok, fok** (Md **fù**)
to bind; to tie

縛住 **bok jyuh**
to tie up; to bind up

縛雞之力 **bok gài jì lihk**
strength for binding a chicken

縝 (縝) **ján** (Md **zhěn**)
fine; close

縝密 **ján maht**
fine; well considered and planned in every respect

縞 **góu** (Md **gǎo**)
plain white raw silk

縞冠 **góu gùn**
plain white cap worn in mourning

縞衣 **góu yì**
plain white clothes worn in mourning

縟 **yuhk** (Md **rù**)
① rick ornament ② excessive formality

縟節 **yuhk jit**
excessive formality

縟禮 **yuhk láih**
excessive ceremony

縢 **tàhng** (Md **téng**)
to bind; to tie to restrict

縢履 **tàhng léih**
shoes for bound feet

縣 (县) **yuhn** (Md **xiàn**)
a county; a prefecture

縣官 **yuhn gùn**
county magistrate

縣城 **yuhn sìhng**
seat of a county government

縗 **chèui** (Md **cuī**)
piece of sack cloth warn on the breast in mourning

縭（褵）**lèih** (Md **lí**)
① a bridal veil ② to tie; to bind

縱 **jung, jùng** (Md **zòng, zōng**)
① vertical; longitudinal ② to allow to move or work freely

縱橫 **jùng wàahng**
the horizontal and the vertical

縱容 **jung yùhng**
to pass over indulgently

縫 **fùhng, fuhng** (Md **féng, fèng**)
① to sew; to stitch ② a suture; a crack

縫製 **fùhng jai**
to make or manufacture

縫紉 **fùhng yahn**
sewing; needlework

縫子 **fuhng jí**
a suture; a crack

縮 **sūk** (Md **suō, sù**)
① to contract; to shorten ② to drawback

縮減 **sūk gáam**
to reduce; to lessen

縮影 **sūk yíng**
a miniature

縲 **lèuih** (Md **léi**)
black rope

縲絏 **lèuih sit**
rope for binding a criminal; confinement

縴（纤）**hin** (Md **qiàn**)
a towrope; a towline

縴夫 **hin fù**
workers who tow boats

縴繩 **hin sìhng**
a towrope; a towline

縵 **maahn** (Md **màn**)
① a plain silk ② plain; unadorned

③ slow

縷 **léuih** (Md **lǔ**)
a thread; a yarn

縷縷 **léuih léuih**
continuous; endless

縷陳 **léuih chàhn**
to state in detail

縹 **pìuh** (Md **piǎo, piāo**)
① light-blue silk ② light-blue ③ dim

縹緲 **pìuh míuh**
distant and dim

縹囊 **pìuh nòhng**
books; silk bag for holding books

縻 **mèih** (Md **mí**)
to tie; to fasten

總 **júng** (Md **zǒng**)
① to gather; to collect ② all; general; total ③ always

總括 **júng kut**
to sum up; to summarize

總是 **júng sih**
always; without exception

總務 **júng mouh**
general affairs

績 **jīk** (Md **jī**)
① to spin ② merit; achievement

績麻 **jīk màh**
to spin hemp

績分 **jīk fàn**
grades; score

績效 **jīk haauh**
results; effects

繁 **fàahn** (Md **fán**)
① many; numerous ② complex; complicated

繁複 **fàahn fūk**
complex; complicated

繁華 **fàahn wàh**
prosperous; flourishing

繁瑣 **fàahn só**
minute and complicated

繃 **bàng** (Md **bēng, běng**)
① tense; taut ② to endure or bear ③ to break open ④ to bind

繃不住 **bàng bāt jyuh**
unable to endure

繃帶 **bàng daai**
a bandage

繆 **miuh, màuh, mauh**
(Md **miǎo, móu, miù**)
① precautions ② a Chinese family name ③ erroneous; false

繆巧 **mauh háau**
trick; ruse

繆誤 **mauh ngh**
error; mistake

繅 **sòu** (Md **sāo**)
to draw (silk from cocoons)

繅繭 **sòu gáan**
to draw silk from cocoon

繅絲 **sòu sì**
to draw silk from cocoon

縧(條) **tòu** (Md **tāo**)
ribbon; flat silk cord

繇 **yàuh, yìuh** (Md **yóu, yáo**)
through; via; by way of

繚 **lìuh** (Md **liáo**)
to wind round

繚亂 **lìuh lyuhn**
disorderly; confuse

繚繞 **lìuh yíu**
winding round and round

繕 **sihn** (Md **shàn**)
① to mend; to repair ② to copy

繕補 **sihn bóu**
to mend

繕寫 **sihn sé**
to transcribe; to copy neatly

織 **jīk** (Md **zhī**)
to weave; to knit

織補 **jīk bóu**
to mend

織布 **jīk bou**
to weave cloth

繙 **fàan** (Md **fān**)
to translate; to interpret

繙譯 **fàan yihk**
to translate; to interpret

繞 **yíu** (Md **rào, rǎo**)
to go around; to encircle

繞道 **yíu douh**
to make a detour

繞過 **yíu gwo**
to pass over a point by detour

繞越 **yíu yuht**
to cross or pass by detour

繡(綉) **sau** (Md **xiù**)
① to embroider ② embroidery

繡補 **sau bóu**
to darn

繡花枕頭 **sau fā jám tàuh**
embroidered pillow

繪(绘、繢) **kúi**
(Md **huì**)
to draw

繪圖 **kúi tòuh**
to draw pictures

繪具 **kúi geuih**
drawing tools

繩(绳) **sìhng**
(Md **shéng**)
① a rope; a cord ② to restrain

繩索 **sìhng sok**
ropes; cords

繩之以法 **sìhng jì yíh faat**
to prosecute according to the law

繫(系)**haih** (Md **xì, jì**)
to connect; to link; to join

繫絆 **haih buhn**
bridle; to hinder

繫獄 **haih yuhk**
to imprison

繭 **gáan** (Md **jiǎn**)
cocoons; chrysalis

繭綢 **gáan chàuh**
pongee

繭絲 **gáan sī**
taxes; levies

繮(韁)**gèung**
(Md **jiāng**)
rein; bridle; halter

繮繩 **gèung sìhng**
reins; bridle

繰(秌)**chìu, sòu**
(Md **qiāo, sāo**)
① a kind of silk ② to draw silk
from cocoon

繳 **gíu, jeuk** (Md **jiǎo,
zhuó**)
① to surrender; to submit ② to
pay ③ a harpoon

繳費 **gíu fai**
to pay fees

繳回 **gíu wùih**
to return

繳械 **gíu haaih**
to surrender arms; to hand
over weapons

繹 **yihk** (Md **yì**)
① to draw silk ② continuous;
uninterrupted ③ to infer

繯 **wàahn** (Md **huán**)
① a noose ② to hang (to death)

繽 **bàn** (Md **bīn**)
① abundant; plentiful ②
disorderly; confused

繽紛 **bàn fàn**
flourishing; thriving

繽亂 **bàn lyuhn**
disorderly; confused

繼(继)**gai** (Md **jì**)
① to continue; to carry on ② to
follow; to inherit

繼續 **gai juhk**
to continue; to last; to go on

繼承 **gai sìhng**
to inherit; to succeed

繼任 **gai yahm**
to succeed to an office

繾 **hín** (Md **qiǎn**)
entangled

繾綣 **hín hyun**
entangled; inseperable

纂 **jyún** (Md **zuǎn**)
① a kind of red cloth ② to compile; to collect

纂輯 **jyún chāp**
to compile

纂修 **jyún sàu**
to edit; to prepare

辮 **bìn** (Md **biàn**)
a braid of hair; a pigtail; a queue

辮髮 **bìn faat**
plaited hair

辮子 **bìn jí**
a pigtail; a queue

續 **juhk** (Md **xù**)
to continue; to extend

續版 **juhk báan**
a reprint

續約 **juhk yeuk**
to renew a contract

纍(累)**lèuih** (Md **léi**)
① strung together ② heavy rope
③ to tie; to bind

纍纍 **lèuih lèuih**
strung together

纍囚 **lèuih chàuh**
prisoner

纏 **chìhn** (Md **chán**)
① to wind round; to bind ② to bother persistently

纏裹 **chìhn gwó**
to wrap up

纏身 **chìhn sàn**
to be delayed

纏繞 **chìhn yíu**
to wind round

纓 **yìng** (Md **yīng**)
① chin strap for holding a hat ② tassel

纓帽 **yìng mouh**
ceremonial hat with red tassesl

纓絡 **yìng lohk**
ornamental fringes on a garment

纖 **chìm** (Md **xiān**)
tiny; minute; fine

纖悉 **chìm sīk**
to know thoroughly

纖細 **chìm sai**
fine, delicate; tiny

纖維 **chìm wàih**
fiber

纘 **jyun** (Md **zuǎn**)
to inherit; to carry on

纘緒 **jyun séuih**
to continue

纜 **laahm** (Md **lǎn**)
a hawser; a cable

纜車 **laahm chè**
cable car

缶部

缶 **fáu** (Md **fǒu**)
a crock with a narrow opening

缸 **gòng** (Md **gāng**)
a cistern; a crock

缺 **kyut** (Md **quē**)
① deficient; lacking; short ③ vacancy; opening

缺乏 **kyut faht**
to lack; to be without

缺德 **kyut dāk**
deficient in the sense of morality

缺陷 **kyut hahm**
defect; shortcoming; handicap

罃 **āng** (Md **yīng**)
long necked bottle

罄 **hing** (Md **qìng**)
to exhaust; to use up

罄竭 **hing kit**
used up; exhausted

罄盡 **hing jeuhn**
to use up

罅 **la** (Md **xià**)
crack; rift; cleft

罅漏 **la lauh**
flaw; fault; defect

罅隙 **la gwīk**
crack; rift; flaw

罌（甖）**àng** (Md **yīng**)
jar with a small mouth

罌粟 **àng sūk**
opium poppy

罍 **lèuih** (Md **léi**)
earthenware wine jar

罐 **gun** (Md **guàn**)
a vessel; a container; a jar; a jug; a can

罐頭 **gun tàuh**
canned goods

罐裝 **gun jòng**
canned

网部

罕 **hón** (Md **hǎn**)
rare; few

罕覯 **hón gùn**
rarely found

罕有 **hón yáuh**
rare

罕物 **hón maht**
a curiosity; a rare thing

罔 **móhng** (Md **wǎng**)
to libel; to slander; to deceive

罔不 **móhng bāt**
there are none that do not

罔效 **móhng haauh**
ineffective; to or of no avail

罟 **gú** (Md **gǔ**)
net

罡 **gòng** (Md **gāng**)
the Taoist name of the Dipper

罡風 **gòng fùng**
winds blowing over high places
(Taoist expressions)

罣 **gwa** (Md **guà**)
① hindrance, obstruction ② a
sieve ③ to be worried; to be
concerned

罣念 **gwa nihm**
to be concerned

罣誤 **gwa ngh**
to be remiss; to be a fault

罪 **jeuih** (Md **zuì**)
sin; crime; offense; fault; evil;
guilt

罪犯 **jeuih fáan**
a criminal; an offender

罪孽 **jeuih yihp**
sin

罪過 **jeuih gwo**
fault; sin

罩 **jaau** (Md **zhào**)
① bamboo basket for catching
fish ② to coop; to cover

罩子 **jaau jí**
a cover; a shade

置 **ji** (Md **zhì**)
① to put; to place ② to establish

置備 **ji beih**
to have (a thing) in convenient
reach

置之不理 **ji jì bāt léih**
to disregard it totally

署 **chyúh** (Md **shǔ**)
① a public ② to arrange ③ to
write down

署理 **chyúh léih**
to administer in an acting
capacity

署名 **chyúh mìhng**
to sign one's name

罰 **faht** (Md **fá**)
to punish; to fine; to penalize

罰欵 **faht fún**
a fine; to fine

罰則 **faht jāk**
penal regulation

罷(罷) **bah** (Md **bā, ba**)
to cease; to stop; to finish

罷免 **bah míhn**
to recall (officials by the
people)

罷工 **bah gùng**
to strike; strike

罷手 **bah sáu**
to discontinue an action

罵(罵) **mah** (Md **mà**)
to swear; to curse

罵人 **mah yàhn**
to call names

罵不絕口 **mah bāt jyuht háu**
to curse unceasingly

罹 **lèih** (Md **lí**)
① sorrow; grief ② to meet (disaster; misfortune)

罹禍 **lèih woh**
to meet disaster

罹難 **lèih naahn**
to fall victim to a disaster

羅 **lòh** (Md **luó**)
① thin, light silk ② net; snare ③ a Chinese family name

羅盤 **lòh pùhn**
a compass

羅列 **lòh liht**
to arrange for display

羅網 **lòh móhng**
net; snare

羆（罴）**bèi** (Md **pí**)
a kind of bear

羆虎 **bèi fú**
fierce animals

羈 **gèi** (Md **jī**)
① bridle ② to confine; to bind

羈絆 **gèi buhn**
to restrain; to confine

羈留 **gèi làuh**
to detain (an offender)

羊部

羊 **yèuhng** (Md **yáng**)
a sheep; a goat

羊毛 **yèuhng mòuh**
wool

羊毛衫 **yèuhng mòuh sāam**
woolen sweater

羊羣 **yèuhng kwàhn**
flock of sheep or goats

羌 **gèung** (Md **qiāng**)
name of an ancient tribe in West China

羌蠻 **gèung màahn**
an ancient barbarian people in West China

羌笛 **gèung dehk**
a kind of flute

美 **méih** (Md **měi**)
beautiful; pretty; good; excellent

美滿 **méih múhn**
happy; sweet (of a life; home, etc.)

美貌 **méih maauh**
a beautiful face

美景 **méih gíng**
beautiful scenery

羑 **yáuh** (Md **yǎu**)
to guide to goodness

羖（羘）**gú** (Md **gǔ**)
a black ram

羔 **gòu** (Md **gāo**)
a lamb

羔羊 **gòu yèuhng**
a lamb

羔皮 **gòu pèih**
lambskin

羚 **lìhng** (Md **líng**)
antelope

羚羊 **lìhng yèuhng**
antelope

羞 **sàu** (Md **xiū**)
① ashamed; shy ② to disgrace; to insult

羞憤 **sàu fáhn**
ashamed and angry

羞愧 **sàu kwáih**
mortified; shamed

羞恥 **sàu chí**
sense of shame

羣(群) **kwàhn**
(Md **qún**)
group; multitude crowd; a flock

羣島 **kwàhn dóu**
group of islands

羣居 **kwàhn gèui**
to live as a group

羣英 **kwàhn yìng**
a large number of brilliant minds

羨 **sihn** (Md **xiàn**)
to envy; to covet

羨慕 **sihn mouh**
to envy; to covet

羨財 **sihn chòih**
to covet wealth

義 **yih** (Md **yī**)
① justice; righteousness ② charity; generosity

義理 **yih léih**
principle; reason

義氣 **yih hei**
spirit of justice; loyalty to friends

義務 **yih mouh**
duty; obligation

羯 **kit** (Md **jié**)
① castrated ram ② name of an ancient barbarian people

羯鼓 **kit gú**
a kind of drum

羯胡 **kit wùh**
an ancient barbarian people

羲 **hèi** (Md **xī**)
Fu Hsi; a legendary ruler who introduced house

羶(膻) **jìn** (Md **shān**)
odor of a sheep or goat

羶氣 **jìn hei**
odor of a sheep or goat

羶腥 **jìn sèng**
odor of mutton

羸 **lèuih** (Md **léi**)
① lean; emaciated ② weak; feeble

羸憊 **lèuih beih**
very weary; exhausted

羸弱 **lèuih yeuhk**
emaciated and weak

羹 **gāng** (Md **gēng**)
thick soup; broth

羹湯 **gāng tòng**
thick soup; broth

羹匙 **gāng chìh**
a spoon

羽部

羽 **yúh** (Md **yǔ**)
feather; plume

羽毛 **yúh mòuh**
feather; plume

羽毛球 **yúh mòuh kàuh**
badminton

羿 **ngaih** (Md **yì**)
name of a legendary archer

翁 **yùng** (Md **wēng**)
① father; father-in-law ② old man

翁姑 **yùng gù**
a woman's parents-in-law

翁婿 **yùng sai**
father-in-law and son-in-law

翅 **chi** (Md **chì**)
wings; fins

翅膀 **chi pòhng**
wings

翎 **lìhng** (Md **líng**)
feather; plume

翎毛 **lìhng mòuh**
feathers; birds

翊 **yihk** (Md **yì**)
flying; to assist respectful

翊戴 **yihk daai**
to assist and support

翊贊 **yihk jaan**
to assist

翊翊 **yihk yihk**
respectful

翌 **yihk** (Md **yì**)
tomorrow

翌朝 **yihk jiu**
tomorrow morning

翌日 **yihk yaht**
tomorrow

習（习） **jaahp** (Md **xí**)
① to learn; to receive training ②
habit; custom

習慣 **jaahp gwaan**
habit; custom

習作 **jaahp jok**
to learn to do

習藝 **jaahp ngaih**
to learn a skill or trade

翔 **chèuhng** (Md **xiǎng**)
① to soar ② detailed

翔集 **chèuhng jaahp**
to gather the essence from many sources

翔盡 **chèuhng jeuhn**
detailed and complete

翟 **dihk, jaahk** (Md **dí, zhái**)
① a kind of pheasant with long tail feathers ② a Chinese family name

翟羽 **dihk yúh**
pheasant feathers

翠 **cheui** (Md **cuì**)
① bluish green ② green jade

翠綠 **cheui luhk**
bluish green

翠玉 **cheui yúk**
blue jade

翡 **féi, feih** (Md **fěi**)
① kingfisher ② emerald

翡翠 **féi cheui**
a kingfisher; emerald

翩 **pìn** (Md **piān**)
to fly swiftly

翩翩 **pìn pìn**
to fly swiftly; elegant; stylish

翩然 **pìn yìhn**
springly; suddenly

翦 **jín** (Md **jiǎn**)
to trim; to cut with scissors

翰 **hohn** (Md **hàn**)
① white horse ② feather

翰林 **hohn làhm**
the literary circle

翰札 **hohn jaat**
letters

翱（翺） **ngòuh** (Md **áo**)
to soar

翳 **ngai** (Md **yì**)
① to screen; to conceal ② haziness of objects due to a weakened vision

翳翳 **ngai ngai**
dim; hazy

翼 **yihk** (Md **yì**)
① wings, fins ② to assist; to help

翼庇 **yihk bei**
to protect; to patronize

翼贊 **yihk jaan**
to assist and support

翹 **kìuh** (Md **qiáo, qiào**)
① long tail feathers ② to raise ③ outstanding

翹楚 **kìuh chó**
man of outstanding ability

翹首 **kìuh sáu**
to raise the head to long eagerly

翻 **fàan** (Md **fān**)
① to fly; to flutter ② to turn; to upset

翻版 **fàan báan**
a reprint of a book

翻譯 **fàan yihk**
to translate; to interpret

翻閱 **fàan yuht**
to thumb through (a book or magazine)

耀 **yiuh** (Md **yào**)
① to shine; to dazzle ② to show off

耀眼 **yiuh ngáahn**
dazzling

耀武揚威 **yiuh móuh yèuhng wài**
to show off one's strength or power

老部

老 **lóuh** (Md **lǎo**)
① old; aged ② always ③ very

老練 **lóuh lihn**
experienced; expert

老遠 **lóuh yúhn**
a very long way

老實 **lóuh saht**
honest; truthful

考 **háau** (Md **kǎo**)
① to test; to examine ② diseased father

考慮 **háau leuih**
to consider; to weigh

考題 **háau tàih**
questions and problems on examination paper

考察 **háau chaat**
to inspect; to examine

耆 **kèih** (Md **qí**)
aged; to be in one's sixties

耆老 **kèih lóuh**
aged person

耆碩 **kèih sehk**
respected old person

耄 **mouh** (Md **mào**)
in an extremely old age

耄齡 **mouh lìhng**
more than 80 or 70 years old

耄勤 **mouh kàhn**
to remain diligent in old age

者 **jé** (Md **zhě**)
① those who; he who ② a particle combining with some words to form adverbials

耋 **diht** (Md **dié**)
in one's eighties

而部

而 **yìh** (Md **ér**)
① and; also; accordingly ② and yet; but

而今 **yìh gàm**
now

而且 **yìh ché**
moreover; besides; in addition

耐 **noih** (Md **nài**)
to bear; to endure; to stand; to insist

耐不住 **noih bāt jyuh**
unable to bear

耐勞 **noih lòuh**
able to endure hard work

耐性 **noih sing**
patience

耍 **sá** (Md **shuǎ**)
to play; to sport

耍把戲 **sá bá hei**
to juggle; to play tricks

耍笑 **sá siu**
to poke fun

耑 **dyùn, jyùn** (Md **duān, zhuān**)
① an end; a tip; a point ② exclusive; concentrated

耒部

耒 **lòih** (Md **lěi**)
wooden handle of a plough

耒耜 **lòih jih**
ploughs

耔 **jí** (Md **zǐ**)
to hoe up earth around a plant

耙 **pàh** (Md **bà, pá**)
a harrow; a drag

耙子 **pàh jí**
a harrow; a drag

耕 **gàang** (Md **gēng**)
to till; to plough; to cultivate

耕種 **gàang jung**
to plough and sow

耕耘 **gàang wàhn**
to till and weed; to cultivate

耗 **houh** (Md **hào**)
to expend; to use up; to waste

耗費 **houh fai**
to expend

耗盡 **houh jeuhn**
to use up; to exhaust

耗時間 **houh sìh gaan**
to consume time

耘 **wàhn** (Md **yún**)
to weed

耘田 **wàhn tìhn**
to weed rice field

耘草 **wàhn chóu**
to remove weeds

耜 **jih** (Md **sì**)
a plough

耦 **ngáuh** (Md **ǒu**)
① to plough side by side ② a couple

耦耕 **ngáuh gàang**
to plough side by side

耦語 **ngáuh yúh**
to have a tête-à-tête

耳部

耳 **yíh** (Md **ěr**)
① ear ② only

耳目 **yíh muhk**
ears and eyes; one's attention

耳聾 **yíh lùhng**
deaf

耶 **yèh** (Md **yé, yē**)
① phrase-final particle for a question ② of Jesus (transliteration)

耶穌基督 **Yèh sōu gēi dūk**
Jesus Christ

耶路撒冷 **Yèh louh saat láahng**
Jerusalem

耽(躭) **dàam** (Md **dān**)
to indulge in; to be addicted to

耽耽 **dàam dàam**
eying greedily

耽誤 **dàam ngh**
to delay; to hinder

耽思 **dàam sì**
to think deeply

耿 **gáng** (Md **gěng**)
① bright ② incorruptible, upright

耿直 **gáng jihk**
honest; upright

耿介 **gáng gaai**
magnificent; upright

聃(聸) **dàam** (Md **dān**)
① another name of Laotse ② a deformed ear

聆 **lìhng** (Md **líng**)
to listen; to hear

聆聽 **lìhng tìng**
to listen to

聆教 **lìhng gaau**
to listen to one's instruction

聆悉 **lìhng sīk**
to learn; to hear

聊 **lìuh** (Md **liǎo**)
① somehow; somewhat ② to rely; to depend ③ to chat

聊天 **lìuh tìn**
to chat

聊賴 **lìuh laaih**
something to live for

聊勝於無 **lìuh sing yù mòuh**
at least better than nothing

聒 **kwut** (Md **guō**)
clamorous; uproarious

聒絮 **kwut seuih**
to keep talking noisly

聒耳 **kwut yíh**
offensive to the ear

聖(圣)**sing**
(Md **shèng**)
① sage ② sacred; holy

聖蹟 **sìng jīk**
relics of a sage

聖旨 **sìng jí**
imperial decree

聘 **ping** (Md **pìn**)
to employ; to engage

聘請 **ping chíng**
to invite for service

聘書 **ping syù**
formal letter of employment

聚 **jeuih** (Md **jù**)
to come or put together; to collect

聚會 **jeuih wuih**
to assemble; to gather to meet

聚積 **jeuih jīk**
to accumulate

聚餐 **jeuih chāan**
to get together for luncheon or dinner

聞 **màhn** (Md **wén**)
① to hear, to have heard ② to learn

聞名天下 **màhn mìhng tìn hah**
world-famous

聞訊 **màhn seun**
to learn of the news

聞所未聞 **màhn só meih màhn**
unheard of

聱 **ngòuh** (Md **áo**)
hard to read or understand

聯(联)**lyùhn** (Md **lián**)
① to connect, to unite ② allied (forces); mutual (guaranty)

聯接 **lyùhn jip**
to joint together, to connect

聯想 **lyùhn séung**
association of ideas

聰(聪)**chùng**
(Md **cōng**)
① clever; bright ② with a good faculty of hearing

聰敏 **chùng máhn**
clever and intelligent

聰穎 **chùng wihng**
clever and bright

聲(声)**sìng** (Md **shēng**)
① sound; voice ② language; tongue ③ reputation

聲明 **sìng mìhng**
to announce; to declare

聲樂 **sìng ngohk**
vocal music

聲譽 **sìng yuh**
reputation; fame

聳(㲎) **súng** (Md **sǒng**)
① to alarm; to warn ② to raise up

聳動 **súng duhng**
to urge; to egg on

聳然 **súng yìhn**
rising in sharp elevation

職(职) **jīk** (Md **zhí**)
① profession; post ② to govern; to direct

職責 **jīk jaak**
one's position and responsibility

職業 **jīk yihp**
profession; occupation

職員 **jīk yùhn**
staff members or employees of a company

聵 **kúi** (Md **kuì**)
① deaf ② stupid and unresponable

聶 **nihp** (Md **niè**)
① to whisper to one's ear ② a Chinese family name

聽(听) **ting** (Md **tīng**)
① to hear; to listen; to obey ② to let

聽命 **ting mihng**
to follow others

聽聞 **ting màhn**
what one has heard

聽其自然 **ting kèih jih yìhn**
to let nature take its course

聾 **lùhng** (Md **lóng**)
deaf; hard of hearing

聾子 **lùhng jí**
a deaf

聾啞 **lùhng ngá**
deaf mute

聿部

聿 **wat** (Md **yù**)
pen; writing brush

肄 **yih** (Md **yì**)
① to study; to learn ② to work hard

肄業 **yih yihp**
to learn; to study

肄習 **yih jaahp**
to practice

肆 **si** (Md **sì**)
① extremely; excessively ② to use to the utmost

肆目 **si muhk**
to stretch one's eyes as far as one can see

肆掠 **si leuhk**
to indulge in looting; robbery

肅 **sūk** (Md **sù**)
① respectful ② solemn

肅敬 **sūk ging**
respectful

肅靜 **sūk jihng**
solemn silence

肅清 **sūk chìng**
to wipe out

肇 **siuh** (Md **zhào**)
① to begin; to start ② to found

肇建 **siuh gin**
to found

肇事 **siuh sih**
to stir up trouble

肉部

肉 **yuhk** (Md **ròu**)
① flesh; physical ② meat animals; meat or pulp of fruit

肉搏 **yuhk bok**
hand-to-hand combat

肉餅 **yuhk béng**
meat cake

肉體 **yuhk tái**
　the body of blood and flesh

肋 **lahk** (Md **lèi**)
　the ribes; the side

肋膜 **lahk mók**
　the pleura

肋骨 **lahk gwāt**
　the ribs

肌 **gèi** (Md **jī**)
　the tissue; the muscles; the flesh

肌膚 **gèi fù**
　the skin and the flesh

肌肉 **gèi yuhk**
　muscles

肘 **jáu, jáau** (Md **zhǒu**)
　① the elbow ② to catch one by
　the elbow

肓 **fòng** (Md **huāng**)
　the vitals; the region between the
　heart and the diaphragm

肖 **chiu** (Md **xiào**)
　to resemble; to be like; similar

肖像 **chiu jeuhng**
　a snapshot

肖子 **chiu jí**
　a good son

肚 **tóuh** (Md **dù, dǔ**)
　the belly; the bowels

肚皮 **tóuh pèih**
　the abdomen; the belly

肛 **gòng** (Md **gāng**)
　the anus

肛門 **gòng mùhn**
　the anus

肝 **gòn** (Md **gān**)
　the liver

肝病 **gòn bihng**
　a liver ailment

肝膽 **gòn dáam**
　intimate; courage

股 **gú** (Md **gǔ**)
　① the thigh ② a section ③ a
　share; stocks

股票 **gú piu**
　stocks

股東 **gú dùng**
　shareholder

肢 **jì** (Md **zhī**)
　① limbs of a person ② legs of
　animals ③ wings of birds

肢體 **jì tái**
　the body

肢骨 **jì gwāt**
　bones of one's limbs

肢解 **jì gáai**
　to dismember

肥 **fèih** (Md **féi**)
　① fat; plump ② plenty ③ fertile

肥胖 **fèih buhn**
　fat

肥沃 **fèih yūk**
　fertile (land)

肥皂 **fèih jouh**
　soap

肩 **gìn** (Md **jiān**)
　① shoulder; to shoulder ② to
　employ

肩膀 **gìn bóng**
　the shoulder

肩負重任 **gìn fuh juhng
yahm**
　to shoulder heavy responsi-
　bility

肪 **fòng** (Md **fáng**)
　fat

肫 **jèun** (Md **zhūn**)
　① sincerely; earnest ② gizzard of
　a fowl

肯 **háng** (Md **kěn**)
　to be willing; to approve

肯定 **háng dihng**
affirmative positive

肯幹 **háng gon**
willing to put in hard work

育 **yuhk** (Md **yù**)
① to beget; to produce; to give birth to ② to raise (children) ③ to educate

育苗 **yuhk mìuh**
to cultivate seedlings

育才 **yuhk chòih**
to cultivate talents

肴(餚) **ngàauh**
(Md **yáo**)
cooked food; especially meat and fish

肺 **fai** (Md **fèi**)
the lung

肺癆 **fai lòuh**
tuberculosis

肺炎 **fai yìhm**
pneumonia

胃 **waih** (Md **wèi**)
the stomach; gizzard (of birds)

胃病 **waih bihng**
a stomach ailment

胃疼 **waih tung**
stomach pain

胄 **jauh** (Md **zhòu**)
① a helmet; a head — gear ② descendants

背 **bui** (Md **bèi**)
① the back; behind ② the reverse side ③ to go against; to rebel ④ to bear

背叛 **bui buhn**
to rebel; to betray

背負 **bui fuh**
to carry on the back

背誦 **bui juhng**
to recite

胎 **tòi** (Md **tāi**)
a fetus; an embryo

胎生 **tòi sàng**
viviparous

胎兒 **tòi yìh**
an unborn baby; a fetus

胖 **buhn** (Md **pàng**)
obese; fat

胖腫 **buhn júng**
general swelling over the body

胖子 **buhn jí**
a fat person

胛 **gaap** (Md **jiǎ**)
the shoulder; the shoulder blades

胚 **pùi** (Md **pēi**)
① a fetus; three months of pregnancy ② tender sprouts of plants

胚胎 **pùi tòi**
to originate form

胚珠 **pùi jyù**
an ovule

胚芽 **pùi ngàh**
a sprout

胝 **dài** (Md **zhī**)
calluses on hands or feet

胞 **bàau** (Md **bāo**)
① the placenta ② children of the same parents

胞子 **bàau jí**
spores (in botany)

胞兄弟 **bàau hìng daih**
brothers by the same parents

胡 **wùh** (Md **hú**)
① reckless; wildly; stupid ② a Chinese family name

胡蝶 **wùh dihp**
butterfly

胡塗 **wùh tòuh**
confused; stupid

胡說 **wùh syut**
wild talk; to talk nonsense

胤 **yahn** (Md **yìn**)
long successions of descendants;
posterity

胤嗣 **yahn jih**
descendants

胥 **sèui** (Md **xū**)
① mutually, together ② to wait
for ③ to assist, to serve in an
advisory role ④ to keep away
from

胭 **yìn** (Md **yān**)
cosmetics; especially referring to
rouge and face powder

胭脂 **yìn jì**
rouge

胭脂虎 **yìn jì fú**
a shrew; a virago

胯 **kwa** (Md **kuà**)
space between the legs

胰 **yìh** (Md **yí**)
the pencreas

胱 **gwòng** (Md **guāng**)
the bladder

胺 **ngòn** (Md **òn**)
NH₃ (in chemistry)

脆 **cheui** (Md **cuì**)
① brittle; hard but easily
breakable ② crisp

脆薄 **cheui bohk**
thin and brittle

脆弱 **cheui yeuhk**
weak; delicate

胴 **duhng** (Md **dōng**)
① the large intestine ② the body;
the trunk

胴體 **duhng tái**
the body; the trunk

胸 **hùng** (Md **xiōng**)
① the chest, the breast ② one's
ambition ③ the mind, as
narrow-minded

胸腹 **hùng fūk**
the chest and belly

胸襟 **hùng kàm**
ambition; mind

能 **nàhng** (Md **néng**)
① can; to be able to ② energy

能力 **nàhng lihk**
energy; power

能量 **nàhng leuhng**
energy (in physics)

能幹 **nàhng gon**
capable; able

脂 **jì** (Md **zhī**)
① the fat of animals ② the gum
or sap of trees ③ cosmetics

脂粉 **jì fán**
rouge and face-powder

脂肪 **jì fòng**
fat of animals or plants

脅(胁、脋) **hip**
(Md **xié**)
① the sides of the trunk from
armpits ② to threaten — with
force

脅迫 **hip bīk**
to threat with force

脅制 **hip jai**
to control with threat of force

脈(脉、𧚄、眿) **mahk**
(Md **mài, mò**)
① the blood vessels, the veins or
arteries ② the pulse ③ mountain
range

脈搏 **mahk bok**
pulse; pulsation

脈岩 **mahk ngàahm**
vein rock

脊 **jek** (Md **jǐ, jí**)
① the spine; the spinal column
② the ridge

脊柱 **jek chyúh**
the vertebra column

脊髓 **jek séuih**
the spinal cord

胳 **gaak** (Md **gē**)
the arms, the armpits

胱 **tiu** (Md **tiǎo**)
sacrificial rites

脫 **tyut** (Md **tuō**)
① to strip; to undress ② to cast off; to escape

脫皮 **tyut pèih**
to cast off the skin

脫離 **tyut lèih**
to break away

脫罪 **tyut jeuih**
to exonerate someone from a charge

脘 **gún** (Md **wǎn**)
the inside of stomach — the gastric cavity

脛(胫) **hìng** (Md **jìng**)
the calf; the part of leg between the knee

脛骨 **hìng gwāt**
the shinebone; the tibia

脖 **buht** (Md **bó**)
the neck

脖領兒 **buht léhng yìh**
the neck or collar of a garment

脖子 **buht jí**
the neck

脩 **sàu** (Md **xiū**)
① to do; to act; restore ② dried meat

脩脯 **sàu fú**
dried meat

脯 **fú, póu** (Md **fú, pú**)
① dried and seasoned meat ② preserved fruits

脹 **jeung** (Md **zhàng**)
① full stomached ② swelling of skin ③ to expand

脹滿 **jeung múhn**
full; inflated

脹率 **jeung léut**
the rate of expansion

脾 **pèih** (Md **pí**)
① the spleen ② temper

脾氣 **pèih hei**
temper or disposition

脾臟 **pèih johng**
the spleen

腆 **tín** (Md **tiǎn**)
① prosperous ② good, virtuous ③ protruding ④ bashful

腆贈 **tín jahng**
rich gifts

腆默 **tín mahk**
to blash and keep silence

腊 **sīk** (Md **xī**)
① dried meat ② very; extremely

腋 **yaht, yihk** (Md **yē**)
the armpits; the part under the forelegs of animals

腋下 **yihk hah**
armpits

腋臭 **yihk chau**
odor emanating from the armpits

腌 **yìm** (Md **yān, ā**)
① to salt; to pickle ② unclean; dirty

腌臢 **yìm jìm**
unclean; dirty

胼 **pìhn** (Md **pián**)
calluses

胼胝 **pìhn dài; pìhn jì**
calluses on the hands and feet

腎 **sahn** (Md **shèn**)
the kidneys; the testicles

腎臟 **sahn johng**
the kidneys

腎結石 **sahn git sehk**
renal culculus

腑 **fú** (Md **fǔ**)
the bowels; the entrails

腑臟 **fú johng**
the bowels; the entrails

腔 **hòng** (Md **qiāng**)
① the cavity ② a tune

腔調 **hòng diuh**
a tune; melody of a tune

腔兒 **hòng yìh**
a cavity in any vessel

腕 **wún** (Md **wàn**)
the wrist

腕力 **wún lihk**
the strength of wrist

腕骨 **wún gwāt**
the wrist bones

腐 **fuh** (Md **fǔ**)
① to decay; rotten ② corrupt;
evil ③ bean-curd

腐敗 **fuh baaih**
corrupt and rotten

腐蝕 **fuh sihk**
to erode; erosion

腐乳 **fuh yúh**
bean cheese

腥 **sìng** (Md **xīng**)
① raw meat ② offensive smell,
especially of fish or blood

腥穢 **sìng wai**
smelly and dirty

腥臭 **sìng chau**
offensive smell of fish, meat,
blood

腮 **sòi** (Md **sāi**)
the cheeks

腦 **nóuh** (Md **nǎo**)
the brain

腦海 **nóuh hói**
the mind; memory

腦膜炎 **nóuh mohk yìhm**
meningitis

腴 **yùh** (Md **yú**)
① plump and soft ② fertile ③
intestines of dogs and hogs

腩 **náahm** (Md **nǎn**)
tender beef

腫 **júng** (Md **zhōng**)
to swell; a swelling; a boil

腫脹 **júng jeung**
to swell; a swelling

腫毒 **júng duhk**
a tumor; a swelling

腰 **yìu** (Md **yāo**)
① the midriff, the waist ② the
kidneys ③ the middle of
something

腰帶 **yìu daai**
a girdle; a waist band

腰骨 **yìu gwāt**
the five lowest pieces of bone
of the spinal column

腱 **gin** (Md **jiàn**)
tendon

腱子 **gin jí**
tendon (of meat animals)

腳（脚）**geuk** (Md **jiǎo**)
① the feet ② the leg or base of
something

腳步 **geuk bouh**
steps; footfalls

腳跡 **geuk jīk**
footprints

腳踏車 **geuk daahp chè**
a bicycle

腸 **chèuhng** (Md **cháng**)
the intestines; the bowels

腸斷 **chèuhng dyuhn**
heart-broken; deeply grieved

腸胃病 **chèuhng waih behng**
disease of stomach and bowels

腹 **fūk** (Md **fū**)
① the belly; under the chest ②
the front part

腹部 **fūk bouh**
the abdominal region; the belly

腹瀉 **fūk se**
diarrhea

腹稿 **fūk góu**
a manuscript in the mind

腺 **sin** (Md **xiàn**)
a gland

腼(靦) **míhn** (Md **miǎn**)
① shy, bashful ② quiet and
graceful

腼腆 **míhn tín**
bashful; shy

腭 **ngohk** (Md **è**)
the roof of the mouth; the palate

腿 **téui** (Md **tuǐ**)
the legs and the thighs

膀 **bóng, pòhng**
(Md **bǎng, páng**)
① the bladder ② to make passes
at

膀胱 **pòhng gwòng**
the bladder

膂 **léuih** (Md **lǚ**)
the spinal column; the backbone

膂力 **léuih lihk**
one's physical strength

膈 **gaak** (Md **gé**)
the diaphragm

膊 **bok** (Md **bó**)
the shoulder, the upper arms

膏 **gòu** (Md **gāo, gào**)
① fat; grease ② ointment; oil ③
fertile; riches ④ to lubricate; to
make smooth

膏壤 **gòu yeuhng**
fertile land

膏油 **gòu yàuh**
grease; to add lubricating oil

膛 **tòhng** (Md **táng**)
① the breast; the chest ② a
cavity

膚 **fù** (Md **fū**)
① the skin; the surface ②
shallow; superficial

膚淺 **fù chín**
shallow; superficial; skin-deep

膚色 **fù sīk**
color of a skin

膜 **mohk** (Md **mó**)
① any thin membrane that pro-
tects internal organs or tissues
in the human body ② to kneel
and worship

膜拜 **mohk baai**
to kneel and worship

膝 **sāt** (Md **xī**)
the knee

膝蓋骨 **sāt koi gwāt**
the kneecap

膝下 **sāt hah**
a respectful address for one's
parents in letters

膠 **gàau** (Md **jiāo**)
① glue; gum ② anything sticky;

to stick on

膠布 **gàau bou**
rubber cloth; plastic cloth

膠水 **gàau séui**
glue

膳（饍）**sihn** (Md **shàn**)
meals; food; provisions

膳費 **sihn fai**
charge for board

膳宿 **sihn sūk**
food and lodging

膨 **pàahng** (Md **péng**)
to expand; to swell

膨脹 **pàahng jeung**
expansion; swelling

膩 **neih** (Md **nì**)
① fatty or greasy (food) ②
smooth ③ bored; tired

膩煩 **neih fàahn**
tired; fed up

膩胃 **neih waih**
(greasy food) to kill one's
appetite

膰 **fàahn** (Md **fán**)
cooked meat for sacrifice or
offering

膺 **yìng** (Md **yīng**)
① the breast of a person ② to
receive; to be given

膺選 **yìng syún**
to be elected

膺任 **yìng yahm**
to be appointed to

膾 **kwúi** (Md **kuài**)
minced meat

膾炙 **kwúi jik, kwúi jek**
minced and roasted — very
tasty

膿 **nùhng** (Md **nóng**)
pus or purulent matter

膿血 **nùhng hyut**
pus and blood

膿瘡 **nùhng chōng**
a boil; an abscess

臀 **tyùhn** (Md **tún**)
the buttocks; the bottom; the
rump

臀部 **tyùhn bouh**
the buttocks; the rump

臂 **bei** (Md **bì, bei**)
the arms (of human being)

臂膀 **bei bóng**
the upper arm

臂助 **bei joh**
a helping hand; help

臆 **yīk** (Md **yì**)
① one's breast; heart; thoughts
② one's personal views or
feelings

臆度 **yīk dohk**
to guess or conjecture

臆斷 **yīk dyun**
to draw conclusion from
conjecture

臊 **sòu, sou** (Md **sāo, sào**)
① ashamed; bashful ② minced
meat

臊得慌 **sòu dāk fòng**
very ashamed

膽 **dáam** (Md **dǎn**)
① the gall ② courage; bravery

膽怯 **dáam hip**
frightened; afraid

膽色 **dáam sīk**
courage and wisdom

膽大心細 **dáam daaih sàm
sai**
brave but cautious

臉 **líhm** (Md **liǎn**)
the face; the cheek

臉色 **líhm sīk**
facial expression

臉紅 **líhm hùhng**
blushing because of embarrass

臉上無光 **líhm seuhng mòuh gwòng**
to lose face

臃 **yúng** (Md **yōng**)
① to swell; a swelling ② fat and clumsy

臃腫 **yúng júng**
fat and clumsy

腋 **gú** (Md **gǔ**)
to expand; to swell

腋脹 **gú jeung**
to expand, expansion; to swell

臍 **chìh** (Md **qí**)
① the navel; the umbilicus ② the under side of a crab

臍帶 **chìh daai**
the umbilical cord

臘 **laahp** (Md **là**)
① the end of the lunar year ② salted and smoked meat, fish, chicken . . . etc.

臘月 **laahp yuht**
the 12th month of the lunar year

臘腸 **laahp chéung**
Chinese sausage made by stuffing salted meat, liver, etc.

臚 **lòuh** (Md **lú**)
① to display; to exhibit ② to forward; to convey

臚列 **lòuh liht**
to display; to arrange in order to exhibit

臚歡 **lòuh fùn**
to express one's joy

臟 **johng** (Md **zàng**)
a general name of all the internal

organs in human being

臢 **jìm** (Md **za**)
dirty; filthy

臠 **lyúhn** (Md **luán**)
① meat chops or cuts ② lean; thin

臣部

臣 **sàhn** (Md **chěn**)
① subjects; to subjugate ② a polite term for "I" (in ancient China)

臣僕 **sàhn buhk**
officials (who serve the king or nation) and servants (who serve the household)

臣服 **sàhn fuhk**
to be subjugated or conquered

卧 (臥) **ngoh** (Md **wò**)
to lie down; to rest

卧病 **ngoh bihng**
bed-ridden on account of illness

卧房 **ngoh fòhng**
bedroom

臧 **jòng** (Md **zāng**)
① good; right; generous ② a slave

臧否 **jòng péi**
yes or no?

臧獲 **jòng wohk**
slaves

臨 (临) **làhm** (Md **lín**)
① to look down from above ② to approach; to descend ③ on the point of; near to ④ to copy; to imitate

臨別 **làhm biht**
at the time of parting

臨帖 **làhm tip**
to copy or imitate calligraphy

臨時 **làhm sìh**
temporary

自部

自 **jih** (Md **zì**)
① self; personal ② from ③ nature

自給自足 **jih kāp jih jūk**
self-sufficient; self-supporting

自然界 **jih yìhn gaai**
the natural world — of animals and plants

自尊 **jih jyùn**
self respect

臬 **yiht** (Md **niè**)
① a rule; a law ② a door-post

臬司 **yiht sì**
the provincial judge in old China

臭 **chau** (Md **chòu, xiù**)
① stinking; offensive-smelling ② very; much; soundly

臭罵 **chau mah**
a stern scolding; to scold soundly

臭名 **chau mìhng**
a notorious reputation

至部

至 **ji** (Md **zhì**)
① to arrive at ② very; extremely; to indicate a superlative degree ③ greatest; best

至親 **ji chàn**
the closest relative

至意 **ji yi**
the best and sincerest intention

至理名言 **ji léih mìhng yìhn**
a proverb of lasting value

致 **ji** (Md **zhì**)
① to send; to present ② to cause to come

致命 **ji mihng**
to sacrifice one's life

致敬 **ji ging**
to pay respect

致辭 **ji chìh**
to deliver a speech

臻 **jèun** (Md **zhēn**)
① the utmost; the best ② to arrive at; to reach

臼部

臼 **kau, káuh** (Md **jiù**)
① a mortar for unhusking rice ② a socket at a bone joint

臼齒 **kau chí**
the morlars (teeth)

臾 **yùh** (Md **yú**)
① a moment; an instant; a little while ② a Chinese family name

舀 **yíuh** (Md **yǎo**)
to ladle out (water)

舁 **yùh** (Md **yú**)
to lift; to raise; to carry

舂 **jùng** (Md **chōng**)
to pound (grain) in order to remove the husk

舂米 **jùng máih**
to pound rice to remove the husk

舅 **káuh** (Md **jiù**)
① maternal uncle (mother's brother) ② brother-in-law (wife's brother)

舅父 **káuh fuh**
mother's brother

舅媽(母) **káuh mā (móuh)**
mother's brother's wife

與 yúh, yuh, yùh (Md yǔ, yù, yú)

① and; with; together with ② to give; to impart ③ to take part in ④ interrogative particle

與眾不同 **yúh jung bāt tùhng**
different from other people

與聞 **yuh màhn**
to participate in the affair

興 hìng, hing (Md xīng, xìng)

① to raise; to propose ② to happen; to start ③ cheerful; happy

興辦 **hìng baahn**
to establish; to found

興衰 **hìng sèui**
rise and fall

興趣 **hìng cheui**
interest; enjoyability

舉 géui (Md jǔ)

① to lift; to raise ② to recommend; to commend ③ manner

舉辦 **géui baahn**
to sponsor; organize

舉薦 **géui jin**
to recommend (a person)

舉止 **géui jí**
deportment; conduct; manner

舊(旧) gauh (Md jiù)

old; ancient; antique; former; past

舊地重遊 **gauh deih chùhng yàuh**
to revisit a place

舊曆 **gauh lihk**
the lunar calendar

舊式 **gauh sīk**
old-style; old-fashioned

舌部

舌 siht (Md shé)

the tongue

舌尖 **siht jìm**
tip of the tongue

舌戰 **siht jin**
verbal confrontation

舍 se, sé (Md shè, shě)

① a house; an inn ② to throw away

舍監 **se gāam**
dormitory super-intendent

舍親 **se chàn**
my relatives

舐 sáai (Md shì)

to lick

舐犢情深 **sáai duhk chìhng sàm**
very affectionate toward one's children

舒 syù (Md shū)

① to unfold; to stretch ② slow; leisurely

舒服 **syù fuhk**
comfortable

舒展 **syù jín**
to unfold; to stretch

舒暢 **syù cheung**
pleasant; comfortable

舔 tím (Md tiǎn)

to lick; to taste

舔乾淨 **tím gòn jihng**
to lick clean

舔一舔 **tím yāt tím**
to taste by licking

舖 pou (Md pù)

a shop; a store

舛部

舛 **chyún** (Md **chuǎn**)
① disorderly; messy; confused; mixed up ② to disobey; to oppose

舛逆 **chyún yihk**
contrary to reason

舛雜 **chyún jaahp**
all mixed up

舛誤 **chyún ngh**
mistake; error

舜 **seun** (Md **shùn**)
① Shun, a legendary ruler said to have ruled around 2200 B.C. ② hibiscus

舜江 **Seun gòng**
name of a river in Chekiang

舞 **móuh** (Md **wǔ**)
① to dance; to prance ② to brandish; to wave ③ to stir up

舞蹈 **móuh douh**
dancing

舞弄 **móuh luhng**
to brandish

舟部

舟 **jàu** (Md **zhōu**)
boat; ship; vessel

舟車勞頓 **jàu gèui lòuh deuhn**
exhausted from a long travel

舢 **sàan** (Md **shān**)
a sampan

舢板 (舨) **sàan báan**
a sampan

航 **hòhng** (Md **háng**)
① ship; boat; vessel ② to navigate

航行 **hòhng hàhng**
to sail; to fly

航程 **hòhng chìhng**
distance of an air or sea trip

航運 **hòhng wahn**
shipping

舨 **báan** (Md **bǎn**)
a sampan

舫 **fóng** (Md **fǎng**)
① two boats lashed side by side ② boats; ships

般 **bùn** (Md **bān**)
intelligence (in Buddism)

般若 **bùn yeuhk**
wisdom (in Buddhism)

舳 **juhk** (Md **zhǔ**)
stern (of a ship)

舳艫 **juhk lòuh**
rectangular boat

舵 **tòh** (Md **duò**)
rudder, helm

舵手 **tòh sáu**
helmsman, steersman

舶 **bohk, baak** (Md **bó**)
ocean going ship

舶來品 **baak lòih bán**
imported goods

舷 **yìhn** (Md **xián**)
bulwarks (or a ship); gunwale

船 (舩、舡) **syùhn** (Md **chuán**)
ship; boat; vessel

船票 **syùhn piu**
ticket for passenger by sea

船家 **syùhn gā**
boat man

船長 **syùhn jéung**
captain or skipper (of a boat)

艇 **tíhng, téhng**
(Md **tǐng**)
long, narrow boat

艄 **sàau** (Md **shāo**)
stern (of a boat)

艄公 **sàau gùng**
boatman

艘 **sáu, sàu** (Md **sōu**)
a numerary adjunct for ships

艙 **chòng** (Md **cāng**)
hold or cabin (of a ship)

艙房 **chòng fòhng**
cabins (of a ship)

艙底 **chòng dái**
bottom of a ship's hold

艟 **tùhng** (Md **chōng**)
ancient warship

艦 **laahm** (Md **jiàn**)
a warship; naval vessel

艦隊 **laahm déui**
a fleet; a naval task force

艦隻 **laahm jek**
naval vessels

艨 **mùhng** (Md **méng**)
ancient warship

艫 **lòuh** (Md **lú**)
bow or prow (of a boat)

艮部

艮 **gan** (Md **gèn, gěn**)
① one of the Eight Diagrams for divination ② tough; resilient ③ straightforward

良 **lèuhng** (Md **liáng**)
good; fine; desirable

良伴 **lèuhng buhn**
good companion

良心 **lèuhng sàm**
conscience

良師 **lèuhng sì**
good teacher

艱 (艰) **gàan** (Md **jiān**)
① difficult; hard laborious ② mourning for one's parents

艱苦 **gàan fú**
trying; hard

艱險 **gàan hím**
difficult and dangerous

色部

色 **sìk** (Md **sè, shǎi**)
① colour; tinge ② facial expression

色盲 **sìk màahng**
colour blindness

色彩 **sìk chói**
colour; tinge

色膽包天 **sìk dáam bàau tìn**
extremely daring in lewdness

艸部

艾 **ngaaih** (Md **ài, yì**)
① moxa ② fine; fair; beautiful good

艾酒 **ngaaih jáu**
moxa wine

艾艾 **ngaaih ngaaih**
stammering

芊 **chìn** (Md **qiān**)
① lush (of glass) ② a Chinese family name

芋 **wuh** (Md **yù**)
taro

芋頭 **wuh tàuh**
taro

芍 **cheuk, jeuk**
(Md **sháo**)
paeonia

芍藥 **cheuk yeuhk**
paeonia

芎 **gùng** (Md **xiōng**)
a kind of herb

芒 **mòhng mòng**
(Md **máng, wáng**)
① Miscanthus sinensis ② sharp
point

芒芒 **mòhng mòhng**
tired; weary

芒果 **mòng gwó**
mango

芝 **jì** (Md **zhī**)
① a kind of purplish fungus
symbolizing nobility ② a kind of
fragrant herb

芝麻 **jì màh**
sesame

芙 **fùh** (Md **fú**)
hibiscus

芙蓉 **fùh yùhng**
hibiscus

芟 **sàam, sàan**
(Md **shān**)
① to mow; to cut down ② to
eliminate

芟除 **sàam chèuih**
to weed out

芟夷 **sàam yìh**
to exterminate

芡 **him** (Md **qiàn**)
chicken-head

芡粉 **him fán**
a kind of starch

芡實 **him saht**
chicken-head

芥 **gaai** (Md **jiè, gài**)
① mustard plant ② tiny

芥菜 **gaai choi**
mustard plant

芥末 **gaai muht**
ground mustard

芩 **kàhm** (Md **qín**)
a kind of herb whose root is
medicinal

芫 **yùhn** (Md **yuán, yán**)
a kind of poisonous plant

芬 **fàn** (Md **fēn**)
fragrance; aroma; sweet smell

芬芳 **fàn fòng**
fragrant; aromatic

芬郁 **fàn yūk**
intense fragrance

芭 **bà** (Md **bā**)
① a fragrant plant ② palmetto
banana

芭蕾舞 **bà lèuih móuh**
ballet

芭蕉 **bà jìu**
plantain

芯 **sàm** (Md **xīn, xìn**)
pith of rushes

芰 **geih** (Md **jì**)
water caltop

芰實 **geih saht**
water caltop

花 **fà** (Md **huā**)
① flower; blossom ② vari-
coloured ③ to spend

花朵 **fà déu**
flowers

花花綠綠 **fà fà luhk luhk**
varicoloured

花錢 **fà chìhn**
to spend money

芳 **fòng** (Md **fāng**)
① sweet smell; fragrant ② honourable; respectable

芳名 **fòng mìhng**
your name

芳香 **fòng hèung**
fragrance; aroma

芳齡 **fòng lìhng**
age (of a young lady)

芷 **jí** (Md **zhǐ**)
angelica

芷若 **jí yeuhk**
angelica

芸 **wàhn** (Md **yún**)
a strong-scented herb

芸香 **wàhn hèung**
a strong-scented herb

芸窗 **wàhn chèung**
a study

芸芸 **wàhn wàhn**
many; numerous

芽 **ngàh** (Md **yá**)
sprout; shoot

芽胞 **ngàh bàau**
spores

芽茶 **ngàh chàh**
bud tea

芹 **kàhn** (Md **qín**)
celery

芹菜 **kàhn choi**
celery

芹獻 **kàhn hin**
a humble gift

芻 (刍) **chò** (Md **chú**)
① to cut grass; to mow ② hay; fodder

芻牧 **chò muhk**
to pasture or graze livestock

芻議 **chò yíh**
my humble view or opinion

苬 **fai, fàt** (Md **fèi, fú**)
small; little; lush; luxuriant

苞 **bàau** (Md **bāo**)
① a variety of rush ② to wrap

苞葉 **bàau yihp**
bract

苞筍 **bàau séun**
tender bamboo shoot in winter

苡 **yíh** (Md **yǐ**)
a kind of plant whose grains are used as food or medicine

苣 **geuih** (Md **qǔ, jù**)
lettuce

苑 **yún** (Md **yuàn**)
a Chinese family name

苓 **lìhng** (Md **líng**)
① a variety of fungus ② tuckahoe

苔 **tòih, tòi** (Md **tái, tāi**)
① moss; lichen ② fur (on the tongue)

苔癬 **tòih sín**
lichen (skin disease)

苔蘚 **tòih sín**
moss and lichen

苕 **tìuh** (Md **tiáo, sháo**)
a plant much used in making brooms

苕帚 **tìuh jáu, tìuh jáau**
a broom

苗 **mìuh** (Md **miáo**)
① sprout ② descendants

苗兒 **mìuh yìh**
sprout; shoot

苗頭 **mìuh tàuh**
first sign of success

苛 **hò** (Md **kē**)
harsh; severe; rigorous; caustic

苛刻 **hò hāak**
harsh; pitiless; merciless

苛求 **hò kàuh**
to be very exacting

苜 **muhk** (Md **mù**)
clover

苜蓿 **muhk sūk**
clover

苟 **gáu** (Md **gǒu**)
① against principle ② careless

苟且 **gáu ché**
against principle

苟言 **gáu yìhn**
careless speech; rash remark

若 **yeuhk** (Md **ruò**)
① if; suppose ② similar to

若不然 **yeuhk bāt yìhn**
if not; otherwise

若干 **yeuhk gòn**
some; a few; several

若果 **yeuhk gwó**
if; provided that

苦 **fú** (Md **kǔ**)
① bitter ② painful; hard ③ earnest; diligent

苦悶 **fú muhn**
bored; low-spirited

苦楚 **fú chó**
pain; suffering

苦衷 **fú chùng**
a reason for doing something not easily understand by others

苧(苎) **chyúh** (Md **zhù**)
ramie; China grass

苧麻 **chyúh màh**
ramie

苯 **bún** (Md **běn**)
benzene

苯胺 **bún ngòn**
aniline

苒 **yíhm** (Md **rǎn**)
lush, delicate

苒苒 **yíhm yíhm**
lush, delicate

苒弱 **yíhm yeuhk**
drooping

英 **yìng** (Md **yīng**)
① flower; leaf ② surpassing; outstanding ③ fine; handsome

英明 **yìng mìhng**
intelligent; wise

英雄 **yìng hùhng**
a hero; a great man

英勇 **yìng yúhng**
brave; heroic

苴 **jèui** (Md **jū**)
① parcel; package ② female plant of the common hemp

苴布 **jèui bou**
sackcloth

苴麻 **jèui màh**
female plant of the common hemp

苻 **fùh** (Md **fú**)
a kind of herb

茁 **jyut** (Md **zhuó**)
① sprouting growing ② vigorous; strong

茁壯 **jyut jong**
vigorous; strong

茁芽 **jyut ngàh**
to sprout

茂 **mauh** (Md **mào**)
① lush; vigorous; strong ② fine; fair

茂密 **mauh maht**
growing densely

茂盛 **mauh sihng**
lush; flourishing

茂才 **mauh chòih**
talented person

范 **faahn** (Md **fàn**)
① the bee ② a Chinese family name

茄 **kèh, gà** (Md **qié, jiā**)
eggplant

茄袋 **kèh doih**
an eggplant-shaped-like

茄子 **kèh jí**
eggplant

茅(茆) **màauh** (Md **máo**)
① couch grass ② a Chinese family name

茅舍 **màauh se**
straw hut; my humble cottage

茅草 **màauh chóu**
straw; thatch

茉 **muht** (Md **mò**)
white jasmine

茉莉 **muht leih**
white jasmine

茶 **chàh** (Md **chá**)
tea

茶博士 **chàh bok sih**
tearoom keeper

茶點 **chàh dím**
refreshment

茶座 **chàh joh**
seats in a tea house

茲 **jì, chìh** (Md **zī, cí**)
① this ② now; here

茲定 **jì dihng**
It is hereby decided

茲因 **jì yàn**
now because

茗 **míhng** (Md **míng**)
tea; tea plant

茗圃 **míhng póu**
tea plantation

茗具 **míhng geuih**
tea set

荔 **laih** (Md **lì**)
lichee

荔枝 **laih jì**
lichee

茜 **sihn, sài** (Md **qiàn, xī**)
madder

茜草 **sihn chóu**
madder

茜素 **sihn sou**
alizarin

茨 **chìh** (Md **cí**)
① to thatch ② a kind of thorny plant

茨菰 **chìh gù**
arrowhead

茫 **mòhng** (Md **máng**)
① vast; boundless ② uncertain

茫茫 **mòhng mòhng**
vast; boundless

茫然不知 **mòhng yìhn bāt jì**
helplessly ignorant; completely in the dark

茯 **fuhk** (Md **fú**)
tuckahoe

茯苓 **fuhk lìhng**
tuckahoe

茱 **jyù** (Md **zhū**)
dogwood

茱萸 **jyù yùh**
dogwood

茵 **yàn** (Md **yīn**)
a cushion; a mat

茵褥 **yàn yuhk**
a mat; a cushion

茸 **yùhng** (Md **róng**)
① soft; fine hair ② untidy; messy

茸茸 **yùhng yùhng**
luxuriant; lush

茹 **yùh** (Md **rú**)
① entangled roots ② to eat; to taste

茹筆 **yùh bāt**
to make writing brushes

茹苦含辛 **yùh fú hàhm sàn**
to undergo all hardships

荀 **sèun** (Md **xún**)
① a kind of herb ② a Chinese family name

荃 **chyùhn** (Md **quán**)
① fragrant herb ② fine cloth

荇 **hahng** (Md **xìng**)
a kind of vegetables

荇菜 **hahng choi**
a kind of vegetables

荏 **yáhm** (Md **rěn**)
soft; weak; fragile

荏弱 **yáhm yeuhk**
soft; weak; fragile

草（艸） **chóu** (Md **cǎo**)
① grass; straw; herb ② draft (of writing) ③ coarse; crude

草皮 **chóu pèih**
young grass cover

草稿 **chóu góu**
a rough draft

草率 **chóu sēut**
careless; perfunctory

荒 **fòng** (Md **huāng**)
① uncultivated; wild ② ridiculous ③ to neglect

荒僻 **fòng pīk**
desolate and remote

荒謬 **fòng mauh**
grossly, absurd

荒廢 **fòng fai**
to neglect; to leave completely unattended to

荷 **hòh, hoh** (Md **hé, hè**)
① lotus; water lily ② load; burden

荷花 **hòh fā**
lotus flower

荷負 **hoh fuh**
to carry; to bear

荸 **buht** (Md **bí**)
water chestnut

荸薺 **buht chàih**
water chestnut

荻 **dihk** (Md **dí**)
a kind of reed

荻花 **dihk fā**
reed flower

荼 **tòuh** (Md **tú**)
① a kind of bitter-tasting vegetables ② to harm; to poison

荼毒 **tòuh duhk**
harm; poison to cause injury

荼炭 **tòuh taan**
suffering of common people

莉 **leih** (Md **lì**)
white jasmine

莊（庄） **jòng** (Md **zhuāng**)
① solemn; dignified ② large farm house ③ village

莊稼 **jòng ga**
farming; crops

莊重 **jòng juhng**
dignified; solemn

莊戶 **jòng wuh**
farmer

莎 **sò, sà** (Md **suō, shā**)
a kind of insect

荽 **sèui** (Md **suī**)
parsley

莓 **mùih** (Md **méi**)
① berries ② moss; lichen

莖 **gìng, hàng** (Md **jìng**)
stalk; stem

莘 **sàn** (Md **shēn, xīn**)
① long ② numerous ③ a kind of plant

莘莘學子 **sàn sàn hohk jí**
students in large numbers

莞 **gùn, wúhn, gún**
(Md **guān, wǎn, guǎn**)
① a kind of herb ② smiling ③ a county in Kwangtung

莞爾 **wúhn yíh**
smiling

東莞 **Dùng gún**
a county in Kwangtung

莠 **yáuh** (Md **yǒu**)
① foxtail (a kind of weed) ② bad; ugly; undesirable

莠民 **yáuh màhn**
wicked people

莠言 **yáuh yìhn**
dirty words

莢 **gaap** (Md **jiá**)
pad

莢果 **gaap gwó**
pad (in botany)

莢錢 **gaap chìhn**
small light coin

莧 **yihn** (Md **xiàn**)
amaranth

莧菜 **yihn choi**
amaranth

莩 **fù, píuh** (Md **fú, piǎo**)
① membrane in stems of rushes or reeds ② carpse of a person who was starved to death

莫 **mohk** (Md **mò**)
① not ② a Chinese family name

莫非 **mohk fèi**
certainly; surely

莫怪 **mohk gwaai**
no wonder that . . .

莫逆之交 **mohk yihk jì gàau**
close friendship

菅 **gàan** (Md **jiān**)
a coarse grass (used for making brushes; brooms)

菁 **chìng, jìng** (Md **jīng**)
① the flower of the leek ② the rape turnip

菁華 **jìng wah**
essence

菁菁 **chìng chìng**
lush or rich growth (of vegetables)

菇 **gù** (Md **gū**)
mushrooms; fungus

莽 **móhng** (Md **mǎng**)
① bushy; weedy ② uncultivated; rude; impolite

莽夫 **móhng fù**
rude fellow

莽撞 **móhng johng**
rude; rough; uncultured

荊 **gìng** (Md **jīng**)
① a thorn; a kind of bramble ② cane for punishment used in ancient china ③ my wife

荊玉 **gìng yuhk**
unpolished jade

荊婦 **gìng fúh**
my wife

荊柴 **gìng chàaih**
a poor family

菊 **gūk** (Md **jú**)
chrysanthemum

菊花 **gūk fā**
　flower of the chrysanthemum

菊花茶 **gūk fā chàh**
　infusion made from dried chrysanthemum

菌 **kwán** (Md **jùn, jūn**)
① fungi; mushrooms ② bacteria

菌柄 **kwán bing**
　mushroom stalk

菌類 **kwán leuih**
　fungi

菑 **jì** (Md **zī**)
① land under cultivation for one year ② to weed grass

菓 **gwó** (Md **guǒ**)
fruits and nuts

菖 **chèung** (Md **chāng**)
sweet flag; calamus

菖蒲 **chèung pòuh**
　sweet flag; calamus

菜 **choi** (Md **cài**)
① vegetables; green ② food eaten with rice or alcoholic drinks

菜蔬 **choi sò**
　vegetables

菜單 **choi dàan**
　menu

菜館 **choi gún**
　restaurant

菠 **bò** (Md **bō**)
spinach

菠菜 **bò choi**
　spinach

菡 **háahm** (Md **hàn**)
another name of water lilly or lotus flower

菩 **pòuh** (Md **pú**)
① a fragrant herb ② the sacred tree of the Buddhism

菩提 **pòuh tàih**
bodhi; knowledge; understanding; perfect

菩薩心腸 **pòuh saat sàm chèuhng**
kind-hearted; compassionate

華 (华) **wàh, wah**
(Md **huá, huà**)
① China ② splendid; majestic ③ luster; glory ④ a Chinese family name

華僑 **wàh kìuh**
　oversea Chinese

華人 **wàh yàhn**
　Chinese people

華陀 **Wàh tòh**
　Hua Tou, a legendary surgeon at the end of the Han Dynasty

菰 (茹) **gù** (Md **gū**)
mushrooms

菱 **lìhng** (Md **líng**)
water-caltrop

菱角 **lìhng gok**
　the water-caltrop

菱形 **lìhng yìhng**
　a rhomb

菲 **fèi, féi** (Md **fēi, fěi**)
① an edible vegetables ② thin; frugal ③ fragrant ④ Philippines

菲薄 **féi bohk**
　thin; to slight

菲酌 **féi jeuk**
　my poor feast (a polite expression)

菲律賓 **Fèi leuht bàn**
　Philippines

菸 **yìn** (Md **yān**)
tobacco leaf

菸草 **yìn chóu**
　tobacco

菸酒 **yìn jáu**
　tobacco and alcoholic drinks

其 **kèih** (Md **qí**)
the stalk of beans

萃 **seuih** (Md **cuì**)
① thick or dense growth of grass ② a group; a set ③ together; to meet

萄 **tòuh** (Md **táo**)
the grape

萊 **lòih** (Md **lái**)
① field lying fallow ② wild weed; to weed ③ a Chinese family name

萊菔 **lòih baahk**
turnip

萊蕪 **lòih mòuh**
a field with dense growth of weed

萋 **chāi** (Md **qī**)
① luxuriant, dense grow of grass ② many, crowded

萋萋 **chāi chāi**
luxuriant growth of grass ② massing of clouds

萌 **màhng** (Md **méng**)
① to bud; to sprout ② to harbor (a thought) ③ the beginning

萌生 **màhng sàng**
to produce; to conceive

萌芽 **màhng ngàh**
the initial stage of something; the bud

萍 **pìhng** (Md **píng**)
① duckweeds ② moving about rootlessly

萍浮 **pìhng fàuh**
to wander about — like duckweed

萍水相逢 **pìhng séui sèung fùhng**
to meet by accident

萎 **wāi, wái** (Md **wēi, wěi**)
① to wither ② ill; sick ③ to fall; to decline

萎謝 **wái jeh**
to wither; to fade (said of flowers)

萎縮 **wái sūk**
to dry up and shrink

萏 **daahm** (Md **dàn**)
another name of water lilly

菟 **tou, tòuh** (Md **tù, tú**)
dodder

菟葵 **tou kwàih**
a kind of mallow

菟絲子 **tou sì jí**
dodder (in botany)

著 **jyu, jeuk** (Md **zhù, zhuó**)
① famous; apparent ② to write; to author

著名 **jyu mìhng**
famous; renowned

著作 **jyu jok**
a writing; a literary work

萬(万) **maahn** (Md **wàn**)
① ten thousand; large number ② all; myraid ③ very; extremely

萬般 **maahn bùn**
all; very; various

萬幸 **maahn hahng**
extremely lucky

萬一 **maahn yāt**
just in case that

萱 **hyùn** (Md **xuān**)
a day-lilly

萱堂 **hyùn tòhng**
mother

萱草 **hyùn chóu**
the day lilly

萵 **wò** (Md **wō**)
lettuce

萵笋 **wò séun**
the lettuce

萼 **ngohk** (Md **è**)
the calys

落 **lohk, laaih** (Md **luò, lào, là**)
① to fall; to descend ② to lose ③ to leave behind

落第 **lohk daih**
to fall in a competitive examination for a job or school admission

落成 **lohk sìhng**
completion (of a new building)

落伍 **lohk ńgh**
backward; over-conservative

葉 **yihp** (Md **yè**)
① a leaf; a petal ② a Chinese family name

葉子 **yihp jí**
the leaves

葉脈 **yihp mahk**
the veins of a leaf

葛 **got** (Md **gé, gě**)
① Pueraria thunbergiana, a creeping edible bean whose fibers can be made into linen-like cloth and whose roots are used in herbal medicine ② a Chinese family name

萸 **yùh** (Md **yú**)
dogwood

葡 **pòuh** (Md **pú**)
① grape; a vine ② short for Portugal

葡萄 **pòuh tòuh**
grapevine; grape

葡萄糖 **pòuh tòuh tóng**
glucose

葡萄牙 **Pòuh tòuh ngàh**
Portugal

董 **dúng** (Md **dǒng**)
① to supervise; to oversea; to rectify ② a Chinese family name

董事 **dúng sih**
a director; a trustee

董事會 **dúng sih wúi**
a meeting of board of directors

葩 **bà, pà** (Md **pā**)
flowers; blossoms in full bloom

葫 **wùh** (Md **hú**)
the calabash or bottle-gourd

葫蘆 **wùh lòuh**
a bottle-gourd; a calabash

葬 **jong** (Md **zàng**)
to bury; inter or consign to grave

葬禮 **jong láih**
a funeral or burial service

葬儀 **jong yìh**
funeral rites

葭 **gà** (Md **jiā**)
① reed; bulrush ② a flute

葭莩 **gà fù**
distant relatives

葯 **yeuhk** (Md **yào**)
① angelica ② to wrap up ③ medicine

葯胞 **yeuhk bàau**
loculus (in botany)

葱 **chùng** (Md **cōng**)
① scallions; onion; leek ② bright green

葱白 **chùng baahk**
pale green

葱頭 **chùng tàuh**
onions

葵 **kwàih** (Md **kuí**)
the sunflower

葵笠 **kwàih lāp**
　a crude palm leaf hat

葵扇 **kwàih sin**
　palm-leaf fan

葷 (荤) **fàn** (Md **hūn**)
① meat and fish diet ② strong smell foods or spices — as onions, leeks, garlic

葷菜 **fàn choi**
　dishes containing meat or fish

葷腥 **fàn sèng**
　meat and fish diet

葸 **sáai** (Md **xǐ**)
① scared; timid ② not pleasant; a displeased look

葺 **chāp** (Md **qì**)
① to repair ② thatched ③ to pile up; to heap together

葺補 **chāp bóu**
　to repair and mend

葺屋 **chāp ngūk**
　a thatched house

蒂 (蔕) **dai** (Md **dì**)
① a footstalk of a flower or fruit; a stem ② a butt (cigaret)

蒂芥 **dai gaai**
　regrets; ill-will or bed feeling

蒙 **mùhng** (Md **méng, měng**)
① to cover; to wrap up ② childish; ignorant stupid ③ to cheat; to deceive

蒙蔽 **mùhng bai**
　to deceive

蒙昧 **mùhng muih**
　ignorant and stupid

蒐 **sáu** (Md **sōu**)
① together; to collect ② to hunt; to search for

蒐羅 **sáu lòh**
　to search aud collect

蒐索 **sáu sok, sáu saak**
　to hunt for; to search for

蒜 **syun** (Md **suàn**)
　the garlic

蒜頭 **syun tàuh**
　garlic head

蒜泥 **syun nàih**
　mashed garlic

蒯 **gwáai, gáai** (Md **kuǎi**)
scirpus, cyperinus var, concolor, a rush, from which many things are weaved

蒲 **pòuh** (Md **pú**)
① various kinds of rush from which mats, bags etc. are made ② a Chinese family name

蒲公英 **pòuh gùng yìng**
　the dandelion

蒲扇 **pòuh sin**
　a rush-leaf fan

蒸 **jìng** (Md **zhēng**)
① steam; to steam ② to evaporate

蒸餅 **jìng béng**
　steamed cake

蒸發 **jìng faat**
　evaporation heat

蒸餾水 **jìng lauh séui**
　distilled water

蒺 **jaht** (Md **jí**)
　the caltrop

蒺藜 **jaht làih**
　the caltrop; caltrap

蓖 **beih** (Md **bì**)
　the castor-oil plant

蓖麻 **beih màh**
　castor-oil plant

蒼 (苍) **chòng** (Md **cāng**)
① green; deep green or blue ②

gray (hair); hoary

蒼白 **chòng baahk**
pale; pallid

蒼蠅 **chòng yìhng**
the fly

蒞 **leih** (Md **lì**)
to arrive

蒿 **hòu** (Md **hāo**)
① plants of the mugwort or artemisia family ② rising vapor

蒿子 **hòu jí**
mugwort or artemisia

蒿廬 **hòu lòuh**
a hut

蓀 **syùn** (Md **sūn**)
a kind of aromatic grass

蓁 **jèun** (Md **zhēn**)
① a wild pepper ② luxuriant

蓁蓁 **jèun jèun**
luxuriant (vegetables)

蓄 **chūk** (Md **xù**)
① to collect; to store, to save ② to sport (long hair or a beard)

蓄髮 **chūk faat**
to grow or sport long hair

蓄意 **chūk yi**
to harbor certain intentions or ideas

蓆（席）**jehk** (Md **xí**)
a mat; especially a straw mat

蓆子 **jehk jí**
a mat; especially a straw mat

蓉 **yùhng** (Md **róng**)
the hibiscus

蓋（盖）**goi, koi**
(Md **gài**)
① to cover; to hide ② a lid; a covering ③ to build; to construct

蓋房子 **goi fòhng jí**
to build a house

蓋世 **goi sai**
surpassing one's generation

蓋上 **goi séuhng**
to cover

蓍 **sì** (Md **shī**)
milfoil; the stalks of which were used in divination in ancient time

蓍草 **sì chóu**
milfoil

蓐 **yuhk** (Md **rù**)
rushes; bed-mat

蓐母 **yuhk móuh**
a midwife

蓐食 **yuhk sihk**
to take meals in bed; breakfast in bed

蓑 **sò** (Md **suō**)
① a raincoat; or a cloak of straw ② to cover with grass

蓑衣 **sò yì**
a coir raincoat

蓓 **púih** (Md **bèi**)
bud; flower-bud

蓓蕾 **púih léuih**
a flower-bud

蓮（莲）**lìhn** (Md **lián**)
① the lotus; water lily ② the clean land (Buddhist paradise)

蓮步 **lìhn bouh**
lady-like steps

蓮花 **lìhn fā**
lotus flower or water lilly

蓮座 **lìhn joh**
the pedestal of a Buddha status

蓬 **pùhng, fùhng**
(Md **péng**)
① over-grown ② flourishing; prospering

蓬勃 **pùhng buht**
rising and flourishing

蓬門 **pùhng mùhn**
houses of the poor; my humble house

蓬鬆 **pùhng sūng**
dishevelled; very loose

蔭 **yam** (Md **yīn, yìn**)
① shade of trees ② shelter; to protect ③ (with) support or blessing of

蔭蔽 **yam bai**
to shelter; to hid in the shade

蔭庇 **yam bei**
to protect; to patronize

蔻 **kau** (Md **kòu**)
cardamon seeds

蔻丹 **kau dàan**
red nail polish

蓿 **sūk** (Md **xu**)
clover; lucerne

蔑 **miht** (Md **miè**)
① to disdain; to slight; to neglect ② without; none

蔑視 **miht sih**
to disdain; to slight

蔑棄 **miht hei**
to despise and cast away

蔓 **maahn** (Md **wàn, màn**)
plants with creeping tendrils or vines

蔓生植物 **maahn sàng jihk maht**
creeping plants

蔓延 **maahn yìhn**
to spread

蔓說 **maahn syut**
windy talk

葡 **baahk** (Md **bo**)
a common name for such edible roots such as turnip; carrot; radish

蔗 **je** (Md **zhè**)
the sugarcane

蔗糖 **je tòhng**
sugar from sugarcane

蔗汁 **je jāp**
sugarcane juice

蔚 **wai, wāt** (Md **wèi, yù**)
① a Chinese family name ② name of a country in Hopei province ③ luxuriant growth; ornamental and colourful

蔚藍 **wai làahm**
sky-blue

蔡 **choi** (Md **cài**)
① a large turtle or tortoise (whose shell was used in divination in ancient China) ② a Chinese family name

蔣(蒋) **jéung**
(Md **jiǎng**)
a Chinese family name

蔴 **màh** (Md **má**)
① hemp ② sesame

蔬 **sò** (Md **shū**)
vegetables; vegetarian diet; vegetable food

蔬菜 **sò choi**
vegetables; greens

蔬果 **sò gwó**
vegetables and fruits

蔬食 **sò sihk**
vegetarian diet; simple food

蕈 **cháhm** (Md **xun**)
① mushrooms; fungus ② mould or mildew

蔽 **bai** (Md **bì**)
① to cover; to cover up ② to hide; to conceal

蔽目 **bai muhk**
to cover the eyes

蔽護 **bai wuh**
to shelter; to protect

蔽塞 **bai sāk**
to block up; stupid or dull

蕃 fàahn (Md fán, fān)

① flourishing, luxuriant growth
② to increase, to multiply ③
numerous

蕃茂 **fàahn mauh**
flourishing and booming

蕃殖 **fàahn jihk**
to bread; to multiply; to
reproduce

蕉 jìu (Md jiāo)

① the banana ② the plantain

蕉園 **jìu yùhn**
a banana plantation

蕉葉 **jìu yihp**
the leaf of a banana plant

蕊 (蕋 、蘂)yéuih (Md ruǐ)

① a flower — bud; unopened
flower ② the stamens or pistills
of a flower

蕎 (荞) kìuh (Md qiáo)

① the buckwheat ② a kind of
herb used in herbal medicine

蕎麥 **kìuh mahk**
buckwheat

蕙 waih (Md huì)

① a species of fragrant grass with
red flowers and black seeds in
early fall ② a species of fragrant
orchid

蕙心 **waih sàm**
a pure heart

蕙質 **waih jāt**
good and pure quality (of a
person)

蕞 jeui (Md zuì)

very small; tiny

蕨 kyut (Md jué)

the bracken

蕩 (荡) dohng

(Md dàng)

① a pond; a pool ② to cleanse
away ③ to shake; unsettled ④ of
loose moral

蕩寇 **dohng kau**
to eliminate bandits

蕩產 **dohng cháan**
to go bankrupt

蕩漾 **dohng yeuhng**
moving, as in ripples

蕪 mòuh (Md wú)

① luxuriant growth of weeds ②
decayed or rotten vegetatables ③
confused; mixed up; in disorder

蕪累 **mòuh leuih**
mixed-up and superfluous

蕭 sìu (Md xiāo)

① quiet; lonely; desolate ② a
Chinese family name

蕭條 **sìu tiuh**
deserted, desolate sluggish

蕭灑 **sìu sá**
elegant stately, and easy (in
one's appearance and manner)

薄 bohk (Md báo, bó)

① thin; light; slight ② to despise;
to slight

薄暮 **bohk mouh**
around sunset

薄禮 **bohk láih**
a meager gift - my humble gift

薄弱 **bohk yeuhk**
weak; fragile

蕾 léuih (Md lěi)

a flower bud; an unopened flower

薇 **mèih** (Md **wēi**)
a kind of fern

薊 **gai** (Md **jì**)
① circium; a kind of thorny plant
② a Chinese family name

薏 **yi** (Md **yì**)
the heart of lotus seed

薐 **lìhng** (Md **léng**)
an old name of spinach

薑 **gèung** (Md **jiāng**)
ginger

薑餅 **gèung béng**
ginger bread

薑汁 **gèung jáp**
ginger juice

薔(蔷) **chèuhng**
(Md **qiáng**)
the roses

薔薇 **chèuhng mèih**
the roses

薙 **tai** (Md **tì**)
① to weed ② to cut (hair); to shave

薙髮 **tai faat**
to cut hair; a hair cut; to shave hair

薙刀 **tai dōu**
a shaving knife

薛 **sit** (Md **xuē**)
① a kind of marsh grass ② a Chinese family name

薦(荐) **jin** (Md **jiàn**)
① to recommend; to offer; to present ② fodder for animals

薦擧 **jin géui**
to recommend a competant person

薦酒 **jin jáu**
to offer wine

薨 **gwàng** (Md **hōng**)
① death of feudal lord ② loud buzzing of insects in flight

薪 **sàn** (Md **xīn**)
① firewood; fuel ② salary; pay ③ grass

薪俸 **sàn fúng**
one's salary or pay

薪工 **sàn gùng**
wages; pay

薅 **hòu** (Md **hāo**)
take away

薩(萨) **saat** (Md **sà**)
① a general name of Buddhist gods or immortals ② a Chinese family name

薯(藷) **syùh** (Md **shǔ**)
yam

薯蕷 **syùh yuh**
yam

薰 **fàn** (Md **xūn**)
① to cauterize; to perfume; to smoke ② warm; hot

薰陶 **fàn tòuh**
to mold a person's character etc.

薰香 **fàn hèung**
perfume; fragrance

蕎(荞) **chàih, cháih**
(Md **jì, qi**)
① caltrap ② water-chestnut

藉 **jihk, je** (Md **jí, jiè**)
① a mat; pad; cushion of grass ② to rely on; to lean on ③ on the excuse or pretext of

藉詞 **jihk chìh**
an excuse; a pretext

藉故 **je gu**
to avail oneself of certain excuse

藍(蓝)làahm (Md lán, la)
① blue; indigo ② a Chinese family name

藍本 làahm bún
a model-book; the original

藍靛 làahm dihn
indigo

藍圖 làahm tòuh
blue print; outline of a project

藏 chòhng, johng (Md cáng, zàng)
① Tibet; Tibetaus ② a storage; a warehouse

藏族 Johng juhk
the Tibetaus

藏藍 johng làahm
a reddish blue

藐 míuh (Md miǎo)
① to slight; to despise ② small; petite

藐小 míuh síu
small; insignificant

藐視 míuh sih
to look down upon; to slight

藕 ngáuh (Md ǒu)
rhizome or rootstock of the lotus

藕斷絲連 ngáuh dyuhn sì lihn
the rootstock is split but the fibers are still joined — the ties are severed but not completely

藜 làih (Md lí)
pigweed

藜羹 làih gāng
coarse food

藜牀 làih chòhng
pigweed bed

藝(艺)ngaih (Md yì)
art; skill; talent; craft

藝名 ngaih mìhng
stage name or screen name (of an entertainer)

藝高膽大 ngaih gòu dáam daaih
the talented or skilled are generally bold

藤(籐)tàhng (Md téng)
rattan

藤椅 tàhng yí
rattan chair

藤條 tàhng tíu
rattan wicker

藥(药)yeuhk (Md yào)
medicine; remedy; drug

藥房 yeuhk fòhng
dispensary

藥丸 yeuhk yún
pill medicine

藩 fàahn (Md fān)
a fence; a hedge; a boundary; a barrier

藩籬 fàahn lèih
a fence; a hedge

藩屬 fàahn suhk
a vessal state

藪 sáu (Md sǒu)
① marsh; swamp ② assembling place

藪澤 sáu jaahk
marsh; swamp

蘊(蕴)wáhn (Md yùn)
① to collect; together ② to store

蘊釀 wáhn yeuhng
to stir up; to foment

蘊藏 wáhn chòhng
to have in store

蘭(兰)leuhn (Md lìn)
① a kind of fragrant herb ② a Chinese family name

蘭石 **leuhn sehk**
rocks used as artillery shells in ancient warfare

蘄 **kèih** (Md **qí**)
a kind of fragrant herb

蘄竹 **kèih jūk**
a variety of bamboo

藹 **ngói, ói** (Md **ǎi**)
① gentle; kind; friendly ② luxuriant; lush

藹然 **ngói yìhn**
glossy; lustrous

藹彩 **ngói chói**
fresh look

藻 **jóu** (Md **zǎo**)
① beautiful; elegant; splendid; gorgeous ② diction; wording

藻類 **jóu leuih**
algae

藻雅 **jóu ngáh**
elegant; graceful

藿 **fok** (Md **huò**)
① leaves of legume ② a kind of medicinal herb

藿香 **fok hèung**
a medicinal herb; ageratum

藿食 **fok sihk**
coarse food

蘅 **hàhng** (Md **héng**)
a fragrant plant

蘅芷 **hàhng jí**
a fragrant plant

蘅蕪 **hàhng mòuh**
a kind of incense

蘆 (芦) **lòuh** (Md **lú**)
① reeds; rushes ② gourds

蘆筍 **lòuh séun**
asparagus

蘆葦 **lòuh wáih**
reeds

蘇 (苏) **sòu** (Md **sū**)
① a kind of thyme ② to come back to life; to revive; to resurrect ③ to awake ④ short for Soviet Russia

蘇息 **sòu sīk**
to rest; to come back to life; to revive

蘇醒 **sòu síng**
to regain conscience; to come to; to awaken

蘋 **pìhng, pàhn**
(Md **píng, pín**)
① duckweed ② apple

蘋果 **pìhng gwó**
apple

蘋果酒 **pìhng gwó jáu**
cider

蘢 (茏) **lùhng** (Md **lóng**)
a kind of tall grass

蘢葱 **lùhng chūng**
luxuriant and beautiful (of vegetation)

蘑 **mòh** (Md **mó**)
a variety of edible mushroom

蘑菇 **mòh gù**
a variety of edible mushroom

蘚 (藓) **sín** (Md **xiǎn**)
moss; lichen

蘚苔 **sín tòih**
moss; lichen

蘚痕 **sín hàhn**
a moss scar

蘭 (兰) **làahn** (Md **lán**)
orchid

蘭花 **làahn fā**
orchid

蘭章 **làahn jèung**
beautiful writtings; your letters (a polite expressions)

蘸 **jaam** (Md **zhàn**)
to dip

蘸筆 **jaam bāt**
to dip a writing brush in ink

蘸濕 **jaam sāp**
to dip

蘿（萝）**lòh** (Md **luo**)
① a kind of creeping plant ②
radish; turnip

蘿蔔 **lòh baahk**
radish; turnip

庄部

虎 **fú** (Md **hǔ**)
① tiger ② fierce; savage

虎口餘生 **fú háu yùh sàng**
to survive a dangerous
experience

虎視眈眈 **fú sih dàam
dàam**
to gaze with the cruel greed of
a tiger

虐 **yeuhk** (Md **nüè**)
cruel; ferocious

虐待 **yeuhk doih**
to maltreat; to torture

虐政 **yeuhk jing**
tyrannical rule

虔 **kìhn** (Md **qián**)
reverent; respectful; pious

虔心 **kìhn sàm**
sincere reverence

虔誠 **kìhn sìhng**
piety; sincerity

處（处、處、処）**chyu,
chyúh** (Md **chù, chǔ**)
① to place oneself in ② to deal
with; to manage

處罰 **chyúh faht**
to punish

處理 **chyúh léih**
to dispose of; to deal with; to
handle

虛 **hèui** (Md **xū**)
① empty; hollow; open ② unreal;
false ③ weak; feeble

虛報 **hèui bou**
to report untruefully

虛心 **hèui sàm**
open-minded (for advice)

虛弱 **hèui yeuhk**
weak; feeble

虜（虏）**lóuh** (Md **lǔ**)
captive; prisoner; to take
prisoner; to capture alive

虞 **yùh** (Md **yú**)
① to worry; to fear ② to expect;
to anticipate ③ a Chinese family
name

號（号）**houh, hòuh**
(Md **hào, háo**)
① designation; title ② order;
command ③ to cry; to shout

號碼 **houh máh**
a number (for identification)

號令 **houh lihng**
a command; an order

號哭 **hòuh hūk**
to weep aloud

虢 **gwīk** (Md **guó**)
name of an ancient feudal state

虧（亏）**kwài** (Md **kuī**)
① to lose; to damage ② to lack;
to want

虧本 **kwài bún**
to suffer losses in business

虧負 **kwài fuh**
to be deficient; to fail

虧心 **kwài sàm**
to go against conscience

虫部

虬（虯）**kàuh** (Md **qiú**)
young dragon

　虬蟠 **kàuh pùhn**
　　curled up like a dragon

　虬龍 **kàuh lùhng**
　　young dragon

虱（蝨）**sāt** (Md **shǐ**)
a louse

　虱子 **sāt jí**
　　a louse

　虱目魚 **sāt muhk yùh**
　　milkfish

虹 **hùhng** (Md **hóng, jiàng**)
rainbow

　虹霓 **hùhng ngàih**
　　rainbow and its reflections

　虹彩 **hùhng chói**
　　colours of rainbow

蚌 **póhng** (Md **bàng, bèng**)
oyster

　蚌殼 **póhng hok**
　　oyster shell

　蚌珠 **póhng jyù**
　　pearl

蚊（蟁）**màn** (Md **wén**)
mosquito; gnat

　蚊香 **màn hēung**
　　mosquito coil

　蚊帳 **màn jeung**
　　mosquito net

　蚊蟲 **màn chùhng**
　　mosquito; gnat

蚪 **dáu** (Md **dǒu**)
tadpole

蚋 **yeuih** (Md **ruì**)
gnat

　蚋翼 **yeuih yihk**
　　wings of gnat — very tiny
　　things

蚓 **yáhn** (Md **yǐn**)
earthworm

蚤 **jóu** (Md **zǎo**)
louse

蚩 **chì** (Md **chī**)
a kind of worm; ignorant; stupid

　蚩拙 **chì jyut**
　　stupid; ignorant

　蚩蚩 **chì chì**
　　ignorance

蚣 **gùng** (Md **gōng**)
centipede

蚯 **yàu** (Md **qiū**)
earthworm

　蚯蚓 **yàu yáhn**
　　earthworm

蚱 **ja** (Md **zhà**)
locust; grasshopper

　蚱蜢 **ja máang**
　　grasshopper

　蚱蟬 **ja sìhm**
　　a variety of cicada

蛀 **jyu** (Md **zhù**)
① worms that eat into woods or
books ② to eat into; to bore

　蛀齒 **jyu chí**
　　decayed tooth

　蛀蟲 **jyu chùhng**
　　worms that eat into woods or
　　books

蛆 **jèui** (Md **qū**)
maggot

蛇 **sèh, yìh** (Md **shé, yí**)
① snake; serpent ② complacement

蛇皮 **sèh pèih**
snake's skin

蛇類 **sèh leuih**
snakes

蛉 **lìhng** (Md **líng**)
a variety of dragonfly

蛋（蛋）**daahn**
(Md **dàn**)
egg

蛋白 **daahn baahk**
the white of an egg

蛋白質 **daahn baahk jāt**
protein; albumen

蛋糕 **daahn gōu**
cake

蛙 **wà** (Md **wā**)
frog

蛙人 **wà yàhn**
frogman

蛔 **wùih** (Md **huí**)
ascarid; round-worm

蛔蟲 **wùih chùhng**
ascarid; round-worm

蛛 **jyù** (Md **zhū**)
spider

蛛絲 **jyù sì**
spider's thread

蛛網 **jyù móhng**
spider's web

蛟 **gàau** (Md **jiāo**)
flood dragon; shark

蛟龍 **gàau lùhng**
flood dragon

蛤 **gahp, hàh** (Md **gé, há**)
① clam ② a toad

蛤蟆 **hàh màh (hā màh)**
a toad

蛤蚌 **gahp póhng**
clam

蛬 **kùhng** (Md **qióng**)
① locust ② cricket

蛬鳴 **kùhng mìhng**
chirping of cricket

蛬蛬 **kùhng kùhng**
anxious

蛭 **jaht** (Md **zhì**)
leech

蛭石 **jaht sehk**
vermiculite

蛹 **yúng** (Md **yǒng**)
chrysalis; pupa

蛹臥 **yúng ngoh**
to live in seclusion

蛻 **teui, seui** (Md **tuì**)
exuviae; to exuviate

蛻變 **teui bin**
to undergo

蛻皮 **teui pèih**
to exuviate

蛾 **ngòh** (Md **é**)
moth

蛾眉 **ngòh mèih**
long, slender eyebrows arched
like the antennae of a moth

蜀 **suhk** (Md **shǔ**)
Shu, an ancient kingdom in what
in Szechwan today

蜂 **fùng** (Md **fēng**)
bee; wasp

蜂蜜 **fùng maht**
honey

蜂房 **fùng fòhng**
beehive

蜃 **sàhn, sáhn** (Md **shèn**)
clams

蜃樓 **sàhn làuh**
mirage

蜆 **hín** (Md **xiǎn**)
a variety of bivalves

蜇 **jit** (Md **zhé, zhē**)
jelly fish

蜊 **lèih** (Md **lí**)
a kind of clam

蜓 **tìhng** (Md **tíng**)
dragonfly

蜈 **ǹgh** (Md **wú**)
centipede

蜈蚣 **ǹgh gùng**
centipede

蜉 **fàuh** (Md **fú**)
ephemera; May fly exphemerid

蜉蝣 **fàuh yàuh**
ephemera; May fly

蜍 **chyùh, chèuih**
(Md **chú**)
toad

蜥 **sīk** (Md **xī**)
lizard

蜥蜴 **sīk yihk**
lizard

蜻 **chìng** (Md **qīng**)
dragonfly

蜻蜓 **chìng tìhng**
dragonfly

蜻蜻 **chìng chìng**
an insect, resembling cicada

蜘 **jì** (Md **zhī**)
spider

蜘蛛 **jì jyù**
spider

蜘蛛網 **jì jyù móhng**
spider's web; cobweb

蜚 **fèi, féi** (Md **fēi, fěi**)
① cockroach ② to fly

蜚蠊 **féi lìhm**
cockroach

蜚語 **fèi yúh**
rumor

蜜 **maht** (Md **mì**)
① honey ② sweet

蜜蜂 **maht fùng**
honey bee

蜜棗 **maht jóu**
date preserves

蜜月 **maht yuht**
honey moon

蜞 **kèih** (Md **qí**)
a variety of small crab

蜢 **máahng** (Md **měng**)
grasshopper

蜮 **wihk** (Md **yù**)
a fabulous tortoise-like creature the sand cast out of whose mouth is believed deadly to humans

蜴 **yihk** (Md **yì**)
lizard

蜷 **kyùhn** (Md **quán**)
to wriggle; to be coiled; to be curled up

蜷曲 **kyùhn kūk**
wriggy; twisted

蜷縮 **kyùhn sūk**
not stretched

蜿 **yùn** (Md **wān**)
to creep; to wriggle

蜿蜒 **yùn yìhn**
creeping; wriggly

蝌 **fò** (Md **kē**)
tadpole

蝌蚪 **fò dáu**
tadpole

蝗 **wòhng** (Md **huáng**)
locust

蝗蟲 **wòhng chùhng**
locust

蝟 **waih** (Md **wèi**)
hedgehog

蝟鼠 **waih syú**
hedgehog

蝟縮 **waih sūk**
to curl up like a hedgehog; to
recoil; to wince

蝠 **fūk** (Md **fú**)
the bat

蝕 **siht, sihk** (Md **shí**)
① to eclipse ② to erode; to eat
up slowly

蝕本 **siht bún**
to suffer loss in business

蝣 **yàuh** (Md **yóu**)
ephemera; May fly

蝰 **kwài** (Md **kuí**)
a kind of snake

蝰蛇 **kwài sèh**
a kind of poisonous snake

蝦（虾）**hà** (Md **xiā**)
shrimp; toad

蝦蟆 **hà màh**
toad

蝦米 **hà máih**
small dried shrimp

蝮 **fūk** (Md **fù**)
a viper

蝮蛇 **fūk sèh**
a viper

蝴 **wùh** (Md **hú**)
butterfly

蝴蝶 **wùh dihp**
butterfly

蝴蝶結 **wùh dihp git**
a bow-tie; a rosette

蝶（蜨）**dihp** (Md **dié**)
butterfly

蝶夢 **dihp muhng**
to dream in sleep

蟊 **màauh** (Md **máo**)
a kind of noxious insect that
feeds on the roots of rice plants

蝸 **wò, wà** (Md **wō**)
snail

蝸牛 **wò ngàuh**
snail

蝸居 **wò gèui**
(my) humble house

蝐 **sīk** (Md **xī**)
polyp

螃 **pòhng** (Md **páng**)
crab

螃蜞 **pòhng kèih**
a kind of crab

螃蟹 **pòhng háaih**
a kind of crab

融 **yùhng** (Md **róng**)
① very bright; glowing burning ②
to melt; to fuse ③ cheerful; joyful

融化 **yùhng fa**
to melt

融洽 **yùhng hāp**
harmonious (said especially of
human relations)

螂 **lòhng (Md láng)**
① mantis ② cicada

螞 **máh, mà, mah
(Md mǎ, mā, mà)**
① ant ② a kind of leech

螞蟻 **máh ngáih**
ant

螞蟥 **mah wòhng**
a kind of leech

螟 **mìhng (Md míng)**
a kind of moth

螟蟲 **mìhng chùhng**
a kind of moth

螟蛾 **mìhng ngòh**
a kind of moth

螢 (萤) **yìhng (Md yíng)**
luminous insect; firefly;
glowworm

螢光板 **yìhng gwòng báan**
fluorescent screen

螢火蟲 **yìhng fó chùhng**
firefly

螣 **tàhng (Md téng)**
a kind of snake which can fly

螫 **sīk (Md shì)**
① a poisonous insect ② to sting

蟊 **màauh (Md máo)**
insects which are injurious to
crops

螯 **ngòuh (Md áo)**
nippers (of crabs, etc.)

螳 **tòhng (Md táng)**
mantis

螳螂 **tòhng lòhng**
mantis

螺 **lòh (Md luó)**
① spiral shell; conch ② spiral

螺貝 **lòh bui**
spiral shell

螺旋 **lòh syùhn**
screw

螺絲釘 **lòh sì dēng**
male screw; external screw

螻 **làuh (Md lóu)**
mole cricket

螻咕 **làuh gù**
mole cricket

螻蟻 **làuh ngáih**
mole cricket and ant —
insignificient creatures

蟀 **sēut (Md shuài)**
cricket (insect)

蟄 (蛰) **jaht (Md zhé)**
to hibernate

蟄伏 **jaht fuhk**
to hibernate; to lie down

蟄居 **jaht gèui**
to live in seclusion

蟆 **màh (Md ma)**
toad

蟋 **sīk (Md xī)**
cricket (insects)

蟋蟀 **sīk sēut**
cricket (insects)

蟑 **jèung (Md zhāng)**
cockroach

蟑螂 **jèung lòhng**
cockroach

螭 **chì (Md chì)**
hornless dragon

螭陛 **chì baih**
steps of the imperial palace

螭魅 **chì meih**
a man eating goblin

蟮 **sihn** (Md **shan**)
earthworm

蟒 **móhng** (Md **mǎng**)
① python ② ceremonial robes worn by mandarins

蟒袍 **móhng pòuh**
ceremonial robes worn by mandarins

蟒蛇 **móhng sèh**
python

蟪 **waih** (Md **huì**)
a kind of bright coloured cicada

蟪蛄 **waih gù**
a kind of bright coloured cicada

蟬 **sìhm** (Md **chán**)
① cicada ② continuous

蟬吟 **sìhm yàhm**
the shrill sound of the cicada

蟬聯 **sìhm lyùhn**
to stay on a position for another term

蟯 (蛲) **yìuh** (Md **náo**)
pinworm

蟲 (虫) **chùhng**
(Md **chóng**)
insects; worms

蟲子 **chùhng jí**
eggs of insects

蟲蝕 **chùhng sihk**
worm eaten

蟛 **pàahng** (Md **péng**)
a kind of crab

蟠 **pùhn** (Md **pán**)
① to coil; to curl up ② to occupy

蟠桃 **pùhn tòuh**
the flat peach; the saucher peach

蟠踞 **pùhn geui**
to occupy

蟹 **háaih** (Md **xiè**)
crab

蟹黃 **háaih wòhng**
crab spawn

蟹箝 **háaih kìhm**
nippers of a crab

蟶 **chìng** (Md **chēng**)
razor clam; razor shell

蟶田 **chìng tìhn**
fields on the seashore where razor shells are cultivated

蟶子 **chìng jí**
razor clam

蟻 (蚁、螘) **ngáih**
(Md **yǐ**)
ant

蟻動 **ngáih duhng**
to swarm or move like ants

蟻穴 **ngáih yuht**
ants' nest

蟾 **sìhm** (Md **chán**)
toad

蟾輪 **sìhm lèuhn**
the moon

蟾彩 **sìhm chói**
moonlight

蠅 **yìhng** (Md **yíng**)
a fly

蠍 (蝎) **kit** (Md **xiē**)
scorption

蠍子 **kit jí**
scorption

蠔 (蚝) **hòuh** (Md **háo**)
oyster

蠟 **laahp** (Md **là**)
wax

蠟筆 laahp bāt
crayon

蠟燭 laahp jūk
candle

蠡 láih (Md lǐ, li)
a calabash

蠡測 láih chāk
to be very naive

蠢 chéun (Md chǔn)
① to wriggle ② stupid

蠢笨 chéun bahn
stupid

蠢材 chéun chòih
a fool; an idiot

蠣 (蛎) laih (Md lì)
oyster

蠣粉 laih fán
lime obtained by burning
oyster shells

蠣房 laih fòhng
oyster shell

蠱 (蛊) gú (Md gǔ)
① poison; harm ② to bewitch

蠱毒 gú duhk
to enchant and injure

蠱惑 gú waahk
to confuse by magic or
witchcraft

蠲 gyùn (Md juān)
① millipede ② clean; pure; bright
③ to remit or remove

蠲潔 gyùn git
to clean; to purify

蠲租 gyùn jòu
to remit rentals

蠹 (蠧、蝥) dou
(Md dù)
① moth ② to embezzle

蠹魚 dou yùh
a kind of silvery worm that
eats clothes, books

蠶 chàahm (Md cán)
silkworm

蠶豆 chàahm dauh
horse bean

蠶繭 chàahm gáan
cocoon of silkworm

蠻 (蛮) màahn
(Md mán)
① barbarous; savage ② very;
fairly

蠻橫 màahn wàahng
barbarous; savage

蠻好 màahn hóu
very good

血部

血 hyut (Md xuè, xiě)
blood

血液 hyut yihk
the blood

血管 hyut gún
a blood vessel

血壓 hyut ngaat
blood pressure

眾 (众、衆) jung
(Md zhòng)
a multitude; crowd; the people;
all; many; numerous

衊 miht (Md miè)
① to stain with blood ② to
slander; to trump up a charge

行部

行 hàhng, hòhng,
hahng (Md xíng, háng)
① to walk; to move; to travel ②
to do; to act; to work ③ a row;
a line ④ a trade

行動 hàhng duhng
to act; conduct

行路 hàhng louh
to walk on the road

行情 **hòhng chìhng**
market prices of certain commodity

衍 **yíhn** (Md **yǎn**)
① to overflow; to spread out ② plenty and abundant

衍繹 **yíhn yihk**
to expound

衍衍 **yíhn yíhn**
to walk fast

衒 **yuhn** (Md **xuàn**)
① to boast; to show off ② to recommand oneself

衒露 **yuhn louh**
to show off one's talent

衒耀 **yuhn yiuh**
to show off; to boast

術 **seuht** (Md **shù**)
① a skill; a feat ② a way or method to do something

術科 **seuht fō**
course offered in school for vocational training or learning of skills; as practical mechanics

術語 **seuht yúh**
professional jargons; technical terms

街 **gàai** (Md **jiē**)
a street; a road in a city

街道 **gàai douh**
street; road in city

街坊 **gàai fōng**
neighbors

街市 **gàai síh**
shopping street

衙 **ngàh** (Md **yá**)
① a government office ② to meet; gather

衙門 **ngàh mùhn**
a government office

衙役 **ngàh yihk**
errand men in a government office

衝(冲) **chùng** (Md **chōng, chòng**)
① to rush; to forge ahead ② a thorough fare

衝動 **chùng duhng**
an impulse; a sudden urge

衝勁 **chùng gihng**
aggressiveness

衝撞 **chùng johng**
to offend; to tread impolitely

衛(卫、衞) **waih** (Md **wèi**)
① to guard; to protect ② a keeper; a person having charge of guarding

衛兵 **waih bìng**
a guard (in military)

衛生 **waih sāng**
sanitation; public health

衡 **hàhng** (Md **héng**)
① to weigh, to measure; to assess; to consider ② horizontal

衡平 **hàhng pìhng**
to weigh and consider in order to uphold justice

衡量 **hàhng leuhng**
to consider; to judge to estimate

衢 **kèuih** (Md **qú**)
a thorough fare; a highway junction

衢道 **kèuih douh**
a sidestreet; crossroad

衢路 **kèuih louh**
a thorough fare

衣部

衣 **yì, yi** (Md **yī, yì**)
① clothing; dress; garment ②

skin or peel of fruits ③ to wear; to dress

衣鉢 **yì but**
teaching, skill handed down from a master to his pupil

衣帽間 **yì mouh gàan**
a cloak room

衣錦還鄉 **yì gám wàahn hèung**
to return home in glory

表 **bíu, bīu** (Md **biǎo**)
① outside; external ② a report to the emperor ③ a watch

表白 **bíu baahk**
to express or state clearly

表面 **bíu mihn**
on the surface; externally

表揚 **bíu yèuhng**
to praise in public

衫 **sàam** (Md **shān**)
a shirt; a garment

衩 **cha** (Md **chà, chǎ**)
slits on the lower part of a gown for freedom of movement

衩衣 **cha yì**
a woman's gown with slits on the sides

衰 **sèui, chèui** (Md **shuāi, cuī**)
① weakening; failing; declining; falling ② order or series — from top downward

衰退 **sèui teui**
falling (energy, strength) weakening (as a result of old age; poor health)

衰落 **sèui lohk**
decline and fall (of a nation, family fortune)

衰弱 **sèui yeuhk**
weak; sickly

袂 **maih** (Md **mèi**)
sleeves

衲 **naahp** (Md **nà**)
① to sow; to mend; to line ② the robe of the monk

衲頭 **naahp tàuh**
a monk's robe

衲子 **naahp jí**
a polite self-reference of a Buddhist monk

衷 **chùng** (Md **zhōng**)
① the bottom of one's heart; honest; sincere ② good and virtuous

衷情 **chùng chìhng**
the feeling or affection in one's heart

衷心感謝 **chùng sàm gám jeh**
to thank sincerely

衾 **kàm** (Md **qīn**)
① a large converlet or quilt ② garments or dress for the deceased

衾枕 **kàm jám**
quilt and pillow

衾單 **kàm dàan**
clothes for the deceased

衿 **gàm, kàm** (Md **qīn**)
① the front of a Chinese gown ② lapel of a Chinese dress worn by the literati in former days

衿契 **gàm kai**
a good friend

袁 **yùhn** (Md **yuán**)
① the graceful look of a flowing robe ② a Chinese family name

袞 **gwán** (Md **gǔn**)
① imperial robe with embroidered dragons ② robes of very high officials

袞命 **gwán mihng**
the offices or appointment of the three highest officials

袞職 **gwán jīk**
the throne; the responsibility of an emperor

袖 **jauh** (Md **xiù**)
① the sleeve ② to hide or put things in sleeve

袖扣 **jauh kau**
cuff links

袖珍本 **jauh jàn bún**
pocket edition

袈 **gà** (Md **jiā**)
cassock or robe of Buddhist monk

袈裟 **gà sà**
the robe of Buddhist monk

袋 **doih** (Md **dài**)
a bag; a sack; a pocket

袋子 **doih jí**
a bag; a pocket

袋鼠 **doih syú**
the kangaroo

袍 **pòuh** (Md **páo**)
a long gown; a robe

袍掛 **pòuh gwa**
long gown topped off with a jacket

袍子 **pòuh jí**
a robe; a long gown

袒 **táan** (Md **tǎn**)
① to bare; to strip ② to protect

袒護 **táan wuh**
to shield or protect; to side with

袒衣 **táan yì**
to dress in a hurry with part of bare flesh showing

襪 **muht, maht** (Md **mò, wà**)
① a stomacher ② stockings; socks

襪腹 **muht fūk**
a stomacher

襪子 **maht jí**
socks; stockings

袤 **mauh** (Md **mào**)
length; lengthwise

袪 **kèui** (Md **qū**)
sleeves; to raise the sleeve

被 **péih, beih** (Md **bèi**)
① bedding; converlet quilt ② to cover; to spread ③ placed before verb to show passive voice

被褥 **péih yuhk**
converlet and mattress

被綁 **beih bóng**
to be kidnapped

被騙 **beih pin**
to be fooled

袱 **fuhk** (Md **fú**)
a bundle wrapped in cloth

裁 **chòih** (Md **cái**)
① to cut paper or cloth with knife or scissors ② to diminish; to deduce ③ to consider; to judge

裁判 **chòih pun**
a judge; a reference

裁縫 **chòih fùhng**
to tailor; to make dress

裁員 **chòih yùhn**
to eliminate unnecessary staff

裂 **liht** (Md **liè, liě**)
① to crack; to break ② to split or divide up

裂縫 **liht fùhng**
a crack or cleavage

裂開 **liht hòi**
　to split; or break apart

袵 **yáhm** (Md **rèn**)
lapel; collar; bedding; sleeves

　袵席 **yáhm jihk**
　　a sleeping place; a sleeping
　　mat

裙 **kwàhn** (Md **qún**)
a skirt; a peticoat; an apron

　裙子 **kwàhn jí**
　　a woman's skirt

　裙帶關係 **kwàhn daai**
　gwàan haih
　　apron-string influence or
　　relationship

裊(褭、嫋) **níuh**
(Md **niǎo**)
① curling up; as smoke ②
around; as sound of music

　裊裊 **níuh níuh**
　　curling up

　裊娜 **níuh nòh**
　　soft and slender

裎 **chìhng** (Md **chéng**)
bare of nude; naked

裏(裡、里) **léuih,**
léih (Md **lǐ**)
① within; inside ② lining of a
dress

　裏面 **léuih mihn**
　　inside; within

　裏衣 **léuih yī**
　　underwear

　裏子 **léih jí**
　　lining of clothing; hat or shoes

袷(祫、夾) **gaap**
(Md **jiá**)
a lined garment or dress

裔 **yeuih** (Md **yì**)
① descendants; posterity ②

remote or border regions

　裔民 **yeuih màhn**
　　the people; the descendants

　裔夷 **yeuih yìh**
　　frontier tribes

裕 **yuh** (Md **yù**)
① abundance; affluent ②
tolerant; lenientp ③ generous

　裕國 **yuh gwok**
　　to enrich the nation

　裕如 **yuh yùh**
　　affluent; rich; well-to-do; in
　　good circumstances

裘 **kàuh** (Md **qiú**)
① furs; any garments ② a
Chinese family name

　裘馬 **kàuh máh**
　　furs and horses

　裘褐 **kàuh hot**
　　to dress economically or
　　simply

補 **bóu** (Md **bǔ**)
① to repair; to patch; to supplement ② to add to; to make up ③
nutritious, nutrient; rich foods

　補品 **bóu bán**
　　foods or medicine of highly
　　nutritious value

　補助 **bóu joh**
　　to subsidize

　補充 **bóu chùng**
　　to supplement; to make up

裝 **jòng** (Md **zhuāng**)
① to fill in or up; to pack ② to
pretend ③ to dress or make up
④ to store; to keep

　裝假 **jòng gá**
　　to pretend; to feign

　裝修 **jòng sàu**
　　to decorate and repair; to
　　equip

裝束 **jòng chūk**
to dress up

裟 **sà** (Md **shā**)
a cassock or robe of a Buddhist monk

裸 **ló** (Md **luǒ**)
to bare; nude; naked

裸體 **ló tái**
naked; nude

裸線 **ló sin**
an uninsulated wire

裨 **bèi, pèih** (Md **bì, pí**)
① to benefit; to supplement ②
small; petty ③ subordinate; to
assist

裨益 **bèi yīk**
to benefit

裨補 **bèi bóu**
to supplement; to aid

裰 **jyut** (Md **duō**)
to mend; to darn; to patch
(clothing)

裯 **chàuh** (Md **chóu**)
bed sheet

裱 **bíu** (Md **biǎo**)
① to mount (painting, calligraphy) ② a scarf

裱工 **bíu gùng**
the work of mounting

裱糊 **bíu wùh**
to paste

裳 **sèuhng** (Md **cháng, shang**)
dress; garment; clothing

裴 **pùih** (Md **péi**)
① the look of flowing gown ② a
Chinese family name

裹 **gwó** (Md **guǒ**)
① to wrap; to bind ② a parcel ③
to surround

裹脚 **gwó geuk**
to bind the feet

裹足不前 **gwó jūk bāt chìhn**
to be afraid to move ahead

裼 **tīk** (Md **tì, xī**)
① to take off one's top garment
② a wrapper or outer garment
worn over a fur

製 **jai** (Md **zhì**)
① to produce; to make; to
manufacture ② to compose;
literary work ③ to cut out
garments and make them

製版 **jai báan**
to make a printing plate

製品 **jai bán**
products; manufactured items

製造 **jai jouh**
to make; to produce

裾 **gèui** (Md **jū**)
the overlap of robe; the hinder
part of a garment

褂 **gwa, kwá** (Md **guà**)
an overcoat; a robe or gown; a
jacket

褂子 **gwa jí**
an overcoat; a garment

複 **fūk** (Md **fù**)
① double; overlapping ② complex; compound ③ to repeat

複雜 **fūk jaahp**
complicated; complex

複賽 **fūk choi**
semi-final

複製品 **fūk jai bán**
a reproduction

褚 **chyú** (Md **chǔ**)
① to recognize; to know ② a bag
③ a Chinese family name

褐 **hot** (Md **hè**)
① coarse woolen cloth ② the poor or destitute ③ brown

褐炭 **hot taan**
brown coal

褐色 **hot sīk**
brown colour

褓（緥）**bóu** (Md **bǎo**)
a swadding cloth

褙 **bui** (Md **bèi**)
to mount (painting or calligraphic work)

褒 **bòu** (Md **bāo**)
to praise; to cite; big; great

褪 **tan, teui** (Md **tùn, tuì**)
① to take off one's clothing ② to fall off; to fade ③ to retreat; to move backward

褪手 **tan sáu**
to hide one's hands in sleeves

褪色 **tan sīk**
color fading

褥 **yuhk** (Md **rù**)
bedding; quilt or coverlet; mattress

褥套 **yuhk tou**
a large bag holding cotton or other fibers used as quilt or mattress

褥子 **yuhk jí**
bedding; coverlet or quilt

褫 **chí** (Md **chǐ**)
① to strip off; to deprive off ② to undress forcibly

褫魄 **chí paak**
to scare someone out of his wits; extremely frightened

褫奪 **chí dyuht**
to deprive of; to strip off

褰 **hīn** (Md **qiān**)
① to lift or raise (one's dress skirt) ② trousers; drawers; pants

褲（袴）**fu** (Md **kù**)
drawers; trousers

褟 **taap** (Md **tā**)
① lace-trimmed hem of a dress; lace of a dress ② a singlet; a thin T-shirt as underwear

褶（襵）**jip** (Md **zhě**)
① a lined garment ② to fold; pleated

褶曲 **jip kūk**
folds (in geology)

褶裙 **jip kwàhn**
a pleated skirt

褸 **láuh, léuih** (Md **lǚ**)
① the collar or lapel of a garment ② tattered; sloppily (dressed)

襄 **sèung** (Md **xiāng**)
① to help; to assist ② to complete

襄辦 **sèung baahn**
to help manage

襄助 **sèung joh**
to help; to assist

褻（亵）**sit** (Md **xiè**)
① underwear ② dirty ③ to slight; to look down ④ intimate

褻瀆 **sit duhk**
to slight; to insult to blaspheme

褻臣 **sit sàhn**
an intimate courtier

襁 **kéuhng** (Md **qiǎng**)
swadding clothes for infant; infancy

襁褓 **kéuhng bóu**
a swadding clothes for infant

襁負 **kéuhng fuh**
infancy; to carry an infant on the back with a broad bandage

襟 **kàm** (Md **jīn**)
① the lapel or collar of a garment or robe ② aspiration; ambition

襟抱 **kàm póuh**
ambition; aspiration

襟懷 **kàm wàaih**
one's feeling; ambition

襖(袄) **óu** (Md **ǎo**)
a coat; a jacket; top garment padded with cotton or lined fur

襠 **dòng** (Md **dāng**)
the crotch or bottom of a pair of trousers; drawers or panties

襤 **làahm** (Md **lán**)
clothes without hem; ragged garments

襤褸 **làahm láuh**
tattered; in rags

襪(袜) **maht** (Md **wà**)
stockings; socks

襪子 **maht jí**
stockings; socks

襪套 **maht tou**
wrappers either worn outside stocking or worm bare footed as a protection from chafing with shoes

襯 **chan** (Md **chèn**)
① inner garments ② to provide a background ③ to give alms

襯托 **chan tok**
to bring into relief

襯裙 **chan kwàhn**
a petticoat

襯衫 **chan sāam**
a shirt

襲 **jaahp** (Md **xí**)
① to put on; to clothe in ② a suit

③ repeated; double

襲奪 **jaahp dyuht**
to take or attack by surprise

襲擊 **jaahp gīk**
to attack by surprise

西部

西 **sài** (Md **xī**)
① the west; western ② Western; European; American ③ a Chinese family name

西部 **sài bouh**
western part (of a territory)

西服 **sài fuhk**
western clothes

要 **yiu, yìu** (Md **yào, yāo**)
① necessary; important ② must; should ③ invite; to request ④ to date

要緊 **yiu gán**
important and urgent

要求 **yìu kàuh**
a demand; a request

覃 **tàahm** (Md **tán, qín**)
① to spread to ② deep and vast ③ a Chinese family name

覃第 **tàahm daih**
vast or extensive residence; your house

覃思 **tàahm sì**
deep and profound thought

覆 **fūk** (Md **fù**)
① to pour out; to overturn ② to reply; to respond ③ to defeat; to destroy

覆敗 **fūk baaih**
to be beaten and destroyed

覆核 **fūk haht**
to re-examine

覆信 **fūk seun**
a letter in reply

覈 **haht** (Md **hé**)
① to test; to examine ② deep; deeply

覈實 **haht saht**
　to examine the fact or truth

覈物 **haht maht**
　fruits that have stones

見 部

見(见) **gin** (Md **jiàn**)
① to see; to perceive; to understand ② to visit; to call on

見禮 **gin láih**
　to salute or greet another upon meeting him

見諒 **gin leuhng**
　to pardon; to forgive

見習 **gin jaahp**
　in-service training; probation

規 **kwài** (Md **guī**)
① regulations; laws; rules ② to plan; to scheme ③ to advise so as to correct

規條 **kwài tìuh**
　items of regulations

規格 **kwài gaak**
　specification (of a manufactured item)

規勸 **kwài hyun**
　to admonish; to give friendly advice

覓(觅、覔) **mihk**
(Md **mì**)
to seek; to search or look for

覓保 **mihk bóu**
　to find a guarantor; to find someone to post a bond

覓索 **mihk sok**
　to seek or search for

視 **sih** (Md **shì**)
① to look at; to observe ② to consider or regard as

視力 **sih lihk**
　eyesight; power of vision

視察 **sih chaat**
　to inspect; to observe

視若無睹 **sih yeuhk mòuh dóu**
　to be undisturbed by what one has seen

覥 **tín** (Md **tiǎn**)
ashamed

覦 **yùh** (Md **yú**)
a strong desire for possession; to covet

親 **chàn, chan** (Md **qīn, qìng**)
① parents; relatives ② to love; intimate ③ personally; in person ④ kiss

親筆 **chàn bāt**
　one's own handwriting

親戚 **chàn chìk**
　relatives

親家 **chan gā**
　relatives as a result of marriage

覬 **gei** (Md **jì**)
to covet; to desire for something belonging to others

覲 **gán** (Md **jìn**)
to have an audience with a chief of state

覲禮 **gán láih**
　rituals performed during audience

覲見 **gán gin**
　to have an audience with a chief of state

覷(觑、覰) **cheui**
(Md **qù**)
to spy on

覷步 **cheui bouh**
　to spy on

覷著眼 cheui jeuhk ngáahn
to narrow one's eyes and gaze at something with great attention

覺 gok, gaau (Md jué, jiào)
① to wake up from sleep; to be conscious of ② to awaken; to realize ③ to tell; to feel ④ a sleep; a nap

覺察 gok chaat
to discover; to realize

覺悟 gok ngh
to become aware; to realize

覽 (览) láahm (Md lǎn)
① to look; to inspect ② to listen

覽古 láahm gú
to tour ancient relics

覽勝 láahm sing
to tour a resort; to visit a scenic spot

觀 (观) gùn, gun (Md guān, guàn)
① to see; to observe; to view ② appearance

觀點 gùn dím
a point of view

觀念 gùn mihm
a concept; an idea

角部

角 gok (Md jiǎo, jué)
① a horn of an animal ② a direction ③ an angle ④ to complete

角度 gok douh
angle; angular measure

角逐 gok juhk
to contest; to jockey

觔 gàn (Md jīn)
sinews or muscular strength

觔斗 gàn dáu
a somersault

觚 gù (Md gū)
① an ancient wine vessel ② an angle ③ a corner

觚牘 gù duhk
correspondence

解 gáai, gaai, haaih (Md jiě, jiè, xiè)
① to untie; to loosen ② to explain ③ to escort (prisoners or goods) from a place to another

解答 gáai daap
explanations or answers to certain questions

解決 gáai kyut
to settle; to conclude

觥 gwàng (Md gōng)
① a wine vessel made of horn in ancient times ② big, great

觥觥 gwàng gwàng
straight forward; honest; upright

觥船 gwàng syùhn
a big wine vessel

觴 sèung (Md shāng)
① a general name of all sorts of wine vessel ② to offer drinks to others

觴豆 sèung dauh
sacrificial wine and food

觴詠 sèung wihng
to compose or chant poems while drinking

觸 jūk (Md chù)
① to touch; to contact ② to move or touch emotionally ③ to offend

觸電 jūk dihn
electric shock

觸怒 jūk nouh
to offend and cause anger

觸覺 jūk gok
the sense of touch

言部

言 **yìhn** (Md **yán**)
① speech; words ② to say; to talk; to mean ③ a language; a dialect

言明 **yìhn mìhng**
to state clearly

言談 **yìhn tàahm**
words and speech

言語 **yìhn yúh**
spoken language; speech

計 **gai** (Md **jì**)
① a scheme; a plot; a trap ② a plan; a program ③ to calculate

計謀 **gai màuh**
a scheme; to scheme

計算 **gai syun**
to calculate; to count

計議 **gai yíh**
to negotiate; to talk; to discuss; to consider

訂 **ding, dihng** (Md **dìng**)
① to draw up or conclude ② to subscribe ③ to edit

訂盟 **ding màhng**
to conclude or sign a treaty of alliance

訂購 **ding kau**
to place a mail order for

訂閱 **ding yuht**
to subscribe to (a publication)

訃 **fuh** (Md **fù**)
a notice announcing the death of a person; an obituary

訃聞 **fuh màhn**
an obituary notice

討 **tóu** (Md **tǎo**)
① to quell; to punish ② to demand; to beg for ③ to study; to research

討論 **tóu leuhn**
to discuss

討好 **tóu hóu**
to please; to carry favor

討債 **tóu jaai**
to demand repayment of a loan

訐 **kit** (Md **jié**)
① to expose another's secret ② to accuse or charge

訐直 **kit jihk**
to blame someone bluntly for his faults

訐揚 **kit yèuhng**
to expose or reveal the faults of another

訊 **seun** (Md **xùn**)
① to ask, to inquire ② information; news

訊問 **seun mahn**
to cross examine; to interrogate

訊聽 **seun ting**
to make inquiry

訌 **hùhng** (Md **hòng**)
confusion; disorder; quarrel

訓 **fan** (Md **xùn**)
① to lecture; to instruct; to teach; to exhort ② lesson

訓勉 **fan míhn**
to exhort and encourage

訓導 **fan douh**
to teach and guide

訓練 **fan lihn**
to train; training

訕 **saan** (Md **shàn**)
① to laugh at ② to slander; to abuse

訕臉 **saan líhm**
brazen; shameless

訕笑 **saan siu**
to laugh or sneer at

訖 **gāt, ngaht** (Md **qì**)
① to come to an end; to con

clude; clear ② until; up to

託 tok (Md tuō)
① to entrust to; to charge with; to rely on ② to ask; to request ③ to use as an excuse

託付 tok fuh
to entrust to

託辭 tok chìh
to make excuse

記 gei (Md jì)
① to remember; to call to mind ② to record; to register

記念 gei nihm
to remember or commemorate

記載 gei joi
to record; a (written) record

記憶 gei yīk
memory; recollection

訏 hèui (Md xū)
① to boast; to brag ② big; great

訟 juhng (Md sòng)
① to bring a dispute to court ② to argue over the right and wrong of something

訟庭 juhng tìhng
a court of law

訟言 juhng yìhn
speak in the public

訛 ngòh (Md é)
① false; fake ② errors; wrong

訛詐 ngòh ja
to extort; to blackmail

訛傳 ngòh chyùhn
false rumors, wrong information

訝 ngah (Md yà)
① surprised; to express surprised ② to welcome or receive

訣 kyut (Md jué)
① to part; to separate ② sorcery; a mystery

訣別 kyut biht
to say good-bye

訣要 kyut yiu
a secret; occult art

訥 naahp (Md nè)
slow-tongue; slow of speech

訥口 naahp háu
slow-tongued; slow of speech

訪 fóng (Md fǎng)
① to visit; to call on ② to inquire about

訪求 fóng kàuh
to seek; to look for

訪親 fóng chàn
to look for relatives

訪問 fóng mahn
to visit; to call upon

設 chit (Md shè)
① to layout; to display ② to establish; to set up ③ to furnish; to provide

設備 chit beih
equipment

設立 chit lahp
to establish; to set up

設計 chit gai
to map out a plan; to plan

許 héui (Md xǔ)
① to promise; to approve ② to expect ③ may be; perhaps ④ to betrothed

許配 héui pui
(of a girl) to betrothed

許諾 héui nohk
to promise

許可 héui hó
to approve; to permit

訩（讻、訩）**hùng**
(Md **xiōng**)
① noisy; loudly arguing ② to be engaged in a lawsuit

訩訩 **hùng hùng**
noisy; loudly arguing

訴 **sou** (Md **sù**)
① to tell; to inform ② to accuse ③ to appeal

訴說 **sou syut**
to tell; to complain

訴訟 **sou juhng**
a lawsuit; to go to law

訴願 **sou yuhn**
to petition to a higher government agency against a decision of a lower office

訶 **hò** (Md **hē**)
to scold or blame in a loud voice

訶護 **hò wuh**
divine protection

訶求 **hò kàuh**
to find fault

訶責 **hò jaak**
to scold; berate

診 **chán** (Md **zhěn**)
to examine; to diagnose

診斷 **chán dyun**
to diagnose (a disease)

診治 **chán jih**
to diagnose and treat

診所 **chán só**
a clinic; a dispensary

詎 **geuih** (Md **jù**)
an interjection indicating surprise

詎料 **geuih liuh**
who could have expected that . . .

詎知 **geuih jì**
unexpected

註 **jyu** (Md **zhù**)
① an explanatory note; a footnote ② to register; to record

註明 **jyu mìhng**
to explain or state clearly

註釋 **jyu sīk**
explanatory note; commentary

註冊 **jyu chaak**
to register

詁 **gú** (Md **gǔ**)
① to explain; explanatory ② to transcribe the classics in everyday language

詁訓 **gú fan**
to transcribe the classics in everyday language

詆 **dái** (Md **dǐ**)
to sensure; to slander; to defame

詆毀 **dái wái**
to defame; to slander

詆謾 **dái maahn**
to slander and insult

詠 **wihng** (Md **yǒng**)
① to sing; to chant ② chirping of birds

詠古 **wihng gú**
to write poems on ancient subjects

詠詩 **wihng sī**
to chant poems

詐 **ja** (Md **zhà**)
① deceitful; false; fake; crafty cunning ② to deceive; to cheat

詐騙 **ja pin**
to swindle

詐降 **ja hòhng**
to fake surrender

詒 **yìh** (Md **yí**)
① words as gift usually given at parting ② to hand down to posterity

詔 **jiu** (Md **zhào**)
① to proclaim; to announce ② to instruct; to teach and direct ③ an imperial decree

詔令 **jiu lihng**
an imperial decree

詔諭 **jiu yuh**
imperial instruction

評 **pìhng** (Md **píng**)
① to comment; to review; to criticize ② to judge; a decision after a comparison

評判 **pìhng pun**
to criticize; to judge

評論 **pìhng leuhn**
to comment; comments

評價 **pìhng ga**
to estimate

詘 **wāt, jēut** (Md **qū**)
① to bend; to crouch ② to yield; to submit

詛 **jo** (Md **zǔ**)
① to curse; to imprecate ② to vow; to pledge; to take oath

詛罵 **jo mah**
to curse and berate

詛咒 **jo jau**
to curse; to swear

詞 **chìh** (Md **cí**)
① words; expressions; phrases ② a part of speech in grammar ③ to talk; speak or tell

詞典 **chìh dín**
a dictionary

詞彙 **chìh wuih**
a glossary; vocabulary

訾 **jí** (Md **zǐ, zī**)
① to blame or censure ② faults; ills ③ to measure; to limit

訾病 **jí bihng**
ills or bane (of the age)

訾議 **jí yíh**
unfavorable criticism

詣 **ngaih** (Md **yì**)
① to go; to arrive; to reach ② achievement; attainment

詣謁 **ngaih yit**
to pay a visit to; to call upon

詡 **héui** (Md **xǔ**)
① to boast; to exaggerate ② to propular; to make widely known

詢 **sèun** (Md **xún**)
① to inquire; to ask ② to deliberate and plan ③ to believe in

詢問 **sèun mahn**
to inquire; to ask

詢問處 **sèun mahn chyu**
an information desk

試 **si** (Md **shì**)
① to try; to experiment; to test ② to use ③ to examine

試辦 **si baahn**
to do something on experimental basis

試驗 **si yihm**
an experiment; to try

詩 **sī** (Md **shì**)
① poetry; poems ② anything or quality as an offspring of pure imagination

詩集 **sī jaahp**
collection of poems

詩意 **sī yi**
poetic quality; romantic atmosphere

詫 **cha** (Md **chà**)
① surprised; to wonder ② to brag; to boast ③ to cheat; to deceive

詫異 **cha yih**
to be surprised

詬 **gau** (Md **gòu**)
① to insult; to shame ② to berate; to abuse

　詬罵 **gau mah**
　　to berate; to abuse

　詬辱 **gau yuhk**
　　to insult; to shame

詭 **gwái** (Md **guǐ**)
① to cheat; to deceive ② cunning; shrewd

　詭辯 **gwái bihn**
　　sophistry; to agrue one's point in a artful clever, sophisticated way

　詭計 **gwái gai**
　　a trick; a trap

詮 **chyùhn** (Md **quán**)
① to explain; to illustrate ② the true or care of something

　詮釋 **chyùhn sīk**
　　to explain

　詮次 **chyùhn chi**
　　to arrange in order

詰 **kit, gāt** (Md **jié, jí**)
① to question; to ask ② to punish; to restrain

　詰責 **kit jaak**
　　to berate; to censure

　詰問 **kit mahn**
　　to demand an explanation angrily

話 **wah** (Md **huà**)
① a talk; speech; words ② language

　話別 **wah biht**
　　to bid farewell

　話題 **wah tàih**
　　topic of conversation

該 **gòi** (Md **gāi**)
① should; ought; obliged ② fated to; preordained

　該備 **gòi beih**
　　complete; nothing lacking

　該當 **gòi dòng**
　　should; ought

詳 **chèuhng** (Md **xiáng**)
① complete; detail ② to interpret

　詳盡 **chèuhng jeuhn**
　　detailed and complete

　詳閱 **chèuhng yuht**
　　to read carefully

詹 **jìm** (Md **zhān**)
① to talk too much; to reach ② a Chinese family name

詼 **fùi** (Md **huī**)
① funny; humorous ② to joke

　詼詭 **fùi gwái**
　　grotesquely funny

　詼諧 **fùi hàaih**
　　funny; comical; to tell joke

詿 **gwa** (Md **guà**)
① error; mistakes ② to cheat; to deceive

　詿誤 **gwa ngh**
　　to be punished for a mistake made by someone else

誄 **lòih** (Md **lěi**)
① writings eulogizing a dead person; a speech in praise of the dead ② to confer a posthumous title ③ to pray for the dead

誅 **jyù** (Md **zhū**)
① to kill; to execute ② to punish

　誅滅 **jyù miht**
　　to eliminate

　誅求 **jyù kàuh**
　　to exact; to demand

誇(夸) **kwà** (Md **kuā**)
① to exaggerate; to boast ② big; great ③ to show off

誇獎 **kwà jéung**
to praise; to extol

誇張 **kwà jèung**
to exaggerate

誠 **sìhng** (Md **chéng**)
① sincere; honest ② true; real

誠懇 **sìhng hán**
sincere; true-hearted

誠實 **sìhng saht**
honest; upright

認 **yihng** (Md **rèn**)
① to recognize; to understand ②
to admit; to acknowledge

認可 **yihng hó**
to approve

認識 **yihng sīk**
to recognize; to understand

認罪 **yihng jeuih**
to plead guilty

誌 **ji** (Md **zhì**)
① to write down; to put down; to
record ② a record

誌慶 **ji hing**
to offer congratulations

誌哀 **ji ngòi**
to condole

誑 **gwóng** (Md **kuáng**)
to deceive; to delude

誑騙 **gwóng pin**
to deceive; to delude

誑誕 **gwóng daan**
to cheat; to deceive

誓 **saih** (Md **shì**)
① to pledge; to vow; to swear ②
to take an oath

誓願 **saih yuhn**
a vow or pledge

誓不兩立 **saih bāt léuhng
lahp**
to vow to fight till oneself or
the other party falls

誕 **daan** (Md **dàn**)
① birth ② preposterous; absurd

誕辰 **daan sàhn**
birthday

誕生地 **daan sàng deih**
birthplace

誘 **yáuh** (Md **yòu**)
① to guide; to lead ② to induce;
to tempt

誘導 **yáuh douh**
to guide; to lead to the right
path

誘騙 **yáuh pin**
to induce by deceit

誚 **chiu** (Md **qiào**)
to blame; to reproach

誚讓 **chiu yeuhng**
to blame; to reproach

語 **yúh, yuh** (Md **yǔ, yù**)
① language; speech ② word;
phrase; expressions; sentences
③ to tell; to inform

語言 **yúh yìhn**
language

語法 **yúh faat**
wording grammar; syntax

誡 **gaai** (Md **jiè**)
to warn; to admonish

誣 **mòuh** (Md **wū**)
to accuse falsely; to bring a false
charge against

誣賴 **mòuh laaih**
to slander; to accuse falsely

誣告 **mòuh gou**
to bring a false charge against

誤 **ngh** (Md **wù**)
① to err ② to mislead; to harm
③ to delay

誤報 **ngh bou**
to report incorrectly

誤事 **ngh sih**
to ruin a plan through mismanagement

誥 **gou** (Md **gào**)
① to grant; to confer ② to rejoin; to order

誥誡 **gou gaai**
an injunction of exhortation

誥贈 **gou jahng**
to bestow

誦 **juhng** (Md **sòng**)
to recite; to intone

誦讀 **juhng duhk**
to read aloud; to recite

誦習 **juhng jaahp**
to learn by reci'ation

誨 **fui** (Md **huì**)
to teach; to instruct; to admonish; to induce

誨人不倦 **fui yàhn bāt gyuhn**
to teach without weariness

說 **syut, seui, yuht**
(Md **shuō, shuì, yuè**)
① to speak; to explain ② to persuade ③ to delight

說明 **syut mìhng**
to explain; to clarify

說謊 **syut fòng**
to tell a lie

說服 **seui fuhk**
to persuade; to convince

課 **fo** (Md **kè**)
① a lesson; a class meeting ② a course ③ a section

課本 **fo bún**
textbook

課程 **fo chìhng**
curriculum

誰 **sèuih** (Md **shuí, shéi**)
① who? whose? ② anyone?

誰能 **sèuih nàhng**
who can? who could?

誰料 **sèuih liuh**
who could have known?

誶 **seuih** (Md **suì**)
to reproach; to scold

誶罵 **seuih mah**
to scold; to reproach

誹 **féi** (Md **fěi**)
to attack; to condemn

誹謗 **féi pong**
to libel; to slander

誼 **yìh, yih** (Md **yì**)
friendship

友誼 **yáuh yìh**
friendship

調 **tìuh, diuh** (Md **tiáo, diào**)
① to mix; to blend ② to regulate; to adjust ③ to move; to shift ④ to tune

調理 **tìuh léih**
to train; to teach

調解 **tìuh gáai**
to mediate

調派 **diuh paai**
to assign

諂 **chím** (Md **chǎn**)
to flatter; to fawn

諂笑 **chím siu**
fawning smile

諂佞 **chím móhng**
to flatter; to toady

諄 **jèun** (Md **zhūn**)
patient or earnest

諄諄 **jèun jèun**
patient or earnest

諄諄教誨 **jèun jèun gaau fui**
to teach and admonish with patience

談 **tàahm** (Md **tán**)
① to talk; to converse; to chat ②
a Chinese family name

談判 **tàahm pun**
negotiation; to negotiate

談論 **tàahm leuhn**
to discuss; to talk about

諉 **wái** (Md **wěi**)
to shirk; to evade; to pass the
back

諉過 v. **ái gwo**
to put the blame upon others

諉為不知 **wái wàih bāt jì**
to pretend not to know

請 **chíng** (Md **qǐng**)
① to request; to ask; to beg ②
please ③ to hire to seek the
service of

請教 **chíng gaau**
to request instruction

請求 **chíng kàuh**
to request; to ask

請願 **chíng yuhn**
to petition

諍 **jang** (Md **zhèng**)
to expostulate; to remonstrate

諍訟 **jang juhng**
to fight a legal battle

諍友 **jang yáuh**
a friend who does not hesitate
to remonstrate

諏 **jàu** (Md **zōu**)
to confer; to consult; to seek the
advice of

諏吉 **jàu gāt**
to pick an auspicious day

諏訪 **jàu fóng**
to consult; to seek the advice
of

諑 **deuhk** (Md **zhuó**)
rumor

諒 **leuhng** (Md **liàng**)
① honest; sincere ② to forgive;
to excuse ③ to conjecture; to
guess

諒必 **leuhng bīt**
most likely; probably

諒解 **leuhng gáai**
to forgive; to be understanding

論 **leuhn, lèuhn** (Md **lùn,
lún**)
① to discuss; to comment ② to
declare; to argue ③ a theory; a
system of thoughts

論斷 **leuhn dyun**
to discuss and judge

論理 **leuhn léih**
to reason; logic

諗 **sám** (Md **shěn**)
① to think of ② to let know ③
to remonstrate ④ to hide; to
conceal

諛 **yùh** (Md **yú**)
to flatter

諛辭 **yùh chìh**
flattering words

諸 **jyù** (Md **zhū**)
all; various

諸多 **jyù dò**
many; numerous

諸位 **jyù wái**
Ladies and Gentlemen

諭 **yuh** (Md **yù**)
to notify; to inform by a directive;
edict

諭知 **yuh jì**
to notify by a directive; edict

諭旨 **yuh jí**
imperial edict

諼 **hyùn** (Md **xuān**)
to deceive; to forget

諝 sèui (Md xū)
① wisdom; sagacity ② clever idea

諜 dihp (Md dié)
① garrulous; valuable ② spying; espionage

諜報 dihp bou
a spy's report

諞 pìhn (Md piǎn)
to quibble; to boast

諞言 pìhn yìhn
to quibble

諞闊 pìhn fut
to show off; to boast

諢 wahn (Md hùn)
ridicule; derision

諢名 wahn mìhng
nickname

諤 ngohk (Md è)
honest speech; frank comments

諤諤 ngohk ngohk
outspoken; honest; magnificent

諦 dai (Md dì)
① attentive; careful ② truth

諦聽 dai ting
to listen attentively

諦視 dai sih
to look attentively

諧 hàaih (Md xiě)
① harmonious; congruous ② to joke; funny

諧和 hàaih wòh
harmony; accord

諧劇 hàaih kehk
farce

諫 gaan (Md jiàn)
to admonish; to remonstrate

諫書 gaan syù
a written admonition to the emperor

諮 jì (Md xī)
① to inquire; to confer; to consult ② an official communication between offices of the same level

諮詢 jì sèun
to inquire and consult

諮議 jì yíh
to confer; to discuss

諱 wáih (Md huì)
① to conceal; to hide ② to avoid

諱飾 wáih sīk
to make a deceptive display; to conceal the truth

諱言 wáih yìhn
to avoid mentioning something

諳 àm (Md ān)
familiar with; skilled in

諳練 àm lihn
skilled in; familiar with

諳算 àm syun
to calculate mentally

諶 sàhm (Md chén)
sincere. honest; candid

諷 fung (Md fěng)
to recite; to chant; to satirize

諷諫 fung gaan
to admonish or remonstrate in a roundabout way

諷刺 fung chi
to satirize; irony

諾 nohk (Md nuò)
① to assent ② to promise; to pledge

諾諾 nohk nohk
yes, yes

諾言 nohk yìhn
a promise; a pledge

謀 màuh (Md móu)
① to scheme; to plan ② to seek;

to try to get

謀面 **màuh mihn**
to meet each other

謀利 **màuh leih**
to seek profit

謀生 **màuh sàng**
to make a living

謁 **yit** (Md **yè**)
to have an audience with; to see (a superior)

謁告 **yit gou**
to ask for leave of absence

謁見 **yit gin**
to have an audience with; to see (a superior)

謂 **waih** (Md **wèi**)
① to tell; to say ② to name; to call ③ to think; to be of the opinion

謂何 **waih hòh**
what can be done about it

諺 **yihn, yihm** (Md **yàn**)
a proverb; an aphorism

諺文 **yihn màhn**
the Korean alphabet

諺語 **yihn yúh**
a proverb; an aphorism

謔 **yeuhk** (Md **xuè**)
① to joke; to jest ② to ridicule; to satirize

謔謔 **yeuhk yeuhk**
cheerful; happy

謔浪 **yeuhk lohng**
to make fun without restraint

謄 **tàhng** (Md **téng**)
to transcribe; to copy

謄本 **tàhng bún**
a transcript

謄寫 **tàhng sé**
to copy; to transcribe

謊 **fòng** (Md **huǎng**)
a lie; to lie

謊言 **fòng yìhn**
a lie

謊騙 **fòng pin**
to cheat; to deceive

謅 **jàu** (Md **zhōu**)
to jest; to joke; to quip

謎（謎、詸）**màih**
(Md **mí**)
puzzle; riddle; conundrum

謎語 **màih yúh**
riddle; conundrum

謎底 **màih dái**
answer to a conundrum

謇 **gín** (Md **ziǎn**)
① to stutter ② to speak out boldly

謇謇 **gín gín**
faithful; loyal

謐 **maht** (Md **mì**)
① silent; quiet; still ② cautious; careful

謐謐 **maht maht**
silent; quiet

謗 **pong** (Md **bàng**)
to slander; to libel

謙 **hìm** (Md **qiān**)
modest; humble; retiring; self-effacing

謙卑 **hìm bèi**
humble; self-depreciating

謚（謚　諡）**si**
(Md **shì**)
to confer posthumous titles

講 **góng** (Md **jiǎng**)
① to speak; to talk ② to pay particular attention to ③ to explain

講論 góng leuhn
to discuss; to expound

講和 góng wòh
to make peace; to conclude peace

謝 jeh (Md xiè)
① to thank ② to decline ③ to fade; to wither

謝罪 jeh jeuih
to apologize

謝恩 jeh yàn
to express thanks for great favor's

謝意 jeh yi
gratitude; appreciation

謠 yìuh (Md yáo)
① rumor ② folk song; song

謠言 yìuh yìhn
unfounded report; rumor

謾 maahn, màahn (Md màn, mán)
to scorn; to disdain to deceive

謾罵 maahn mah
to revile scornfully

謾天謾地 màahn tìn màahn deih
to revile scornfully

謨 mòuh (Md mó)
① plan; course of action ② to have no, without

謨信 mòuh seun
treacherous; sly; cunning

謫 (讁) jaahk (Md zhé)
① to blame; to reproach ② to punish ③ fault ④ to exile

謫奸 jaahk gàan
to punish the wicked

謫居 jaahk gèui
to live in exile

謬 mauh (Md miù)
① incorrect; wrong ② absurd; unreasonable

謬論 mauh leuhn
absurd statement

謬誤 mauh ngh
error; inaccuracy

謳 ngàu (Md ōu)
to sing; to chant

謳歌 ngàu gō
to sing in praise; to glorify

謹 gán (Md jǐn)
① cautious; careful; attentive ② respectful; reverent

謹防 gán fòhng
to guard carefully against

謹呈 gán chìhng
presented respectfully by . . .

謹愼 gán sahn
cautious; prudent

譏 gèi (Md jī)
to ridicule; to jeer

譏諷 gèi fung
to ridicule

譏笑 gèi siu
to laught at; to make fun of

譁 wà (Md huá)
noise; tumult; hubbub

譁笑 wà siu
noisy laughters

譁然 wà yìhn
uproarious; tumultuous

證 (证 証) jing (Md zhèng)
① to prove; to testify ② evidence; proof; testimony

證明 jing mìhng
to prove; to certify

證據 jing geui
evidence; proof

證人 jing yàhn
a witness

譎 **kyut** (Md **jué**)
① to cheat; to deceive ② wily; artful

譎詭 **kyut gwái**
　unpredictable

譎諫 **kyut gaan**
　to admonish by hints

譖 **jam** (Md **zèn**)
to slander

譖人 **jam yàhn**
　to slander others

譖言 **jam yìhn**
　slanderous remarkers

識 **sīk, ji** (Md **shí, zhì**)
① to know; to recognize ② opinion; view ③ to record; to remember

識別 **sīk biht**
　to discern; to identify

識破 **sīk po**
　to see through

譚 **tàahm** (Md **tán**)
① to talk; to converse ② a Chinese family name

譜 **póu** (Md **pǔ**)
① a register; a record ② score ③ to compose (a song)

譜子 **póu jí**
　a musical score

譜號 **póu houh**
　musical notes

議 **yíh** (Md **yì**)
① to discuss; to argue ② argumentative writing

議定 **yíh dihng**
　to arrive at a decision after discussion

議程 **yíh chìhng**
　agenda

譟 **chou** (Md **zào**)
① noise of a crowd ② to slander

警 **gíng** (Md **jǐng**)
① to guard; to keep watch ② to warn; to alert

警察 **gíng chaat**
　policeman

警備 **gíng beih**
　to keep watch

警告 **gíng gou**
　to warn; a warning

譫 **jìm** (Md **zhān**)
talkative

譬 **pei** (Md **pì**)
① to liken; to compare ② a simile

譬如 **pei yùh**
　suppose; for instance

譬喻 **pei yuh**
　a simile

譯 **yihk** (Md **yì**)
to translate

譯述 **yihk seuht**
　to translate freely

譯音 **yihk yàm**
　a transliteration

譭 **wái** (Md **huǐ**)
to slander

譭謗 **wái pong**
　to slander

譴 **hín** (Md **qiǎn**)
to reproach; to reprimand

譴責 **hín jaak**
　to reprimand

譴訶 **hín hò**
　to scold

護 **wuh** (Md **hù**)
to protect; to shelter

護庇 **wuh bei**
　to shelter; to cover up

護照 **wuh jiu**
　a passport

護衞 **wuh waih**
to guard; to escort

譽 **yuh** (Md **yù**)
fame; glory

譽滿全球 **yuh múhn chyùhn kàuh**
world famous

名譽 **mìhng yuh**
prestige

讀 **duhk, dauh** (Md **dú, dòu**)
① to read; to study ② pauses in a sentence

讀本 **duhk bún**
a reader (for a course)

讀音 **duhk yàm**
pronunication

句讀 **geui dauh**
pauses in a sentence

讅 **sám** (Md **shěn**)
to know; to be aware

變 (变) **bin** (Md **biàn**)
① to change; to alter to transform ② uncommon

變態 **bin taai**
abnormality

變通 **bin tùng**
to adapt oneself

變遷 **bin chìn**
evolution; change

讎 (讐) **chàuh** (Md **chóu**)
① enemy; rival ② to collate; to compare

讎敵 **chàuh dihk**
enemy; foe

讎視 **chàuh sih**
to regard with hostility

讕 **làahn** (Md **lán**)
to abuse; to revile; to slander

讕言 **làahn yìhn**
abusive words

讒 (谗) **chàahm** (Md **chán**)
to misrepresent; to slander; to defame

讒謗 **chàahm pong**
to defame; to slander

讒害 **chàahm hoih**
to incriminate by false charges

讓 (让) **yeuhng** (Md **ràng**)
① to give away; to let; to allow ② to turnover

讓步 **yeuhng bouh**
to give way; to make concession

讓賢 **yeuhng yìhn**
to yield one's position to a more talented person

讖 **cham** (Md **chèn**)
prophecy; omens

讖語 **cham yúh**
a prophetic remark made casually which later comes true

讙 **fùn** (Md **huān**)
to be noisy; clamor

讙呼 **fùn fù**
to give a cheer; to cheer

讚 **jaan** (Md **zàn**)
to command; to praise; to applaud

讚賞 **jaan séung**
to praise; to command

讚揚 **jaan yèuhng**
to glorify

讞 **yihn** (Md **yàn**)
to judge at a court of law

讜(谠)**dóng** (Md **dǎng**)
to speak out boldly

讜論 **dóng leuhn**
outspoken statement

讜言 **dóng yìhn**
outspoken remarks

谷部

谷 **gūk, yuhk** (Md **gǔ, yù**)
① a valley; a waterway between two mountains ② a hollow; a pit ③ a Chinese family name

谷底 **gūk dái**
the bottom of a valley

谷飲 **gūk yám**
to live like a hermit

谿 **kut** (Md **huō, huò**)
① to crack or break open ② to give up ③ to open up; clear

谿命 **kut mihng**
at the expense of one's life

谿免 **kut míhn**
to exempt from

谿然 **kut yìhn**
open and clear

谿 **kài, hàih** (Md **xī**)
① a valley; a gorge ② a stream; a creek

豆部

豆 **dauh** (Md **dòu**)
beans and peas

豆腐 **dauh fuh**
bean curd

豆芽 **dauh ngàh**
bean sprouts as a vegetable

豆漿 **dauh jèung**
soybean milk

豈 **héi** (Md **qǐ**)
① an interrogative particle implying a conflicting or dissenting view — how; what ② harmonious; happy

豈不 **héi bāt**
Wouldn't it result in . . .

豈能 **héi nàhng**
How can . . . ?

豉 **sih** (Md **chǐ**)
fermented bean

豌 **wún** (Md **wān**)
peas; garden peas

豌豆 **wún dauh**
garden peas

豌豆糕 **wún dauh gōu**
a small sweetened cake made of mashed peas

豎(竖、竪) **syuh**
(Md **shù**)
① to erect; to set up ② upright; perpendicular; verticle; to stand up

豎立 **syuh lahp**
to erect

豎琴 **syuh kàhm**
the harp

豐 **fùng** (Md **fēng**)
① abundant; luxuriant; fruitful; plenty ② a crop; a harvest

豐沛 **fùng pui**
copious or plentiful

豐富 **fùng fu**
abundant; copious

豐收 **fùng sàu**
a rich harvest

豔(艳、艷) **yihm**
(Md **yàn**)
① plump; voluptuous ② beautiful

豔福 **yihm fūk**
good fortune or success in love affairs

艷麗 **yihm laih**
radiantly beautiful

豕部

豕 **chí** (Md **shǐ**)
pig; hog

豕牢 **chí lòuh**
a pigsty; pigpen

豕心 **chí sàm**
greedy; avaricious

豚 **tyùhn** (Md **tún**)
a small pig

豚犬 **tyùhn hyún**
bad sons

豚肩 **tyùhn gìn**
pig's legs

象 **jeuhng** (Md **xiàng**)
① an elephant; ivory ② a potrait;
an image

象牙 **jeuhng ngàh**
ivory; elephant tusk

象棋 **jeuhng kèih**
Chinese chess game

豢 **waahn** (Md **huàn**)
① to feed animals with grains ②
to tempt people with profit

豢養 **waahn yéuhng**
to feed; to rear

豢圈 **waahn yúh**
an animal barn or stable

豪 **hòuh** (Md **háo**)
① a person outstanding in
intelligence or talent ② a leader

豪邁 **hòuh maaih**
straightforward and carefree

豪華 **hòuh wàh**
luxurious; swanky

豪爽 **hòuh sóng**
bold and generous

豬 **jyù** (Md **zhū**)
a pig

豬肉 **jyù yuhk**
pork

豬油 **jyù yàuh**
lard

豫 **yuh** (Md **yù**)
① comfort; to beat easy ② to get
ready or prepared ③ to travel; to
make an excursion

豳 **bàn** (Md **bīn**)
① name of a state in Chou
Dynasty ② name of a mountain
in Shensi

豸部

豸 **jih** (Md **zhì**)
reptiles without feet

豹 **paau** (Md **bào**)
① leopard; panther; wild cat ②
a Chinese family name

豹略 **paau leuhk**
a military commander

豹子 **paau jí**
a leopard; panther

豺 **chàaih** (Md **chái**)
① a ravenous beast; akin to the
wolf ② wickedly; cunning

豺狼 **chàaih lòhng**
ravenous and cruel beasts

豺虎 **chàaih fú**
cruel bandits

貂 **dìu** (Md **diāo**)
the sable; the marten; mink

貂皮 **dìu pèih**
sable skin

貅 **yàu** (Md **xiū**)
a kind of animal like tiger; a fierce
and courageous soldier

貉 **hohk** (Md **hé, háo**)
a badger; a racoon dog; a fox like
animal

貉絨 **hohk yùhng**
　badger skin (fur)

貉子 **hohk jí**
　a young badger

貌 **maauh** (Md **mào**)
① facial appearance ② general
appearance; manner; form

貌美 **maauh méih**
　beautiful

貌相 **maauh seung**
　to judge someone by his
　appearance only

狸（狸）**lèih** (Md **lí**)
a fox-like animal

狸貓 **lèih māau**
　a cat-like animal

狸奴 **lèih nòuh**
　a cat

貓 **māau** (Md **māo, máo**)
the cat

貓頭鷹 **māau tàuh yìng**
　the owl

貓眼石 **māau ngáahn sehk**
　cat's-eye; or cymophane

貔 **pèih** (Md **pí**)
a fierce animal of the panther
family

貔虎 **pèih fú**
　fierce and courageous soldiers

貔休 **pèih yàu**
　a kind of fierce wild beast

貝部

貝 **bui** (Md **bèi**)
① shells; cowries ② precious;
valuable

貝母 **bui móuh**
　fritillary

貝殼 **bui hok**
　sea-shells

負 **fuh** (Md **fù**)
① defeated; beaten; to loose; to
fail ② to bear; to carry ③ to be
proud ④ to owe

負擔 **fuh dàam**
　an obligation; a burden

負責 **fuh jaak**
　to be responsible

負債 **fuh jaai**
　to be in debt

貞 **jìng** (Md **zhēn**)
① chastity of a woman ② pure;
virtuous ③ devotion

貞節 **jìng jit**
　tenacity to hold on to one's vir-
　tuous way

貞淑 **jìng suhk**
　pure and chaste

貢 **gung** (Md **gòng**)
① to offer tribute ② to recommand ③ to contribute

貢品 **gung bán**
　items offered as tribute

貢獻 **gung hin**
　to offer or to contribute

財 **chòih** (Md **cái**)
wealth· riches

財寶 **chòih bóu**
　money and jewels

財政 **chòih jing**
　finance; financial adminis-
　tration

財產 **chòih cháan**
　property

貧 **pàhn** (Md **pín**)
① poverty; poor ② deficiency;
lack ③ stingy; tightfisted

貧病 **pàhn bihng**
　impoverished and in poor
　health

貧乏 **pàhn faht**
　wanting; deficient

貧血 **pàhn hyut**
anaemia

貨 **fo** (Md **huò**)
① commodities; goods ② money; currency

貨幣 **fo baih**
currency; money

貨價 **fo ga**
the price of a commodity

貨運 **fo wahn**
shipment of commodities

販 **faan** (Md **fàn**)
① to buy and sell; to deal in ② a seller

販賣 **faan maaih**
to sell; to peddle

販子 **faan jí**
a seller; a peddler

貪(贪) **tàam** (Md **tān**)
① to covet; greedy ② to hope or wish for

貪圖 **tàam tòuh**
to hope; desire or long for

貪心 **tàam sàm**
greed; cupidity

貫 **gun** (Md **guàn**)
① to string on a thread ② to pierce through

貫通 **gun tùng**
to have a thorough understanding

貫注 **gun jyu**
to concentrate one's attention to

責 **jaak** (Md **zé**)
① one's duty; obligation ② to demand; to punish

責罰 **jaak faht**
to punish; a punishment

責任 **jaak yahm**
duty; responsibility; obligation

貶 **bín** (Md **biǎn**)
① to reduce or lower ② to dismiss; to send away

貶價 **bín ga**
to reduce price

貶值 **bín jihk**
to devaluate

貯 **chyúh** (Md **zhù**)
to store up; to save up; to deposit

貯備金 **chyúh beih gàm**
reserve fund

貯蓄 **chyúh chūk**
to store up

貯存 **chyúh chyùhn**
to stockpile; to deposit

貳 **yih** (Md **èr**)
① deputy ② to suspect; to doubt

貳心 **yih sàm**
a rebellious mind

貳言 **yih yìhn**
a different view

貴 **gwai** (Md **guì**)
① high-price; honorable ② expensive; costly ③ to treat with respect

貴賓 **gwai bàn**
distinguished guests

貴庚 **gwai gāng**
How old are you? (a polite expression)

貴重 **gwai juhng**
precious; rare; valuable

貽 **yìh** (Md **yí**)
① to give to; to present to ② to hand down; to pass on to

貽害 **yìh hoih**
to bring trouble to another

貽贈 **yìh jahng**
to present a gift

買 **máaih** (Md **mǎi**)
to buy; to purchase; to win over

買賣 **máaih maaih**
sell and buy; line of business

買方 **máaih fòng**
buyer

貸 **taai** (Md **dài**)
① to loan; to lend ② the credit side in book keeping

貸方 **taai fòng**
the credit in book-keeping

貸款 **taai fún**
a loan of money

貺 **fong** (Md **kuàng**)
① to give or bestow a gift ② to be favored with

貺臨 **fong làhm**
to be honored by your presence

貲 **jì** (Md **zī**)
same as 資

費 **fai, bei** (Md **fèi**)
① to spend; to waste; to used up ② a Chinese family name

費力 **fai lihk**
taking a lot of exertion

費解 **fai gáai**
difficult to understand

費用 **fai yuhng**
expenses; costs

貼 **tip** (Md **tiē**)
① to paste; to stick up ② to make up the deficiency ③ proper

貼補 **tip bóu**
to make up the deficiency

貼廣告 **tip gwóng gou**
to paste up posters

貼切 **tip chit**
proper; appropriate

貿 **mauh** (Md **mào**)
① to trade; to barter ② mixed ③ rashly

貿貿然 **mauh mauh yìhn**
rashly; without consideration

貿易 **mauh yihk**
trade; to trade

賀 **hoh** (Md **hè**)
① to congratulate; to send a present ② a Chinese family name

賀禮 **hoh láih**
a congratulatory present

賀儀 **hoh yìh**
money sent as token of one's congratulation

賁 **bei, bàn** (Md **bì, bēn**)
① to adorn; ornamental ② bright; luminous ③ to forge ahead

賁然 **bei yìhn**
bright and brilliant

賁如 **bei yùh**
richly adorn

賃 **yahm** (Md **lìn**)
to rent; to hire

賃借 **yahm je**
to hire; to borrow

賃租 **yahm jòu**
to rent

賄 **kwúi, fúi** (Md **huì**)
① to bribe ② money; wealth

賄賂 **kwúi louh**
to bribe

賄選 **kwúi syún**
to try to win in an election by means of bribery

賂 **louh** (Md **lù**)
to send gift; to bribe

賄賂 `**kwúi louh**
to bribe

賅 **gòi** (Md **gāi**)
provided for; included in; all inclusive

資 **jì** (Md **zī**)
① money; wealth; property ② natural endowment ③ to aid; to

help

資本 **jì bún**
capital

資歷 **jì lihk**
qualifications and experience

資助 **jì joh**
to help another with money

賈 **gá, gú** (Md **jiǎ, gǔ**)
① a Chinese family name ② a merchant; a businessman ③ to buy; to trade

賈利 **gú leih**
to make profit

賈勇 **gú yúhng**
with courage to spare

賊 **chaahk** (Md **zéi**)
① a thief; a burglar ② rebel

賊匪 **chaahk féi**
rebels; bandits

賊心 **chaahk sàm**
a crooked mind; a wicked and suspicious mind

賑 **jan** (Md **zhèn**)
to relieve or give aid to the distressed; to support

賑糧 **jan lèuhng**
relief food or grains

賑災 **jan jòi**
to relief the afflicted area

賒 **sè** (Md **shē**)
① to buy or sell on credit ② distant; faraway ③ slowly; to put off

賒貸 **sè taai**
credit

賒貨 **sè fo**
to get goods on credit

賓 **bàn** (Md **bīn**)
① a guest; a visitor ② to obey; to submit

賓禮 **bàn láih**
the courtesy on the part of a guest

賓客 **bàn haak**
guests and visitors

賙 **jàu** (Md **zhōu**)
to give; to aid; to relieve

賙濟 **jàu jai**
to relieve the needy

賜 **chi** (Md **cì**)
① to bestow or confer on an inferior ② favors; good grace

賜福 **chi fūk**
to bless

賜教 **chi gaau**
your instruction; your advice (a polite expression)

賞 **séung** (Md **shǎng**)
① to reward; to bestow; to grant ② to appreciate; to enjoy ③ to respect

賞罰 **séung faht**
to reward and punish

賞識 **séung sīk**
to appreciate the virtues in a person or thing

賞賜 **séung chi**
to bestow money or present for an inferior

賠 **pùih** (Md **péi**)
① to compensate; to make up for a lose due to one's fault ② to offer ③ to lose money

賠本 **pùih bún**
to lose money in business

賠款 **pùih fún**
an indemnity for damages

賠罪 **pùih jeuih**
to apologize

賡 **gàng** (Md **gēng**)
to continue; to carry on

賡續 **gàng juhk**
　to continue

賡酬 **gàng chàuh**
　to write poems to each other
　as a means of communication

賢 **yìhn** (Md **xián**)
　① capable; able; talented ②
　good; worthy; virtuous ③ to
　admire; to praise

賢明 **yìhn mìhng**
　capable and virtuous

賢達 **yìhn daaht**
　wise and virtuous

賢妻良母 **yìhn chài lèuhng
　móuh**
　a dutiful wife and loving
　mother

賣 **maaih** (Md **mài**)
　① to sell; to betray ② to show
　off; to flaunt

賣力 **maaih lihk**
　to work as a laborer; to work
　hard willingly

賣國 **maaih gwok**
　to betray one's country

賣唱 **maaih cheung**
　to live in singing

賤 **jihn** (Md **jiàn**)
　① cheap; inexpensive; ②
　worthless; inferior ③ to look
　down

賤貨 **jihn fo**
　a tramp; a slut

賤軀 **jihn kèui**
　my body; my health

賦 **fu** (Md **fù**)
　① tax; revenue ② troops; army
　③ to bestow; to give

賦閒 **fu hàahn**
　to be out of employment

賦稅 **fu seui**
　farm tax and excise taxes

賦有 **fu yáuh**
　endowed or gifted with

質 **jāt, ji,** (Md **zhì**)
　① matter; substance ② one's
　disposition or temperament;
　quality ③ to question

質料 **jāt líu**
　quality; raw material

質問 **jāt mahn**
　to interrogate

質詢 **jāt sèun**
　to interpellate

賬 **jeung** (Md **zhàng**)
　① accounts ② debts ③ credits;
　loans

賬目 **jeung muhk**
　accounts; details of accounts

賬單 **jeung dāan**
　bills; invoices

賴 **laaih** (Md **lài**)
　① to rely on; to depend on ② to
　accuse without ground or
　evidence

賴賬 **laaih jeung**
　to repudiate account; (debts,
　etc.)

賴以為生 **laaih yíh wàih
　sàng**
　to rely on something or
　someone for a living

賭 **dóu** (Md **dǔ**)
　① to gamble; to bet ② to
　compete

賭博 **dóu bok**
　to gamble; gambling

賭氣 **dóu hei**
　to do something out of spite

賺 **jaahn** (Md **zhuàn,
　zuàn**)
　to earn; to make money

賺錢 **jaahn chìhn**
　to earn money; to make profit

購 **fuh** (Md **fù**)
to help another with money in financing a funeral

購儀 **fuh yìh**
money presented to another for financing a funeral

購贈 **fuh jahng**
donation to another for financing a funeral

購 **kau** (Md **gòu**)
to buy; to purchase; to hire

購備 **kau beih**
to purchase beforehand

購買 **kau máaih**
to buy

賽 **choi** (Md **sài**)
① to compete; to contest ② to rival; to surpass

賽跑 **choi páau**
to run a race on foot

賽車 **choi chè**
car race

贅 **jeui** (Md **zhuì**)
① useless; superfluous ② repetition; to repeat ③ to meet; to congregate

贅述 **jeui seuht**
repetitious statement

贅子 **jeui jí**
to sell one's son to someone as a slave

贗 **ngaahn** (Md **yàn**)
counterfeit; fake

贗本 **ngaahn bún**
an imitation of a book

贗品 **ngaahn bán**
a counterfeit; an imitation

贈 **jahng** (Md **zèng**)
to send (gifts); to confer; to bestow

贈品 **jahng bán**
a gift; a present

贈言 **jahng yìhn**
words of advice

贊 **jaan** (Md **zàn**)
① to assist; to aid ② to praise; to command

贊助 **jaan joh**
to support; to sponsor

贊揚 **jaan yèuhng**
to glorify; to praise

贍 **sihm, sihn** (Md **shàn**)
① to provide; to supply ② abundance; plenty

贍養 **sihm yéuhng**
to provide with means of support

贍足 **sihm jūk**
abundant; plenty

贏 **yìhng** (Md **yíng**)
to win; to gain; profit

贏得 **yìhng dāk**
to win (honour; privilege)

贏錢 **yìhng chìhn**
to win money by gambling

贓(贓) **jòng** (Md **zāng**)
① bribe ② stolen goods; loot

贓證 **jòng jing**
plunder as evidence of theft or graft

贓物 **jòng maht**
stolen goods; plunder

贖 **suhk** (Md **shú**)
to redeem; to ransom; to buy; to atone for

贖款 **suhk fún**
a ransom

贖身 **suhk sàn**
to buy freedom (from slavery, prostitution)

贛 **gam, gung** (Md **gàn**)
alternative name of Kiangsi Province

贛江 **Gam gòng**
the Kam River in Kiangsi Province

赤部

赤 **chik** (Md **chì**)
red; bare; naked sincere

赤膽 **chik dáam**
sincere loyalty

赤脚 **chik geuk**
bare feet

亦字 **chik jih**
deficit; loss

赦 **se** (Md **shè**)
to pardon; to excuse; to forgive

赦免 **se míhn**
to pardon (an offender)

赦罪 **se jeuih**
to pardon (a criminal)

赧 **náahn** (Md **nǎn**)
to turn red from shame or embarrassment

赧愧 **náahn kwáih**
to be ashamed

赧然 **náahn yìhn**
ashamed; blushing

赫 **hāak** (Md **hè**)
① bright; growing brilliant; glorious ② angry; indigant

赫怒 **hāak nouh**
angry; furious

赫然 **hāak yìhn**
looking angry

赭 **jé** (Md **zhě**)
① red ② hematite

赭面 **jé mihn**
to dye the face red

赭石 **jé sehk**
hematite

走部

走 **jáu** (Md **zǒu**)
① to walk; to go on foot ② to run; to go swiftly ③ to leave; to depart

走避 **jáu beih**
to run away from

走遍 **jáu pin**
to travel all over

走獸 **jáu sau**
beasts

赳 **gáu** (Md **jiū**)
valiant; gallant

赳赳 **gáu gáu**
valiant; gallant

赴 **fuh** (Md **fù**)
to go out; to proceed to

赴會 **fuh wuih**
to go to a meeting

赴約 **fuh yeuk**
to leave for an engagement

起 **héi** (Md **qǐ**)
① to begin; to start ② to rise; to get up ③ to happen; to occur

起碼 **héi máh**
at least

起居 **héi gèui**
one's everyday life at home

起誓 **héi saih**
to make an oath; to swear

趁 **chan** (Md **chèn**)
to take advantage of; to avail oneself of

趁機會 **chan gèi wuih**
to take advantage of an opportunity

趁早 **chan jóu**
to act before it is too late

超 **chìu** (Md **chāo**)
① to jump over; to fly across ②
to be more than ③ to excell; to
surpass

超齡 **chìu lìhng**
to be over the specified age

超卓 **chìu cheuk**
surpassing

超載 **chìu joi**
overloading

越 **yuht** (Md **yuè**)
① to go beyond; to go across ②
even more; the more

越發 **yuht faat**
even more; the more

越權 **yuht kyùhn**
to act without authorization

越過 **yuht gwo**
to go beyond

趙 (赵) **jiuh** (Md **zhào**)
① name of an ancient feudal
state ② a Chinese family name

趙璧 **jiuh bik**
a famous precious stone
belonging to the state of Chao
during the age of Civil Wars

趕 **gón** (Md **gǎn**)
① to pursue; to catch up; to
overtake ② to drive; to expel

趕不上 **gón bāt séuhng**
unable to catch up with

趕開 **gón hòi**
to drive away

趕緊 **gón gán**
quickly; with no loss of time

趣 **cheui** (Md **qù**)
interest; fun; interesting; funny

趣事 **cheui sih**
amusing incident

越味 **cheui meih**
fun; interest

趟 **tong** (Md **tàng**)
an auxiliary noun for verbs
meaning "to walk", "to journey"

趟子 **tong jí**
a round trip between two
localities

趨 (趋、趍) **chèui**
(Md **qū**)
① to go quickly; to hasten ② to
incline; to tend

趨勢 **chèui sai**
trend; to go after man of power

趨向 **chèui heung**
tendency; trend

趲 (趱) **jáan** (Md **zǎn**)
to hurry; to hasten; to urge

趲路 **jáan louh**
to hurry in a journey

趲行 **jáan hàhng**
to travel hurriedly

足部

足 **jūk** (Md **zú**)
foot; base; sufficient; enough

足跟 **jūk gàn**
the heel

足夠 **jūk gau**
enough; sufficient

足智多謀 **jūk ji dò màuh**
wise and resourceful

趴 **pà** (Md **pā**)
to prostrate oneself; to lie face
downward

趴下 **pà hah**
to prostrate oneself

趴著 **pà jeuhk**
lying flat on the ground

趵 **paau** (Md **bào**)
to jump; to leap

趵突泉 **Paau daht chyùhn**
a renowned spring at Chinan

趾 **jí** (Md **zhǐ**)
toe; foot prints

趾骨 **jí gwāt**
phalanx (of the foot)

趾高氣揚 **jí gòu hei yèuhng**
elated and proud

跗 **fù** (Md **fū**)
① back of the foot ② to sit cross-legged

跗骨 **fù gwāt**
tarsal bone

跗坐 **fù joh**
to sit cross-legged

跂 **kéih, kèih** (Md **qí, qì**)
① an extra toe ② crawling ③ to stand on tiptoe

跂望 **kéih mohng**
to wait on tiptoe

跂想 **kéih séung**
to expect auxiously

跋 **baht** (Md **bá**)
to travel; to postscript

跋涉 **baht sip**
to travel over land and water

跋刺 **baht chi**
sound of fish jumping or birds flying up

跌 **dit** (Md **diē**)
to stagger; to fall; to drop; to stumble

跌傷 **dit sèung**
to get injured by a fall

跌跤 **dit gàau**
to have a fall

跌價 **dit ga**
to cut price

跎 **tòh** (Md **tuó**)
to miss one's footing; to stumble

跑 **páau** (Md **pǎo, páo**)
to run; to run away; to flee

跑步 **páau bouh**
to run

跑道 **páau douh**
track; runway

跑開 **páau hòi**
to get out of the way

跖 **jek** (Md **zhí**)
① sole (of the foot) ② name of a notorious robber

跗 **fù** (Md **fū**)
the instep

跗骨 **fù gwāt**
tarsus; tarsal bone

跗蹠 **fù jik**
tarsi and metatarsi

跚 **sàan** (Md **shān**)
to walk unsteadily

跛 **bài, bó** (Md **bǒ**)
① lame; crippled ② to lean; to be partial

跛脚 **bài geuk**
lame; crippled

距 **kéuih** (Md **jù**)
distance

距離 **kéuih lèih**
distance

距今 **kéuih gàm**
ago

跨 **kwà** (Md **kuà**)
① to take a stride ② to sit astride on; to straddle; to ride

跨馬 **kwà máh**
to mount a horse

跨海 **kwà hói**
to cross the sea

跨越 **kwà yuht**
to stride over

跟 **gàn** (Md **gēn**)
① the heel ② to follow; to attend upon ③ and

跟兒 **gàn yìh**
the heel

跟班 **gàn bàan**
attendant

跟踪 **gàn jùng**
to follow others track

踩 **cháai, chói** (Md **căi**)
to trample; to tread on

踩扁 **cháai bín**
to trample flat

踩水 **cháai séui**
to tread water

跣 **sín** (Md **xiǎn**)
bare footed

跣子 **sín jí**
slippers

跣足 **sín jūk**
barefooted

跪 **gwaih** (Md **guì**)
to kneel

跪拜 **gwaih baai**
to kowtow

跪地 **gwaih deih**
to kneel on the ground

踝 **yaih** (Md **zhuǎi**)
waddling

路 **louh** (Md **lù**)
way; road; path

路標 **louh bīu**
a road sign

路程 **louh chìhng**
distance to be traveled

跳 **tiu** (Md **tiào**)
to jump; to leap

跳過 **tiu gwo**
to jump over or across

跳舞 **tiu móuh**
to dance

跺 (踩) **dó** (Md **duò**)
to stamp the feet

跺脚 **dó geuk**
to stamp the feet

跤 **gàau** (Md **jiāo**)
a stumble; a fall

跼 **guhk** (Md **jú**)
bent; contracted

跼促 **guhk chūk**
narrow-minded; ill at ease; uneasy

趄 **jit** (Md **xué**)
① to go on one leg ② to loiter around

趄探 **jit taam**
to spy; to peep

趄轉 **jit jyun**
to whirl; to turn

踐 **chíhn** (Md **jiàn**)
to tread upon; to trample; to fulfil; to carry out

踐踏 **chíhn daahp**
to trample

踐約 **chíhn yeuk**
to honoɪ an agreement; to fulfil promise

踏 **daahp** (Md **tà, tā**)
to step upon; to tread upon; to trample

踏板 **daahp báan**
foot board; footrest

踏實 **daahp saht**
practical; realistic

踝 **wáh** (Md **huái**)
ankle

踝子骨 **wáh jí gwāt**
anklebone

踞 **geui** (Md **jù**)
to squat; to crouch; to occupy

跐 **chìh** (Md **chí**)
to hesitate
跐躇 **chìh chyùh**
to hesitate

踢 **tek** (Md **tī**)
to kick
踢開 **tek hòi**
to kick open; to kick out of the way
踢球 **tek kàuh**
to kick a ball; to play football

踔 **cheuk** (Md **chuō**)
to go across; to go beyond; very high
踔絕 **cheuk jyuht**
very high; very far
踔遠 **cheuk yúhn**
very high; very far

踩 (踹) **chói** (Md **cǎi**)
to tread upon; to step upon; to trample
踩高蹺 **chói gòu hìu**
to walk on stilts

踹 **cháai** (Md **chuài**)
to tread; to trample
踹踏 **cháai daahp**
to trample; to tread

踴 (踊) **yúng** (Md **yǎng**)
to jump; to leap; to rise
踊貴 **yúng gwai**
rise of price
踴躍 **yúng yeuhk**
joyful; happy

踰 **yùh** (Md **yú**)
① to pass over; to go beyond ② excessive; overly
踰年 **yùh nìhn**
the following year
踰越 **yùh yuht**
to go beyond

踱 **dohk** (Md **duó**)
to stroll; to walk slowly
踱來踱去 **dohk lòih dohk heui**
to stroll to and fro

踵 **júng, dúng** (Md **zhǒng**)
① the heel ② to follow ③ to call personally at
踵接 **júng jip**
so crowded that the people move with their toes on the heels of others
踵謝 **júng jeh**
to thank in person

踽 **géui** (Md **jǔ**)
to walk alone
踽踽 **géui géui**
walking alone

蹀 **dihp** (Md **dié**)
to stamp the feet
蹀足 **dihp jūk**
to stamp the feet

蹁 **pìhn** (Md **pián**)
walking unsteadily
蹁躚 **pìhn sìn**
to walk unsteadily

蹂 **yàuh** (Md **róu**)
① to tread upon; to trample ② to tread out grain
蹂踐 **yàuh chíhn**
to trample
蹂躪 **yàuh leuhn**
to trample; to devastate

蹄 (蹏) **tàih** (Md **tí**)
hoof
蹄筋 **tàih gàn**
tendon of Achilles
蹄形磁石 **tàih yìhng chìh sehk**
horseshoe magnet

蹄子 **tàih jí**
hoof

蹈 **douh** (Md **dǎo**)
① to tread; to trample ② to follow; to persue

蹈覆轍 **douh fūk chit**
to repeat a mistake someone has previously made

蹈火赴湯 **douh fó fuh tòng**
to brave all possible difficulties

蹇 **gín** (Md **jiǎn**)
① lame; crippled ② slow ③ weak; feeble

蹇連 **gín lìhn**
difficult to travel

蹇滯 **gín jaih**
not proceeding smoothly

蹉 **chò** (Md **cuō**)
a failure; a miss

蹉跌 **chò dit**
failure; slip

蹉跎 **chò tòh**
to slip and fall

蹋 **daahp** (Md **tà**)
to tread on

蹋地 **daahp deih**
to stamp the feet

蹊 **hàih** (Md **xī, qī**)
① path; footpath ② to tread

蹊徑 **hàih ging**
a narrow path

蹊蹺 **hàih hìu**
extraordinary; strange

蹌 **chòng** (Md **qiàng**)
walking unsteadily

蹌蹌 **chòng chòng**
walking rapidly

蹣 **mùhn** (Md **pán**)
① to jump over ② to limp

蹣跚 **mùhn sàan**
limping

蹙 **chūk** (Md **cù**)
① to contract; to draw together ② urgent ③ sad; sorrow

蹙眉 **chūk mèih**
to knit the brows

蹙蹙 **chūk chūk**
drawn together; wrinkled

蹤(踪) **jùng** (Md **zōng**)
① footprint; track ② to follow; to keep track of

蹤踪 **jùng jīk**
track; trace

蹤由 **jùng yàuh**
origin and development

蹢 **jaahk, dīk** (Md **dí, zhí**)
① hoof ② faltering; hesitate

蹢躅 **jaahk juhk**
faltering; hesitate

蹠 **jik** (Md **zhí**)
① to tread on; to step on ② sole (of the foot)

蹠骨 **jik gwāt**
metatarsus

蹦 **bahng** (Md **bèng**)
to skip; to caper; to trip; to jump

蹦跳 **bahng tiu**
skipping; capering

蹲 **dèun, chyùhn** (Md **dūn, cún**)
to squat; to crouch

蹲踞 **dèun geui**
to squat

蹲下去 **dèun hah heui**
to squat

蹩 **biht** (Md **bié**)
to limp

蹩脚 **biht geuk**
  lame; inferior in quality

蹬 **dahng** (Md **dēng**)
  ① to tread on; to step on ②
deprived of power or influence

蹴(踀) **chūk** (Md **cù**)
  ① to tread on ② to kick ③
respectful

  蹴然 **chūk yìhn**
    respectful; uneasy; nervous

蹶 **kyut** (Md **jué, juě**)
  ① to tread ② to stumble and fell

  蹶然 **kyut yìhn**
    standing up from fright; rising
suddenly from fear

  蹶子 **kyut jí**
    a horse's backward kick with
its hind hoof

蹺(蹺、蹻) **hìu**
(Md **qiāo**)
  to raise the feet

  蹺捷 **hìu jiht**
    able to move quickly and
easily; agile

  蹺蹊 **hìu hàih**
    extraordinary; strange

躁 **chou** (Md **zào**)
  ① irritable; hot tempered ②
restless; uneasy

  躁急 **chou gāp**
    impatient; uneasy

  躁率 **chou sēut**
    impatient and careless

躅 **juhk** (Md **zhú**)
  to falter; to hesitate

躇 **chyùh** (Md **chú**)
  to hesitate

蠆(躉) **dán** (Md **dǔn**)
  ① a whole batch or amount ② to
buy or sell whole-sale

躉船 **dán syùhn**
  a lighter (for loading or
unloading larger ship)

躉售 **dán sauh**
  to sell wholesale

躊(踌) **chàuh**
(Md **chóu**)
  ① hesitant ② complacent

  躊躇 **chàuh chyùh**
    to hesitate; complacent

  躊佇 **chàuh chyú**
    to falter; to hesitate

躋 **jài** (Md **jī**)
  to go up; to rise; to ascend

躍 **yeuhk** (Md **yuè**)
  to jump; to leap; to bound; to
spring

  躍動 **yeuhk duhng**
    to move actively

  躍進 **yeuhk jeun**
    to leap forward; to make rapid
progress

  躍起 **yeuhk héi**
    to leap up; to jump up

躕(蹰) **chyùh** (Md **chú**)
  to falter; to hesitate

躑(踯) **jaahk** (Md **zhí**)
  to falter; to hesitate

  躑躅 **jaahk juhk**
    to falter; to hesitate

躚 **sìn** (Md **xiān**)
  to turn round and round

  躚躚 **sìn sìn**
    turning round and round

躡(蹑) **nihp** (Md **niè**)
  ① to tread on; to step over ② to
follow; to persue ③ to walk
lightly

  躡蹀 **nihp dihp**
    walking with mincing steps

躡足 **nihp jūk**
to step upon another's foot

躪 **leuhn** (Md **lìn**)
to trample; to devastate; to overrun; to lay waste to a place

身部

身 **sàn** (Md **shēn**)
① body; trunk ② one's ownperson

身份 **sàn fán**
one's status or position

身體 **sàn tái**
the body; health

身心 **sàn sàm**
body and mind

躬(躳) **gùng** (Md **gōng**)
① in person; personally ② to bend (the body)

躬臨 **gùng làhm**
to be present personally

躬身 **gùng sàn**
to bend the body in respect

躲(躱) **dó** (Md **duǒ**)
to hide; to escape; to avoid

躲避 **dó beih**
to ward off

躲懶 **dó láahn**
to shun work

躲藏 **dó chòhng**
to hide oneself

躺 **tóng** (Md **tǎng**)
to be in a lying position; to lie down

躺下 **tóng hah**
to lie down

躺椅 **tóng yí**
a couch; a sofa

軀(躯) **kèui** (Md **qū**)
body; trunk

軀體 **kèui tái**
body

軀幹 **kèui gon**
trunk (of the human anatomy)

車部

車(车) **chè, gèui**
(Md **chē, jū**)
① vehicle; wheel ② name of a chessman in a kind of Chinese chess ③ a Chinese family name

車牌 **chè pàaih**
license plate

車馬費 **gèui máh fai**
transportation allowances

軋(轧) **jaat** (Md **yà, zhá**)
① to crush; to grind ② to crowd; to joint

軋傷 **jaat sèung**
to run over and injure

軋碎 **jaat seui**
to crush to pieces

軌 **gwái** (Md **guǐ**)
① rut; track; path ② rule; regulation

軌範 **gwái faahn**
pattern; model; rule

軌道 **gwái douh**
railway track

軍(军) **gwàn** (Md **jūn**)
① military; of war ② corps

軍隊 **gwàn déui**
armed forces

軍事 **gwàn sih**
military affairs

軒 **hìn** (Md **xuān**)
① carriage formerly used by high officials ② balcony ③ open; wide; high

軒敞 **hìn chóng**
open; wide

軒然 **hìn yìhn**
　smiling delighted

軒昂 **hìn ngòhng**
　high; lofty

軔 **yahn** (Md **rèn**)
　① skid (for checking the motion
　of a vehicle) ② to block; to check
　③ soft

軟(软　輭) **yúhn**
　(Md **ruǎn**)
　① soft; tender; plastic ② gentle;
　mild ③ weak; feeble

軟禁 **yúhn gam**
　to put under house arrest

軟心腸 **yúhn sàm chèuhng**
　soft-hearted

軟弱 **yúhn yeuhk**
　weak; feeble

軫 **chán, ján** (Md **zhěn**)
　① wooden bumper at the rear of
　a cart ② very much; deeply

軫念 **chán nihm**
　to remember with deep
　emotion

軫恤 **chán sēut**
　to pity deeply

軸 **juhk** (Md **zhóu, zhòu**)
　① axis; pivot ② scroll

軸心 **juhk sàm**
　axis

軻 **ò** (Md **kē**)
　① a kind of axle ② name of
　Mencius

軻峩 **ò ngòh**
　lofty

軼 **yaht** (Md **yì**)
　① to excell; to surpass ② to be
　scattered; to go loose

軼羣 **yaht kwàhn**
　to be outstanding

軼事 **yaht sih**
　anecdote

較 **gaau** (Md **jiào**)
　① to compare ② in a greater or
　lesser degree; more or less

較量 **gaau leuhng**
　to compare in a contest

較勝一籌 **gaau sing yāt
chàuh**
　better by one degree; a little
　better

軾 **sīk** (Md **shì**)
　① horizontal front bar on a cart
　② leaning board in a sedan chair

載 **joi, jói** (Md **zài, zǎi**)
　① (of vehicles) to carry (loads) ②
　to record ③ year

載明 **joi mìhng**
　to record clearly

載運 **joi wahn**
　to transport

軽 **ji** (Md **zhì**)
　the lower rear of a chariot

輋(輋) **chèh** (Md **shē**)
　used as a name of a place

輒(辄、輙) **jip**
　(Md **zhé**)
　① sides of a chariot ② arbitrary
　③ then; in the case

輔 **fuh** (Md **fǔ**)
　① human cheek bones ② to
　assist; to help

輔導 **fuh douh**
　to assist and guide

輔幣 **fuh baih**
　coins of small denominations

輕 **hìng** (Md **qīng**)
　① light; easy to carry ② simple;
　easy ③ mild; gentle; soft

輕便 **hìng bihn**
handy; convenient

輕易 **hìng yih**
easy

輕視 **hìng sih**
to look down upon

輓 **wáahn** (Md **wǎn**)
① to draw or pull ② to mourn

輓聯 **wáahn lyùhn**
funeral scrolls

輓近 **wáahn gahn**
lately; recently

輜 (輺) **jì** (Md **zī**)
① curtained carriage ② wagon for supplies

輥 **gwán** (Md **gǔn**)
pivot; driving shaft

輛 **leuhng** (Md **liàng**)
numerary adjunct for vehicles

輝 (辉、煇) **fāi**
(Md **huī**)
light; luster; brilliance

輝煌 **fāi wòhng**
magnificent; splendid; glorious

輝映 **fāi yíng**
to emit and reflect light

輟 **jyut** (Md **chuò**)
to stop; to halt; to suspend

輟學 **jyut hohk**
to drop out of school

輟耕 **jyut gàang**
to stop ploughing

輦 **líhm** (Md **niǎn**)
① handcart ② king's carriage

輦夫 **líhm fù**
a porter

輦道 **líhm douh**
the emperor's road

輩 **bui** (Md **bèi**)
① rank; grade ② generation

輩份 **bui fahn**
difference in seniority

輩兒 **bui yìh**
a generation

輪 **lèuhn** (Md **lún**)
① wheel ② to alternate ③ majestic; stately

輪軸 **lèuhn juhk**
wheel and axle

輪值 **lèuhn jihk**
to go on duty in turn

輯 **chāp** (Md **jí**)
① friendly ② to collect; to gather

輯睦 **chāp muhk**
friendliness

輯要 **chāp yiu**
an outline; a summary

輸 **syù** (Md **shū**)
① to transport; to convey ② to hand in; to submit ③ to lose (in a game)

輸送 **syù sung**
to transport

輸血 **syù hyut**
blood transfusion

輸錢 **syù chín**
to lose money in gambling

輻 **fūk** (Md **fú**)
spokes (of wheel)

輻聚 **fūk jeuih**
to gather

輻射 **fūk seh**
radiation; to radiate

輾 **jín** (Md **zhǎn**)
to turn over; to roll over

輾轉 **jín jyún**
to roll about; to take a round-about course

輾斃 **jín baih**
　to be run over by a vehicle and
　got killed

輿 **yùh** (Md **yú**)
　① carriage; vehicle ② sedan chair
　③ the land; the earth

輿馬 **yùh máh**
　the carriage and the horse

輿論 **yùh leuhn**
　public opinion

輿地 **yùh deih**
　the land; the earth

轂（轂）**gūk** (Md **gǔ**)
hub (of a wheel) wheel

轂轆 **gūk lūk**
　wheel

轂下 **gūk hah**
　the capital

轄（轄、鎋）**haht**
(Md **xiá**)
　① linchpin ② to govern; to
　manage

轄下 **haht hah**
　under the command or
　jurisdiction of

轄治 **haht jih**
　to govern; to rule

轅 **yùhn** (Md **yuán**)
　① shafts (of a cart) ② the
　magistrate's office or residence

轅門 **yùhn mùhn**
　outer gate of a commander's
　residence

轅下駒 **yùhn hah kèui**
　a horse between the shafts —
　to be under-restraint

轉 **jyún, jyun**
（Md **zhuǎn, zhuàn**）
　① to turn; to shift ② to
transport; to transfer ③ indirect;
roundabout

轉播 **jyún bo**
　to relay a broadcast

轉捩點 **jyún liht dím**
　turning point

轉一轉 **jyun yāt jyun**
　to take a short walk; to take
　a turn

轆 **lūk** (Md **lù**)
　① wheel ② a capstan

轆轤 **lūk lòuh**
　a capstan; a pulley for drawing
　water from a well

轇 **gàau** (Md **jiū**)
　① dispute ② disorder

轇輵 **gàau got**
　dispute; disorder

轍 **chit** (Md **zhé**)
ruts; wheel tracks

轍迹 **chit jīk**
　wheel tracks; ruts

轎（轿）**giuh, gíu**
（Md **jiào**）
sedan-chair; palankeen

轎夫 **giuh fù**
　sedan-chair bearer

轎子 **giuh jí**
　sedan-chair palankeen

轔 **lèuhn** (Md **lín**)
　① noise of wheels; rumbling of
vehicles ② wheels

轔轔 **lèuhn lèuhn**
　rumbling of vehicles

轕 **got** (Md **gé**)
dispute; disorder

轟（轰）**gwàng**
（Md **hōng**）
　① noise; uproar ② grant;
magnificent

轟動 **gwàng duhng**
　to cause an uproar; to create

a sensation

轟炸 **gwàng ja**
to bomb

轡（轡）**bei (Md pèi)**
reins; bridle

轡勒 **bei laahk**
reins and bit

轤 **lòuh (Md lú)**
① pulley for drawing water ②
Windlass; capstan

辛部

辛 **sàn (Md xīn)**
① bitter; acid ② hard; laborious
③ a Chinese family name

辛勞 **sàn lòuh**
great care or effort

辛勤 **sàn kàhn**
hard-working; diligent

辛酸 **sàn syùn**
hardships; the bitters of life

辜 **gù (Md gū)**
① sin; crime; guilt ② to be
negligent in an obligation ③ a
Chinese family name

辜負 **gù fuh**
to fail to live up to

辜月 **gù yuht**
the eleventh month of the
lunar year

辟 **pīk, bīk (Md pì, bì)**
① moarch ② to summon; to call
③ remote; inaccessible

辟邪 **pīk chèh**
to ward off evils

辟引 **bīk yáhn**
to summon to court

辟匿 **pīk līk**
remote; out of the way

辣 **laaht (Md là)**
pungent; hot

辣手 **laaht sáu**
cruel means; drastic means

辣味 **laaht meih**
piquancy; peppery

辦 **baahn (Md bàn)**
① to manage; to handle ② to try
and punish

辦報 **baahn bou**
to publish a newspaper

辦法 **baahn faat**
means; schemes

辦理 **baahn léih**
to handle; to manage

辨 **bihn (Md biàn)**
to distinguish; to identify; to
recognize

辨白 **bihn baahk**
to distinguish clearly

辨認 **bihn yihng**
to identify; to recognize

辭（辞、辝）**chìh**
(Md cí)
① words; phrase ② to decline ③
to leave; to depart

辭令 **chìh lihng**
diplomatic speech

辭行 **chìh hàhng**
to say good-bye to

辭職 **chìh jīk**
to resign from one's post

辯 **bihn (Md biàn)**
to debate; to argue

辯駁 **bihn bok**
to defend and refute

辯論 **bihn leuhn**
to debate; a debate

辰部

辰 **sàhn (Md chén)**
① 7:00 − 9:00 a.m. ② time ③
fortune; luck

辰星 **sàhn sìng**
morning star

辰砂 **sàhn sà**
cinnabar

辱 **yuhk** (Md **rǔ**)
① to disgrace; to insult ② to condescend

辱罵 **yuhk mah**
to abuse and insult

辱臨 **yuhk làhm**
to condescend to come to such a humble place

農（农、辳）**nùhng**
(Md **nóng**)
agriculture; farming

農民 **nùhng màhn**
farmer

農田 **nùhng tìhn**
agricultural fields

農場 **nùhng chèuhng**
farm

辵部

迂 **yù** (Md **yū**)
① impractical; unrealistic; trite ② roundabout; indirect

迂腐 **yù fuh**
trite; stale

迂迴曲折 **yù wùih kūk jit**
having many turns and curves; not straighforward

迄 **ngaht** (Md **qì**)
up to; till

迄今 **ngaht gàm**
up to now

迄未 **ngaht meih**
not until now; not yet

迅 **seun** (Md **xùn**)
swift; rapid sudden

迅雷 **seun lèuih**
sudden clap and thunder

迅速 **seun chūk**
quick; rapid; swift

迎 **yìhng** (Md **yíng**)
to receive; to greet to meet; to welcome

迎敵 **yìhng dihk**
to meet enemy in battle

迎接 **yìhng jip**
to receive; to greet

迎頭趕上 **yìhng tàuh gón séuhng**
to try hard to catch up

近 **gahn** (Md **jìn**)
① near or close (in space and time) ② intimate; to approach

近鄰 **gahn lèuhn**
close neighbor

近日 **gahn yaht**
lately; recently

近似 **gahn chíh**
similar to; resembling

迓 **ngah** (Md **yà**)
to go out to meet or receive

返 **fáan** (Md **fǎn**)
① to go back; to return ② to send back; to give back

返國 **fáan gwok**
to return from abroad

返魂 **fáan wàhn**
to come back to life; to resurrect

迕 **ngh** (Md **wǔ**)
to meet; to oppose

迕逆 **ngh yihk**
to oppose; delinquent in filial piety

迢 **tìuh** (Md **tiáo**)
far; distant

迢迢 **tìuh tìuh**
faraway

迢遙 **tìuh yìuh**
    far; distant

迴(迥) **gwìng**
(Md **jiǒng**)
far

迴異 **gwìng yih**
    great difference

迴遠 **gwìng yúhn**
    faraway; remote

迦 **gà** (Md **jiā**)
a character used in transliteration

迦納 **Gà naahp**
    Ghana

迪 **dihk** (Md **dí**)
① to advance; to progress ② to
enlighten

迪吉 **dihk gàt**
    lucky; going well

迫(廹) **bāak, bīk**
(Md **pò, pǎi**)
① to press; to force ② urgent;
imminent

迫害 **bīk hoih**
    to oppress cruelly

迫促 **bāak chūk**
    urgent; pressed for time

迫擊砲 **bīk gīk paau**
    mortar

迭 **diht** (Md **dié**)
① to alternate ② repeated;
frequently ③ to stop

迭擊 **diht gīk**
    to attack by turns

迭用 **diht yuhng**
    to use alternately

述 **seuht** (Md **shù**)
① to give an account of; to
explain ② to follow; to continue

述職 **seuht jīk**
    to report in person the perfor-
    mance of one's official duties

述說 **seuht syut**
    to give an account of; to
    narrate

迤(迆) **yíh, yìh** (Md **yǐ,
yí**)
to move away; connected

迴(回、廻) **wùih**
(Md **huí**)
① to turn; to rotate; to revolve ②
zigzag; winding

迴避 **wùih beih**
    to avoid meeting another

迴旋 **wùih syùhn**
    to turn round and round; to
    circle

迷 **màih** (Md **mí**)
① indistinct; dim ② to bewitch;
to charm

迷途 **màih tòuh**
    to get lost

迷惑 **màih waahk**
    to misguide; to confuse

迷信 **màih seun**
    superstition

迹(跡、蹟) **jīk** (Md **jī**)
footprints; traces

迹象 **jīk jeuhng**
    signs; marks

追 **jèui** (Md **zhuī**)
① to chase; to pursue ② to drive;
to expel ③ to demand insistently

追悼 **jèui douh**
    to commemorate (the dead)

追求 **jèui kàuh**
    to seek; to pursue

追隨 **jèui chèuih**
    to follow a leader

逢 **pòhng** (Md **páng**)
a Chinese family name

退 teui (Md tuì)
① to retreat; to withdraw to regress ② to bow out; to retire ③ to send back; to give back

退保 **teui bóu**
to return a bond

退步 **teui bouh**
to regress; to fall backwards

退休 **teui yàu**
to retire from active life

送 sung (Md sòng)
① to send; to deliver ② to present; to give ③ to see off; to send off

送到 **sung dou**
to send to

送別 **sung biht**
to see a person off

送禮 **sung láih**
to send gifts

逃 tòuh (Md táo)
to run away; to flee; to escape; to avoid

逃避 **tòuh beih**
to run away from

逃亡 **tòuh mòhng**
to escape; to flee

逃生 **tòuh sàng**
to flee for one's life

逅 hauh (Md hòu)
to meet unexpectedly

逆 yihk, ngaahk (Md nì)
① to oppose; to go against ② beforehand ③ inverse; converse

逆風 **ngaahk fùng**
head wind; against wind

逆叛 **yihk buhn**
to rebel

迻 yìh (Md yí)
to shift; to transfer

迻譯 **yìh yihk**
to translate

逍 sìu (Md xiāo)
to wander in a leisurely manner

逍遙 **sìu yìuh**
to loiter about

逍遙法外 **sìu yìuh faat ngoih**
to remain out of the law's reach

透 tau (Md tòu)
① to pass through ② to let out ③ thorough; complete

透明 **tau mìhng**
transparent

透風 **tau fùng**
to let the wind through

透徹 **tau chit**
thorough

逐 juhk (Md zhú)
① to chase; to follow ② to drive off; to expel ③ little by little

逐漸 **juhk jihm**
gradually; by degrees

逐出 **juhk chēut**
to drive out; to expel

逑 kàuh (Md qiú)
① to pair; to match ② to collect; to draw together

途 tòuh (Md tú)
way; road

途經 **tòuh gìng**
to pass through

途徑 **tòuh ging**
way; road

逕 ging (Md jìng)
① a path ② direct

逕庭 **ging tìhng**
very unlike; quite different

逕寄 **ging gei**
to mail directly to . . .

逖(逷) **tīk** (Md **tì**)
far; distant

逗 **dauh** (Md **dòu**)
① to stay; to linger ② to stir; to rouse

逗弄 **dauh luhng**
to make fun of; to tease

逗留 **dauh làuh**
to stay; to linger

這(这) **je** (Md **zhè, zhèi**)
this; such

這麼 **je mō**
so; thus; this way

這裏 **je léuih**
here; this place

這年 **je nìhn**
this year

通 **tùng** (Md **tōng, tòng**)
① to go; move ② to communicate to exchange ③ to lead to

通道 **tùng douh**
passage; way

通信 **tùng seun**
communication; correspondence

通行 **tùng hàhng**
to travel through

逛 **kwaang** (Md **guàng**)
to stroll; to rumble; to wander about

逛街 **kwaang gāai**
to stroll down the street; to do window shopping

逛一逛 **kwaang yāt kwaang**
to go for a walk

逝 **saih** (Md **shì**)
to pass; to be gone; to depart

逝世 **saih sai**
to pass away; to die

逝止 **saih jí**
going and staying

逞 **chíng** (Md **chěng**)
① to indulge in ② to use up ③ to display; to show off

逞能 **chíng nàhng**
to display or show off one's ability

逞强 **chíng kèuhng**
to bully; to throw one's weight around

速 **chūk** (Md **sù**)
① quick; speed ② to invite

速度 **chūk douh**
velocity; speed

速成 **chūk sìhng**
to attain goals within a short time

造 **jouh** (Md **zào**)
① to make; to do; to create; to build ② to arrive at; to reach

造反 **jouh fáan**
to rebel; to rise up against

造就 **jouh jauh**
to educate

造酒 **jouh jáu**
to brew alcoholic beverage

逡 **sèun** (Md **qūn**)
to withdraw; to retreat; to move back

逡巡 **sèun chèuhn**
to hesitate or waver

逢 **fùhng** (Md **féng**)
① to meet; to come across ② to happen; to fall in with

逢迎 **fùhng yìhng**
to receive (a guest)

逢凶化吉 **fùhng hùng fa gāt**
to turn bad luck into good fortune

連 **lìhn** (Md **lián**)
① to connect; to joint ② together with ③ a Chinese family name

連忙 **lìhn mòhng**
promptly; quickly

連同 **lìhn tùhng**
together with; in addition to

連續 **lìhn juhk**
successive; continuous

逮 **daih** (Md **dài, dǎi**)
① to reach ② to be after; to hunt ③ to catch

逮捕 **daih bouh**
to make arrest

逮住 **daih jyuh**
to catch (a thief or a ball)

週 **jàu** (Md **zhōu**)
a week; a period

週末 **jàu muht**
weekend

週年 **jàu nìhn**
a full year; an anniversary

週全 **jàu chyùhn**
complete and perfect

進(进) **jeun** (Md **jìn**)
① to go ahead; to advance ② to improve ③ to offer

進兵 **jeun bìng**
to march troops forward

進修 **jeun sàu**
to study; to learn

進級 **jeun kāp**
to get promoted

逵 **kwàih** (Md **kuí**)
a thorough fare

逶 **wài** (Md **wēi**)
winding; curved

逶迤 **wài yìh**
winding (river; road) ② long; distant

逴 **cheuk** (Md **chuō**)
far and high

迸 **bing** (Md **bèng**)
① to catter; to explode ② to crack; to spit out

迸淚 **bing leuih**
tears pouring out

迸裂 **bing liht**
to crack; to spit

逸 **yaht** (Md **yì**)
① to flee; to escape ② to rusticate ③ ease; leisure ④ to let loose

逸樂 **yaht lohk**
enjoyment of an easy life

逸才 **yaht chòih**
outstanding talent

逾 **yùh** (Md **yú**)
① to exceed; to passover ② to transgress ③ added; more

逾期 **yùh kèih**
to exceed a time limit

逾越 **yùh yuht**
to pass over; to do what one is not supposed to do

逼(偪) **bīk** (Md **bī**)
① to press; to compel ② to close in; to draw near

逼迫 **bīk bāak**
urgent; to compel

逼眞 **bīk jàn**
almost real (of acting; performance)

逼近 **bīk gahn**
to close in; to draw near

遁(遯) **deuhn** (Md **dùn**)
① to run away; to escape ② to conceal oneself

遁形 **deuhn yìhng**
to become invisible

遁走 **deuhn jáu**
to flee; to take to one's heels

遂 **seuih** (Md **suì, suí**)
① to have things one's way ② successful ③ to proceed to

遂令 **seuih lihng**
to order thereupon

遂願 **seuih yuhn**
to have one's wish fulfilled

遄 **chyùhn** (Md **chuán**)
swiftly; quickly

遄返 **chyùhn fáan**
to hurry back

遄死 **chyùhn séi**
to die very quickly

遇 **yuh** (Md **yù**)
① to meet; to run into; to come across; to treat ② opportunity; luck

遇著 **yuh jeuhk**
to meet; to encounter

遇難 **yuh naahn**
to get killed in an accident

遊 **yàuh** (Md **yóu**)
① to travel; to roam ② to study under ③ to freely wield

遊覽 **yàuh láahm**
to tour; sightseeing

遊蕩 **yàuh dohng**
to fool around

遊學 **yàuh hohk**
to study abroad

運 **wahn** (Md **yùn**)
① to move; to revolve; to transport; to ship ② to utilize; to make use of

運動 **wahn duhng**
sports; physical exercise

運輸 **wahn syù**
transportation

運用 **wahn yuhng**
to employ; to make use of

遍(徧) **pin** (Md **biàn**)
① a time, as "you must read it ten times in order to understand it" ② everywhere; all over

遍地 **pin deih**
everywhere

遍告 **pin gou**
to announce to all

過(过) **gwo** (Md **guò, guō**)
① to pass; to pass by; ② to surpass ③ too much ④ mistake

過路 **gwo louh**
to pass by; to transit

過錯 **gwo cho**
mistakes; faults

過半 **gwo bun**
more than a half

遏 **aat, ngaat** (Md **è**)
① to curb; to stop; to check; to prevent ② to harm; to hurt

遏制 **aat jai**
to restrain; to check

遏阻 **aat jó**
to curb; to arrest

遑 **wòhng** (Md **huáng**)
hurry; anxious

遑急 **wòhng gāp**
scared and in a hurry

遑遑 **wòhng wòhng**
disturb; jittery

遐 **hàh** (Md **xiá**)
① distant ② a long time ③ to vanish; to cast off

遐布 **hàh bou**
to spread far and wide

遐迹 **hàh jīk**
matters and stories of ancient people

遒 **chàuh** (Md **qiú**)
① strong; forceful ② to come to an end

遒美 **chàuh méih**
forceful and graceful

遒勁 **chàuh gihng**
forceful

道 **douh** (Md **dào**)
① a road; a path ② a method; a way ③ to say; to speak

道路 **douh louh**
a road

道德 **douh dāk**
morality; moral

道賀 **douh hoh**
to offer congratulation

達 **daaht** (Md **dá**)
① to reach; to arrive at ② to inform; to tell ③ intelligent; understanding; reasonable

達到 **daaht dou**
to reach; to attain

達成 **daaht sìhng**
to succeed in; to accomplish

違 **wàih** (Md **wéi**)
① to disobey; to go against ② to be disregard ③ to avoid

違背 **wàih bui**
to defy; to disobey

違法 **wàih faat**
to be against law

違失 **wàih sāt**
faults; errors

遜 **seun** (Md **xùn**)
① humble; modest ② not as good as ③ respectful and compliant

遜色 **seun sīk**
inferior to; not as good as

遜位 **seun waih**
to abdicate

遘 **gau** (Md **gòu**)
to come across; to meet; to encounter

遘患 **gau waahn**
to meet with trouble; to meet with bad luck

遙 **yìuh** (Md **yáo**)
far; distant

遙遠 **yìuh yúhn**
far and remote

遙遙領先 **yìuh yìuh líhng sìn**
to be far ahead

遛 **làuh** (Md **liù**)
to hang around; to roam

遞 **daih** (Md **dì**)
① to hand; to pass over to ② to substitute; to alternate

遞交 **daih gàau**
to hand over; to deliver

遞增 **daih jàng**
to increase progressively

遠 **yúhn** (Md **yuǎn**)
① far; distant ② deep; profound

遠行 **yúhn hàhng**
to travel to a distant place

遠見 **yúhn gin**
plan; a farsighted view

遠離 **yúhn lèih**
to depart for a distant place

遢 **taap** (Md **ta**)
careless; untidy

遣 **hín** (Md **qiǎn**)
① to send ② to forget

遣送 **hín sung**
to send away

遣悶 **hín muhn**
to drive away melancholy; to kill time

遭 jòu (Md **zāo**)

to meet with; to incur; to be victimized

遭遇 jòu yuh
to meet with disaster calamity

遭害 jòu hoih
to be murdered or assassinated

適 sīk (Md **shì**)

① just; right; exactly ② comfortable ③ to match; to adapt

適合 sīk hahp
suitable; to fit

適應 sīk ying
to adapt; to adjust

適當 sīk dong
proper; fit

遮 jè (Md **zhē**)

① to shade; to cover ② to block; to intercept

遮蔽 jè bai
to cover up; to screen

遮瞞 jè mùhn
to hide the truth

遮擋 jè dóng
to block

遨 ngòuh, ngouh
(Md **áo**)

to travel for pleasure

遨遊 ngòuh yàuh
to ramble

遲 chìh (Md **chí**)

① late ② slow ③ to delay

遲到 chìh dou
to come or arrive late

遲鈍 chìh deuhn
stupid; clumsy

遲延 chìh yìhn
to delay

遴 lèuhn (Md **lín**)

① to select carefully ② a Chinese

family name

遴選 lèuhn syún
to select; to pick

遴派 lèuhn paai
to appoint a person after careful selection

遵 jèun (Md **zūn**)

① to obey; to follow ② to observe; to abide

遵命 jèun mihng
to obey orders

遵照 jèun jiu
to follow; to observe

遵守 jèun sáu
to abide; to keep (promise)

遷 chìn (Md **qiān**)

① to remove; to move ② to change

遷就 chìn jauh
to compromise; to accommodate

遷居 chìn gèui
to move to a new address

遷怒 chìn nouh
to shift one's anger from one person to another

選 syún (Md **xuǎn**)

① election; choice ② to choose; to elect

選拔 syún baht
to pick the better one from a group of people

選擇 syún jaahk
a choice; to choose

選派 syún paai
to nominate

遺 wàih, waih (Md **yí, wěi**)

① to lose; to miss ② things lost; an omission due to negligence

遺漏 wàih lauh
to omit or miss

遺棄 **wàih hei**
to cast away; to desert

遺囑 **wàih jūk**
will of a dead person

遼 **lìuh** (Md **liáo**)
① far, distant ② the Liao River

遼闊 **lìuh fut**
vast; distant

遼遠 **lìuh yúhn**
far away or distant

避 **beih** (Md **bì**)
to hide; to avoid

避免 **beih míhn**
to avoid; to prevent something from happening

避難 **beih naahn**
to escape calamity

避暑 **beih syú**
to run away from summer heat

邁 **maaih** (Md **mài**)
① to pass; to exceed ② to go on a long journey ③ old age

邁進 **maaih jeun**
to forge ahead

邁步 **maaih bouh**
to take a step

遽 **geuih** (Md **jù**)
① hurriedly; suddenly ② scared; frightened

遽然 **geuih yìhn**
suddenly

遽步 **geuih bouh**
to walk hurriedly

邀 **yiu** (Md **yāo**)
① to request; to invite ② to intercept

邀請 **yiu chíng**
to invite

邀宴 **yiu yin**
to invite to a feast

邂 **haaih** (Md **xiè**)
to meet without prior engagement

邂逅 **haaih hauh**
to chance to meet

還(还) **wàahn**
(Md **huán, hái**)
① to come back; to return ② to give back; to repay ③ yet; still

還債 **wàahn jaai**
to repay a debt

還是 **wàahn sih**
this . . . or . . .; still

邅 **jìn** (Md **zhān**)
very difficult to proceed

邇 **yíh** (Md **ěr**)
① recently; lately ② near; close to

邇來 **yíh lòih**
recently

邃 **seuih** (Md **suì**)
① deep; far ② profound; depth

邃蜜 **seuih maht**
abstruse and fall

邃古 **seuih gú**
the remote pass

邈 **míuh** (Md **miǎo**)
① far; distant ② to look down upon

邈視 **míuh sih**
to despise; to look down upon

邈然 **míuh yìhn**
remote; distant

邊 **bìn** (Md **biān**)
① side; edge; hem ② near to; to boader on

邊界 **bìn gaai**
the national boundary

邊緣 **bìn yùhn**
the edge

邏 **lòh** (Md **luó**)
to inspect; to patrol

邏輯 **lòh chāp**
logic

邐 **léih** (Md **lǐ**)
continuous and meandering

邑部

邑 **yāp** (Md **yì**)
a city; a town; a state

邑紳 **yāp sàn**
gentry

邑人 **yāp yàhn**
people of the same country or district

邙 **mòhng** (Md **máng**)
name of a hill Loyang in Honan Province

邛 **kùhng** (Md **qióng**)
① a hill ② illness; ailment

邛水 **Kùhng séui**
name of a county in Kweichow Province; name of a river in Szechwan Province

邕 **yùng** (Md **yōng**)
① peaceful; harmony ② to cultivate

邕邕 **yùng yùng**
harmonious; peaceful

邠 **bàn** (Md **bīn**)
name of an anicent state in today's Shensi Province

邠如 **bàn yùh**
flourishing or booming; culturally

那 **náh** (Md **nà, nèi**)
that; those; which

那般 **náh bùn**
that way

那時 **náh sìh**
at that moment

那個 **náh go**
which one

邦 **bòng** (Md **bāng**)
a country; a nation

邦交 **bòng gàau**
international relations; diplomatic relations

邦國 **bòng gwok**
a nation; a country

邪 **chèh** (Md **xié**)
① evil; wicked ② pertaining to sorcery

邪魔 **chèh mò**
devils; demons

邪惡 **chèh ngok**
evil and the wicked

邵 **siuh** (Md **shào**)
a Chinese family name

邯 **hòhn** (Md **hán**)
① name of a county in Hopeh Province ② name of a river in Chingfai and a hill in Hopeh

邱 **yàu** (Md **qiū**)
① a hill ② a Chinese family name

邸 **dái** (Md **dǐ**)
residence of a prince or nobility

邸第 **dái daih**
residence of lords and nobility

邢 **yìhng** (Md **xíng**)
a Chinese family name

郁 **yūk** (Md **yù**)
adorned; beautiful

郁烈 **yūk liht**
permeated with strong aroma

郁穆 **yūk muhk**
harmonious and refined

郇 **sèun** (Md **xún, huán**)
① name of an ancient state in today's Shansi Province ② a Chinese family name

郊 **gàau** (Md **jiāo**)
① suburbs of a city ② a ceremony for offering sacrifice to the Heaven and Earth

　郊區 **gàau kèui**
　　suburban area

　郊遊 **gàau yàuh**
　　outing

　郊祀 **gàau jih**
　　to offer sacrifice to the Heaven and Earth

郝 **kok** (Md **hǎo**)
a Chinese family name

郎 **lòhng** (Md **láng**)
① an official rank in former days ② a man ③ the husband; the bean

　郎舅 **lòhng káuh**
　　brothers-in-law

　郎君 **lòhng gwàn**
　　it is used to address a man

郡 **gwahn** (Md **jùn**)
a political division in ancient China; a prefecture

　郡城 **gwahn sìhng**
　　a prefectural city

　郡主 **gwahn jyú**
　　a princess

郢 **yíhng** (Md **yǐng**)
name of the capital of the state of Chu, in today's Hupeh Province

郤 **gwīk** (Md **xì**)
a Chinese family name

郗 **chì** (Md **xī**)
① a Chinese family name ② name of a town in the Chou Dynasty

部 **bouh** (Md **bù**)
① a section; a department ② a volume

　部門 **bouh mùhn**
　　a class; a section

　部隊 **bouh déui**
　　troops; a military unit

　部位 **bouh waih**
　　location

郵 **yàuh** (Md **yóu**)
① a post office; postal ② to deliver letters

　郵包 **yàuh bāau**
　　a postal parcel

　郵差 **yàuh chàai**
　　postman

　郵船 **yàuh syùhn**
　　mail boat; a luxurious passenger liner

郭 **gwok** (Md **guō**)
① the outer part of anything ② a Chinese family name

　郭外 **gwok ngoih**
　　beyond the outer city wall

都 **dòu** (Md **dū, dōu**)
① a large town ② beautiful, elegant ③ all; altogether

　都市 **dòu síh**
　　a city

　都是 **dòu sih**
　　all; no exception

鄂 **ngohk** (Md **è**)
① brink; edge ② short for Hupeh Province

鄆 **wahn** (Md **yùn**)
① name of an ancient town in Shantung Province ② a Chinese family name

鄉 **hèung** (Md **xiāng**)
① rural; country; village ② one's native place

鄉民 **hèung màhn**
villagers; country folks

鄉談 **hèung tàahm**
local dialects

鄉音 **hèung yàm**
native accent

廎 **tòhng** (Md **táng**)
name of town in Shantung Province

鄔 **wù** (Md **wū**)
① a Chinese family name ② name of various place in ancient times

鄒 **jàu** (Md **zōu**)
① a Chinese family name ② name of a state in the period of the Warring States

鄙 **péi** (Md **bǐ**)
① despicable; mean ② remote; out of the way ③ to despise; to scorn

鄙人 **péi yàhn**
I (self depreciatory way of referring to oneself)

鄙賤 **péi jihn**
lowly; humble

鄞 **ngàhn** (Md **yín**)
name of a county in Chekiang

鄧 **dahng** (Md **dèng**)
① a Chinese family name ② name of an ancient state in what is today's Hupeh

鄭 **jehng** (Md **zhèng**)
① formal; solemn ② a Chinese family name

鄭重 **jehng juhng**
careful; cautious; solemn

鄯 **sihn** (Md **shàn**)
name of a region in Chinese Turkestan

鄰 **lèuhn** (Md **lín**)
① neighboring ② neighborhood neighbor

鄰國 **lèuhn gwok**
neighboring country

鄰舍 **lèuhn se**
neighbor

鄰近 **lèuhn gahn**
located near by

鄱 **pòh** (Md **pó**)
Poyang, name of a county in Kiangsi

鄲 **dàan** (Md **dān**)
① a Chinese family name ② name of a county in Hupeh

鄴 **yihp** (Md **yè**)
① an ancient name for a part of what is today's Honan ② a Chinese family name

鄺 **kwong** (Md **kuàng**)
a Chinese family name

酆 **fùng** (Md **fēng**)
① a Chinese family name ② name of a county in Szechwan

酈 **lihk** (Md **lì**)
① ancient name of a part what is Honan today ② a Chinese family name

酉部

酉 **yáuh** (Md **yǒu**)
① 5:00 − 7:00 p.m. ② the tenth of the twelve Terrestial Branches

酊 **dìng, díng** (Md **dīng, dǐng**)
drunk; intoxicated

酋 **chàuh, yàuh** (Md **qiú**)
chief of a clan or tribe

酋長 **yàuh jéung**
chieftain

酌 **jeuk** (Md **zhuó**)
① to weigh and consider ② to pour

酌量 **jeuk leuhng**
to weigh and consider

酌減 **jeuk gáam**
to make considered reduction

配 **pui** (Md **pèi**)
① to match; to mate ② to fit; to suit ③ a spouse; a partner

配藥 **pui yeuhk**
to dispense medicine

配眼鏡 **pui ngáahn geng**
to get the right lenses for one's eyeglass

配偶 **pui ngáuh**
spouse

酒 **jáu** (Md **jiǔ**)
alcoholic drink; wine; liquor

酒肴 **jáu ngàauh**
wine and delicacies

酒保 **jáu bóu**
bar-tender

酒後失言 **jáu hauh sāt yìhn**
to say something wrong when drunk

酖 **dàam, jahm** (Md **dān, zhèn**)
addicted to alcoholic drinks; poisonous wine

酖酖 **dàam dàam**
enjoying comfort

酖毒 **jahm duhk**
harm; poison

酗 **yu** (Md **xù**)
to lose temper when drunk

酗酒 **yu jáu**
to indulge in excessive drinking

酗訟 **yu juhng**
to accuse each other when drunk

酢 **johk, chou** (Md **zuò, cù**)
to pour wine for the host

酣 **hàhm** (Md **hān**)
① to enjoy intoxicants ② as much as one wants

酣眠 **hàhm mìhn**
to sleep soundly

酣娛 **hàhm yùh**
to enjoy oneself to one's heart's content

酥 **sòu** (Md **sū**)
① crisp; fresh ② brittle

酥餅 **sòu béng**
a kind of crisp biscuit

酥酪 **sòu lok**
cream cheese

酩 **míhng** (Md **mǐng**)
drunk; intoxicated

酩酊大醉 **míhng díng daaih jeui**
dead drunk

酪 **lok** (Md **lào**)
① alcoholic drinks ② animal milk ③ fruit jam

酪酸 **lok syùn**
butyric acid

酪酥 **lok sòu**
cream cheese

酬(酧、醻)**chàuh** (Md **chóu**)
to request; to toast

酬報 **chàuh bou**
to reward

酬勞 **chàuh lòuh**
to reward service

酵 **gaau, hàau** (Md **jiào**)
yeast; leaven

酵母 **gaau móuh**
yeast; leaven

酵素 **hàau sou**
enzyme

酷 **huhk** (Md **kù**)
① strong ② cruel; relentless

酷刑 **huhk yìhng**
torture

酷熱 **huhk yiht**
torturing heat

酷似 **huhk chíh**
to resemble very closely

酸 **syùn** (Md **suān**)
① sour; acid ② sad; sorrowful ③ jealous; envious

酸痛 **syùn tung**
to ache from overexertion (of muscles)

酸溜溜 **syùn làuh làuh**
sour; sad; jealous

酹 **laaih, lyut** (Md **lèi**)
to make a libation

酹地 **laaih deih**
to make a libation; to pour wine in a libation

醃 (腌) **yìm** (Md **yān**)
to salt; to pickle

醃肉 **yìm yuhk**
salted meat

醃菜 **yìm choi**
pickled vegetable

醇 **sèuhn** (Md **chún**)
① strong wine; rich wine ② pure; unadulterated ③ gentle; gracious

醇酒 **sèuhn jáu**
rich wine

醇粹 **sèuhn séuih**
pure; unadulterated

醇朴 **sèuhn pok**
gentle and honest

醉 **jeui** (Md **zuì**)
① drunk; intoxicated ② charmed; infatuated

醉鄉 **jeui hèung**
paradise, or utopia, of drunkenness

醉意 **jeui yi**
slightly drunk

醋 **chou** (Md **cù**)
vinegar

醋酸 **chou syùn**
acetic acid

醋意 **chou yi**
jealousy

醄 **tòuh** (Md **táo**)
drunk

醍 **tàih** (Md **tí**)
① cream of milk ② a kind of reddish wine

醍醐 **tàih wùh**
clarified butter; purity of a man's character

醐 **wùh** (Md **hú**)
clarified butter (symbol of Buddhist wisdom or truth)

醒 **síng** (Md **xǐng**)
① to awake ② to recover from drunkenness

醒眼 **síng ngáahn**
to attract attention

醒悟 **síng ngh**
to awake (from errors, illusions)

醞 **wan** (Md **yùn**)
to brew; to ferment

醞釀 **wan yeuhng**
to brew (wine); disturbance (of

a storm) to begin to form

醜 **cháu** (Md **chǒu**)
① ugly; bad ② shameful

醜名 **cháu mìhng**
bad reputation

醜陋 **cháu lauh**
ugly; bad looking

醫 **yì** (Md **yī**)
① to cure, to treat (disease) ②
a doctor; a physician

醫治 **yì jih**
medical treatment

醫生 **yì sāng**
doctor; a surgeon; a physician

醫藥 **yì yeuhk**
healing, drugs

醪 **lòuh** (Md **láo**)
unstrained wine

醬 **jeung** (Md **jiàng**)
① soybean sauce, soy ② fruit in
the form of paste

醬油 **jeung yàuh**
soybean sauce; soy

醬瓜 **jeung gwā**
cucumbers pickled in soybean
sauce

醮 **jiu** (Md **jiào**)
① religious service ② wedding;
marriage

醴 **láih** (Md **lǐ**)
① sweet wine ② sweet spring

醴泉 **láih chyùhn**
sweet spring or fountain

醺 **fàn** (Md **xūn**)
drunk; intoxicated

醺酣 **fàn hàhm**
warm weather; balmy

醺醺 **fàn fàn**
inebriated

釀 (酿) **yeuhng**
(Md **niàng**)
① to brew; to ferment ② to take
shape or form slowly ③ wine

釀蜜 **yeuhng maht**
to make honey

釀造 **yeuhng jouh**
to brew

釁 (衅) **yan, yahn**
(Md **xìn**)
① to anoint with blood ② rift
(between people)

釁端 **yan dyūn**
cause of a fight

釁隙 **yan kwīk**
rift (between groups of people)

采部

采 **chói, choi** (Md **cǎi,
cài**)
① to collect; to pick up ② fief

采辦 **chói baahn**
to select and purchase

采集 **chói jaahp**
together or collect

采地 **choi deih**
fief

釉 **yauh** (Md **yòu**)
glaze (on pottery)

釉子 **yauh jí**
glaze

釉灰 **yauh fùi**
substance used to produce
glaze

釋 **sīk** (Md **shì**)
① to explain ② to relieve

釋放 **sīk fong**
to set free

釋去重負 **sīk heui juhng
fuh**
to be relieve of a heavy
responsibility

里部

里 **léih** (Md **lǐ**)
① a neighborhood ② a unit of linear measure

重 **chúhng, juhng, chùhng** (Md **zhòng, chóng**)
① heavy ② important ③ repeat

重量 **chúhng leuhng**
weight

重要 **juhng yiu**
important

重複 **chùhng fūk**
to repeat

野 **yéh** (Md **yě**)
① country side; field ② wild; uncultured

野蠻 **yéh màahn**
uncivilized

野地 **yéh deih**
wilderness

野獸 **yéh sau**
wild beast

量 **lèuhng, leuhng** (Md **liáng, liàng**)
① to measure ② quantity

量度 **lèuhng dohk**
to measure; to estimate

量入為出 **lèuhng yahp wàih chēut**
to regulate expenses according to income

釐 (厘) **lèih** (Md **lí**)
① unit of linear measure ② to measure ③ to reform

釐定 **lèih dihng**
to formulate

釐正 **lèih jing**
to correct

金部

金 **gàm** (Md **jīn**)
① gold ② metal ③ money; wealth

金牌 **gàm pàaih**
gold medal

金科玉律 **gàm fò yuhk leuht**
a golden rule

金玉滿堂 **gàm yuhk múhn tòhng**
to have one's house filled with riches

釘 **dèng, dìng** (Md **dīng, dìng**)
① nail ② to look steadily ③ to fasten

釘子 **dèng jí**
nails

釘書 **dèng syù**
to bind books

釘住 **dèng jyuh**
to nail securely

釜 **fú** (Md **fǔ**)
① a kettle ② an ancient unit of capacity

釜底抽薪 **fú dái chàu sàn**
to make water stop boiling by pulling firewood from under the kettle — to remove the ultimate cause of trouble

釜中魚 **fú jùng yùh**
fish in a kettle — doomed

針 (鍼) **jàm** (Md **zhēn**)
pin; needle

針線 **jàm sin**
needle and thread; needle work

針對 **jàm deui**
to aim directly at

釗 **chìu** (Md **zhāo**)
to encourage

釣 **diu** (Md **diào**)
① to fish ② to tempt; to lure

釣竿 **diu gòn**
fishing pole

釣名 **diu mìhng**
to angle for fame

釧 **chyun, chyùn**
(Md **chuàn**)
armlet; bracelet

釵 **chàai** (Md **chāi**)
a kind of hair pin

釵光鬢形 **chàai gwòng ban yíng**
a gathering of richly dressed women

鈉 **naahp** (Md **nà**)
sodium; natrium

鈉玻璃 **naahp bō lēi**
sodium glass

鈍 **deuhn** (Md **dùn**)
blunt; dull

鈍漢 **deuhn hon**
stupid fellow

鈍角 **deuhn gok**
an obtuse angle

鈔 **chàau** (Md **chāo**)
① to copy; to transcribe ② bank notes

鈔票 **chàau piu**
bank notes

鈔寫 **chàau sé**
to copy or transcribe by hand

鈞 **gwàn** (Md **jūn**)
① unit of weight ② you, your (in addressing a superior in a letter)

鈞衡 **gwàn hàhng**
to evaluate a person's abilities

鈞啟 **gwàn kái**
a conventional phrase used in the envelope address of a letter to a superior

鈕 **náu** (Md **nǐu**)
① buttons ② a Chinese family name

鈕扣 **náu kau**
buttons

鈕孔 **náu húng**
button hole

鈣 **koi** (Md **gài**)
calcium

鈣片 **koi pín**
calcium tablet

鈣質 **koi jāt**
calcium content

鈴 **lìhng** (Md **líng**)
bells

鈴聲 **lìhng sìng**
the tinkle of bells

鈸 **baht** (Md **bó**)
cymbals

鈿 **tìhn, dihn** (Md **tián, diàn**)
filigree

鉀 **gaap** (Md **jiǎ**)
potassium

鉑 **bohk** (Md **bó**)
① thin sheet of metal ② platinum

鉗(箝) **kìhm** (Md **qián**)
① forceps; tongs ② to hold with tongs

鉗子 **kìhm jí**
tongs, forceps

鉗制 **kìhm jai**
to keep under control with forceps

鉛 **yùhn** (Md **qiān, yán**)
lead

鉛筆 **yùhn bāt**
pencil

鉛球 **yùhn kàuh**
shot (thrown in shot-put)

鉢(缽) **but** (Md **bō**)
① earthernware basin or bowl ②
Buddhist priest's rice bowl

鉢盂 **but yùh**
earthernware basin

鉤(鈎) **ngàu** (Md **gōu**)
① a hook ② to hook; to probe

鉤搭 **ngàu daap**
to seduce; secret alliance

鉤心鬥角 **ngàu sàm dau gok**
to strain the wits of each other

鉤子 **ngàu jí**
a hook

鈺 **yuhk** (Md **yù**)
a hard variety of gold

鈾 **yàuh** (Md **yóu**)
uranium

銀 **ngàhn** (Md **yín**)
① silver ② money; wealth

銀行 **ngàhn hòhng**
bank

銀器 **ngàhn hei**
silverware

銀幣 **ngàhn baih**
silver coin

鉸 **gáau** (Md **jiǎo**)
① scissors ② hinges

鉸刀 **gáau dōu**
scissors; shears

鉸鏈 **gáau lín**
hinges

銅 **tùhng** (Md **tóng**)
copper; bronze; brass

銅像 **tùhng jeuhng**
bronze statue

銅牌 **tùhng pàaih**
bronze medal

銓 **chyùhn** (Md **quán**)
to weigh; to evaluate qualifications in selecting officials

銓敘 **chyùhn jeuih**
to select and appoint officials

銓擇 **chyùhn jaahk**
to evaluate and select

銖 **jyù** (Md **zhū**)
an ancient unit of weight

銖鈍 **jyù deuhn**
dull knives and spears

銖衣 **jyù yì**
extremely light garment

銘 **mìhng, míhng**
(Md **míng**)
① to inscribe; to imprint; ②
inscriptions

銘感 **mìhng gám**
to remember with gratitude

銘刻 **mìhng hāk**
to engrave

銘誌 **mìhng ji**
to record or to commemorate

銜 **hàahm** (Md **xián**)
① bit; title ② to hold in the
mouth ③ to harbor; to follow

銜接 **hàahm jip**
to connect

銜命 **hàahm mihng**
to follow an order

銜冤 **hàahm yùn**
to have a chance of airing
one's grievance

銬 **kaau** (Md **kào**)
manacles-handcuffs

鉻 **gok** (Md **gè**)
chromium

銥 **yì** (Md **yī**)
iridium

銳 **yeuih** (Md **ruì**)
① sharp; keen; acute ②
intelligent; clever

銳敏 **yeuih máhn**
keen; acute

銳利 **yeuih leih**
sharp; pointed

銳氣 **yeuih hei**
dash; vigor; aggressiveness

銷 **sìu** (Md **xiāo**)
to melt; to sell; to cancel

銷售 **sìu sauh**
to sell

銷鎔 **sìu yùhng**
to melt

銷假 **sìu ga**
to begin work after a leave of
absence or vacation

銻 **tài** (Md **tī**)
antimony

鋁 **léuih** (Md **lǔ**)
aluminium

鋁錠 **léuih ding**
aluminium ingot

鋃 **lòhng** (Md **láng**)
① chains for prisoners ② tolling
of a bell

鋃鐺 **lòhng dòng**
chains for prisoners

鋃鐺入獄 **lòhng dòng yahp
yuhk**
to be jailed

鋅 **sàn** (Md **xīn**)
zinc

鋅板 **sàn báan**
zinctype

鋅白 **sàn baahk**
zinc white

鋌 **tíhng** (Md **tǐng**)
① to rush ② large arrow

鋌而走險 **tíhng yìh jáu hím**
to be forced to break the law

鋏 **gaap** (Md **jiá**)
① pincers; tongs ② sword

鋒 **fùng** (Md **fēng**)
① sharp point ② van guard

鋒銳 **fùng yeuih**
sharp; keen

鋒芒畢露 **fùng mòhng bāt
louh**
to show one's abilities;
intelligent; knowledge

鋤(耡) **chòh** (Md **chú**)
① a hoe ② to hoe

鋤頭 **chòh tàuh**
a hoe

鋤强扶弱 **chòh kèuhng fùh
yeuhk**
to eliminate the bullies and
help the down-trodden

鋪 **pòu, pou** (Md **pū, pù**)
① to lay in order; to spread; to
arrange ② a store

鋪路 **pòu louh**
to surface a road

鋪設 **pòu chit**
to arrange

鋪戶 **pou wuh**
shops; stores

銹(鏽) **sau** (Md **xiù**)
rust

銼 **cho** (Md **cuò**)
① a pan ② to file; to make
smooth with a file

銼刀 **cho dōu**
a file (a steel tool)

鋸 **geui** (Md **jù**)
① a saw ② to saw

鋸齒 **geui chí**
teeth of a saw

鋸木 geui muhk
to saw wood

鋼 gong (Md gāng)
steel

鋼筆 gong bāt
fountain pen

鋼琴 gong kàhm
piano

鋼筋 gong gàn
steel bars

錄（录）luhk (Md lù)
① to copy; to take down to accept ② a record

錄用 luhk yuhng
to accept for employment

錄音 luhk yàm
to record sound

錄下 luhk hah
to record

錐 jèui (Md zhuī)
① an awl ② to pierce

錐子 jèui jí
an awl

錐指 jèui jí
a very limited outlook

錘 chèuih (Md chuí)
① to hammer ② an ancient weapon

錘鍊 chèuih lihn
to forge; to train

錙 jì (Md zī)
an ancient unit of weight

錙銖 jì jyù
very small quantity

錚（铮）jàng (Md zhēng)
① clang of metal ② gongs

錚錚 jàng jàng
clang of metal; upright

錠 ding (Md dìng)
① a kind of ancient utensil ② ingot of gold or silver ③ a tablet (medicine)

錠劑 ding jài
medicine in tablet form

錢 chìhn (Md qián)
① money; cash ② a unit of weight ③ a Chinese family name

錢財 chìhn chòih
wealth; money riches

錢債 chìhn jaai
debts

錦 gám (Md jǐn)
① brocade ② brilliant and beautiful

錦標 gám bīu
championship; trophy

錦上添花 gám seuhng tìm fà
to give something or someone additional splendor

錕 gwàn (Md kūn)
name of a precious sword

錫 sek, sik (Md xī)
① tin ② to bestow

錫蘭 Sek làahn
Ceylon

錫命 sek mihng
to bestow life

錮 gu (Md gù)
① to run metal into cracks ② to confine

錮疾 gu jaht
chronic complaint

錯 cho, chok (Md cuò)
① wrong; mistakes ② untidy; disorderly complicated

錯過 cho gwo
to miss; to let a chance slip by

錯誤 cho ngh
error; fault

錯綜複雜 **chok jùng fūk jaahp**
very complicated

錳 **máahng** (Md **měng**)
manganese

錶 **bīu** (Md **biǎo**)
watch

錶帶 **bīu daai**
band of wrist watch

錶殼 **bīu hok**
watch case

錨 **màauh** (Md **máo**)
an anchor

鍋 **wò** (Md **guō**)
cooking pot, pan

鍋蓋 **wò goi**
cover of a cooking pot

鍋爐 **wò lòuh**
a boiler

鍍 **douh** (Md **dù**)
to plate; to gilt

鍍金 **douh gàm**
to plate with gold

鍍銀 **douh ngàhn**
to plate with silver

鍛 **dyun** (Md **duàn**)
to melt; to refine; to forge

鍛鐵 **dyun tit**
wrought iron

鍛鍊 **dyun lihn**
to forge; to temper; to train

鍾 **jùng** (Md **zhōng**)
① a kind of wine container ② to concentrate ③ a Chinese family name

鍾情 **jùng chìhng**
to fall in love

鍾愛 **jùng ngoi**
to love deeply

鍥 **kit** (Md **qiè**)
to carve

鍥薄 **kit bohk**
merciless; pitiless

鍥而不捨 **kit yìh bāt sé**
to carve without rest

鍬(鍫、鍪) **chìu** (Md **qiāo**)
① a spade ② a shovel

鍇 **káai** (Md **kǎi**)
refined iron

鍊 **lihn** (Md **liàn**)
to practice; to train

鍵 **gihn** (Md **jiàn**)
key to a door or on a musical instrument

鍵盤 **gihn pùhn**
keyboard (on a piano, typewriter)

鎂 **méih** (Md **měi**)
magnesium

鎂光燈 **méih gwòng dàng**
magnesium light

鎖 **só** (Md **suǒ**)
① a lock; fetters; chains ② to lock

鎖鏈 **só lín**
chains

鎖門 **só mùhn**
to lock a door

鎖骨 **só gwāt**
collar bone

鎊 **bohng** (Md **bàng**)
sterling pound

鎧 **hói** (Md **kǎi**)
armor

鎧馬 **hói máh**
horse protected by coat of mail

鎧甲 **hói gaap**
armor; coat of mail

鎬 **houh** (Md **gǎo, hào**)
① bright ② a kind of hoe

鎬鎬 **houh houh**
brilliant; bright

鎮 **jan** (Md **zhèn**)
① to subdue; to put down; to suppress ② a town

鎮定 **jan dihng**
self-composed; calm

鎮壓 **jan ngaat**
to put down; to suppress

鎰 (镒) **yaht** (Md **yì**)
an ancient unit of weight

鎳 **nīp** (Md **niè**)
nickel

鎳幣 **nīp baih**
nickel coin

鎢 **wù** (Md **wū**)
tungsten; wolfram

鎢絲 **wù sì**
tungsten filaments

鏃 **juhk** (Md **zú**)
arrowhead

鏈 (鍊) **lihn** (Md **liàn**)
chain

鏈著 **lihn jeuhk**
chained

鏈鎖反應 **lihn só fáan ying**
chain reaction

鎩 (铩) **saat** (Md **shā**)
① a lance ② to shed

鏹 (镪) **kéuhng**
(Md **qiǎng, qiāng**)
① money; wealth ② corrosive

鏹水 **kéuhng séui**
corrosive acid

鏖 **òu** (Md **áo**)
to fight hard

鏖兵 **òu bìng**
to engage in hard fighting

鏖戰 **òu jin**
to engage in hard fighting

鏗 **hàng** (Md **kēng**)
① clang of metal; twang of a string ② to strike; to smash

鏗鏘 **hàng chēung**
tinkle; clang

鏘 **chèung** (Md **qiāng**)
tinkle; clang

鏘鏘 **chèung chèung**
tinkle; clang

鏟 (铲、剷) **cháan**
(Md **chǎn**)
① shovel; scoop ② to shovel; to uproot

鏟除 **cháan chèuih**
to eliminate; to uproot

鏟子 **cháan jí**
shovel; scoop

鏡 **geng** (Md **jìng**)
a mirror; lens glass

鏡頭 **geng tàuh**
lens of a camera

鏡子 **geng jí**
mirror; lens

鏢 **bìu** (Md **biāo**)
① javelin; harpoon ② a guard; an escort

鏢客 **bìu haak**
hired escort

鏢局 **bìu guhk**
an establishment which provides escorts or bodyguards for fee

鏤 **lauh** (Md **lòu**)
to carve; to engraved

鏤刻 **lauh hāk**
to engrave

鏤花 **lauh fā**
to engrave a design of flowers

鐘 **jùng** (Md **zhōng**)
bell; clock

鐘點 **jùng dím**
hour

鐘樓 **jùng làuh**
bell tower

鐘鳴鼎食 **jùng mìhng díng sihk**
to enjoy affluence

鐐 **lìuh** (Md **liào**)
fetters

鐐銬 **lìuh kaau**
fetters; manacles

鐗 **gaan, gáan** (Md **jiàn, jiǎn**)
protective metal on the axis of a wheel

鐙 **dang** (Md **dèng**)
a kind of cooking vessel in ancient times

鐲 (鉥) **juhk** (Md **zhuó**)
① a kind of bell used in the army in ancient time ② bracelet

鐲子 **juhk jí**
bracelet; armlet

鐫 **jyùn** (Md **juān**)
to carve; to be demoted

鐫刻 **jyùn hāk**
to engrave; to carve

鐮 **lìhm** (Md **lián**)
a sickle

鐮刀 **lìhm dōu**
a sickle

鐵 (铁) **tit** (Md **tiě**)
① iron ② strong; firm ③ cruel; merciless

鐵門 **tit mùhn**
iron gate

鐵定 **tit dihng**
definitely

鐵石心腸 **tit sehk sàm chèuhng**
a cold heart; an unfeeling heart

鐶 **wàahn** (Md **huán**)
a ring

鐸 (铎) **dohk** (Md **duó**)
① a large bell ② a Chinese family name

鐺 **dòng, chàang** (Md **dāng, chēng**)
① a heater ② a pan for frying; a shallow pot

鐳 **lèuih** (Md **léi**)
① radium ② a pot; a jar

鐳錠 **lèuih dihng**
radium

鑊 **wohk** (Md **huò**)
a cauldron for cooking

鑊烹 **wohk pāang**
to cook a criminal in a cauldron

鑄 **jyu** (Md **zhù**)
① to melt metal; to mint ② to make a commit

鑄鐵 **jyu tit**
cast iron

鑄造 **jyu jouh**
to educate; to cast; to mint

鑑 (鑒、鉴) **gaam** (Md **jiàn**)
① a mirror ② an example serving as a rule or warning ③ to mirror; to reflect ④ to study; to examine

鑑定 **gaam dihng**
to examine; to judge

鑑賞 **gaam séung**
　to examine and appriciate

鑒察 **gaam chaat**
　to examine and study

鑠 **seuk** (Md **shuò**)
　① to melt metals with fire or heat
　② to wear off ③ shining

鑠鑠 **seuk seuk**
　brilliant; lustrous

鑠石流金 **seuk sehk làuh gàm**
　to melt stone and turn metal into fluid — extremely heat

鑣 **bìu** (Md **biǎo**)
　① bit for a horse ② to ride on a horse

鑫 **yàm** (Md **xīn**)
used in names only, with a connotation of prospering or good profit

鑰 **yeuhk** (Md **yuè, yào**)
a key, a lock

鑰匙 **yeuhk sìh**
　a key

鑲 **sèung** (Md **xiāng**)
　① to inlay; to set ② to border, to hem

鑲邊 **sèung bīn**
　to edge or hem

鑲牙 **sèung ngàh**
　to fill in an artificial tooth

鑾 **lyùhn** (Md **luán**)
bells around the neck of a horse

鑾鈴 **lyùhn lìhng**
　bells hung on the imperial carriage

鑾駕 **lyùhn ga**
　carriage used by the emperor

鑼 **lòh** (Md **luó**)
a gong

鑼鼓 **lòh gú**
　gong and drum

鑽 **jyun, jyùn** (Md **zuàn, zuān**)
　① to pierce; to dig through ② to gain (profit)

鑽探 **jyun taam**
　to investigate

鑽研 **jyun yìhn**
　to study thoroughly

鑽井 **jyun jéng**
　to drill a well

鑿 **johk** (Md **záo, zuò**)
　① an instrument for boring wood ② to bore; to chisel ③ real true

鑿鑿 **johk johk**
　real; indisputable

鑿開 **johk hòi**
　to cut open; to bore through

長部

長(长) **jéung, chèuhng** (Md **zhǎng, cháng**)
　① senior, old; eldest ② long, good

長輩 **jéung bui**
　an elder

長進 **jéung jeun**
　to make progress

長途 **chèuhng tòuh**
　a long distance

長期 **chèuhng kèih**
　a long time

門部

門(门) **mùhn** (Md **mén**)
　① door, gate ② family ③ a set of; a school ④ a profession

門鈴 **mùhn lìhng**
　the door bell

門第 **mùhn daih**
family standing

門生 **mùhn sàng**
pupils or disciples

閂(閅、橎) **sàan**
(Md **shuān**)
① latch or bolt of a door ② to
bolt

閃 **sím** (Md **shǎn**)
① to flash ② to avoid; to cast
away ③ to twist

閃電 **sím dihn**
lightning

閃避 **sím beih**
to dodge quickly

閃耀 **sím yiuh**
to sparkle; to twinkle

閉 **bai** (Md **bì**)
to close; to block up

閉幕 **bai mohk**
to close (a show or meeting)

閉塞 **bai sāk**
to block up

開 **hòi** (Md **kāi**)
① to open; to start ② to drive

開辦 **hòi baahn**
to start or open (a shop,
school)

開支 **hòi jì**
expenses

開罪 **hòi jeuih**
to offend another

間 **gàan, gaan**
(Md **jiān, jiàn**)
① the space between ② a leak;
a space ③ to divide

間斷 **gaan dyuhn**
suspended

間接 **gaan jip**
indirect

閏 **yeuhn** (Md **rùn**)
① with surplus ② extra

閏年 **yeuhn nìhn**
a leap year

閏月 **yeuhn yuht**
an intercalary month

閒 **hàahn** (Md **xián**)
① quiet; calm ② spare time

閒談 **hàahn tàahm**
idle talk; to chat

閒心 **hàahn sàm**
a peaceful or easy mood

閑 **hàahn** (Md **xián**)
① a bar; a fence ② to defend ③
calm, quiet; peaceful

閑靜 **hàahn jihng**
peaceful and calm at mind

閑習 **hàahn jaahp**
to be well-versed in

閘 **jaahp** (Md **zhá**)
① a lock; a floodgate ② a brake;
a device

閘板 **jaahp báan**
sluice

閘門 **jaahp mùhn**
a flood gate

閣 **gok** (Md **gé**)
a room; a chamber an attic

閣樓 **gok láu**
an attic; a garret

閣下 **gok hah**
your excellency, you (a polite
expression)

閡 **haht** (Md **hé**)
blocked; seperated

閤 **hahp, gap** (Md **hé, gé**)
① to close ② a small side door

閥 **faht** (Md **fá**)
① the left wing of a door ② an
influential family

閨 **gwāi** (Md **guī**)
① a small door ② feminine

閨房 **gwāi fòhng**
the private room of a house where women live

閨秀 **gwāi sau**
a well-educated girl brought up in a good family

閩 **màhn** (Md **mǐn**)
another name of Fukien Province

閩南 **Màhn nàahm**
the southern part of the Fukien province

閩江 **Màhn gòng**
the Ming River in Fukien Province

閫 **kwán** (Md **kǔn**)
① threshold ② feminine

閫德 **kwán dāk**
feminine virtues

閫令 **kwán lihng**
a woman's order

閭 **lèuih** (Md **lú**)
① a community of 25 families ② gate of a village ③ to meet

閭里 **lèuih léih**
neighborhood

閭閭 **lèuih lèuih**
the people; the rural community

閱 **yuht** (Md **yuè**)
to read; to review; to inspect; to observe

閱讀 **yuht duhk**
to read

閱兵 **yuht bìng**
to inspect troops

閻 (閆、閰) **yìhm**
(Md **yán**)
① a village gate ② a Chinese family name

閻羅王 **yìhm lòh wòhng**
the king of Hell

閹 **yìm** (Md **yān**)
① to castrate ② a eunuch

閹雞 **yìm gài**
a capon

閹寺 **yìm jí**
a eunuch

閼 **ngaat, yin** (Md **è, yān**)
① to block up; to stop up ② formal wife of the Chieftain of Hsiung Nu in the Han Dynasty

閼塞 **ngaat sāk**
to block up; to stop up

閽 **fàn** (Md **hūn**)
① a door or gate ② a gate keeper

閽人 **fàn yàhn**
a gate keeper

闃 **gwīk** (Md **qù**)
quiet, without people around

闃然 **gwīk yìhn**
quiet

闇 **ngám** (Md **àn**)
① to shut the door ② dark ③ evening; night

闇劣 **ngám lyut**
stupid and useless

闇練 **ngám lihn**
to be familiar with

闈 **wàih** (Md **wéi**)
① side-door in a palace ② living quarters of the queen and the imperial concubines

闆 (板) **báan** (Md **bǎn**)
the boss; the owner

闊 **fut** (Md **kuò**)
broad; wide; rich; separate

闊別 **fut biht**
separated for a long time

闊綽 **fut cheuk**
　Lavish; throwing money around

闋 **kyut** (Md **què**)
to shut; to retire empty

闌 **làahn** (Md **lán**)
① a door curtain; a fence ② to separate; to block up

闌干 **làahn gòn**
　fence or railing

闌尾炎 **làahn méih yìhm**
　appendicitis

闐 **tìhn** (Md **tián**)
to fill; to fill to the brim

闐溢 **tìhn yaht**
　to fill to the brim

闐闐 **tìhn tìhn**
　flourishing

闓 **hói** (Md **kǎi**)
to open

闔 **hahp** (Md **hé**)
① to shut; to close ② all; whole

闔府 **hahp fú**
　your whole family

闕 **kyut** (Md **què, quē**)
① a watch-tower outside the palace gate in ancient China ② faults; errors

闕失 **kyut sāt**
　a mistake or error

闕如 **kyut yùh**
　lacking or wanting deficient

闖 **chóng, chong**
(Md **chuǎng, chuàng**)
① to rush in all of a sudden ② to cause

闖禍 **chóng woh**
　to cause misfortune

闖江湖 **chóng gòng wùh**
　to roam about to make a living

關 (关、関) **gwàan**
(Md **guān**)
① to shut; to close ② a frontier pass; a customs house ③ related; to negotiate

關閉 **gwàan bai**
　to close

關係 **gwàan haih**
　relation; relationship

關心 **gwàan sàm**
　to be concerned about

闡 **jín, chín** (Md **chǎn**)
① to make clear ② evident

闡明 **jín mìhng**
　to clarify; to make clear

闡究 **jín gau**
　to study and expound

闥 (闼) **taat** (Md **tà**)
a door, fast

闢 **pīk** (Md **pì**)
① to develop; to open up ② to rid; to do away with

闢墾 **pīk hán**
　to open up land for farming

闢謠 **pīk yìuh**
　to clearify rumored reports

阜部

阜 **fauh** (Md **fù**)
a small hill; the continent

阜陵 **fauh lìhng**
　a mound

阡 **chìn** (Md **qiān**)
① paths on a farm ② the path leading to a grave

阡表 **chìn bíu**
　a tomb tablet

阡陌 **chìn mahk**
　paths on a farmland

阨（阸）ngāk (Md è)
a strategic position, a precarious position

阨窮 ngāk kùhng
difficulty

阨塞 ngāk choi
a strategic place

阪 báan (Md bǎn)
slope of a hill; hillside

阪田 báan tìhn
a hillside farm field

阮 yún (Md ruǎn)
① an ancient musical instrument
② a Chinese family name

阱（穽）jihng (Md jǐng)
a trap; a snare

防 fòhng (Md fáng)
① to defend; to resist; to prepare for ② a Chinese family name

防備 fòhng beih
to get ready or prepared

防腐 fòhng fuh
to preserve (food)

防衛 fòhng waih
to defend; to guard

阻 jó (Md zǔ)
① to prevent; to stop; to separate; to hinder ② difficulty

阻擋 jó dóng
to stop; to be in the way

阻滯 jó jaih
impeded; blocked

阻塞 jó sāk
to block up

阿 a, ngò (Md ā, ē)
① to favor; to rely on ② slender and beautiful ③ a prefix to name

阿媚 ngò meih
to flatter

阿順 ngò seuhn
to flatter and be obsequious

阿門 a mùhn
Amen

陀 tòh (Md tuó)
craggy; rugged terrain

陀螺 tòh lòh
a top (a toy)

陂 bèi, pèih, bò (Md bēi, pí, pō)
① a water pond ② steep and craggy ③ name of a city in Wupei Province

陂塘 bèi tòhng
a pond

陂陀 bò tòh
craggy; steep

附（坿）fuh (Md fù)
① to rely on; dependent on; to attach; to send along with; to add to ② near

附和 fuh woh
to agree with

附件 fuh gín
an enclosure

附近 fuh gahn
around; nearby

陋 lauh (Md lòu)
① narrow and small ② ugly ③ poor; low; mean

陋習 lauh jaahp
bad habits

陋巷 lauh hohng
a narrow, dirty alley

陌 mahk (Md mò)
① paths in the rice field ② a road; a street

陌路 mahk louh
a stranger

陌生 mahk sàng
unfamiliar

降 **gong, hòhng**
(Md **jiàng, xiáng**)
① to decend; to lower; to drop;
to decline ② to surrender

降福 **gong fūk**
  to bless

降落 **gong lohk**
  to land

降服 **hòhng fuhk**
  to surrender to the new master

限 **haahn** (Md **xiàn**)
① a boundary; a line; a limit ②
to specify; to fix

限定 **haahn dihng**
  to fix (a deadline); to specify
  (qualification of a person)

限制 **haahn jai**
  to restrict

陔 **gòi** (Md **gāi**)
steps; grades; scale

陘 (陉) **yìhng** (Md **xíng**)
a deep valley; a defile

陛 **baih** (Md **bì**)
wide and high steps in the palace

陛下 **baih hah**
  your Majesty

陛見 **baih gin**
  to have an audience with the
  emperor

陝 (陕) **sím** (Md **shǎn**)
① short for Shensi Province ②
a Chinese family name

陝西 **Sím sài**
  Shensi Province

陞 **sìng** (Md **shēng**)
① to ascend; to promote ② a
Chinese family name

陟 **jīk** (Md **zhì**)
to mound; to ascend; to advance;
to promote

陟降 **jīk gong**
  to promote and demote

陟罰 **jīk faht**
  to promote; to reward and
  punish

陡 (阧) **dáu** (Md **dǒu**)
① suddenly ② steep

陡壁 **dáu bik**
  a steep bank

陡覺 **dáu gok**
  to feel all of a sudden

院 **yún** (Md **yuàn**)
① a courtyard ② a hall; a court;
a college; a hospital

院子 **yún jí**
  a yard

院宇 **yún yúh**
  the house and the yard

陣 (阵) **jahn** (Md **zhèn**)
① a column or row ② to battle;
to go to war

陣亡 **jahn mòhng**
  to be killed in action

陣雨 **jahn yúh**
  occasional showers

除 **chèuih** (Md **chú**)
to divide; to rid of; to remove; to
deduct; to change

除名 **chèuih mìhng**
  to strike one's name off the list

除害 **chèuih hoih**
  to get rid of evils

除數 **chèuih sou**
  a division

陪 **pùih** (Md **péi**)
to accompany; to repay

陪伴 **pùih buhn**
  to keep company

陪罪 **pùih jeuih**
  to apologize

陲 **sèuih** (Md **chuí**)
border; frontier

陰(阴)**yàm** (Md **yīn**)
① cloudy; shady ② cunning and crafty ③ feminine ④ the hell

陰謀 **yàm màuh**
a plot; a secret scheme

陰暗 **yàm ngam**
dim; gloomy

陰間 **yàm gàan**
the Hades; the hell

陳(陈)**chàhn**
(Md **chén**)
① to display; to state ② old; preserved for a long time ③ a Chinese family name

陳列 **chàhn liht**
to arrange and display

陳舊 **chàhn gauh**
old; worn out

陳述 **chàhn seuht**
to tell; to state

陵 **lìhng** (Md **líng**)
① a high mound ② a tomb of an emperor ③ to offend; to outrage ④ a Chinese family name

陵墓 **lìhng mouh**
a tomb

陵居 **lìhng gèui**
to live on the highland

陶 **tòuh** (Md **táo**)
① to make pottery ② happy; joyful ③ a Chinese family name

陶器 **tòuh hei**
earthware

陶醉 **tòuh jeui**
very happy

陶冶 **tòuh yéh**
to mold; to cultivate

陷 **haahm** (Md **xiàn**)
① to sink; to fall ② to harm another

陷沒 **haahm muht**
to sink

陷害 **haahm hoih**
to harm another

陷阱 **haahm jihng**
a trap

陸(陆)**luhk** (Md **lù, liù**)
① land; continent ② land transportation ③ a Chinese family name

陸路 **luhk louh**
by land; high way

陸軍 **luhk gwàn**
the army

陽(阳)**yèuhng**
(Md **yáng**)
① the sun ② positive ③ musculine ④ a Chinese family name

陽光 **yèuhng gwòng**
sunshine

陽曆 **yèuhng lihk**
solar calendar

隅 **yùh** (Md **yú**)
a conner; an angle

隅目 **yùh muhk**
angry eyes

隅中 **yùh jùng**
approaching noontime

隆 **lùhng** (Md **lóng**)
flourishing; glorious; abundant

隆恩 **lùhng yàn**
great kindness

隆重 **lùhng juhng**
impressive and solemn

隈 **wùi** (Md **wēi**)
a bend in the hills or river; a cover

隋 **chèuih** (Md **suí**)
① name of a dynasty ② a Chinese family name

隊 **deuih** (Md **duì**)
a group; a team

隊伍 **deuih ńgh**
troops in ranks

隊員 **deuih yùhn**
members of a team

隍 **wòhng** (Md **huáng**)
the dry Moat of a city

城隍廟 **sìhng wòhng miu**
temple of the city god

階 (阶 堦) **gàai**
(Md **jiē**)
① a way leading to the main hall
② a flight of steps ③ grade of rank

階段 **gàai dyuhn**
a stage or phrase

階層 **gàai chàhng**
sub-divisions within a class of people

隗 **wàih, ngáih** (Md **wěi, kuí**)
① high; lofty ② a Chinese family name

隔 **gaak** (Md **gé**)
① to separate; to divide ②
blocked ③ a partition

隔膜 **gaak mohk**
the diaphragm; no communication

隔絕 **gaak jyuht**
blocked; separated

隔音 **gaak yàm**
soundproof

隕 **wáhn** (Md **yǔn**)
to fall; to die

隕命 **wáhn mihng**
to die

隕星 **wáhn sìng**
a meteor

隘 **aai, ngaai** (Md **ài**)
① a strategic pass ② narrow ③
difficult; urgent

隘路 **aai louh**
a narrow road

隘險 **aai hím**
of great strategic value

隙 **gwīk** (Md **xì**)
① a crack; an opportunity ②
spare time ③ dispute; complaint

隙地 **gwīk deih**
vacant lot

際 (际) **jai** (Md **jì**)
① at the time; on the occasion
of ② a border ③ opportunity

際會 **jai wuih**
to meet

際遇 **jai yuh**
opportunity

障 **jeung** (Md **zhàng**)
① to separate; to screen ② to
defend; to guard

障蔽 **jeung bai**
to screen of

障礙 **jeung ngoih**
obstacles

隨 **chèuih** (Md **suí**)
① to follow; to listen to; to accompany ② a Chinese family
name

隨筆 **chèuih bāt**
to write as one's thought
rambles

隨時 **chèuih sìh**
any time

隨從 **chèuih chùhng**
entourage; attendants

隧 **seuih** (Md **suì**)
① a tunnel ② to turn ③ a
Chinese family name

隧道 **seuih douh**
a tunnel

隩 **yūk, ou** (Md **yù**)
① a bend of a stream ② warm

險 **hím** (Md **xiǎn**)
① dangerous, difficult; cunning; mean ② a strategic pass ③ nearly

險境 **hím gíng**
dangerous situation

險些 **hím sè**
almost; nearly

險詐 **hím ja**
treacherous

隱（隐）**yán** (Md **yǐn**)
① hidden; concealed ② dark ③ to retire; to reject public life

隱瞞 **yán mùhn**
to hide the truth

隱居 **yán gèui**
to retire from public life

隰 **jaahp** (Md **xí**)
① low; marshy land ② newly open farmland ③ a Chinese family name

隴（陇）**lúhng** (Md **lǒng**)
a grave; a mound

隴畝 **lúhng máuh**
rural community; the farm

隶部

隸（隶）**daih** (Md **lì**)
① to belong to ② servants, slaves ③ a type of Chinese calligraphy

隸書 **daih syù**
clerical style of Chinese calligraphy

隸屬 **daih suhk**
to be attached to

佳部

佳 **jèui** (Md **zhuī**)
a general name of a short tail birds such as pigeons

隻 **jek** (Md **zhī**)
① a numerary adjunct for hen, pigeon, bird etc ② single; alone

隻立 **jek lahp**
to stand alone

隻身 **jek sàn**
alone; all by oneself

隼 **jéun** (Md **sǔn**)
a falcon

雀 **jeuk** (Md **què, qiāo, qiǎo**)
① a general name of a small bird ② freckled

雀斑 **jeuk bàan**
freckled

雀躍 **jeuk yeuhk**
to jump up with joy

雄 **hùhng** (Md **xióng**)
① masculine ② heroes ③ to win; to triumph

雄辯 **hùhng bihn**
a forceful presentation of one's points in a debate

雄心 **hùhng sàm**
ambition

雁 **ngaahn** (Md **yàn**)
the wild goose

雁帛 **ngaahn baahk**
letters; correspondence

雁戶 **ngaahn wuh**
a transient resident

雅 **ngáh** (Md **yǎ**)
① refined; elegant, graceful ② usually; often

雅致 **ngáh ji**
refined taste

雅俗共賞 **ngáh juhk guhng séung**
to appeal to both the sophisticated and the simple-minded — arts, performance etc.

集 **jaahp** (Md **jí**)
① to gather; together ② a collection of works

集合 **jaahp hahp**
to gather together

集訓 **jaahp fan**
to train many people at the same place and same time

集思廣益 **jaahp sì gwóng yīk**
to canvass various opinions and benefit from them

雇（僱）**gu** (Md **gù**)
to employ

雇主 **gu jyú**
the employer

雇員 **gu yùhn**
the employee

雍 **yùng** (Md **yōng**)
① harmony; peaceful ② to block up ③ a Chinese family name

雍睦 **yùng muhk**
harmonious or friendly

雍容 **yùng yùhng**
majestic; stately appearance

雉 **jih** (Md **zhì**)
a pleasant

雉雞 **jih gài**
a pleasant

雉經 **jih gìng**
to commit suicide by hanging

雌 **chì** (Md **cí, cī**)
① feminine; woman like ② weak; retiring ③ to expose; to show

雌雄莫辨 **chì hùhng mohk bihn**
unable to distinguish the sex identity

雌威 **chì wài**
the tantrum of a shrew

雋（隽）**syúhn, jeun** (Md **juàn, jùn**)
① fat meat ② good looking; talented; outstanding

雋楚 **jeun chó**
outstanding; extra-ordinary

雋譽 **jeun yuh**
good reputation

雎 **jèui** (Md **jū**)
① a kind of waterfowl ② to hesitate; to avoid

雒 **lohk** (Md **luò**)
① name of a river ② to brand (an animal)

雕（彫）**dìu** (Md **diāo**)
① to carve; to engrave ② an eagle ③ to weaken

雕琢 **dìu deuk**
to cut and polish

雕塑 **dìu sou**
to cut wood or clay for a statue

雕蟲小技 **dìu chùhng síu geih**
a petty skill

雖（虽、雖）**sèui** (Md **suī**)
① although; even though ② to push away

雖然 **sèui yìhn**
even though

雖則 **sèui jāk**
even if

雙（双、雙）**sèung** (Md **shuāng**)
a pair; a couple; two; even

雙倍 **sèung púih**
double; twice the number

雙管齊下 **sèung gún chàih hah**
to do two things simultaneously in order to attain an objective

雛 **chò, chòh** (Md **chú**)
① a very yound bird ② a small kid of toddler

雛鳳 **chò fúng**
bright and promising children

雛菊 **chò gūk**
daisy

雜(杂、襍) **jaahp** (Md **zá**)
① mixed; assorted ② petty and numerous

雜費 **jaahp fai**
miscellaneous expenses

雜亂 **jaahp lyuhn**
confused and disorderly

雜誌 **jaahp ji**
magazine; a journal

雞(鸡、鷄) **gài** (Md **jī**)
chickens

雞皮 **gài pèih**
the shriveled skin of the aged

雞犬不寧 **gài hyún bāt nìhng**
great disturbance — not even chickens and dogs are left in peace

離(离) **lèih** (Md **lí**)
① to leave; to depart ② to distant from

離別 **lèih biht**
to separate; to leave

離譜 **lèih póu**
too far away from what is normal

離棄 **lèih hei**
to desert

難(难) **nàahn, naahn** (Md **nán, nàn**)
① difficult; hard; unpleasant ② disaster; calamity

難怪 **nàahn gwaai**
no wonder that

難受 **nàahn sauh**
to feel bad

難民 **naahn màhn**
refugees

雨部

雨 **yúh** (Md **yǔ**)
rain; rainy

雨量 **yúh leuhng**
rainfall

雨季 **yúh gwai**
the rainy season

雪 **syut** (Md **xuě**)
① snow ② to clean; to wash

雪花 **syut fā**
snowflakes

雪白 **syut baahk**
snow-white

雪恨 **syut hahn**
to avenge one's grudge

霧 **fàn** (Md **fēn**)
mist; fog

雲(云) **wàhn** (Md **yún**)
① clouds ② short for Yunnan Province ③ a Chinese family name

雲霄 **wàhn siu**
the sky; very high

雲彩 **wàhn chói**
clouds illuminated by the rising or setting sun

雲霧 **wàhn mouh**
clouds and fog

零 **lìhng** (Md **líng**)
① zero ② fraction; small amount

零賣 **lìhng maaih**
retail sales

零落 **lìhng lohk**
desolate and scattered

零用錢 **lìhng yuhng chìhn**
pocket money

雷 **lèuih** (Md **léi**)
① thunder ② fuse ③ a Chinese family name

雷電 **lèuih dihn**
lightning and thunder

雷霆 **lèuih tìhng**
great wrath

雷同 **lèuih tùhng**
similar; exactly the same

電 (电) **dihn** (Md **diàn**)
① electricity; power ② short for cable or telegram

電報 **dihn bou**
a cable or telegram

電力 **dihn lihk**
electric power

電腦 **dihn nóuh**
computer; electric brain

雹 **bohk** (Md **báo**)
hail

雹子 **bohk jí**
hail; hailstone

需 **sèui** (Md **xū**)
① to need; to require ② expenses; provisions

需求 **sèui kàuh**
to need; to require

需要品 **sèui yiu bán**
necessities

震 **jan** (Md **zhèn**)
① to shake; to tremor; to shock ② scared; terrified

震驚 **jan gìng**
greatly surprised

震慄 **jan leuht**
trembling from fear

震災 **jan jòi**
disaster caused by an earthquake

霄 **sìu** (Md **xiāo**)
① the skies; clouds and mist ② to exhaust

霄壤 **sìu yeuhng**
heaven and earth

霄外 **sìu ngoih**
beyond the sky

霆 **tìhng** (Md **tíng**)
a sudden peal of thunder

霆擊 **tìhng gìk**
as quickly as lightning

霈 **pui** (Md **pèi**)
① rains; torrential rain ② good graces

霈然 **pui yìhn**
plentiful

霉 **mùih** (Md **méi**)
musty; moldly; damp

霉天 **mùih tìn**
damp days; rainy days

霉爛 **mùih laahn**
moldy and rotten

霍 **fok** (Md **huò**)
① very rapidly; suddenly; in a flash ② a Chinese family name

霍亂 **fok lyuhn**
cholera

霍然 **fok yìhn**
rapidly; suddenly

霍閃 **fok sím**
a lightning

霎 **saap** (Md **shà**)
① an instant; very short time ② twinkle of an eye

霎時 **saap sih**
in a very short moment

霎眼 **saap ngáahn**
　to wink

霏 **fèi** (Md **fēi**)
　the falling of snow and rain

霏霏 **fèi fèi**
　to snow or rain hard

霑 **jìm** (Md **zhān**)
　① soaked; damp; to moisten ②
　imbibed; drunk

霑沐 **jìm muhk**
　to be soaked

霑染 **jìm yíhm**
　to get affected by a com-
　municable disease

霓 **ngàih** (Md **ní**)
　a rainbow; a coloured cloud

霓虹燈 **ngàih hùhng dāng**
　the neon light

霖 **làhm** (Md **lín**)
　copious rain falling continuously

霖霖 **làhm làhm**
　incessant raining

霖雨 **làhm yúh**
　pouring rain; graces

霜 **sèung** (Md **shuāng**)
　① frost ② white and powdery-
　like hoarfrost ③ coolness; grave

霜鋒 **sèung fùng**
　sharp; gleaming blades

霜雪 **sèung syut**
　frost and snow; snow white

霞 **hàh** (Md **xiá**)
　coloured; low-hanging clouds;
　rosy clouds

霞片 **hàh pin**
　muti-coloured glaze of a
　porcelain ware

霞蔚 **hàh wai**
　splendid

霧 **mouh** (Md **wù**)
　fog; mist; vapor

霧氣 **mouh hei**
　fog or mist

霧塞 **mouh sāk**
　mentally blinded

霪 **yàhm** (Md **yín**)
　to rain cats and dogs for a long
　time

霪雨 **yàhm yúh**
　incessant rain

霰 **sin** (Md **xiàn**)
　sleet; snow and rain

霰石 **sin sehk**
　aragonite

露 **louh, lauh** (Md **lù,
lòu**)
　① dew ② uncovered; exposed ③
　to appear; to show

露珠 **louh jyù**
　dew drops

露宿 **louh sūk**
　to stay overnight in open field

霹 **pīk** (Md **pī**)
　thunders

霸 **ba** (Md **bà**)
　① to rule by might rather than
　right ② outstanding

霸據 **ba geui**
　to occupy by force

霸王 **ba wòhng**
　the leader of feudal lords

霽(霁) **jai** (Md **jì**)
　① to stop raining; to clear up ②
　to stop being angry

霽威 **jai wài**
　to stop anger

霽月 **jai yuht**
　a clear moon after rain;
　open-minded

霾 **màaih** (Md **mái**)
① cloudy; misty; foggy ② a dust-storm

靂 (雳)**lihk, līk** (Md **lì**)
thunder

靄 **ngói, ói** (Md **ǎi**)
① mild; peaceful; kind; friendly ② cloudy

靄靄 **ngói ngói**
luxuriant growth; to do one's very best; cloudy

靈 (灵)**lìhng** (Md **líng**)
① spirit; spiritual; the soul ② wonderful; excellent ③ clever; with quick reflex

靈敏 **lìhng máhn**
clever; skillful

靈感 **lìhng gám**
inspiration

靈驗 **lìhng yihm**
to come true with unbelievable accuracy

青部

青 **chìng, chèng** (Md **qīng**)
① green; blue; black ② young; youth

青天 **chìng tìn**
blue sky

青春 **chìng chèun**
one's youth

青翠 **chìng cheui**
fresh green

青蛙 **chìng wà**
frog

靖 **jihng** (Md **jìng**)
safe; peaceful; quiet

靖亂 **jihng lyuhn**
to quell uprisings

靖言 **jihng yìhn**
insincere words; sweet talk

靚 **jihng, leng** (Md **jìng, liàng**)
① to doll up ② still; quiet

靚衣 **jihng yì**
beautiful dresses

靚妝 **jihng jòng**
fully dressed and ornamented

靜 **jihng** (Md **jìng**)
calm; quiet; peaceful; harmonious

靜寂 **jihng jihk**
quiet; tranquility

靜默 **jihng mahk**
silence

靜養 **jihng yéuhng**
to rest or convalence without disturbance

靛 **dihn** (Md **diàn**)
indigo colour; any blue dyes

靛白 **dihn baahk**
indigo white

靛藍 **dihn làahm**
indigo blue

非部

非 **fèi** (Md **fēi**)
① negative; not to be ② faults; mistakes

非法 **fèi faat**
illegal; unlawful

非常 **fèi sèuhng**
extraordinary; very

非議 **fèi yíh**
to censure; to dispute

靠 **kaau** (Md **kào**)
① to rely on; to depend on ② near to; keep to (the left or right) as driving

靠得住 **kaau dāk jyuh**
reliable; dependable

靠墊 **kaau jin**
a back cushion

靠近 **kaau gahn**
near to; to approach

靡 **méih** (Md **mí, mǐ**)
① to disperse ② negative ③ to waste

靡敝 **méih baih**
decline; to get weak

靡費 **méih fai**
to waste; wasteful

面部

面(靣) **mihn** (Md **miàn**)
① face of a person ② surface; side

面目 **mihn muhk**
face; appearance

面積 **mihn jīk**
area

面試 **mihn si**
an oral quiz; an interview

靦(靦) **tín** (Md **tiǎn, miǎn**)
ashamed and embarrassed

靦然 **tín yìhn**
feature of one's face

靦顏 **tín ngàahn**
shame-faced

靨(靨) **yip** (Md **yè**)
dimples in the face

革部

革 **gaak, gīk** (Md **gé, jí**)
① hides; leather ② to get rid of ③ to reform; to change ④ urgent; dangerous

革命 **gaak mihng**
a revolution

革除 **gaak chèuih**
to get rid of

革職 **gaak jīk**
to fire

靴(鞾) **hèu** (Md **xuē**)
boots

靴子 **hèu jí**
boots

靴底 **hèu dái**
soles of boots

靶 **bá** (Md **bǎ**)
the target

靶場 **bá chèuhng**
a shooting range

靶子 **bá jí**
a target

靳 **gan** (Md **jìn**)
① stingy ② a Chinese family name

靼 **táan, daat** (Md **dá**)
the Tartars

鞋 **hàaih** (Md **xié**)
shoes; footware

鞋店 **hàaih dim**
a shoeshop

鞋油 **hàaih yáu**
shoepolish

鞍 **ngòn** (Md **ōn**)
saddle

鞍子 **ngòn jí**
a saddle

鞏 **gúng** (Md **gǒng**)
① to tie with thongs ② firm; strong ③ a Chinese family name

鞏膜 **gúng mók**
sclerotic coat

鞏固 **gúng gu**
strong; secure; well guarded

鞘 **chiu, sàau** (Md **qiào, shāo**)
a scabbard; a sheath

鞠 **gūk** (Md **jū**)
① to bow; to raise ② a ball ③ young ④ a Chinese family name

鞠躬 **gūk gùng**
　to bow

鞠子 **gūk jí**
　a child

鞠養 **gūk yéuhng**
　to raise kids

鞭 **bìn** (Md **biān**)
① a whip; a lash ② a string of firecrackers

鞭打 **bìn dá**
　to flog with a whip

鞭刑 **bìn yìhng**
　flogging

鞭長莫及 **bìn chèuhng mohk kahp**
　beyond one's influence

鞦 **chàu** (Md **qīu**)
a swing; a crupper

鞦韆 **chàu chìn**
　a swing

韃(鞑) **daaht** (Md **dá**)
Tartars

韃靼 **daaht daat**
　Tartars

韆 **chìn** (Md **qiān**)
a swing

韋部

韋(韦) **wàih, wáih**
(Md **wéi**)
① leather; tanned leather ② a Chinese family name

韋衣 **wàih yì**
　hunting clothes; simple clothes

韋帶 **wàih daai**
　a leather girdle worn by a commoner

韌(韧、靭) **yahn**
(Md **rèn**)
soft but tough; elastic

韌帶 **yahn daai**
　ligament

韌性 **yahn sing**
　tenacity

韓 **hòhn** (Md **hán**)
① a fence ② name of two feudal states in late Chou Dynasty ③ short for the Republic of Korea ④ a Chinese family name

韙(韪) **wáih** (Md **wěi**)
right; proper

韜(韬、弢) **tòu**
(Md **tāo**)
① scabbard; swords ② military strategy ③ to conceal

韜筆 **tòu bāt**
　to let the pen idle — to write no more

韜略 **tòu leuhk**
　military strategy

韜晦 **tòu fui**
　to conceal

韞 **wan** (Md **yùn**)
to hide; to conceal

韭部

韭(韮) **gáu** (Md **jiǔ**)
scallion; leeks; Chinese chive

韭黃 **gáu wòhng**
　yellow, tender leeks or scallion

韭菜 **gáu choi**
　leeks or scallion

音部

音 **yàm** (Md **yīn**)
sound; voice; tones; musical notes

音標 **yàm bīu**
phonetic signs

音符 **yàm fùh**
notes (in music)

音信 **yàm seun**
news

音樂 **yàm ngohk**
music

韶 **sìuh** (Md **sháo**)
beautiful; excellent

韶光 **sìuh gwòng**
beautiful scenes in the spring; best years of one's life

韻 **wáhn** (Md **yùn**)
① rhymes; harmony of sound ② refined; elegant ③ vowels

韻母 **wáhn móuh**
vowels

韻律 **wáhn leuht**
rhyme scheme; rhythm

響 (响) **héung**
(Md **xiǎng**)
① a sound; an echo ② loud sound

響亮 **héung leuhng**
loud and clear

響應 **héung ying**
to respond; to rise in support

頁部

頁 (页、箓) **yihp**
(Md **yè**)
a page; a sheet

頁次 **yihp chi**
page number

頂 **díng** (Md **dǐng**)
① the top of anything ② topmost; extremely ③ to carry on one's head; to substitute

頂點 **díng dím**
the topmost; the utmost

頂替 **díng tai**
to represent; to take someone's place

頂撞 **díng johng**
to offend with words

頃 (顷) **kíng** (Md **qǐng**)
① a moment ② about 15.13 acres; a hectare ③ to lean toward one side; to incline

頃刻 **kíng hāk**
in a short moment

頃步 **kíng bouh**
half a step

項 **hohng** (Md **xiàng**)
① the back of the neck ② item; article; kind ③ a Chinese family name

項目 **hohng muhk**
an item

項領 **hohng líhng**
the neck; the collar

順 **seuhn** (Md **shùn**)
① to follow; to submit to; to cause to surrender ② obedient; agreeable; smooth

順理 **seuhn léih**
reasonable; logical

順利 **seuhn leih**
smoothly; easy

順從 **seuhn chùhng**
to obey

須 **sèui** (Md **xū**)
① to have to; must ② necessary ③ probably

須知 **sèui jì**
should know

須要 **sèui yiu**
to have to; must

頌 **juhng** (Md **sòng**)
① to praise ② a hymn

頌讚 **juhng jaan**
to praise

頌詞 **juhng chìh**
　　a message of praise

預 **yuh** (Md **yù**)
　① beforehand; advance ② to prepare

預備 **yuh beih**
　　to prepare

預防 **yuh fòhng**
　　to prevent beforehand

預期 **yuh kèih**
　　to expect

頑 **wàahn** (Md **wán**)
　stupid; ignorant; stubborn; naughty

頑皮 **wàahn pèih**
　　naughty

頑鈍 **wàahn deuhn**
　　foolish; stupid

頑固 **wàahn gu**
　　stubborn

頒 **bàan** (Md **bān**)
　① to grant; to distribute ② to proclaim; to make public

頒布 **bàan bou**
　　to proclaim

頒發 **bàan faat**
　　to bestow; to award

頓(顿) **deuhn, duhk** (Md **dùn, dú**)
　① to stop; to stamp (the foot); to arrange ③ immediately

頓筆 **deuhn bāt**
　　to stop writing

頓時 **deuhn sìh**
　　promptly; immediately

頓悟 **deuhn ngh**
　　to realize suddenly

領 **líhng** (Md **lǐng**)
　① the neck; the collar ② to lead; to receive; to understand

領導 **líhng douh**
　　to lead

領取 **líhng chéui**
　　to get; to receive

領悟 **líhng ngh**
　　to comprehand

頗 **pó** (Md **pō**)
　① somewhat; rather ② quite; very

頗多 **pó dò**
　　rather many

頗久 **pó gáu**
　　for quite a while

頡 **git, kit** (Md **jié, xié**)
　to deduct; to omit

頡頏 **kit hòhng**
　① to match; to contest ② haughty

頭 **tàuh** (Md **tóu**)
　① the head ② the top; the first; the chief; the boss

頭等 **tàuh dáng**
　　first class

頭顱 **tàuh lòuh**
　　the head

頭獎 **tàuh jéung**
　　the first prize

頤 **yìh** (Md **yí**)
　① the cheeks ② to rear ③ a Chinese family name

頤神 **yìh sàhn**
　　to have a mental relaxation

頤養 **yìh yéuhng**
　　to nourish

頰 **gaap** (Md **jiá**)
　the cheeks; the jaw

頰骨 **gaap gwāt**
　　the cheek-bone

頷 **háhm, hahm** (Md **hàn**)
　① the chin; the jaw ② a slight nod of the head

頷首 **háhm sáu**
to nod the head — a sign of approval

頸 **géng** (Md **jǐng**)
the neck; the throat

頸項 **géng hohng**
the front and back of the neck

頹(穨) **tèuih** (Md **tuí**)
① disintegrated; ruined to crumbled ② withered, weakened ③ bald ④ to descend ⑤ a Chinese family name

頹喪 **tèuih song**
discouraged, ruined, beaten

頹然 **tèuih yìhn**
submissive, pliant

頻 **pàhn** (Md **pín**)
① successive; frequently ② urgent

頻煩 **pàhn fàahn**
frequent; busy

頻率 **pàhn léut**
frequency

顆 **fó** (Md **kē**)
a drop; a grain

顆粒 **fó nāp**
a drop; a grain

額 **ngaahk** (Md **é**)
① the forehead ② a fix amount; a quota; a horizontal tablet

額骨 **ngaahk gwāt**
the frontal bone

額外 **ngaahk ngoih**
extra; beyond the set amount

題 **tàih** (Md **tí**)
① the forehead ② a sign; a topic ③ to sign; to write

題目 **tàih muhk**
the title of a speech

題字 **tàih jih**
to write on something

顎 **ngohk** (Md **è**)
the jowl; the high cheek-boned

顎骨 **ngohk gwāt**
the jaw bones

顏 **ngàahn** (Md **yán**)
① face; feature ② reputation ③ colours ④ a Chinese family name

顏面 **ngàahn mihn**
face; honor

顏色 **ngàahn sīk**
colour

願(愿) **yuhn** (Md **yuàn**)
① to be willing ② a vow

願意 **yuhn yi**
to be willing

願望 **yuhn mohng**
one's wish

顛(顛) **dìn** (Md **diān**)
① the top; the highest spot ② to fall; to upset ③ upside down; mad

顛沛 **dìn pui**
to fall in one's attempt

顛倒 **dìn dóu**
upside down

類 **leuih** (Md **lèi**)
① a kind; a class ② similar; alike

類別 **leuih biht**
classification

類推 **leuih tèui**
to reason by analogy

類似 **leuih chíh**
to resemble; similar to

顧 **gu** (Md **gù**)
① to look at; to gaze; to mind; to care for ② however ③ a Chinese family name

顧盼 **gu paan**
to look around

顧念 **gu nihm**
to care for

顧忌 **gu geih**
fear

顥 **houh** (Md **hào**)
bright; hoary; white

顫 **jin** (Md **chàn, zhàn**)
to tremble; to shake; unsteady

顫抖 **jin dáu**
to tremble; to shiver

顫動 **jin duhng**
to shake

顯 **hín** (Md **xiǎn**)
① evident; clear ② well-known ③ to expose

顯明 **hín mìhng**
evident; clear

顯貴 **hín gwai**
bigwigs

顯赫 **hín hāak**
outstanding; glorious

顰 **pàhn** (Md **pín**)
to frown; to knit one's brows

顰眉 **pàhn mèih**
to knit the brows

顱 **lòuh** (Md **lú**)
the skull; the forehead

顱骨 **lòuh gwāt**
the skull

顴 **kyùhn** (Md **quán**)
the cheek-bone

顴骨 **kyùhn gwāt**
the cheek-bone

風部

風 (风) **fùng** (Md **fēng**)
① wind; gust; breeze ② education; influence ③ customs; style

風暴 **fùng bouh**
a storm

風度 **fùng douh**
manner; carriage

風趣 **fùng cheui**
interesting; humorous

颱 **tòih** (Md **tái**)
typhoon; hurricane

颱風 **tòih fùng**
typhoon; hurricane

颯 **saap** (Md **sà**)
① the sound of wind ② weakened; failing

颯然 **saap yìhn**
the sound of the wind; leaves felled by strong winds

颯沓 **saap daahp**
crowded; numerous; abundant

颳 (刮) **gwaat** (Md **guā**)
wind blowing

颳風 **gwaat fùng**
wind blowing

颶 **geuih** (Md **jù**)
a hurricane; a gale; strong gusts at sea

颶風 **geuih fùng**
hurricane; gale

颺 (风易) **yèuhng**
(Md **yáng**)
① blown about by the wind ② to fly; to scatter

颼 **sáu** (Md **sōu**)
① blown about by wind ② the swishing sound of a fast-flying object

飄 (飄、飃) **pìu**
(Md **piāo**)
① to blow; to move with the wind; to float ② a cyclone

飄蕩 **pìu dohng**
to drift along without fixed lodging

飄忽 **pìu fāt**
to float in the air hither and thither

飄然 **pìu yìhn**
gracefully; flying

飆 (大風、飈、飇) **bìu**
(Md **biāo**)
violent winds

飛部

飛 (飞) **fèi** (Md **fēi**)
① to fly; to hang in the air ②
quickly; rapidly

飛奔 **fèi bàn**
to run very fast

飛行 **fèi hàhng**
to fly; as a plane

飛禽 **fèi kàhm**
birds

食部

食 **sihk, jih** (Md **shí, sì**)
① to eat ② food; salary

食物 **sihk maht**
foodstuff

食言 **sihk yìhn**
to break one's promise

食慾不振 **sihk yuhk bāt
jan**
poor appetite

飢 (饥) **gèi** (Md **jī**)
hungry; hunger

飢渴 **gèi hot**
hungry and thirsty

飢荒 **gèi fòng**
famine

飧 (殮) **syùn** (Md **sūn**)
cooked food; supper

飩 **tàn** (Md **tún**)
stuffed dumplings

飪 (饪、餁) **yahm**
(Md **rèn**)
to cook

飭 (饬) **chīk** (Md **chì**)
① severe ② respectful ③ to
arrange; to order

飭辦 **chīk baahn**
to instruct a subordinate to do
something

飭拿 **chīk nàh**
to give orders for the arrest of

飭查 **chīk chàh**
to order an investigate

飯 (饭) **faahn** (Md **fàn**)
① cooked rice ② a meal

飯店 **faahn dim**
a restaurant

飯碗 **faahn wún**
rice bowl; one's job

飲 **yám, yam** (Md **yǐn,
yìn**)
① to drink; to swallow ② to
make animal drink

飲品 **yám bán**
beverages; drinks

飲恨 **yám hahn**
to swallow grievance

飲泣 **yám yāp**
to weep in deep sorrow

飼 **jih** (Md **sì**)
to feed; to raise

飼料 **jih liuh**
animal feeds

飼養 **jih yéuhng**
to raise; to breed

飴 **yìh** (Md **yí**)
syrup; jell-like sugar made from
grains

飽 **báau** (Md **bǎo**)
① to eat to the full ② satisfied

飽暖 **báau nyúhn**
well-fed and well-clothed

飽滿 **báau múhn**
well-stacked; full; plump

飽嘗 **báau sèuhng**
　　to experience (bitterness; hardship) to the fullest extent

飾 **sīk** (Md **shì**)
　　① to ornament; to polish ② to excuse oneself on a pretext ③ clothing and dresses

飾詞 **sīk chìh**
　　an excuse

飾物 **sīk maht**
　　jewels and ornaments

餂 **tíhm** (Md **tiǎn**)
　　to obtain by hook

餃 **gáau** (Md **jiǎo**)
　　stuffed dumpling

餃子 **gáau jí**
　　stuffed dumpling

餉 **héung** (Md **xiǎng**)
　　① pay; provisions ② to entertain with food

餉賓 **héung bàn**
　　to entertain guests with food

餉銀 **héung ngàhn**
　　military expenditure

養 (养) **yéuhng**
(Md **yǎng**)
　　① to grow; to raise ② to bear a child; to support ③ to educate; to nurse

養病 **yéuhng bihng**
　　to recuperate; to nurse a disease

養家 **yéuhng gà**
　　to support one's family

養老 **yéuhng lóuh**
　　to retire and enjoy the fruit of one's work in the past

餌 **neih** (Md **ěr**)
　　① a bait ② food ③ to eat

餌敵 **neih dihk**
　　to set a trap for the enemy

餐 (湌、飡) **chāan**
(Md **cān**)
　　① a meal; food ② to eat

餐廳 **chāan tēng**
　　a restaurant; a dining room

餐具 **chāan geuih**
　　a dinner set

餑 **buht** (Md **bō**)
　　cakes; fancy baked foods

餑餑 **buht buht**
　　cakes; pies; tarts

餒 **noih, néuih** (Md **něi**)
　　① hungry; to starve ② decay of fish ③ lacking in confidence

餓 **ngoh** (Md **è**)
　　① hungry; hunger ② greedy; covetous

餓倒 **ngoh dóu**
　　to collapse from hunger

餓狼 **ngoh lòhng**
　　a greedy and covetous person

餘 (余) **yùh** (Md **yú**)
　　① remaining; the rest ② surplus

餘地 **yùh deih**
　　spare space; alternative

餘欵 **yùh fún**
　　remaining fund; balance

餘興 **yùh hing**
　　entertainment program

餛 **wàhn** (Md **hún**)
　　stuffed dumpling with delicate flour wrapping; ravioli

餛飩 **wàhn tàn**
　　stuffed dumpling with delicate flour wrapping

餞 (饯) **jin** (Md **jiàn**)
　　① a farewell dinner or luncheon ② to send off ③ to present as gift

餞別 **jin biht**
　　to entertain a parting friend

with feast

餅 **béng** (Md **bǐng**)
① cakes; cookies; biscuits ②
anything roundish

　餅乾 **béng gòn**
　　biscuits or crackers

　餅餌 **béng neih**
　　steamed cakes of rice or wheat
　　flour

館(舘) **gún** (Md **guǎn**)
① a house; a guest house ② an
official residence

　館長 **gún jéung**
　　a superintendent

　館子 **gún jí**
　　a restaurant

餡 **háahm, háam**
(Md **xiàn**)
anything serving as stuffing for
dumplings

餬 **wùh** (Md **hú**)
congee; porridge; paste

　餬口 **wùh háu**
　　to make a bare living

　餬紙 **wùh jí**
　　to paste paper

餵(餧) **wai** (Md **wèi**)
to feed; to raise

　餵奶 **wai náaih**
　　to feed a baby with milk;
　　breast-feeding

　餵養 **wai yéuhng**
　　to raise; to rear

餽(饋) **gwaih** (Md **kuì**)
① to present as gift ② to offer
food to a superior

　餽贈 **gwaih jahng**
　　to present as gift

餾 **lauh** (Md **liù, liú**)
① to steam ② distilled (water)

饅 **maahn** (Md **mán**)
steamed dumplings

　饅頭 **maahn tàuh**
　　steamed dumplings

饈 **sàu** (Md **xiū**)
① to eat; to offer ② a meal

饉 **gán** (Md **jǐn**)
famine; hunger

饌(餪、籑) **jaahn**
(Md **zhuàn**)
① to prepare food ② to eat and
drink

　饌具 **jaahn geuih**
　　food vessels

饑(饥) **gèi** (Md **jī**)
① year of famine ② hunger

　饑荒 **gèi fòng**
　　famine

　饑饉 **gèi gán**
　　starvation; famine

饒(饶) **yìuh** (Md **ráo**)
① plentiful; abundant ② to
forgive

　饒恕 **yìuh syu**
　　to forgive; to pardon

　饒裕 **yìuh yuh**
　　abundance

饗(饟) **héung**
(Md **xiáng**)
① to give a big party ② a
sacrificial ceremony

饔 **yùng** (Md **yōng**)
① to eat cooked food ②
breakfast ③ to slaughter animals

　饔餐 **yùng syùn**
　　breakfast and supper

饕 **tòu** (Md **tāo**)
a fierce person; a greedy and
gluttonous person

饜 **yim** (Md **yàn**)
full-stomached; sufficient

饜食 **yim sihk**
to eat to repletion

饜事 **yim sih**
plenty to do

饞 (馋) **chàahm**
(Md **chán**)
piggish; greedy

饞勞 **chàahm lòuh**
to be piggish about good food

饞嘴 **chàahm jéui**
gluttonous

首部

首 **sáu** (Md **shǒu**)
① the head; the king; the chief ②
the first; the capital

首都 **sáu dòu**
capital city

首腦 **sáu nóuh**
the boss; the chief

首飾 **sáu sīk**
jewelry

馗 **kwàih** (Md **kuí**)
a road; a path

香部

香 **hèung** (Md **xiāng**)
① sweet-smelling; fregrant ②
tasty; delicious ③ incense; spice

香甜 **hèung tìhm**
sweet; delicious

香料 **hèung liuh**
spice

香燭 **hèung jūk**
incense and candles

馥 **fūk** (Md **fù**)
fregrance; aroma

馥郁 **fūk yūk**
powerfully fragrant

馨 **hìng** (Md **xīn**)
fragrant; aroma

馨香 **hìng hèung**
fragrant; aroma

馬部

馬 (马) **máh** (Md **mǎ**)
① horse ② a Chinese family
name

馬匹 **máh pāt**
horses

馬力 **máh lihk**
horsepower

馭 (驭) **yuh** (Md **yù**)
① to drive a carriage ② to govern;
to rule

馮 (冯) **fùhng** (Md **féng**)
a Chinese family name

馱 (驮) **tòh** (Md **tuó,
duò**)
to carry a load on the back

馱不動 **tòh bāt duhng**
too heavy to carry on the back

馳 **chìh** (Md **chí**)
① to go swiftly; to rush ② to
exert; to spread

馳名 **chìh mìhng**
to spread one's fame

馳馬 **chìh máh**
to go swiftly on horse back

馴 **sèuhn** (Md **xún**)
① tame; obedient ② to tame; to
put under control

馴良 **sèuhn lèuhng**
docile; obedient

馴服 **sèuhn fuhk**
to tame; to subdue

駁 **bok** (Md **bó**)
① to rebut; to disprove ② to
transport; to ship

駁斥 **bok chīk**
　　to rebut; to refute

駁船 **bok syùhn**
　　lighter (in a harbor)

駐 **jyu** (Md **zhù**)
　　to halt; to remain; to station

駐守 **jyu sáu**
　　to station troops at a place for
　　defence purpose

駐顏 **jyu ngàahn**
　　to preserve a youthful
　　complexion

駑 **nòuh** (Md **nú**)
　　① old; worn-out horse ②
　　incompetent; stupid

駑馬 **nòuh máh**
　　old; worn-out horse

駑鈍 **nòuh deuhn**
　　incompetent; incapable

駒 **kèui** (Md **jū**)
　　① young and fleet-footed horse
　　② the sun

駒光 **kèui gwòng**
　　fleeting time

駒齒 **kèui chí**
　　youth

駕 **ga** (Md **jià**)
　　① to ride; to drive ② to excel; to
　　surpass ③ the emperor

駕臨 **ga làhm**
　　to give the honor of your visit

駕駛 **ga sái**
　　to drive; to control; to pilot

駙 **fuh** (Md **fù**)
　　① an extra horse harnessed by
　　the side of the team ② swift

駙馬 **fuh máh**
　　an ancient official title;
　　imperial son-in-law

駛 **sái** (Md **shǐ**)
　　① to run (a vehicle); to sail ②
fast

駛船 **sái syùhn**
　　to sail a ship

駛近 **sái gahn**
　　to approach (said of vehicles)

駝 **tòh** (Md **tuó**)
　　① camel ② hunchbacked ③ to
　　carry on the back

駝背 **tòh bui**
　　hunchbacked

駝峯 **tòh fùng**
　　hump of camel

駟 **si** (Md **sì**)
　　a team of four horses

駟馬難追 **si máh nàahn
jèui**
　　even with a team of four
　　horses; it is difficult to over-
　　take carelessly uttered words

駭 **haaih** (Md **hài**)
　　① to terrify; to frighten ② to
　　marvel; to wonder

駭怕 **haaih pa**
　　scared; frightened

駭浪 **haaih lohng**
　　awful waves

駭異 **haaih yih**
　　surprised; amazed

駱 **lohk** (Md **luò**)
　　① white horse with black name
　　② camel ③ a Chinese family
name

駱駝 **lohk tòh**
　　camel

騁 **chíng** (Md **chěng**)
　　① to go swiftly; to speed ② to
　　exert; to develop

騁馳 **chíng chìh**
　　to go at full speed

騁望 **chíng mohng**
　　to look as far as one can see

駿 jeun (Md **jùn**)
① fine horse; swift horse ②
great; outstanding

駿馬 **jeun máh**
fine horse

駿逸 **jeun yaht**
outstanding surpassing

騎 kèh (Md **qí**)
to ride a horse; to sit

騎兵 **kèh bìng**
mounted troops

騎馬 **kèh máh**
to ride a horse

騎牆 **kèh chèuhng**
to sit on the fence; uncom-
mitted between two opposing
forces

騅 jèui (Md **zhuī**)
a piebald horse

駢 pìhn, pìhng
(Md **piǎn**)
① a pair of horses ② to stand;
lie; go side by side

駢體文 **pìhn tái màhn**
an euphuistic antithetic
style of writing

駢肩 **pìhng gìn**
shoulders beside shoulders

騖 mouh (Md **wù**)
① to rush; to speed ②
unrestrained

騖外 **mouh ngoih**
to depart from one's proper
role

騖遠 **mouh yúhn**
impractically ambitious

騙 pin (Md **piàn**)
to cheat; to deceive

騙局 **pin guhk**
fraud; trickery

騙取 **pin chéui**
to obtain by fraud

騫 hìn (Md **qiān**)
to raise high; to fly; to pull up

騫騰 **hìn tàhng**
to soar high

騫舉 **hìn géui**
to soar

騭 jāt (Md **zhì**)
① stallion ② to go up ③
predestined

騰 tàhng (Md **téng**)
to jump; to rear; to go up; to fly;
to turn over

騰達 **tàhng daaht**
to prosper; to thrive

騰空 **tàhng hùng**
to fly in the sky

騶 jàu (Md **zōu**)
official in charge of driving
carriage

騶卒 **jàu jēut**
servant

騷 sòu (Md **sāo**)
to disturb; to worry

騷動 **sòu duhng**
disturbance; unrest

騷擾 **sòu yíu**
to disturb

騾 (驘) lèuih, lòh
(Md **luó**)
a mule

騾馬 **lèuih máh**
a mule

騾車 **lèuih chè**
mule cart

驀 mahk (Md **mò**)
① sudden ② to mount the horse

驀然 **mahk yìhn**
all of a sudden

驃 **piu, bīu** (Md **piào, biāo**)
① horse with yellowish white colour ② valiant

驅 (驱、敺) **kèui** (Md **qū**)
① to go before other ② to drive; to urge

驅逐 **kèui juhk**
　to drive out; to get rid of

驅使 **kèui sí**
　to order (a person) about

驕 (骄) **gìu** (Md **jiāo**)
① untamed; disobedient ② proud

驕傲 **gìu ngouh**
　proud; haughty

驕陽 **gìu yèuhng**
　hot sunshine

驍 (骁) **hìu** (Md **xiāo**)
① having courage; brave ② fine horse

驍將 **hìu jeung**
　valiant general

驍勇 **hìu yúhng**
　valiant; brave

驗 **yihm** (Md **yàn**)
to test; to examine; to verify; to prove

驗血 **yihm hyut**
　blood test

驗算 **yihm syun**
　to check computations

驚 **gìng** (Md **jīng**)
① to surprise; to amaze; to terrify; to frighten ② marvel; afraid

驚慌 **gìng fòng**
　to be frightened

驚訝 **gìng ngah**
　to be surprised

驛 **yihk** (Md **yì**)
courier station

驛馬車 **yihk máh chè**
　a stagecoach

驛站 **yihk jaahm**
　courier station

驟 **jaauh, jauh** (Md **zhòu**)
① to gallop ② swift; sudden

驟然 **jaauh yìhn**
　suddenly

驟雨 **jaauh yúh**
　sudden rainstorm

驢 (驴) **lòuh, lèuih** (Md **lú**)
an ass; a donkey

驢駒 **lòuh kèui**
　young donkey

驢車 **lòuh chè**
　donkey cart

驥 **kei** (Md **jì**)
① very fast horse ② man of outstanding ability

驥足 **kei jūk**
　great talent

骨部

骨 **gwāt** (Md **gǔ, gú**)
① bone ② framework

骨骼 **gwāt gaak**
　frame of the body

骨節 **gwāt jit**
　joints (of bones)

骰 **sīk, tàuh** (Md **tóu**)
dice

骰子 **sīk jí**
　dice

骯 **òng, hòhng** (Md **ōng**)
dirty; filthy

骯髒 **òng jòng**
dirty; filthy

骷 **fù** (Md **kū**)
human skeleton

骷髏 **fù lòuh**
human skeleton

骸 **hàaih, hòih** (Md **hói**)
① shinbone ② skeleton

骸骨 **hàaih gwāt**
skeleton

骼 **gaak** (Md **gé**)
bone; skeleton

骾(鯁) **gáng** (Md **gěng**)
fish bone etc.; stick in the throat

髀 **béi** (Md **bì**)
① buttock ② hipbone

髀骨 **béi gwāt**
hipbone

髏(髅) **lòuh** (Md **lóu**)
human skeleton

髓 **séuih** (Md **suǐ**)
marrow; pith; essence

髒 **jòng** (Md **zāng**)
dirty; filthy

髒土 **jòng tóu**
dirty soil

髒心 **jòng sàm**
impure heart

體 **tái** (Md **tǐ, tī**)
① body ② shape ③ entity

體諒 **tái leuhng**
to be understanding;
sympathetic

體裁 **tái chòih**
style or form of writing

體育 **tái yuhk**
physical education

髑 **duhk** (Md **dú**)
human skull

高部

高 **gòu** (Md **gāo**)
① high; tall ② noble ③ a Chinese
family name

高潮 **gòu chìuh**
high tide; climax

高峯 **gòu fùng**
peak; summit; climax

高雅 **gòu ngáh**
elegant; noble

髟部

髦 **mòuh** (Md **máo**)
① mane ② man of talent

髦俊 **mòuh jeun**
man of talent

髦士 **mòuh sih**
man of talent

髣 **fóng** (Md **fǎng**)
like; similar

髣髴 **fóng fāt**
like; similar

髫 **tìuh** (Md **tiáo**)
① children's hair style with hair
hanging down the forehead ②
youngster; child

髫年 **tìuh nìhn**
childhood; youth

髴 **fāt** (Md **fú**)
like; similar

髮 **faat** (Md **fà**)
① hair (covering human's head)
② hair's breadth

髮髻 **faat gai**
hair tied in a knot

髮妻 **faat chài**
first wife

髭 **jì** (Md **zī**)
moustaches

髻 **gai** (Md **jì**)
a coiffure with a topknot

鬏 (髹) **yàu** (Md **xiū**)
① a kind of dark-red paint ② to paint

鬆 **sùng** (Md **sōng**)
① loose; lax ② to relax

鬆懈 **sùng haaih**
to relax efforts

鬆脆 **sùng cheui**
crisp and soft (of food)

鬃 **jùng** (Md **zōng**)
① topknot of a lady's headdress ② mane

鬈 **kyùhn** (Md **quán**)
① fine hair ② curled hair

鬍 **wùh** (Md **hú**)
beard

鬍子 **wùh jí**
beard

鬚 (須) **sòu** (Md **xū**)
① beard; whiskers ② awn

鬚眉 **sòu mèih**
beard and eyebrows

鬚生 **sòu sàng**
bearded character (in Chinese opera)

鬟 **wàahn** (Md **huán**)
① to dress the hair in a coiled knot ② female servant

鬢 **ban** (Md **bìn**)
hair on the temples

鬢班 **ban bàan**
hair turning gray at the temples

鬢霜 **ban sèung**
temples covered with white hair

鬥部

鬥 (斗 、鬪 、鬦)
dau (Md **dòu**)
to struggle

鬧 (閙) **naauh** (Md **nào**)
① to disturb; to trouble ② noisy ③ to have (disasters, sickness, etc.)

鬧病 **naauh bihng**
to get sick

鬧事 **naauh sih**
to cause trouble

鬧市 **naauh síh**
busy shopping district

鬨 (哄) **huhng**
(Md **hòng**)
① uproar; noise ② dispute; quarrel

鬨堂 **huhng tòhng**
to fill a room with roars

鬩 (阋) **yīk** (Md **xì**)
to quarrel; to conflict

鬩牆 **yīk chèuhng**
to quarrel within the family

鬯部

鬯 **cheung** (Md **chàng**)
sacrificial spirit

鬯酒 **cheung jáu**
sacrificial spirit

鬱 **wāt** (Md **yù**)
① tulip; plum ② help in check ③ luxuriant

鬱悶 **wāt muhn**
to have pent-up

鬱金香 **wāt gàm hèung**
tulip

鬱郁 **wāt yūk**
fragrant; sweet-smelling

鬲部

鬲 **lihk, gaak** (Md **lì, gé**)
① name of ancient state ② a kind of caldon ③ to separate

鬻 **yuhk** (Md **yù**)
① to sell; to bring up ② young; childish

鬻子 **yuhk jí**
merchant; young child

鬻文 **yuhk màhn**
to write for pay

鬼部

鬼 **gwái** (Md **guǐ**)
① spirits; ghosts ② cunning; crafty

鬼魂 **gwái wàhn**
ghosts; spirits of dead

鬼才 **gwái chòih**
genius in an unorthodox way

魁 **fùi** (Md **kuí**)
① chief; head ② tall; big

魁星 **fùi sìng**
the god of literature

魁梧 **fùi ngh**
tall and robust

魂 **wàhn** (Md **hún**)
soul; spirit

魂魄 **wàhn paak**
soul

魂不附體 **wàhn bāt fuh tái**
frightened out of one's wits

魄 **paak, tok, bohk**
(Md **pà, tuò, bó**)
① vigor; life ② form; shape

魄力 **paak lihk**
guts; courage to plunge ahead in big things

魄散 **paak saan**
unnerved

魅 **meih** (Md **mèi**)
① mischievous spirit ② to charm

魅力 **meih lihk**
glamor; attractiveness

魅惑 **meih waahk**
to bewitch

魉(魎) **léuhng**
(Md **liǎng**)
a kind of monster

魍 **móhng** (Md **wǎng**)
a kind of monster

魍魉 **móhng léuhng**
a kind of monster

魏 **ngaih** (Md **wèi**)
① lofty; magnificent ② a Chinese family name

魑 **chì** (Md **chī**)
a mountain demon resembling a tiger

魑魅 **chì meih**
evil spirit

魔 **mò** (Md **mó**)
witch; devil

魔鬼 **mò gwái**
devil; evil spirit

魔術 **mò seuht**
magic

魘(魇) **yím** (Md **yǎn**)
nightmare

魘魅 **yím meih**
to kill by magic

魚部

魚 **yùh** (Md **yú**)
fish

魚塘 **yùh tòhng**
fish pond

魚鱗 **yùh lèuhn**
scales (of fish)

魚雁 **yùh ngaahn**
letters

魯 **lóuh** (Md **lǔ**)
① stupid; dull ② a Chinese family name

魯莽 **lóuh móhng**
rude; uncivil

魯鈍 **lóuh deuhn**
dull; slow-witted

魷 **yàuh** (Md **yáu**)
cuttle fish

魷魚 **yàuh yùh**
cuttle fish

鮑 **bàau, baauh**
(Md **bào**)
① abalone ② salted fish ③ a Chinese family name

鮑魚 **bàau yùh**
abalone; salted fish

鮫 **gàau** (Md **jiāo**)
shark

鮫魚 **gàau yùh**
shark

鮭 **gwài** (Md **guī**)
salmon

鮮 **sìn, sín** (Md **xiān, xiǎn**)
① fresh; new ② delicious; tasty ③ rare; few

鮮味 **sìn meih**
fresh favor

鮮有 **sín yáuh**
seldom to have

鯀（鮌）**gwán** (Md **gǔn**)
large fish

鯉 **léih** (Md **lǐ**)
① carp ② letters

鯉魚 **léih yùh**
common carp

鯉素 **léih sou**
letters

鯇 **wáahn** (Md **huàn**)
grass carp

鯊 **sà** (Md **shā**)
shark

鯊魚 **sà yùh**
shark

鯨 **kìhng** (Md **jīng**)
whale

鯨波 **kìhng bò**
huge waves

鯨油 **kìhng yàuh**
whale oil

鯤 **gwàn** (Md **kūn**)
① a kind of legendary fish said to be thousands of miles long ② roe

鯪 **lìhng** (Md **líng**)
① carp ② dace

鯿 **bìn** (Md **biān**)
fresh-water bream

鯽 **jīk** (Md **jì**)
gold carp

鰍（鰌）**chàu** (Md **qiū**)
loach

鰓 **sòi** (Md **sāi**)
gills of a fish

鰣 **sìh** (Md **shǐ**)
Reeves' shad

鰥 **gwàan** (Md **guān**)
① a kind of huge predatory fish ② widower; bachelor

鰥夫 **gwàan fù**
widower; bachelor

鰭 **kèih** (Md **qí**)
fins

鰻 **màahn** (Md **mán**)
eels

鰵 **máhn** (Md **mǐn**)
cod

鰾 **píuh** (Md **biào**)
① maw of a fish ② fish glue
　鰾膠 **píuh gàau**
　　fish glue

鱔 **síhn** (Md **shàn**)
eels

鱖 **gwai** (Md **guì**)
mandarin fish

鱗 **lèuhn** (Md **lín**)
scales of fish
　鱗甲 **lèuhn gaap**
　　hard scales of crocodiles
　鱗爪 **lèuhn jáau**
　　scales and claws

鱷 **ngohk** (Md **è**)
crocodiles
　鱷魚 **ngohk yùh**
　　crocodiles

鱸 **lòuh** (Md **lú**)
perch; bass

鳥部

鳥 **níuh** (Md **niǎo**)
bird
　鳥槍 **níuh chēung**
　　a fowling piece
　鳥獸散 **níuh sau saan**
　　to disperse in confusion like
　　birds or beasts

鳧 **fùh** (Md **fǔ**)
wild duck
　鳧水 **fùh séui**
　　to swim

鳩 **kàu, gàu** (Md **jiū**)
① pigeon ② to collect
　鳩合 **kàu hahp**
　　to gather together
　鳩居 **kàu gèui**
　　my humble house

鳳 **fuhng** (Md **fèng**)
male phoenix
　鳳蝶 **fuhng dihp**
　　a kind of butterfly
　鳳梨 **fuhng lèih**
　　pineapple
　鳳求凰 **fuhng kàuh wòhng**
　　courtship

鳴 **mìhng** (Md **míng**)
to sing; to make sounds
　鳴不平 **mìhng bāt pìhng**
　　to complain against
　鳴謝 **mìhng jeh**
　　to express gratitude
　鳴冤 **mìhng yùn**
　　to complain of unfairness

鳶 **yùn, yíu** (Md **yuān**)
a kite (a bird); a kite (a toy)

鴆 **jahm** (Md **zhèn**)
① a kind of venomous bird ②
poisoned bird
　鴆媒 **jahm mùih**
　　to slander
　鴆酒 **jahm jáu**
　　poisoned wine

鴇 **bóu** (Md **bǎo**)
① a bird resembling the wild
goose ② prostitute, procuress
　鴇母 **bóu móuh**
　　procuress
　鴇兒 **bóu yìh**
　　prostitute

鴉（鴉、鵶）ngà (Md yā)

crow; raven

鴉片 ngà pin
opium

鴉雀無聲 ngà jeuk mòuh sìng
so quiet that not a single voice can be heard

鴕 tòh (Md tuó)
ostrich

鴕鳥 tòh níuh
ostrich

鴛 yùn (Md yuān)
male of the mandarin duck

鴛鴦 yùn yèung
mandarin duck; a couple in love

鴛侶 yùn léuih
a spouse

鴣 gù (Md gú)
a kind of pigeon

鴦 yèung (Md yāng)
female of mandarin duck

鴨 ngaap (Md yā)
duck

鴨掌 ngaap jéung
webs on ducks' feet

鴨嘴筆 ngaap jéui bāt
drawing pen; ruling pen

鴿 gap (Md gē)
dove; pigeon

鴿子 gap jí
dove; pigeon

鴿子傳書 gap jí chyùhn syù
transmission of messages by homing pigeons

鴻 hùhng (Md hóng)
① wild swan ② great; huge; large

鴻圖 hùhng tòuh
great plan

鴻恩 hùhng yàn
great favor or kindness

鵑 gyùn (Md juān)
the cuckoo

鵝（鵞）ngòh (Md é)
goose; gander

鵝毛被 ngòh mòuh péih
bedding stuffed with goose down

鵝卵石 ngòh léun sehk
pebbles

鵠 gūk, huhk (Md gǔ, hú)
① swan ② standing quietly ③ target

鵠立 huhk lahp
to stand on the lookout

鵠候 huhk hauh
to await eagerly

鵠的 gūk dīk
target; bull's eyes

鵬 pàahng (Md péng)
a fabulous bird supposed to be the greatest of all kinds

鵬圖 pàahng tòuh
great ambition

鵬程萬里 pàahng chìhng maahn léih
years of great promise

鵪 àm (Md ān)
quail

鵪鶉 àm sèuhn (àm chèun)
quail

鵰（雕）dìu (Md diāo)
a bird of prey

鵲 cheuk, jeuk (Md què)
magpie

鵲報 **cheuk bou**
the magpie's good news

鵲起 **cheuk héi**
to rise at an opportune time

鶉 **sèuhn, chèun (Md chún)**
quail

鶉居 **sèuhn gèui**
to be without a fixed home

鶩 **mouh (Md wù)**
ducks

鶴 **hohk (Md hè)**
crane

鶴立 **hohk lahp**
to expect eagerly

鶴唳 **hohk leuih**
cries of crane

鶯 **ngàng (Md yīng)**
greenfinch; Chinese oriole

鶯歌 **ngàng gō**
songs of the oriole

鶻 **waht, gwāt (Md hú, gú)**
① a kind of pigeon ② a kind of bird of prey

鶻突 **waht daht**
muddle-headed; confused

鷓 **je (Md zhè)**
partridge

鷓鴣 **je gū**
partridge

鷗 **ngàu (Md ōu)**
gull

鷦 **jìu (Md jiāo)**
wren

鷦鷯 **jìu lìuh**
wren; the tailor bird

鷯 **lìuh (Md liáo)**
wren

鷲 **jauh (Md jiù)**
eagle

鷺 **louh (Md lù)**
egret

鷺鷥 **louh sī**
egret

鷸 **waht (Md yù)**
snipe

鷸蚌相爭 **waht póhng sèung jàng**
a quarrel which benefits only a third party

鷹 **yìng (Md yīng)**
hawk; eagle

鷹犬 **yìng hyún**
falcons and dogs used in hunting

鷹視 **yìng sih**
fierce look

鸚 **yìng (Md yìng)**
parrot

鸚哥 **yìng gō**
parrot

鸝 **lèih (Md lí)**
Chinese oriole

鸞 **lyùhn (Md luán)**
a fabulous bird related to the phoenix

鸞鳳和鳴 **lyùhn fuhng wòh mìhng**
harmony in marriage

鸞旗 **lyùhn kèih**
imperial flag

鹵部

鹵(卤、滷) **lóuh**
(Md **lǔ**)
① alkaline ② natural salt ③ rude; unfined

鹵莽 **lóuh móhng**
rude; rash

鹵水 **lóuh séui**
alkaline

鹹(咸) **hàahm**
(Md **xián**)
salty; salted

鹹水 **hàahm séui**
saline water

鹹魚 **hàahm yùh**
salted fish

鹽(盐) **yìhm** (Md **yán**)
salt

鹽田 **yìhm tìhn**
salt garden

鹽池 **yìhm chìh**
salt pond

鹿部

鹿 **luhk** (Md **lù**)
deer; stag; doe

鹿角 **luhk gok**
antlers

鹿死誰手 **luhk séi sèuih sáu**
who is to kill the deer? — who will win

麋 **mèih** (Md **mí**)
a kind of deer

麋黎 **mèih làih**
old; aged

麋沸 **mèih fai**
disturbance; unrest

麒 **kèih** (Md **qí**)
male of a fabulous animal resembling the deer

麒麟 **kèih lèuhn**
a fabulous animal resembling the deer said to appear only in time of peace and prosperity

麓 **lūk** (Md **lù**)
foot of hill or mountain

麇 **kwàhn** (Md **qún**)
a species of roe

麇集 **kwàhn jaahp**
to flock together

麗 **laih** (Md **lì, lí**)
beautiful; elegant

麗質 **laih jāt**
beauty (especially femine)

麗文 **laih màhn**
elegant writing

麝 **seh** (Md **shè**)
musk deer

麝香 **seh hèung**
musk

麟 **lèuhn** (Md **lín**)
female of fabulous animals resembling the deer

麟麟 **lèuhn lèuhn**
bright; brilliant

麟兒 **lèuhn yìh**
a fine son

麥部

麥 **mahk** (Md **mài**)
① wheat; barley ② a Chinese family name

麥片 **mahk pin**
oat meal

麥芽 **mahk ngàh**
malt

麩(麸、𪌊) **fù** (Md **fū**)
bran

麩素 **fù sou**
gluten

麩酸 **fù syùn**
glutanic acid

麪（面、麵）**mihn**
(Md **miàn**)
flour; noodle

麪包 **mihn bāau**
bread

麪粉 **mihn fán**
flour

麵（麴、曲 糀 ）
gūk, kūk (Md **gū**)
ferment for brewing

麴錢 **gūk chìhn**
tax paid by brewers

麻部

麻 **màh** (Md **má**)
hemp; sesame

麻痺 **màh bei**
paralysis

麻醉 **màh jeui**
to anesthetize

麻煩 **màh fàahn**
troublesome

麼 **mò** (Md **mó, me**)
① tiny ② an interrogative particle

麾 **fài** (Md **huī**)
① flag; banner ② to lead

麾節 **fài jit**
flags; banners

麾軍 **fài gwàn**
to lead an army

黃部

黃 **wòhng** (Md **huáng**)
① yellow ② a Chinese family name

黃金時代 **wòhng gàm sìh doih**
golden age

黃熱病 **wòhng yiht behng**
yellow fever

黌（黉）**hùhng**
(Md **hóng**)
school

黌教 **hùhng gaau**
schooling

黌舍 **hùhng se**
school building

黍部

黍 **syú** (Md **shǔ**)
a variety of millet

黍米 **syú máih**
millet grain

黍子 **syú jí**
a variety of millet

黎 **làih** (Md **lí**)
① many; numerous ② black; dark ③ a Chinese family name

黎明 **làih mìhng**
dawn; daybreak

黎老 **làih lóuh**
aged person

黏 **nìhm, nìm** (Md **nián**)
① to stick ② sticky; glutinous

黏膜 **nìm mók**
mucous membrane

黏土 **nìm tóu**
clay

黏住 **nìhm jyuh**
to stick

黑部

黑 **hāk** (Md **hēi**)
black; dark; evil; gloomy

黑暗 **hāk ngam**
darkness, dark

黑市 **hāk síh**
black market

黑幕 **hāk mohk**
what is done under a cover; a dark secret

黔 **kìhm** (Md **qián**)
① black ② Kweichow

黔首 **kìhm sáu**
the people; multitude

默 **mahk** (Md **mò**)
silent; quiet; still

默許 **mahk héui**
permission

默契 **mahk kai**
tacit understanding

默默無言 **mahk mahk mòuh yìhn**
wordless; speechless

點 (点) **dím** (Md **diǎn**)
① dot; spot; point ② hours ③ to select; to light

點名 **dím mìhng**
to make a roll call

點火 **dím fó**
to light a fire

點綴 **dím jeui**
to embellish

黛 **doih** (Md **dài**)
a bluish-black material used by ancient women to blacken their eyebrows

黛蛾 **doih ngòh**
beautiful eyebrows of a woman

黜 **jēut** (Md **chù**)
to reject; to dismiss; to demote

黜免 **jēut míhn**
to dismiss from office

黜斥 **jēut chīk**
to dispel

黜升 **jēut sìng**
promotion

黝 **yáu** (Md **yǎu**)
bluish black

黝黝 **yáu yáu**
gloomy; dark

黠 **haht** (Md **xiá**)
① smart; clever ② crafty; cunning

黠吏 **haht leih**
crafty; evil official

黠慧 **haht wai**
clever; smart

黨 (党) **dóng** (Md **dǎng**)
① party; gang; faction ② relatives ③ to associate

黨派 **dóng paai**
faction; parties

黨章 **dóng jèung**
party regulations

黯 **ám** (Md **àn**)
① pitch dark ② miserable; dismal

黯然失色 **ám yìhn sāt sīk**
gloomy; dismal

黯慘 **ám cháam**
gloomy; dismal

黴 (霉) **mèih** (Md **méi**)
① mold; mildew ② germs; fungs ③ dirty

黴爛 **mèih laahn**
decaying and mildew cover

黴菌 **mèih kwán**
fungs; mold fungs

黷 **duhk** (Md **dú**)
to corrupt; to be rash about

黷武 **duhk móuh**
to use military might rashly

黹部

黹 **jí** (Md **zhǐ**)
needlework

黻 **fāt** (Md **fú**)
a kind of embroidered design on ancient robe

黽部

黽（黾）**máhn** (Md **mǐn**)
to strive; to endeavor

黽勉 **máhn míhn**
to strive; to endeavor

鼇（鰲）**ngòuh** (Md **áo**)
huge sea turtle

鼇頭 **ngòuh tàuh**
top successful candidate in a civil service examination under the former system

鼈（鱉）**biht** (Md **biē**)
a kind of freshwater turtle

鼎部

鼎 **díng** (Md **dǐng**)
① huge tripod of bronze with two ears; heavy three legged caldron
② vigorous; thriving ③ triangular

鼎力 **díng lihk**
great strength

鼎立 **díng lahp**
to develop a triangular balance of power

鼐 **náaih** (Md **nài**)
huge tripod caldon

鼓部

鼓 **gú** (Md **gǔ**)
① drums ② to drum; to arouse

鼓動 **gú duhng**
to rouse; to stir up

鼓勵 **gú laih**
to encourage

鼓掌 **gú jéung**
to clap the hands

鼕 **dùng** (Md **dōng**)
the rattle of drums

鼙 **pèih** (Md **pí**)
a kind of war drum

鼙鼓 **pèih gú**
a kind of war drum

鼠部

鼠 **syú** (Md **shǔ**)
mouse; rat; rodent

鼠輩 **syú bui**
mean fellow

鼠膽 **syú dáam**
cowardice

鼠窟 **syú fāt**
rat hole

鼬 **yauh** (Md **yòu**)
weasel

鼬鼠 **yauh syú**
weasel

鼯 **ǹgh** (Md **wú**)
flying squirrel

鼯鼠 **ǹgh syú**
flying squirrel

鼯鼠技窮 **ǹgh syú geih kùhng**
at one's wit's end

鼷 **hàih** (Md **xī**)
mouse

鼻部

鼻 **beih** (Md **bí**)
① nose ② first

鼻孔 **beih húng**
nostril

鼻祖 **beih jóu**
founder; originator

鼻音 **beih yàm**
nasal sounds

鼾 **hohn, hòhn** (Md **hān**)
to snore

鼾睡 **hohn seuih**
heavy sleep

鼾聲如雷 **hohn sìng yùh lèuih**
to snore terribly

齊部

齊(齐) **chàih** (Md **qí**)
① equal; uniform ② to set in order ③ name of a dynasty ④ a Chinese family name

齊備 **chàih beih**
everything ready

齊名 **chàih mìhng**
equal in fame

齊家 **chàih gà**
to govern one's family

齋(斋) **jàai** (Md **zhāi**)
① pure; respectful ② vegetarian meal ③ room for study

齋堂 **jàai tòhng**
dining room in a Buddhist temple

齋心 **jàai sàm**
to purify the mind

齎 **jài** (Md **jī**)
① to present; to offer ② to harbor; to entertain

齎恨 **jài hahn**
to harbor hatred

齎送 **jài sung**
to present; to offer

齏(齑) **jài** (Md **jī**)
① pulverized powdered ② seasoning in powder form

齒部

齒 **chi** (Md **chǐ**)
① teeth ② age ③ to speak; to mention

齒根 **chí gàn**
root of a tooth

齒輪 **chí lèuhn**
cogwheel

齒音 **chí yàm**
dental sounds

齟 **jéui** (Md **jǔ**)
irregular teeth

齟齬 **jéui yúh**
irregular teeth; to disagree

齠 **tìuh** (Md **tiáo**)
to shed the milk teeth

齠年 **tìuh nìhn**
the age of shedding the milk teeth — childhood

齠容 **tìuh yùhng**
handsome; youth look

齡 **lìhng** (Md **líng**)
one'a age

齣 **chēut** (Md **chū**)
a numerary adjunct for plays

齦 **ngàhn, hán** (Md **yín, kěn**)
gums of the teeth

齧(嚙、啮) **ngaht, yiht** (Md **niè**)
to gnaw; to bite

齧斷 **ngaht dyuhn**
to bite off

齪 **chūk** (Md **chuò**)
① narrow; small ② dirty

齬 **yúh** (Md **yú**)
① uneven teeth ② to disagree

齷 **ngāk** (Md **wò**)
① narrow; small ② dirty

齷齪 **ngāk chūk**
narrow; small; dirty

龍部

龍 (龙) **lùhng** (Md **lóng**)
① dragon ② imperial ③ a
Chinese family name

龍馬 **lùhng máh**
old but strong

龍爭虎鬥 **lùhng jàng fú dau**
fierce battle between giants

襲 **gùng** (Md **gōng**)
a Chinese family name

龕 **hàm** (Md **kān**)
niche for an idol

龜部

龜 (龟) **gwài** (Md **guī**)
tortoise; turtle

龜貝 **gwài bui**
tortoise shell used as money
in ancient times

龠部

龠 **yeuhk** (Md **yuè**)
① a kind of flute ② a kind of
measuring vassel

Brief Introduction to Cantonese Pronunciation

In pronouncing a syllable in Cantonese, three elements must be taken into account, namely, an <u>initial</u>, a <u>final</u> and a <u>tone</u>. The initial includes whatever is before the main vowel, the final includes the main vowel and whatever follows it and the tone is the voice pitch for the syllable. For the syllable, "ngáak", then, the initial is <u>ng</u>, the final is <u>aak</u> and the tone is high-rising.

Initials

An initial is the starting-off sound of a word.

Of the nineteen initials in Cantonese, ch, p, t k and kw are aspirated while b, d, g, gw and j are unaspirated. The aspirated ch is articulated between the English ch and ts.

1. Aspirated stops: I.E.
    P   T   K   CH   KW

2. Non-aspirated stops: I.E.
    B   D   G   J   GW

3. Nasals: I.E.
    M   N   NG

4. Fricative and Continuants: I.E.
    F   L   H   S

5. Semi-Vowels: I.E.
    Y   W

Finals

A final is the concluding sound of a word and there are fifty one of these. The main vowel is the key part of the Cantonese final. The vowels may be either long or short and this affects the pronunciation.

1. Finals starting with "A"

    A
    | AAI | AI |
    | AAU | AU |
    | AAM | AM |
    | AAN | AN |
    | AANG | ANG |
    | AAP | AP |
    | AAT | AT |
    | AAK | AK |

2. Finals starting with "E"

    | E | EI | ENG | EK | | |
    | EU | EUI | EUNG | EUT | EUN | EUK |

3. Finals starting with "I"

    | I | IU | IM | IN | ING |
    | IP | IT | IK | | |

4. Finals starting with "O"

    | O | OI | ON | OU | ONG | OT | OK |

5. Finals starting with "U"

    | U | UI | UN | UNG | UT | UK |

6. Finals starting with "Y"

    | YU | YUN | YUT |

The vowels in the underlined finals are shorter. The endings P T K are pronounced without any burst of air.

Tones

The student of Cantonese will be well aware of the importance of tones in conveying meaning. Basically, there are seven tones which, in the Yale system, are represented by the use of diacritics and by the insertion of h for the three low tones.

The following chart will illustrate the seven tones:

1	2	3	4	5	6	7
High Falling	High Rising	Mid Level	High Level	Low Falling	Low Rising	Low Level
chàng	cháng	chang	chāng	chàhng	cháhng	chahng
bàai	báai	baai	bāai	bàaih	báaih	baaih

Below is a chart describing the relative differences between the seven tones:

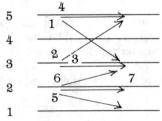

Brief Introduction to
Chinese Pronunciation in Pinyin

The Roman Alphabet, by and large, is the norm for writing Western European and North american Languages, whereas the Chinese Language uses ideographic symbols. A person unfamiliar with these symbols but who wishes to write down the Chinese sounds according to the way they are heard has to use a phonetic seight commonly termed Romanization.

Over the countries several Romanization systems have and are been applied to the Mandarin Chinese Language, which is now the standard for the whole country. The most popular current system is the Pinyin Romanization and to date it has proved to be one of the most conducive to the learning of Chinese Pronunciation

A syllable in Pinyin consists three elements (1) an initial or the beginning sound, (2) a final, the ending of a syllable, (3) a tone which characterizes the whole syllable.

(1)   Initials: There are 21 initials which are listed as below:

b	p	m	f	d	t	n	l
g	k	h	j	q	x		
zh	ch	sh	r	z	c	s	

(2) Finals: The following table consists of 36 finals:

	i (yì)	u (w)	ü (yu)
a	ia	ua	
o		uo	
e			
er			
ê	iê		üê
ai		uai	
ei		uei (ui)	
ao	iao		
ou	iou (iu)		
an	ian	uan	üan
en	in	uen	ün
ang	iang	uang	
eng	ing	ueng (ong)	üeng (iong)

(3) Tones: In Beijing dialect there are four tones. The four tones are:

1. ā   high and level
2. á   high and rising/mid-rising
3. ǎ   low and dipping
4. à   falling

Comparative Chart of
Four Romanization Systems

Initials

Yale	IPA	Sidney Lau	Meyer-Wempe
p	p'	p	p'
b	p	b	p
t	t'	t	t'
d	t	d	t
k	k'	k	k'
g	k	g	k
ch	tʃ'	ch	ch', ts'
j	tʃ	j	ch, ts
kw	k'w	kw	k'w
gw	kw	gw	kw
m	m	m	m
n	n	n	n
ng	ŋ	ng	ng
f	f	f	f
l	l	l	l
h	h	h	h
s	ʃ	s	s, sh
y	j	y	i, y
w	w	w	oo, w

Finals

Yale	IPA	Sidney Lau	Meyer-Wempe
a	a:	a	a
aai	a:i	aai	aai
aau	a:u	aau	aau
aam	a:m	aam	aam
aap	a:p	aap	aap
aan	a:n	aan	aan
aat	a:t	aat	aat
aang	a:ŋ	aang	aang
aak	a:k	aak	aak
ai	ai	ai	ai
au	au	au	au
am	am	am	am, om
ap	ap	ap	ap, op
an	an	an	an
at	at	at	at
ang	aŋ	ang	ang
ak	ak	ak	ak
e	ɛ	e	e
eng	ɛ:ŋ	eng	eng
ek	ɛ:k	ek	ek
ei	ei	ei	ei
eu	oe:	euh	oeh
eung	oe:ŋ	eung	eung
euk	oe:k	euk	euk
eui	oei	ui	ui
eun	oen	un	un
eut	oet	ut	ut

Finals

Yale	IPA	Sidney Lau	Meyer-Wempe
i	i:	i	i
iu	i:u	iu	iu
im	i:m	im	im
ip	i:p	ip	ip
in	i:ŋ	in	in
it	i:t	it	it
ing	iŋ	ing	ing
ik	ik	ik	ik
o	o	oh	oh
oi	o:i	oi	oi
on	o:n	on	on
ot	o:t	ot	ot
ong	o:ŋ	ong	ong
ok	o:k	ok	ok
ou	ou	o	o
u	u	oo	oo
ui	u:i	ooi	ooi
un	u:n	oon	oon
ut	u:t	oot	oot
ung	u:ŋ	ung	ung
uk	u:k	uk	uk
yu	y:	ue	ue
yun	y:n	uen	uen
yut	y:t	uet	uet

Tones

Yale		Sidney Lau		Meyer-Wempe	
high falling	à	high falling 1	a^1	upper even	a
high rising	á	middle rising 2	a^2	upper rising	á
middle level	a, at	middle level 3	a^3	upper going	à
				middle entering	àt
high level	ā, āt	high level 1^0	a^{1^0}	upper even	a
				upper entering	at
low falling	àh	low falling 4	a^4	low even	a̠
low rising	áh	low rising 5	a^5	lower rising	ă
low level	ah, aht	low level 6	a^6	lower going	â
				lower entering	ât